**Politics, Economics, and Society
in the Two Germanies,
1945-75**

Politics, Economics, and Society in the Two Germanies, 1945-75

A BIBLIOGRAPHY
OF ENGLISH-LANGUAGE WORKS

Compiled by
Anna J. Merritt and Richard L. Merritt

with the assistance of
Kathleen Kelly Rummel

UNIVERSITY OF ILLINOIS PRESS
Urbana   Chicago   London

© 1978 by the Board of Trustees of the University of Illinois
Manufactured in the United States of America

Library of Congress Cataloging in Publication Data
Merritt, Anna J.
  Politics, economics, and society in the
two Germanies, 1945-75.

  1. Germany, West — Politics and government —
Bibliography. 2. Germany, West — Economic
conditions — Bibliography. 3. Germany, West —
Social conditions — Bibliography. 4. Germany,
East — Politics and government — Bibliography.
5. Germany, East — Economic conditions — Bibliog-
raphy. 6. Germany, East — Social conditions —
Bibliography. I. Merritt, Richard L., joint
author. II. Rummel, Kathleen Kelly, joint
author. III. Title.
Z7165.G3M47 [JN3971.A2] 016.3091′43′087
ISBN 0-252-00684-4   77-26853

To
Arnold H. Price and Robert Wolfe

who have labored to make Germany more
accessible for American scholarship

INTRODUCTION

The three decades since 1945 have seen the reemergence of Germany — not one Germany, but two! — on the center stage of world politics. The worldwide trauma of World War II, the postwar struggle between East and West for control over Germany, the birth and growth of the Federal Republic of Germany (FRG) in the West and the German Democratic Republic (GDR) in the East, economic solidification, potentially violent conflict over such issues as the Berlin wall and the eastern territories of the prewar Germany, détente, and the politics of recognition — all these events and more have captured the attention of statesmen, journalists, and scholars alike, producing a flood of literature both analytic and polemical in both English and other languages.

And yet, curiously enough, many of the most interesting English-language analyses are in out-of-the-way places, tucked away in obscure scholarly journals or as chapters in books with innocuous, uninformative titles. In teaching undergraduate courses on German politics and graduate seminars on comparative politics, and simply in trying to perform research on postwar Germany, we increasingly felt the need for some sort of guide to the mass and mazeways of such publications. The present bibliography is one consequence of this felt need.

The bibliography began simply enough. Over the course of years, and in the most unsystematic fashion imaginable, we gathered some titles on note cards and slips of paper and in short bibliographies produced for other purposes. These were made available to students writing term papers, who in turn uncovered some items of which we were not aware. By 1969, with about 500 titles in hand, we employed an undergraduate student, Philip S. Yocum, to spend the summer in the University of Illinois's magnificent library to dig out any that we had missed, in the expectation that we could prepare a mimeographed bibliography for local distribution. By the end of the summer, Yocum had provided us with an additional 500 titles — and also with the realization that there were plenty more where these had come from.

After pausing for thought, we plunged ahead anyway. Two years later Kathleen Kelly Rummel spent several months at the Library of Congress checking existing references and adding almost 2,000 more. Thinking the task finally completed, we then initiated a final check and search at the University of Illinois. With assistance from Barbara Tinsley we systematically went through almost 500 social science, intellectual, and other journals. The result is the present listing of 8,548 items.

Principles of Selection

The focus of the bibliography — postwar German politics, economics, and society — is clearly broad. Under this rubric might fall any item that had anything whatever to do with Germans or Germany since 1945. It would be the rare book on international relations, for instance, that would fail to touch, at least in passing, on "the German problem." Similarly, there was also the question of brief articles in news magazines, discussions of scientific or technological accomplishments, and novels or short stories. A major task facing us as bibliographers, then, was to define limits. That is, what sort of item should be included and what excluded?

Our basic inclination was inclusivity. We did, however, set some general limits. First, we sought to include only analyses, whether descriptive, evaluative, or theoretic, of political, economic, or social relevance. Items on technological developments, art, science, and other topics were omitted unless they somehow bore directly on that theme. Reluctantly, we also decided to exclude fiction. Thus, the translations of works by Wolfgang Borchert, Guenter Grass, Uwe Johnson, Guenter Herburger, Christa Wolf, and many others that can provide the English-speaking reader with excellent insights into contemporary German life are not listed. We also ignored novels, often perspicacious, by such foreign writers as John Le Carré. To the extent that scholars and others have discussed the politically relevant aspects of this body of literature, we have tried to include their analyses.

A second limitation was the decision to exclude political studies that did not deal substantially with Germany. We listed what we considered to be the most important items — for example, memoirs of a statesman who dealt with German problems extensively in his professional life, or studies in international politics or foreign policy that focus in detail upon Germany as a case study — but to have added every book listing Germany in its index would have posed a very difficult task indeed. As a practical matter, but also to help readers particularly interested in the two Germanies, we chose to be selective rather than exhaustive.

The defining characteristic of substantive centrality is clearly discretionary and open to question. Where it proved to be most difficult to apply was in items on NATO or the European Community. By definition, any such item deals with the FRG, however generally or specifically, but a bibliography on NATO or the European Community would be as large as or perhaps larger than the present one. The same principle holds for the position of the GDR in the Soviet bloc, the Warsaw Treaty Organization, and COMECON. Again we had little choice but to be selective in a discretionary fashion. We have opted, when in doubt, to list the item in question, but it is quite likely that we have failed to include some of substantial importance.

Third, even given the above limitations we did not try to be exhaustive. We excluded articles in such news magazines as *Newsweek* and *Time.* References to these can be found easily in *The Readers' Guide to Periodical Literature.* Nor did we include newspaper articles, however substantial they might be. Again, the reader interested in following current events in the two Germanies can consult well-organized indices to the *New York Times, The Times* (London), the *Christian Science Monitor,* and the *Wall Street Journal.* Summaries are presented in such publications as *Facts on File, Deadline Data on World Affairs,* and *Keesing's Archives.* Finally, there are numerous periodical publications dealing specifically with Germany whose articles we did not list but which should be of considerable value to those who want to follow German developments on a continuing basis.

Periodicals on Germany

Among these publications are periodical reports published by the occupation forces in the first postwar decade, official organs of the FRG and GDR, other publications supported if not sponsored by the German governments, and a smaller number issued by private associations. Only a few of these — noted in the descriptions below by the phrase "articles listed" — were searched thoroughly for articles to be included in this bibliography.

The first group includes those publications which were published in the immediate postwar period by the occupying powers. Official gazettes containing laws, decrees, and other official matters, which appeared in English-language editions, were:

Official Gazette of the Control Council for Germany, which began publication on 29 October 1945 in Berlin at (irregular) monthly intervals.

Control Commission Gazette, Germany (British Zone), also started in 1945. Its title varied: Nos. 1-3, *Military Government Gazette, Germany, 21st Army Group;* Nos. 4-28, *Military Government Gazette, Germany, British Zone of Control;* Nos. 29-35, *Military Government Gazette, Germany (British Zone).*

Military Government Gazette, Germany, United States Area of Control, published by the Office of the Military Government, United States (OMGUS) from 1 June 1946 to 21 September 1949.

Official Gazette of the Allied High Commission for Germany, published at (irregular) monthly intervals in Bonn-Mehlem starting 23 September 1949 and ending in 1953; 126 issues in all.

A number of monthly and weekly reports also appeared:

Military Government Weekly Field Report, published by the U.S. Army; appeared sixteen times between July and October 1945.

Information Control Review (originally *Information Control Intelligence Summary*), published weekly by OMGUS between 5 July 1945 and 23 November 1946; there were sixty-nine issues. On 30 November 1946 it was renamed *Information Control Weekly Review;* under this title thirty-eight more issues were published.

Weekly Information Bulletin, published by OMGUS in Frankfurt; appeared weekly from 28 July 1945 until 1953 (with a biweekly interval in 1948-49).

Monthly Report of the Military Governor, published by the Military Government of Germany, U.S. Zone, in Berlin starting July 1945; includes "functional reports" which appeared on a bimonthly basis from April 1946 to 1949; there are also various "annexes" with the same numbering as the reports, each dealing with a specific topic.

Report on Germany, published by the U.S. High Commission for Germany (HICOG) from Washington, Government Printing Office, between 1949 and 1952.

British Zone Review, a monthly review of activities in the British Zone published in Hamburg by Information Services Division; appeared between 29 September 1945 and 20 September 1949.

With the end of the occupation period, a great many publications emerged in both the FRG and the GDR that dealt with economic and political developments as well as topics of general interest. From the FRG, publications concerned with general and political problems include:

Aussenpolitik: German Foreign Affairs Review, published quarterly since 1970 by Uebersee Verlag, Hamburg; comprises translations of articles selected from the monthly publication of the same name, published under the auspices of the Deutsches Institut fuer Auswaertige Politik. Articles listed.

The Bulletin, Weekly Survey of German Affairs, published since 1953 by the Press and Information Office of the Government of the Federal Republic of Germany at Bonn; the "official" newsletter.

Bulletin on German Questions, published monthly since 1948 by Gamma Publications, London.

Central Europe Journal, has appeared monthly since 1951 from Atlantic Forum, Bonn.

German Tribune, Weekly Review of the German Press, published weekly since 1952 by F. Reinecke Verlag, Hamburg; contains articles translated from FRG newspapers and news magazines. Quarterly supplement has longer articles.

German Social Report, Monthly Bulletin of News and Background Information on Social Affairs, published in Bonn since 1963; renamed *Inter Nationes* in 1971.

Modern Law and Society, Review of German-Language Research Contributions on Law, Political Science, and Sociology, has appeared semi-annually since 1968 from Tuebingen.

New German Critique: An Interdisciplinary Journal of German Studies, published since 1973 by the German Department, University of Wisconsin, Milwaukee; three issues per year. Original articles and translations offer a critical approach to German politics, economics, and society.

News from Germany, a monthly published since 1946 by the Social Democratic Party of Germany (SPD).

Overseas Review, published monthly since 1949 by the Uebersee Verlag, Hamburg.

Other useful sources, ones that deal more with cultural than political and social matters, are:

Cultural News from Germany, published monthly since 1958 by Inter Nationes, Bonn.

German Life and Letters, has appeared quarterly since 1936 from Blackwell and Mott, Oxford.

Hallo Friends, published bimonthly since 1964 by Deutsche Welle, Cologne; Deutsche Welle is the FRG's overseas radio station.

Publications from the FRG concerned with economic issues include:

Deutsche Bundesbank, Monthly Report, published in Frankfurt; started in 1951 as *Monthly Report of the Bank Deutscher Laender.*

Economic Report from Germany, a survey published since 1958 by the Deutsches Industrieinstitut in Cologne.

German American Trade News, published since 1952 by the German American Chamber of Commerce in New York City.

German Economic Review: An English Language Quarterly on German Economic Research and Current Developments, edited by the Gesellschaft fuer Wirtschafts- und Sozialwissenschaften — Verein fuer Socialpolitik, Bonn, since 1963. Contains scholarly articles in translation and listings of other relevant items.

German International: The Independent Monthly News Magazine for Politics, Economics, Science and Overseas Development, published monthly since 1957 by Heinz Moeller Verlag, Bonn.

Germany: The Magazine of the Federal Republic, a quarterly published in Bonn by the Uebersee Verlag from 1956 to 1964; absorbed by *German International.*

Handbook of Economic Statistics, prepared by the Economic Affairs Section of the American Embassy, Bonn; continues series begun in OMGUS period.

Inter-Economics, monthly, published since 1968 by the Institut fuer Wirtschaftsforschung, Hamburg.

Wirtschaftsdienst: A Monthly Review of Economic Policy, Kiel, since 1950.

A more extensive listing of 150 English-language journals on West German politics, economics, language, and science appeared in *The Bulletin,* 20:6 (8 February 1972), 43, and 20:7 (22 February 1972), 51-52.

GDR English-language publications containing useful information for the foreign observer include:

Democratic German Report, a biweekly appearing since 1952 from Berlin.

Documents on the Policy of the German Democratic Republic, begun in 1966 and published by the Verlag Zeit im Bild, Dresden.

Foreign Affairs Bulletin, contains extracts from the weekly German-language *Aussenpolitische Korrespondenz;* published biweekly since 1961 by the Press Department of the Ministry of Foreign Affairs.

GDR Review: Magazine from the German Democratic Republic, published monthly in seven languages since 1956 by the Verlag Zeit im Bild, Dresden.

German Export, published semimonthly since 1953 by the Chamber of Foreign Trade in Berlin.

German Foreign Policy, published quarterly from 1961 through 1974 in Berlin. Contains listing of other articles.

Organization of the Bibliography

All 8,548 items in the bibliography are organized in two different ways. First, we have divided them into a number of discrete categories according to their primary focus. The broad groupings are six in number: (1) general, comprising bibliographies and information on demography, geography, and historical background of the two Germanies; (2) the occupation years, specifically 1945-49 but also the High Commission era (1949-55) insofar as its occupation aspects are concerned; (3) political structures and processes in the FRG and GDR; (4) economic structures and processes in the two Germanies; (5) the social systems of East and West Germany, including the politically relevant aspects of social policy, education, culture, and the arts; and (6) foreign policy issues, including relations of the two Germanies with their respective blocs, the "German question," and the status of Berlin.

Individual items are not double-listed. This means that we had to make hard judgments about the single most appropriate category for each entry. In some cases this posed no serious problem. In others, such as an article on women in the labor force, we had to examine the item to see whether it was more about the status of women or about the labor force. To mitigate somewhat the consequences of this kind of decision, we have cross-listed other relevant categories after each section's or subsection's title. These cross-listings merely direct the reader's attention to the fact that related items may be located in categories other than the one the reader is examining at the time.

Second, the volume contains an author listing. Each item, which has been assigned a discrete number, is listed after the name(s) of its author(s). The listing itself contains 5,116 individual and corporate authors.

Systematic searching for new entries was halted in early 1975. Articles and books published since then were included if they came our way, but nothing was added after summer 1976. As with any bibliography, this one, too, will have unfortunate gaps. It did not come to our attention until after the final printout had been produced, for instance, that we had neglected E. F. Penrose's excellent volume, *Economic Planning for the Peace* (Princeton,

N.J.: Princeton University Press, 1953). Every user of the bibliography will undoubtedly find other works of importance that have been omitted. We regret the presence of such lapses, and particularly the absence of items printed since our cutoff date. In a real sense, however, no bibliography can ever come to a final end; there comes a time when its compilers must simply call a halt and hope that further supplements may make their efforts even more useful.

Acknowledgments

Many individuals and institutions assisted us in preparing this bibliography. The source of funds for research assistance and keypunching was the Research Board of the University of Illinois at Urbana-Champaign. The Institute of Communications Research and the Department of Political Science at the University of Illinois at Urbana-Champaign provided funds for computer time and programming. West Germany's Federal Ministry for Inner-German Relations, at the suggestion of Professor Peter Christian Ludz of the University of Munich, generously subsidized publication costs.

Collecting and organizing the bibliographic entries were time-consuming tasks. Philip S. Yocum, Kathleen Kelly Rummel, and Barbara Tinsley assisted us in combing through libraries; and Arnold Price, head of the Slavic and Central European Division of the Library of Congress, provided valuable counsel and numerous references. Our colleagues at the University of Illinois at Urbana-Champaign — Hans J. Brems of the Department of Economics, Fred S. Coombs of the Department of Educational Policy Studies, and Ralph Reisner of the College of Law — helped us to categorize some groups of entries.

The most difficult part of our task turned out to be producing a computer printout with the entries in a useful form. Our original intention to include a Key Word In Context (KWIC) index, which ran afoul of changing programs and machines, had to be abandoned, but not after great cost in terms of time and other resources. In the process of developing such an index, however, we encountered many friendly people who helped in various ways. Frances L. Sykes supervised a good part of the keypunching. Marilyn Gode-von Aesch and Richard Roistacher wrote programs that got us under way. Marion Carter and Leslie Lareau, of the Social Science Quantitative Laboratory at the University of Illinois at Urbana-Champaign, gave us a mini-course on the care and feeding of computers. And Steven Seitz of the Department of Political Science managed to resurrect a set of files that were allegedly lost forever.

After we had abandoned the idea of a KWIC index, Stuart M. Pellish arrived on the scene to enter the section headings. He and Robert Kolstad subsequently performed a miraculous last-minute rescue, just as the Digital Computer Laboratory was about to switch machines again (which would have required rewriting all our programs), by convincing the computer that it really did want to number each of the entries sequentially.

Of basic importance was the cooperation of library staffs at Yale University's Sterling Memorial Library, Harvard University's Widener Library, the Library of Congress, and, particularly, the University Library of the University of Illinois at Urbana-Champaign. Many individuals, who must go unnamed here, provided services as gracious and helpful as the facilities of their institutions are extensive.

Without this assistance the bibliography could not have been completed. To all who helped we are grateful, but each we absolve of any blame for errors of omission, commission, judgment, or categorization.

Anna J. Merritt
Richard L. Merritt

CONTENTS

A. General — 1
   A.1. Bibliographies: General, FRG, GDR — 1
   A.2. Descriptions and Travel Guides — 1
   A.3. Handbooks — 2
      A.3.1. General — 2
      A.3.2. FRG — 2
      A.3.3. GDR — 2
   A.4. History (see also D.3.5; N.7.4) — 2

B. Geography — 3
   B.1. General: FRG and GDR — 4
   B.2. FRG — 4
      B.2.1. Locational Studies — 4
      B.2.2. Regional and Urban Planning — 5
   B.3. GDR — 5

C. Demography — 5
   C.1. Characteristics and Statistics — 5
      C.1.1. General — 5
      C.1.2. FRG — 6
      C.1.3. GDR — 6
   C.2. National Character Assessments (see also F.1.1) — 6
   C.3. Population Movements — 8
      C.3.1. Displaced Persons — 8
      C.3.2. Movements across Boundaries — 9

D. Allied Occupation — 12
   D.1. Wartime Planning and Development — 12
      D.1.1. Wartime Proposals — 12
      D.1.2. Wartime Planning — 13
      D.1.3. Relevant Military Developments — 15
   D.2. Military Occupation — 16
      D.2.1. General (see also I.2.1) — 16
      D.2.2. Four-Power Control — 18
      D.2.3. American Zone — 19
      D.2.4. British Zone — 22
      D.2.5. French Zone — 22
      D.2.6. Soviet Zone — 22
   D.3. Punishment, Restitution, and Rehabilitation (see also I.2) — 23
      D.3.1. War Crimes Trials — 23
      D.3.2. Denazification (see also F.2.4) — 27
      D.3.3. Compensation to Nazi Victims (see also O.3.2) — 28
      D.3.4. Re-Education (see also N.1.3) — 29
      D.3.5. Postwar Views on Nazi Era (see also A.4; N.7.4) — 30
   D.4. Breakdown of Four-Power Cooperation (see also Q.1) — 31
      D.4.1. Disunity on Germany's Future, 1946-47 (see also D.2.2) — 31
      D.4.2. Bizonal Administration, 1947-48 — 32
      D.4.3. Division of Germany (see also D.2.6) — 32
      D.4.4. Re-Establishment of Self-Government (see also E.1; E.3.6) — 34

E. FRG: Governmental Framework — 35
E.1. Creation of FRG — 35
- E.1.1. Western Allies and Parliamentary Council — 35
- E.1.2. Basic Law — 35
- E.1.3. Analyses of Basic Law (see also E.3.2) — 36
- E.1.4. Federalism and Political Theory (see also E.3.4) — 36
- E.1.5. General Treatises — 37

E.2. Political Institutions and Processes (see also H.2) — 38
- E.2.1. Election Laws and Behavior (see also F.1.3; F.4; F.5) — 38
- E.2.2. Coalitions and Cabinets (see also F.2) — 39
- E.2.3. Bundestag and Legislative Behavior (see also F.5) — 39
- E.2.4. Bundesrat — 40
- E.2.5. Public Administration and Civil Service (see also E.3.3.1) — 40
- E.2.6. State and Local Government (see also B.2.1; D.4.4) — 41

E.3. Legal System (see also H.3) — 42
- E.3.1. General — 42
  - E.3.1.1. Legal System — 42
  - E.3.1.2. Jurisprudence — 43
  - E.3.1.3. Legal Profession — 43
- E.3.2. Constitutional Law — 43
  - E.3.2.1. Constitutional Court — 43
  - E.3.2.2. Constitutional Law — 44
  - E.3.2.3. Civil and Political Liberties — 44
  - E.3.2.4. Restrictions on Political Activity — 44
  - E.3.2.5. Emergency Provisions — 45
- E.3.3. Institutional Functions — 45
  - E.3.3.1. Administrative Process — 45
  - E.3.3.2. Civil Procedures and Courts — 45
  - E.3.3.3. Judicial Review — 46
  - E.3.3.4. Conflict of Laws — 46
- E.3.4. Other — 46
  - E.3.4.1. Business Law: General — 46
  - E.3.4.2. Commercial Law; Contracts — 47
  - E.3.4.3. Corporation Law — 47
  - E.3.4.4. Regulation of Business (see also I.6.5) — 47
  - E.3.4.5. Criminal Law (see also L.5.8) — 48
  - E.3.4.6. Family Law (see also L.1.3) — 49
  - E.3.4.7. International Law — 49
  - E.3.4.8. Labor Law (see also I.7) — 49
  - E.3.4.9. Other Legal Issues — 49

E.4. Military (see also 0.4) — 49
- E.4.1. Domestic Aspects of Rearmament Debate — 49
- E.4.2. Military Organization — 50
- E.4.3. Civilian Control Procedures — 51
- E.4.4. Nuclear Weapons Issue — 51
- E.4.5. Other Military Issues (see also E.3.2.5) — 52
- E.4.6. Intelligence Activities — 52

F. FRG: Politics and Political Behavior — 53
F.1. Political Attitudes — 53
- F.1.1. Personality Characteristics and Social Attitudes (see also C.2) — 53
- F.1.2. Public Opinion and Political Attitudes — 53
- F.1.3. Party Identification (see also E.2.1.; F.4; F.5) — 55

F.1.4. Opinion on International Affairs	55
F.2. Political Leadership	56
F.2.1. General	56
F.2.2. Political Biographies	57
F.2.3. Konrad Adenauer	58
F.2.4. Former Nazis in Political Positions? (see also D.3.2; F.4.7)	59
F.3. Interest Groups	60
F.4. Political Parties (see also E.2.1; F.1.3)	60
F.4.1. General	60
F.4.2. Christian Democratic Union (CDU)	62
F.4.3. Social Democratic Party (SPD)	62
F.4.4. Minor Parties	64
F.4.5. Free Democratic Party (FDP)	64
F.4.6. Communist Parties (KPD and DKP)	64
F.4.7. Extreme Nationalism and Neo-Nazi Parties	65
F.4.8. National Democratic Party (NPD)	66
F.5. General Political Surveys	66
F.5.1. 1949-53: 1st Legislative Period	66
F.5.2. 1953-57: 2nd Legislative Period	68
F.5.3. 1957-61: 3rd Legislative Period	69
F.5.4. 1961-65: 4th Legislative Period	70
F.5.5. 1965-66: 5th Legislative Period	72
F.5.6. 1966-69: Grand Coalition	72
F.5.7. 1969-72: 6th Legislative Period	73
F.5.8. 1972-74: 7th Legislative Period	74
G. GDR: Government and Politics	**74**
G.1. Political Framework	74
G.1.1. Constitutional Developments	74
G.1.2. Political Leadership	75
G.1.3. Ideological Developments and Disputes	75
G.2. Political Structures and Processes (see also H.2)	76
G.2.1. Institutions and Processes	76
G.2.2. SED and Other Political Parties	76
G.2.3. National People's Army	77
G.2.4. Youth and Youth Movements	77
G.3. Legal System (see also H.3)	78
G.3.1. Codes and Procedures	78
G.3.2. Structures	79
G.3.3. Western Criticism	80
G.4. General Political Developments	80
G.4.1. Initial Phases, 1949-53	80
G.4.2. Uprising in June 1953	81
G.4.3. Consolidation, 1954-66	81
G.4.4. Since 1967	84
H. FRG-GDR: Political Comparisons	**85**
H.1. General	85
H.2. Political Structures and Processes	85
H.3. Legal Systems	86
I. FRG: Economic System	**86**
I.1. Data and Models	86
I.1.1. Economic Statistics	86

I.1.2. Econometric Models	87
I.1.3. Forecasting	87
I.2. Occupation Controls, 1945-48 (see also D.3)	87
I.2.1. Allied Economic Policy	87
I.2.2. Economic Disarmament	89
I.2.3. Reparations	90
I.2.4. Overseas Assets and External Debts	91
I.3. General Developments and Problems (see also K.1)	91
I.3.1. Occupation Period, 1945-48	91
I.3.2. Currency Reform and Aftermath	92
I.3.3. Marshall Plan Assistance	92
I.3.4. Economic Recovery, 1949-55	93
I.3.5. Prosperity, 1955–	94
I.4. Domestic Economy and Government	96
I.4.1. Money and Banking	96
I.4.2. Fiscal Policy and Public Finance	97
I.4.3. Planning and Economic Policy	98
I.5. Agriculture and Natural Resources	99
I.5.1. Agricultural Sector	99
I.5.2. Land Tenure and Reform	100
I.5.3. Fishing, Forestry, Natural Resources	100
I.6. Industry and Business	101
I.6.1. Industrial Organization and Production	101
I.6.2. Ruhr as an Industrial Area	102
I.6.3. Energy Production	103
I.6.4. Business	103
I.6.5. Business Regulation (see also E.3.4.4)	104
I.6.6. Management; Business Executives	104
I.6.7. Cooperatives	105
I.7. Labor Movements and Issues (see also E.3.4.8)	105
I.7.1. Workers and Labor Market	105
I.7.2. Trade Unions	106
I.7.3. Law and Policymaking	108
I.7.4. Labor-Management Relations; Codetermination	108
I.7.5. Foreign Workers	110
I.7.6. Other Labor Questions	110
I.8. Transportation and Shipping	111
I.9. International Economics	111
I.9.1. International Trade	111
I.9.2. Trade with USSR and Soviet Bloc (see also K.2)	113
I.9.3. Exchange Rates	113
I.9.4. Balance of Payments	114
I.9.5. International Capital Movements	115
I.9.6. Development Assistance (see also O.3)	116
I.9.7. Eastern Charges of Neo-Imperialism	117
J. GDR: Economic System	**117**
J.1. General, 1948-63 (see also K.1)	117
J.2. New Economic System	118
J.3. Agriculture	119
J.4. Industrial Organization and Production	120
J.5. Labor	121
J.6. Foreign Trade (see also K.2)	121
J.7. Comecon; Soviet Bloc Trade	121

K. FRG-GDR Economic Comparisons and Transactions	**122**
K.1. General	122
K.2. Intra-German Trade	123
L. Social Structure and Policy	**123**
L.1. FRG: Social Structure	123
L.1.1. General	123
L.1.2. Community Studies	123
L.1.3. Family (see also E.3.4.6)	124
L.1.4. Women: Roles and Status	124
L.1.5. Youth and Youth Movements (see also F.1.1)	125
L.2. GDR: Social Structure	126
L.3. FRG-GDR: Social Structure	126
L.4. Religion	126
L.4.1. FRG: General (see also N.2.7)	126
L.4.2. FRG: Judaism; Attitudes to Jews (see also D.3.3; O.3.2)	127
L.4.3. GDR: General	129
L.4.4. FRG-GDR Comparisons	129
L.5. FRG: Social Policy	130
L.5.1. General	130
L.5.2. Social Security, Pensions	130
L.5.3. Social Benefits for Workers	130
L.5.4. Social Services and Welfare	131
L.5.5. Public Health; Health Insurance	131
L.5.6. Children and Child-Care	131
L.5.7. Housing	132
L.5.8. Criminology and Rehabilitation (see also E.3.4.5)	132
L.5.9. Environmental Control	132
L.6. GDR: Social Policy	133
L.6.1. General	133
L.6.2. Public Health	133
L.6.3. Criminology and Rehabilitation	133
L.7. FRG-GDR Comparisons	133
M. Communications	**134**
M.1. FRG	134
M.1.1. General	134
M.1.2. Newspapers and Periodicals	134
M.1.3. Conservative Press	135
M.1.4. Press Freedom; Spiegel Affair	135
M.1.5. Radio and Television	136
M.2. GDR	136
M.3. FRG-GDR Comparisons	137
N. Education and Culture	**137**
N.1. FRG: Education	137
N.1.1. General	137
N.1.2. Comparative Perspective	138
N.1.3. Reconstruction under Allied Occupation (see also D.3.4)	138
N.1.4. Planning and Policymaking	140
N.1.5. Educational Reform	140
N.1.6. Teachers and Teacher Training	141
N.1.7. Other Developments	142

- N.2. FRG: Schools and Curricula — 142
  - N.2.1. Preschools and Elementary Schools — 142
  - N.2.2. Lower and Upper Secondary Schools — 142
  - N.2.3. Vocational Training; Industrial Education — 143
  - N.2.4. Adult and Permanent Education — 144
  - N.2.5. Curriculum and Textbooks — 144
  - N.2.6. Educational Technology — 145
  - N.2.7. Religion and Education — 145
- N.3. FRG: Universities — 145
  - N.3.1. Universities: General — 145
  - N.3.2. University Reform — 147
  - N.3.3. Teaching and Administrative Personnel — 147
  - N.3.4. University Students — 147
  - N.3.5. Student Protest — 148
  - N.3.6. Educational and Cultural Exchange — 149
- N.4. FRG: University Programs and Research — 150
  - N.4.1. Humanities, Area Studies, Education — 150
  - N.4.2. Law — 150
  - N.4.3. Social Sciences — 151
  - N.4.4. Sciences and Technical Education — 152
  - N.4.5. Research Organization, Archives, Libraries — 153
- N.5. GDR: Education — 153
  - N.5.1. General — 153
  - N.5.2. Higher Education and Research — 154
- N.6. FRG-GDR: Comparative Education — 155
- N.7. FRG: Cultural Developments — 155
  - N.7.1. General Culture and the Arts — 155
  - N.7.2. Literature — 156
  - N.7.3. Drama and Theater — 157
  - N.7.4. Recent History in Literature and Drama (see also A.4; D.3.5) — 157
- N.8. GDR: Cultural Developments — 157
  - N.8.1. General Culture and the Arts — 157
  - N.8.2. Literature — 158
  - N.8.3. Drama and Theater; Brecht — 158
- N.9. FRG-GDR: Cultural Comparisons — 159

O. FRG: Foreign Policy — 159
- O.1. General (see also E.3.4.7; F.1.4; I.9) — 159
  - O.1.1. Allied High Commission — 159
  - O.1.2. Policymaking Processes — 160
  - O.1.3. Cultural Policy — 161
  - O.1.4. Foreign Policy, 1949-55; Sovereignty and Rearmament — 161
  - O.1.5. Foreign Policy, 1955– — 163
  - O.1.6. Eastern and Socialist Views: Militarism — 165
- O.2. United States and West Europe (see also O.5) — 168
  - O.2.1. North Atlantic Area — 168
  - O.2.2. United States — 168
  - O.2.3. West Europe — 171
  - O.2.4. United Kingdom — 172
  - O.2.5. France — 173
  - O.2.6. France: Saar Question — 174
  - O.2.7. Other European Countries — 175
- O.3. Other Regions and Organizations (see also I.9.6; I.9.7) — 175

O.3.1. Middle East	175
O.3.2. Israel (see also D.3.3; L.4.2)	175
O.3.3. Africa	176
O.3.4. Asia; Oceania	176
O.3.5. Latin America	176
O.3.6. International Organizations (see also E.3.4.7)	176
O.4. Defense and Détente	177
O.4.1. National Security Policy (see also O.1.6)	177
O.4.2. Rearmament within EDC, 1949-54 (see also E.4)	177
O.4.3. NATO (see also O.2.1)	179
O.4.4. Arms Limitation	180
O.4.5. European Security	181
O.5. Western European Integration	182
O.5.1. General Trends	182
O.5.2. Schuman Plan (ECSC)	183
O.5.3. European Community (EEC)	184
O.6. FRG and Soviet Bloc (see also I.9.2; Q.1)	185
O.6.1. Eastern Policy to 1966	185
O.6.2. Eastern Policy, 1966–	186
O.6.3. Soviet Union	188
O.6.4. Poland	189
O.6.5. Oder-Neisse Territories	191
O.6.6. Czechoslovakia	193
P. GDR: Foreign Policy	**193**
P.1. Institutions and Policies	193
P.2. USSR, Warsaw Pact, Other Socialist States (see also J.7)	195
P.3. Defense, Security, Arms Control	196
P.4. Third World	197
P.5. International Organizations	197
Q. FRG-GDR: The German Problem	**198**
Q.1. German Problem: Unity (see also D.4)	198
Q.1.1. Between East and West, 1949-55	198
Q.1.2. Declining Hopes for Unity, 1955-61	200
Q.1.3. New Status Quo, 1961-69	202
Q.1.4. Divided Germany, 1969–	205
Q.2. Conflicting FRG-GDR Claims	205
Q.2.1. FRG: Sole Representation	205
Q.2.2. GDR: Recognition	206
Q.3. FRG-GDR Relations	206
Q.4. FRG-GDR Foreign Policy: Comparisons	207
R. Berlin	**208**
R.1. General, East and West	208
R.2. Legal Context	209
R.3. Access to East and West Berlin	210
R.4. Social and Political Issues	210
R.5. Economic Issues	211
R.6. Blockade and Division, 1948-58	211
R.7. Soviet Ultimatum and the Wall, 1958-69	213
R.8. Normalization, 1969–	217
Author Listing	**219**

A. General

A.1. Bibliographies: General, FRG, GDR

1. Boeninger, Hildegard R. The Hoover Library Collection on Germany Since 1945. Hoover Institute and Library on War, Revolution, and Peace, Collection Survey, No. 2, Pt. 4. Stanford: Stanford University Press, 1955, 56 P.

2. Childs, James Bennett. German Democratic Republic Official Publications, with Those of the Preceding Zonal Period, 1945-1958: A Survey. Washington: Library of Congress, Reference Department, Serial Division, 1960-61, 4 Vols., 1448 P.

3. Childs, James Bennett. German Federal Republic Official Publications, 1949-1957, With Inclusion of Preceding Zonal Official Publications: A Survey. Washington: Library of Congress, Reference Department, Serial Division, 1958, 887 P. 7,500 Items.

4. Childs, James Bennett. Government and Official Publications in a People's Democracy. Library Science Today: Ranganathan Festschrift. Ed. Prithvi Nath Kaula. Bombay: Asia Publishing House, 1965, Pp. 163-170. on GDR; Republished (Updated) as 11-Page Pamphlet, Washington, 1968

5. Epstein, Fritz Theodor. East Germany: A Selected Bibliography. Washington: Library of Congress, Slavic and Central European Division, 1959, 55 P., 325 Items.

6. Epstein, Klaus. The Current West German Scene. Modern Age. 11:2 (Spring 1967), 161-175.

7. German Society for Foreign Policy, Research Institute. Schriftum Ueber Deutschland, 1918-1963: Ausgewaehlte Bibliographie Zur Politik Und Zeitgeschichte. Bonn: Inter Nationes, 2D Ed., 1964, 292 P.

8. Horecky, Paul East Central and Southeast Europe: A Handbook of Library and Archival Resources in North America. Santa Barbara, Calif.: American Bibliographical Center-Clio Press, 1975.

9. Horecky, Paul L., Editor. East Central Europe: A Guide to Basic Publications. Chicago: University of Chicago Press, 1969, 956 P., Esp. Pp. 361-440. 350 Items.

10. Imperial War Museum, Foreign Documents Centre. Repositories in the German Federal Republic. London: Imperial War Museum, Foreign Documents Centre, 1966, 12 P.

11. Inter Nationes. Dokumentationen Ueber Deutschland: Auswahl Amtlicher Und Von Amtlicher Seite Gefoerderter Publikationen. Bonn: Inter Nationes, 2D Ed., 1964, 198 P.

12. Inter Nationes. The Reunification of Germany: A Necessity for World Peace. Bonn: Inter Nationes, 1961, 15 P.

13. Inter Nationes, Editor. Bibliography of Paperbound Books Translated From the German and of Works on Germany. Bonn: Inter Nationes, 4Th Ed., 1967.

14. Kehr, Helen, Compiler. After Hitler: Germany, 1945-1963. London: Vallentine, Mitchell, 1963, 261 P. Prepared for Wiener Library Collection, London; 3,000 Items.

15. Mason, John Brown. Government, Administration, and Politics in East Germany: A Selected Bibliography. American Political Science Review. 53:2 (June 1959), 507-523.

16. Mason, John Brown. Government, Administration and Politics in West Germany: A Selected Bibliography. American Political Science Review. 52:2 (June 1958), 513-530.

17. Moennig, Richard. Bibliography of Paperbound Books Translated From the German and of Works on Germany. Bonn: Inter Nationes, 2D Ed., 1965, 61 P.

18. Moennig, Richard. Deutschland Und Die Deutschen Im Englischsprachigen Schriftum, 1948-1955: Eine Bibliographie. Boettingen: Vandenhoeck & Ruprecht, 1957, 147 P. Lists 3,863 Books and 97 Newspapers and Magazines.

19. Moennig, Richard. Translations From the German: English, 1948-1964. Goettingen: Vandenhoeck & Ruprecht, 2D Ed., 1968, 509 P.

20. Price, Arnold H. East Germany: A Selected Bibliography. Washington: Library of Congress, 1967, 133 P., 833 Entries.

21. Price, Arnold H. The Federal Republic of Germany: A Selected Bibliography of English-Language Publications, With Emphasis on the Social Sciences. Washington: Library of Congress, Government Printing Office, 1972, 63 P.

22. Price, Arnold H. Germany: Recent Bibliographies and Reference Works. Quarterly Journal of Current Acquisitions, Library of Congress. 20:1 (December 1962), 21-29.

23. US, Department of Commerce, Bureau of the Census. Bibliography of Social Science Periodicals and Monograph Series: Soviet Zone of Germany, 1948-1963. Washington: Foreign Social Science Bibliographies Series P-92, No. 21, Government Printing Office, 1965, 190 P.

A.2. Descriptions and Travel Guides

24. Boas International Publishing Company. Germany, 1945-1954. Schaan, Liechtenstein: Boas International, 1954, 738 P.

25. Boehle, Bernd. Handy Guide to Western Germany: A Reference Book for Travel in the German Federal Republic. Gutersloh: Bertelsmann, 1956, 488 P.

26. Clark, Sydney Aylmer. All the Best in Germany and Austria. New York: Dodd, Mead, 1961, 559 P. Travel Book.

27. Cole, John Alfred. Germany, My Host. New York: Abelard-Schumann, 1957, 284 P. Social Life and Customs.

28. Douglas, A. Vibert. East Germany Through a Tourist's Eyes. Queen's Quarterly. 76:1 (Spring 1969), 66-73.

29. Engel, Lyle Kenyon. West Germany. New York: Cornerstone Library, Simon and Schuster, 1973, 192 P.

30. Farrell, Ralph B. Tisch, J. Herman. St. Leon, R. P. Stowell, J. D. German-Speaking Countries Today and Yesterday. Sydney: Novak, 1966, 229 P.

31. Gatterman, A., and Others. Travel Guide: German Democratic Republic. Leipzig: Veb Edition, 1962, 358 P.

32. Harlinghausen, C. Harald Merleker, Hartmuth. Christie, Donald M. Germany. Geneva: Nagel, 3D Ed., 1968, 863 P.

33. Hasenclever, Walter, Editor. Perspective of Germany. New York: Intercultural Publications, With the Atlantic Monthly, 1957, 94 P.

34. Hess, Peter. Notes on a Journey Through East Germany. Swiss Review of World Affairs. 20:9 (December 1970), 4-6.

35 Homze, Alma. Homze, Edward. Germany: The Divided Nation. Camden: Nelson, 1970, 223 P.

36 Leipold, L. Edmond. Come Along to East Germany. Minneapolis: Denison, 1969, 146 P.

37 A Little Journey Through the GDR. Dresden: Zeit Im Bild, 1965, 83 P.

38 Mikes, George. Ueber Alles: Germany Explored. London: Wingate, 1953, 148 P.

39 Ogrizek, Dore. Germany. New York: McGraw-Hill, 1956, 414 P.

40 Pilkington, Roger. Small Boat to the Skagerrak. New York: St. Martin's, 1960, 232 P.

41 Prittie, Terence C. F. Germany. New York: Time-Life Books, 1968, 176 P.

42 Putnam, John J. East Germany: The Struggle to Succeed. National Geographic Magazine. 146:3 (September 1974), 295-329.

43 Sankaran, S. A Peep Into a People's State: A Little Journey Through the Madras: Mallikai Pathippakam, 1969, 110 P.

44 Searle, Ronald. Huber, Heinz. Haven'T We Met Before Somewhere? Germany From the Inside and Out. New York: Viking, 1966, 190 P.

45 Seger, Gerhart H. Come Along to Germany. Minneapolis: Dennison, 1966, 146 P.

46 Seger, Gerhart H. Germany. Grand Rapids: Fideler, 1972, Xii and 158 P.

47 Stars and Stripes. Cities of Germany. Darmstadt: Stars and Stripes, Rev. Ed., 1972, 152 P.

48 Thonger, Richard. A Calendar of German Customs. London: Wolff, 1966, 126 P.

49 Wohlrabe, Raymond A. Krusch, Werner. The Land and the People of Germany. Philadelphia: Lippincott, 1957, 118 P.

A.3. Handbooks

A.3.1. General

50 Radcliffe, Stanley. Twenty-Five Years on: The Two Germanies. London: Harrap, 1972, 254 P.

A.3.2. FRG

51 Arntz, Helmut. Facts About Germany. Bonn: Press and Information Office, 5Th Ed., 1964, 381 P.

52 Arntz, Helmut. Germany at a Glance. Bonn: Press and Information Office, 11Th Ed., 1969, 47 P.

53 Arntz, Helmut. Germany in a Nutshell. Wiesbaden: Press and Information Office, 7Th Ed., 1967, 144 P.

54 Arntz, Helmut. Germany in Brief. Bonn: Press and Information Office, 4Th Ed., 1968, 140 P.

55 Arntz, Helmut, Editor. Germany Reports. Wiesbaden: Franz Steiner, for the Press and Information Office of the Federal Government, 4Th Ed., 1966.

56 Atlantic Bridge. Meet Germany. Hamburg: Atlantik-Bruecke, 13Th Ed., 1969, 138 P.

57 American University, Foreign Areas Study Division. U.S. Army Area Handbook for Germany. Washington: Department of the Army, Headquarters, 2D Ed., 1964, 955 P.

58 Calmann, John, Editor. Western Europe: A Handbook. New York: Praeger, 1967, 679 P., Esp. Pp. 61-77.

59 FRG, German Diplomatic Mission. Handbook of German Affairs. Washington: German Diplomatic Mission, Press Office, 1954, 174 P.

60 FRG, Press and Information Office The Federal Republic of Germany at a Glance. Bonn: Press and Information Office, 1970, 56 P.

61 FRG, Press and Information Office The German Federal Government. Hamburg: Nordpress, for the Press and Information Office, 1970, 93 P. Biographical Sketches of Cabinet Members and State Secretaries in the Brandt Government.

62 Merkatz, Hans Joachim Von. Metzner, Wolfgang. Germany Today: Facts and Figures. Frankfurt: Metzner, 1954, 413 P.

63 Royce, Hans. Germany at a Glance. Cologne: German American Trade Promotion Co., 1952, 32 P.

A.3.3. GDR

64 Arndt, Herbert, and Others. Introducing the German Democratic Republic. Dresden: Zeit Im Bild, 2D Rev. Ed., 1971, 255 P.

65 FRG, Federal Ministry for All-German Affairs. The Soviet Zone of Occupation: The Facts. Bonn: Federal Ministry for All-German Affairs, 1960, 31 P.

66 Friedrich, Carl J., Editor. The Soviet Zone of Germany. New Haven: Human Relations Area Files, Hraf-34, Harvard-1 Subcontractor's Monograph, 1956, 646 P.

67 GDR. German Democratic Republic Outline. Dresden: Zeit Im Bild, 1967, 60 P.

68 Goettingen Research Committee. Eastern Germany: A Handbook. Wuerzburg: Holzner, 1960-63, 3 Vols., 856 P. Vol. 1, Law; Vol. 2, History; Vol. 3, Economy.

69 Keefe, Eugene K. Area Handbook for East Germany. Washington: Government Printing Office, 1972, 329 P.

70 Meet the GDR. Dresden: Zeit Im Bild, 1966, 91 P.

71 Rosenkrantz, Heinz. The Truth About Life in the German Democratic Republic. Berlin (East): Society for Cultural Relations With Foreign Countries of the GDR, 1955, 40 P.

72 Sharp, Elke, Editor. Meyer, Ingeborg, Editor. Freyar, Helmut, Editor. GDR: 300 Questions, 300 Answers. Dresden: Zeit Im Bild, 1968, 317 P. Earlier Editions Published By Committee for German Unity.

73 Society for Cultural Relations With Foreign Countries. Facts About the German Democratic Republic--Pocket Guide. Leipzig: Veb, 1961, 96 P.

74 Society for Cultural Relations With Foreign Countries. German Democratic Republic: Political and Social Activities. Berlin (East): Gesellschaft Fuer Kulturelle Verbindungen Mit Dem Ausland, 1957, 48 P.

75 US, Department of State. Moscow's European Satellites: A Handbook. Washington: Department of State Publication 5914, Government Printing Office, 1955, 52 P.

A.4. History (See Also D.3.5; N.7.4)

76 Milatz, Alfred, Editor. Vogelsang, Thilo, Editor. Hochschulschriften Zur

Neueren Deutschen Geschichte: Eine Bibliographie. Bonn: Kommission Fuer Geschichte Des Parlamentarismus Und Der Politischen Parteien, and Institut Fuer Zeitgeschichte, 1956, 142 P. Lists 1925 Completed Theses and 400 in Progress, 1945-55.

77   Price, Arnold H. German History: A Review of Some Recent Publications. Quarterly Journal of the Library of Congress. 23:2 (April 1966), 138-146.

78   Childs, David. Germany Since 1918. New York: Harper and Row, 1971, 208p.

79   Crawley, Aidan. The Spoils of War: The Rise of Western Germany Since 1945. Indianapolis: Bobs-Merrill, 1973, 315 P.

80   Dill, Marshall. Germany: A Modern History. Ann Arbor: University of Michigan Press, 1970, 490 P.

81   Dunlop, Sir John Kinninmont. A Short History of Germany. London: Wolff, 4Th Ed., 1968, 182 P.

82   Ebenstein, William. The German Record: A Political Portrait. New York and Toronto: Farrar & Rinehart, 1945, 334 P.

83   Ernst, Fritz. The Germans and Their Modern History. New York: Columbia University Press, 1966, 164 P.

84   Falk, Minna Regina. History of Germany: From the Reformation to the Present Day. New York: Philosophical Library, 1957, 438 P.

85   Fitzgibbon, Constantine. A Concise History of Germany. New York: Viking, 1973, 192 P.

86   Flenley, Ralph. Modern German History. New York: Dutton, 1968, 4Th Ed., 503 P.

87   Gredel, Zdenka J. M. The Problem of Continuity in German History as Seen By West German Historians Between 1945 and 1953. Ph.D. Thesis, State University of New York at Buffalo, 1969, 229 P.

88   Grosser, Alfred. Germany in Our Time: A Political History of the Postwar Years. New York: Praeger, 1971, 378 P.

89   Hawgood, John Arkas. The Evolution of Germany. London: Methuen, 1955, 206 P.

90   Herzfeld, Hans. Germany: After the Catastrophe. Journal of Contemporary History. 2:1 (1967), 79-91.

91   Iggers, Georg C. The German Conception of History: The National Tradition of Historical Thought From Herder to the Present. Middletown: Wesleyan University Press, 1968, 363 P.

92   Jaksch, Wenzel. Europe's Road to Potsdam. New York: Praeger, 1963, 498 P., Esp. Pp. 391-439.

93   Koehl, Robert. Zeitgeschichte and the New German Conservatism. Journal of Central European Affairs. 20:2 (July 1960), 131-157.

94   Kohn, Hans. German History: Some New German Views. Boston: Beacon, 1954, 224 P.

95   Kohn, Hans. Re-Thinking Recent German History. Review of Politics. 14:3 (July 1952), 325-345.

96   Kosok, Paul. Modern Germany: A Study of Conflicting Loyalties. New York: Russell and Russell, 1969, 348 P. Social Conditions.

97   Loewenstein, Prince Hubertus Zu. A Basic History of Germany. Bonn: Inter Nationes, 1965, 192p.

98   Mann, Golo. The History of Germany Since 1789. New York: Praeger, 1968, 547 P.

99   Maurois, Andre. An Illustrated History of Germany. London: Bodley Head, 1966, 296 P.

100 Meyer, Henry Cord. Five Images of Germany: Half a Century of American Views on German History. Washington: Service Center for Teachers on History, 2D Ed., 1966, 57 P.

101 Morgan, Roger P. Germany 1870-1970: A Hundred Years of Turmoil. London: Macdonald, 1970, 127 P. Based on Bbc's Tv Series "Germany 1870-1970".

102 Moses, John A. The Crisis in West German Historiography: Origins and Trends. Historical Studies. 13:52 (April 1969), 445-459.

103 Pinnow, Hermann. History of Germany: People and State Through a Thousand Years. Freeport, N.Y.: Books for Libraries, 1970, 473 P.

104 Pinson, Koppel S. Modern Germany: Its History and Civilization. New York: Macmillan, 2D Ed., 1966, 682 P.

105 Pois, Robert A. Friedrich Meinecke and German Politics in the Twentieth Century. Ph.D. Thesis, University of Wisconsin, 1965, 187 P.

106 Rodes, John E. Germany, a History. New York: Holt, Rinehart and Winston, 1964, 703 P.

107 Rodes, John E. The Quest for Unity: Modern Germany, 1848-1970. New York: Holt, Rinehart and Winston, 1971, 432 P., Esp. Pp. 306-397.

108 Russell, Francis. The Horizon Concise History of Germany. New York: American Heritage Publishing Company, 1973, 217 P.

109 Ryder, A. J. Twentieth-Century Germany: From Bismarck to Brandt. New York: Columbia University Press, 1973, Xviii and 656 P.

110 Schalk, Adolph. The Germans. Englewood Cliffs: Prentice-Hall, 1971, 521 P.

111 Simon, Walter M. Germany: a Brief History. New York: Random House, 1966, 366 P.

112 Snell, John L. Recent German History in German Universities, 1945-1953; Research Report. Journal of Central European Affairs. 14:2 (June 1954), 174-180.

113 Snyder, Louis L. Basic History of Modern Germany. Princeton: Van Nostrand, 1957, 192 P.

114 Snyder, Louis L. Documents of German History. New Brunswick: Rutgers University Press, 1958, 619 P., Esp. Pp. 493-580.

115 Taylor, A. J. P. The Course of German History: A Survey of the Development of Germany Since 1815. New York: Capricorn Books, 1946, 1962, 231 P.

116 Tenbrock, Robert-Hermann. A History of Germany. Munich: Hueber; and Paderborn: Schoeningh, 1968, 335 P.

117 Treue, Wolfgang. Germany Since 1848: History of the Present Times. Bonn-Bad Godesberg: Inter Nationes, 1969, 122 P.

118 Vermeil, Edmond. The German Scene, Social, Political, and Cultural, 1890 to The Present Day. London: Harrap, 1956, 288 P.

119 Wucher, Albert. Contemporary German Historiography. Orbis. 10:4 (Winter 1967), 1298-1309.

B. Geography

B.1. General: FRG and GDR

120 Dickinson, Robert E. Germany: A General and Regional Geography. New York: Dutton, 2D Ed., 1964, 716 P.

121 Dickinson, Robert E. Germany's Frontiers. World Affairs (London). 1:3 (July 1947), 262-277.

122 Dickinson, Robert E. The Regions of Germany. London: Kegan Paul, 1945, 175 P.

123 Gutkind, Erwin A. Urban Development in Central Europe. International History of City Development. Vol. 1. London: Free Press of Glencoe, 1964, 491 P.

124 Pounds, Norman J. G. The Economic Pattern of Modern Germany. London: John Murray, 2D Ed., 1966, 133 P.

125 Pounds, Norman J. G., Editor. Europe, with Focus on Germany. Grand Rapids: Fideler, 1965, 340 P.

126 Samuel, Richard H. Hajdu, J. G. The German Speaking Countries of Central Europe. Sydney: Angus and Robertson, 1969, 31 P.

127 Sinnhuber, Karl A. Germany: Its Geography and Growth. London: Murray, 2Nd Ed., 1970, 128 P.

128 Streumann, Charlotte, Editor. Economic Regionalization. Bad Godesberg: Bundesforschungsanstalt Fuer Landeskunde Und Raumordnung, 1968, 380 P. Bibliography of German-Language Publications.

B.2. FRG

B.2.1. Locational Studies

129 Alexander, Lewis M. Recent Changes in the Benelux-German Boundary. Geographical Review. 43:1 (January 1953), 69-76. History of Present Boundary, Postwar Adjustments, Future.

130 Barnum, H. Gardiner. Market Centers and Hinterland in Baden-Wuerttemberg. Chicago: University of Chicago, 1966, 173 P.

131 Buckholts, Paul Omar. A Political Geography of the Federal Republic of Germany. Ph.D. Thesis, Harvard University, 1957.

132 Clare, G. P. Bonn: Federal Capital. Contemporary Review. 182:1044 (December 1952), 344-348.

133 Cologne the Western Commercial Metropolis. Cologne: Industrie- Und Handelskammer, 1950, 256 P.

134 Deml, Ferdinand. Baden-Wuerttemberg--Dialectics and Dynamics. Central Europe Journal. 22:1-2 (January-February 1974), 1-32.

135 Deml, Ferdinand. Rhineland-Palatinate--Heartland of Europe. Central Europe Journal. 22:4 (May-June 1974), 97-102.

136 Dickinson, Robert E. Braunschweig Industrial Area. Economic Geography. 34:3 (July 1958), 249-263.

137 Dickinson, Robert E. City and Region: A Geographical Interpretation. London: Routledge, 1964, 588 P.

138 Fischer, Helmut. Munich--Ten Years After the War: Glimpses of the Reconstruction of a City Known the World Over. Munich: Department of Reconstruction, 1955, 54 and 34 P. A Report on Building Activities in 1954.

139 Gilbert, Edmund W. The University Town in England and West Germany: Marburg, Goettingen, Heidelberg, and Tuebingen, Viewed Comparatively With Oxford and Cambridge. Chicago: University of Chicago, Department of Geography, Research Paper No. 71, 1961, 74 P.

140 Goppel, Alfons. Bavaria--A Liberal, Constitutional State. Central Europe Journal. 22:3 (March-April 1974), 49-52.

141 Hahn, C. H. The Economic and Geographical Aspects of the Location of the Volkswagenwerk at Wolfsburg. Cahiers De Bruges. 8:2 (1958), 59-64.

142 Hall, Peter. The World Cities. New York: Mcgraw-Hill, 1966, 256 P., Esp. Pp. 122-157. Regional Treatment of Rhine/Ruhr Area.

143 Harris, Alan. Matzat, Wilhelm. The Aachen Coal Field. Economic Geography. 35:2 (April 1959), 164-171.

144 Hurter, Edwin. Borderland Bavaria. Swiss Review of World Affairs. 3:5 (August 1953), 16-18. Special Problems of Area Cut Off From Natural Hinterland Through Partition of Germany.

145 Isbary, Gerhard. Central Places and Local Service Areas; on Quantifying the Central Places in the Federal Republic of Germany. Bad Godesberg: Bundesforschungsanstalt Fuer Landeskunde Und Raumordnung, 1967, 141 P.

146 Joesten, Joachim. This Is Hamburg in 1960: A Close-Up. Great Barrington, Mass.: Joachim Joesten, New Germany Reports No. 45, January 1960, 14 P.

147 Klugmann, Werner. Facts and Figures About the Port of Hamburg. Hamburg: Okis Sattelmaier, 1966, 155 P.

148 Langley, Robert S. The Industrial Region of Stuttgart, Germany. Ph.D. Thesis, Northwestern University, 1961, 491 P.

149 Meynen, E. Official and Private Cartography in Germany. Geographical Journal. 126:3 (September 1960), 369-370.

150 Moenkemeier, Karl-Ludwig. Hamburg--An Up-to-Date Port. Intereconomics. No. 6 (June 1970), 196-198.

151 Pounds, Norman J. G. Lorraine and the Ruhr. Economic Geography. 33:2 (April 1957), 149-162.

152 West Germany. Focus. 16:3 (November 1965), 1-6.

153 Robinson, G. W. S. Exclaves. Annals of the Association of American Geographers. 49:3 (September 1959), 283-295.

154 Rugg, Dean S. Alexandria, Virginia and Bad Godesberg, West Germany: A Comparative Study in Urban Geography. Ph.D. Thesis, University of Maryland, 1962, 282 P.

155 Savory, Douglas L. Heligoland Past and Present. Contemporary Review. 191:1097 (May 1957), 273-278.

156 Schmidt, Helmut. Hamburg and the Other North Sea Ports. Hamburg: Holler, 1951, 11 P.

157 Schulz, Peter. A Viability Concept: Isolated West-Berlin as a Case Study. Ph.D. Thesis, University of Illinois at Urbana-Champaign, 1971, 160 P.

158 Shaffer, Ralph G. A Geographic Study of Tourism on the Coasts of Schleswig-Holstein, Germany. Ph.D. Thesis, Syracuse University, 1958, 207 P.

159 Spilker, Hans. Prospects of the North German Coast. Intereconomics. No. 12 (December 1970), 389-392.

160 Stoltenberg, Gerhard. Schleswig-

Holstein--Historical Land With European Future. Central Europe Journal. 22:5 (July-August 1974), 141-144.

161 Thoman, Richard S. Recent Methodological Contributions to German Economic Geography. Annals of the Association of American Geographers. 48:1 (March 1958), 92-96.

162 Treuner, Peter. The Spatial Distribution of New Establishments: Sectoral aspects. German Economic Review. 12:1 (1974), 83-92.

163 Tussler, Anthony J. B. Alden, A. J. L. A Map Book of West Germany. London: Macmillan, 1972, 72 P.

164 US, Department of State, Office of the Geographer. Belgium-Germany Boundary. Washington: Department of State, Office of the Geographer, International Boundary Study No. 7, Government Printing Office, 1961, 5 P.

165 US, Department of State, Office of the Geographer. Denmark-Germany Boundary. Washington: Department of State, Office of the Geographer, International Boundary Study No. 81, Government Printing Office, 1968, 8 P.

166 US, Department of State, Office of the Geographer. Germany-Netherlands Boundary. Washington: Department of State, Office of the Geographer, International Boundary Study No. 31, Government Printing Office, 1964, 11 P.

167 US, Office of Geography. Germany--Federal Republic and West Berlin: Official Standard Names Approved By the U.S. Board on Geographic Names. Washington: Board on Geographic Names, Gazetteer No. 47, Government Printing Office, 1960, 2 Vols.

168 Urbscheit, Peter W. The Dutch-German Borderland Geography and Interaction: A Case Study Within the Framework of West-European Integration. Ph.D. Thesis, University of Waterloo, 1973.

169 Weigend, Guido G. The Problem of Hinterland and Foreland as Illustrated By the Port of Hamburg. Economic Geography. 32:1 (January 1956), 1-16.

170 Wolf, Simon. Hamburg Today. Contemporary Review. 197 (May 1960), 271-274.

B.2.2. Regional and Urban Planning

171 Biehl, Dieter. Hussmann, Eibe. Schnyder, Sebastian. Determinants of Regional Development Potential. 13:2 (1975), 117-134.

172 Bielfeldt, Claus. Rural Development in the Wiedau-Bongsiel Region of the "Program Nord" Area. Paris: Oecd, 1966, 113 P.

173 FRG. First Government Report on Regional Planning in the Federal Republic of Germany. Bonn?: N.P., 1965, 16 P.

174 FRG, Bundestag. Federal Law Concerning Regional Planning (Raumordnungsgesetz) of 8 April 1965. Bonn: Bundestag, 1965, 13 P.

175 FRG, Federal Ministry of the Interior. Regional Planning in the Federal Republic of Germany. Bonn: Bundesministerium Des Innern, Referat Oeffentlichkeitsarbeit, 1968, 39 P.

176 Fair, Thomas J. D. Report on Regional Planning in Britain, the Netherlands, and Germany. Commerce and Industry. 14:9 (May 1956), 596-622.

177 Continuity in the Rebuilding of Bombed Cities in Western Europe. American Journal of Sociology. 61:5 (March 1956), 463-469.

178 Greene, Ernest Thomas. Politics and Geography in Postwar German City Planning. Ph.D. Thesis, Princeton University, 1958, 367 P. A Field Study of Four German Cities: Hannover, Cologne, Kiel, and Trier.

179 Greene, Ernest Thomas. Politics and Planning for Reconstruction in Western Germany. Urban Studies. 1:1 (May 1964), 71-78.

180 Greene, Ernest Thomas. West German City Reconstruction: Two Case Studies. Sociological Review. 7:2 (December 1959), 231-244.

181 Grotewold, Andreas. Sublett, Michael. The Effect of Import Restrictions on Land Use: The United Kingdom Compared With West Germany. Economic Geography. 43:1 (January 1967), 64-70.

182 Hemdahl, Reuel G. Cologne and Stockholm: Urban Planning and Land-Use Controls. Metuchen, N.J.: Scarecrow, 1971, 334 P.

183 Mueller, Eberhard. Social System of Building-Land Law. German Economic Review. 13:1 (1975), 83-88.

184 Munich, Reconstruction Department. Munich After World War II: An Official Report. Munich: Reconstruction Department, 1948, 30 P.

185 Rose, Richard, Editor. The Management of Urban Change in Britain and Germany. Beverly Hills, Calif.: Sage, 1974, 270 P.

186 Rugg, Dean S. Selected Areal Effects of Planning Processes Upon Urban Development in the Federal Republic of Germany. Economic Geography. 42:4 (October 1966), 326-335.

187 Wesserle, Andreas Roland. The City and the State: Urban and Regional Planning and Administration in West Germany. Ph.D. Thesis, Southern Illinois University, 1972, 418 P.

188 Wierling, L. Functions and Competences of the Ruhr Planning Association. Studies in Comparative Local Government. 3:1 (Summer 1969), 47-52.

B.3. GDR

189 Wallace, J. Allen. An Annotated Bibliography on the Climate of East Germany. Washington: U.S. Weather Bureau, 1963, 50 P.

190 Pounds, Norman J. G. Eastern Europe. London: Longmans, 1969, 912 P.

191 US, Office of Geography. Germany--Soviet Zone and East Berlin: Official Standard Names Approved By the United States Board on Geographic Names. Washington: Board of Geographic Names, Gazetteer No. 43, Government Printing Office, 1959, 487 P.

192 Villmow, Jack R. A Regional Analysis of East German Industrialization in the 1950's. Canadian Slavic Studies. 1:3 (Autumn 1967), 424-460.

C. Demography

C.1. Characteristics and Statistics

C.1.1. General

193 Beveridge, William H., Lord. The War Hitler Won--The War of Numbers. New York Times Magazine. (18 August 1946), 11+. Population Growth Relative to Other Countries.

194 Kokot, Jozef. The Demography of Germany and Poland. Poland and Germany. 4:13 (July 1960), 21-35.

195 Kostanick, Huey Louis. The German Plea for Lebensraum. Current History. 28:164 (April 1955), 193-199.

196 Peck, Reginald. The West Germans: How They Live and Work. New York: Praeger, 1970, 183 P.

197 Sauermann, Heinz. Demographic Changes in Postwar Germany. Annals of the American Academy of Political and Social Science. 260 (November 1948), 99-107.

198 US, Office of Strategic Services, Research & Analysis Bran. The Projected Population of Germany, 1945 to 1975. Washington: Office of Strategic Services, Research and Analysis Branch, R & a No. 2359, 1945, 21 P.

199 US, Omgus, Civil Administration Division. The Population of Germany. N.P.: Omgus, Civil Administration Division, March 1947, 10 P.

C.1.2. FRG

200 Allied High Commission, Central Statistical Office. Statistical Developments in Germany, December, 1953. Washington: Department of State, Public Services Division, Liaison Officer for German Affairs, 1954, 21 and 5 P.

201 FRG, Federal Statistical Office. Census Program 1961. Stuttgart: Kohlhammer, 1961, 42 P.

202 FRG, Federal Statistical Office. Considerations on the Census Programme, 1960. Stuttgart: Kohlhammer, Studies on Statistics No. 4, 1957, 26 P.

203 FRG, Federal Statistical Office. Federal Statistics: The Activities of the Federal Statistical Office and the Statistics Processed By the Supreme Federal Authorities. Stuttgart: Kohlhammer, 1954, 88 P.

204 FRG, Federal Statistical Office. Fertility, Mortality, Age Structure, and Population Development. Stuttgart: Kohlhammer, 1969, 23 P.

205 FRG, Federal Statistical Office. The German Microcensus. Stuttgart: Kohlhammer, 1969, 90 P.

206 FRG, Federal Statistical Office. German Sample Surveys. Stuttgart: Kohlhammer, 1959, 19 P.

207 FRG, Federal Statistical Office. Handbook of Statistics for the Federal Republic of Germany. Stuttgart: Kohlhammer, Triennial, 1961+.

208 FRG, Federal Statistical Office. Housing Sample Surveys 1957 and 1960. Stuttgart: Kohlhammer, 1961, 32 P.

209 FRG, Federal Statistical Office. Life Tables, 1960/62. Stuttgart: Kohlhammer, 1966, 32 P.

210 FRG, Federal Statistical Office. Number and Structure of Households and Families: Results of a Special Compilation Within the Framework of the Micro-Census, October, 1957. Stuttgart: Kohlhammer, 1960, 14 P.

211 FRG, Federal Statistical Office. Outlines of the Population and Occupation Census, 1961. Stuttgart: Kohlhammer, Studies on Statistics No. 17, 1965, 62 P.

212 FRG, Federal Statistical Office. Planning the 1970 Population Census. Stuttgart: Kohlhammer, Studies on Statistics No. 21, 1968, 42 P.

213 FRG, Federal Statistical Office. Population and Occupation Census, 1961. Stuttgart: Kohlhammer, 1965, 62 P.

214 FRG, Federal Statistical Office. Sample Surveys in German Federal Statistics. Stuttgart: Kohlhammer, 1961.

215 FRG, Federal Statistical Office. Survey of German Federal Statistics, 1958. Stuttgart: Kohlhammer, 1959, 127 P. Published Also in Subsequesnt Years With Same Title.

216 Kirk, Dudley. Economic and Demographic Developments in Western Germany. Population Index. 24:1 (January 1958), 3-21.

217 Myers, Paul F. Mauldin, W. Parker. Population of the Federal Republic of Germany and West Berlin. Washington: Government Printing Office, 1952, 95 P.

218 Powell, Nicolas. Western Germany: The Human Scene. Geographical Magazine. 27:5 (September 1954), 211-221.

219 Schwarz, Karl. Influence of Changes in Fertility and Mortality on the Development and Age Structure of the Population. Stuttgart: Kohlhammer, 1969, 23 P.

220 UK, CCG, Internal Affairs & Communication Division. Population and Occupational Census of the British Zone of N.P.: Control Commission for Germany (Be), Internal Affairs and Communication Division, 1946.

221 US, Omgus, Civil Administration Division. Population Changes, 1947, U.S. Zone of Germany. N.P.: Omgus, Adjutant General, 1948, 52 P.

222 US, Omgus, Civil Administration Division. Population of the U.S. Zone of Germany. N.P.: Omgus, Civil Administration Division, November 1947, 2 Vols.

C.1.3. GDR

223 GDR, State Central Administration for Statistics. East German Statistical Yearbook, 1955. Berlin?: State Central Administration for Statistics, C.1956, 585 P.

224 GDR, State Central Administration for Statistics. Statistical Pocket Book of the German Democratic Republic. Berlin: Veb Deutscher Zentralverlag, 1959+.

225 GDR, State Central Administration for Statistics. Translation and Glossary of 1957 Statistical Yearbook of the German Democratic Republic. New York: U.S. Joint Publications Research Service, 766-D, 1959, 733 P. Also 1958 Yearbook, Jprs 1155-D, 1960, 584 P.

226 K. G. Demographic Decline in East Germany. Poland and Germany. 2:6 (September 1958), 39-41.

227 Stolper, Wolfgang F. Population Movements and Labor Force in the Sbz. Cambridge: Massachusetts Institute of Technology, Center For International Studies, 1956, 73 P.

C.2. National Character Assessments (See Also F.1.1)

228 Adler, Hans. Berlin Apartment House: Clinical Notes on the Average German Mind. 1:7 (May 1946), 54-56.

229 Albertson, Ralph. You Believe in War / (to the Germans). World Affairs. 108:1 (March 1945), 17-18.

230 Anderson, H. Foster. Reflections on the German Character. Fortnightly, 172:1027 (July 1952), 9-15.

231 Ansbacher, Heinz L. Lasting and Passing Aspects of German Military Psychology. Sociometry. 12:4 (November 1949), 301-312.

232 Bailey, George. Germans: The Biography of an Obsession. New York: World, 1972, 409 P.

233 Bloch, Enid Greenberg. The Inverse Cultures: Politics Versus Philiosophy in America and Germany. Ph.D. Thesis, Cornell University, 1973, 223 P.

234 Bluecher Von Wahlstatt, Kurt. Know Your Germans. London: Chapman & Hall, 1951, 188 P.

235 Borgese, Giuseppe Antonio. Considerations on Germany. Common Cause. 1:10 (May 1948), 374-381. Musings About Character and Politics.

236 Bossenbrook, William J. The German Mind. Detroit: Wayne State University Press, 1961, 469 P.

237 Bossenbrook, William J. German Nationalism and Fragmentation. Mid-Twentieth Century Nationalism. Ed. William J. Bossenbrook.

238 Brett-Smith, Richard N. B. Contemporary German Nationalism. Cambridge Journal. 3:7 (April 1950), 417-431.

239 Brickner, Richard M. Is Germany Incurable?. Philadelphia and New York: Lippincott, 1943, 318 P.

240 Daniell, Raymond. The Real German Problem Is the People. New York Times Magazine. (16 March 1947), 11+.

241 Dicks, Henry V. Personality Traits and National Socialist Ideology: A War-Time Study of German Prisoners of War. Human Relations. 3:2 (May 1950), 111-154.

242 Dicks, Henry V. Some Psychological Studies of the German Character. Psychological Factors of Peace and War. Ed. T. H. Pear. New York: Philosophical Library, 1950, Pp. 193-218.

243 Enzensberger, Hans Magnus. Am I German?. Encounter. 22:4 (April 1964), 16-18. Question of Nationalism.

244 Glaser, Kurt. The So-Called German Mind. Antioch Review. 9:2 (June 1949), 146-162.

245 Gooch, George P., Editor. The German Mind and Outlook. London: Chapman & Hall, 1945, 225 P.

246 Gordon-Finlayson, R. The German Plague. Royal United Service Institution Journal. 90:560 (November 1945), 463-468.

247 Griffiths, Eldon W. Retrospect on Germany. Yale Review. 39:1 (September 1949), 96-107. An English View of Nationalism in Contemporary Germany.

248 Grossmann, Kurt R. "So You Too Are a German-Baiter?". New Europe. 5:1 (January 1945), 27-28.

249 Gruson, Sydney. Lewis, Flora. Have the Germans Learned?. New York Times Magazine. (29 January 1961), 8+.

250 Hauser, Heinrich. The German Talks Back. New York: Holt, 1945, 215 P.

251 Heuss, Theodor. German Character and History. Atlantic. 199:3 (March 1957), 103-109.

252 Jones, Alan G. The Germans: An Englishman's Notebook. London: Pond, 1968, 247 P.

253 Kohn, Hans. The Mind of Germany: The Education of a Nation. New York: Scribner's, 1960, 370 P.

254 Kohn, Hans. Nationalism. Current History. 30:176 (April 1956), 213-216.

255 Kohn, Hans. The Problem of German Nationalism. Contemporary Review. 189:1085 (May 1956), 261-266.

256 Krieger, Leonard. The German Idea of Freedom: History of a Political Tradition. Boston: Beacon, 1957, 540 P.

257 Lewis, Flora. Hans Schmidt Lives to Work. New York Times Magazine. (24 May 1959), 15+. FRG's Work Ethic.

258 Lougee, Robert W. German Romanticism and Political Thought. Review of Politics. 21:4 (October 1959), 631-645.

259 Lowenthal, Richard. The Germans Feel Like Germans Again. New York Times Magazine. (6 March 1966), 36+.

260 Lowie, Robert H. Toward Understanding Germany. Chicago: University of Chicago Press, 1954, 396 P.

261 Mann, Thomas. Germany and the Germans. Washington: Library of Congress, 1945, 20 P.

262 Mann, Thomas. Germany and the Germans. Yale Review. 35:2 (December 1945), 223-241.

263 Mayer, Milton. They Thought They Were Free: The Germans, 1933-45. Chicago: University of Chicago Press, 1955, 346, Esp. Pp. 289-344.

264 Mccormick, John. Frozen Country. Kenyon Review. 22:1(Winter 1960), 32-59.

265 Middleton, Drew. Germans Today: Doleful and Angry. New York Times Magazine. (16 September 1945), 10+.

266 Middleton, Drew. Hans Schmidt: Portrait of a "Kleiner Mann". New York Times Magazine. (17 July 1949), 14+.

267 Middleton, Drew. Hopes--and Doubts--About the Germans. New York Times Magazine. (9 March 1952), 11+.

268 Middleton, Drew. Key to Peace or War--75,000,000 Germans. New York Times Magazine. (13 November 1949), 12+.

269 Money-Kyrle, Roger Ernle. Some Aspects of State and Character in Germany. Psychoanalysis and Culture. Eds. George B. Wilbur and Warner Muensterberger. New York: International Universities Press, 1951, Xii and 462 P.

270 Muggeridge, Malcolm. Then and Now: The Germans and the English. Encounter. 22:4 (April 1964), 20-22.

271 Owen, Francis. The Germanic People: Their Origin, Expansion, and Culture. New York: Bookman, 1960, 317 P.

272 Picton, Harold. The Ordinary German: A Gathering of Memories. London: St. Botolph, 1948, 104 P.

273 Prittie, Terence C. F. Passing of Work-Obsessed Germany. New York Times Magazine. (21 April 1963), 41+.

274 Pross, Harry. Reflections on German Nationalism, 1866-1966. Orbis. 10:4 (Winter 1967), 1148-1156.

275 Rippley, Lavern J. of German Ways. Minneapolis: Dillon, 1970, 301 P.

276 Rodnick, David. Postwar Germans: An Anthropologist's Account. New Haven: Yale University Press, 1948, 233 P.

277 Ross, Albion. Germany--Report on a Perplexing People. New York Times Magazine. (3 April 1955), 9+.

278 Rovan, Joseph. Germany. New York: Viking, 1959, 191 P.

279 Schaffner, Bertram. Father Land: A Study of Authoritarianism in the German Family. New York: Columbia University Press, 1948, 203 P.

280 Sebald, Hans. Studying National Character Through Comparative Content Analysis. Social Forces. 40:4 (May 1962), 318-322. German and American School Song Books Published in 1940.

281 Shays, Eugene. German Prisoners of War in the U.S.--Observations of a Soldier. Fourth International. 6:12 (December 1945), 366-371.

282 Sibert, Edwin L. The German Mind: Our Greatest Problem. New York Times Magazine. (17 February 1946), 7+. Two Elements--Reason and Fanaticism--and Re-Education.

283 Sigel, Roberta S. What Germans Think--and Why: The Authoritarian Pattern From the Cradle on. Commentary. 12:3 (September 1951), 278-284.

284 Snyder, Louis L. German Nationalism: The Tragedy of a People. Harrisburg: Stackpoole, 1952, 322 P.

285 Snyder, Louis L. Hans Kohn on Germany. Orbis. 10:4 (Winter 1967), 1327-1340.

286 Speier, Hans. The Future of German Nationalism. Social Research. 14:4 (December 1947), 421-445. Comment By Kurt Riezler, Pp. 445-454.

287 Spitzer, H. M. Keys to the German Character. World Affairs. 108:4 (December 1945), 261-263.

288 Stern, Fritz. The Fragmented People That Is Germany. Commentary. 19:2 (February 1955), 137-146.

289 Tempel, Gudrun. The Germans: An Indictment of My People; a Personal History and a Challenge. New York: Random House, 1963, 172 P.

290 Thompson, Carol L. The German Military Tradition. Current History. 28:164 (April 1955), 199-204.

291 Tureen, Louis L. Palmer, James O. Some Group Differences in Personal Values Between American Soldiers and German Prisoners of War. Journal of Social Psychology. 42:2 (November 1955), 305-313.

292 Verba, Sidney. Germany: The Remaking of Political Culture. Political Culture and Political Development. Ed. Lucian W. Pye and Sidney Verba. Princeton: Princeton University Press, 1965, Pp. 130-170.

293 Verrina (Pseud.). The German Mentality. London: Allen & Unwin, 2D Ed., 1946, 344 P.

294 Viereck, Peter. Metapolitics: The Roots of the Nazi Mind. New York: Capricorn Books, 1961, 364 P., Esp. Pp. I-XXVII

295 Waldeck, Rosie Goldschmidt. Meet Mr. Blank: The Leader of Tomorrow's Germans. New York: Putnam's, 1943, 179 P.

296 Webster, Donald H. The German Attitude as a Factor in Maintaining the Peace in Europe. Proceedings of the Institute of World Affairs. 21:2 (December 1945), 48-52.

C.3. Population Movements

C.3.1. Displaced Persons

297 Conover, Helen F., Editor. The Displaced Persons Analytical Bibliography. Washington: Library of Congress, European Affairs Division, 81St Congress, 2D Session, House Report No. 1687, 1950, 82 P.

298 Agar, Herbert. The Saving Remnant: An Account of Jewish Survival. New York: Viking, 1960, Xi and 269 P. on American Jewish Joint Distribution Committee.

299 American Ort Federation. Ort in the U.S. Zone, Germany. , November 1948, 47 P.

300 Ansbacher, Heinz L. The Problem of Interpreting Attitude Survey Data: A Case Study of the Attitude of Russian Workers in Wartime Germany. Public Opinion Quarterly. 14:1 (Spring 1950), 126-138.

301 Bentwich, Norman D. They Found Refuge: An Account of British Jewry's Work for Victims of Nazi Oppression. London: Cresset, 1956, 227 P.

302 Berger, Joseph A. Displaced Persons: A Human Tragedy of World War II. Social Research. 14:1 (March 1947), 45-58.

303 Boudin, Anna P. New Problems for Old. Ort Economic Review. 7:3 (March 1948), 20-25. Schooling for Dps.

304 Brand, Joel. Desperate Mission. New York: Criterion Books, 1958, 310 P.

305 Carey, Jane Perry Clark. The Role of Uprooted People in European Recovery. Washington: National Planning Association, Pamphlet No. 64, 85 P.

306 Chamberlain, Joseph P. The Fate of Refugees and Displaced Persons. Proceedings of the Academy of Political Science. 22:2 (January 1947), 192-202.

307 Cobb, Alice. War's Unconquered Children Speak. Boston: Beacon, 1953, 244 P.

308 Dawidowicz, Lucy S. The War Against the Jews, 1933-1945. New York: Holt, Rinehart & Winston, 1975, 460 P.

309 Dickson, Alec. Displaced Persons. National Review. 129:777 (November 1947), 382-392; and 129:778 (December 1947), 490-493.

310 Displaced-Persons Resettlement Program. Department of State Bulletin. 19:482 (26 September 1948), 411-412.

311 Drutmann, D. The Displaced Jews in the American Zone of Germany. Jewish Journal of Sociology. 3:2 (December 1961), 261-263.

312 Frenkiel, Leon. Ort in Germany. Ort Economic Review. 7:4 (June 1948), 42-52.

313 The Future of Displaced Persons in Europe. Department of State Bulletin. 17:419 (13 July 1947), 86-95.

314 Gringauz, Samuel. Ort Perspectives Among the Dp's. Ort Economic Review. 7:4 (June 1948), 16-41.

315 Gringauz, Samuel. Our New German Policy and the Dp's--Why Immediate Resettlement Is Imperative. Commentary. 5:6 (June 1948), 508-514.

316 Handlin, Oscar. A Continuing Task: The American Jewish Joint Distribution Committee, 1914-1964. New York: Random House, 1965, Vi and 118 P.

317 Hilldring, John H. Position on Resettlement of Displaced Persons. Department of State Bulletin. 16:415 (15 June 1947), 1162-1166.

318 Hoehn, Elfriede. Sociometric Studies on the Adjustment Process of Displaced Persons. International Social Science Bulletin. 7:1 (1955), 22-29.

319 Jewish Black Book Committee. The Black Book: The Nazi Crime Against the Jewish People. New York: Duell, Sloan and Pearce, 1946, 560 P.

320 Johnson, Alvin. Places for Displaced Persons. Yale Review. 36:3 (March 1947), 394-404.

321 Kaplan, Louis L. Schuchat, Theodor. Justice--Not Charity: A Biography of Harry Greenstein. New York: Crown, 1967, Xiii and 176 P. Greenstein Was Director, Welfare Division, Unrra.

322 Keller, Franklin J. The Miracle of Ort Among the Dp's. Ort Economic Review. 7:4 (June 1948), 3-15.

323 Klemme, Marvin. The Inside Story of Unrra: An Experience in Internationalism. New York: Lifetime, 1949, 307 P.

324 Lvovitch, David. Ort and the Rehabilitation of Jewish Life in Europe. Ort Economic Review. 5:3-4 (March-June 1946), 24-33. Interaction of Ort, Unrra, and Omgus.

325 Marks, Edward B., Jr. The "Hard Core" Dp's. Survey (Pennsylvania). 85:9 (September 1949), 481-486. Pending Liquidation of Iro.

326 Newman, Jean J. Ort and the Jewish Dp's in Germany. Ort Economic Review. 5:3-4 (March-June 1946),7-12.

327 Papanek, Ernst. They Are Not Expendable: The Homeless and Refugee Children in Germany. Social Services Review. 20:3 (September 1946), 312-319.

328 Proudfoot, Malcolm J. The Anglo-American Displaced Persons Program for Germany and Austria. American Journal of Economics and Sociology. 6:1 (October 1946), 35-54.

329 Role of American Voluntary Agencies in Germany and Austria. Washington: American Council on Education, 1951, 22 P.

330 Samuels, Gertrude. Children Who Have Known No Childhood. New York Times Magazine. (9 March 1947), 12+. Dp Children.

331 Samuels, Gertrude. Passport to Nowhere: A Dp Story. New York Times Magazine. (19 September 1948), 14+.

332 Shils, Edward A. Social and Psychological Aspects of Displacement and Repatriation. Journal of Social Issues. 2:3 (August 1946), 3-18.

333 Smith, Marcus J. The Harrowing of Hell: Dachau. Albuquerque: University of New Mexico Press, 1972, 291 P. US Army Doctor Describes Fight to Save 32,000 Survivors.

334 Srole, Leo. Why the Dp's Can'T Wait: Proposing an International Plan of Rescue. Commentary. 3:1 (January 1947), 13-24.

335 T. B. Relief Work With Displaced Persons in Germany. World Today. 1:3 (September 1945), 135-144.

336 US, Displaced Persons Commission. Memo to America: The Dp Story. Washington: Government Printing Office, 1952, 376 P.

337 US, Hicog. Displaced Populations: Welfare, Assistance and Problems in Germany Today. Frankfurt: Hicog, 1950, 45 P.

338 Vida, George. From Doom to Dawn: A Jewish Chaplain's Story of Displaced Persons. New York: David, 1967, 146 P.

339 Walinsky, Louis J. Current Ort Work in Germany and Austria. Ort Economic Review. 7:3 (March 1948), 26-49.

340 Walinsky, Louis J. Ort Work in Germany--1947. Ort Economic Review. 7:1 (September 1947), 7-14.

341 Wilson, Roger Cowan. Quaker Relief: An Account of the Relief Work of the Society of Friends. London: Allen & Unwin, 1952, 373 P.

C.3.2. Movements Across Boundaries

342 Agreement By the Allied Control Council in Berlin on the Transfer of the German Population, 20Th November, 1945. Poland and Germany. 5:4 (October-December 1961), 30-31.

343 App, Austin J. History's Most Terrifying Peace. San Antonio: Austin J. App, 1947, 109 P. Expellees and Refugees.

344 Barley, Delbert. Refugees in Germany: Relationships Between Refugees and the Indigenous Population of a Rural Black Forest Community. Ph.D. Thesis, University of Pennsylvania, 1957, 277 P. Barton, Betty. The Problem of 12 Million German Refugees in Today's Germany. Philadelphia: American Friends Service Committee, 1949, 39 P.

345 Bentwich, Norman D. The Rescue and Achievement of Refugee Scholars: The Story of Displaced Scholars and Scientists, 1933-1952. The Hague: Nijhoff, 1953, 107 P.

346 Bieri, Ernst. Expellees and Refugees in West Germany. Swiss Review of World Affairs. 3:4 (July 1953), 16-20.

347 Bouman, Pieter Jan. Beijer, G. Oudegeest, J. J. The Refugee Problem in Western Germany. The Hague: Nijhoff, 1950, 49 P.

348 Braun, Joachim Freiherr Von. Germany's Eastern Border and Mass Expulsions. American Journal of International Law. 58:3 (July 1964), 747-750. Von Braun Is Director of the Goettingen Research Institute: Response By Gelberg, 59:3 (July 1965), 590-593.

349 Brown, Macalister. Expulsion of German Minorities From Eastern Europe: The Decision at Potsdam and Its Background. Ph.D. Thesis, Harvard University, 1953.

350 Brozek, Andrsej. Former German Refugees in the Gfr--in the Light of the 1961 Census and the Statistical Year-Books of 1967 and 1968. Poland and Germany. 12:3-4 (July-December 1968), 18-34.

351 C. A. M. Heirs of Potsdam: The Tragedy of Expelled Germans. World Today. 4:10 (October 1948), 446-453.

352 Germany's New People. Survey. 85:3 (March 1949), 145-148. The Influx of Refugees.

353 Chablani, S. P. The Rehabilitation of Refugees in the Federal Republic of Germany. Weltwirtschaftliches Archiv. 79:2 (1957), 281-304.

354 Claude, Inis L., Jr. The International Treatment of the Problem of National Minorities. Ph.D. Thesis, Harvard University, 1949.

355 Claude, Inis L., Jr. National Minorities: An International Problem. Cambridge: Harvard University Press, 1955, 248 P.

356 Committee Against Mass Expulsions. Men Without the Rights of Man. New York: Committee Against Mass Expulsion, 1948, 32 P.

357 Edding, Friedrich. The Refugees as a Burden, a Stimulus, and a Challenge to the West German Economy. The Hague: Nijhoff, 1951, 53 P.

358 FRG, Federal Ministry for All-German Affairs. Every Fifth Person. Bonn: Federal Ministry for All-German Affairs, 1962, 32 P.

359 FRG, Federal Ministry for Expellees. American Public Opinion on the German Expellee Problem: 5 Reports, November 1950-January 1951. Bonn: Federal Ministry for Expellees, 1951.

360 FRG, Federal Ministry for Expellees. The German Expellee Problem. Bonn: Federal Ministry for Expellees, 1951, 44 P. Lecture Delivered at International Conference Called By Leagus of Red Cross Societies, Hanover, 9-14 April 1951.

361 After Ten Years: A European Problem--Still No Solution. Frankfurt: Wirtschaftsdienst, 1957, 64 P.

362 FRG, Federal Ministry for Expellees. Care and Help for Expellees, Refugees, Victims of Material War Damage, Evacuees, Prisoners of War and Civilian Prisoners, Repatriated Persons, Non-German Refugees. Bonn: Federal Ministry for Expellees, Refugees and War Victims, Rev. Ed., 1964, 86 P.

363 FRG, Federal Ministry for Expellees, Refugees & War Victim Escapes From the Soviet Zone: Their Causes and Course, Integration of Refugees. Bonn: Federal Ministry for Expellees, Refugees and War Victims, 6Th Ed., 1964, 20 P.

364 FRG, Federal Ministry for Expellees, Refugees & War Victim Flight From the Soviet Zone. Bonn: Federal Ministry for Expellees, Refugees and War Victims, 5Th Ed., C.1961, 10 P.

365 FRG, Federal Ministry for Expellees, Refugees & War Victim The Right to the Homeland, the Law of God: Three Sermons Preached to Men and Women Whose Homeland Had Been Taken From Them. Guenzburg: Jantsch, for Federal Ministry for Expellees, Refugees and War Victims, 1957, 21 P.

366 FRG, Federal Ministry for Expellees, Refugees & War Victim Some Facts About Expellees in Germany, 1949. Bonn: Federal Ministry for Expellees, 1951, 8 P. Published Annually Under Various Titles Through 1956.

367 FRG, Federal Ministry for Federal Aff., Expellees, Refugee Zone Limit Lower-Saxony. Hanover: Federal Ministry for Federal Affairs, Expellees and Refugees, 1966, 40 P.

368 FRG, Federal Ministry for the Marshall Plan. Germany's Expellee Problem. Bonn: Federal Ministry for the Marshall Plan, 1950, 151 P.

369 FRG, Federal Ministry of Finance. Refugee Burdens and Defence Contribution: Two Burdens That Complement and Limit One Another. Hameln: Niemeyer,1951, 22p.

370 FRG, Federal Statistical Office. Statistical Pocket-Book on Expellees in the Federal Republic of Germany and West Berlin. Wiesbaden: Federal Statistical Office, 1953, 115 E.

371 Frei, Otto. Migration Between the Two Germanies. Swiss Review of World Affairs. 10:9 (December 1960), 12-14.

372 Friedman, Samy. Expropriation in International Law. London: Stevens, 1953, 236 P.

373 Goettingen Research Committee. Documents of Humanity During the Mass Expulsions. Comp. K. O. Kurth. New York: Harper, 1954, 184 P.

374 Goettingen Research Committee. Emigration--A Means of Solving the German Problem?. Goettingen: Goettingen Research Committee, 1950, 10 P.

375 Goettingen Research Committee. European Achievements in the Homelands of the German Expellees. Kitzingen: Holzner, 1954, 24 P.

376 Harris, Chauncy D. Wuelker, Gabriele. The Refugee Problem of Germany. Economic Geography. 29:1 (January 1953), 10-25.

377 Held, Colbert C. Refugee Industries in West Germany After 1945. Economic Geography. 32:4 (October 1956), 316-335.

378 Holler, Joanne E. The German Expellees: A Problem of Integration. Washington: George Washington University, Population Research Project, 1963, 45p.

379 Hurley, Neil. Refugees Reach Berlin. Social Order. 9:5 (May 1959), 234-240.

380 Institute for the Study of Public Affairs. Europe and the German Refugees. Frankfurt: Institut Zur Foerderung Oeffentlicher Angelegenheiten, 1952, 94 P.

381 Jaenicke, Wolfgang A. Refugees: Bavaria, 1947. Annals of the American Academy of Political and Social Science. 260 (November 1948), 108-114.

382 Jaenicke, Wolfgang, Editor. From Scratch. Munich: N.P., 1952, 23 P. Picture Report on Bavarian Industries Built Up By Expellees.

383 Jenkis, Helmut W. Problems of the Refugees in Western Germany. Cahiers De Bruges. 4:3 (October 1954) 207-216.

384 Kee, Robert. Refugee World. London: Oxford University Press, 1961, 153 P., Esp. Pp. 5-100.

385 Kee, Robert. The Refugees. Encounter. 16:4 (April 1961), 26-36.

386 Kertesz, Stephen. The Expulsion of the Germans From Hungary: A Study in Post-War Diplomacy. Review of Politics. 15:2 (April 1953), 179-208.

387 Kokot, Jozef. The Economic Aspects of the Resettlement of German Population after the Second World War. Polish Western Affairs. 5:1 (1964), 92-119.

388 Kokot, Jozef. Re-Settlement and Integration in Post-War Germany. Poland and Germany. 7:1-2 (January-June 1963), 18-30.

389 Kulischer, Eugene M. Europe on the Move: War and Population Changes, 1917-1947. New York: Columbia University Press, 1948, 377 P.

390 Kulischer, Eugene M. Population Transfer. South Atlantic Quarterly. 45:4 (October 1946), 403-414.

391 Lane, Stephen K. The Integration of the German Expellees: A Case Study of Bavaria, 1945-1969. Ph.D. Thesis, Columbia University, 1972, 185 P.

392 Lattimore, Bertram Gresh. The Assimilation of German Expellees Into the West German Policy and Society Since 1945: A Case Study of Schleswig-Holstein. Ph.D. Thesis, Fletcher School of Law and Diplomacy, 1972.

393 Lattimore, Bertram Gresh. The Assimilation of German Expellees Into the West German Policy and Society Since 1945: A Case Study of Eutin, Schleswig-Holstein. The Hague: Martinus Nijhoff, 1974, Xiv and 158 P.

394 Leiser, Ernest. Germany's Stepchildren. This Is Germany. Ed. Arthur Settel. New York: Sloane, 1950, Pp. 195-209. on Refugees.

395 Lemmer, Ernst. German Refugees and Conditions in the Soviet Zone of Germany. Washington: German Embassy, Press Office, 1958, 19 P.

396 Lohr, George. Why They Return to East Germany. New World Review. 28:6 (June 1960), 14-17.

397 Lukaschek, Hans. The Expellees in the German Federal Republic and Their Importance to Europe. Bonn: Federal

Ministry for Expellees, 1950, 15 P.

398 Lukaschek, Hans. The German Expellees: A German Focal Problem. Bonn: Federal Ministry for Expellees, 2D Ed., 1952, 35 P.

399 Luza, Radomir. The Transfer of the Sudeten Germans: A Study of Czech-German Relations, 1933-1962. New York: New York University Press, 1964, 365 P.

400 Martin, Denis. March of Millions. This Is Germany. Ed. Arthur Settel. New York: Sloane, 1950, Pp. 210-225.

401 Marton, J. H. Sudeten Industries in the Western Zone. Contemporary Review. 175:998 (February 1949), 99-102.

402 Meissner, Alfred. The Transfer of Germans From Czechoslovakia. Fortnightly. 159:952 (April 1946), 250-253.

403 Melby, Everett K. The Refugees in Western Germany. Ph.D. Thesis, University of Chicago, 1954.

404 Mueller, Ernst F. Attitudes Toward Westbound Refugees in the East German Press. Journal of Conflict Resolution. 14:3 (September 1970), 311-333.

405 Neumann, Sigmund. The New Crisis Strata in German Society. Germany and the Future of Europe. Ed. Hans J. Morgenthau. Chicago: University of Chicago Press, 1951, Pp. 25-39.

406 Nieduszynski, T. The Resettlement of German Refugees. Poland and Germany. 1:2 (Summer 1957), 21-31.

407 Oberlaender, Theodor, Editor. The Expellees Are Working. Graefeling Near Munich: Verlag Fuer Planung Und Aufbau, 1951, 103 P. Picture Report of Expellees' Reconstruction Work in Bavaria.

408 Old Liberal. The Case of the Sudeten Germans. Contemporary Review. 168:956 (August 1945), 79-82.

409 Paikert, G. C. The German Exodus: A Selective Study on the Post-World War II Expulsion of German Populations and Its Effects. The Hague: Nijhoff, 1962, 97 P.

410 Palmer, Martha Ellen. The Institutional Impact of the Distribution of the Economic Activities of Expellees in Hessen, Federal Republic of Germany, From 1945 to 1958. Ph.D. Thesis, Michigan State University, 1967, 178 P.

411 Radspieler, Tony. The Ethnic German Refugee in Austria, 1945-1954. The Hague: Nijhoff, 1955, 197 P.

412 Raymond, Jack. Over the Green Border From East Germany. New York Times Magazine. (27 August 1950), 12+. Refugees.

413 Read, James M. Magna Carta for Refugees. New York: United Nations, Dept. of Public Information, 1953, 54 P.

414 Reimann, Horst. The Refugee and His Country of Refuge: Integration Problems in the German Federal Republic. International Journal of Comparative Sociology. 2:1 (March 1961), 70-80.

415 Resettlement of the Expellees and Refugees in the Federal Republic of Germany and Austria. International Labour Review. 68:2 (August 1953), 166-185.

416 Rosenthal, Harry K. The Assimilation and Integration of the German Expellees. Polish Review. 8:1 (Winter 1963), 78-111.

417 Rothfels, Hans. Frontiers and Mass Migrations in Eastern Central Europe. Review of Politics. 8:1 (January 1946), 37-67. Comment By Oscar Halecki, 8:2 (April 1946), 255-256. Oder-Neisse Territories.

418 Ruff, Gunther Hermann. The Impact of the Refugees on the West German Economy: A Study in Refugee Integration. Ph.D. Thesis, Harvard University, 1956.

419 Salwin, Lester N. Uncertain Nationality Status of German Refugees. Minnesota Law Review. 30:5 (April 1946), 372-394.

420 Schechtman, Joseph B. The Lesson of German Resettlement. Midstream. 5:2 (Spring 1959), 56-66.

421 Schechtman, Joseph B. Postwar Population Transfers in Europe, 1945-1955. Philadelphia: University of Pennsylvania Press, 1963, 417 P.

422 Schechtman, Joseph B. Resettlement of Transferred Volksdeutsche in Germany. Journal of Central European Affairs. 7:3 (October 1947), 262-284.

423 Schieder, Theodor, Editor. Documents on the Expulsion of the Germans From Eastern-Central Europe. Bonn: Federal Ministry for Expellees, Refugees and War Victims, 1960-1961. 4 Vols., 1518 P. (1) the Expulsion of the German Population From the Territories East of the Oder-Neisse Line, 1960, 370 P.; (2) the Fate of the Germans in Hungary, 1961, 214 P.; (3) the Fate of The Germans in Rumania, 1961, 355 P.; (4) the Expulsion of the German Population From Czechoslovakia, 1961, 579 P.

424 Schoenberg, Hans W. Germans From the East: A Study of Their Migration, Resettlement, and Subsequent Group History, 1945-1961. Ph.D. Thesis, School of Advanced International Studies, Johns Hopkins University, 1968, 653 P.

425 Schoenberg, Hans W. Germans From the East: A Study of Their Migration, Resettlement and Subsequent Group History Since 1945. The Hague: Nijhoff, 1971, 366 P.

426 Schwarz, Leo Walder. Refugees in Germany Today. New York: Twayne, 1957, 172 P.

427 Sternberg, Charles. The German Refugees and Expellees. Journal of International Affairs. 7:1 (1953), 35-41.

428 Swanstrom, Edward E. Pilgrims of the Night: A Study of Expelled Peoples. New York: Sheed and Ward, 1950, 114 P.

429 Taeuber, Irene B. Postwar Emigration From Germany and Italy. Annals of the American Academy of Political and Social Science. 262 (March 1949), 82-91.

430 Technical Assistance Commission on Integration of Refugees. The Integration of Refugees Into German Life. Bonn: Technical Assistance Commission on the Integration of the Refugees in the German Republic, 1951, 109 P. Also: Appendix, 1951, 118 P. US, Department of Commerce, Bureau of Foreign Commerce. Impact of the Currect Influx of Refugees on the West German Economy. N.P.: Department of Commerce, Bureau of Foreign Commerce, Office of Economic Affairs, 1953.

431 US, Department of State, Office of Public Affairs. Flight From "Paradise": The East German Exodus; Background. Washington: Department of State Publication 5091, Government Printing Office, 1953, 7 P.

432 US, Economic Cooperation Administration. The Integration of Refugees Into German Life.

Washington: National Planning Association, 1951, 2 Vols. Report Submitted to FRG Chancellor, 21 March 1951, By Eca Technical Assistance Commission on the Integration of Refugees in the German Republic.

433 US, Hicog, Office of Labor Affairs. The Problem of Refugees and Expellees in Western Germany. Frankfurt: Hicog, Office of Labor Affairs, 1949, 12 and 6 P.

434 US, Omgus, Civil Administration Division. Population Transfers. N.P.: Omgus, Civil Administration Division, November 1947, 12 P. Return of German Prisoners of War.

435 US, Omgus, Pw & Dp Division. Refugees and Expellees. N.P.: Omgus, 1947, 18 P.

436 Transfer of the German Population From Poland: Legend and Reality. Warsaw: Western Press Agency, 1966, 55 + 1 P.

437 Vernant, Jacques. The Refugee in the Post-War World. New Haven: Yale University Press, 1953, 827 P.

438 Wildenmann, Rudolf. The Integration of the German Refugees. Confluence. 2:4 (December 1953), 37-48.

439 World Council of Churches, Refugee Division. Report From Hamburg: A Survey of the German Problem in 1949. Geneva: World Council of Churches, Refugee Division, 1949, 32 P.

440 Worsley, R. H. M. Mass Expulsions. Twentieth Century. 139:828 (February 1946), 90-96.

D. Allied Occupation

D.1. Wartime Planning and Development

D.1.1. Wartime Proposals

441 Flenley, Ralph. Post-War Problems: A Reading List. Toronto: The Canadian Institute of International Affairs, 1943, 62 P.

442 Albrecht-Carrie, Rene. Croce and the German Problem. South Atlantic Quarterly. 44:3 (July 1945), 260-271.

443 American Historical Association. Can the Germans Be Re-Educated?. Washington: War Department, 1945, 46 P.

444 American Historical Association. What Shall Be Done About Germany After the War?. Washington: War Department, 1944, 24 P.

445 Balling, Francis C. The Problem of Post-War Germany. Journal of Central European Affairs. 5:1 (April 1945), 45-55.

446 Barach, Alvan L. Brickner, Richard M. Cameron, D. Ewen. Hendrick, Ives. Millet, John A. P. Lowrey, Lawson G. (Chairman). American Journal of Orthopsychiatry. 15:3 (July 1945), 381-441.

447 Beck, Maximilian. Notes on the Re-Education of Germany. Harvard Educational Review. 15:3 (May 1945), 226-229.

448 Benes, Edward. Postwar Germany and Central-Eastern Europe. New Europe. 3:6 (June 1943), 17-18.

449 Boehm, Eric H. The "Free Germans" in Soviet Psychological Warfare. Public Opinion Quarterly. 14:2 (Summer 1950), 285-295. Soviet-Organized "Free Germany Committee" in Moscow, 1943.

450 Brecht, Arnold. Federalism and Regionalism in Germany: The Division of Prussia. London: Oxford University Press, 1945, 202 P.

451 Brehm, Eugen. A Democratic Foreign Policy. After Nazism--Democracy? a Symposium By Four Germans. Ed. Kurt Hiller. London: Lindsay Drummond, 1945, Pp. 166-199.

452 Bundschuh, Wilhelm. Prussia Must Die So the World May Live. New Europe. 3:7-8 (July-August 1943), 22-24.

453 Burridge, Trevor David. The British Labour Party and the "German Question" During The Second World War, 1939-45. Ph.D. Thesis, Mcgill University, 1973.

454 Carthago, D. E. (Pseudonym). Partitioning Germany to Make a Third War Impossible. London: Molloy, 1945, 16 P.

455 E. P. W. Germany and European Reconstruction. World Today. 1:1 (July 1945), 23-29.

456 Eaton, J. W. The Treatment of Post-War Germany. Queen's Quarterly. 51:3 (Autumn 1944), 233-243.

457 Ebenstein, William. Can Germany Be Democratic After the War?. Dalhousie Review. 24:1 (April 1944), 60-63.

458 Eliot, George F. Problems in Occupying Germany. New York: World Wide Broadcasting Foundation, Beyond Victory Program No. 100, 1945, 6 P.

459 Flenley, Ralph, Editor. The Treatment of Postwar Germany. Toronto: Ryerson Press, 1943, 67 P.

460 Foerster, Friedrich. Germany and the Coming Peace. New Europe. 3:7-8 (July-August 1943), 5-9.

461 "Free German" Committees. Jewish Comment. 2:15 (12 May 1944), 1-4.

462 Free German Movement in Great Britain, Editor. Free Germans in the French Maquis: The Story of the Committee "Free Germany" in the West. London: I.N.G. Publications, 1945, 24 P.

463 The Future of East Prussia. New Masses. 51:9 (30 May 1944), 15-16.

464 German Labor Delegation in U.S.A. What Is to Be Done With Germany: Prerequisites of Democracy in Germany: A Declaration. New York: German Labor Delegation in U.S.A., 1945, 6 P.

465 Grossmann, Kurt R. German Political Emigration's True Task. New Europe. 3:12 (December 1943), 21-22.

466 Grossmann, Kurt R. Peace and the German Problem. New Europe. 3:2 (February 1943), 9-12.

467 Guradze, Heinz. Recent Changes in German Governmental Organization. American Political Science Review. 39:1 (February 1945), 97-100.

468 Gurian, Waldemar. on the Future of Germany. Review of Politics. 7:1 (January 1945), 3-14.

469 Hadsel, Winifred N. Allied Governments in London: War Efforts and Peace Aims. Foreign Policy Reports. 18:19 (15 December 1942), 250-259.

470 Hagen, Paul. Germany After Hitler. New York: Farrar & Rinehart, 1944, 240 P.

471 Hager, Johannes. The Federalist Solution for Germany. Central European Observer. 21:11 (26 May 1944), 161-162.

472 Herz, Carl. Foundations for a Democratic Germany. Fabian Quarterly. No. 43 (October 1944), 12-16.

473 Hiller, Kurt, Editor. After Nazism--Democracy? a Symposium By Four Germans. London: Drummond, 1945, 204

474 Hiller, Kurt. The Problem of Constitution. After Nazism--Democracy? a Symposium By Four Germans. Ed. Kurt Hiller. London: Drummond, 1945, Pp. 9-77.

475 Jaeger, Hans. The Free German Committee in London. Free Europe. 8:106 (3 December 1943), 190.

476 Jaeger, Hans. A New Form of Democracy. After Nazism--Democracy? a Symposium By Four Germans. Ed. Kurt Hiller. London: Lindsay Drummond, 1945, Pp. 129-165.

477 Jerome, V. J. The Treatment of Defeated Germany. New York: New Century, 1945, 107 P.

478 Joesten, Joachim. The Rhineland Question. Elmhurst, L.I.: Joachim Joesten, European Report No. 2, 1945, 23 P.

479 Kahn, Siegbert. The National Committee "Free Germany": Background, Tasks, Men. London: I.N.G. Publications, 1943, 11 P.

480 Kantorowicz, Alfred. "Free Germany" in Moscow: A Weapon of Psychological Warfare. Free World. 7:2 (February 1944), 149-156.

481 Kohn, Hans. Russia and Germany in the Post-War World. Ort Economic Review. 4:2 (November 1944), 39-47.

482 Lach, Donald F. What They Would Do About Germany. Journal of Modern History. 17:3 (September 1945), 227-243. Discusses Books and Articles on Postwar Treatment.

483 Lamont, Thomas W. The Problem of Germany: Some of Its Complexities. International Conciliation. No. 407 (January 1945), 40-46.

484 Lerner, Max. Paulding, C. G. Pauck, Wilhelm. The Moral Regeneration of Germany. University of Chicago Round Table. No. 376 (3 June 1945), 1-15. Radio Discussion.

485 London International Assembly. Council for Education in World Citizenship. Education and the United Nations. Washington: American Council on Public Affairs, 1943, 54 P. Considers Inter Alia Re-Education of Postwar Germany.

486 Lowenfeld, Andreas F. The Free Germany Committee: An Historical Study. Review of Politics. 14:3 (July 1952), 346-366.

487 Lowrey, Lawson G. to Make the Germans Men of Peace. New York Times Magazine. (17 June 1945), 12+. Psychiatrist Prescribes Possible Cure for German Problem.

488 Maccurdy, John T. Germany, Russia, and the Future. London: Cambridge University Press, 1944, 140 P.

489 Mead, Nelson P. Germany in the Postwar World. School and Society. 61:1587 (26 May 1945), 337-340.

490 Merker, Paul. Germany Today and Germany Tomorrow. London: I.N.G. Publications, 1943, 57 P.

491 Motherwell, Hiram. Germany. Cleveland: Western Reserve University Press, 1944, 39 P.

492 Moulton, Harold. Marlio, Louis. The Control of Germany and Japan. Washington: Brookings Institution, 1944, 116 P.

493 Neumann, Sigmund. Transition to Democracy in Germany?. Political Science Quarterly. 59:3 (September 1944), 341-362.

494 Poland, Ministry of Preparatory Work Concerning Peace Conf. Economic Problems of Postwar Germany. London: Ministry of Preparatory Work Concerning the Peace Conference, January 1945, Various Pagination.

495 Poland, Ministry of Preparatory Work Concerning Peace Conf. The Political Future of Germany. London: Ministry of Preparatory Work Concerning the Peace Conference, Information Note No. 4, October 1944, 54 P.

496 Pollock, James K. The Role of the Public in a New Germany. American Political Science Review. 39:3 (June 1945), 464-473.

497 Royal Institute of International Affairs. The Problem of Germany: An Interim Report. Oxford: Oxford University Press, 1945, 92 P.

498 Scheurig, Bodo. Free Germany: The National Committee and the League of German Officers. Middletown: Wesleyan University Press, 1969, 311 P.

499 Schultz, Walter D. Democracy, Freedom, Socialism. After Nazism, Democracy: A Symposium By Four Germans. Ed. Kurt Hiller. London: Drummond, 1945, Pp. 78-128

500 Schwarzschild, Leopold. Occupy Germany for Fifty Years. New York Times Magazine. (1 July 1945), 8+.

501 Seger, Gerhart H. Marck, Siegfried K. Germany: to Be or Not Be?. New York: Rand School Press, 1943, 190 P.

502 Sollman, William F. Germany's Crime and Salvation. New Europe. 5:2-3 (February-March 1945), 17-19.

503 Tabouis, Genevieve. The Future German Government. Knickerbocker Weekly. 4:26 (21 August 1944), 28-29.

504 Thompson, Carol L. Ersatz German Revolutions: Will Germany Be Able to Set Up a Republic After the War?. Current History. 5:28 (December 1943), 327-334.

505 Troughten, Ernest R. It's Happening Again. London: Gifford, 1944, 111 P.

506 Union of Democratic Control. Report on Germany. London: Union of Democratic Control, April 1945, 14 P.

507 Vansittart, Robert G. V., Lord. Bones of Contention. London: Hutchinson, 1945, 146 P.

508 Vansittart, Robert G. V., Lord. Germany's Third Try. Atlantic Monthly. 176:2 (August 1945), 43-46.

509 Vansittart, Robert G. V., Lord. The Problem of Germany: A Discussion. International Affairs (London). 21:3 (July 1945), 313-324.

510 Viner, Jacob. The Treatment of Germany. Foreign Affairs. 23:4 (July 1945), 567-581.

511 Weber, August. A New Germany in a New Europe. London: Lindsay Drummond, 1945, 208 P.

512 Weymouth, Anthony, Editor. Germany: Disease and Treatment: Based on the Memoranda of The Post-War Policy Group. London: Hutchinson, 1945, 132 P.

513 Wolff, Max. Germany's Tomorrow. Social Education. 8:7 (November 1944), 312-316.

D.1.2. Wartime Planning

514 Allen, Diane M. Development of Postwar Policy in Germany. Western Political Quarterly. 17:1 (March 1964), 109-116.

515 Alperowitz, Gar. Atomic Diplomacy: Hiroshima and Potsdam. New York: Vintage, 1967.

516 Arrangements for Control of Germany By Allied Representatives. Department of State Bulletin. 12:311 (10 June 1945), 1051-1055.

517 Balfour, Michael. Another Look at "Unconditional Surrender". International Affairs (London). 46:4 (October 1970), 719-736.

518 Beitzell, Robert, Editor. Tehran, Yalta, Potsdam: The Soviet Protocols. Hattiesburg, Miss.: Academic International, 1973, 349 P.

519 Blum, John M. From the Morgenthau Diaries: Iii. Years of War, 1941-1945. Boston: Houghton Mifflin, 1967, 526 P.; Esp. Pp. 327-420, 451-464.

520 Cecil, Robert. Potsdam and Its Legends. International Affairs (London). 46:3 (July 1970), 455-465.

521 Chase, John L. The Development of the Morgenthau Plan Through the Quebec Conference. Journal of Politics. 16:2 (May 1954), 324-359.

522 Chase, John L. The Development of the United States Policy Toward Germany During World War II. Ph.D. Thesis, Princeton University, 1952.

523 Clayton, William L. Security Against Renewed German Aggression. Washington: Department of State Publication 2366, Government Printing Office, 1945, 38 P.

524 Clemens, Diane Shaver. Yalta. New York: Oxford University Press, 1970, 356 P., Esp. Pp. 137-177.

525 Commager, Henry Steele. Was Yalta a Calamity? Concessions to Reality. New York Times Magazine. (3 August 1952), 1+.

526 Dean, Vera Micheles. European Agreements for Post-War Reconstruction. Foreign Policy Reports. 18:1 (15 March 1942), 2-12.

527 Donnisor, F. S. V. Civil Affairs and Military Government Central Organization and Planning. London: H. M. Stationery Office, 1966, 400 P.

528 Dorn, Walter L. The Debate Over American Occupation Policy in Germany in 1944-1945. Political Science Quarterly. 72:4 (December 1957), 481-501.

529 Dudgeon, Ruth A. Yalta, Twenty-Five Years Later. Indiana Social Studies Quarterly. 23:2 (Autumn 1970), 7-16.

530 Fainsod, Merle. The Development of American Military Government Policy During World War II. American Experiences in Military Government in World War II. Ed. Carl J. Friedrich and Associates. New York: Rinehart, 1948, Pp. 23-51.

531 Feis, Herbert. Between War and Peace: The Potsdam Conference. Princeton: Princeton University Press, 1960, 367 P.

532 Feis, Herbert. Churchill, Roosevelt, Stalin: The War They Waged and the Peace They Sought. Princeton: Princeton University Press, 1957, 692 P.

533 Gabriel, Ralph H. Military Government and the Will of the Victors. Virginia Quarterly Review. 21:3 (July 1945), 331-339.

534 Gaddis, John Lewis. The United States and the Origins of the Cold War, 1941-1947. New York: Columbia University Press, 1972, 382 P.

535 Giere, Eggert W. A Case Study in Institutional Aspects of Foreign Policy Making: The American Policy Toward Germany From 1942 to 1945. Ph.D. Thesis, University of Washington, 1958, 231 P.

536 Halle, Louis J. Our War Aims Were Wrong. New York Times Magazine. (22 August 1965), 12+.

537 Harriman W. Averell. Abel, Elie. Special Envoy to Churchill and Stalin, 1941-1946. New York: Random House, 1975, 477 P.

538 Hermens, Ferdinand A. Evaluating the Potsdam Plan. American Journal of Economics and Sociology. 6:2 (January 1947), 181-193.

539 Holborn, Hajo. American Planning of the Military Government of Germany During World War II. Germany and Europe: Historical Essays By Hajo Holborn. Garden City: Doubleday, 1970, Pp. 253-282.

540 Holborn, Louise W., Editor. War and Peace Aims of the United Nations: From Casablanca to Tokyo Bay. Boston: World Peace Foundation, 1948, 1278 P.

541 Hull, Cordell. The Memoirs of Cordell Hull. New York: Macmillan, 1948, 2 Vols., 1804 P., Esp. Vol. 2, Pp. 1570-1582, 1602-1622.

542 Ivanyi, B. G. Bell, Alan. Route to Potsdam: The Story of the Peace Aims, 1939-1945. London: Wingate, 1945, 112 P.

543 Kelsen, Hans. The Legal Status of Germany According to the Declaration of Berlin. American Journal of International Law. 39:3 (July 1945), 518-526.

544 Keplicz, Klemens. Potsdam: Twenty Years After. Warsaw: Zachodnia Agencja Prasowa, 1965, 129 P.

545 The Politics of War: The World and United States Foreign Policy, 1943-1945. New York: Random House, 1968, 685 P.

546 Krieger, Leonard. The Inter-Regnum in Germany: March-August, 1945. Political Science Quarterly. 64:4 (December 1949), 507-532.

547 Krieger, Leonard. The Potential for Democratization in Occupied Germany: A Problem in Historical Projection. Public Policy, Vol. 17. Ed. John D. Montgomery and Albert O. Hirschman. Cambridge: Harvard University Press, 1968, Pp. 27-58.

548 Kubek, Anthony. The Evolution of the "Treasury Plan" for Postwar Germany: An Introduction to the Morgenthau Diary on Germany. Morgenthau Diary (Germany). U.S. Senate, Committee on the Judiciary, Subcommittee to Investigate the Administration of the Internal Security Act and other Internal Security Laws. Washington: Committee Print: 90Th Congress, 1St Session, 2 Vols, 1967, Pp. 1-81.

549 Leahy, William D. I Was There. New York: Whittlesey, 1950, 527 P., Esp. Pp. 291-429.

550 Litchfield, Edward H. Political Objectives and Legal Bases of Occupation Government. Governing Postwar Germany. Ed. Edward H. Litchfield and Associates. Ithaca: Cornell University Press, 1953, Pp. 3-18.

551 Mccormick, Anne O'Hare. Two Mighty Tests for the Big Three. New York Times Magazine. (15 July 1945), 5+. Forthcoming Potsdam Conference.

552 Mckelvey, Raymond D. The Big Power Conferences. Proceedings of the Institute of World Affairs. 21:2 (December 1945), 143-148.

553 Mee, Charles L., Jr. Meeting at Potsdam. New York: M. Evans and Company, 1975, Xiv and 370 P.

554 Miksche, Ferdinand O. Unconditional Surrender: The Roots of a World War Iii. New York: Faber and Faber, 1952,

468 P.

555 Moltmann, Guenter. Yalta Conference. Marxism, Communism and Western Society: A Comparative Encyclopedia. Ed. C. D. Kernig. New York: Herder and Herder, 1973, Vol. 8, Pp. 397-399.

556 Morgenthau, Henry, Jr. Germany Is Our Problem. New York: Harper & Brothers, 1945, 239 P.

557 Morrow, Felix. "Big Three" Differences in Germany. Fourth International. 6:6 (June 1945), 174-177.

558 Mosely, Philip E. Dismemberment of Germany: The Allied Negotiations From Yalta to Potsdam. Foreign Affairs. 28:3 (April 1950), 487-498.

559 Mosely, Philip E. The Occupation of Germany: New Light on How the Zones Were Drawn. Foreign Affairs. 28:4 (July 1950), 580-604.

560 Ogmore, Lord. A Journey to Berlin, 1944-45. Contemporary Review. 206:1138 (January 1965), 25-30; 206:1139 (February 1965), 85-90; and 206:1130 (March 1965), 150-156.

561 Pan, Stephen C. Y. Legal Aspects of the Yalta Agreement. American Journal of International Law. 46:1 (January 1952), 40-59.

562 Schlauch, Wolfgang. American Policy Toward Germany, 1945. Journal of Contemporary History. 5:4 (1970), 113-128.

563 Sharp, Tony. The Wartime Alliance and the Zonal Division of Germany. Oxford: Clarendon Press, 1975, xii and 220 P.

564 Sherwood, Robert E. Roosevelt and Hopkins, an Intimate History. New York: Harper, 1948, 979 P., Esp. Pp. 832-916.

565 Shneiderman, Samuel L. Morgenthau's Blueprint for Germany. Midstream. 13:5 (May 1967), 56-62.

566 Snell, John L. Illusion and Necessity: The Diplomacy of Global War, 1939-1945. Boston: Houghton Mifflin, 1963, 229 P., Esp. Pp. 172-191.

567 Snell, John L., Editor. The Meaning of Yalta: Big Three Diplomacy and the New Balance of Power. Baton Rouge: Louisiana State University Press, 1956, 239 P.

568 Snell, John L. Wartime Origins of the East-West Dilemma Over Germany. New Orleans: Hauser, 1959, 268 P.

569 Stettinius, Edward R. Roosevelt and the Russians: The Yalta Conference. Garden City: Doubleday, 1949, 367 P.

570 Stimson, Henry L. Bundy, Mcgeorge. on Active Service in Peace and War. New York: Harper, 1948, 698 P., Esp. Pp. 553-611. Strang, William, Lord. Home and Abroad. London: Deutsch, 1956, 320 P., Esp. Pp. 199-238.

571 Strang, William, Lord. Prelude to Potsdam: Reflections on War and Foreign Policy. International Affairs (London). 46:3 (July 1970), 441-454.

572 UK, Foreign Office. UK, Ministry of Economic Warfare, Economic Advisory Board. Germany Basic Handbook. London: H.M. Stationery Office, 1944-45, 18 Vols.

573 UK, Foreign Office. UK, Ministry of Economic Warfare, Economic Advisory Board. Germany Zone Handbook. London: H.M. Stationery Office, 1944-45, 8 Vols.

574 US, Department of State. The Axis in Defeat: A Collection of Documents on the American Policy Toward Germany and Japan. Washington: Department of State Publication 2423, Government Printing Office, 1945, 118 P.

575 US, Department of State. Making the Peace Treaties, 1941-1947. Washington: Department of State Publication 2774, Government Printing Office, February 1947, 150 P. Subtitle: A History of the Making of the Peace Beginning With Atlantic Charter, the Yalta and Potsdam Conferences, and Culminating in the Drafting of Peace Treaties With Italy, Bulgaria, Hungary, Rumania, and Finland.

576 US, Department of State, Historical Division. The Conference of Berlin: The Potsdam Conference, 1945. Washington: Department of State Publication 7015, Government Printing Office, 1960, 2 Vols.

577 US, Department of State, Historical Division. Conferences at Cairo and Tehran, 1943. Washington: Department of State Publication 7187, Government Printing Office, 1961, 932 P.

578 US, Department of State, Historical Division. The Conferences at Malta and Yalta, 1945. Washington: Department of State Publication 6199, Government Printing Office, 1955, 1032 P.

579 US, Department of the Army, European Command, Hist. Div. Planning for the Occupation of Germany. Frankfurt: U.S. Army, European Command, Office of the Chief Historian, 1947, 200 P.

580 US, Omgus. The United States Program for the Occupation of Germany, 15 September 1945. Berlin-Tempelhof: Druckhaus Tempelhof, 1945, 16 P.

581 US, Office of Strategic Services. The Administrative Separation of Austria From Germany. Washington: War Department Pamphlet No. 31-229, Government Printing Office, 1945, 72 P.

582 US, Senate, Committee on the Judiciary. Morgenthau Diary (Germany). Washington: Senate, Committee on the Judiciary, Subcommittee to Investigate the Administration of the Internal Security Act and Other Internal Security Laws, Government Printing Office, 1967, 2 Vols., 1643 P.

583 Wagner, Wolfgang. The Partitioning of Germany: A History of the Soviet Expansion Up to the Cleavage of Germany, 1918-1945. Stuttgart: Deutsche Verlags-Anstalt, 1959, 240 P.

584 Wagner, Wolfgang. Potsdam Agreement. Marxism, Communism and Western Society: A Comparative Encyclopedia. Ed. C. D. Kernig. New York: Herder and Herder, 1973, Vol. 6, Pp. 422-426.

585 White, Nathan I. Harry Dexter White-- Loyal American. Waban, Mass.: Bessie (White) Bloom, 1956, 415 P., Esp. Pp. 205-215.

586 Wilmot, Chester. Was Yalta a Calamity? Sacrifice of Principles. New York Times Magazine (3 August 1952), 1+.

D.1.3. Relevant Military Developments

587 Ambrose, Stephen E. Eisenhower and Berlin, 1945: The Decision to Halt at the Elbe. New York: Norton, 1967, 119 P.

588 Bethell, Nicholas. The Last Secret: The Delivery to Stalin of Over Two Million Russians By Britain and the United States. New York: Basic Books, 1974, 224 P.

589 Chuikov, Vasilii Ivanovich. The Fall of Berlin. New York: Holt, Rinehart

and Winston, 1968, 261 P.

590 Churchill, Winston S. The Second World War: Triumph and Tragedy. Boston: Houghton Mifflin, 1953, 800 P., Esp. Pp. 329-676.

591 Eisenhower, Dwight D. Crusade in Europe. Garden City: Doubleday, 1948, 559 P.

592 Epstein, Julius. Operation Keelhaul: The Story of Forced Repatriation From 1944 to the Present. Old Greenwich: Devin-Adair, 1973, Xiv and 255 P.

593 Irving, David. The Destruction of Dresden. New York: Holt, Rinehart and Winston, 1964, 255 P.

594 Kirst, Hans Hellmut. Germany '45: The Day the Americans Came. New York Times Magazine. (2 May 1965), 26+.

595 Norden, Albert. Doomsday or Day of Liberation?. German Foreign Policy (GDR). 4:2 (1965), 91-98.

596 Sevruk, Vladimir, Compiler. How Wars End: Eye-Witness Accounts of the Fall of Berlin. Moscow: Progress Publishers, 1969, 336 P.

597 Steinert, Marlis G. 23 Days: The Final Collapse of Nazi Germany. New York: Walker, 1969, 326 P.

598 Strawson, John. The Battle for Berlin. New York: Charles Scribner's Sons, 1974, Viii and 182 P.

599 Strong, Anna Louise. The Drive That Took Berlin. Soviet Russia Today. 14:2 (June 1945), 16-21.

600 Stueck, Hans-Jurgen. How Hitler's War Ended--for a German Boy. New York Times Magazine. (27 June 1965), 8+.

601 US, Strategic Bombing Survey. Over-All Report (European War). Washington: Government Printing Office, 30 September 1945, 109 P.

602 Ziemke, Earl F. The Soviets' Lost Opportunity--Berlin in February 1945. Military Review. 49:6 (June 1969), 45-53.

D.2. Military Occupation

D.2.1. General (See Also I.2.1)

603 Albrecht-Carrie, Rene. The German Problem Can Be Simple. Social Education. 9:8 (December 1945), 355-358.

604 Anderson, Mosa. Germany and Europe's Future. London: National Council, Peace Aims Pamphlet No. 35, 1946, 16 P.

605 Aurelius, Marcus (Pseud. for Walter Ernest Padley). Am I My Brother's Keeper?. London: Gollancz, 1945, 32 P.

606 Berger, Hans. Do Germans Have Rights?. New Masses. 56:6 (7 August 1945), 5-6.

607 Berkes, Ross N. Germany in Defeat. Proceedings of the Institute of World Affairs. 22 (1947), 42-46.

608 Beveridge, William H., Lord. An Urgent Message From Germany. London: Pilot Press, 1946, 24 P.

609 Bonn, Moritz J. Wandering Scholar: Autobiography. New York: Day, 1948, 403 P.

610 Bourke-White, Margaret. "Dear Fatherland, Rest Quietly": A Report on the Collapse of Hitler's "Thousand Years". New York: Simon and Schuster, 1946, 175 P.

611 Boyle, Kay. The Smoking Mountain: Stories of Germany During the Occupation. New York: Knopf, 1963, 260 P.

612 Brockway, Fenner. German Diary, April 28-May 11, 1946. London: Gollancz, 1946, 148 P.

613 Civis Germanicus. A German Exile Returns. Contemporary Review. 171:976 (April 1947), 217-220.

614 Daniell, Raymond. At Our Knees--or at Our Throats. New York Times Magazine. (27 May 1945), 8+.

615 Daniell, Raymond. The Long Road Ahead for Germany. New York Times Magazine. (19 May 1946), 9+.

616 Dickopf, Karl. 1945--Turning Point in German History: End or Continuity?. Indiana Social Studies Quarterly. 23:2 (Autumn 1970), 60-80.

617 Doeblin, Alfred. Germany Is No More: Life Among the Ruins. Commentary. 2:3 (September 1946), 227-232.

618 Duggan, Stephen. Europe's Slum: Germany. Institute of International Education News Bulletin. 21:5 (February 1946), 3-5.

619 Ebenstein, William. Common Sense on the German Problem. Dalhousie Review. 25:3 (October 1945), 284-291.

620 Eichler, Willi. Federalism and Separatism: The Future of Germany. Socialist Commentary. 11 (August 1946), 426-428.

621 F. G. Germany Revisited: Some Impressions After Two Years. World Today. 3:9 (September 1947), 424-431.

622 Fraser, Lindley. Germany in Eclipse. Current Affairs (London). No. 16 (16 November 1946), 1-19.

623 G. K. Y. Germany in Defeat. World Today. 2:2 (February 1946), 66-78.

624 The Germans: A European Policy. Soundings. No. 2 (March-April 1947), 2-6.

625 Germany and the Peace. Proceedings of the Institute of World Affairs. 21:5 (December 1945), 170-172.

626 Gilbert, Felix. Mitteleuropa: The Final Stage. Journal of Central European Affairs. 7:1 (April 1947), 58-67.

627 Gilbert, Horace N. Germany and the Peace. Proceedings of the Institute of World Affairs. 21:2 (December 1945), 170-176.

628 Glasgow, George. Potsdam and After. Contemporary Review. 168:957 (September 1945), 145-151.

629 Gollancz, Victor. Germany Revisited. London: Gollancz, 1947, 39 P.

630 Gollancz, Victor. in Darkest Germany. Hinsdale: Regnery, 1947, 252 P.

631 Guthrie, Edwin R. Propaganda and the Peace. Proceedings of the Institute of World Affairs. 21:4 (August 1945), 81-85.

632 Hermens, Ferdinand A. Potsdam or Peace: The Choice Before US. Chicago: Human Events Associates, Human Events Pamphlets No. 13, 1946, 30 P.

633 Hirsch, Felix Edward. Germany After Two Lost Wars: The Deeper Problems of Reconstruction. 13:73 (September 1947), 149-192.

634 Hommen, Willi. A Letter From Germany. Fortnightly. 164:979 (July 1948), 104-109.

635 Hopkins, L. Thomas. Democracy in Germany, If.... Teachers College Record. 49:1 (October 1947), 10-18.

636 Jebens, F. Germany in Defeat. Royal United Service Institution Journal. 90:559 (August 1945), 307-310.

637 Keyserlingk, Robert W. The German Situation Today. International Journal. 2:1 (Winter 1946-47), 26-36.

638 Kirkpatrick, Clifford. Sociological Principles and Occupied Germany. American Sociological Review. 11:1 (February 1946), 67-78.

639 Knauth, Percy. Germany in Defeat. New York: Knopf, 1946, 233 P.

640 Lasky, Melvin J. Report on the German Intelligentsia. Partisan Review. 14:6 (November-December 1947), 616-624.

641 Long, Tania. This Is Berlin--Without Hitler. New York Times Magazine. (22 July 1945), 9+.

642 Ludwig, Emil. Germany in 1945: A Pessimistic Prediction. Free Europe. 12:154 (2 November 1945), 107-108.

643 Lunau, Heinz. The Germans on Trial. New York: Storm, 1948, 180 P. A Passionately Pro-German Plea, Asserting That the Tragedy Of Nazism Could Have Happened to Any Other Civilized Nation.

644 Lutz, Ralph H. Peace Arrangements for Europe. Proceedings of the Institute of World Affairs. 21:2 (December 1945), 156-166.

645 Lutz, Ralph H. The Political Heritage of the War. Proceedings of the Institute of World Affairs. 22:3 (June 1946), 21-28.

646 Mccormick, Anne O'Hare. Germany, Weak, Is Still a Great Problem. New York Times Magazine. (16 December 1945), 5+.

647 Mccormick, Anne O'Hare. Thoughts on Visiting Hitler's Chancellery. New York Times Magazine. (21 March 1948), 11+.

648 Madariaga, Salvador De. Victors, Beware!. London: Jonathan Cape, 1946, 304 P., Esp. Pp. 143-151.

649 Mead, A.R. How Shall We Treat Defeated Enemies?. Social Education. 13:4 (April 1949), 187-190.

650 Menck, Clara. Germany Today. Review of Politics. 8:3 (July 1946), 354-380.

651 Mende, Tibor. Europe's Suicide in Germany. London: St. Botolph, 1946, 100 P.

652 Morgenthau, Hans J. Shils, Edward A. Wilson, O. Meredith. Do We Fail a Second Time in Germany?. University of Chicago Round Table. No. 400 (18 November 1945), 1-18. Radio Discussion.

653 Morgenthau, Henry, Jr. Postwar Treatment of Germany. Annals of the American Academy of Political and Social Science. 246 (July 1946), 125-129.

654 Mosley, Leonard O. Report From Germany. London: Gollancz, 1945, 125 P.

655 National Conference on the Occupied Countries. Report, 1949-1950. Washington: American Council on Education Studies, 1950, 2 Vols. Vol. I: Cultural Relations; Vol. II: Responsibilities of Voluntary Agencies.

656 National Peace Council, London. The German Crisis. London: National Peace Council, Peace Aims Pamphlet No. 37, 1946, 20 P.

657 Parker, Margaret. Population Problems in Germany and Italy. Current History. 9:48 (August 1945), 112-117.

658 Patch, Buel W. Future of Germany. Editorial Research Reports. (23 October 1946), 717-738.

659 Peters, William. in Germany Now. London: Progress, 1946, 115 P.

660 Raymond, Jack. Der Kleine Mann. This Is Germany. Ed. Arthur Settel. New York: Sloane, 1950, Pp. 149-160. Attitudes Toward Occupiers.

661 Richardson, Justin. Germany--Is Our Occupation Really Necessary?. National Review. 126:759 (May 1946), 382-388.

662 Roepke, Wilhelm. The German Dust-Bowl. Review of Politics. 8:4 (October 1946), 511-527.

663 Roepke, Wilhelm. New Germans Must Shape the New Germany. New York Times Magazine. (13 October 1946), 11+.

664 Rust, William. Where Is Germany Going?. London: N.P., 1946, 15 P. By Editor of the "Daily Worker."

665 Schimansky, Stefan. Vain Victory. London: Gollancz, 1946, 172 P.

666 Schmidt, Dana Adams. Land of Questions Without Answers. New York Times Magazine. (26 May 1946), 18+.

667 Schuetz, Wilhelm Wolfgang. Germany After the Potsdam Conference. London Quarterly of World Affairs. 11:3 (October 1945), 191-200.

668 Schuetz, Wilhelm Wolfgang. Germany: Democracy or Autocracy?. London Quarterly of World Affairs. 12:3 (October 1946), 203-210.

669 Germany Revisited. Contemporary Review. 168:960 (December 1945), 339-343.

670 Schumacher, Kurt. Germany's Aims. Canadium Forum. 27:318 (July 1947), 79-80.

671 Shirer, William L. End of a Berlin Diary. New York: Knopf, 1947, 369 P.

672 Shuster, George N. What Is Germany Thinking?. Germany--Nation or No-Man's Land. Ed. James P. Warburg. New York: Foreign Policy Association, Headline Series No. 60, November-December 1946, Pp. 55-61.

673 Smith, Rennie. Concerning Germany. Quarterly Review. 284:570 (October 1946), 504-520.

674 Spender, Stephen. European Witness. London: Hamish Hamilton, 1946, 241 P.

675 Spender, Stephen. Germany in Europe. Fortnightly. 159:954 (June 1946), 401-407.

676 Stern, James. The Hidden Damage. New York: Harcourt, Brace, 1947, 406 P.

677 Stone, Shepard. Report on the Mood of Germany. New York Times Magazine. (26 January 1947), 8+.

678 Tomberg, Valentin. Trends of Opinion in Germany Today. Dublin Review. 220:441 (Autumn 1947), 86-96.

679 Trevor-Roper, Hugh R. The Strange Vacuum That Is Germany. New York Times Magazine. (6 July 1947), 8+.

680 Valentin, Veit. Germany After Twelve Years. Contemporary Review. 169:961 (January 1946), 10-14.

681 Vansittart, Robert G. V., Lord. Events and Shadows. London: Hutchinson, 1947, 208 P.

682 Walker, Patrick Gordon. The Lid Lifts. London: Gollancz, 1945, 96 P.

683 Waln, Nora. Can the Nazis Learn?. Atlantic Monthly. 176:5 (November 1945), 45-49.

684 Waln, Nora. Return to Germany. Atlantic Monthly. 176:4 (October 1945), 43-45.

685 White, William L. Report on the Germans. New York: Harcourt, Brace, 1947, 260 P.

686 Wiener Library. Europe 1945/46. London: Wiener Library, 1946, 3 Vols. Allied Occupation as Mirrored in the German Press; and Report on a Recent Journey to Germany By L. W. Bondy.

687 Wilson, Francesca M. 1946. New York: Penguin, 1947, 253 P.

688 Winternitz, Josef. German Workers Unite. Labour Monthly. 28:4 (April 1946), 115-119.

D.2.2. Four Power Control

689 Almond, Gabriel A., Editor. The Struggle for Democracy in Germany. Chapel Hill: University of North Carolina Press, 1949, 345 P.

690 Arrangements for Control of Germany By Allied Representatives. Department of State Bulletin. 13:328 (7 October 1945), 515-521.

691 Balfour, Michael, Mair, John. Four-Power Control in Germany and Austria, 1945-1946. New York: Oxford University Press, 1956, 390 P.

692 Belgion, Montgomery. Victor's Justice: A Letter Intended to Have Been Sent to a Friend Recently in Germany. Hinsdale: Regnery, 1949, 187 P.

693 Collins, Henry H., Jr. The Elections in Germany Since V-E Day. Soviet Russia Today. 17:5 (September 1948), 13-14, 27.

694 De Mendelssohn, Peter. What Price Co-Operation--Resistance and Collaboration in Occupied Germany. This Is Germany. Ed. Arthur Settel. New York: Sloane, 1950, Pp. 293-308.

695 Draper, William H., Jr. Military Government in Germany. Columbia Journal of International Affairs. 2:1 (Winter 1948), 39-40.

696 Legal Problems of German Occupation. Michigan Law Review. 47:1 (November 1948), 11-22.

697 Fried, John H. E. Transfer of Civilian Manpower From Occupied Territory. American Journal of International Law. 40:2 (April 1946), 303-331. National Socialist Deportation of Non-Germans in Support of The German War Effort and the Transference of Germans as a Labor Force for Reconstruction Work.

698 Friedmann, Wolfgang G. The Allied Military Government of Germany. London: Stevens, 1947, 362 P.

699 Friedmann, Wolfgang G. The Military Government of Germany. Fortnightly. 161:964 (April 1947), 233-239; and 161:965 (May 1947), 320-329.

700 Germany Under Allied Control. Round Table. 35:140 (September 1945), 314-319; and 36:141 (December 1945), 20-25.

701 Greaves, Rex E. Seborer, Stuart J. The Occupied Germany of Postwar Europe. Education. 69:3 (November 1948), 162-166.

702 H. H. Allied Administration in Germany: An American View. World Today. 4:4 (April 1948), 160-173.

703 Hadsel, Winifred N. Allied Military Rule in Germany. Foreign Policy Reports. 21:16 (1 November 1945), 222-231.

704 Harvey, C. P. Quadripartite Control in Germany. National Review. 128:769 (March 1947), 203-213.

705 Hemken, Ruth, Editor. Sammlung Der Vom Alliierten Kontrollrat Und Der Amerikanischen Militaerregierung Erlassenen Proklamationen, Gesetze, Verordnungen, Befehle, Direktiven. Stuttgart: Deutsche Verlagsanstalt, 1946-49, 30 Vols.

706 Herman, Frederick. The Victors and the Vanquished: The Quest for Security as Illustrated By the Three Allied Occupations of Territory of The Defeated Power--France, 1815-1818; Germany, 1918-1929; and Germany, 1945-. Ph.D. Thesis, Fletcher School of Law and Diplomacy, 1954.

707 Hoffman, Lawrence A. Germany: Zones of Occupation. Department of State Bulletin. 14:354 (14 April 1946), 599-607.

708 Kreinheder, Walter R. Military Government in Occupied Germany. Military Review. 26:2 (May 1946), 67-70.

709 Loewenstein, Karl. Political Reconstruction in Germany, Zonal and Interzonal. Change and Crisis in European Government. Ed. James K. Pollock. New York: Rinehart, 1947, Pp. 29-43.

710 Mcinnis, Edgar. Hiscocks, Richard. Spencer, Robert A. The Shaping of Postwar Germany. London: Dent, 1960, 195 P.

711 Mason, John Brown. The Hitler Nightmare and Postwar Reconstruction. Foreign Governments--The Dynamics of Politics Abroad. Ed. Fritz Morstein Marx. New York: Prentice-Hall, 1952, Pp. 327-354, Esp. Pp. 344-349 on FRG and 349-354 on GDR.

712 Merkl, Peter H. Allied Strategies of Effecting Political Change and Their Reception in Occupied Germany. Public Policy, Vol. 17. Ed. John D. Montgomery and Albert O. Hirschman. Cambridge: Harvard University Press, 1968, Pp. 59-103.

713 Montgomery, John D. Forced to Be Free: The Artificial Revolution in Germany and Japan. Chicago: University of Chicago Press, 1957, 210 P.

714 Nadelmann, Kurt H. The Legal Status of Germany. American Journal of International Law. 40:4 (October 1946), 811-817.

715 Nobleman, Eli E. Quadripartite Military Government Organization and Operations in Germany. American Journal of International Law. 41:3 (July 1947), 650-655.

716 The Occupation of Germany. Proceedings of the Institute of World Affairs. 25:5 (December 1948), 35-40.

717 Pollock, James K. Germany Under Military Occupation. Change and Crisis in European Government. Ed. James K. Pollock. New York: Rinehart, 1947, Pp. 45-61.

718 Pollock, James K. Meisel, James H. Germany Under Occupation: Illustrative Materials and Documents. Ann Arbor: Wahr, 1947, 306 P.

719 Potter, Pitman B. Legal Bases and Character of Military Occupation in Germany and Japan. American Journal of International Law. 43:2 (April 1949), 323-325.

720 Rheinstein, Max. The Legal Status of Occupied Germany. Michigan Law Review. 47:1 (November 1948), 23-40.

721 Ruhm Von Oppen, Beate. Documents on Germany Under Occupation, 1945-1954. London and New York: Oxford University Press, 1955, 660 P.

722 Schuetz, Wilhelm Wolfgang. Interregnum in Germany. World Affairs (London). 1:3 (July 1947), 253-261.

723 Schwada, John W. Policy of the Western Allies Toward Post-War Germany: Development and Evolution, 1941-1949. Ph.D. Thesis, University of Texas, 1951.

724 Schwelb, Egon. The Legal Status of Germany. American Journal of International Law. 40:4 (October 1946), 811-812.

725 Spackman, Ellis L. Allied Military Government Policies in Germany. Proceedings of the Institute of World Affairs. 22 (1947), 75-76.

726 Templer, G. W. R. Military Government in Germany. Royal United Service Institution Journal. 91:561 (February 1956), 17-37.

727 Thomas, Elbert D. The Problems of German Military Control. Proceedings of the Institute of World Affairs. 21:4 (August 1945), 39-41.

728 Tripathi, Krishna Dev. Occupation Policy of the Allies in Vanquished Germany. Indian Journal of Political Science. 16:2 (April-June 1955), 124-133.

729 US, Department of State, Office of Public Affairs. Germany--Unfinished Business: Background Information. Washington: Government Printing Office, 1946, 23 P.

730 US, Omgus, Civil Administration Division. Freedom of Movement Within Germany. N.P.: Omgus, November 1947.

731 US, Omgus, Military Governor. German Territorial Organization. N.P.: Omgus, Adjutant General, November 1946, 22 P. Texts and Graphics.

732 Whipple, William, Jr. A Review of Military Government in Germany. Military Review. 27:1 (April 1947), 13-27.

733 Whyte, Anne. Quadripartite Rule in Berlin: An Interim Record of the First Year of the Allied Control Authority. International Affairs (London). 23:1 (January 1947), 30-41.

734 X. Y. Z. The Allied Zones of Occupation in Germany: Their Economic Features Compared. World Today. 1:1 (July 1945), 13-23.

D.2.3. American Zone

735 Allied Forces, Supreme Headquarters, Chief of Staff. Handbook for Military Government. Fort Gordon: US Army Civil Affairs School, 1962.

736 Anspach, Ernest. The Nemesis of Creativity: Observations on Our Occupation of Germany. Social Research. 19:4 (December 1952), 403-429.

737 Bach, Julian, Jr. America's Germany: An Account of the Occupation. New York: Random House, 1946, 310 P.

738 Benson, George C. S. Howe, Mark Dewolfe. Military Government Organizational Relationships. American Experiences in Military Government in World War II. Ed. Carl J. Friedrich and Associates. New York: Rinehart, 1948, Pp. 52-69.

739 Bettany, A. Guy. With the Americans in Germany. World Affairs (London). 1:4 (October 1947), 409-418.

740 Blumenson, Martin, Editor. The Patton Papers, 1940-1945. Boston: Houghton Mifflin, 1974, Xx and 889 P.

741 Brandt, Karl. Germany Is Our Problem. Washington and Chicago: Human Events, 1946, 18 P.

742 Brandt, Karl. Is There Still a Chance for Germany? America's Responsibility. Hinsdale: Regnery, 1948, 46 P.

743 Byrnes, James F. All in One Lifetime. New York: Harper & Brothers, 1958, 432 P., Esp. Pp. 252-386.

744 Byrnes, James F. Speaking Frankly. New York and London: Harper, 1947, 324 P.

745 Christen, Peter. From Military Government to State Department. Erding, Germany: Wagner, 1950. How a German Employee Sees the Work of the U.S. Military Government and the State Department in a Small Bavarian Town: Its Successes and Its Handicaps.

746 Clark, Dale. Conflicts Over Planning at Staff Headquarters. American Experiences in Military Government in World War II. Ed. Carl J. Friedrich and Associates. New York: Rinehart, 1948, Pp. 211-237.

747 Clark, William. Goodman, Thomas H. American Justice in Occupied Germany: United States Military Government Courts. American Bar Association Journal. 36:6 (June 1950), 443-447.

748 Clay, Lucius D. Achievements of Military Government in 1948. Department of State Bulletin. 20:506 (13 March 1949), 324-326.

749 Clay, Lucius D. Decision in Germany. Garden City: Doubleday, 1950, 522 P.

750 Clay, Lucius D. Easterly, B. Germany--Four Years of Occupation. Army Information Digest. 4:6 (June 1949), 3-12.

751 Coles, Harry L. Weinberg, Albert K. Civil Affairs: Soldiers Become Governors. Washington: Department of the Army, Office of the Chief of Military History, 1964.

752 Daniell, Raymond. Are We Making Headway in Germany?. New York Times Magazine. (14 December 1947), 7+.

753 Daniell, Raymond. We Talk Tough, But We Act Soft. New York Times Magazine. (7 October 1945), 5+. American Occupation Policy.

754 Davidson, Eugene. The Death and Life of Germany: An Account of the American Occupation. New York: Knopf, 1959, 422 P.

755 Davis, Franklin M., Jr. Come as a Conqueror: The United States Army's Occupation of Germany, 1945-1949. New York: Macmillan, 1967, 271 P.

756 Dean, Vera Micheles. Will U.S. Civil Corps Replace Occupation Army in Germany?. Foreign Policy Bulletin. 25:4 (9 November 1945), 1-2.

757 Debevoise, Eli Whitney. The Occupation of Germany: United States Objectives and Participation. Journal of International Affairs. 8:2 (1954), 166-184.

758 Dittmar, Henry G. The American Zone. Contemporary Review. 173:987 (March 1948), 154-157.

759 Dos Passos, John. Tour of Duty. Boston: Houghton Mifflin, 1946, 336 P., Esp. Pp. 243-336.

760 Dunner, Joseph. Information Control in the American Zone of Germany, 1945-1946. American Experiences in Military Government in World War II. Ed. Carl J. Friedrich and Associates. New York: Rinehart, 1948, Pp. 276-291.

761 Edwards, Morris O. A Case Study of Military Government in Germany During and After World War II. Ph.D. Thesis, Georgetown University, 1957.

762 Fahy, Charles. The Lawyer in Military Government of Germany. Department of State Bulletin. 15:384 (10 November 1946), 852-859.

763 Fairman, Charles. Some New Problems of the Constitution Following the Flag. Stanford Law Review. 1:4 (June 1949), 587-645. American Occupation of Germany.

764 Frederiksen, Oliver J. The American Military Occupation of Germany, 1945-1953. Karlsruhe: Headquarters, United States Army, Europe: Historical Division, 1953, 222 P.

765 Freidin, Seymour. Bailey, George. The Experts. New York: Macmillan, 1968, 398 P.

766 Friedrich, Carl J. Military Government and Democratization: A Central Issue of American Foreign Policy. American Experiences in Military Government in World War II. Ed. Carl J. Friedrich and Associates. New York: Rinehart, 1948, Pp. 3-22.

767 Friedrich, Carl J. Organizational Evolution in Germany, 1945-1947. American Experiences in Military Government in World War II. Ed. Carl J. Friedrich and Associates. New York: Rinehart, 1948, Pp. 197-210.

768 Friedrich, Carl J. The Three Phases of Field Operations in Germany, 1945-1946. American Experiences in Military Government in World War II. Ed. Carl J. Friedrich and Associates. New York: Rinehart, 1948, Pp. 238-252.

769 Friedrich, Carl J., and Associates. American Experiences in Military Government in World War II. New York: Rinehart, 1948, 436 P.

770 Fuller, Leon W. The Problem of German Political Revival. Department of State Bulletin. 14:353 (7 April 1946), 547-552.

771 Galbraith, John Kenneth. Is There a German Policy? What Are Its Aims? What Are the Plans for Achieving Them? Here Is the Story of How Major Policy Was Made and What It Is. Fortune. 35:1 (January 1947), 126-127 and 184-192.

772 Gardner, Lloyd C. America and the German "Problem," 1945-1949. Politics and Policies of the Truman Administration. Ed. Barton J. Bernstein. Chicago: Quadrangle, 1970, Pp. 113-148.

773 Gimbel, John. American Military Government and the Education of a New German Leadership. Political Science Quarterly. 83:2 (June 1968), 248-267.

774 Gimbel, John. The American Occupation of Germany: Politics and the Military, 1945-1949. Stanford: Stanford University Press, 1968, 335 P.

775 Gimbel, John. The Artificial Revolution in Germany: A Case Study. Political Science Quarterly. 76:1 (March 1961), 88-104.

776 Gimbel, John. A German Community Under American Occupation: Marburg, 1945-52. Stanford: Stanford University Press, 1961, 259 P.

777 Gimbel, John. On the Implementation of the Potsdam Agreement: An Essay on U.S. Postwar German Policy. Political Science Quarterly. 87:2 (June 1972), 242-269.

778 Glaser, Kurt. Organization and Methods of Control. Governing Postwar Germany. Ed. Edward H. Litchfield and Associates. Ithaca: Cornell University Press, 1953, Pp. 294-306.

779 Haeger, Robert. No More Conquerors. This Is Germany. Ed. Arthur Settel. New York: Sloane, 1950, Pp. 1-22.

780 Hammond, Paul Y. Directives for the Occupation of Germany: The Washington Controversy. American Civil-Military Decisions: A Book of Case Studies. Ed. Harold Stein. Birmingham: University of Alabama Press, 1963, Pp. 311-460.

781 Handy, Mary. The Development of American Policy Towards Postwar Germany, With Special Reference to the Field of Public Affairs. Dr.Phil. Thesis, Heidelberg University, 1954, 383 P.

782 Harwood, Ralph. Case History of a German Town. This Is Germany. Ed. Arthur Settel. New York: Sloane, 1950, Pp. 177-194. Effects of the Occupation on a Small Town.

783 Heath, Kathryn G. Army Civilian Personnel Policy and Problems in the United States Zone of Germany, With Special Reference to Indigenous Personnel, 1947-1948. Ph.D. Thesis, American University, 1951.

784 Heneman, Harlow J. American Control Organization in Germany. Public Administration Review. 6:1 (Winter 1946), 1-9.

785 Heymann, Hans, Jr. Tron, Rene A. Martin, James Stewart. Villard, Oswald Garrison. Pollock, James K. Briefs, G. A. Farley, Miriam S. Round Table on American Occupation. Columbia Journal of International Affairs. 2:1 (Winter 1948), 41-58.

786 Hilldring, John H. What Is Our Purpose in Germany?. Annals of the American Academy of Political and Social Science. 255 (January 1948), 77-83.

787 Holborn, Hajo. American Military Government: Its Organization and Policies. Washington: Infantry Journal Press, 1947, 243 P.

788 Hutton, Oram C. Conqueror's Peace: A Report to the American Stockholders. Garden City: Doubleday, 1947, 92 P.

789 Johnston, Howard W. United States Public Affairs Activities in Germany, 1945-1955. Ph.D. Thesis, Columbia University, 1956, 341 P.

790 Kahn, Arthur D. Betrayal: Our Occupation of Germany. N.P., 2D Ed., 1950, 224 P.

791 Karsteter, William R. 1948 Historical Report: Mg/Hist/I/D. N.P.: Omg Greater Hesse, C.1949, 563 P.

792 Kyre, Martin. Kyre, Joan. Military Occupation and National Security. Washington: Public Affairs Press, 1968, 198 P.

793 Litchfield, Edward H., and Associates. Governing Postwar Germany. Ithaca: Cornell University Press, 1953, 661 P.

794 Long, Tania. Goering's Home Town--Under American Rule. New York Times Magazine. (3 June 1945), 9+.

795 Lunden, Walter A. United States Army Supervision of Civil Prisons in Bavaria. Journal of Criminal Law. 38:4 (November 1947), 358-368.

796 Mccloy, John J. American Occupation Policies in Germany. Proceedings of the Academy of Political Science. 21:4 (January 1946), 540-541.

797 Maginnis, John J. Military Government Journal: Normandy to Berlin. Ed. Robert A. Hart. Amherst: University of Massachusetts Press, 1971, 351 P.

798 Martin, James Stewart. All Honorable Men. Boston: Little, Brown, 1950, 326 P.

799 Marx, Walter J. Consular Services for German Nationals. Department of State Bulletin. 20:514 (8 May 1949), 575-578.

800 Mason, Edward S. Has Our Policy in

Germany Failed?. Foreign Affairs. 24:4 (July 1946), 579-590.

801 Mason, John Brown. Training American Civilian Personnel for Occupation Duties. American Journal of International Law. 40:1 (January 1946), 180-181.

802 Middleton, Drew. "Uncommon Clay": Our Ruler in the Reich. New York Times Magazine. (15 July 1945), 10+.

803 Military Control Directive for Germany. Current History. 13:73 (September 1947), 166-172.

804 Military Government of Germany: Directive to the Commander in Chief of the United States Forces of Occupation. Department of State Bulletin. 13:330 (21 October 1945), 596-607.

805 Miller, Robert W., Editor. United States Policy Towards Germany, 1945-1955: U.S. Government Documents on Germany. Frankfurt: Forschungsinstitut Der Deutschen Gesellschaft Fuer Auswaertige Politik, 1956, 40 P.

806 Muhlen, Norbert. America and American Occupation in German Eyes. Annals of the American Academy of Political and Social Science. 295 (September 1954), 52-61.

807 Neumann, Robert G. Political Intelligence and Its Relation to Military Government. American Experiences in Military Government in World War II. Ed. Carl J. Friedrich and Associates. New York: Rinehart, 1948, Pp. 70-85.

808 Nichol, David M. The Hard Peace. This Is Germany. Ed. Arthur Settel. New York: Sloane, 1950, Pp. 226-248. US Occupation Policy.

809 Nobleman, Eli E. American Military Government Courts in Germany. American Journal of International Law. 40:4 (October 1946), 803-811. Annals of the American Academy of Political and Social Science. 267 (January 1950), 87-97.

810 Norman, Albert. The Media of Public Education in Postwar Germany: A Year of United States Government, 1945-1946. Ph.D Thesis, Clark University, 1949, 138 P.

811 O'Brien, William V. The Constitution of the United States and the Occupation of Germany. World Polity: A Yearbook of Studies in International Law and Organization. 1 (1957), 61-107.

812 Padover, Saul K. Psychologist in Germany: The Story of an American Intelligence Officer. London: Phoenix House, 1946, 320 P.

813 Russ, William A., Jr. American Military Government After Two Wars. Social Studies. 38:5 (May 1947), 207-217.

814 Schloss, Bert P. The American Occupation of Germany, 1945-1952: An Appraisal. Ph.D. Thesis, University of Chicago, 1955.

815 Smith, Jean Edward, Editor. The Papers of General Lucius D. Clay, Germany 1945-1949. Bloomington: Indiana University Press, 1974, 2 Vols., 1216 P.

816 US, Department of State. American Policy in Occupied Areas. Washington: Department of State Publication 2794, Government Printing Office, 1947, 31 P.

817 US, Department of State. Occupation of Germany: Policy and Progress, 1945-46. Washington: Department of State Publication 2783, Government Printing Office, 1947, 241 P.

818 US, Department of State. What We Are Doing in Germany, and Why. Washington: Department of State Publication 2621, Government Printing Office, 1946, 4 P.

819 US, Department of State, Office of Public Affairs. Directive Regarding the Military Government of Germany. Washington: Department of State Publication 2913, Government Printing Office, 11 July 1947, 23 P. Directive By State, War and Navy Departments to Gen. Clay.

820 US, Department of the Army, Civil Affairs Division. Civil Affairs and Military Government in Europe: Background Summary. Washington: Department of the Army, Civil Affairs Division, Reports and Analysis Branch, C.1948, 30 P.

821 US, Department of the Army, Civil Affairs Division. Field Operations of Military Government Units. Washington: Department of the Army, Civil Affairs Division, January 1949, 217 P.

822 US, Department of the Army, Civil Affairs Division. Key Personnel: U.S. Military Government in Germany. Washington: Department of the Army, Civil Affairs Division, Reports and Analysis Branch, 1948, 14 P.

823 US, Department of the Army, Civil Affairs Division. Military Government Relations. Washington: Department of the Army, Civil Affairs Division, 25 April 1947, 27 P.

824 US, Department of the Army, European Command, Hist. Div. Military Government in Munich, 1945-1947. Karlsruhe?: U.S. Army, European Command, Historical Division, 1951, 26 P.

825 US, Department of the Army, Public Information Division. The Three R's of Occupied Germany: Rebuilding a Peaceful Industry, Rehabilitating a Peaceful Economy, Re-Educating a Defeated Enemy. Washington: Department of the Army, Public Information Division, Government Printing Office, 1948, 38 P.

826 US, Omgus. Confiscation of Literature and Material of a Nazi and Militaristic Nature. Berlin: Omgus, Ag 007 (Cs), 1946, 33 P.

827 US, Omgus. Law for Liberation From National Socialism and Militarism, With Annex and Regulations. Wiesbaden: Wiesbadener Verlag, 1946, 89 P.

828 US, Omgus. Status Report on Military Government of Germany, U.S. Zone. Berlin: Omgus, 1946, 45 P.

829 US, Omgus, Armed Forces Division. Demilitarization. N.P.: Omgus, 1947, 6 P.

830 US, Omgus, Civil Administration Division. The Civil Administration of U.S. Zone, Germany. N.P.: Omgus, C.1948, 49 P.

831 US, Omgus, Control Office. Comparative Readings in Basic U.S. Policy Directives on Germany. N.P.: Omgus, Control Office, Program Control Branch, November 1947, 37 P.

832 US, Omgus, Control Office. Organization Manual, U.S. Military Government in Germany. Berlin: Omgus, Control Office, 1946, 141 P.

833 US, Omgus, Information Services Division. Report to Smith-Mundt Committee. N.P.: Omgus, September 1947.

834 US, Omgus, Legal Division. Enactments and Approved Papers of the Control Council and Coordinating Committee. N.P.: Omgus, Legal Division, Legal Advice Branch, Drafting Section, 9

Vols., 1945-30 June 1948.

835   US, Omgus, Military Governor. German and Military Government Courts, 1946. Berlin: Omgus, January 1947, 25 P. Statistical Review.

836   US, Omgus, Military Governor. Monthly Report of the Military Governor. N.P.: Omgus, August 1945 to August-20 September 1949. 50 Issues, Accompanied By 48 Functional Reports and 29 Statistical Appendices.

837   US, Omgus, Military Governor. Omgus: Facts You Want to Know. Berlin: Omgus, Headquarters Command, I & E Section, 1946, 22 P.

838   US, Omgus, Omg Berlin. A Four Year Report, July 1, 1945-September 1, 1949. Berlin: Omgus, Berlin Sector, Public Relations, Statistical, and Historical Branch, 1949, 127 P.

839   US, Senate, Committee on Foreign Relations. A Decade of American Foreign Policy: Basic Documents, 1941-49. Washington: Senate Document No. 123, Government Printing office, 1950, 1381 P.

840   United States Policy on German Youth Activities. Department of State Bulletin. 16:398 (16 February 1947), 294-298.

841   Zink, Harold. American Military Government in Germany. New York: Macmillan, 1947, 272 P.

842   Zink, Harold. American Military Government Organization in Germany. Journal of Politics. 8:3 (August 1946), 329-349.

843   Zink, Harold. American Occupation Policies in Germany. Review of Politics. 9:3 (July 1947), 284-296.

844   Zink, Harold. A Political Scientist Looks at Military Government in the European Theater of Operations. American Political Science Review. 40:6 (December 1946), 1097-1112.

845   Zink, Harold. The United States in Germany, 1944-1955. Princeton: Van Nostrand, 1957, 374 P.

D.2.4. British Zone

846   Bentwich, Norman D. German Snapshots. Contemporary Review. 172:983 (November 1947), 275-277.

847   Bentwich, Norman D. Germany: The British Zone. Fortnightly. 158:947 (November 1945), 311-314.

848   Birley, Robert. The German Problem and the Responsibility of Britain. London: S.C.M. Press, 1947, 32 P.

849   Bonn, Moritz J. The British in Germany. Fortnightly. 168:1007 (November 1950), 292-298.

850   Butler, Harold. Peace or Power. London: Faber and Faber, 1947, 269 P.

851   Derrick, Michael. The Task in Germany: Impressions of the British Zone. Soundings. No. 26 (May 1949), 27-37.

852   Dickens, Arthur G. Luebeck Diary. London: Gollancz, 1947, 349 P.

853   Donnison, F. S. V. Civil Affairs and Military Government: North-West Europe, 1944-1946. London: H. M. Stationery Office, 1961, 518 P.

854   Ebsworth, Raymond. Restoring Democracy in Germany: The British Contribution. New York: Praeger, 1960, 222 P.

855   Eden, Anthony. Hynd, John B. The British Zone in Germany. British Speeches of the Day. 4:10 (December 1946), 721-739. Debate, House of Commons, London, 14 November 1946.

856   Gorer, Geoffrey. The British Zone of Germany. Fortnightly. 160:960 (December 1946), 381-387.

857   Harvey, C. P. Control Commission for Germany: My Experiences in the Legal Division. National Review. 127:765 (November 1946), 379-387.

858   Hynd, John B. British Administration in Germany. British Speeches of the Day. 4:9 (November 1946), 664-667.

859   Pakenham, Lord. Born to Believe: An Autobiography. London: Jonathan Cape, 1953, 254 P., Esp. Pp. 163-200.

860   Schilling, Frederick K., Jr. Germany and Her Future: British Opinion and Policy, 1939-1947. Ph.D. Thesis, Indiana University, 1954, 697 P.

861   Smallwood, Russell. Our Changing Approach to the German. Contemporary Review. 170:969 (September 1946), 138-141.

862   UK, CCG. Monthly Report. London: H.M. Stationery Office, 1945-1949.

863   UK, CCG. Progress of Demilitarisation in the British Zone of Occupation. Berlin: Control Commission for Germany (Be), 1946.

864   Voigt, Fritz A. Pax Britannica. London: Constable, 1949, 576 P., Esp. Ch. 2.

865   What We Saw in Germany. London: S.P.C.K., 1948, 32 P. Report By British Churchwomen to the Control Commission for Germany.

866   Woodman, D. R. Note on the Origins of British Military Governmemt in North-West Europe. Public Administration. 24:1 (Spring 1946), 41-43.

867   Woodman, D. R. The Organisation of Control in the British Zone of Germany. Public Administration. 24:3 (Autumn 1946), 171-175.

D.2.5. French Zone

868   Callender, Harold. What Kind of Europe?--The Question for Paris. New York Times Magazine. (28 July 1946), 5+.

869   Fontaine, Andre. Potsdam: A French View. International Affairs (London). 46:3 (July 1970), 466-474.

870   Fraser, Geoffrey. Crotch, W. Walter. The French Plan for Germany. Contemporary Review. 171:975 (March 1947), 139-145.

871   Mackie, Norman S., Jr. French National Security and the Postwar Treatment of Germany, 1944-1948. Ph.D. Thesis, Columbia University, 1960, 361 P.

872   Simmons, Stephen. The French Zone of Germany. Contemporary Review. 173:990 (June 1948), 336-339.

873   Strausz-Hupe, Robert. France and the Future German State. Yale Review. 38:2 (Winter 1948), 313-326.

874   Willis, F. Roy. The French in Germany, 1945-1949. Stanford: Stanford University Press, 1962, 308 P.

875   Willis, F. Roy. The French Zone of Occupation in Germany, 1945-1949. Ph.D. Thesis, Stanford University, 1959, 300 P.

D.2.6. Soviet Zone

876   A Berlin Correspondent. The Russian Zone of Germany. Fortnightly. 163:973 (January 1948), 19-23.

877   Croan, Melvin. Soviet Uses of the Doctrine of the "Parliamentary Road" to Socialism: East Germany, 1945-

1946. American Slavic and East European Review. 17:3 (October 1958), 302-315.

878 Davis, Jerome. Soviet Administration of Eastern Germany. Soviet Russia Today. 17:5 (September 1948), 11-12, 29-30.

879 Dewhurst, C. H. Close Contact. London: Allen & Unwin, 1954, 173 P. Report By Former Chief of British Mission to Soviet Forces Of Occupation in Germany.

880 Ernst, A. The Other Germany. Contemporary Review. 174:995 (November 1948), 306-309.

881 Fischer, Alfred Joachim. The Eastern Zone of Germany. World Affairs (London). 3:3 (July 1949), 259-268.

882 Fischer, Alfred Joachim. The Russian Zone in Germany. Contemporary Review. 174:993 (September 1948), 142-147.

883 Fraenkel, Heinrich. Berlin and the Russian Zone. Political Quarterly. 18:4 (October 1947), 323-330.

884 Glaser, Kurt. Governments of Soviet Germany. Governing Postwar Germany. Ed. Edward H. Litchfield and Associates. Ithaca: Cornell University Press, 1953, Pp. 152-183.

885 Joesten, Joachim. Soviet Rule in Eastern Germany: The Political System of the Soviet Zone. Great Barringtor, Mass.: Joachim Joesten, New Germany Reports No. 9, March 1949, 20 P.

886 Knop, Werner Gustav John. Prowling Russia's Forbidden Zone: A Secret Journey Into Soviet Germany. New York: Knopf, 1949, 200 P.

887 Krisch, Henry. German Politics Under Soviet Occupation. New York: Columbia University Press, 1974.

888 Kuby, Erich. The Russians and Berlin, 1945. New York: Hill and Wang, 1968, 372 P.

889 League of Culture for Democratic Regeneration of Germany. The League of Culture in Berlin: A Memorandum. Berlin (East): Aufbau, 1948, 63 P.

890 Leonhard, Wolfgang. Child of the Revolution. Chicago: Regnery, 1958, 447 P.

891 Leskov, Vlas. The Administration of Foreign Trade, 1946-49. Soviet Economic Policy in Postwar Germany. Ed. Robert Slusser. New York: Research Program on the Ussr, 1953, Pp. 61-77.

892 Loewenthal, Fritz. News From Soviet Germany. London: Gollancz, 1950, 344 P.

893 Nettl, Peter. Inside the Russian Zone, 1945-1947. Political Quarterly. 19:3 (July 1948), 201-233.

894 Nevsky, Viacheslav. Soviet Agricultural Policy in Eastern Germany, 1945-1949. Soviet Economic Policy in Postwar Germany. Ed. Robert Slusser. New York: Research Program on the Ussr, 1953, Pp. 87-126.

895 P. N. Eastern Germany: A Survey of Soviet Policy, 1945-50. World Today. 6:7 (July 1950), 297-308.

896 Raphael, Joan. Political Trends in the Soviet Zone of Germany. Columbia Journal of International Affairs. 2:2 (Spring 1948), 60-63.

897 Rudolph, Vladimir. The Agencies of Control: Their Organization and Policies. Soviet Economic Policy in Postwar Germany. Ed. Robert Slusser. New York: Research Program on the Ussr, 1953, Pp. 18-36.

898 Rudolph, Vladimir. The Execution of Policy, 1945-47. Soviet Economic Policy in Postwar Germany. Ed. Robert Slusser. New York: Research Program on the Ussr, 1953, Pp. 36-61.

899 Schaffer, Gordon. Russian Zone of Germany. London: Allen and Unwin, 1947, 192 P.

900 Schaffer, Gordon. Will the Eastern Zone Collapse?. New Central European Observer. 2:2 (22 January 1949), 15.

901 Slusser, Robert M., Editor. Soviet Economic Policy in Postwar Germany: A Collection of Papers By Former Soviet Officials. New York: Research Program on the U.S.S.R., Studies on the U.S.S.R. No. 3, 1953, 184 P.

902 Sorio, Georges. Through the Iron Curtain. Soviet Russia Today. 15:9 (January 1947), 9, 32. French Poet/Journalist Describes Soviet Zone.

903 Trevor-Roper, Hugh R. Is Russia Falling Between Two Plans?. New York Times Magazine. (18 July 1948), 9+. Difficulty Finding German Policy to Satisfy Both Germans and Satellites.

904 US, Omgus, Civil Administration Division. Government and Its Administration in the Soviet Zone of Germany. N.P.: Omgus, Civil Administration Division, November 1947, 44 P.

905 US, Omgus, Economics Division. Reciprocal Deliveries By the Ussr. N.P.: Omgus, November 1947.

906 US, Omgus, Economics Division. Socialization in the Soviet Zone. N.P.: Omgus, Adjutant General, 1947, 6 P.

907 US, Omgus, Finance Division. Financial Exploitation of German Resources By the Ussr. N.P.: Omgus, Adjutant General, 1947, 6 P.

908 Voigt, Fritz A. Eastern Germany. Twentieth Century. 139:829 (March 1946), 97-101.

909 Yershov, Vassily. Confiscation and Plunder By the Army of Occupation. Soviet Economic Policy in Postwar Germany. Ed. Robert Slusser. New York: Research Program on the Ussr, 1953, Pp. 1-14.

D.3. Punishment, Restitution, and Rehabilitation (See Also I.2)

D.3.1. War Crimes Trials

910 Addison, Lord. War Criminals. Fortnightly. 157:941 (May 1945), 285-289.

911 American Historical Association. What Shall Be Done With the War Criminals?. Washington: War Department, 1944, 44 P.

912 Andrus, Burton C. I Was the Nuremberg Jailer. New York: Coward-Mccann, 1969, 210 P.

913 Anspacher, John M. The German Guilt. This Is Germany. Ed. Arthur Settel. New York: Sloane, 1950, Pp. 116-135. War Crimes Trials and Denazification.

914 Appleman, John A. Military Tribunals and International Crimes. Indianapolis: Bobbs-Merrill, 1954, 421 P.

915 April, Nathan. An Inquiry Into the Juridical Basis for the Nuernberg War Crimes Trial. Minnesota Law Review. 30:5 (April 1946), 313-331.

916 Bar-Zohar, Michel. The Avengers. New York: Hawthorn, 1969, 279 P.

917 Barrister-at-Law. The Trial of the Nazis. Fortnightly. 158:945 (September 1945), 176-181.

918 Beck, Earl Ray. Verdict on Schacht: A Study in the Problem of Political "Guilt". Tallahassee: Florida State University, 1955, 201 P.

919 Benton, Wilbourn E., Editor. Grimm, Georg, Editor. Nuremberg: German Views of the War Trials. Dallas: Southern Methodist University Press, 1955, 232 P.

920 Bird, Eugene K. Prisoner #7: Rudolf Hess. New York: Viking, 1974.

921 Bonhoeffer, Emmi. Auschwitz Trials: Letters From an Eyewitness. Richmond: John Knox, 1967, 61 P.

922 Bonn, Moritz J. The Crime of War and the Soviets. Contemporary Review. 173:988 (April 1948), 207-211.

923 Bosch, William J. Judgment on Nuremberg: American Attitudes Toward the Major War Crimes Trials. Ph.D. Thesis, University of North Carolina at Chapel Hill, 1966, 689 P.

924 Bosch, William J. Judgment on Nuremberg: American Attitudes Toward the Major German War-Crime Trials. Chapel Hill: University of North Carolina Press, 1970, 272 P.

925 Brand, G. The War Crimes Trials and the Laws of War. British Year Book of International Law. 26 (1949), 414-427.

926 Bundestag Debate on the Statute of Limitations Extension. German Politics. Ed. Donald Schoonmaker. Lexington: Heath, 1971, Pp. 205-211.

927 Calvocoresm, Peter. German Officers' Corps. National Review. 130:780 (Febuary 1948), 120-128.

928 Calvocoressi, Peter. Nuremberg: The Facts, the Law and the Consequences. New York: Macmillan, 1948, 176 P.

929 Carmichael, Joel. The Eichmann Case: Reactions in Germany. Midstream. 7:3 (Summer 1961), 13-27.

930 Cherne, Leo. Why Punish War Criminals?. Ort Economic Review. 4:4 (June 1945), 16-23.

931 Clark, Delbert. The Fabulous Farben Empire Faces Trial. New York Times Magazine. (10 August 1947), 12+.

932 Cohn, Kurt. Crimes Against Humanity. German Foreign Policy (GDR). 6:2 (1967), 160-167. FRG Statute of Limitations for Nazi Crimes.

933 Cowles, Willard B. Trials of War Criminals (Non-Nuremberg). American Journal of International Law. 42:2 (April 1948), 299-319.

934 Daniell, Raymond. "So What?" Say the Germans of Nuremberg. New York Times Magazine. (2 December 1945), 5+.

935 Daskiewicz, Krystyna. Prescription of Nazi Crimes in the German Federal Republic in Relation to Law-Keeping. Polish Western Affairs. 12:1 (1971), 87-115.

936 Dautricourt, Joseph Y. Crime Against Humanity: European Views on Its Conception and Its Future. Journal of Criminal Law. 40:2 (July-Auguest 1949), 170-175.

937 Davidson, Eugene. The Trial of the Germans: An Account of the Twenty-Two Defendants Before the International Military Tribunal at Nuremberg. New York: Macmillan, 1966, 636 P.

938 Davidson, Eugene. The West German Statute of Limitations. Modern Age. 9:2 (Spring 1965), 114-118.

939 Dodd, Thomas J. The Nuernberg Trials. Journal of Criminal Law and Criminology. 37:5 (January-February 1947), 357-367.

940 Doenitz, Karl. Memoirs: Ten Years and Twenty Days. Cleveland: World, 1959, 500 P.

941 Doman, Nicholas. Political Consequences of the Nuremberg Trial. Annals of the American Academy of Political and Social Science. 246 (July 1946), 81-90.

942 Dreyfuss, Allan. Again Schacht Comes Out on Top. New York Times Magazine. (2 November 1952), 16+.

943 Du Bois, Josiah E. Generals in Grey Suits: The Directors of the International "I.G. Farben" Cartel, Their Conspiracy and Trial at Nuremberg. London: Bodley Head, 1953, 373 P.

944 Ehard, Hans. The Nuremberg Trial Against the Major War Criminals and International Law. American Journal of International Law. 43:2 (April 1949), 223-245.

945 FRG, Federal Ministry of Justice. The Prosecution Since 1945 of National Socialist Crimes By Public Prosecutors and Courts in the Territory of the Federal Republic of Germany. Duesseldorf: Leiner-Druck, for Federal Ministry of Justice, 1962, 19 P. Compiled in Collaboration With Laender Judicial Authorities.

946 Farago, Ladislas. Aftermath: Martin Bormann and the Fourth Reich. New York: Simon and Schuster, 1974, 479 P.

947 Farnsworth, Clyde A. Sleuth With 6 Million Clients: Simon Wiesenthal. New York Times Magazine. (2 February 1964), 11+.

948 Federn, Robert. Peace, Prosperity, International Order. London: Williams and Norgate, 1945, 167 P., Esp. Ch. 8. Punishment of War Crimes.

949 Fehl, Philipp. The Ghosts of Nuremberg. Atlantic Monthly. 229:3 (March 1972), 70-80.

950 Finch, George A. The Nuremberg Trial and International Law. American Journal of International Law. . 41:1 (January 1947), 20-37.

951 Fishman, Jack. The Seven Men of Spandau. New York: Rinehart, 1954, 276 P.

952 Friedmann, Tuviah. The Hunter. New York: Macfaddan, 1961, 286 P. Autobiographical Account of Search for Adolf Eichmann and Other Nazi War Criminals.

953 Fry, Geoffrey K. The Sachsenhausen Concentration Camp Case and the Convention of Ministerial Responsibility. Public Law. 15:3 (Autumn 1970), 336-357.

954 Gallagher, Richard. Nuremberg: The Third Reich on Trial. New York: Avon, 1961, 255 P.

955 Gilbert, Gustave Mark. Nuremberg Diary. New York: Farrar, Straus, 1947, 471 P.

956 Glassgold, A. C. The Spirit Will Rise: The Miracle of Landsberg. Ort Economic Review. 6:3 (March 1947), 12-18. on Displaced Persons.

957 Glueck, Sheldon. The Nuernberg Trial and Aggressive War. Harvard Law Review. 49:3 (February 1946), 396-456.

958 Glueck, Sheldon. The Nuremberg Trial and Aggressive War. New York: Knopf, 1946, 121 P.

959 Goerner, Gunter. Drawing Conclusions From the Wilhelmstrasse Trial. German Foreign Policy (GDR). 1:3 (1962), 327-334.

960 Goerner, Gunter. Schumann, Guenter.

War Crimes and Crimes Against Humanity. German Foreign Policy (GDR). 8:3 (1969), 177-194. FRG's Statute of Limitations, Refusal to Punish.

961 Goodhart, A. L. Questions and Answers Concerning the Nuremberg Trials. International Law Quarterly. 1:4 (Winter 1947), 525-531.

962 Halley, Fred G., Compiler. Preliminary Inventory of the Records of the United States Counsel for the Prosecution of Axis Criminality. Washington: National Archives Publication No. 49-29, Government Printing Office, 1949, 182 P.

963 Hankey, Baron Maurice Pascal Alers. Politics, Trials, and Errors. Chicago: Regnery, 1950, 150 P. Allied Policy of Unconditional Surrender and the Resulting War Crimes Trials.

964 Harris, Whitney R. Tyranny on Trial: The Evidence at Nuremberg. Dallas: Southern Methodist University Press, 1954, 608 P.

965 Heller, Maxine J. The Treatment of the Defeated War Leaders. Ph.D. Thesis, Columbia University, 1965, 500 P.

966 Heydecker, Joe Julius. The Nuremberg Trial: A History of Nazi Germany as Revealed Through the Testimony at Nuremberg. Cleveland: World, 1962, 398 P.

967 Hirsch, Felix Edward. Lessons of Nuremberg. Current History. 11:62 (October 1946), 312-318.

968 Hogan, Willard N. War Criminals. South Atlantic Quarterly. 45:4 (October 1946), 415-424.

969 Honig, Frederick. German Industrialists on Trial. World Affairs (London). 3:2 (April 1949), 175-186.

970 Honig, Frederick. Powers Behind the Nazi Throne: "The Ministries Case". World Affairs (London). 4:2 (April 1950), 209-223. The Trial of 21 Nazi Officials.

971 Honig, Frederick. War Crimes Trials: Lessons for the Future. International Affairs (London). 26:4 (October 1950), 522-532.

972 Jackson, Robert H. The Case Against the Nazi War Criminals: Opening Statement for the United States of America, and Other Documents. New York: Knopf, 1946, 217 P.

973 Jackson, Robert H. Justice Jackson Weighs Nuremberg's Lessons. New York Times Magazine. (16 June 1946), 12+.

974 Jackson, Robert H. Nuernberg. Common Cause. 3:6 (January 1950), 284-294.

975 Jackson, Robert H. The Nuernberg Case. New York: Knopf, 1947, 269 P.

976 Jackson, Robert H. Nuremberg in Retrospect: Legal Answer to International Lawlessness. American Bar Association Journal. 35:10 (October 1949), 813-816.

977 Jackson, William Eldred. Putting the Nuremberg Law to Work. Foreign Affairs. 25:4 (July 1947), 550-565.

978 Janeczek, Edward John. Nuremberg Judgement in the Light of International Law. Geneva: Graduate Institute of International Studies, University of Geneva, 1949, 142 P.

979 Jaspers, Karl. Augstein, Rudolf. No Statute of Limitations for Genocide. Midstream. 12:2 (February 1966), 3-18. Interview in "Der Spiegel".

980 Jaworski, Leon. After Fifteen Years. Houston: Gulf, 1961, 155 P. Reflections on Nuremberg.

981 Kahn, Leo. Achievement and Failure at Nuremberg. Bulletin of the Wiener Library. 25:24 (1972), 21-29.

982 Kaul, Friedrich Karl. About the Auschwitz Trials in Frankfurt/Main. Law and Legislation in the German Democratic Republic. No. 1 (1967), 65-72.

983 Kaul, Friedrich Karl. and Once Again: The Non-Application of the Statute of Limitations to Nazi War Crimes. Law and Legislation in the German Democratic Republic. No. 2 (1966), 31-33.

984 Kelley, Douglas M. 22 Cells in Nuremberg: A Psychiatrist Examines the Nazi Criminals. New York: Greenberg, 1947, 245 P.

985 Kelsen, Hans. Will the Judgment in the Nuremberg Trial Constitute a Precedent in International Law?. International Law Quarterly. 1:2 (Summer 1947), 153-171.

986 Kempner, Robert M. W. Impact of Nuremberg on the German Mind. New York Times Magazine. (6 October 1946), 8+.

987 Kempner, Robert M. W. The Nuremberg Trials as Sources of Recent German Political and Historical Materials. American Political Science Review. 44:2 (June 1950), 447-459.

988 Kenny, John P. Moral Aspects of Nuremberg. Baltimore: Carrol, Thomistic Studies No. 2, 1949, 168 P.

989 Klafkowski, Alfons. The Nuremberg Principles and the Development of International Law. Warsaw: Zachodnia Agencja Prasowa, 1966, 55 P.

990 Klafkowski, Alfons. The Prosecution of Nazi Criminals as a Problem of International Law. Polish Western Affairs. 5:2 (1964), 266-274.

991 Klarsfeld, Beate. Wherever They May Be! New York: Vanguard Press, 1975.

992 Knieriem, August Von. The Nuremberg Trials. Chicago: Regnery, 1959, 561 P.

993 Konvitz, Milton R. Will Nuremberg Serve Justice?. Commentary. 1:3 (January 1946), 9-15.

994 Kramer, Yale. Even-Handed Justice. Common Cause. 3:6 (January 1950), 284-314. About Nuremberg Trials.

995 Lawyer. War Crimes and International Law. Fortnightly. 158:946 (October 1945), 228-233.

996 Lekschas, John. Renneberg, Joachim. on the Necessity and Legal Obligation to Prosecute and Punish War and Nazi Crimes. Law and Legislation in the German Democratic Republic. No. 2 (1964), 51-62.

997 Lekschas, John. Renneberg, Joachim. Schulz, Joachim. Crimes Against Peace, War Crimes and Crimes Against Humanity Are Imprescriptible. Law and Legislation in the German Democratic Republic. No. 1 (1968), 5-33.

998 Leo, Gerhard. International Aspects of the Eichmann Trial. German Foreign Policy (GDR). 1:1 (1962), 31-37.

999 Leonhardt, Hans. The Nuremberg Trial: A Legal Analysis. Review of Politics. 11:4 (October 1949), 449-476.

1000 Leventhal, Harold. Harris, Sam. Wollsey, John M., Jr. Farr, Warren F. The Nuernberg Verdict. Harvard Law Review. 60:6 (July 1947), 857-907.

1001 Levi, Edward H. Meltzer, Bernard D. Reel, A. Frank. Were the War Crimes Trials Successful?. University of Chicago Round Table. No. 600 (18 September 1949), 1-13. Radio Discussion.

1002 Low, David. Portrait of the Master Race in the Dock. New York Times Magazine. (23 December 1945), 6+.

1003 Lozier, Marion E. Nuremberg: A Reappraisal. Columbia Journal of Transnational Law. 2:1 (1963), 22-33.

1004 Mallard, William D., Jr. Nuremberg--A Step Forward?. International Lawyer. 4:4 (July 1970), 673-681.

1005 Middleton, Drew. The Silent, Forgotten Seven of Spandau. New York Times Magazine. (20 July 1952), 10+.

1006 Morgan, John H. The Great Assize: An Examination of the Law of the Nuremberg Trials. London: Murray, 1948, 44 P.

1007 Morgan, John H. Nuremberg and After. Quarterly Review. 285:572 (April 1947), 319-336; and 285:574 (October 1947), 605-625.

1008 Morgenthau, Hans J. Nuremberg Trial. Politics in the Twentieth Century: Decline of Democratic Politics. Ed. Hans J. Morgenthau. Chicago: University of Chicago Press, 1962, Pp. 377-379.

1009 Murray, Michael Patrick. A Study in Public International Law: Comparing the Trial of Adolf Eichmann in Jerusalem with the Trial of the Major German War Criminals at Nuremberg. S.J.D. Thesis, George Washington University, 1973, 362 P.

1010 Naumann, Bernd. Auschwitz: A Report on the Proceedings Against Robert Karl Ludwig Mulka and Others Before the Court at Frankfurt. New York: Praeger, 1966, 433 P.

1011 Neumann, Franz L. The War Crimes Trials. World Politics. 2:1 (October 1949), 135-147.

1012 Neumann, Robert G. Neutral States and the Extradition of War Criminals. American Journal of International Law. 45:3 (July 1951), 495-508.

1013 Niebergall, Fred. Brief Survey Concerning the Records of the War Crime Trials in Nuernberg, Germany. Law Library Journal. 42:2 (May 1949), 87-90.

1014 Nuremberg in Retrospect: Towards an International Criminal Law. Round Table. 37:145 (December 1946), 22-28.

1015 O'Donnell, James P. The Devil's Architect: Albert Speer. New York Times Magazine. (26 October 1969), 45+.

1016 Pritt, Denis N. Shall Nazi Criminals Go Free?. New World Reivew. 33:4 (April 1965), 16-17.

1017 Pritt, Denis N. Shall War Criminals Go Free?. Labour Monthly. 51 (July 1969), 329-332.

1018 Pritt, Denis N. The Trial of War Criminals. Political Quarterly. 16:3 (July-September 1945), 195-204.

1019 Przybylski, Peter. Bonn's Concealed Amnesty for Nazi and War Criminals--A Menace to European Security. German Foreign Policy (GDR). 8:4 (1969), 243-256.

1020 Radin, Max. Justice at Nuremberg. Foreign Affairs. 24:3 (April 1946), 369-384.

1021 Radin, Max. War Crimes and the Crime of War. Virginia Quarterly Review. 21:4 (Autumn 1945), 497-516.

1022 Reed, Douglas. The Prisoner of Ottawa: Otto Strasser. London: Jonathan Cape, 1953, 271 P., Esp. Pp. 223-255. Inability to Return to Germany.

1023 Rie, Robert. The War Crimes Trials. American Journal of International Law. 48:3 (July 1954), 470-474. Review of Book By August Von Knieriem.

1024 Schick, F. B. The Nuremberg Trial and the International Law of the Future. American Journal of International Law. 41:4 (October 1947), 770-794.

1025 Schoenbaum, David. Nazi Murders & German Politics. Commentary. 39:6 (June 1965), 72-77.

1026 Shabecoff, Philip. The Last Prisoner of Spandau: Rudolf Hess. New York Times Magazine. (28 August 1966), 28+.

1027 Spiropoulos, Jean. Report on the Nuremberg Principles. American Bar Association Journal. 36:6 (June 1950), 505-508.

1028 Stevens, E. H., Editor. Trial of Nikolaus Von Falkenhorst. London: Hodge, 1949, 278 P.

1029 Stimson, Henry L. The Nuremberg Trial: Landmark in Law. Foreign Affairs. 25:2 (January 1947), 179-189.

1030 Taylor, Telford. Final Report to the Secretary of the Army on the Nuernberg War Crimes Trials Under Control Council Law No. 10. Washington: Government Printing Office, 15 August 1949, 346 P.

1031 Taylor, Telford. Nuremberg and Vietnam: An American Tragedy. Chicago: Quadrangle and the New York Times, 1970, 224 P.

1032 Taylor, Telford. Nuremberg Trials: War Crimes and International Law. International Conciliation. No. 450 (April 1949), 241-371.

1033 Taylor, Telford. Nuremberg War Crimes Trials: An Appraisal. Proceedings of the Academy of Political Science. 23:3 (May 1949), 19-34.

1034 Tomlinson, A. K. War Crimes and the Law. Poland and Germany. 5:1 (January-March 1961), 18-28.

1035 Trevor-Roper, Hugh R. The Lasting Effects of the Nuremberg Trial. New York Times Magazine. (20 October 1946), 15+.

1036 US, Chief of Counsel for Prosecution of Axis Criminality. Nazi Conspiracy and Aggression: Opinion and Judgment. Washington: Government Printing Office, 1947, 190 P.

1037 US, Department of State. Trial of War Criminals. Washington: Department of State Publication 2420, Government Printing Office, 1945, 89 P.

1038 US, Hicog. Landsberg: A Documentary Report. Frankfurt: Hicog, 1951, 30 P.

1039 US, Omgus. Trial of Members of Criminal Organizations. N.P.: Omgus, Adjutant General, C.1947, 48 P.

1040 US, Omgus, Military Tribunals. Trials of War Criminals Before the Nuernberg Military Tribunals Under Control Council Law No. 10, Nuernberg, October 1946-April 1949. Washington: Government Printing Office, 1949-53, 15 Vols.

1041 Wade, D. A. L. A Survey of the Trials of War Criminals. Royal United Service Institute Journal. 96:581 (February 1951), 66-70.

1042 Wechsberg, Joseph. Wiesenthal, Simon. The Murderers Among US: The Simon Wiesenthal Memoirs. New York: McGraw-Hill, 1967, 340 P.

1043 Wechsler, Herbert. The Issues of the Nuremberg Trial. Political Science Quarterly. 62:1 (March 1947), 11-26.

1044 Weir, Patricia Ann Lyons. The German War-Crimes Trials, 1949 to Present:

Repercussions of American Involvement. Ph.D. Thesis, Ball State University, 1973, 563 P.

1045 Weiss, Martin. The World Does Not Want to Live With Nazi Murderers. German Foreign Policy (GDR). 4:3 (1965), 217-224.

1046 Wells, Leon W. Living Ghosts of the Concentration Camps. New York Times Magazine. (26 January 1964), 13+. Onetime Inmate Returns to FRG to Confront Former Jailers.

1047 West, Rebecca (Pseud. of Cicily Isabel Fairfield Andrews). A Train of Powder. New York: Viking, 1955, 310 P., Esp. Pp. 1-72, 115-161, 231-250.

1048 Winfield, P. H. War Crimes and the Future of International Law. Fortnightly. 159:951 (March 1946), 163-169.

1049 Woetzel, Robert K. The Nuremberg Trials in International Law, With a Postlude on the Eichmann Case. New York: Praeger, 1962, 317 P.

1050 Wright, Lord. That the Guilty Shall Not Escape: War Crimes Trials. New York Times Magazine. (13 May 1945), 6+.

1051 Wright, Quincy. The Law of the Nuremberg Trial. American Journal of International Law. 41:1 (January 1947), 38-72.

1052 Wright, Quincy. The Nuremberg Trial. Annals of the American Academy of Political and Social Science. 246 (July 1946), 72-80.

1053 Wright, Quincy. War Criminals. American Journal of International Law. 39:2 (April 1945), 257-285.

1054 Zimmermann, Rolf. The West German Attack on the Principles on Nuremberg. German Foreign Policy (GDR). 1:2 (1962), 204-214.

D.3.2. Denazification (See Also F.2.4)

1055 Arndt, Hans-Joachim. The Questionnaire and the Information Program: Reflections on the Impact of America on Germany. Confluence. 2:3 (September 1953), 82-94.

1056 Berkes, Ross N. Denazification and Reeducation in Germany. World Affairs Interpreter. 17:2 (July 1946), 189-195.

1057 Carmichael, Joel. No German Policy Is Possible: The Denazification Policy in The American Zone. South Atlantic Quarterly. 46:1 (January 1947), 1-11.

1058 Denazification. Social Research. 14:1 (March 1947), 59-74. Letter From a German Anti-Nazi Lawyer; Comment By Karl Loewenstein, 14:3 (September 1947), 365-369.

1059 Fitzgibbon, Constantine. Denazification. London: Joseph, 1969, 222 P.

1060 Friedrich, Carl J. Denazification, 1944-1946. American Experiences in Military Government in World War II. Ed. Carl J. Friedrich and Associates. New York: Rinehart, 1948, Pp. 253-275.

1061 Gimbel, John. American Denazification and German Local Politics, 1945-1949: A Case Study in Marburg. American Political Science Review. 54:1 (March 1960), 83-105.

1062 Griffith, William E. Denazification in the United States Zone of Germany. Annals of the American Academy of Political and Social Science. 267 (January 1950), 68-76.

1063 Griffith, William E. The Denazification Program in the United States Zone of Germany. Ph.D. Thesis, Harvard University, 1950, 2 Vols.

1064 Havens, R. M. Note on Effect of Denazification Upon Property Rights in Germany. Southern Economic Journal. 13:2 (October 1946), 158-161.

1065 Herz, John H. The Fiasco of Denazification in Germany. Political Science Quarterly. 63:4 (December 1948), 569-594.

1066 Jones, Russell. Freedom on the Auction Block. This Is Germany. Ed. Arthur Settel. New York: Sloane, 1950, Pp. 136-148. Denazification.

1067 Kormann, John G. U.S. Denazification Policy in Germany, 1944-1950. Bad Godesberg-Mehlem: Office of the U.S. High Commissioner for Germany, Historical Division, 1952, 153 P.

1068 Levy, David M. New Fields of Psychiatry. New York: W. W. Norton & Company, 1947, 171 P., Esp. Pp. 105-161. Personnel Screening for Omgus Employment.

1069 Massing, Paul. Is Every German Guilty?. Commentary. 3:5 (May 1947), 442-446.

1070 Merritt, Anna J. Germans and American Denazification. Communications in International Politics. Ed. Richard L. Merritt Urbana: University of Illinois Press, 1972, Pp. 361-383.

1071 Napoli, Joseph F. Denazification From an American's Viewpoint. Annals of the American Academy of Political and Social Science. 264 (July 1949), 115-123.

1072 Plischke, Elmer. Denazification Law and Procedure. American Journal of International Law. 41:4 (October 1947), 807-827.

1073 Plischke, Elmer. Denazifying the Reich. Review of Politics. 9:2 (April 1947), 153-172.

1074 Roth, Guenther. Wolff, Kurt H. The American Denazification of Germany: A Historical Survey and an Appraisal. Columbus: Ohio State University, Department of Sociology and Anthropology, 1954, 49 P.

1075 Salomon, Ernst Von. Fragebogen: The Questionnaire. Garden City: Doubleday, 1955, 525 P.

1076 Stone, Shepard. "I Had to Join--I Was Never a Good Nazi": Denazification. New York Times Magazine. (15 December 1946), 12+.

1077 Straeter, Artur. Denazification. Annals of the American Academy of Political and Social Science. 260 (November 1948), 43-52.

1078 US, Omgus, Civil Administration Division. Denazification in the Four Zones of Germany. N.P.: Omgus, November 1947.

1079 US, Omgus, Civil Administration Division. A Summary of Denazification: The Year 1948 and 1 January to 30 June 1949. Berlin: Omgus, Civil Administration Division, 1949, 51 P.

1080 US, Omgus, Omg Hesse, Public Safety Section. Land Greater Hesse Removal List: Persons Removed or Excluded From Public Office or Positions of Importance in Quasi-Public or Private Enterprise. N.P.: Omg Greater Hesse, Public Safety Section, Special Branch, 1946, 410 P.

1081 US, Office of Strategic Services. Dissolution of the Nazi Party and Its Affiliated Organizations; De-Nazification of Important Business Concerns in Germany. Washington: War Department Pamphlet No. 31-110A, Government Printing Office, 1945, 193 P.

1082 Wood, Cecil, Editor. Shell, Curtis, Editor. German Denazification Law and All Implementations: American Directives. Munich: Omg Bavaria, Special Branch, 1947.

1083 Zink, Harold. The American Denazification Program in Germany. Journal of Central European Affairs. 6:3 (October 1946), 227-240.

D.3.3. Compensation to Nazi Victims (See Also O.3.2)

1084 American Federation of Jews From Central Europe. Former Jewish Communal Property in Germany: A Questionnaire Survey. New York: American Jewish Committee, American Federation of Jews From Central Europe, 1947, 38 P.

1085 American Jewish Joint Distribution Committee. European Legislation on Declarations of Death. Paris: American Jewish Joint Distribution Committee, 1949, 200 P., Esp. Pp. 79-94.

1086 American Jewish Joint Distribution Committee. Report of Activities in the United States Zone of Occupation for the Year 1947. Munich: American Jewish Joint Distribution Committee, 1947, 38 P.

1087 Axis Victims League. Restitution Legislation in Germany: Proposals to Remedy Defects. New York: Axis Victims League, April 1948, 8 P.

1088 Bentwich, Norman D. German Restitution and Reparation. Fortnightly. 171:1021 (January 1952), 31-36.

1089 Bentwich, Norman D. Germany's Restitution and Compensation Account. Contemporary Review. 201 (June 1962), 298-301.

1090 Bentwich, Norman D. International Aspects of Restitution and Compensation for Victims of the Nazis. British Year Book of International Law. 32 (1955-56), 204-217.

1091 Bentwich, Norman D. Nazi Spoliation and German Restitution: The Work of the United Restitution Office. Year Book of the Leo Baeck Institute. 10 (1965), 204-224.

1092 Bentwich, Norman D. U.R.O.: The United Restitution Office. London: U.R.O., 1954, 16 P.

1093 Breslauer, Walter. Goldschmidt, F. The Work of the Council of Jews From Germany in the Sphere of Indemnification. London: Council of Jews From Germany, 1966, 31 P.

1094 Callmann, H. William. United States Taxation of Income Arising From Restitution of Property Seized By Nazis. Journal of Accountancy. 89:4 (April 1950), 318-328.

1095 Chmielewski, Mieczyslaw. National Discrimination in the German Federal Compensation Law. Poland and Germany. 4:12 (April 1960), 17-23.

1096 Chmielewski, Mieczyslaw. The Problem of Compensation for Victims of National Persecution. Polish Affairs (London). No. 2 (February 1958), 11-20.

1097 Cohn, Ernst J. The Board of Review. International and Comparative Law Quarterly. 4:4 (October 1955), 492-507.

1098 Conference on Jewish Material Claims Against Germany. Annual Reports. New York: Conference on Jewish Material Claims Against Germany, 1954 Through 1961.

1099 Conference on Jewish Material Claims Against Germany. Five Years Later (Activities, 1954-1958). New York: Conference on Jewish Material Claims Against Germany, 1959, 87 P.

1100 Council for Protection of Rights and Interests of Jews. Draft of an Indemnification Law for Germany. London: Council for the Protection of the Rights and Interests of Jews From Germany, 1947, 11 P.

1101 Council for Protection of Rights and Interests of Jews. Memoradum to the Signatory Powers of the Final Act of the Paris Conference on Reparation. London: Council for the Protection of the Rights and Interests of Jews From Germany, 1946, 6 P.

1102 FRG. The German Federal Compensation Law (Beg) and Its Implementary Regulations. New York: Institute of Jewish Affairs, World Jewish Congress, 1957, 119 P. 1956 Law on Compensation for Victims of Nazi Persecution.

1103 FRG. The German Federal Supplementary Law for the Compensation of Victims of National Socialist Persecution (Beg) of September 18, 1953. New York: Institute of Jewish Affairs, 1954, 41 P.

1104 Goldschmidt, Siegfried. Legal Claims Against Germany: Compensation for Losses Resulting From Anti-Racial Measures. New York: Dryden, 1945, 213 P.

1105 Institute of Jewish Affairs. Information on Restitution and Related Subjects. New York: Institute of Jewish Affairs, 1952, 11 P.

1106 Institute of Jewish Affairs. The Institute Anniversary Volume, 1941-1961. New York: Institute of Jewish Affairs, 1962, 336 P.

1107 Institute of Jewish Affairs, The West German Federal Legislation in the Field of Compensation to Victims of Nazi Persecution. New York: Institute of Jewish Affairs, 1956, 54 P.

1108 Jewish Restitution Successor Organization. After Five Years, 1948-1953. Nuremberg: Jewish Restitution Successor Organization, 1953, 32 P. Report on Restitution of Identifiable Property in U.S. Zone.

1109 Jewish Restitution Successor Organization. Report on the Restitution of Jewish Property in the U.S. Zone of Germany. Nuremberg: Jewish Restitution Successor Organization, 1949.

1110 Jewish Trust Corporation for Germany. Annual Reports. London: Jewish Trust Corporation for Germany, 1951-57, 7 Vols.

1111 Kapralik, Charles I. The History of the Work of the Jewish Trust Corporation for Germany. London: Jewish Trust Corporation for Germany, 1971, Xv and 121 P.

1112 Kapralik, Charles I. Reclaiming the Nazi Loot: The History of the Work of the Jewish Trust Corporation for Germany. London: Jewish Trust Corporation for Germany, 1962, 199 P.

1113 Karasik, Monroe. Problems of Compensation and Restitution in Germany and Austria. Law and Contemporary Problems. 16:3 (Summer 1951), 448-468.

1114 Kosovac, Nikola Dz. Compensation of Yugoslav Victims of Nazism; Legal and Moral Obligation of the Federal German Republic. Belgrade: Federation of Yugoslav Journalists, 1964, 76 P.

1115 Marx, Hugo. The Case of the German Jews Vs. Germany: Legal Basis for The Claims Against Germany By the German Jews. New York: Egmont, 1944, 124 P.

1116 Robinson, Jacob. Friedman, Philip.

Guide to Jewish History Under Nazi Impact. New York: Yad Washem Martyrs' and Heroes' Memorial Authority (Jerusalem) and Yivo Institute for Jewish Research, 1960, 425 P., Esp. Pp. 176-221, 283-294. 3,684 Items.

1117 Robinson, Nehemiah. Compensation Legislation in Germany. New York: Institute of Jewish Affairs, 1950, 45 P.

1118 Robinson, Nehemiah. Indemnification and Reparations. New York: Institute of Jewish Affairs, 1944, 302 P. Four Supplements, 1945-1949.

1119 Robinson, Nehemiah. Problems of European Reconstruction. Quarterly Journal of Economics. 60:1 (November 1945), 1-55.

1120 Robinson, Nehemiah. Reparations, Restitution, Compensation. The Institute Annual, 1956. New York: Institute of Jewish Affairs, 1957, Pp. 5-54.

1121 Robinson, Nehemiah. Reparation and Restitution in International Law as Affecting Jews. Jewish Yearbook of International Law, 1948. Ed. Nathan Feinberg and J. Stoyanovsky. Jerusalem: Mass, 1949, 186-205.

1122 Robinson, Nehemiah. Restitution Legislation in Germany. New York: Institute of Jewish Affairs, 1950, 59 P.

1123 Robinson, Nehemiah. Ten Years of German Indemnification. New York: Conference on Jewish Material Claims Against Germany, 1964, 79 P.

1124 Robinson, Nehemiah. War Damage Compensation and Restitution in Foreign Countries. Law and Contemporary Problems. 16:3 (Summer 1951), 347-376.

1125 Robinson, Nehemiah. The West German Federal Legislation in the Field of Compensation to Victims of Nazi Persecution. New York: Institute of Jewish Affairs, 2D Ed., 1956, 53 P.

1126 Rowson, Sefton W. D. The Abolition of Nazi and Fascist Anti-Jewish Legislation By British Military Administration of the Second World War. Jewish Yearbook of International Law, 1948. Ed. Nathan Feinberg and J. Stoyanovsky. Jerusalem: Mass, 1949, Pp. 261-268.

1127 Scheir, Ernest. Settlement of World War II Claims. International Lawyer. 1:3 (April 1967), 444-456.

1128 Schwarz, Leo Walder. Summary Analysis of Ajdc Program in the U.S. Zone of Occupation, Germany. Menorah Journal. 35:2 (Spring 1947), 217-239.

1129 Schwerin, Kurt. German Compensation for Victims of Nazi Persecution. Northwestern University Law Review. 67:4 (September-October 1972), 479-527.

1130 UK, CCG. Law No. 59: Restitution of Identifiable Property to Victims of Nazi Oppression. London: H.M. Stationery Office, 1949, 20 P.

1131 UK, O'sullivan Committee. Report on the Progress Made in the Disposal of Internal Restitution Claims in the British Zone of Germany, 30Th June, 1951. London: H.M. Stationery Office, 59-117, 1951, 33 P.

1132 US, Omgus. Law No. 59: Restitution of Identifiable Property. N.P.: Omgus, 1947, 42 P.

1133 US, Omgus, Military Governor. Property Control: History, Policies, Practices and Procedures of the United States Area of Control, Germany. N.P.: Omgus, Adjutant General, November 1948, 71 P.

1134 US, Omgus, Military Governor. Property Control in the U.S.-Occupied Area of Germany, 1945-1949. N.P.: Hicog, July 1949, 90 P.

1135 United Restitution Organisation. Federal Idemnification Law: Implementary Regulations. London: United Restitution Organisation, 1957, 40 P.

1136 United Restitution Organisation. Federal Indemnification Law, 29 June 1956. London: United Restitution Organisation, 1956, 81 P.

1137 Weis, George. The Ordinance Supplementing the Law Concerning Missing Persons, Declarations of Death and the Determination of the Time of Death. Legal Adviser, Jewish Relief Unit, 1947, 22 P.

1138 Wengler, Wilhelm. Conflict of Laws Problems Relating to Restitution of Property in Germany. International and Comparative Law Quarterly. 11:4 (October 1962), 1131-1152.

1139 Wiener Library. Jewry and Germany: Reconciliation of Interests: The Approach to Reparations, a Survey of Developments, 1949-1952. London: Wiener Library, 1952, 18 P.

1140 Wiener Library. Restitution: European Legislation to Redress the Consequences of Nazi Rule. London: Wiener Library, 1946, 198 P.

1141 World Jewish Congress. The Convention on the Declaration of Death of Missing Persons. New York: World Jewish Congress, 1950, 12 P.

D.3.4. Re-Education (See Also N.1.3)

1142 Benton, Arthur. A Long-Range Policy on German Re-Education. School and Society. 64:1655 (September 1946), 181-183.

1143 Bidwell, Percy Wells. Reeducation in Germany: Emphasis on Culture in the French Zone. Foreign Affairs. 27:1 (October 1948), 68-85.

1144 Brailsford, H. N. The Re-Education of Germany. Contemporary Review. 168:956 (August 1945), 70-75.

1145 Colvin, Ian. Exporting Democracy to Germany. National Review. 129:774 (August 1947), 109-117.

1146 Colwell, Ernest C. D'Arms, Edward F. Stoddard, George D. Are We Re-Educating the Germans and the Japanese?. University of Chicago Round Table. No. 436 (28 July 1946), 1-18. Radio Discussion.

1147 Cook, F. G. Alletson. Democratic Abc's for Nazi Pw's. New York Times Magazine. (11 November 1945), 8+. Army School for German Pow's on Democracy.

1148 Cramer, Frederick H. Re-Education in Germany: An American Experiment. Forum. 104:2 (October 1945), 114-119.

1149 Dean, Vera Micheles. Allies Must Push Social Transformation of Germany. Foreign Policy Bulletin. 25:5 (16 November 1945), 1-2.

1150 Duggan, Stephen. Problems of Postwar International Education: The Reeducation of the Germans. Institute of International Education News Bulletin. 21:1 (October 1945), 3-5.

1151 Ehrmann, Henry W. Experiment in Political Education: The Prisoner-of-War Schools in the United States. Social Research. 14:3 (September 1947), 304-320.

1152 Evans, Frederic. The Re-Education of Germany. Political Quarterly. 16:1 (January-March 1945), 21-30.

1153 Hocking, William Ernest. Experiment in Education: What We Can Learn From

Teaching Germany. Chicago: Regnery, 1954, 303 P.

1154 Keohane, Robert E. Dilemmas of German Re-Education: Reflections Upon an Experiment Noble in Purpose. School Review. 57:8 (October 1949), 405-415.

1155 Knappen, Marshall M. and Call It Peace: America's Dangerous Blunders in Re-Educating the Germans. Chicago: University of Chicago Press, 1947, 213 P.

1156 Landeen, William M. United States Policy in the Re-Education of Germany. Proceedings of the Institute of World Affairs. 23 (1947), 141-149.

1157 Levi, Werner. Is Germany Being Democratized?. Fortnightly. 165:985 (January 1949), 8-15.

1158 Mcgrath, Earl J. Merriam, Charles E. Smith, Thomas V. Are We Re-Educating for Democracy in Germany?. University of Chicago Round Table. No. 459 (5 January 1947), 1-20. Radio Discussion.

1159 Martin, Kingsley. Re-Education of Germany. Political Quarterly. 15:2 (April 1944), 135-148.

1160 Menck, Clara. The Problem of Reorientation. The Struggle for Democracy in Germany. Ed. Gabriel A. Almond. Chapel Hill: University of North Carolina Press, 1949, Pp. 281-307.

1161 Middleton, Drew. Only a Start in Re-Educating the Germans. New York Times Magazine. (31 March 1946), 10+.

1162 Mulhern, James. Re-Educating the Germans. World Affairs Interpreter. 19:3 (October 1948), 250-275.

1163 Neumann, Franz L. Re-Educating the Germans: The Dilemma of Reconstruction. Commentary. 3:6 (June 1947), 517-525.

1164 Newman, James R. How We Began the Re-Education of Nazi Germany. American School Board Journal. 112:2 (February 1946), 33-34.

1165 Peak, Helen. Some Psychological Problems in the Re-Education of Germany. Journal of Social Issues. 2:3 (August 1946), 26-38.

1166 Pundt, Alfred C. Re-Educating the New Germany. Journal of Higher Education. 19:7 (October 1948), 350-360.

1167 Richter, Werner. Re-Educating Germany. Chicago: University of Chicago Press, 1945, 227 P.

1168 Riess, Curt. We Must Win Another Battle in Germany: Re-Education. New York Times Magazine. (20 May 1945), 5+.

1169 Russell, William F. Reeducation in Germany: Teaching Germans to Teach Themselves. Foreign Affairs. 27:1 (October 1948), 68-77.

1170 Russell, William F. Reeducation of the Germans. Education Digest. 12:1 (September 1946), 12-16.

1171 Russell, William F. The Re-Education of the Germans. Teachers College Record. 47:6 (March 1946), 345-353.

1172 Shuster, George N. German Re-Education: Success or Failure?. Proceedings of the Academy of Political Science. 23:3 (May 1949), 12-18.

1173 Smith, Thomas V. The Re-Education of Conquered Peoples. Proceedings of the National Conference of Social Work: Selected Papers, Seventy-Fourth Annual Meeting, San Francisco, April 13-19, 1947. New York: Columbia University Press, 1948, Pp. 25-38.

1174 Stonborough, John. Can Germany Be Re-Educated?. National Review. 128:768 (February 1947), 125-137.

1175 Traxler, Arthur E. The Re-Education of German Youth: What Kind of a Job Are We Doing?. School and Society. 69:1798 (4 June 1949), 393-398.

1176 US, Department of State, Division of Research for Europe. The Progress of Reeducation in Germany. Washington: Department of State, Office of Intelligence Research, Oir Report 4237, 1947, 111 P.

1177 Wickham, Denis A. Re-Educating the Nazi Child. Contemporary Review. 169:965 (May 1946), 302-306.

1178 Zook, George F. Japan and Germany: Problems in Reeducation. International Conciliation. No. 427 (January 1947), 1-40.

D.3.5. Postwar Views on Nazi Era (See Also A.4; N.7.4)

1179 Baade, Hans W. Hoggan's History: A West German Case in the Judicial Evaluation of History. American Journal of Comparative Law. 16:3 (1968), 391-404. on David L. Hoggan's Book, Der Erzwungene Krieg: Die Ursachen Und Urheber Des 2. Weltkriegs.

1180 Becker, Howard. Intellectuals, Concentration Camps and Black Propaganda: An Interview With Alfred Weber. American Journal of Economics and Sociology. 10:1 (January 1951), 139-143.

1181 Bettany, A. Guy. The Lessons of the Nazi Concentration Camps. London Quarterly of World Affairs. 11:2 (July 1945), 119-123.

1182 Bettelheim, Bruno. Returning to Dachau--The Living and the Dead. Commentary. 21:2 (February 1956), 144-151.

1183 Boehle, Karl-Heinz. Immortal Testament. Dresden: Zeit Im Bild, 1968, 64 P. Concentration Camps, Prisoners, Monuments.

1184 Denny, Harold. The World Must Not Forget. New York Times Magazine. (6 May 1945), 8+. Opening of Concentration Camps.

1185 Dorpalen, Andreas. Hitler, Twelve Years After. Review of Politics. 19:4 (October 1957), 486-506.

1186 Fitzgibbon, Constantine. Again the Issue of German Guilt. New York Times Magazine. (18 August 1963), 17+. Growing German Acceptance of Responsiblity for Nazi Crimes.

1187 Frankel, Theodore. The Good German of Auschwitz. Midstream. 6:3 (Summer 1960), 16-24.

1188 Grenfell, Russell. Unconditional Hatred: German War Guilt and the Future of Europe. New York: Devin-Adair, 1954, 273 P.

1189 Heller, Bernard. Dawn or Dusk?. New York: Bookman's, 1961, 314 P. Discusses German Guilt.

1190 Heym, Stefan. But the Hitler Legend Isn't Dead. New York Times Magazine. (20 January 1946), 8+.

1191 Janowitz, Morris. German Reactions to Nazi Atrocities. American Journal of Sociology. 52:1 (July 1946), 141-146.

1192 Jaspers, Karl. Augstein, Rudolf. The Criminal State and German Responsibility: A Dialogue. Commentary. 41:2 (February 1966), 33-39. Interview in "Der Spiegel".

1193 Jouhy, Ernest. German Youth and German History. Commentary. 29:4 (April 1960), 308-314. Especially With Regard to Anti-Semitism.

1194 Kalow, Gert. The Shadow of Hitler: A Critique of Political Consciousness. London: Rapp & Whiting, 1968, 144 P.

1195 Knees, Adalbert. German Resistance-- to-Day. Contemporary Issues. 1:1 (Summer 1948), 25-37. Follow-Up Reports in 1:2 (Winter 1948), 57-101; 1:3 (Spring 1949), 217-232; and 1:4 (Autumn 1949), 302-335.

1196 Kraus, Wolfgang H. The German Resistance Movement. Journal of Social Issues. 2:3 (August 1946), 50-69. Anti-Nazi Resistance; Current Attitudes to Occupation.

1197 Kuebler, Jeanne. War Guilt Expiation. Editorial Research Reports. (February 1965), 143-160.

1198 Lewis, Flora. What German Youth Knows About Hitler. New York Times Magazine. (7 June 1959), 12+.

1199 Luchsinger, Fred. The Forgotten Third Reich. Swiss Review of World Affairs. 9:11 (February 1960), 3-4. Vergangenheitsbewaeltigung: Problems With and Lack Thereof.

1200 Pachter, Henry M. Germany Looks in the Mirror of History. World Politics. 13:4 (July 1961), 633-641.

1201 Peterson, Hans Joachim. The Post-War German View of Franklin Delano Roosevelt. Ph.D. Thesis, University of Denver, 1966, 220 P.

1202 Rothfels, Hans. The Political Legacy of the German Resistance Movement. Bad Godesberg: Inter Nationes, 1969, 23 P.

1203 Sagalowitz, Benjamin. Carmel at Dachau. Swiss Review of World Affairs. 16:2 (May 1966), 14-18.

1204 Samuels, Gertrude. German Democracy-- A Reporter's Notebook. New York Times Magazine. (5 January 1964), 17+. Current German Views on Burden of Past (Nazi) History.

1205 Schoenbaum, David. What West German Boys Say About Hitler. New York Times Magazine. (9 January 1966), 30+.

1206 Taylor, Telford. Re-Educating Germany With Nazi History. New York Times Magazine. (28 May 1950), 8+.

1207 Tomlinson, A. K. Watching Germany. Poland and Germany. 3:7 (January 1959), 22-31. How Are They Dealing With Their Nazi Past?.

1208 Trevor-Roper, Hugh R. The Germans Reappraise the War. Foreign Affairs. 31:2 (January 1953), 225-237.

1209 Whitney, Craig R. Papa, Who Was Hitler? New York Times Magazine. (28 October 1973), 24+.

1210 Wires, Richard. German Anti-Revisionism and the Responsibility Question. Indiana Social Studies Quarterly. 21:3 (Winter 1968-69), 46-60.

D.4. Breakdown of Four-Power Cooperation (See Also C.1)

D.4.1. Disunity on Germany's Future, 1946-47 (See Also D.2.2)

1211 American Jewish Committee. The Peace Treaty With Germany: Recommendations. New York: American Jewish Committee, 1947, 13 P.

1212 American Jewish Committee. Towards Peace and Equity: Recommendations. New York: American Jewish Committee, 1946, 152 P.

1213 Berkes, Ross N. Germany: Test Tube of Peace. American Scholar. 16:1 (Winter 1946-47), 46-56. The Problem of Four-Power Administration.

1214 Bevin, Ernest. Peace Conference. Vital Speeches. 13:3 (15 November 1946), 85-92.

1215 Bidault, Georges. Agreement on Germany: Key to World Peace. Foreign Affairs. 24:4 (July 1946), 271-278.

1216 Byrnes, James F. American Policy on Germany. International Conciliation. No. 424 (October 1946), 469-480. Speech at Stuttgart, 6 September 1946.

1217 Byrnes, James F. Paris Peace Conference. Washington: Department of State, Publication 2682, Conference Series 90, Government Printing Office, 1946, 14 P.

1218 Churchill, Winston S. Sinews of Peace, Post-War Speeches. Ed. Randolph S. Churchill. Boston: Houghton Mifflin, 1947, 256 P.

1219 Colvin, Ian. Germany Towards Chaos. National Review. 127:762 (August 1946), 109-113.

1220 Colvin, Ian. The Road to Nihilism. National Review. 127:763 (September 1946), 215-217. Allied Confusion Over the Future of Germany.

1221 Dean, Vera Micheles. Will Germany Again Play East and West Against Each Other?. Foreign Policy Bulletin. 25:48 (13 September 1946), 1-2.

1222 Dean, Vera Micheles. Work of Foreign Ministers Offers Hope for Peace Settlement. Foreign Policy Bulletin. 26:6 (22 November 1946), 1-2.

1223 Denmark, Ministry for Foreign Affairs. Memorandum Containing the Views of the Royal Danish Government Regarding the Future Settlement of Germany. Copenhagen: Ministry for Foreign Affairs, 1947, 30 P.

1224 Dorpalen, Andreas. The Split Occupation of Germany. Virginia Quarterly Review. 22:4 (Autumn 1946), 581-597.

1225 Dulles, Allen Welsh. Alternatives for Germany. Foreign Affairs. 25:3 (April 1947), 421-432.

1226 Glazebrook, G. Det. The Settlement of Germany. International Journal. 2 (Spring 1947), 132-143.

1227 Gollancz, Victor. on Reconciliation: Two Speeches. London: Gollancz, 1948, 60 P.

1228 Heilperin, Michael A. The "Redefinition" of Germany and Europe's Peace. International Journal. 2 (Winter 1946-47), 16-25.

1229 Hirsch, Felix Edward. The German Balance Sheet: Reflections on the Eve of the Big Four Conference in Moscow. Current History. 12:67 (March 1947), 205-211.

1230 Johnson, Alvin. Two Sides of the German Problem. Yale Review. 36:1 (September 1946), 38-45.

1231 Kelsen, Hans. Is a Peace Treaty With Germany Legally Possible and Politically Desirable?. American Political Science Review. 41:6 (December 1947), 1188-1193.

1232 Mason, Edward S. Reflections on the Moscow Conference. International Organization. 1:3 (September 1947) 475-487.

1233 Mende, Tibor. Germany and Allied Unity. Contemporary Review. 170:969 (September 1946), 148-152.

1234 Milliken, Robert. Germany and the Coming Peace. Dalhousie Review. 26:4 (January 1947), 459-464.

1235 Molotov, Viacheslav Mikhailovich. The Future of Germany: Two Statements Made in Paris. London: Soviet News, 1946, 24 P.

1236 Molotov, Viacheslav Mikhailovich. Speeches and Statements Made at the Moscow Session of the Council of Foreign Ministers, March 10-April 24, 1947. London: Soviet News, 1947, 124 P.

1237 Morgenthau, Hans J. Shuster, George N. Toynbee, Arnold J. The Moscow Conference and the Future of Europe. University of Chicago Round Table. No. 470 (23 March 1947), 1-20. Radio Discussion.

1238 Pick, Frederick Walter. The German Problem. Contemporary Review. 172:984 (December 1947), 336-339.

1239 Pick, Frederick Walter. Peacemaking in Perspective. Journal of Central European Affairs. 6:4 (January 1947), 337-350; and 7:2 (July 1947), 162-196.

1240 Pick, Frederick Walter. Peacemaking in Perspective: From Potsdam to Paris. Oxford: Pen-in-Hand, 1950, 251 P.

1241 Reimann, Karl. Towards the Solution of the German Problem. Dublin Review. 219:438 (July 1946), 9-20.

1242 The System of Three: A Proposition for the Realization of Total Democracy in State, Economy and Culture. Hamburg: N.P., 1947, 61 P.

1243 Warburg, James P. Germany: Bridge or Battle Ground. New York: Harcourt, Brace, 1947, 386 P.

1244 Warburg, James P. Germany--Nation or No-Man's Land. New York: Foreign Policy Association, Headline Series No. 60, November-December 1946, Pp. 3-54.

1245 Whyte, Anne. The Future of Germany. London: Fabian, 1947, 26 P.

1246 Wilcox, Francis C. The United Nations and the Peace Treaties. Annals of the American Academy of Political and Social Science. 257 (May 1948), 175-183.

1247 Wyndham, E. H. The Military Situation in Europe. Army Quarterly. 52:1 (April 1946), 12-17.

D.4.2. Bizonal Administration, 1947-48

1248 Anglo-American Agreement Regarding Germany: General Summary of Agreement; Text of Agreement. Department of State Bulletin. 17:443 (28 December 1947), 1262-1267.

1249 Bevin, Ernest. Byrnes, James F. Anglo-American Statement on German Zones Merger. Current History. 12:1 (January 1947), 69-73.

1250 Bi-Zonal Reorganization for Germany. World Report. 2:24 (17 June 1947), 36-37. Text of US-UK Agreement, 29 May 1947.

1251 Britain, France and Germany. Economist. 151:5371 (3 August 1946), 161-162. British Government's Decision to Accept the United States' Offer to Effect an Economic Fusion Between the American Zone and Other Zones in Germany.

1252 Draper, William H., Jr. Havighurst, Robert J. Riddy, Donald C. Taylor, John W. What Should America Do Now in Bizonia?. University of Chicago Round Table. No. 516 (8 February 1948), 1-30. Radio Discussion.

1253 Economic Integration of U.S. and U.K. Zones in Germany. Department of State Bulletin. 15:389 (15 December 1946), 1102-1104.

1254 The Government of Bizonia: Western Germany Since the Conference. Round Table. 38:150 (March 1948), 559-565.

1255 Montagu, Ivor. Bi-Zonal Germany. Labour Monthly. 29:6 (June 1947), 175-178.

1256 Seborer, Stuart J. Droller, Gerard. Bizonal Germany, 1947-1948: The Interrelation of Internal Economic Progress and Foreign Trade, a Study. Washington: Department of the Army, Civil Affairs Division, Washington Analysis Branch, 1949, 34 P.

1257 Slover, Robert H. The Bizonal Economic Administration of Western Germany. Ph.D. Thesis, Harvard University, 1950, 277 P.

1258 UK, Foreign Office. Memorandum of Agreement Between His Majesty's Government in The United Kingdom and the Government of the United States Concerning the British and American Zones of Occupation in Germany, New York, December 2, 1946. London: H.M. Stationery Office, Cmd. 6984, 1946, 5 P.

1259 US, Omgus, Civil Administration Division. The Evolution of Bizonal Organization. N.P.: Omgus, Civil Administration Division, 2D Ed., 1948, 115 P.

1260 US, Omgus, Military Governor. Documents on Bizonal Economic Organization. N.P.: Omgus, June 1947.

1261 US, Omgus, Military Governor. UK, CCG, Military Governor. Statistical Handbook of Bizonal Recovery of Programs for Fiscal Years 1948/49, 1949/50, 1952/53 and Summary of Economic Progress US/UK Occupied Areas of Germany. N.P.: US and UK Military Governors, January 1949.

D.4.3. Division of Germany (See Also D.2.6)

1262 Royal Institute of International Affairs. Select Reference and Reading List on the German Problem. London: H. M. Stationery Office, 1947, 52 P.

1263 Acheson, Dean G. The Current Situation in Germany. Department of State Bulletin. 20:514 (8 May 1949), 585-588.

1264 Blow, Jonathan. Germany Approaches the Cross-Roads: Influence of the Western Powers and of Russia. Quarterly Review. 285:571 (January 1947), 152-167.

1265 Cassidy, Velma Hastings. Germany, 1947-1949: The Story in Documents. Washington: Department of State, Office of Public Affairs, Division of Historical Policy Research, Government Printing Office, 1950, 631 P.

1266 Clark, Joseph. The German Problem and Big Three Unity. Political Affairs. 26:3 (March 1947), 204-215.

1267 The Cockpit of Germany. Soundings. No. 18 (September 1948), 1-4.

1268 Colvin, Ian. London-Berlin-Moscow. National Review. 128:770 (April 1947), 275-278.

1269 Davidson, Basil. Germany: What Now? Potsdam, 1945-Partition, 1949. London: Frederick Muller, 1950, 268 P.

1270 Dittmar, Henry G. Germany and the Peace to Come. Proceedings of the Institute of World Affairs. 25:5 (December 1948), 136-142.

1271 Eisler, Robert. Hart, Eric G. Winning the Peace: A Comprehensive Policy. London: Muller, 1948, 270 P.

1272 Fay, Sidney B. The German Balance Sheet: The Struggle Between Russia and The West for Germany. Current History. 15:84 (August 1948), 65-71.

1273 Fay, Sidney B. What Future for Germany?. Current History. 15:88

(December 1948), 321-328.

1274 Friedrich, Carl J. The Peace Settlement With Germany--Economic and Social. Annals of the American Academy of Political and Social Science. 257 (May 1948), 129-141.

1275 Friedrich, Carl J. The Peace Settlement With Germany--Political and Military. Annals of the American Academy of Political and Social Science. 257 (May 1948), 119-128.

1276 The German Problem Can Be Settled. New Central European Observer. 1:5 (10 July 1948), 49.

1277 Havighurst, Robert J. Pollock, James K. Schultz, Theodore W. The Problem of Germany. University of Chicago Round Table. No. 543 (15 August 1948), 1-14. Radio Discussion.

1278 Higgins, Marguerite. Obituary of a Government--The Story of the East-West Breakup in Germany. This Is Germany. Ed. Arthur Settel. New York: Sloane, 1950, Pp. 309-328.

1279 Hill, Russell. Struggle for Germany. New York: Harper and Row, 1947, 260 P.

1280 Howe, Quincy. Ashes of Victory: World War II and Its Aftermath. New York: Simon & Schuster, 1972, 542 P.

1281 Hughes, Richard D. Soviet Foreign Policy and Germany, 1945 to 1948. Ph.D. Thesis, Claremont Graduate School, 1964, 293 P.

1282 Joesten, Joachim. Germany: What Now?. Chicago and New York: Ziff-Davis, 1948, 331 P.

1283 Johnson, Julia E., Compiler. The Dilemma of Postwar Germany. New York: Wilson, Reference Shelf, Vol. 20, No. 3, 1948, 304 P.

1284 Knudson, Charles A. One or More Germanies: The Economics of Partition. International Journal. 3 (Winter 1947-48), 56-66.

1285 Kulski, Wladyslaw W. Problem of the Heartland of Europe. Journal of Central European Affairs. 7:3 (October 1947), 253-261.

1286 Maguire, Robert F. The Unknown Art of Making Peace: Are We Sowing the Seeds of World War III?. American Bar Association Journal. 35:11 (November 1949), 905-909.

1287 Mann, F. A. The Present Legal Status of Germany. International Law Quarterly. 1:3 (Autumn 1947), 314-335.

1288 Maynard, Peter. Western Germany: Challenge to Peace. New Central European Observer. 1:1 (15 May 1948), 2-3.

1289 Middleton, Drew. Moscow's Aim: A Germany Bound to Russia. New York Times Magazine. (23 March 1947), 7+.

1290 Middleton, Drew. The Struggle for Germany. Indianapolis: Bobbs-Merrill, 1949, 304 P.

1291 Murphy, Robert. Diplomat Among Warriors. Garden City: Doubleday, 1964, 470 P.

1292 N. M. German Reactions to the Moscow Conference. World Today. 3:6 (June 1947), 277-285.

1293 Neumann, Franz L. Soviet Policy in Germany. Annals of the American Academy of Political and Social Science. 263 (May 1949), 165-179.

1294 Poland, Embassy. Poland, Germany and European Peace: Official Documents. London and Washington: Polish Embassy Printing Office, 1949, 116 P.

1295 Price, Hoyt. Schorske, Carl E. The Problem of Germany. New York: Council on Foreign Relations, 1947, 161 P.

1296 Richards, Paul. Spotlight on Germany. New York: New Century, 1948, 46 P.

1297 Rostow, Eugene V. Germany: A Warning. New York Times Magazine. (6 June 1948), 9+. Unity Will Permit Germany to Threaten World's Peace Again.

1298 Rostow, Eugene V. The Partition of Germany and the Unity of Europe. Virginia Quarterly Review. 23:1 (Winter 1947), 18-33.

1299 Sale-Harrison, Leonard. The Coming Great Northern Confederacy; or, the Future of Russia and Germany. Wheaton: Van Kampen, 16Th Ed., 1948, 103 P.

1300 Schorske, Carl E. The Dilemma in Germany. Virginia Quarterly Review. 24:1 (December 1948), 29-42.

1301 Schwarzenberger, Suse. Trends of Thought in Germany. World Affairs (London). 2:1 (January 1948), 40-48.

1302 Smith, Walter Bedell. My Three Years in Moscow. Philadelphia: Lippincott, 1950, 346 P., Esp. 211-260.

1303 Soviet Violations of Treaty Obligations. Department of State Bulletin. 18:466 (6 June 1948), 738-744.

1304 Stirk, S. D. Germany and Russia. Public Affairs. 11:3 (July 1948), 176-181.

1305 Strasser, Otto. Germany in a Disunited World. Eastbourne: Lifestream Controversy Series No. 1, 1947, 31 P.

1306 Strasser, Otto. What to Do in Germany Now. Dalhousie Review. 28:2 (July 1948), 154-157.

1307 Strauss, Harold. The Division and Dismemberment of Germany From the Casablanca Conference (January 1943) to the Establishment of the East German Republic (October 1949). Ambilly: Les Presses De Savoie, 1952, 240 P.

1308 Thorp, Willard L. The Future of Germany. Department of State Bulletin. 18:454 (14 March 1948), 353-355.

1309 US, Office of Political Adviser for Germany. Certain International and U.S. Policy Documents Regarding Germany. N.P.: Office of Political Adviser for Germany, 1949, 294 P.

1310 US, Omgus, Civil Administration Division. Chronologic Tables on Western Germany, 1947-1948. Berlin: Omgus, Civil Administration Division, Cfm Secretariat, 1949, 2 Vols., 332 P.

1311 US, Omgus, Civil Administration Division. Documented Chronology on Political Developments Regarding Germany. N.P.: Omgus, Civil Administration Division, January 1949, 178 P.

1312 US, Omgus, Civil Administration Division. Documented Chronology on Western Germany. Berlin: Omgus, Civil Administration Division, 1949, 101 P.

1313 US, Omgus, Civil Administration Division. Soviet Propaganda Practices in Germany. N.P.: Omgus, November 1947, 2 Vols.

1314 US, Omgus, Civil Administration Division. Summary of Multipartite Agreements and Disagreements on Germany. Berlin: Omgus, Civil Administration Division, Cfm Secretariat, 2D Ed., 1948, 2 Vols., 469 P.

1315 Utley, Freda. The High Cost of Vengeance. Chicago: Regnery, 1949,

310 P.

1316 The Warsaw Conference and the German Problem. New Central European Observer. 1:5 (10 July 1948), 50.

1317 Wells, Roger Hewes. The German Problem in 1948. Western Political Quarterly. 2:2 (June 1949), 208-216.

1318 Wheeler-Bennett, John. Nicholls, Anthony. The Semblance of Peace: The Political Settlement After the Second World War. New York: St. Martin's, 1972, 873 P.

1319 Winternitz, Josef. Germany--The Storm Centre. Labour Monthly. 30:8 (August 1948), 236-240.

1320 Zander, Ernst. Concerning Germany and World Development. Contemporary Issues. 1:1 (Summer 1948), 3-19.

1321 Zbinden, Hans. Whither Germany? Reflections of a Swiss on the Future of Germany and Europe. Hinsdale: Regnery, 1948, 90 P.

D.4.4. Re-Establishment of Self-Government (See Also E.1; E.3.6)

1322 Almond, Gabriel A. German Political Parties. Germany and the Future of Europe. Ed. Hans J. Morgenthau. Chicago: University of Chicago Press, 1951, Pp. 89-99.

1323 Barnes, Samuel H. Grace, Frank. Pollock, James K. Sperlich, Peter W. The German Party System and the 1961 Federal Election. American Political Science Review. 56:4 (December 1962), 899-914.

1324 Bell, Daniel. Paris, Berlin, and London: Decline of Political Parties. New Leader. 54:20 (October 1960), 79-83.

1325 Bergstraesser, Ludwig. Political Parties in Germany. Contemporary Review. 172 (August 1947), 75-79.

1326 Cassidy, Velma Hastings. The Beginnings of Self-Government in the American Zone of Germany. Department of State Bulletin. 16:397 (9 Febrary 1947), 223-233.

1327 Fay, Sidney B. Germany: Self-Government. Current History. 11:64 (December 1946), 500-506.

1328 Fleming, William. German Post-War Constitutions: What Chance for a Democratic Germany?. Current History. 14:80 (April 1948), 219-223; and 14:81 (May 1948), 289-292.

1329 Guradze, Heinz. The Laenderrat: Landmark of German Reconstruction. Western Political Quarterly. 3:2 (June 1950), 190-213.

1330 Hill, J. W. F. Local Government in Western Germany. Political Quarterly. 20:3 (July-September 1949), 256-264.

1331 Ingrams, Harold. Building Democracy in Germany. Quarterly Review. 285:572 (April 1947), 208-222.

1332 Joesten, Joachim. The Strange Ways of German Democracy. Antioch Review. 7:1 (March 1947), 17-22.

1333 Jones, Howard Palfrey. Wells, Roger Hewes. Germany Faces Democracy: Self-Government Gradually Returning. National Municipal Review. 35:10 (November 1946), 514-520.

1334 Kybal, M. Bavaria's New Constitution. World Affairs Interpreter. 18:2 (July 1947), 290-296.

1335 Litchfield, Edward H. Emergence of German Governments. Governing Postwar Germany. Ed. Edward H. Litchfield and Associates. Ithaca: Cornell University Press, 1953, Pp. 19-54.

1336 Local Government in Bizonia. Planning (P.E.P.) 14:277 (23 January 1948), 209-228.

1337 Marshall, A. H. Local Government in Bizonia. Public Administration. 26:3 (Autumn 1948), 188-190.

1338 Meyerhoff, Hans. The Reconstruction of Government and Administration. The Struggle for Democracy in Germany. Ed. Gabriel A. Almond. Chapel Hill: University of North Carolina Press, 1949, Pp. 185-220.

1339 Miller, Robert W. The South German Laenderrat: The Origins of Postwar German Federalism. Ph.D. Thesis, University of Michigan, 1960, 194 P.

1340 Neumann, Franz L. Military Government and the Revival of Democracy in Germany. Columbia Journal of International Affairs. 2:1 (Winter 1948), 3-20.

1341 Neumann, Robert G. New Constitutions in Germany. American Political Science Review. 42:3 (June 1948), 448-468.

1342 Provisional Advisory Council. N.P., 1946, 36 P.

1343 R. O. W. Administration in Germany: Reconstruction By Military Government. World Today. 1:2 (August 1945), 52-61.

1344 Robson, William A. Local Government in Occupied Germany. Political Quarterly. 16:4 (October-December 1945), 277-287.

1345 Saltzman, Charles E. A Positive Achievement of the American Military Government in Germany. Columbia Journal of International Affairs. 2:1 (Winter 1948), 37-38. Reestablishment of Government in Laender.

1346 Steinmetz, Hans. The Problems of the Landrat: A Study of County Government in the U.S. Zone of Germany. Journal of Politics. 11:2 (May 1949), 318-334.

1347 UK, CCG. Progress Towards German Reconstruction: Opening of the Landtag of North Rhine-Westphalia, 2 October 1946. Duesseldorf: Schwann, 1946, 39 P.

1348 UK, Foreign Office. Report on Some Methods Used to Assist Local Government and The Civil Service in the British Zone of Germany. London: H.M. Stationery Office, Cmd. 7804, 1949, 8 P.

1349 US, Omgus, Civil Administration Division. Comparative Federal Election Systems. N.P.: Omgus, Civil Administration Division, 1947, 12 P.

1350 US, Omgus, Civil Administration Division. Constitutions of Bavaria, Hesse and Wuerttemberg-Baden. N.P.: Omgus, Civil Administration Division, 1947, 74 P.

1351 US, Omgus, Civil Administration Division. Constitutions of the German Laender. Berlin: Omgus, Civil Administration Division, 1947, 243 P.

1352 US, Omgus, Civil Administration Division. Governmental Organization in the Occupied Zones of Germany. N.P.: Omgus, Civil Administration Division, 1947, 22 P.

1353 US, Omgus, Civil Administration Division. Land and Local Government in the U.S. Zone of Germany. N.P.: Omgus, Adjutant General, 1947, 111 P.

1354 US, Omgus, Civil Administration Division. Provisional German Government. N.P.: Omgus, Adjutant General, 1947, 11 P.

1355 US, Omgus, Education and Cultural Relations Division. Recommendations for Assignment of Powers and Functions to German Governmental

Levels. N.P.: Omgus, July 1946.

1356 US, Omgus, Manpower Division. Land Labor Ministries in the U.S. Zone. N.P.: Omgus, January 1947, 23 P.

1357 US, Omgus, Military Governor. Central German Agencies. N.P.: Omgus, Adjutant General, May 1946, 15 P.

1358 US, Omgus, Military Governor. Elections in Germany. Berlin: Omgus, Rev. Ed., March 1947, 22 P.

1359 Wells, Roger Hewes. Local Government. Governing Postwar Germany. Ed. Edward H. Litchfield and Associates. Ithaca: Cornell University Press, 1953, Pp. 57-83.

1360 Wells, Roger Hewes. State Government. Governing Postwar Germany. Ed. Edward H. Litchfield and Associates. Ithaca: Cornell University Press, 1953, Pp. 84-116.

E. FRG : Governmental Framework

E.1. Creation of FRG

E.1.1. Western Allies and Parliamentary Council

1361 Beloff, Max. If We End the Occupation of Germany--. New York Times Magazine. (7 November 1948), 9+.

1362 Berger, Stephen D. The Development of Legitimating Ideas: Intellectuals and Politicians in West Germany, 1945-1949. Sozialwissenschaftliches Jahrbuch Fuer Politik, Vol. 3.

1363 Ed. Rudolf Wildenmann. Munich and Vienna: Guenter Olzog Verlag, 1972, Pp. 9-173.

1364 Brecht, Arnold. Re-Establishing German Government. Annals of the American Academy of Political and Social Science. 267 (January 1950), 28-42.

1365 Dietrich, Hermann R. Creating a New State: German Problems, 1945-1953. Cologne: Comel, 1953, 67 P.

1366 Dulles, Allen Welsh. Germany: A Formula. New York Times Magazine. (6 June 1948), 8+.

1367 Fay, Sidney B. Germany, Spring, 1949: The Hopes and Despairs of the New Season. Current History. 16:93 (May 1949), 262-266.

1368 Friedrich, Carl J. The Legacies of the Occupation of Germany. Public Policy, Vol. 17 Ed. John D. Montgomery and Albert O. Hirschman. Cambridge: Harvard University Press, 1968, Pp. 1-26.

1369 Friedrich, Carl J. West German States Draft Plans for Constitution. Foreign Policy Bulletin. 28:2 (22 October 1948), 2-3.

1370 Golay, John Ford. The Founding of the Federal Republic of Germany. Chicago: University of Chicago Press, 1958, 299 P.

1371 Guerster, Eugene. Prospects for Democracy in Germany. South Atlantic Quarterly. 47:4 (October 1948), 445-458.

1372 Hart, Adrian Liddell. The Growth of a New Germany. Twentieth Century. 145:864 (February 1949), 77-85.

1373 Hartmann, Frederick H. Settlement for Germany. Yale Review. 39:2 (December 1949), 240-254.

1374 Hirsch, Felix Edward. From Weimar to Bonn: Western Germany on the Way to a New Constitution. Current History. 15:87 (November 1948), 269-273.

1375 Hirschmann, Ira A. The Embers Still Burn. New York: Simon and Schuster, 1949, 272 P. Postwar Ferment in Europe and the Middle East, and the Disastrous American "Get-Soft-With-Germany" Policy.

1376 London Conference Recommendations on Germany. Department of State Bulletin. 18:468 (20 June 1948), 807-813.

1377 Maynard, Peter. Six Power "Agreement" on Germany. New Central European Observer. 1:4 (26 June 1948), 40-41.

1378 Mclaughlin, Kathleen. Birth of a State. This Is Germany. Ed. Arthur Settel. New York: Sloane, 1950, Pp. 329-345.

1379 Merkl, Peter H. The Emergent Federal System of Western Germany. Ph.D. Thesis, University of California, Berkeley, 1959.

1380 Merkl, Peter H. The Origin of the West Germany Republic. New York: Oxford University Press, 1963, 269 P.

1381 Military Security Board for Western Zones of Germany. Department of State Bulletin. 20:502 (13 February 1949), 195-197.

1382 The Occupation Statute (10 April 1949). Current History. 16:93 (May 1949), 294-295.

1383 Occupation Statute for Germany, 1949. American Journal of International Law. 43:Suppl. (October 1949), 172-174. Text Approved at Washington, D.C., 8 April 1949; in Force, 21 September 1949.

1384 The Paris Conference of the Council of Foreign Ministers. Department of State Bulletin. 21:522 (4 July 1949), 857-861. Results of the Sixth Session, 23 May-20 June, 1949.

1385 The Place of Western Germany in World Affairs in 1949. Dalhousie Review. 28:4 (January 1949), 355-362.

1386 Poage, Oren J. The Creation of a Western German Federal Republic as a Result of the Cold War. M.A. Thesis, Georgetown University, 1950, 271 P.

1387 Six-Power Accord on Western Germany. Current History. 15:84 (August 1948), 105-108. London Conference Communique, 7 June 1948.

1388 UK, Foreign Office. Memorandum on the Measures Agreed By the United Kingdom, United States, and French Foreign Ministers on the Programme for Germany, With Annexes, Washington, 6-8Th April 1949. London: H.M. Stationery Office, Cmd. 7677, 1949, 31 P.

1389 US, Omgus, Civil Administration Division. Distribution of Governmental Powers Between Federal, State and Local Government. N.P.: Omgus, Adjutant General, 1947, 20 P.

1390 US, Omgus, Civil Administration Division. Summary of U.S. Statements and Proposals on German Government. Berlin: Omgus, Civil Administration Division, Cfm Secretariat, 1948, 142 P.

1391 Ullmann, Richard K. The Struggle for Representative Institutions in Germany. Parliamentary Affairs. 3:2 (Spring 1950), 321-338.

1392 West German Notebook. New Central European Observer. 2:1 (18 January 1949), 6-7.

1393 Yakoubian, Arsen Lionel. Western Allied Occupation and Development of German Democracy, 1945-1951. Ph.D. Thesis, New York University, 1951.

E.1.2. Basic Law

1394 FRG. Basic Law for the Federal Republic of Germany: Adopted at Bonn By the Parliamentary Council,

September 1948-May 1949. Bonn: Carthaus, 1949, 37 P.

1395 FRG. The Basic Law for the Federal Republic of Germany: Amendments as of November 15, 1968. New York: German Information Center, C.1968, 63 P.

1396 FRG. Basic Law for the Federal Republic of Germany: Promulgated By the Parliamentary Council on 23 May 1949, as Amended Up to and Including 29 January 1969. Bonn: Foreign Office, Linguistic Section, 1969, 156 P.

1397 FRG. The Bonn Constitution With Amendments: Basic Law for the Federal Republic of Germany. New York: Bernard, 1955, 66 P.

1398 FRG, German Information Center. The Basic Law of the Federal Republic of Germany; Amendments as of December 31, 1962. New York: German Information Center, 1962, 62 P.

1399 FRG, Press and Information Office. Basic Law for the Federal Republic of Germany. Bonn: Press and Information Office, 1971, 162 P. as Amended Up to 31 May 1971.

1400 FRG, Press and Information Office. The Bonn Constitution, With Amendments. New York: Bernard, 1958, 66 P.

1401 US, Department of State, Office of Public Affairs. The Bonn Constitution: Basic Law for the Federal Republic of Germany. Washington: Department of State Publication 3526, Government Printing Office, 1949, 52 P.

1402 US, Omgus, Civil Administration Division. Draft Basic Law (Provisional Constitution). Berlin: Omgus, Civil Administration Division, 1949, as Passed By Main Committee of Parliamentary Council in First Reading, 11 November to 10 December 1948.

1403 The Western German Constitution. Current History. 16:94 (June 1949), 346-361.

E.1.3. Analyses of Basic Law (See Also E.3.2)

1404 Born, Moritz J. A Constitution for Germany. Contemporary Review. 174:995 (November 1948), 270-274.

1405 Brecht, Arnold. The New German Constitution. Social Research. 16:4 (December 1949), 425-473.

1406 Constantopoulos, Demetrios S. The Relation of the Law of Nations and the New Constitution of Germany. Revue Hellenique De Droit International. 5:1-2 (January-June 1952), 42-62.

1407 Dash, Shreeram Chandra. Comparison of the Fundamental Features of the Constitution of India With Those of the Constitutions of the United States, United Kingdom, Weimar Germany, and West German Federal Republic. Dr.Phil. Thesis, Free University of Berlin, 1954, 490 P.

1408 Eichler, Willi. Testing Time at Bonn: The Basic Law. Socialist Commentary. 13 (June 1949), 135-137.

1409 Friedrich, Carl J. The Political Theory of the New Democractic Constitutions. Review of Politics. 12:2 (April 1950), 215-224.

1410 Friedrich, Carl J. Rebuilding the German Constitution. American Political Science Review. 43:3 (June 1949), 461-482; and 43:4 (August 1949), 704-720.

1411 Friedrich, Carl J. Spiro, Herbert J. The Constitution of the German Federal Republic. Governing Postwar Germany. Ed. Edward H. Litchfield and Associates. Ithaca: Cornell University Press, 1953, Pp. 117-151.

1412 Graham, Malbone Watson. The New Fundamental Law for the Western German Federal Republic. American Journal of International Law. 43:3 (July 1949), 494-498.

1413 Kauper, Paul G. The Constitutions of West Germany and the United States: A Comparative Study. Michigan Law Review. 58:8 (June 1960), 1091-1184.

1414 Lanhoff, Arthur. The German (Bonn) Constitution With Comparative Glances at The French and Italian Constitutions. Tulane Law Review. 24:1 (October 1949), 1-50.

1415 Lewis, Harold O. New Constitutions in Occupied Germany. Washington: Foundation for Foreign Affairs, Foundation Pamphlet No. 6, 1948, 145 P.

1416 Mann, Golo. Constitutions in the Making: Western Germany. Common Cause. 3:5 (December 1949), 262-267.

1417 Ostwald, Walter. The West German Constitution. Contemporary Review. 183:1051 (May 1953), 289-292.

1418 Popova, T. The Constitutional Structure of the German Federal Republic. International Affairs (Moscow). (June 1957), 86-93.

1419 Preuss, Lawrence. International Law in the Constitutions of the Laender in the American Zone of Germany. American Journal of International Law. 41:4 (October 1947), 888-899.

1420 Schmid, Karl. The Work of Bonn. World Affairs (London). 3:4 (October 1949), 358-367. Discussion of Functions of Basic Law: to Create Order for Frg in Transitional Period.

1421 Simons, Hans. The Bonn Constitution and Its Government. Germany and the Future of Europe. Ed. Hans J. Morgenthau. Chicago: University of Chicago Press, 1951, Pp. 114-130.

1422 US, Omgus, Civil Administration Division. Documents on the Creation of the German Federal Constitution. Berlin: Omgus, Civil Administration Division, 1949, 154 P.

1423 US, Omgus, Civil Administration Division. German Constitutional Proposals. N.P.: Omgus, Civil Administration Division, C.1948, 178 P.

E.1.4. Federalism and Political Theory (See Also E.3.4)

1424 Amen, Mary Zelime. The Theory of Consensus: A Theoretical Framework and Its Application to the Development of Political Consensus in the Federal Republic of Germany. Ph.D. Thesis, University of Texas at Austin, 1971, 193 P.

1425 Berger, Peter L. Kellner, Hansfried. Arnold Gehlen and the Theory of Institutions. Social Research. 32:1 (Spring 1965), 110-115.

1426 Bergstraesser, Arnold. Man and Society. United Asia. 19:6 (November-December 1967), 294-303.

1427 Buckhout, Gerard Lee. The Concept of the State in Modern Germany. Ph.D. Thesis, Northwestern University, 1962, 198 P.

1428 Butz, Otto. Modern German Political Theory. Garden City: Doubleday, 1955, 72 P., Esp. Pp. 67-69.

1429 Dahrendorf, Ralf. Conflict and Liberty: Some Remarks on the Social Structure of German Politics. British Journal of Sociology. 14:3 (September 1963), 197-211.

1430 Dahrendorf, Ralf. Society and Democracy in Germany. Garden City: Doubleday, 1967, 482 P.

1431 Frye, Charles E. The Third Reich and the Second Republic: National Socialism's Impact Upon German Democracy. Western Political Quarterly. 21:4 (December 1968), 668-680.

1432 Hartjens, Peter G. Varieties of Democratic Political Development: The German Experience. Ph.D. Thesis, University of North Carolina at Chapel Hill, 1972, 424 P.

1433 Hoepker, Wolfgang. Ten States or Five? Boundary Reform Is Not a Panacea. German Tribune Quarterly Review. No. 14 (29 April 1971), 12-16.

1434 King, Anthony. Ideas, Institutions and the Policies of Governments: A Comparative Analysis. British Journal of Political Science. 3:3 (July 1973), 291-313; and 3:4 (October 1973), 409-423. Canada, France, FRG, UK, US.

1435 Mantell, David Mark. The Potential for Violence in Germany. Journal of Social Issues. 27:4 (1971), 101-112.

1436 Mason, John Brown. Federalism--The Bonn Model. Constitutions and Constitutional Trends Since World War II: An Examination of Significant Aspects of Postwar Public Law With Particular Reference to the New Constitutions of Western Europe. Ed. Arnold J. Zurcher. New York: New York University Press, 1951, Pp. 134-153.

1437 Merkl, Peter H. Executive-Legislative Federalism in West Germany. American Political Science Review. 53:3 (September 1959), 732-741.

1438 Neumann, Sigmund. Trends Toward Statism in Western Europe. Proceedings of the Academy of Political Science. 24:1 (May 1950), 13-22.

1439 Preece, Rodney J. C. The Budget as Law in the German Federal Republic. Political Studies. 16:1 (February 1968), 94-96.

1440 Ridley, F. F. Chancellor Government as a Political System and the German Constitution. Parliamentary Affairs. 19:4 (Autumn 1966), 446-461.

1441 Rogowski, Ronald Lynn. Social Structure and Stable Rule: A General Theory. Princeton: Princeton University, Center of International Studies, Technical Report No. 3, September 1969, 108 P.

1442 Rogowski, Ronald Lynn. Social Structure and Stable Rule: The German Case. Ph.D. Thesis, Princeton University, 1970, 301 P.

1443 Rudolf, Walter. Present Problems of German Federalism. Indian Journal of Political Science. 30:4 (October-December 1969), 331-342.

1444 Sachar, Abram L. The Course of Our Times. New York: Knopf, 1972, 635 P., Esp. Pp. 324-336, 474-485.

1445 Sawer, G. Federalism in West Germany. Public Law. 6:1 (Spring 1961), 26-44.

1446 Schram, Glenn N. Government Without Politics: The West German Rechtsstaat. Ph.D. Thesis, Indiana University, 1967, 207 P.

1447 Schram, Glenn N. Ideology and Politics: The Rechtsstaat Idea in West Germany. Journal of Politics. 33:1 (February 1971), 133-157.

1448 Schultes, Karl. German Politics and Political Theory. Political Quarterly. 28:1 (January-March 1957), 40-48.

1449 Seifritz, Adelbart. Federalism in West Germany. United Asia. 19:6 (November-December 1967), 311-314.

1450 Ulbricht, Paul Wolfgang. Complicating Factors in the Political Evolution of the Federal Republic of Germany. Ph.D. Thesis, University of Washington, 1965, 274 P.

1451 Zawadzki, Sylwester. Some Aspects of the West German Doctrine of a "Social Legal State". Polish Western Affairs. 7:1 (1966), 20-47.

E.1.5. General Treatises

1452 Balfour, Michael. West Germany. New York: Praeger, 1968, 344 P.

1453 Bethell, Jethro, Editor. Germany: A Companion to German Studies. London: Methuen, 5Th Ed., 1955, 578 P.

1454 Boelling, Klaus. Republic in Suspense: Politics, Parties and Personalities in Postwar Germany. New York: Praeger, 1964, 276 P.

1455 Boutros, Samir R. The Supremacy of the Polity; Britain and Germany: Towards an Assessment of Some Contemporary Approaches in Comparative Politics. Ph.D. Thesis, Wayne State University, 1975.

1456 Bracher, Karl Dietrich. Germany's Second Democracy--Structures and Problems. Democracy in a Changing Society. Ed. Henry W. Ehrmann. New York: Praeger, 1964, Pp. 117-148.

1457 Bramsted, Ernest K. Germany. New York: Prentice-Hall, 1972, 278 P.

1458 Crane, Wilder W., Jr. The Government of the Federal Republic of Germany. Government and Politics: An Introduction to Political Science. Ed. Alex N. Dragnich and John C. Wahlke. New York: Random House, 1966, Pp. 148-182.

1459 Deutsch, Karl W. Politics and Government: How People Decide Their Fate. Boston: Houghton Mifflin, 2Nd Ed., 1974, Esp. Pp. 464-496.

1460 Deutsch, Karl W. Breitling, Rupert. The German Federal Republic. Modern Political Systems: Europe. 3D Ed. Ed. Roy C. Macridis and Robert E. Ward. Englewood Cliffs: Prentice-Hall, 1972, Pp. 309-473.

1461 Dragnich, Alex N. The Government of the Federal Republic of Germany. Government and Politics: An Introduction to Political Science. 2D Ed. Ed. John C. Wahlke and Alex N. Dragnich. New York: Random House, 1971, Pp. 156-192.

1462 Dragnich, Alex N. Major European Governments. Homewood: Dorsey, 1966, Pp. 253-332.

1463 Edinger, Lewis J. Politics in Germany: Attitudes and Processes. Boston: Little, Brown, 1968, 360 P.

1464 Elkins, Thomas Henry. Germany. New York: Praeger, 2D Ed., 1968, 334 P.

1465 Finer, Herman. The Government of Germany. The Major Governments of Modern Europe. New York: Harper & Row, 1962, Pp. 388-539.

1466 Finer, Herman. Government of Greater European Powers: A Comparative Study of the Governments and Political Culture of Great Britain, France, Germany and the Soviet Union. New York: Holt, 1956, 931 P.

1467 Gibbon, Monk. Western Germany. London: Batsford, 1955, 306 P.

1468 Goldman, Guido. The German Political System. Patterns of Government: The Major Political Systems of Europe. 3D Ed. Ed. Samuel H. Beer and Adam B. Ulam. New York: Random House, 1973,

Pp. 471-593.

1469 Goldman, Guido. The German Political System. New York: Random House, 1974, X and 228 P.

1470 Grosser, Alfred. The Federal Republic of Germany: A Concise History. New York: Praeger, 1964, 150 P.

1471 Harbeson, John W. German Government. Germany: Comparative Culture and Government. Ed. William O. Westervelt. Skokie: National Textbook, 1970, Pp. 19-35.

1472 Heidenheimer, Arnold J. The Governments of Germany. New York: Crowell, 3D Ed., 1971, 335 P.

1473 Heidenheimer, Arnold J. Heclo, Hugh. Adams, Carolyn Teich. Comparative Public Policy: The Politics of Social Choice in Europe and America. New York: St. Martin's Press, 1975, 288 P.

1474 Herz, John H. German Government and Politics From the Textbook Author's Viewpoint. Teaching Postwar Germany in America: Papers and Discussions. Ed. Louis F. Helbig and Eberhard Reichmann. Bloomington: Indiana University, Institute of German Studies, 1972, Pp. 77-82.

1475 Herz, John H. The Government of Germany. New York: Harcourt Brace Jovanovich, 2D Ed., 1972, 208 P.

1476 Hiscocks, Richard. Democracy in Western Germany. London: Oxford University Press, 1957, 324 P.

1477 Holborn, Louise W., Editor. Herz, John H., Editor. Carter, Gwendolen M., Editor. Documents of Major Foreign Powers: A Sourcebook on Great Britain, France, Germany, and the Soviet Union. New York: Harcourt, Brace & World 1968, 381 P., Esp. Pp. 169-280.

1478 Holt, Stephen C. Six European States: The Countries of the European Community and Their Political Systems. New York: Taplinger, 1970, 414 P., Esp. Pp. 111-188.

1479 Jacobs, Walter Darnell. Zink, Harold. Germany. Modern Governments. Princeton: Van Nostrand, 3D Ed., 1966, Pp. 353-468.

1480 Lane, John C. Pollock, James K. Source Materials on the Government and Politics of Germany. Ann Arbor: Wahrs, 1964, 404 P.

1481 Leonhardt, Rudolf Walter. This Germany: The Story Since the Third Reich. Greenwich: New York Graphic Society, 1964, 275 P.

1482 Loewenstein, Karl. The Government and Politics of Germany--Germany Since 1945. Governments of Continental Europe. Ed. James Shotwell. New York: Macmillan, 1952, Pp. 479-664.

1483 Mayntz, Renate. Scharpf, Fritz W. Policy-Making in the German Federal Bureaucracy. New York: Elsevier, 1975, 180 P.

1484 Merkl, Peter H. Germany: Yesterday and Tomorrow. New York: Oxford University Press, 1965, 366 P.

1485 Midgley, John. Germany. London: Oxford University Press, 1968, 128 P.

1486 Mookerjee, Girija K. Pohekar, G. S. Contemporary Germany. Bombay: United Asia Publications, 1968, 222 P.

1487 Moore, Charles Henry, Editor. Ueber Deutschland: A Reader on German Affairs. Oxford and New York: Pergamon, 1972, 247 P.

1488 Morgan, Roger P. Modern Germany. London: Hamilton, 1966, 128 P.

1489 Neumann, Robert G. European and Comparative Government. New York: Mcgraw-Hill, 3D Ed., 1960, 886 P., Esp Pp. 371-496.

1490 Neumann, Robert G. The Government of the German Federal Republic. New York: Harper and Row, 1966, 192 P.

1491 Neumann, Sigmund. Germany. European Political Systems. Ed. Taylor C. Cole. New York: Knopf, 2D Ed., 1960, Pp. 323-451.

1492 Neven-Du Mont, Juergen. After Hitler: A Report on Today's West Germans. New York: Pantheon, 1970, 319 P.

1493 Nova, Fritz. Contemporary European Governments. Baltimore: Helicon, 1963, 720 P.

1494 Plischke, Elmer. Contemporary Governments of Germany. New York: Houghton Mifflin, 2D Ed., 1969, 281 P.

1495 Plischke, Elmer. Hille, Hans J. The West German Federal Government. Bad Godesberg-Mehlem: Office of the U.S. High Commissioner for Germany, Historical Division, 1952, 182 P.

1496 Pollock, James K., Editor. German Democracy at Work: A Selective Study. Ann Arbor: University of Michigan Press, 1955, 208 P.

1497 Pollock, James K. Thomas, Homer. Germany in Power and Eclipse: The Background of German Development. New York: Van Nostrand, 1952, 661 P.

1498 Roberts, Geoffrey K. West German Politics. New York: Taplinger, 1972, 206 P.

1499 Rothman, Stanley. European Society and Politics. Indianapolis: Bobbs-Merrill, 1970, 931 P.

1500 Schoonmaker, Donald O., Editor. German Politics. Lexington: Heath, 1971, 238 P.

1501 Settel, Arthur, Editor. This Is Germany. New York: Sloane, 1950, 429 P.

1502 Sontheimer, Kurt. The Government and Politics of West Germany. New York: Praeger, 1972, 208 P.

1503 Spiro, Herbert J. The German Political System. Patterns of Government: The Major Political Systems of Europe. 2D Ed. Ed. Samuel H. Beer and Adam B. Ulam. New York: Random House, 1962, Pp. 463-592.

1504 Stahl, Walter, Editor. The Politics of Postwar Germany. New York: Praeger, 1963, 480 P.

1505 Tilford, Roger B. Preece, Rodney J. C. Federal Germany: Political and Social Order. Chester Springs, Pa.: Dufour, 1969, 176 P.

1506 Wildenmann, Rudolf. Towards a Sociopolitical Model of the German Federal Republic. Sozialwissenschaftliches Jahrbuch Fuer Politik, Vol. 4. Ed. Rudolf Wildenmann. Munich: Guenter Olzog Verlag, 1975.

E.2. Political Institutions and Processes (See Also H.2)

E.2.1. Election Laws and Behavior (See Also F.1.3; F.4; F.5)

1507 Conradt, David P. Electoral Law Politics in West Germany. Political Studies. 18:3 (September 1970), 341-356.

1508 Diederich, Nils. Germany. International Guide to Electoral Statistics. Ed. Stein Rokkan and Jean Meyriat. The Hague and Paris: Mouton, 1969, Pp. 128-162.

1509 Edinger, Lewis J. Electoral Politics

and Voting Behavior in Western Germany. World Politics. 13:3 (April 1961), 471-484.

1510 Edinger, Lewis J. Luebke, Paul. Grass-Roots Electoral Politics in the German Federal Republic: Five Constituencies in the 1969 Election. Comparative Politics. 3:4 (July 1971), 463-498.

1511 Fisher, Stephen L. The Wasted Vote Thesis: West German Evidence. Comparative Politics. 5:2 (January 1973), 293-300.

1512 Kirchheimer, Otto. Price, Arnold H. Analysis and Effects of the Elections in Western Germany. Department of State Bulletin. 21:537 (17 October 1949), 563-573.

1513 Kitzinger, Uwe W. The West German Electoral Law. Parliamentary Affairs. 11:2 (Spring 1958), 220-238.

1514 Mchargue, Daniel S. The Voting Machinery. German Democracy at Work: A Selective Study. Ed. James K. Pollock. Ann Arbor: University of Michigan Press, 1955, Pp. 79-102.

1515 Merkl, Peter H. Comparative Study and Campaign Management: The Brandt Campaign in Western Germany. Western Political Quarterly. 15:4 (December 1962), 681-704.

1516 Pollock, James K. The Electoral System of the Federal Republic of Germany: A Study in Representative Government. American Political Science Review. 46:4 (December 1952), 1056-1068.

1517 Pollock, James K. The West German Electoral Law of 1953. American Political Science Review. 49:1 (March 1955), 107-130.

1518 Pridham, Geoffrey. A 'Nationalization' Process? Federal Politics and the State Elections in West Germany. Government and Opposition. 8:4 (Autumn 1973), 455-472.

1519 Scammon, Richard M. Postwar Elections and Electoral Processes. Governing Postwar Germany. Ed. Edward H. Litchfield and Associates. Ithaca: Cornell University Press, 1953, Pp. 500-533.

1520 Scheuch, Erwin K. Wildenmann, Rudolf. The Professionalization of Party Campaigning. European Politics: A Reader. Ed. Mattei Dogan and Richard Rose. Boston: Little, Brown and Company, 1971, Pp. 296-300.

1521 Schoenbaum, David. A Voting District Reverses Itself. German Politics. Ed. Donald C. Schoonmaker. Lexington: Heath, 1971, Pp. 61-72.

1522 Stiefbold, Rodney P. The Significance of Void Ballots in West German Elections. American Political Science Review. 59:2 (June 1965), 391-407.

1523 Urwin, Derek W. Germany: Continuity and Change in Electoral Politics. Electoral Behavior: A Comparative Handbook. Ed. Richard Rose. Riverside, N.J.: The Free Press, 1973, Pp. 109-170.

1524 Collester, Jerry B. Coalition Politics in the German Federal Republic: Extensions of Empirical Theory. Ph.D. Thesis, Indiana University, 1969, 277 P.

E.2.2. Coalitions and Cabinets (See Also F.2)

1525 A Critique of the Cabinet By "A High-Ranking Political Official". European Political Institutions: A Comparative Government Reader. 2D Ed. Ed. William G. Andrews. Princeton: Van Nostrand, 1966, Pp. 525-527.

1526 Dyson, Kenneth H. F. The German Federal Chancellor's Office. Political Quarterly. 45:3 (July-September 1974), 364-371.

1527 Dyson, Kenneth H. F. Planning and the Federal Chancellor's Office in the West D German Federal Government. Political Studies. 21:3 (September 1973), 348-362.

1528 Kirchheimer, Otto. Majorities and Minorities in Western European Governments. Western Political Quarterly. 12:2 (June 1959), 492-510.

1529 Morkel, Arnd. The Cabinet Reform. International Journal of Politics. 2:2-3 (Summer-Fall 1972), 10-50.

1530 Sternberger, Dolf. Forms and Formation of Coalition Government With Special Reference to Post-War Germany. Public Policy. Vol. 4. Ed. Carl J. Friedrich and John Kenneth Galbraith. Cambridge: Graduate School of Public Administration, 1953, Pp. 159-179.

E.2.3. Bundestag and Legislative Behavior (See Also F.5)

1531 Bathurst, Maurice E. Legislation in the Federal Republic of Germany. International Comparative Law Quarterly. 1:1 (January 1952), 40-53.

1532 Brinkers, Helmut. Ombudsman. Bonn: Bundestag, Research Section, 1970, 116 P.

1533 The Bundestag: Legislation in the German Federal Republic. Bonn: Beinhauer, 7Th Ed., 1962, 32 P.

1534 Dishaw, Frank H. Roll Call Vote Deviancy of the CDU/Csu Praktion in the West German Bundestag. Sozialwissenschaftliches Jahrbuch Fuer Politik, Vol. 2. Muenchen and Wien: Olzog, 1971, Pp. 539-561.

1535 Dorr, Harold M. Bretton, Henry L. Legislation. Governing Postwar Germany. Ed. Edward H. Litchfield and Associates. Ithaca: Cornell University Press, 1953, Pp. 207-235.

1536 Fishel, Jeff. Parties, Candidates and Recruitment: West Germany and the United States. Ph.D. Thesis, University of California, Los Angeles, 1971, 1971, 409 P.

1537 Fishel, Jeff. Parliamentary Candidates and Party Professionalism in Western Germany. Western Political Quarterly. 25:1 (March 1972), 64-80.

1538 Fishel, Jeff. on the Transformation of Ideology in European Political Systems: Candidates for the West German Bundestag. Comparative Political Studies. 4:4 (January 1972), 406-437.

1539 Foster, Charles R. Romoser, George K. Parliamentary Reform in West Germany. Parliamentary Affairs. 21:1 (Winter 1967-68), 69-74.

1540 Frankland, E. Gene. Cross-National Determinants of Parliamentary Career Advancement: Britain and West Germany. Ph.D. Thesis, University of Iowa, 1973, 195 P.

1541 Gehrig, Norbert. Tomorrow's Government: The Function of Parliamentary Opposition. German Tribune Quarterly Review. No. 13 (18 February 1971), 9-12.

1542 Gerstenmaier, Eugen. The Parliament of the Federal Republic. European Political Institutions: A Comparative Government Reader. 2D Ed. Ed. William G. Andrews. Princeton: Van Nostrand, 1966, Pp. 421-432.

1543 Hennis, Wilhelm. Reform of the Bundestag: The Case for General Debate. Modern Parliaments: Change or Decline?. Ed. Gerhard Loewenberg.

Chicago and New York: Aldine-Atherton, 1971, Pp. 65-79.

1544 Johnson, Nevil. Questions in the Bundestag. Parliamentary Affairs. 16:1 (Winter 1962-63), 22-34.

1545 Kirchheimer, Otto. The Composition of the German Bundestag, 1950. Western Political Quarterly. 3:4 (December 1950), 590-601.

1546 Koenig, Peter-Michael. Parliamentarianism in the Federal Republic. German Tribune Quarterly Review. No. 15 (26 August 1971), 6-8.

1547 Litov, M. Social and Party Composition of the Bundestag. International Affairs (Moscow). (February 1968), 106-109.

1548 Loewenberg, Gerhard. Parliament in the German Political System. Ithaca: Cornell University Press, 1966, 463 P.

1549 Loewenberg, Gerhard. Parliamentarism in Western Germany: The Functioning of the Bundestag. American Political Science Review. 55:1 (March 1961), 87-102.

1550 Prittie, Terence C. F. The Federal German Parliament. Parliamentary Affairs. 8:2 (Spring 1955), 235-239.

1551 Prittie, Terence C. F. How Far Does the German Parliament Govern?. Parliamentary Affairs. 10:1 (Winter 1956-57), 57-62.

1552 Rueckert, George L. Parliamentary Party Cohesion in the West German Bundestag. Ph.D. Thesis, University of Wisconsin, 1962, 402 P.

1553 Rueckert, George L. Crane, Wilder W., Jr. CDU Deviancy in the German Bundestag. Journal of Politics. 24:3 (August 1962), 477-488.

1554 Schramm, Friedrich K. The Bundeshaus: The Work of the German Bundestag and Bundesrat. Bonn: Beinhauer, 4Th Ed., 1958, 32 P.

1555 Steffani, Winfried. Congress and Bundestag. Comparative Political Parties: Selected Readings. Ed. Andrew J. Milnor. New York: Crowell, 1969, Pp. 288-309.

1556 Trossmann, Hans. The German Bundestag: Organization and Operation. Darmstadt: Neue Darmstadter Verlagsanstalt, 1965, 156 P.

1557 US, Department of State, Office of Intelligence Research. The Composition of the German Bundestag, 1950: Intelligence Report. Washington: Department of State, Office of Intelligence Research, Oir Report No. 5334, 1950, 19 P.

1558 US, Hicog, Foreign Relations Division. Germany's Parliament in Action: The September 1949 Debate on the Government's Statement of Policy. Washington: Hicog, Office of Political Affairs, Foreign Relations Division, Cfm & Research Branch; Government Printing Office, 1950, 112 P.

1559 Ullmann, Richard K. King-Hall, Sir William Stephen Richard. German Parliaments: A Study of the Development of Representative Institutions in Germany. New York: Praeger, 1954, 162 P.

1560 Van Hoek, Kees. Bonn and Its Parliament. Contemporary Review. 177:1014 (June 1950), 332-338.

1561 Watson, Gerald G. Recruitment and Representation: A Study of the Social Backgrounds and Political Career Patterns of Members of the West German Bundestag, 1949-1969. Ph.D. Thesis, University of Florida, 1971, 218 P.

1562 Watson, Gerald G. Recruitment and Representation: Socio-Political Selection Of Bundestag Members in the Federal Republic of Germany, 1949-1969. Sozialwissenschaftliches Jahrbuch Fuer Politik, Vol. 4. Ed. Rudolf Wildenmann. Munich: Guenter Olzog Verlag, 1975.

E.2.4. Bundesrat

1563 Hughes, Christopher. The German Federal Council. Parliamentary Affairs. 13:2 (Spring 1960), 248-255.

1564 Neunreither, Karlheinz. Federalism and West German Bureaucracy. Political Studies. 7:3 (October 1959), 233-245.

1565 Neunreither, Karlheinz. Politics and Bureaucracy in the West German Bundesrat. American Political Science Review. 53:3 (September 1959), 713-731.

1566 Pfitzer, Albert. The German Bundesrat. Bonn: Press and Information Office, 2D Ed., 1962, 32 P.

1567 Pinney, Edward Lee. Federalism, Bureaucracy, and Party Politics in Western Germany: The Role of the Bundesrat. Chapel Hill: University of North Carolina Press, 1963, 268 P.

1568 Pinney, Edward Lee. Latent and Manifest Bureaucracy in the West German Parliament: The Case of the Bundesrat. Midwest Journal of Political Science. 6:2 (May 1962), 149-164.

1569 Pinney, Edward Lee. The Role of the Bundesrat in Legislation in the Federal Republic of Germany. Ph.D. Thesis, University of North Carolina, 1960, 329 P.

E.2.5. Public Administration and Civil Service (See Also E.3.3.1)

1570 Armstrong, John A. The European Administrative Elite. Princeton: Princeton University Press, 1973, 406 P.

1571 Baade, Hans W. West Germany's "Brownlow Committee": The First Report. Law and Contemporary Problems. 35:3 (Summer 1970), 626-665.

1572 Bader, Helmut. Brompton, Henry. Remedies Against Administrative Abuse in Central Europe, the Soviet Union, and Communist East Europe (Ombudsmen and Others). Annals of the American Academy of Political and Social Science. 377 (May 1968), 73-86.

1573 Brecht, Arnold. Civil Service Reform in Germany. Personnel Administration. 9:3 (January 1947), 1-14.

1574 Brecht, Arnold. Personnel Management. Governing Postwar Germany. Ed. Edward H. Litchfield and Associates. Ithaca: Cornell University Press, 1953, Pp. 263-293.

1575 Brecht, Arnold. What Is Becoming of the German Civil Service?. Public Personnel Review. 12:2 (April 1951), 83-91.

1576 Chapman, Brian. The Profession of Government: The Public Serivce in Europe. London: Allen and Unwin, 1959, 352 P.

1577 Chaput De Saintonge, Rolland A. A. Public Administration in Germany. London: Weidenfeld & Nicolson, 1961, 371 P. Regional and Local Administration in Rhineland-Palatinate.

1578 Cole, R. Taylor. The Democratization of the German Civil Service. Journal of Politics. 14:1 (February 1952), 3-18.

1579 Cullity, John P. The Growth of Governmental Employment in Germany. Ph.D. Thesis, Columbia University, 1964, 246 P.

1580 Cullity, John P. The Growth of Governmental Employment in Germany, 1882-1950. Zeitschrift Fuer Die Gesamte Staatswissenschaft. 123:2 (April 1967), 201-217.

1581 Eckes, Wolfgang. The Recruitment of Higher Federal Public Officials in Germany. Cahiers De Bruges. 7:2 (1957), 44-49.

1582 Fiedler, Ewald. Budget Administration and Law. International Review of Administrative Sciences. 25:2 (1959), 193-200.

1583 Grauhan, Rolf-Richard. Green, Georg W. Linder, Wolf. Strubelt, Wendelin. Policy Analysis Illustrated By the Problem of Urbanization. German Political Studies, Vol. 1. Ed. Klaus Von Beyme. Beverly Hills: Sage Publications, 1974, Pp. 141-182.

1584 Hanf, Kenneth I. The Higher Civil Service in West Germany: Administrative Leadership and the Policy Process. Ph.D. Thesis, University of California, Berkeley, 1968, 435 P.

1585 Harris, Richard L. The Government Bureaucracies of West Germany and Italy. Philippine Journal of Public Administration. 9:3 (July 1965), 209-220.

1586 Heady, Bruce. The Civil Service as an Elite in Britain and Germany. International Review of Administrative Sciences. 38:1 (1972), 41-48.

1587 Herz, John H. German Officialdom Revisited: Political Views and Attitudes of the West German Civil Service. World Politics. 7:1 (October 1954), 63-83.

1588 Herz, John H. Political Views of the German Civil Service. Santa Monica: Rand Corporation, P-528-Rc, 1954, 123 P.

1589 Herz, John H. Political Views of the West German Civil Service. West German Leadership and Foreign Policy. Ed. Hans Speier and W. Phillips Davison. Evanston and White Plains: Row, Peterson, 1957, Pp. 96-135.

1590 Hochschwender, Karl A. The Politics of Civil Service Reform in West Germany. Ph.D. Thesis, Yale University, 1962, 296 P.

1591 Jacob, Herbert. German Administration Since Bismarck: Central Control Versus Local Autonomy. New Haven: Yale University Press, 1963, 224 P.

1592 Jochimsen, Reimut. Establishing and Developing an Integrated Project Planning and Coordinating System for the West German Federal Government. International Journal of Politics. 2:2-3 (Summer-Fall 1972), 51-77.

1593 Jochimsen, Reimut. Problems of Establishing an Integrated Planning System for Goal-Setting and Co-Ordination Within the Federal Government. International Review of Administrative Sciences. 38:2 (1972), 181-192.

1594 Johnson, Nevil. The Profession of Government. Public Administration. 37:3 (Autumn 1959), 293-298. Review of Book of Same Title By Brian Chapman.

1595 Kaltefleiter, Werner. Modernization of the Bureaucracy: West Germany. International Journal of Politics. 2:2-3 (Summer-Fall 1972), 5-9.

1596 Kempner, Robert M. W. Police Administration. Governing Postwar Germany. Ed. Edward H. Litchfield and Associates. Ithaca: Cornell University Press, 1953, Pp. 403-418.

1597 Lompe, Klaus. The Role of Scientific Planning in the Governmental Process: the West German Experience. American Journal of Economics and Sociology. 29:4 (October 1970), 369-387.

1598 Lompe, Klaus. Scientific Counselling in Policy-Making in the Federal Republic of Germany: The Contemporary Situation. International Review of Administrative Sciences. 35:1 (January 1969), 2-10.

1599 Meghen, P.J. Public Administration in Germany. Administration (Dublin). 10:1 (Spring 1962), 50-69.

1600 Moro Serrano, Sebastian. Promotion in the Career Civil Service. International Review of Administrative Sciences. 25:2 (1959), 160-166.

1601 Morstein Marx, Fritz. German Administration and the Speyer Academy. Public Administration Review. 27:5 (December 1967), 403-410.

1602 Normanton, E. L. The Accountability and Audit of Governments: A Comparative Study. New York: Praeger, 1966, 452 P. Financial Administration in UK, US, France, and FRG.

1603 Peters, Hans. Administrative Decentralization. International Review of Administrative Sciences. 25:2 (1959), 150-154.

1604 Schirrmacher, Herbert. State and Local Public Administration. International Review of Administrative Sciences. 25:2 (1959), 142-149.

1605 Sisson, Charles H. The Spirit of British Administration and Some European Comparisons. London: Faber and Faber, 1959, 162 P.

1606 Spanner, Hans. Non-Contentious Administrative Procedure. International Review of Administrative Sciences. 25:2 (1959), 167-172.

1607 Taussig, Andrew J. The Impact of European Communities Upon German Ministries. Ph.D. Thesis, Harvard University, 1971.

1608 Theis, Adolf. Basic Problems of Government Organization. Aussenpolitik. 24:2 (1973), 217-230.

1609 Theis, Adolf. Governmental Reorganization. Aussenpolitik. 22:3 (1971), 338-351.

1610 Theis, Adolf. Political Planning in Western Democracies. Aussenpolitik. 21:4 (1970), 434-454.

1611 Ule, Carl Hermann. German Administrative Jurisdiction. International Review of Administrative Sciences. 25:2 (1959), 173-183.

1612 US, Omgus, Civil Administration Division. Public Service in Germany. Frankfurt: Omgus, Civil Administration Division, 1948, 72 P.

1613 Wallich, Henry C. The American Council of Economic Advisors and the German Sachverstaendigenrat: A Study of the Economics of Advice. Quarterly Journal of Economics. 82:3 (August 1968), 349-379.

1614 Warnecke, Steven. Reform, Codetermination and the German Bureaucracy: The Dilemmas of Democratization. Ph.D. Thesis, Columbia University, 1967, 261 P.

E.2.6. State and Local Government (See Also B.2.1; D.4.4)

1615 Aiker, Michael. Comparative Cross-National Research on Subnational Units in Western Europe: Problems, Data Sources, and a Proposal. Journal of Comparative Administration. 4:4 (February 1973), 437-471.

1616 Berkley, George E. Crisis and Change: West German Federalism Faces Alterations, With Mounting Pressure for Increased Centralization. National Civic Review. 59:4 (April 1970), 198-203.

1617 Culver, Lowell W. Land Elections in West German Politics. Western Political Quarterly. 19:2 (June 1966), 304-336.

1618 Culver, Lowell W. Land Elections in West German Politics: A Study of the Postwar Elections in the West German Laender, 1946-1965. Ph.D. Thesis, University of Southern California, 1967, 503 P.

1619 Dolive, Linda Landers. Electoral Politics at the Local Level in the German Federal Republic. Ph.D. Thesis, University of Florida, 1972, 171 P.

1620 Drummond, Stuart. The Laender and German Federal Politics. Political Studies. 16:1 (February 1968), 89-94.

1621 Gillen, J. F. J. State and Local Government in West Germany, 1945-1953: With Special Reference to the U.S. Zone and Bremen. Frankfurt: Office of the U.S. High Commissioner for Germany, Historical Division, Office of Executive Secretary, 1953, 131 P.

1622 Hensel, Walther. The City Manager System in Germany. Studies in Comparative Local Government. 1:2 (Winter 1967), 22-32.

1623 Hensel, Walther. The Council-Manager Plan in Germany. Public Management. 43:1 (January 1961), 2-5.

1624 Jones, Howard Palfrey. New German Charter. National Municipal Review. 38:8 (September 1949), 386-392.

1625 Koetter, Herbert. The Rural Municipality, Municipal Administration and the Rural Community in the Federal Republic of Germany. German Economic Review. 1:2 (1963), 127-139.

1626 Luchsinger, Fred. "Atomic Death" in Western Germany. Swiss Review of World Affairs. 8:5 (August 1958), 6-8. Landtag Election in North Rhine-Westphalia.

1627 Muralt, Anton Von. The Bavarian Way. Swiss Review of World Affairs. 2:3 (June 1952), 11-13.

1628 Naumann, Hans Guenther. An Attempt at Participation: The Munich Forum. Studies in Comparative Local Government. 4:2 (Winter 1970), 53-55.

1629 Nolting, Orin F. Europe's Manager Plans. National Civic Review. 48:3 (March 1959), 123-127. Finland, FRG, Ireland, Norway, Sweden.

1630 Pollock, James K. A Sensible Approach: West Germany Uses Nonpartisan Commission, Legal Guidelines, to Achieve Its Fair Reapportionment. National Civic Review. 54:7 (July 1965), 357-361.

1631 Pommerening, H. E. Local Self-Government in West Germany. Quarterly Journal of Local Self-Government Institute (Bombay). 25:2 (October 1954), 299-306.

1632 Preece, Rodney J. C. Land Elections in the German Federal Republic. Harlow: Longmans, 1968, 95 P.

1633 Warren, Roland L. Citizen Participation in Community Affairs in Stuttgart, Germany. Social Forces. 36:4 (May 1958), 322-329.

1634 Watson, Gerald G. The Structure of Opportunity in West German State Politics: the Case of Lower Saxony. Sozialwissenschaftliches Jahrbuch Fuer Politik, Vol. 3. Ed. Rudolf Wildenmann. Munich and Vienna: Guenter Olzog Verlag, 1972, Pp. 367-391.

1635 Watt, Donald C. The Baden-Wuerttemberg Elections. World Today. 24:6 (June 1968), 222-225.

1636 Weinberger, Bruno. The Changing Financial Relationship Between State and Municipality. Studies in Comparative Local Government. 1:1 (Summer 1967), 5-17.

1637 Weinberger, Bruno. Local Government Taxes in Germany and Their Future. Studies in Comparative Local Government. 3:2 (Winter 1969), 25-28.

1638 Wells, Roger Hewes. Arising From the Ruins. National Municipal Review. 45:2 (February 1956), 66-71.

1639 Wells, Roger Hewes. German State and Local Government. American Political Science Review. 50:4 (December 1956), 1112-1115.

1640 Wells, Roger Hewes. The States in West German Federalism: A Study in Federal-State Relations, 1949-1960. New Haven: College and University Press, 1961, 148 P.

1641 Wollmann, Hellmut. Cities in West Germany Face Emerging Crisis. National Civic Review. 60:9 (October 1971), 492-496.

1642 Ziebill, Otto. The German Towns' Council and the Municipal Economic Activity. Annals of Collective Economy. 24:1 (January-March 1953), 41-45.

E.3. Legal System (See Also H.3)

E.3.1. General

E.3.1.1. Legal System

1643 Cohn, Ernst J. Manual of German Law: I. General Introduction, Civil Law. Dobbs Ferry: Oceana, 2D Ed., 1968, 324 P.

1644 Cohn, Ernst J., Editor. Manual of German Law, II. Dobbs Ferry: Oceana, 2D Ed., 1971, 329 P.

1645 Forrester, Ian S. Ilgen, Hans-Michael. The German Legal System. South Hackensack: Rothman, 1972, 25 P.

1646 Graue, Eugen Dietrich. Nonjusticiable Issues Under German Law. American Journal of Comparative Law. 3:1 (Winter 1954), 97-98.

1647 Heyde, Wolfgang. The Administration of Justice in the Federal Republic of Germany. Bonn: Press and Information Office, 1971, 150 P.

1648 International Commission of Jurists. The Rule of Law in the Federal Republic of Germany. The Hague: International Commission of Jurists, German National Section, 1958, 41 P.

1649 Leibholz, Gerhard. Politics and Law. Leyden: Sythoff, 1965, 339 P.

1650 Loewenstein, Karl. Justice. Governing Postwar Germany. Ed. Edward H. Litchfield and Associates. Ithaca: Cornell University Press, 1953, Pp. 236-262.

1651 Loewenstein, Karl. Law and the Legislative Process in Occupied Germany. Yale Law Journal. 57:5 (March 1948), 724-760; and 57:6 (April 1948), 994-1022.

1652 Loewenstein, Karl. Reconstruction of

the Administration of Justice in American-Occupied Germany. Harvard Law Review. 61:3 (February 1948), 419-467.

1653 Mehren, Arthur T. Von. The Judicial Process: A Comparative Analysis. American Journal of Comparative Law. 5:2 (Spring 1956), 197-228.

1654 Mehren, Arthur T. Von. Judicial Process in the United States and Germany. Rechtsvergleichung Und Internationales Privatrecht: Festschrift Fuer Ernst Rabel. Ed. Hans Doelle, Max Rheinstein, and Konrad Zweigert. Tuebingen: Mohr, 1954, Pp. 68-98.

1655 Mueller, Gebhard. German System of Law. United Asia. 19:6 (November-December 1967), 343-345.

1656 Rheinstein, Max. The Approach to German Law. Indiana Law Journal. 34:4 (Summer 1959), 546-558.

1657 Rheinstein, Max. German Law in Transition. Common Cause. 1:8 (February 1948), 301-306.

1658 Rockwell, Alvin J. Post-War Problems in Occupied Germany: American Democracy Versus Russian Democracy. American Bar Association Journal. 36:5 (May 1950), 359-362. Rebuilding German Law.

1659 Rupp, Hans G. Government Under Law in Germany. Annales De La Faculte De Droit D'Istanbul. 9:12 (1959), 100-112.

1660 Schneider, Hans, Editor. A Reference Guide to the Public Law of the Federal Republic of Germany. Munich: Beck, 2D Ed, 1964, 136 P.

1661 Sweigert, William T. The Legal System of the Federal Republic of Germany. Hastings Law Journal. 11:1 (August 1959), 7-22.

1662 Weiden, Paul L. The Impact of Occupation on German Law. Wisconsin Law Review. No. 3 (May 1947), 332-356.

1663 Zirn, Georg-August. Administration of Justice in Germany. Annals of the American Academy of Political and Social Science. 260 (November 1948), 32-42.

E.3.1.2. Jurisprudence

1664 Bodenheimer, Edgar. Significant Developments in German Legal Philosophy Since 1945. American Journal of Comparative Law. 3:3 (Summer 1954), 379-396.

1665 Burin, Frederic Siegfried. The Rule of Law in German Constitutional Thought: A Study in Comparative Jurisprudence. Ph.D. Thesis, Columbia University, 1952, 321 P.

1666 Dietze, Gottfried. Natural Law in the Modern European Constitutions. Natural Law Forum. 1 (1956), 73-91.

1667 Engisch, Karl. Recent Developments of German Legal Philosophy: A Report and Appraisal (1964-1966). Ottawa Law Review. 3:1 (Fall 1968), 47-78.

1668 Hahn, H. J. Trends in the Jurisprudence of the German Federal Constitutional Court. American Journal of Comparative Law. 16:4 (1968), 570-579.

1669 Heydte, Freiherr Von Der. Natural Law Tendencies in Contemporary German Jurisprudence. Natural Law Forum. 1 (1956), 115-121.

1670 Hippel, Ernst Von. The Role of Natural Law in the Legal Decisions of the German Federal Republic. Natural Law Forum. 4 (1959), 106-118.

1671 Leibholz, Gerhard. Judicial Power and the Authority of the State in the Federal Republic of Germany. Journal of the International Commission of Jurists. 4:2 (Summer 1963), 243-251.

1672 Rommen, Heinrich. Natural Law Decisions of the Federal Supreme Court and of The Constitutional Courts in Germany. Natural Law Forum. 4 (1959), 1-25.

E.3.1.3. Legal Profession

1673 Cohn, Ernst J. The German Attorney: Experiences With a Unified Profession. International and Comparative Law Quarterly. 9:4 (October 1960), 580-599; and 10:1 (January 1961), 103-122.

1674 Schram, Glenn N. The Recruitment of Judges for the West German Federal Courts. American Journal of Comparative Law. 21:4 (Fall 1973), 691-711.

1675 Weyrauch, Walter O. The Personality of Lawyers: A Comparative Study of Subjective Factors in Law, Based on Interviews With German Lawyers. New Haven: Yale University Press, 1964, 316 P.

E.3.2. Constitutional Law

E.3.2.1. Constitutional Court

1676 Baade, Hans W. Social Science Evidence and the Federal Constitutional Court of West Germany. Journal of Politics 23:3 (August 1961), 421-461.

1677 Blumenwitz, Dieter. The Federal Constitutional Court of Germany and Foreign Affairs. German Unity: Documentation and Commentaries on the Basic Treaty. Ed. Frederick W. Hess. Kansas City: Park College, Governmental Research Bureau, 1974, Pp. 11-22.

1678 Cole, R. Taylor. The Bundesverfassungsgericht, 1956-1958: An American Appraisal. Jahrbuch Des Oeffentlichen Rechts Der Gegenwart. Vol. 8. Ed. Gerhard Leibholz. Tuebingen: Mohr (Paul Siebeck), 1959, Pp. 29-47.

1679 Cole, R. Taylor. Three Constitutional Courts: A Comparison. American Political Science Review. 53:4 (December 1959), 963-984.

1680 Cole, R. Taylor. The West German Federal Constitutional Court: An Evaluation After Six Years. Journal of Politics. 20:2 (May 1958), 278-307.

1681 Dirnecker, Rupert. The Karlsruhe Decision and the Constitutionality of the Basic Treaty. Ed. Frederick W. Hess. Kansas City: Park College, Governmental Research Bureau, 1974, Pp. 65-90.

1682 Kommers, Donald P. The Federal Constitutional Court in the West German Political System. Frontiers of Judicial Research. Ed. Joel B. Grossman and Joseph Tanenhaus. New York: Wiley, 1969, Pp. 73-132.

1683 Lane, John C. The Constitutional Court of the German Federal Republic. Ph.D. Thesis, Columbia University, 1960, 313 P.

1684 Massing, Otwin. The Federal Constitutional Court as an Instrument of Social Control. German Political Studies, Vol. 1. Ed. Klaus Von Beyme. Beverly Hills: Sage Publications, 1974, Pp. 215-252.

1685 Mcwhinney, Edward. Constitutionalism in Germany and the Federal Constitutional Court. Leyden: Sythoff, 1962, 71 P.

1686 Mehren, Arthur T. Von.

Constitutionalism in Germany--The First Decision of the New Constitutional Court. American Journal of Comparative Law. 1:1-2 (Winter-Spring 1952), 70-94.

1687 Mueller, Gebhard. The Federal Constitutional Court of the Federal Republic of Germany. Journal of the International Commission of Jurists. 6:2 (Winter 1965), 191-218.

1688 Nadelmann, Kurt H. Non-Disclosure of Dissents in Constitutional Courts: Italy and West Germany. American Journal of Comparative Law. 13:2 (Spring 1964), 268-276.

1689 Reich, Donald R. Court, Comity, and Federalism in West Germany. Midwest Journal of Political Science. 7:3 (August 1963), 197-228.

1690 Rupp, Hans G. The Federal Constitutional Court in Germany: Scope of Its Jurisdiction and Procedure. Notre Dame Lawyer. 44:4 (April 1969), 548-559.

1691 Rupp-Von Bruenneck, Wiltraut. Germany: The Federal Constitutional Court. American Journal of Comparative Law. 20:3 (Summer 1972), 387-403.

E.3.2.2. Constitutional Law

1692 Arndt, Adolf. Status and Development of Constitutional Law in Germany. Annals of the American Academy of Political and Social Science. 260 (November 1948), 1-9.

1693 Dietze, Gottfried. Unconstitutional Constitutional Norms? Constitutional Developments in Postwar Germany. Virginia Law Review. 42:1 (January 1956), 1-22.

1694 Ferencz, Benjamin B. Supreme Court Bars Claims of Forced Laborers. American Journal of Comparative Law. 15:3 (1966-67), 561-566.

1695 Forsthoff, Ernst. The Dualism of Rule of Law and Welfare State in the Constitutional Law of the Federal Republic of Germany. Annales De La Faculte De Droit D'Istanbul. 9:12 (1959), 326-349.

1696 Friauf, Karl Heinrich. Techniques for the Interpretation of Constitutions in German Law. Proceedings of the Fifth International Symposium on Comparative Law. Ottawa: University of Ottawa Press, 1968, Pp. 9-22. 2

1697 Kutscher, Hans. The Role of the Bundesverfassungsgericht in Insuring Equality Under the Law. Jahrbuch Des Oeffentlichen Rechts Der Gegenwart. Vol. 9. Ed. Gerhard Leibholz, Tuebingen: Mohr, 1960, Pp. 197-201.

1698 Leibholz, Gerhard. Equality as a Principle in German and Swiss Constitutional Law. Journal of Public Law. 3:1 (Spring 1954), 156-166.

1699 Leibholz, Gerhard. The Federal Constitutional Court in Germany and the "Southwest Case". American Political Science Review. 46:3 (September 1952), 723-731.

1700 Lewan, Kenneth M. The Significance of Constitutional Rights for Private Law: Theory and Practice in West Germany. International and Comparative Law Quarterly. 17:3 (July 1968), 571-601.

1701 Mcwhinney, Edward. Federal Constitutional Law and the Treaty-Making Power: German-Vatican Concordat of 1933. Canadian Bar Review. 35:7 (August-September 1957), 842-848.

1702 Mcwhinney, Edward. Judicial Restraint and the West German Constitutional Court. Harvard Law Review. 75:1 (November 1961), 5-38.

E.3.2.3. Civil and Political Liberties

1703 Barnet, Richard J. The Protection of Constitutional Rights in Germany. Virginia Law Review. 45:7 (November 1959), 1139-1164.

1704 Castberg, Frede. Freedom of Speech in the West: A Comparative Study of Public Law in France, the United States, and Germany. New York: Oceana, 1960, P. 296-406.

1705 Committee for the Protection of Human Rights of the GDR. Memorandum on the Violation of Human Rights in West Germany. Berlin (East): Committee for the Protection of Human Rights, 1961, 55 P.

1706 Cordes, Bernhard H. Freedom of Opinion. American Journal of Comparative Law. 12:1 (Winter 1963), 94-95.

1707 Doehring, Karl. Non-Discrimination and Equal Treatment Under the European Human Rights Convention and the West German Constitution, With Particular Reference to Discrimination Against Aliens. American Journal of Comparative Law. 18:2 (1970), 305-325.

1708 FRG, Foreign Office. Information From Governments Relating to Prevention of Discrimination and Protection of Minorities. New York: United Nations, E/Cn.4/Sub.2/122:Add.40, 1952, 76 P. FRG Report to Un Secretary General, 4 October 1951.

1709 Foster, Charles R. Stambuk, George. Judicial Protection of Civil Liberties in Germany. Political Studies. 4:2 (June 1956), 190-194.

1710 Gallatin, Judith. Adelson, Joseph. Legal Guarantees of Individual Freedom: A Cross-National Study of the Development of Political Thought. Journal of Social Issues. 27:2 (1971), 93-108.

1711 The General Law Relating to Privacy. International Social Science Journal. 24:3 (1972), 440-446.

1712 Hays, Arthur Garfield. Civil Liberties in Germany. Survey. 85:1 (Janaury 1949), 6-11.

1713 International Commission of Jurists. Justice Enslaved: A Collection of Documents on the Abuse of Justice for Political Ends. The Hague: International Commission of Jurists, 1955, 535 P.

1714 Kamlah, Ruprecht B. The Invasion of Privacy By Electronic Listening Devices in The United States and Germany. Proceedings of the Eighth International Symposium on Comparative Law. Ottawa: University of Ottawa Press, 1971, Pp. 161-196.

1715 Krause, Harry D. The Right to Privacy in Germany--Pointers for American Legislation?. Duke Law Journal. 1965:3 (Summer 1965), 481-530.

1716 Lehman, Jon A. The Right of Privacy in Germany. New York University Journal of International Law & Politics.1:1 (April 1968), 106-127.

1717 Mueller, Rudolf. Weitzel, Heinz. Weisner, Gerhard. Legal Status of Foreigners in the Federal Republic of Germany. Frankfurt: European League for Economic Cooperation, 1955, 176 P.

1718 Rich, Bennett M. Civil Liberties in Germany. Political Science Quarterly. 65:1 (March 1950), 68-85.

E.3.2.4. Restrictions on Political Activity

1719 Communist Party of Germany. The

Karlsruhe Trial for Banning the Communist Party of Germany. London: Lawrence and Wishart, 1956, 127 P.

1720 FRG, Federal Constitutional Court. Action Against the Communist Party of Germany. Washington: Gerd Pfeiffer and Hans-George Strickert, 1957, 372 P.

1721 Kirchheimer, Otto. Political Justice: The Use of Legal Procedures for Political Ends. Princeton: Princeton University Press, 1961, 452 P.

1722 Klein, Peter. The Vracaric Case. German Foreign Policy (GDR). 1:2 (1962), 190-196. Arrest in Munich of Former Yugoslav Partisan.

1723 Klenner, Hermann. Human Rights in Germany--A Review of the Past Fifteen Years. German Foreign Policy (GDR). 3:6 (1964), 413-420.

1724 M. R. Office for the Protection of the Constitution on Trial. German Foreign Policy (GDR). 2:6 (1963), 451-456.

1725 Mcwhinney, Edward. The German Federal Constitutional Court and the Communist Party Decision. Indiana Law Journal. 32:3 (Spring 1957), 295-310.

1726 Pfeiffer, Gerd, Editor. Strickert, Hans-Georg, Editor. Outlawing the Communist Party: A Case History. New York: Bookmailer, 1957, 227 P. Decision of First Senate of Federal Constitutional Court.

1727 Sheldon, Charles H. Public Opinion and High Courts: Communist Party Cases in Four Constitutional Systems. Western Political Quarterly. 20:2 (June 1967), 341-360.

E.3.2.5. Emergency Provisions

1728 Baikalov, A. Ragnov, V. Emergency Legislation in West Germany. International Affairs (Moscow). (April 1967), 73-76.

1729 A Bundestag Debate: The Emergency Powers Bill. European Political Institutions: A Comparative Government Reader. 2D Ed. Ed. William G. Andrews. Princeton: Van Nostrand, 1966, Pp. 411-421.

1730 Meister, Roland. War Preparations Through Emergency Legislation. German Foreign Policy (GDR). 1:6 (1962), 629-635.

1731 Pfannenschwarz, Karl. Schneider, Theodor. The Draft Laws of the West German Government for the Establishment of a Military Dictatorship. Law and Legislation in the German Democratic Republic. No. 2 (1963), 35-49.

1732 Preece, Rodney J. C. Federal German Emergency Powers' Legislation. Parliamentary Affairs. 22:3 (Summer 1969), 216-225.

1733 Przybylski, Peter. "Fallex 66"--Milestone on the Road to Emergency Dictatorship. German Foreign Policy (GDR). 6:1 (1967), 22-35.

1734 Recent Emergency Legislation in West Germany. Harvard Law Review. 82:8 (June 1969), 1704-1737.

1735 Schweitzer, C. C. Emergency Powers in the Federal Republic of Germany. Western Political Quarterly. 22:1 (March 1969), 112-121.

E.3.3. Institutional Functions

E.3.3.1. Administrative Process

1736 Bachof, Otto. German Administrative Law, With Special Reference to the Latest Developments in the System of Legal Protection. International and Comparative Law Quarterly. 2:3 (July 1953), 368-382.

1737 Bachof, Otto. Special Administrative Tribunals. International Review of Administrative Sciences. 25:2 (1959), 184-192.

1738 Beguin, J. C. The Suspensive Effect of Appeals for Annulment in German Administrative Law. International Review of Administrative Sciences. 39:4 (1973), 394-412.

1739 Evans, Roger Warren. French and German Administrative Law, With Some English Comparisons. International and Comparative Law Quarterly. 14:4 (October 1965), 1104-1123.

1740 Feld, Werner J. The German Administrative Courts. Tulane Law Review. 36:3 (April 1962), 495-506.

1741 Pakuscher, Ernst K. Administrative Law in Germany--Citizen V. State. American Journal of Comparative Law. 16:3 (1968), 309-331.

1742 Pakuscher, Ernst K. Control of the Administration in the Federal Republic of Germany. International and Comparative Law Quarterly. 21:3 (July 1972), 452-471.

1743 Schindler, M. Judicial Review of Administrative Acts in Germany. British Journal of Administrative Law. 2:4 (July 1956), 113-120.

1744 Taylor, Richard W. Nordheim, Manfred Von. Petitions Committees and Grievance Resolution in the Federal Republic of Germany. Midwest Review of Public Administration. 7:4 (October 1973), 215-228.

1745 Werner, Fritz. Recent Trends in Administrative Law. International Review of Administrative Sciences. 25:2 (1959), 137-141.

E.3.3.2. Civil Procedures and Courts

1746 Amram, Philip W. The Dissenting Opinion Comes to the German Courts. American Journal of Comparative Law. 6:1 (Winter 1957), 108-111.

1747 Baur, Fritz. Present German Practices in the Application for Temporary Relief: Attachment and Temporary Restraining Orders. American Journal of Comparative Law. 14:2 (Spring 1965), 247-265.

1748 Cohn, Ernst J. Dissenting Opinions in German Law. International and Comparative Law Quarterly. 6:4 (October 1957), 540-543.

1749 Cohn, Ernst J. Law of Civil Procedure. Manual of German Law, II. 2D Ed. Ed. Ernst J. Cohn. Dobbs Ferry: Oceana, 1971, Pp. 162-260.

1750 Fleming, John G. Distant Shock in Germany (and Elsewhere). American Journal of Comparative Law. 20:3 (Summer 1972), 485-491.

1751 Herrmann, Joachim. The Rule of Compulsory Prosecution and the Scope of Prosecutorial Discretion in Germany. University of Chicago Law Review. 41:3 (Spring 1974), 468-505.

1752 Hertel, Duido. Organization and Functions of the Federal Audit Court in Germany. Federal Accountant. 11:1 (September 1961), 12-24.

1753 Hillhouse, A. M. Copeman, H. W. M. Tax Courts in Western Germany. Public Finance. 8:3 (1953), 259-282.

1754 Hoegen, Dieter L. Required Joinder of Claims: A Comparative Study of the American and the German Law. Michigan Law Review. 55:6 (April 1957), 799-844; and 55:7 (May 1957), 967-984.

1755 Kaplan, Benjamin. Mehren, Arthur T. Von. Schaefer, Rudolf. Phases of German Civil Procedure. Harvard Law

Review. 71:7 (May 1958), 1193-1268; and 71:8 (June 1958), 1443-1472.

1756 Langbein, John H. Controlling Prosecutorial Discretion in Germany. University of Chicago Law Review. 41:3 (Spring 1974), 439-467.

1757 Nadelmann, Kurt H. The Judicial Dissent: Publication Vs. Secrecy. American Journal of Comparative Law. 8:4 (Autumn 1959), 415-432.

1758 Rupp, Hans G. Judicial Conflicts of Interest in the Federal Republic of Germany. American Journal of Comparative Law. 18:4 (1970), 716-725.

1759 Schubert, Richard S. Compensation Under New German Legislation on Expropriation. American Journal of Comparative Law. 9:1 (Winter 1960), 84-94.

1760 Toussaint, Hergard. Conciliation Proceedings in the Federal Republic of Germany, Switzerland, Austria, Scandinavia, England and the United Sates. International Social Science Bulletin. 10:4 (1958), 616-625.

1761 Weyrauch, Walter O. The Art of Drafting Judgments: A Modified German Case Method. Journal of Legal Education. 9:3 (1957), 311-331.

E.3.3.3. Judicial Review

1762 Bader, Helmut. The Impact of the American Doctrine of Judicial Review Upon Austrian and German Constitutional Law. Ph.D. Thesis, University of Southern California, 1957.

1763 Dietze, Gottfried. Judicial Review in Europe. Michigan Law Review. 55:4 (February 1957), 539-566.

1764 Kommers, Donald P. Judicial Review in Italy and West Germany. Jahrbuch Des Oeffentlichen Rechts Der Gegenwart. Vol. 20. Ed. Gerhard Leibholz. Tuebingen: Mohr, 1971, Pp. 111-133.

1765 Nagel, Heinrich. Judicial Review in Germany. American Journal of Comparative Law. 3:2 (Spring 1954), 233-241.

1766 Pakuscher, Ernst K. Judicial Review of Executive Acts in Economic Affairs in Germany. Journal of Public Law. 20:1 (January 1971), 273-329.

1767 Rupp, Hans G. Judicial Review in the Federal Republic of Germany. American Journal of Comparative Law. 9:1 (Winter 1960), 29-47.

E.3.3.4. Conflict of Laws

1768 Cohn, Ernst J. Conflict of Laws. Manual of German Law, II. 2D Ed. Ed. Ernst J. Cohn. Dobbs Ferry: Oceana, 1971, Pp. 94-161.

1769 Graue, Eugen Dietrich. Recognition of Foreign Expropriations. American Journal of Comparative Law. 3:1 (Winter 1954), 93-95.

1770 Juenger, Friedrich K. The German Constitutional Court and the Conflict of Laws. American Journal of Comparative Law. 20:2 (Spring 1972), 290-298.

1771 Steefel, Ernest C. Recognition of Mexican Divorces in Germany. International Lawyer. 1:2 (January 1967), 206-209.

1772 Wengler, Wilhelm. Choice of Law and Forum in Contracts: Germany and Other European Countries. Proceedings of the Sixth International Symposium on Comparative Law. Ottawa: University of Ottawa Press, 1969, Pp. 189-211.

E.3.4. Other

E.3.4.1. Business Law: General

1773 Arthur Andersen and Company. Tax and Trade Guide, Germany. Chicago: Arthur Andersen and Company, 2D Ed., 1968, 109 P.

1774 Bohndorf, Michael T. Law of Bankruptcy. Manual of German Law, II. Ed. Ernst J. Cohn. Dobbs Ferry: Oceana, 1971, Pp. 261-275.

1775 Broder, Simon. A Comparative Study of the United States Patent Office and The German Patent Office. Ph.D. Thesis, American University, 1960, 268 P.

1776 Broder, Simon. The United States Patent Office and the German Patent Office: A Comparative Study. New York: Vantage, 1964, 227 P.

1777 Ernst and Ernst. West Germany: A Digest of Principal Taxes. New York: Ernst and Ernst, 1970, 111 P.

1778 FRG. Added Value Tax Law. Intro. By H. Karsten Schmidt, Wulf H. Doeser, Christoph Bellstedt. Chicago: Commerce Clearing House, 1967, 146 P.

1779 FRG. German Patent Law, Utility Model Law and Trade Mark Law. Cologne: Heymann, for J. Detlev Frhr. Von Uexkuell, 1963, 128 P.

1780 FRG. German Patent Law, Utility Model Law and Trade Mark Law: Text of 2Nd January 1968. Cologne: Heymann, for J. Detlev Frhr. Von Uexkuell, 1968, 145 P.

1781 Federation of British Industries. Taxation in Western Europe, 1964: A Guide for Industrialists. London: Federation of British Industries, 6Th Ed., October 1964, Pp. 108-128.

1782 Foreign Tax Law Association. West German Income Tax Service. Gainesville: Foreign Tax Law Association, 1970+.

1783 Gumpel, Henry J. Boettcher, Carl. Taxation in the Federal Republic of Germany. Chicago: Commerce Clearing House, 1963, 932 P.

1784 Gumpel, Henry J. Revision of the Tax Convention Between the U.S. and Federal Republic of Germany Signed September 17, 1965. Taxes. 44:6 (June 1966), 383-408.

1785 Landwehrmann, Friedrich. Legislative Development of International Corporate Taxation in Germany: Lessons for and From the United States. Harvard International Law Journal. 15:2 (Spring 1974), 238-297.

1786 Moss, John J., Editor. Commercial, Trademark, and Patent Law of the German Democratic Republic Today. Cambridge: Linguistic Systems, Inc., 1968, 221 P.

1787 Mueller, Rudolf. Steefel, Ernest C. Doing Business in Germany: A Legal Manual. Frankfurt: Knapp, 1960, 158 P.

1788 Mueller-Freienfels, Wolfram. Law of Agency. American Journal of Comparative Law. 6:2-3 (Spring-Summer 1957), 165-188.

1789 Mueller-Freienfels, Wolfram. Legal Relations in the Law of Agency: Power of Agency and Commercial Certainty. American Journal of Comparative Law. 13:2 (Spring 1964), 193-215; and 13:3 (Summer 1964), 341-359.

1790 Niehus, Rudolf J. The Revised U.S.-German Double Taxation Treaty--A German View. Bulletin for International Fiscal Documentation (Amsterdam).20:10 (October 1966), 397-412.

1791 Wallace, Donald O., Editor. West Germany Income Tax Service. Hempstead: Foreign Tax Law

Association, 1953.

E.3.4.2. Commercial Law; Contracts

1792 Cartwright, Hilary. The Law of Obligations in England and Germany. International and Comparative Law Quarterly. 13:4 (October 1964), 1316-1348.

1793 Crauford, W. G. Differences Between the English and the German Law Relating to Negotiable Instruments. International and Comparative Law Quarterly. 6:3 (July 1957), 418-441.

1794 Daniels, William G. The German Law of Sales. American Journal of Comparative Law. 6:4 (Autumn 1957), 470-502.

1795 Dawson, John P. Negotiorum Gestio: The Altruistic Intermeddler. Harvard Law Review. 74:5 (March 1961), 817-865; and 74:6 (April 1961), 1073-1129.

1796 Dawson, John P. Specific Performance in France and Germany. Michigan Law Review. 57:4 (February 1959), 495-538.

1797 Giles, C. C. Commercial Law. Manual of German Law, II. Ed. Ernst J. Cohn. Dobbs Ferry: Oceana, 1971, Pp. 3-93.

1798 Graue, Eugen Dietrich. Delimitation of Unjust Enrichment Claims. American Journal of Comparative Law. 3:1 (Winter 1954), 95-97.

1799 Mehren, Arthur T. Von. Civil-Law Analogues to Consideration: An Exercise in Comparative Analysis. Harvard Law Review. 72:6 (April 1959), 1009-1078.

1800 Riegert, Robert A. Unilateral Mistake Under the West German Civil Code and Some Comparisons. International Lawyer. 5:2 (April 1971), 312-323.

1801 Zweigert, Konrad. Aspects of the German Law of Sale. International and Comparative Law Quarterly. Suppl. Publ. No. 9 (1964), 1-15.

E.3.4.3. Corporation Law

1802 Berger, Don. Shareholder Rights Under the German Stock Corporation Law of 1965. Fordham Law Review. 38:4 (May 1970), 687-742.

1803 Bodungen, Thilo Von. The Defective Corporation in American and German Law. American Journal of Comparative Law. 15:1-2 (1966-67), 313-330.

1804 FRG. Commercial laws of Western Germany: Laws on Stock Corporations and Stock Partnerships. Deer Park: Foreign Tax Law Association, 1960, 191 P.

1805 FRG. Domestic and Foreign Investment Company Laws of the Federal Republic of Germany and Related Tax Laws. Munich?: N.P., C.1971, 76 P.

1806 FRG. German Stock Corporation Act. Chicago: Commerce Clearing House, 1967, 299 P.

1807 FRG. GmbH: German Law Concerning the Companies With Limited Liability. Intro. By Rudolf Mueller. Frankfurt: Knapp, 1967, 47 P.

1808 Falkenhausen, Bernhard Freiherr Von. Steefel, Ernst C. Shareholders' Rights in German Corporations. American Journal of Comparative Law. 10:4 (Autumn 1961), 407-431; and 11:2 (Spring 1962), 248.

1809 Mueller, Rudolf, Editor. Galbraith, Evan G., Editor. The German Stock Corporation Law. Frankfurt: Knapp, 1966, 502 P.

1810 Shilling, Neil. Myth and Reality in the French and German Close Corporation. Harvard International Law Club Journal. 6:1 (Winter 1964), 1-71.

1811 Williams, Lowell. The Social Responsibility of Corporations: A Comparative Analysis Under the Corporation Laws of the United States and the Federal Republic of Germany. Columbia Journal of Transnational Law. 11:1 (Winter 1972), 104-123.

E.3.4.4. Regulation of Business (See Also I.6.5)

1812 Bieberstein, Joerg. The German Cartel Law and Its Administration: Role of the Federal Cartel Office in Regard to the Eec Anti-Trust Provisions. International and Comparative Law Quarterly. 12:3 (July 1963), 850-885.

1813 Braunthal, Gerard. The Struggle for Cartel Legislation. Cases in Comparative Politics. Ed. James B. Christoph. Boston and Toronto: Little, Brown, 1965, Pp. 241-255.

1814 Bridge, F. H. S. The Antecedents of the Proposed German Law Against Restraints of Competition. International and Comparative Law Quarterly. 3:2 (April 1953), 348-351.

1815 Damm, Walter. National and International Factors Influencing Cartel Legislation in Post-War Germany. Ph.D. Thesis, University of Chicago, 1958, 285 P.

1816 Duerrhammer, Wilhelm. The German Cartel Law and Concentration. Cartel. 12:1 (January 1962), 24-27.

1817 FRG, Federal Insurance Supervisory Service. Supervision of Private Insurance in Germany. Paris: Organisation for Economic Cooperation and Development, 1963, 41 P.

1818 Fabricus, Fritz. The German Companies Act of 1965. Journal of Business Law. 10:3 (July 1957), 274-281.

1819 Fikentscher, Wolfgang. Proposed Antitrust Legislation and Price Discrimination. American Journal of Comparative Law. 2:4 (Autumn 1953), 523-533.

1820 Graupner, Rudolf. The Law Relating to Restrictive Trade Practices in West Germany and in the Treaty Establishing the European Economic Community. International and Comparative Law Quarterly. Suppl. Publ. No. 2 (1961), 41-55.

1821 Griesbach, Bernard. The German Policy on Competition Within the Scope of General Economic Policy. Antitrust Bulletin. 14:2 (Summer 1969), 449-472.

1822 Guenther, Eberhard. Cartel Policy in Germany. German Economic Review. 2:1 (1964), 16-24.

1823 Guenther, Eberhard. Cartel Policy in Germany. Cartel. 14:4 (October 1964), 160-166.

1824 Hurter, Edwin. Anti-Cartel Law Debate in West Germany. Swiss Review of World Affairs. 3:1 (April 1953), 7-9.

1825 Joliet, Rene. The Rule of Reason in Antitrust Law: American, German, and Common Market Laws in Comparative Perspective. The Hague: Nijhoff, 1967, 198 P.

1826 Kuehne, Karl. Co-Operation and Cartel Legislation in Western Germany. Cartel. 4:3 (July 1954), 91-98.

1827 Kuehne, Karl. The West German Cartel Bill. Cartel. 6:2 (April 1956), 48-54.

1828 Lacey, David C. The Law on Cartels in the Federal Republic of Germany and West Berlin (Amended). Washington: Bureau of International Commerce,

Government Printing Office, 1966, 63 P.

1829 Mankiewicz, R. H. Products Liability--A Judicial Breakthrough in West Germany. International and Comparative Law Quarterly. 19:1 (January 1970), 99-117.

1830 Mestmaecher, E. J. The Relation of the Law of Unfair Competition to the Law on Restraint of Competition in Germany. Unfair Competition: Some Comparative Aspects of the Laws of the United States, Germany, France, and the United Kingdom. Ed. Dennis C. Thompson. London: British Institute of International and Comparative Law, 1966, Pp. 17-27.

1831 Steefel, Ernest C. A Comparative Survey of Products Liability Law as Applied to Motor Vehicles: Germany. International Lawyer. 2:1 (October 1967), 130-133.

1832 Steindorff, E. Restrictive Practices Laws of Germany. International and Comparative Law Quarterly. Suppl. Publ. No. 4 (1962), 28-39.

1833 Thal, Steven H. The Existence of the Rule of Reason in the German Law Against Trade Restraints: A Case Study Analysis. New York University Journal of International Law & Politics. 3:2 (Winter 1970), 278-305.

1834 Treeck, Joachim. Joint Research Ventures and Antitrust Law in the United States, Germany and the European Economic Community. New York University Journal of International Law & Politics. 3:1 (Spring 1970), 18-55.

1835 Trescher, Karl. The New German Cartel Law. Cartel. 8:1 (January 1958), 12-17.

1836 West German Regulation of Foreign Mutual Fund Distributions. New York University Journal of International Law & Politics. 3:2 (Winter 1970), 323-342.

E.3.4.5. Criminal Law (See Also L.5.8)

1837 Auerbach, Philipp. Criminal Law and Criminality in Germany of Today. Annals of the American Academy of Political and Social Science. 260 (November 1948), 131-136.

1838 Bennett, James V. Notes on the German Legal and Penal System. Journal of Criminal Law and Criminology. 37:5 (January-February 1947), 368-376.

1839 Binavince, Emilio. The Doctrine of Mens Rea in Germany. Proceedings of the Fourth International Symposium on Comparative Law. Ottawa: University of Ottawa Press, 1967, Pp. 143-163.

1840 Casper, Gerhard. Zeisel, Hans. Lay Judges in the German Criminal Courts. Journal of Legal Studies. 1:1 (January 1972), 135-191.

1841 Clemens, Walter R. The Exclusionary Rule Under Foreign Law: Germany. Journal of Criminal Law, Criminology, and Police Science. 52:3 (September-October 1961), 277-282.

1842 Clemens, Walter R. Police Detention and Arrest Privileges Under Foreign Law: Germany. Journal of Criminal Law, Criminology, and Police Science. 51:4 (November-December 1960), 421-426.

1843 Clemens, Walter R. Police Interrogation Privileges and Limitations Under Foreign Law: Germany. Journal of Criminal Law, Criminology, and Police Science. 52:1 (May-June 1961), 59-63.

1844 Clemens, Walter R. The Privilege Against Self-Incrimination Under Foreign Law: Germany. Journal of Criminal Law, Criminology, and Police Science. 51:2 (July-August 1960), 172-175.

1845 Eichler, Wolfgang. German Criminal Jurisdiction. International and Comparative Law Quarterly. 5:4 (October 1956), 542-548.

1846 Eser, Albin. The Politics of Criminal Law Reform. American Journal of Comparative Law. 21:2 (Spring 1973), 245-262.

1847 FRG. The German Code of Criminal Procedure. Charlottesville: Judge Advocate General's School, Usareur Manual No. 550-155, 1955, 146 P.

1848 FRG. The German Code of Criminal Procedure. Introduction By Eberhard Schmidt. South Hackensack: Rothman, 1965, 235 P.

1849 FRG. The German Draft Penal Code. Intro. By Eduard Dreher. South Hackensack: Rothman, 1966, 253 P.

1850 FRG. The German Penal Code of 1871. Intro. By Horst Schroeder. South Hackensack: Rothman, 1961, 177 P.

1851 Fletcher, George P. Two Kinds of Legal Rules: A Comparative Study of Burden-of-Persuasion Practices in Criminal Cases. Yale Law Review. 77:5 (April 1968), 880-935.

1852 James, Eldon R., Editor. The Statutory Criminal Law of Germany, With Comments. Washington: Library of Congress, 1947, 276 P. Translation of 1871 Penal Code With Amendments and Allied Laws Nos. 1 and 11 and Proclamation No. 3.

1853 Jescheck, Hans-Heinrich. The Discretionary Powers of the Prosecuting Attorney in West Germany. American Journal of Comparative Law. 18:3 (1970), 508-517.

1854 Jescheck, Hans-Heinrich. Germany. The Accused: A Comparative Study. Ed. J. A. Coutts. London: Stevens & Sons, British Institute Studies in International and Comparative Law No. 3, 1966, Pp. 246-256.

1855 Jescheck, Hans-Heinrich. Principles of German Criminal Procedure in Comparison With American Law. Virginia Law Review. 56:2 (March 1970), 239-253.

1856 Mcwhinney, Edward. Court Jurisdiction in Germany and the Otto John Case Decision. Indiana Law Journal. 32:3 (Spring 1957), 310-312.

1857 Mueller, Gerhard O. W. Kroeger, Wilhelm. The Meeting of Two Police Ideas: Anglo-German Experiments in West Germany. Journal of Criminal Law, Criminology, and Police Science. 51:2 (July-August 1960), 257-262.

1858 Oidtman, Christoph Von, Editor. Reade, Arthur E. E., Editor. German Penal Code of 1871 Amended to May 1950 as Effective in the British Occupation Zone and Sector. Bielefeld: British Control Commission for Germany, 1950, 103 P.

1859 Opoku, Kwame. Delictual Liability in German Law. International and Comparative Law Quarterly. 21:2 (April 1972), 230-269.

1860 Pfannenschwarz, Karl. The Norms of High Treason, Endangerment of the State and Treason Laid Down in the West German Government Draft for a New Criminal Code. Law and Legislation in the German Democratic Republic. No. 2 (1962), 22-42.

1861 Przybylski, Peter. The Reform of West Germany's Penal Law--A Challenge of Democracy and Peaceful Coexistence. German Foreign Policy (GDR). 5:3 (1966), 223-236.

1862 Robinson, Cyril D. Arrest, Prosecution and Police Power in the

Federal Republic of Germany. Duquesne University Law Review. 4:2 (Winter 1965), 225-302.

1863 Schoerke, Adolf. Criminal Law and Criminality in Germany of Today. Annals of the American Academy of Political and Social Science. 260 (November 1948), 137-143.

1864 Schram, Glenn N. The Obligation to Prosecute in West Germany. American Journal of Comparative Law. 17:4 (1969), 627-632.

1865 Weber, Hans. On the Violations of International Law and of the Constitution in the "Major Reform of Criminal Law" in West Germany. Law and Legislation in the German Democratic Republic. No. 1 (1963), 29-49.

1866 Zimmer, Thomas M. The German Narcotics Law. Military Law Review. 53 (August 1971), 165-184.

E.3.4.6. Family Law (See Also L.1.3)

1867 Bohndorf, Michael T. The New Illegitimacy Law in Germany. International and Comparative Law Quarterly. 19:2 (April 1970), 299-308.

1868 Bohndorf, Michael T. Recent Developments in German Divorce Law. International and Comparative Law Quarterly. 19:4 (October 1970), 705-710.

1869 Ficker, Hans. A Survey of Marriage and Educational Counseling in the Federal Republic of Germany. Annales De La Faculte De Droit D'Istanbul. 9:13 (1960), 82-98.

1870 Fricke, Weddig. Divorce in German Law. American Journal of Comparative Law. 8:4 (Autumn 1959), 508-515.

1871 Grobe, Hans. Family Courts for Germany?. Journal of Family Law. 2:2 (July 1962), 157-160.

1872 Kahn-Freund, O. A New Development in German Matrimonial Property Law. International and Comparative Law Quarterly. 2:4 (October 1953), 611-614.

1873 Leyser, J. "Equality of the Spouses" Under the New German Law. American Journal of Comparative Law. 7:2 (Spring 1958), 276-287.

1874 Mueller-Freienfels, Wolfram. Family Law and the Law of Succession in Germany. International and Comparative Law Quarterly. 16:2 (April 1967), 409-445.

1875 Purcell, David W. A Comparison of the Community Property Systems of France, Germany, and Texas. Texas Law Review. 34:7 (October 1956), 1065-1081.

1876 Turner, J. Neville. Divorce: Australian and German "Breakdown" Provisions Compared. International and Comparative Law Quarterly. 18:4 (October 1969), 896-930.

E.3.4.7. International Law

1877 Allen, Claud G. Revision of German War-Time Judgments Under the Bonn-Paris Agreement. International and Comparative Law Quarterly. 5:1 (January 1956), 40-60.

1878 Domke, Martin. Immunity of Foreign States From German Jurisdiction. American Journal of International Law. 48:2 (April 1954), 302-304.

1879 Hamburg, Superior Court. Interlocutory Decision in Case Concerning Chilean Nationalization of El Teniente Mine. International Legal Materials. 13:5 (September 1974), 1115-1125.

1880 International Court of Justice. Judgments in the Fisheries Jurisdiction Cases: United Kingdom v. Iceland; Federal Republic of Germany v. Iceland. International Legal Materials. 13:5 (September 1974), 1090-1114.

1881 International Court of Justice. North Sea Continental Shelf Cases: Pleadings, Oral Arguments, Documents. Leiden: Sythoff, 1968, 2 Vols.

1882 Knoke, Karl Hermann. Law of the Sea Conference--Caracas Session. Aussenpolitik. 25:4 (1974), 418-428.

1883 Mann, F. A. The U.S. Treaty of Commerce With Germany and the German Constitution. American Journal of International Law. 65:4 (September 1971), 793-795.

1884 Plischke, Elmer. Reactivation of Prewar German Treaties. American Journal of International Law. 48:2 (April 1954), 245-264.

E.3.4.8. Labor Law (See Also I.7)

1885 Cole, R. Taylor. The Role of Labor Courts in Western Germany. Journal of Politics. 18:3 (August 1956), 479-498.

1886 Mcpherson, William H. Basic Issues in German Labor Court Structure. Labor Law Journal. 5:6 (June 1954), 439-452.

1887 Ramm, Th. Collective Agreements in Germany. International and Comparative Law Quarterly. Suppl. Publ. No. 5 (1962), 9-12.

E.3.4.9. Other Legal Issues

1888 Bohndorf, Michael T. Law of Nationality. Manual of German Law, II. Ed. Ernst J. Cohen. Dobbs Ferry: Oceana, 1971, Pp. 276-280.

1889 Fulda, Carl H. Prospective Overruling of Court Decisions in Germany and the United States. American Journal of Comparative Law. 13:3 (Summer 1964), 438-441.

1890 Heldrich, Andreas. Compensating Non-Economic Losses in the Affluent Society. American Journal of Comparative Law. 18:1 (1970), 22-30.

1891 Hink, Heinz R. Some Aspects of Public Liability in France and Germany. Ph.D. Thesis, University of Washington, 1957, 430 P.

1892 Meyer, Alex. The Development and Present State of German Air Law. Journal of Air Law and Commerce. 23:2 (Spring 1956), 188-204.

1893 Rinck, Gerd. Recent Developments in German Air Law. Journal of Air Law and Commerce. 23:4 (Autumn 1956), 479-489.

1894 Sommerich, Otto C. Busch, Benjamin. The German First Heir: Owner or Life Tenant?. American Journal of Comparative Law. 11:1 (Winter 1962), 92-95.

E.4. Military (See Also O.4)

E.4.1. Domestic Aspects of Rearmament Debate

1895 Brass, Paul. The Campaign Against Remilitarisation in Retrospect. Contemporary Issues. 8:28 (August-September 1956), 257-275.

1896 De Mendelssohn, Peter. The German Military Mind. Political Quarterly. 23:2 (April-June 1952), 182-190. A Survey of Recent Military Writings Covering Past, Present, and Future of German Army.

1897 Douglas, William A. The K.P.D.

Against Rearmament: The Role of the West German Communist Party in the Soviet Campaign Against West German Rearmament, 1949-1953. Ph.D. Thesis, Princeton University, 1964, 384 P.

1898 Dowell, Jack D. The Politics of Accommodation: German Democracy and Rearmament. Washington State University, Research Studies. 31:1 (March 1963), 1-17.

1899 Europa-Archiv. The Attitude of the Christian Churches Toward a German Defense Contribution. Santa Monica: Rand Corporation, Rm-927, 1952, 31 P.

1900 Europa-Archiv. German Labor Unions and the Question of German Participation in European Defense. Santa Monica: Rand Corporation, Rm-929, 1952, 46 P.

1901 Europa-Archiv. German Veterans Organizations and the Defense Contribution. Santa Monica: Rand Corporation, Rm-928, 1952, 47 P.

1902 Europa-Archiv. German Youth and Its Attitude Toward a German Defense Contribution. Santa Monica: Rand Corporation, Rm-926, 1952, 46 P.

1903 Europa-Archiv. The Ideological Groups in Germany and Their Attitude Toward The Defense Contribution. Santa Monica: Rand Corporation, Rm-930, 1952, 31 P.

1904 Fliess, Walter. German Opinion on Defence. Socialist Commentary. 15 (January 1951), 22-23.

1905 Grossmann, Kurt R. Peace Movements in Germany. South Atlantic Quarterly. 49:3 (July 1950), 292-302.

1906 Hirsch, Felix Edward. Growing German Pacifism. Current History. 20:114 (February 1951), 77-82.

1907 Jungclas, Georg. We Say "No" to Remilitarization--Revolutionary Germany Speaks. Fourth International. 12:2 (March-April 1951), 63-64.

1908 Magathan, Wallace C. The Politics of German Rearmament, 1949-1953: A Study of Some of the Limits to Executive Power in the Government of the Federal Republic of Germany. Ph.D. Thesis, Princeton University, 1961, 492 P.

1909 Nenno, William C. The SPD and West German Rearmament, 1949-1959. Ph.D. Thesis, Georgetown University, 1964.

1910 R. S. The West German Political Parties and Rearmament. World Today. 9:2 (February 1953), 53-64.

1911 Speier, Hans. German Rearmament and Atomic War: The Views of German Military and Political Leaders. Evanston and White Plains: Row, Peterson, 1957, 272 P.

1912 Speier, Hans. German Rearmament and the Old Military Elite. Santa Monica: Rand Corporation, P-458, 1953, 30 P.

1913 Speier, Hans. German Rearmament and the Old Military Elite. World Politics. 6:2 (January 1954), 147-168.

1914 Street, Jessie. Peace Movement Grows in West Germany. New Central European Observer. 5:18 (20 August 1952), 279.

1915 Vigers, T. W. The German People and Rearmament. International Affairs (London). 27:2 (April 1951), 151-155.

1916 Winzer, Otto. West German Working Class Fights Remilitarization. International Affairs (Moscow). (July 1955), 24-35.

1917 Zander, Ernst. The Campaign Against Remilitarisation in Germany. Contemporary Issues. 6:23 (May-June 1955), 170-214; and 7:27 (May-June 1956), 186-235.

E.4.2. Military Organization

1918 Albright, Raymond J. The Defense Ministry of the Federal Republic of Germany: A Study of Organizational Patterns for Creating and Controlling Military Power in West Germany, 1949-1960. Ph.D. Thesis, Harvard University, 1960, 468 P.

1919 Angelfort, Jupp. Is the Bundeswehr Really a "Paper Army"?. World Marxist Review: Problems of Peace and Socialism. 12:8 (August 1969), 72-74.

1920 Bailey, George. A New Army for the New Germany. Reporter. 25:2 (20 July 1961), 20-24.

1921 Baldwin, Hanson W. Communique on the New German Army. New York Times Magazine. (1 December 1957), 24+.

1922 Baudissin, Wolf Graf Von. The New German Army. Foreign Affairs. 34:1 (October 1955), 1-13.

1923 Brauer, Max. for a German Citizens' Army. New Leader. 38:10 (7 March 1955), 5-6.

1924 Bredow, W. Von. The West German Bundeswehr as an Institution for Political Education. On Military Ideology. Ed. Morris Janowitz and Jacques Van Doorn. Rotterdam: Rotterdam University Press, 1971.

1925 Colby, Reginald. The Birth of the New German Army. Quarterly Review. 295:611 (January 1957), 22-35.

1926 Feldman, K. Frank. New German Army. Contemporary Review. 186:1068 (December 1954), 327-330.

1927 FRG, Federal Ministry of Defense. White Paper 1970 on the Security of the Federal Republic of Germany and on the State of the German Federal Armed Forces. Bonn: Federal Ministry of Defense, 1970, 212 P.

1928 FRG, Federal Ministry of Defense. White Paper 1971/1972: The Security of the Federal Republic of Germany and the Development of the Federal Armed Forces. Bonn: Press and Information Office, 1972, 228 P.

1929 FRG, Press and Information Office. The Bundeswehr: Partner in the Western Alliance. Bonn: Press and Information Office, 3D Ed., 1963, 46 P.

1930 Geyr, Leo Freiherr Von. Some Comments on the Rebuilding of the German Bundeswehr. Royal United Service Institute Journal. 110:639 (August 1965), 271-277.

1931 Herbst, Josef. The New Model Bundeswehr--Army of the Federal Republic of Germany. Army Information Digest. 20:1 (January 1965), 40-51.

1932 Herrmann, K. The Activation of the Federal Defense Forces (Bundeswehr). Army Quarterly. 74:1 (April 1957), 33-39.

1933 Joesten, Joachim. The Bundeswehr Today: West German's Armed Forces in 1960-1961. New York: Joachim Joesten, New Germany Reports No. 50, October 1960, 16 P.

1934 Joy, James L. West German Perceptions of the Wehrmacht. Ph.D. Thesis, University of Denver, 1971, 182 P.

1935 Kelleher, Catherine M. Political-Military Systems: Comparative Perspectives. Beverly Hills: Sage, 1975, 300 Pp.

1936 Kitchen, Martin. Military History of Germany. London: Weidenfelt & Nicholson, 1975, 392 P.

1937 Loewenstein, Prince Hubertus Zu. The German Bundeswehr. Modern Age. 5:3

(Summer 1961), 281-289.

1938 Luchsinger, Fred. The New German Armed Forces. Swiss Review of World Affairs. 8:8 (November 1958), 3-5.

1939 Muhlen, Norbert. The New Army of a New Germany. Orbis. 1:3 (Fall 1957), 278-290.

1940 Paget, Reginald. What Sort of an Army Will Germany Have?. Twentieth Century. 157:935 (January 1955), 8-14.

1941 Rudoi, G. The Bundeswehr--Instrument of Revanche and Aggression. International Affairs (Moscow). (April 1959), 82-86.

1942 Ruge, Friedrich. The Reconstruction of the German Navy, 1956-1961. Proceedings of the United States Naval Institute. 88:7 (July 1962), 52-65.

1943 Ruge, Friedrich. The Postwar German Navy and Its Mission. Proceedings of the United States Naval Institute. 83:10 (October 1957), 1034-1043.

1944 Schloenbach, Knut. Studies on the Structure of the Armed Forces with the Aid of Simulation. German Economic Review. 11:4 (1973), 361-368. Quantitative Methods of Analysis Used By Force Structure Commission.

1945 Suchenwirth, Richard. Command and Leadership in the German Air Force. Maxwell Air Force Base, Ala.: Air University, Aerospace Studies Institute, Historical Division, 1969, 351 P.

1946 Waldman, Eric. The Goose Step Is Verboten: The German Army Today. New York: Free Press, 1964, 294 P.

E.4.3. Civilian Control Procedures

1947 Boenau, Arthur Bruce. Civilian Control of the Military By the West German Government, 1949-1957. Ph.D. Thesis, Columbia University, 1964, 534 P.

1948 Chaplin, Dennis. West German Army Ombudsman. Royal United Service Institution Journal. 117:665 (March 1972), 61-64.

1949 Lohse, Egon. West Germany's Military Ombudsman. The Ombudsman, Citizen's Defender. Ed. Donald C. Rowat. London: Allen & Unwin, 1968, Pp. 119-126.

1950 Moe, George R. A Survey of Politically Significant Innovations in the German Bundeswehr. Ph.D. Thesis, American University, 1966, 343 P.

1951 Moritz, Gunther. The Administration of Justice Within the Armed Forces of the German Federal Republic. Military Law Review. 7 (January 1960), 1-22.

1952 Ridley, F. F. The Parliamentary Commissioner for Military Affairs in the Federal Republic of Germany. Political Studies. 12:1 (February 1964), 1-20.

1953 Ritter, Gerhard. The Military and Politics in Germany. Journal of Central European Affairs. 17:3 (October 1957), 259-271.

1954 Roghmann, Klaus. Armed Forces and Society in West Germany: Program and Reality, 1955-1970. on Military Intervention. Ed. Morris Janowitz and Jacques A. A. Van Doorn. Rotterdam: Rotterdam University Press, 1971.

1955 Roghmann, Klaus. Sodeur, Wolfgang. The Impact of Military Service on Authoritarian Attitudes: Evidence From West Germany. American Journal of Sociology. 78:2 (September 1972), 418-433.

1956 Secher, H. Pierre. The Bundeswehr: A New Phase in Civil-Military Relations in The FRG. Teaching Postwar Germany in America: Papers and Discussions. Ed. Louis F. Helbig and Eberhard Reichmann. Bloomington: Indiana Univeristy, Institute of German Studies, 1972.

1957 Secher, H. Pierre. Controlling the New German Military Elite: The Political Role of the Parliamentary Defense Commissioner in the Federal Republic. Proceedings of the American Philosophical Society. 109:2 (9 April 1965), 63-84.

1958 Shirk, Paul R. The German Defense Commissioner. Military Review. 47:2 (February 1967), 54-60.

1959 Singer, Rudolf. Indignation at Inhumanity. German Foreign Policy (GDR). 4:2 (1965), 122-126. Training in FRG Bundeswehr.

1960 Smith, Willard E. Political Education in the West German Bundeswehr: A Cast of Civil-Military Relations. Ph.D. Thesis, University of Nebraska, 1965, 377 P.

1961 Sutton, John L. The Personnel Screening Committee and Parliamentary Control of the West German Armed Forces. Journal of Central European Affairs. 19:4 (January 1960), 389-401.

1962 Warnke, Rudolf. The Problem of Social Integration in the Armed Forces as Demonstrated in the Deutsche Bundeswehr. The Armed Services and Society: Alienation, Management, and Integration. Ed. J. N. Wolfe and John Erickson. Edinburgh: Edinburgh University Press, 1970, Pp. 43-64.

1963 Wieck, Hans-Georg. Policy Planning Council in the Defence. Aussenpolitik. 25:2 (1974), 177-191.

1964 Wieser, Theodor. Army and Society in West Germany. Swiss Review of World Affairs. 18:9 (December 1968), 7-9.

E.4.4. Nuclear Weapons Issue

1965 Arzumanyan, A. European Security and the Atomic Arming of the Federal Republic of Germany. International Affairs (Moscow). (July 1961), 44-49.

1966 Bader, W. B. Nuclear Weapons Sharing and the German Problem. Foreign Affairs. 44:4 (July 1966), 693-700.

1967 Baumann, Otto. Germans Against Atomic Death. Labour Monthly. 40 (July 1958), 331-335.

1968 Baumann, Otto. Popular Movement Against Atomic Death. World Marxist Review: Problems of Peace and Socialism. 1:3 (November 1958), 64-67.

1969 Braunthal, Gerard. Direct and Representative Democracy in West Germany: The Atomic Armament Issue. Canadian Journal of Economics and Political Science. 25:3 (August 1959), 313-323.

1970 Close, Richard B. Nuclear Weapons and West Germany. Ph.D. Thesis, University of Massachusetts, 1967, 228 P.

1971 Committee for the Protection of Human Rights of the GDR. Alarming Facts; a Document on the Persecution of Nuclear War Opponents. Berlin (East): Committee for the Protection of Human Rights, 1961, 31 P.

1972 Doernberg, Stefan. Bonn's Atomic Ambitions. International Affairs (Moscow). (March 1965), 9-13.

1973 Edinger, Lewis J. Atomic Blackmail and German Democracy. South Atlantic Quarterly. 57:3 (Summer 1958), 311-324.

1974 Hinterhoff, Eugene. Germany and Nuclear Weapons. Poland and Germany. 8:4 (October-December 1964), 7-18.

1975 Ilyin, V. Bonn's Nuclear Ambitions. International Affairs (Moscow). (May 1968), 24-29.

1976 Kelleher, Catherine M. German Nuclear Dilemmas, 1955-1965. Ph.D. Thesis, Massachusetts Institute of Technology, 1967.

1977 Kelleher, Catherine M. The Issue of German Nuclear Armament. Proceedings of the Academy of Political Science. 29:2 (November 1968), 95-107.

1978 Klein, Peter. Atom Free Zones in the Whole World. German Foreign Policy (GDR). 3:1 (1964), 59-70.

1979 Klein, Peter. Bonn's Struggle Against Non-Proliferation of Nuclear Weapons. German Foreign Policy (GDR). 6:5 (1967), 385-393.

1980 Kowalewski, Jerzy. West Germany's Striving for Nuclear Armaments. Warsaw: Zachodnia Agencja Prasowa, 1963, 110 P.

1981 Krusche, Heinz. The Striving of the Kiesinger-Strauss Government for Nuclear Weapons Is a Threat to European Security. German Foreign Policy (GDR). 6:2 (1967), 152-160.

1982 Mahncke, Dieter M. Nuclear Participation: The Federal Republic of Germany and Nuclear Weapons, 1954-1966. Ph.D. Thesis, School of Advanced International Studies, Johns Hopkins University, 1968, 326 P.

1983 Mendershausen, Horst. Will West Germany Go Nuclear?. Orbis. 16:2 (Summer 1972), 411-434.

1984 Mendershausen, Horst. Will West Germany Try to Get Nuclear Arms--Somehow?. Santa Monica: Rand Corporation, P-4649, May 1971, 32 P.

1985 Schaffer, Gordon. H-Bomb for Adenauer?. Labour Monthly. 39:6 (June 1957), 259-262.

E.4.5. Other Military Issues (See Also E.3.2.5)

1986 Albrecht, Ulrich. The Costs of Armamentism. Journal of Peace Research. 10:3 (1973), 265-283.

1987 Benecke, Theodor. Military Technology in West Germany. Military Review. 47:8 (August 1967), 41-46.

1988 Dammer, H. W. Training the New German Army. Army Information Digest. 12:12 (December 1957), 36-42.

1989 Dernburg, H. J. Rearmament and the German Economy. Foreign Affairs. 33:4 (July 1955), 648-662.

1990 Economic Implications of German Rearmament. World Today. 11:3 (March 1955), 117-129.

1991 Educating German Army Officers. Military Review. 46:4 (April 1966), 65-67.

1992 Forstmeier, Friedrich. The Image of the German Officer. Royal United Service Institution Journal. 114:656 (December 1969), 52-55.

1993 Grieves, Forest L. Der Bundesgrenzschutz--Overlooked Strength?. Military Review. 53:2 (February 1973), 53-64.

1994 Herwig, Holger H. An Introduction to Military Archives in West Germany. Military Affairs. 36:4 (December 1972), 121-124.

1995 Hoffmann, Walther G. The Share of Defence Expenditure in Gross National Product (Gnp)--An International and Diachronic Comparison. German Economic Review. 7:4 (1969), 295-307.

1996 Hurter, Edwin. Germany's Financial Defense Contribution: Facts, Figures and Rumors. Swiss Review of World Affairs. 4:11 (February 1955), 5-6. 4

1997 Hurter, Edwin. West Germany: Economic Aspects of Rearmament. Swiss Review of World Affairs. 5:4 (July 1955), 3-7.

1998 Institute for Finances and Taxes. Bases for Assessing West European Defense Contributions. Bonn: Institut Finanzen Und Steuern, 1953, 43 P.

1999 Institute for Finances and Taxes. Defense Contribution and Tax Burden. Bonn: Institut Finanzen Und Steuern, 1953, 23 P.

2000 Institute for Occupation Affairs. Occupation Costs--Are They a Defence Contribution?. Tuebingen: Mohr, for Institut Fuer Besatzungsfragen (Tuebingen), 1951, 68 P.

2001 Mikhailov, Vladimir Ivanovich. West Germany as an Arms Factory. International Affairs (Moscow). (February 1964), 19-23.

2002 Russett, Bruce M. The Economic Impact of German Rearmament. Williamstown: Williams College, April 1957, 44 P.

2003 Schmidt, Helmut. Military Expenditure in a Free Market Economy. Intereconomics. No. 1 (January 1968), 28-29.

2004 Schmoelders, Guenter. The Impact of the Rearmament on Western Germany. Public Finance. 7:1-2 (1952), 100-114.

2005 Waldman, Eric. German Home Defense Troops. Military Reveiw. 46:5 (May 1966), 84-90.

2006 Zeimer, Siegfried. Charisius, Albrecht. Bundeswehr Crisis. German Foreign Policy (GDR). 6:1 (1967),56-64.

E.4.6. Intelligence Activities

2007 Birdwood, C. B. Germany's Information Services. Twentieth Century. 143:853 (March 1948), 142-146.

2008 Cookridge, E. H. Gehlen: Spy of the Century. New York: Random House, 1972, 402 P.

2009 Delmer, Sefton. Black Boomerang: An Autobiography. London: Secker & Warburg, 1962, Vol. 2, 320 P., Esp. Pp. 255-295. Former UK Secret Service Agent's Defense of Otto John.

2010 Frischauer, Willi. The Man Who Came Back: The Story of Otto John. London: Muller, 1958, 276 P.

2011 GDR, Committee for German Unity. What Dr. John Really Said. Berlin: Committee for German Unity, 1954, 39 P. Dr. Otto John's Reasons for Leaving FRG; Report of Press Conference, 11 August 1954.

2012 Gehlen, Reinhard. The Service: Memoirs of General Reinhard Gehlen. New York: World, 1972, 386 P.

2013 Hoehne, Heinz. Zolling, Hermann. The General Was a Spy: The Truth About General Gehlen and His Spy Ring. New York: Coward, Mccann & Geoghegan, 1972, 347 P.

2014 Joesten, Joachim. The Frame-Up of Captain Kauffman. New York: Joachim Joesten, New Germany Reports Nos. 60-61, September-October 1963, 26 P. US Officer Accused of Treason By Former GDR Agent.

2015 Joesten, Joachim. Germany's "Secret Service Jungle": Background to the Dr. John Scandal. New York: Joachim Joesten, New Germany Reports No. 28,

September 1954, 19 P.

2016 John, Otto. Twice Through the Lines: The Autobiography of Otto John. New York: Harper & Row, 1973.

2017 Luchsinger, Fred. Aims and Methods of Communist Infiltration in Germany. Swiss Review of World Affairs. 9:7 (October 1959), 7-9.

2018 Mader, Julius. Anti-National Machinations of the Bonn "Office for the Protection of the Constitution". German Foreign Policy (GDR). 2:5 (1963), 374-385.

2019 Mader, Julius. The West German Intelligence Service. International Affairs (Moscow). (May 1964), 72-75.

F.FFG: Politics and Political Behavior

F.1. Political Attitudes

F.1.1. Personality Characteristics and Social Attitudes (See Also C.2)

2020 Alfert, Elizabeth. A Multiple Score Personality Test Administered to German and Austrian Students: Cross-Cultural Vs. Intra-Cultural Differences. Journal of Social Psychology. 50:1 (August 1959), 37-46.

2021 Becker, Joerg. Racism in Children's and Young People's Literature in the Western World. Journal of Peace Research. 10:3 (1973), 295-303.

2022 Cohn, Thomas S. Carsch, Henry. Administration of the F Scale to a Sample of Germans. Journal of Abnormal and Social Psychology. 49:3 (July 1954), 471.

2023 Culver, Wallace W. A Study of Social Attitudes of German and American High School Students as Related to Authoritarianism. Ph.D. Thesis, Pennsylvania State College, 1951, 285 P.

2024 Dicks, Henry V. Licensed Mass Murder: A Socio-Psychological Study of Some Ss Killers. New York: Basic Books, 1972, Xiii and 283 P.

2025 Eysenck, Hans J. Primary Social Attitudes: A Comparison of Attitude Patterns in England, Germany, and Sweden. Journal of Abnormal and Social Psychology. 48:4 (October 1953), 563-568.

2026 Harrelson, Lawrence E. A Guttman Facet Analysis of Attitudes Toward the Mentally Retarded in the Federal Republic of Germany: Content, Structure and Determinants. Ph.D. Thesis, Michigan State University, 1970, 328 P.

2027 Kaldegg, A. Responses of German and English Secondary School Boys to a Projection Test. British Journal of Psychology. 39 (September 1948), 30-53.

2028 Mcclelland, David C. Sturr, J. F. Knapp, R. H. Wendt, H. W. Obligations to Self and Society in the United States and Germany. Journal of Abnormal and Social Psychology. 56:2 (March 1958), 245-255.

2029 Mcgranahan, Donald V. A Comparison of Social Attitudes Among American and German Youth. Journal of Abnormal and Social Psychology. 41:3 (July 1946), 245-257.

2030 Metraux, Rhoda Bubendey. The Consequences of Wrongdoing: An Analysis of Story Completions By German Children. Childhood in Contemporary Cultures. Ed. Margaret Mead and Martha Wolfenstein. Chicago: University of Chicago Pres, 1956, Pp. 306-323.

2031 Ogletree, Earl J. A Cross-Cultural Examination of the Creative Thinking Ability of Public and Private School Pupils in England, Scotland, and Germany. Journal of Social Psychology. 83:2 (April 1971), 301-302.

2032 Ogletree, Earl J. A Cross-Cultural Exploratory Study of the Creativeness of Steiner and State School Pupils in England, Scotland, and Germany. Ph.D. Thesis, Wayne State University, 1967.

2033 Pipping, Knut. Report on the Unesco Study "Attitudes of the German Youth Toward Authority". Transactions of the Second World Congress of Sociology. London: International Sociological Association, 1954, Vol. 1, Pp. 120-124.

2034 Plog, Stanley C. The Disclosure of Self in the United States and Germany. Journal of Social Psychology. 65:2 (April 1965), 193-203.

2035 Rieder, Guenther. Bringmann, Wolfgang. Stereotyped Attitudes Toward the Aged in West Germany and The United States. Journal of Social Psychology. 76:2 (December 1968), 267-268.

2036 Schirokauer, Arnold. Spitzer, L. German Words, German Personality and Protestantism Again. Psychiatry. 12:2 (May 1949), 185-187.

2037 Spindler, G. Dearborn. American Character Revealed By the Military. Psychiatry. 11:3 (August 1948), 275-281.

2038 Stoodley, Bartlett H. Normative Attitudes of Filipino Youth Compared With German and American Youth. American Sociological Review. 22:5 (October 1957), 553-561.

2039 Strickland, Richard C. Mobility and Achievement of Selected Dependent Junior High School Pupils in Germany. Ph.D. Thesis, Miami University, 1970, 125 P.

2040 Sundberg, Norman D. The Use of the Mmpi for Cross-Cultural Personality Study: A Preliminary Report on the German Translation. Journal of Abnormal and Social Psychology. 52:2 (March 1956), 281-283.

2041 Szalai, Sandor. The Use of Time: Daily Activities of Urban and Suburban Populations in Twelve Countries. The Hague: Mouton, 1972, Xii and 858 P.

2042 Thomae, Hans. Ageing and Problems of Adjustment. International Social Science Journal. 15:3 (1963), 366-376.

2043 Thorner, Isidor. German Words, German Personality and Protestantism. Psychiatry. 8:4 (November 1945), 403-417. See Also Arnold Schirokauer and L. Spitzer, Psychiatry, 12:2 (May 1949), 185-187.

2044 Triandis, Harry. Davis, Earl. Takezawa, Shin-Ichi. Some Determinants of Social Distance Among American, German, and Japanese Students. Journal of Personality and Social Psychology. 2:4 (October 1965), 540-551.

2045 US, Omgus, Information Control Division. German Youth and Adults View Individual Responsibility. International Journal of Opinion and Attitude Research. 2:2 (Summer 1948), 230-236.

2046 Williams, John E. Carter, Dorothy Jean. Connotations of Racial Concepts and Color Names in Germany. Journal of Social Psychology. 72:1 (June 1967), 19-26.

F.1.2. Public Opinion and Political Attitudes

2047 Abramson, Paul. Social Class and Political Change in Western Europe: A Cross-National Longitudinal Analysis. Comparative Political Studies. 4:2 (July 1971), 131-156.

2048 Almond, Gabriel A. Verba, Sidney. The Civic Culture: Political Attitudes and Democracy in Five Nations. Princeton: Princeton University Press, 1963, 562 P.

2049 Bendix, Reinhard. Compliant Behavior and Individual Personality. American Journal of Sociology. 58:3 (November 1952), 292-303.

2050 Boynton, G. Robert. Loewenberg, Gerhard. The Development of Public Support for Parliament in Germany, 1951-59. British Journal of Political Science. 3:2 (April 1973), 169-189.

2051 Burstein, Paul. Social Structure and Individual Political Participation in Five Countries. American Journal of Sociology. 77:6 (May 1972), 1067-1110. Usa, UK, FRG, Italy, Mexico.

2052 Cantril, Hadley. The Pattern of Human Concerns. New Brunswick: Rutgers University Press, 1965, 427 P.

2053 Cassidy, Paul J. West German Political Cultures: A Test of the Substantive and Methodological Utility of the Political Culture Approach. Ph.D. Thesis, University of North Carolina, 1969, 258 P.

2054 Chandler, William Mayhew. The Socialization of Democratic Attitudes in Germany. Ph.D. Thesis, University of North Carolina, 1971, 285 P.

2055 Comfort, Louise K. Openness to Political Conflict in Britain and Germany: An Inquiry Into Causal Relationships. Ph.D. Thesis, Yale University, 1975.

2056 Crespi, Leo P. Germans View the U.S. Reorientation Program. International Journal of Opinion and Attitude Research. 5:2 (Summer 1951), 179-190; and 5:3 (Fall 1951), 335-346.

2057 Crespi, Leo P. The Influence of Military Government Sponsorship in German Opinion Polling. International Journal of Opinion and Attitude Research. 4:2 (Summer 1950), 151-178. Comment By Frederick W. Williams and Rejoinder By Crespi, 4:3 (Fall 1950), 415-418.

2058 Davison, W. Phillips. Trends in West German Public Opinion, 1946-1956. West German Leadership and Foreign Policy. Ed. Hans Speier and W. Phillips Davison. Evanston: Row, Peterson, 1957, Pp. 282-304.

2059 Dennis, Jack. Lindberg, Leon N. Mccrone, Donald J. Stiefbold, Rodney P. Political Socialization to Democratic Orientations in Four Western Systems. Comparative Political Studies. 1:1 (April 1968), 71-101. U.S.A., Britain, Italy, and Germany.

2060 Di Palma, Giuseppe. Disaffection and Participation in Western Democracies: The Role of Political Oppositions. Journal of Politics. 31:4 (November 1969), 984-1010.

2061 Enzensberger, Hans Magnus. A German Poet Assaults the Polls. Atlas. 10:5 (November 1965), 273-275. Criticizes German Poll-Takers and Their Predictions.

2062 Erhard, Ludwig. Problems Put to Public Opinion Experts. Allensbach and Bonn: Verlag Fuer Demoskopie, Allensbacher Schriften No 8, 1962, 25 P.

2063 FRG. Press and Information Office. Public Opinion. Bonn: Press and Information Office, 1971, 81 P.

2064 Feldman, K. Frank. Will the Fallen Monarchs Return?. Contemporary Review. 187:1071 (March 1955), 182-186.

2065 Gillespie, James M. Allport, Gordon W. Youth's Outlook on the Future: A Cross-National Study. New York: Doubleday, 1955, 61 P.

2066 Grossack, Martin. A Study of Attitudes Toward American Policy in Germany. Public Opinion Quarterly. 16:3 (Fall 1952), 440-442.

2067 Hadley, Guy. Public and Parliament in West Germany. Parliamentary Affairs. 9:2 (Spring 1956), 224-229.

2068 Halpern, Henry. Soviet Attitude Toward Public Opinion Research in Germany. Public Opinion Quarterly. 13:1 (Spring 1949), 117-118.

2069 Hartmann, Heinz. Institutional Immobility and Attitudinal Change. Comparative Politics. 2:4 (July 1970), 579-592.

2070 Hess, Robert D. Socialization of Attitudes Toward Political Authority: Some Cross-National Comparisons. International Social Science Bulletin. 15:4 (1963), 542-559.

2071 Katona, George. Survey Research in Germany. Public Opinion Quarterly. 17:4 (Winter 1954), 471-480.

2072 Kecskemeti, Paul. Leites, Nathan C. Some Psychological Hypotheses on Nazi Germany. Journal of Social Psychology. 26 (November 1947), Pp. 141-184; 27 (February 1948), Pp. 91-117; 27 (May 1948), Pp. 240-270; 28 (August 1948), 141-164. See Response By Reinhard Bendix, "Compliant Behavior and Individual Personality," American Journal of Sociology, 58:3 (November 1952), 292-303.

2073 Kellerer, Hans. Opinion and Attitude Research in Western Germany and West Berlin. International Journal of Opinion and Attitude Research. 5:4 (Winter 1951-52), 511-518.

2074 Kirkpatrick, Clifford. Reactions of Educated Germans to Defeat. American Journal of Sociology. 54:1 (July 1948), 36-47.

2075 Kirschhofer, Andreas Von. The Germans on Themselves: Public Opinion Polls Reveal Changing Attitudes. Modern World. 6 (1968), 99-110.

2076 Lamm, Hans. An Opinion Poll in Western Germany--Every Fifth Person Wants to Become a World Citizen. Common Cause. 3:2 (September 1949), 92-94.

2077 Luchsinger, Fred. Public Opinion in Germany Today. Swiss Review of World Affairs. 13:4 (July 1963), 11-12.

2078 Luebke, Paul. Political Attitudes in a West German Factory: A Political-Sociological Analysis of Chemical Workers. Ph.D. Thesis, Columbia University, 1975.

2079 Mende, Tibor. Public Opinion in Germany. Fortnightly. 160:955 (July 1946), 34-41.

2080 Mendershausen, Horst. Troop Stationing in Germany: German Public Opinion. Santa Monica: Rand Corporation, Rm-6172-Pr, November 1969, 34 P.

2081 Merritt, Anna J., Editor. Merritt, Richard L., Editor. Public Opinion in Occupied Germany: The Omgus Surveys, 1945-1949. Urbana: University of Illinois Press, 1970, 328 P.

2082 Merritt, Anna J. Merritt, Richard L. Public Opinion in Semisovereign Germany: The Hicog Surveys, 1949-1955. Urbana: University of Illinois Press, 1976.

2083 Merritt, Richard L. Political

Perspectives in Germany: The Occupation Period, 1945-1949. Social Science Information. 8:2 (April 1969), 129-140.

2084 Meszaros, Joseph W. Chancellor Popularity in the Federal Republic of Germany From 1950-1069: A Time Series Analysis. Ph.D. Thesis, University of Iowa, 1974.

2085 Moore, William W. Some German Attitudes Toward U.S. Occupation. Columbia Journal of International Affairs. 2:1 (Winter 1948), 76-82.

2086 Neumann, Erich Peter. Public Opinion in Germany, 1961. Allensbach and Bonn: Verlag Fuer Demoskopie, Allensbacher Schriften No. 6, 1961, 71 P.

2087 Noelle, Elisabeth, Editor. Neumann, Erich Peter, Editor. The Germans: Public Opinion Polls, 1947-1966. Allensbach and Bonn: Verlag Fuer Demoskopie, 1967, 630 P.

2088 Noelle, Elisabeth. Schmidtchen, Gerhard. The Significance of Opinion Surveys in Public Life. International Social Science Journal. 14:2 (1962), 283-302.

2089 Noelle-Neumann, Elisabeth. The Spiral of Silence: A Theory of Public Opinion. Journal of Communication. 24:2 (Spring 1974), 43-51.

2090 Powell, Charles A. Social Participation and Political Behavior in West Germany. Ph.D. Thesis, University of Oregon, 1965, 450 P.

2091 Terhune, Kenneth W. An Examination of Some Contributing Demographic Variables in a Cross-National Study. Journal of Social Psychology. 59:2 (April 1963), 209-219. US, FRG, Norway.

2092 Verba, Sidney. Organizational Membership and Democratic Consensus. Journal of Politics. 27:3 (August 1965), 467-497.

2093 Verba, Sidney. Political Participation and Strategies of Influence: A Comparative Study. Acta Sociologica. 6:1-2 (1962), 22-52.

2094 Wildenmann, Rudolf. Germany 1930/1970--The Empirical Findings. Sozialwissenschaftliches Jahrbuch Fuer Politik, Vol. 2. Munich and Vienna: Olzog, 1971, Pp. 13-60.

2095 Ylvisaker, Hedvig. Experience in the Time International Survey: The Special Problem in Germany. Public Opinion Quarterly. 12:4 (Winter 1948-49), 718-720.

2096 Ylvisaker, Hedvig. Crespi, Leo P. German Attitudes and the Prospects for Democracy. International Journal of Opinion and Attitude Research. 4:2 (Summer 1950), 2-8.

F.1.3. Party Identification (See Also E.2.1; F.4; F.5)

2097 Baker, Kendall L. The Acquisition of Partisanship in Germany. American Journal of Political Science. 18:3 (August 1974), 569-584.

2098 Baker, Kendall L. Political Participation, Political Efficacy, and Socialization in Germany. Comparative Politics. 6:1 (October 1973), 73-98.

2099 Brantley, Susan K. Voting Stability and Party Identification in the United States and West Germany. Ph.D. Thesis, University of Iowa, 1974.

2100 Dennis, Jack. Mccrone, Donald J. Preadult Development of Political Identification in Western Democracies. Comparative Political Studies. 3:2 (July 1970), 243-263.

2101 Hartenstein, Wolfgang. Liepelt, Klaus. Party Members and Party Voters in W. Germany. Acta Sociologica. 6:1-2 (1962), 43-52.

2102 Janowitz, Morris. Segal, David R. Social Cleavage and Party Affiliation: Germany, Great Britain, and the United States. American Journal of Sociology. 72:6 (May 1967), 601-618.

2103 Klingemann, Hans D. Testing the Left-Right Continuum on a Sample of German Voters. Comparative Political Studies. 5:1 (April 1972), 93-106.

2104 Linz, Juan J. Cleavage and Consensus in West German Politics: The Early Fifties. Party Systems and Voter Alignments: Cross-National Perspectives. Ed. Seymour M. Lipset and Stein Rokkan. New York: Free Press, 1967, Pp. 283-321.

2105 Linz, Juan J. The Social Bases of West German Politics. Ph.D. Thesis, Columbia University, 1960, 2 Vols., 945 P.

2106 Rokkan, Stein. Citizens, Elections, Parties: Approaches to the Comparative Study of the Processes of Development. New York: Mckay, 1970, 470 P.

2107 Rokkan, Stein. Party Preferences and Opinion Patterns in Western Europe: A Comparative Analysis. International Social Science Bulletin. 7:4 (1955), 575-596. Belgium, UK, France, Netherlands, Norway, Sweden, FRG.

2108 Schleth, Uwe. Weede, Erich. Causal Models on West German Voting Behavior. Sozialwissenschaftliches Jahrbuch Fuer Politik, Vol. 2. Munich and Vienna: Guenter Olzog Verlag, 1971, Pp. 73-97.

2109 Segal, David R. Classes, Strata and Parties in West Germany and the United States. Comparative Studies in Society and History. 10:1 (October 1967), 66-84.

2110 Segal, David R. Social Structural Bases of Political Partisanship in West Germany and the United States. Public Opinion and Politics. Ed. William J. Crotty. New York: Holt, Rinehart & Winston, 1969, Pp. 216-235.

2111 Zohlnhoefer, Werner. Party Identification in the Federal Republic of Germany and The United States. The Democratic Political Process. Ed. Kurt L. Shell. Waltham: Blaisdell, 1969, Pp. 148-158.

F.1.4. Opinion on International Affairs

2112 Anderson, Nels. Opinion on Europe. European Yearbook. 5 (1959), 143-160. Belgium, France, FRG, Netherlands.

2113 Brouwer, Marten. International Contacts and Integration-Mindedness. Polls. 1:2 (Summer 1965), 1-11.

2114 Brouwer, Marten. Some Data From a Six-Country Split Ballot Survey on European Military Co-Operation Anno 1951. Gazette. 5:2 (1959), 249-264.

2115 Bruner, Jerome S. Perlmutter, Howard. Compatriot and Foreigner: A Study of Impression Formation in Three Countries. Journal of Abnormal and Social Psychology. 55:2 (1957), 253-260. France, U.S.A., and Germany.

2116 Buchanan, William. Stereotypes and Tensions as Revealed By the Unesco International Poll. International Social Science Bulletin. 3:3 (1951), 515-528.

2117 Buchanan, William. Cantril, Hadley. How Nations See Each Other: A Study in Public Opinion. Urbana: University of Illinois Press, 1953, 220 P.

2118 Gallup International. Public Opinion and the European Community. Journal of Common Market Studies. 2:2 (November 1963), 101-126.

2119 German Polls of 1959 on Rearmament, Atomic Energy, Nuclear Weapons, the Balance of World Power, and Prospects of Peace. Santa Monica: Rand Corporation, T-123, 1960, 12 P.

2120 Haavelsrud, Magnus. Views on War and Peace Among Students in West Berlin Public Schools. Journal of Peace Research. No. 2 (1970), 99-120.

2121 Inglehart, Ronald. An End to European Integration?. American Political Science Review. 61:1 (March 1967), 91-105.

2122 Inglehart, Ronald. Public Opinion and Regional Integration. Regional Integration: Theory and Research. Ed. Leon N. Lindberg and Stuart A. Scheingold. Cambridge: Harvard University Press, 1971, Pp. 160-191.

2123 Inglehart, Ronald. The Socialization of "Europeans". Ph.D. Thesis, University of Chicago, 1967.

2124 Konieczny, Jozef. The Attitude to Foreigners in the G.F.R. in Connection With The Postulate to "Live Down the Past". Polish Western Affairs. 4:1 (1963), 223-263.

2125 Kriesberg, Louis. German Public Opinion and the European Coal and Steel Community. Public Opinion Quarterly. 23:1 (Spring 1959), 28-42.

2126 Mander, John. Through German Eyes: The British Image. Twentieth Century. 173:1023 (Autumn 1964), 98-105.

2127 Merritt, Richard L. Public Opinion and Foreign Policy in West Germany. Sage International Yearbook of Foreign Policy Studies, Vol. 1. Ed. Patrick J. Mcgowan. Beverly Hills: Sage, 1973, Pp. 255-274.

2128 Merritt, Richard L. Visual Representation of Mutual Friendliness. Western European Perspectives on International Affairs: Public Opinion Studies and Evaluations. Ed. Richard L. Merritt and Donald J. Puchala. New York: Praeger, 1968, Pp. 111-141.

2129 Merritt, Richard L., Editor. Puchala, Donald J., Editor. Western European Perspectives on International Affairs: Public Opinion Studies and Evaluations. New York: Praeger, 1968, 552 P.

2130 Milyukova, Valentina. West German Opinion and a Peace Treaty. International Affairs (Moscow). (May 1959), 85-87.

2131 Neumann, Erich Peter. How Do the West Germans Feel About Nato in 1969?. Allensbach: Verlag Fuer Demoskopie, Allensbacher Schriften No. 10, 1969, 67 P.

2132 Puchala, Donald J. The Common Market and Political Federation in Western European Public Opinion. International Studies Quarterly. 14:1 (March 1970), 32-59.

2133 Puchala, Donald J. Factor Analysis in International Survey Research. Western European Perspectives on International Affairs: Public Opinion Studies and Evaluations. Ed. Richard L. Merritt and Donald J. Puchala. New York: Praeger, 1968, Pp. 142-172. French and West German Views of Each Other and World, 1954.

2134 Rabier, Jacques-Rene. The European Idea and National Public Opinion. Government and Opposition. 2:3 (April-July 1967), 443-454.

2135 Reigrotski, Erich. Anderson, Nels. National Stereotypes and Foreign Contacts. Public Opinion Quarterly. 23:4 (Winter 1959-60), 515-528. French and German Views of Selves and Each Other.

2136 Sharif, Regina S. Ostpolitik and German Public Opinion, 1964-1972. Ph.D. Thesis, American University, 1974.

2137 Shepherd, Robert James. Public Opinion and European Integration. Lexington: Heath-Lexington, 1975, Xiii and 249 Pp.

2138 Williams, Frederick W. German Opinion and American Isolationism. Public Opinion Quarterly. 11:2 (Summer 1947), 179-188.

2139 Willick, Daniel H. Public Interest in International Affairs: A Cross-National Study. Social Science Quarterly. 50:2 (September 1969), 272-285. FRG, UK, France, Japan, Italy.

F.2. Political Leadership

F.2.1. General

2140 Bertsch, Herbert. Top People in Bonn (A-Z): A Documentation. Dresden: Zeit Im Bild, 1965, 93 P.

2141 Dahrendorf, Ralf. Who Governs Germany?. Government and Opposition. 2:1 (October 1966), 119-132.

2142 Dombrowski, Erich Franz Otto. German Leaders of Yesterday and Today. Freeport: Books for Libraries, 1967, 335 P.

2143 Edinger, Lewis J. Continuity and Change in the Background of German Decision-Makers. Western Political Quarterly. 14:1 (March 1961), 17-36.

2144 Edinger, Lewis J. Post-Totalitarian Leadership: Elites in the German Federal Republic. American Political Science Review. 54:1 (March 1960), 58-82.

2145 Edinger, Lewis J. Searing, Donald D. Social Background in Elite Analysis; a Methodological Inquiry. American Political Science Review. 61:2 (June 1967), 428-445.

2146 FRG, German Information Center. Biographical Sketches: Ministers, Parliamentary State Secretaries, Bundestag Leaders. New York: German Information Center, 1969, 11 P.

2147 Free, Lloyd A. Six Allies and a Neutral: A Study of the International Outlooks of Political Leaders in the United States, Britain, France, West Germany, Italy, Japan and India. Glencoe: Free Press, 1959, 210 P.

2148 GDR, Committee for German Unity. Introducing the West German State Secretaries. Berlin: Committee for German Unity, 1963, 31 P.

2149 Heidenheimer, Arnold J. The Chanceller Effect in the Federal Republic. German Politics. Ed. Donald O. Schoonmaker. Lexington: Heath, 1971, Pp. 100-108.

2150 Herzog, Dietrich. The Structure of Elites in Post-War German Political Parties. Transactions of the Sixth World Congress of Sociology. Geneva: International Sociological Association, 1966, Vol. 4, Pp. 243-268.

2151 Indian Institute of Public Opinion. The Structure of Opinion of Members of Parliament: A Seven Nation Study. Monthly Public Opinion Surveys. 3:9 (June 1958), 1-36.

2152 Joesten, Joachim. Who's Who in German Politics Today: Western Germany. Great Barrington, Mass.: Joachim Joesten, New Germany Reports No. 7, January 1949, 22 P.

2153 Kliemann, Horst G., Editor. Taylor, Stephen S., Editor. Who's Who in Germany. New York: Intercontinental, 3D Ed., 1964, 1,955 and 145 P.

2154 Laumann, Edward O. Pappi, Franz Urban. New Directions in the Study of Community Elites. American Sociological Review. 38:2 (April 1973), 212-230.

2155 Laumann, Edward C. Verbrugge, Lois M. Pappi, Franz Urban. A Causal Modelling Approach to the Study of a Community Elite's Influence Structure. American Sociological Review. 39:2 (April 1974), 162-174.

2156 Lerner, Daniel. Interviewing European Elites. Polls. 2:1 (1966), 1-7.

2157 Lerner, Daniel. Gorden, Morton. Euratlantica: Changing Perspectives of the European Elites. Cambridge: M.I.T. Press, 1969, 447 P.

2158 Putnam, Robert D. The Political Attitudes of Senior Civil Servants in Britain, Germany, and Italy. The Mandarins of Western Europe: The Political Role of Top Civil Servants. Ed. Mattei Dogan. New York: John Wiley & Sons, Halsted Press Division, Sage Publications, 1975, Pp. 87-127.

2159 Saur, Karl-Otto, Editor. Who's Who in German Politics: A Bibliographical Guide to 4,500 Politicians in the Federal Republic of Germany. New York: Bowker, 1971, 342 P.

2160 Schleth, Uwe. Once Again: Does It Pay to Study Social Background in Elite Analysis?. Sozialwissenschaftliches Jahrbuch Fuer Politik, Vol. 2. Munich and Vienna: Guenter Olzog Verlag, 1971, Pp. 99-118.

2161 Searing, Donald D. Two Theories of Elite Consensus: Tests With West German Data. Midwest Journal of Political Science. 15:3 (August 1971), 442-474.

2162 Swiridoff, Paul. Portraits From German Political Life. Pfullingen: Neske, 1968, 228 P.

2163 US, Omgus, Information Control Division. German Militarism: A Study of Militaristic Tendencies in Germany Today, as Revealed By the Attitudes of Opinion Leaders. N.P.: Omgus, Information Control Division, Research Branch, 1948, 11 P.

2164 Who's Who in Germany. Ottobrunn: Who's-Who-Book-and-Publishing, 1972, 2 Vols., 1779 P. 15,500 Biographies; Information on 2400 Organizations.

F.2.2. Political Biographies

2165 Aust, Hans Walter. The Next Federal Chancellor. German Foreign Policy (GDR). 2:5 (1963), 345-348.

2166 Binder, David. The Other German: Willy Brandt's Life and Times. New York: New Republic, 1975, 66 Pp.

2167 Binder, David. Willy Brandt's Wanderjahre Are Finished. New York Times Magazine. (30 November 1969), 34+.

2168 Bolesch, Hermann Otto. Leicht, Hans Dieter. Willy Brandt: A Portrait of the German Chancellor. Tuebingen and Basel: Erdmann, 1971, 84 P.

2169 Brandt, Willy. In Exile: Essays, Reflections, and Letters, 1933-1947. Philadelphia: University of Pennsylvania Press, 1971, 280 P.

2170 Brandt, Willy. Peace: Writings and Speeches of the Nobel Peace Prize Winner, 1971. Bonn: Neue Gesellschaft, 1971, 176 P.

2171 Braun, Joachim. Gustav Heinemann: The Committed President. London: Wolff, 1972, 279 P.

2172 Brecht, Arnold. The Political Education of Arnold Brecht: An Autobiography, 1884-1970. Princeton: Princeton University Press, 1970, 544 P.

2173 Childs, David. A German Socialist Leader: Herbert Wehner. Socialist Commentary. (November 1963), 15-17.

2174 Cooper, Elias. The Ghost of the Third Reich. Midstream. 13:2 (February 1967), 36-41. Kiesinger's Past.

2175 Doering, Guenter. Schmidt, Max. A Spokesman of the Trusts. German Foreign Policy (GDR). 5:4 (1966), 273-280. Heinrich Luebke on Tour in Africa.

2176 Drath, Viola Herms. Willy Brandt: Prisoner of His Past. Radnor, Pa.: Chilton, 1975, 357 P.

2177 Edinger, Lewis J. Kurt Schumacher: A Study in Personality and Political Behavior. Stanford: Stanford University Press, 1965, 390 P.

2178 Epstein, Klaus. A New Biography of Schumacher. World Politics. 18:4 (July 1966), 727-734.

2179 Gaus, Guenter. Ludwig Erhard as Chancellor. European Political Institutions: A Comparative Government Reader. 2D Ed. Ed. William G. Andrews. Princeton: Van Nostrand, 1966, Pp. 513-525.

2180 Harpprecht, Klaus. Willy Brandt: Portrait and Self-Portrait. Los Angeles: Nash, 1971, 300 P.

2181 Heinrich Luebke, President of the West German Federal Republic in the Service of Bonn Neo-Colonialism: A Documentation. Dresden: Zeit Im Bild, 1966, 79 P.

2182 Hill, Leonidas E. Ernst Von Weizsaecker, 1882-1951: A Study in German Diplomacy. Ph.D. Thesis, Harvard University, 1963.

2183 Hirsch, Felix Edward. William Sollman: Wanderer Between Two Worlds. South Atlantic Quarterly. 52:2 (April 1953), 207-227.

2184 Hoeping, Hubert. Brandt at Half-Time. Intereconomics. No. 10 (October 1971), 292-293.

2185 Hotham, David. The Return of Franz Josef Strauss. New York Times Magazine. (23 March 1969), 36+.

2186 Hynd, John B. Willy Brandt: A Pictorial Biography. Compiled and Edited By John Parker and Eugene Prager. London: Lincolns-Prager, 1966, 148 P.

2187 Joesten, Joachim. Erich Ollenhauer: A Pen-Portrait of the Social-Democratic Leader. Great Barrington, Mass.: Joachim Joesten, New Germany Reports No. 35, July 1957, 19 P.

2188 Joesten, Joachim. Ludwig Erhard: The Man Behind the German Boom. Great Barrington, Mass.: Joachim Joesten, New Germany Reports No. 36, August 1957, 17 P.

2189 Kellerman, Barbara. Willy Brandt: Portrait of the Leader as a Young Politician. Ph.D. Thesis, Yale University, 1975.

2190 Kiesinger, Kurt-Georg. Spiegel Interview, 1967. German Politics. Ed. Donald C. Schoonmaker. Lexington: Heath, 1971, Pp. 139-146.

2191 Leiser, Ernest. Germany's Would-Be Strong Man: Franz Josef Strauss. New York Times Magazine. (1 June 1958), 10+.

2192 Lewis, Flora. Candidate to Fill Adenauer's Shoes: Ludwig Erhard. New York Times Magazine. (26 April 1959), 13+.

2193 Lewis, Flora. "Franz Josef"--German Question Mark. New York Times Magazine. (1 May 1960), 19+.

2194 Lewis, Flora. The Hard-Bitten Herr Schumacher. New York Times Magazine. (31 July 1949), 10+.

2195 Lewis, Flora. More Germans Listen to a New Voice: Gerhard Schroeder. New York Times Magazine. (14 October 1962), 28+.

2196 O'Donnell, James P. "The Chopper Chancellor" Awaits Air Force One; Kurt Georg Kiesinger. New York Times Magazine. (16 February 1969), 26+.

2197 Olsen, Arthur J. Erhard Finally Moves Toward the Summit. New York Times Magazine. (5 May 1963), 20+.

2198 Olsen, Arthur J. "Herr Bundeskanzler" Comes to See US: Ludwig Erhard. New York Times Magazine. (7 June 1964), 24+.

2199 Prittie, Terence C. F. Willy Brandt: Portrait of a Statesman. New York: Schocken Books, 1974, 356 P.

2200 Schmitt, Hans A. Ludwig Erhard: Another Bismarck?. Current History. 50:297 (May 1966), 257-262+.

2201 Webb, Robert N. Ludwig Erhard. Leaders of Our Time. New York: Watts, Series 2, 1965, 152 P.

2202 Whiteside, Andrew G. Ernst Von Salomon: A Study in Frustrated Conservatism. South Atlantic Quarterly. 56:2 (April 1957), 234-246.

2203 Wiedemeyer, Wolfgang. Walter Scheel, Foreign Minister, Federal Republic of Germany. Bonn: Press and Information Office, 1971, 30 P.

F.2.3. Konrad Adenauer

2204 Adenauer, Konrad. Memoirs, 1945-53. Chicago: Regnery, 1965, 478 P.

2205 Alexander, Edgar. Adenauer and the New Germany: The Chancellor of the Vanquished. New York: Farrar, Straus and Cudahy, 1957, 300 P.

2206 Augstein, Rudolf. Konrad Adenauer. London: Secker and Warburg, 1964, 128 P.

2207 Eyck, Frank. Dr. Adenauer Is Eighty. Contemporary Review. 189:1081 (January 1956), 6-9.

2208 Eyck, Frank. Dr. Adenauer's Waning Power. Contemporary Review. 190:1087 (July 1956), 5-8.

2209 Handler, M. S. Adenauer's Formula for Vitality. New York Times Magazine. (11 September 1955), 12+.

2210 Handler, M. S. The German With the European Idea: Konrad Adenauer. New York Times Magazine. (13 September 1953), 12+.

2211 Hirsch, Felix Edward. Stresemann and Adenauer: Two Great Leaders of German Democracy in Times of Crisis. Studies in Diplomatic History and Historiography. Ed. Arshag O. Sarkissian. New York: Barnes & Noble, 1961, Pp. 266-280.

2212 Jacobi, Claus. Germany's Great Old Man. Foreign Affairs. 33:2 (January 1955), 239-249.

2213 Joesten, Joachim. Adenauer and Erhard: The Facts Behind the Presidential Hassle. Great Barrington, Mass.: Joachim Joesten, New Germany Reports No. 43, August 1959, 18 P.

2214 Joesten, Joachim. Konrad Adenauer: The Man and His Work, a Political Pen Portrait. New York: Joachim Joesten, New Germany Reports No. 20, October 1952, 21 P.

2215 Joesten, Joachim. Revolt Against Adenauer: The "Breakers" of Bonn. New York: Joachim Joesten, New Germany Reports No. 29, October 1954, 16 P.

2216 Johnston, W. H. Dr. Adenauer. Contemporary Review. 188:1078 (October 1955), 218-222.

2217 Johnston, W. H. Dr. Adenauer's Second Term. Fortnightly. 174:1042 (October 1953), 219-225.

2218 Kellen, Konrad. Adenuaer at 90. Foreign Affairs. 44:2 (January 1966), 275-290.

2219 Lewis, Flora. Adenauer's Rx for Vitality. New York Times Magazine. (21 August 1960), 23+.

2220 Lewis, Flora. "Der Alte" at 83: Symbol of a New Germany. New York Times Magazine. (4 January 1959), 10+.

2221 Lewis, Flora. The Iron-Willed Chancellor. New York Times Magazine. (21 June 1959), 6+.

2222 Livneh, Eliezer. Konrad Adenauer--A Self-Portrait. Midstream. 13:1 (January 1967), 14-25.

2223 Luchsinger, Fred. The Adenauer Era. Swiss Review of World Affairs. 13:8 (November 1963), 1-3.

2224 Mann, Golo. Bismarck and Adenauer. Encounter. 22:4 (April 1964), 19-20.

2225 Mclaughlin, Kathleen. Head Man of the New German State: Konrad Adenauer. New York Times Magazine. (18 September 1949), 11+.

2226 Merkl, Peter H. Equilibrium, Structure of Interests and Leadership: Adenauer's Survival as Chancellor. American Political Science Review. 56:3 (September 1962), 634-650.

2227 Meyer, Erich. Rising Revolt Against Adenauer. Labour Monthly. 37:3 (March 1955), 122-126.

2228 Middleton, Drew. Adenauer, and Germany, at a Turning Point. New York Times Magazine. (11 May 1952), 11+.

2229 Middleton, Drew. Adenauer of Germany--A Balance Sheet. New York Times Magazine. (9 July 1950), 15+.

2230 Neumann, Erich Peter. Noelle, Elisabeth. Statistics on Adenauer: Portrait of a Statesman. Allensbach and Bonn: Verlag Fuer Demoskopie, 1962, 152 P.

2231 Nicholls, Anthony. Adenauer. The History Makers: Leaders and Statesmen of the 20Th Century. Ed. Lord Frank A. P. Longford and John Wheeler-Bennett. New York: St. Martin's, 1973, Pp. 172-196.

2232 Olsen, Arthur J. "Gaullist" Adenauer Challenges Erhard. New York Times Magazine. (26 July 1964), 11+.

2233 Preece, Rodney J. C. Konrad Adenauer and the German Chancellorship. Contemporary Review. 211:1219 (August 1967), 85-88.

2234 Prittie, Terence C. F. Konrad Adenauer, 1876-1967. Chicago: Cowles, 1971, 334 P.

2235 Stern-Rubarth, Edgar. Dr. Adenauer. Contemporary Review. 181:1034 (February 1952), 75-78.

2236 Webb, Robert N. Konrad Adenauer. Leaders of Our Time. New York: Watts, Series 1, 1964, Pp. 3-11.

2237 Weymar, Paul. Adenauer, His Authorized Biography. New York: Dutton, 1957, 509 P.

2238 Wighton, Charles. Adenauer: A Critical Biography. New York: Coward-McCann, 1964, 389 P.

F.2.4. Former Nazis in Political Positions? (See Also D.3.2; F.4.7)

2239 Ainsztein, Reuben. The Bandera-Oberlaender Case. Midstream. 6:2 (Spring 1960), 17-25.

2240 Allemann, Fritz Rene. Brown Shadows: Letter From Bonn. Encounter. 22:4 (April 1964), 84-85. Former Nazis in Government.

2241 Allen, Charles R. Heusinger of the Fourth Reich. New York: Marzani & Munsell, 1963, 320 P.

2242 Baur, Walter. The Prevention of the Revival of Nazism and the Prosecution of Nazi and War Crimes Are Indispensable Precepts of International Law. Law and Legislation in the German Democratic Republic. No. 1 (1971), 32-38.

2243 Chamberlin, William Henry. Germany's Former Nazi Judges: Do They Thrive in West Germany?. Modern Age. 7:1 (Winter 1962-63), 33-38.

2244 Dahl, Guenther. What Steps Does the Federal Government Take Against Nazi Criminals at Large in West Germany?. Law and Legislation in the German Democratic Republic. No. 1 (1960), 57-64.

2245 Drozdzynski, Aleksander. Zaborowski, Jan. Oberlaender: A Study in German East Policies. Poznan and Warsaw: Wydawnictwo Zachodnie, 1960, 324 P.

2246 Foth, Carlos. Ender, Gerhard. On the Reinstatement of Hitler's Bloodstained Judges in the Federal German Republic. Law and Legislation in the German Democratic Republic. No. 2 (1962), 43-70.

2247 Foth, Carlos. Ender, Gerhard. Twenty Years Later. Law and Legislation in the German Democratic Republic. No. 2 (1965), 5-21. Nazi War Criminals in FRG; Statute of Limitations.

2248 FRG, Federal Ministry of Defense. The Communist Defamation Campaign Against General Trettner: a Case in Point. Cologne: Markus, 1964, 40 P.

2249 GDR, Committee for German Unity. Freedom and Democracy at the Mercy of 1000 Nazi Judges: Documents Unmask a Further 200 West German Jurists Who Served Hitler. Berlin: Committee for German Unity, 1959, 24 P.

2250 GDR, Committee for German Unity. Globke: Adenauer's State Secretary and the Extermination of the Jews. Berlin: Committee for German Unity, 1960, 120 P.

2251 GDR, Committee for German Unity. Hitler's Diplomats Serve the Aggressive Foreign Policy of West German Militarism. Berlin: Committee for German Unity, c.1958, 28 P.

2252 GDR, Committee for German Unity. Hitler's Special Judges--Pillars of the Adenauer Government. Berlin: Committee for German Unity, 1957, 31 P.

2253 GDR, Committee for German Unity. Murderers at Large in West Germany. Berlin: Committee for German Unity, 1958, 31 P.

2254 GDR, Committee for German Unity. Terror Justice in the Bonn State: 44 More Bonn Judges Exposed as Nazi Executioners. Berlin: Committee for German Unity, 1957, 25 P.

2255 GDR, Committee for German Unity. The Truth About Oberlaender: Brown Book on the Criminal Fascist Past of Adenauer's Minister. Berlin: Committee for German Unity, 1960, 223 P.

2256 GDR, Committee for German Unity. We Accuse: 800 Nazi Judges--Bastions of Adenauer's Militarist Regime. Berlin: Committee for German Unity, 1959, 182 P.

2257 GDR, Committee for German Unity. Yesterday Hitler's Bloodstained Judges--Today Bonn's Legal Elite. Berlin: Committee for German Unity, 1957, 40 P.

2258 GDR, Supreme Court. In the Name of the Peoples, in the Name of the Victims: Excerpts From the Protocol of the Trial Held Against Bonn State Secretary Hans Globke. Berlin: Press Centre Globke Trial, 1963, 63 P.

2259 Institute for International Politics and Economics. The Incorrigibles. Prague: Orbis, 1960, 73 P.

2260 Joesten, Joachim. Dr. Naumann's Conspiracy: Pattern of the World-Wide Crypto-Nazi Plot. New York: Joachim Joesten, New Germany Reports No. 23, August 1953, 18 P.

2261 Joesten, Joachim. Justice on Trial: The Fraenkel Scandal and Related Issues. New York: Joachim Joesten, New Germany Reports No. 58, October 1962, 14 P. Former Nazi Judge, Later FRG Chief Public Prosecutor.

2262 Lohr, George. Galaxy of Nazis--Who Are the Men Around Adenauer?. New World Review. 28:9 (October 1960), 34-38.

2263 Mader, Julius. Nazi Officers in Bonn's Diplomatic Service. German Foreign Policy (GDR). 4:5 (1965), 357-367.

2264 Maynard, Peter. Remove the German War-Makers. New Central European Observer. 1:2 (29 May 1948), 16-17.

2265 Miller, Moses. Nazis Preferred: The Renazification of Western Germany. New York: New Century, 1950, 31 P.

2266 National Front of Democratic Germany. Brown Book: Nazi and War Criminals in the Federal Republic and in West Berlin: State Apparatus, Economy, Administration, Armed Forces, Judiciary, Science. Dresden: Zeit Im Bild, 2D Ed., c. 1968, 446 P.

2267 National Front of Democratic Germany. White Book on the War Crimes of Heinz Trettner, Inspector-General of the Bundeswehr. Dresden: Zeit Im Bild, 1964.

2268 Norden, Albert. War and Nazi Criminals in the Federal Republic of Germany. German Foreign Policy (GDR). 4:4 (1965), 259-268.

2269 Palgleish, Donald D. The Nazi "Past" in the Communist Cause. Ph.D. Thesis, University of Colorado, 1963, 683 P.

2270 Samuels, Gertrude. Wanted: 1,000 Nazis Still at Large. New York Times Magazine. (28 February 1965), 26+.

2271 Sterling, Eleonore. West Germany's Second Denazification. Chicago Jewish Forum. 17:3 (Spring 1959), 167-169.

2272 Tetens, Tete Harens. The New Germany and the Old Nazis. New York: Random House, 1961, 286 P.

2273 Tomlinson, A. K. Swastikas, Judges and Ministers. Poland and Germany. 4:12 (April 1960), 24-37.

2274 Union of Anti-Fascist Fighters. Criminals on the Bench. Prague: Orbis, 1960, 138 P. Documents on Crimes Committed in Occupied Czechoslovakia By 230 Nazi Judges and Prosecutors Active in FRG Legal System.

2275 Wiener Library. The Naumann Plot: Evidence From the Impounded

Documents. London: Wiener Library, 1953, 11 P.

2276 Zaborowski, Jan. Dr. Hans Globke, the Good Clerk. Warsaw: Zachodnia Agencja Prasowa, 1962, 166 P.

F.3. Interest Groups

2277 Almond, Gabriel A. The Political Attitudes of German Business. World Politics. 8:2 (January 1956), 157-186.

2278 Almond, Gabriel A. The Politics of German Business. Santa Monica: Rand Corporation, Rm-1506-Rc, 1955, 116 P.

2279 Almond, Gabriel A. The Politics of German Business. West German Leadership and Foreign Policy. Ed. Hans Speier and W. Phillips Davison. Evanston and White Plains: Row, Peterson, 1957, Pp. 195-241.

2280 Bird, Dillard E. The Development of Management Associations in Germany. Frankfurt: Omgus, Manpower Division, Visiting Expert Series No. 12, October 1949, 35 P.

2281 Braunthal, Gerard. The Federation of German Industry in Politics. Ithaca: Cornell University Press, 1965, 389 P.

2282 Braunthal, Gerard. West German Trade Unions and Disarmament. Political Science Quarterly. 73:1 (March 1958), 82-99.

2283 Bunn, Ronald F. Codetermination and the Federation of German Employers' Associations. Midwest Journal of Political Science. 2:3 (August 1958), 278-297.

2284 Bunn, Ronald F. Employers' Associations and Collective Bargaining in the German Federal Republic. Southwestern Social Science Quarterly. 46:2 (September 1965), 154-163.

2285 Bunn, Ronald F. The Federation of German Employers' Associations: A Political Interest Group. Western Political Quarterly. 13:3 (September 1960), 652-669.

2286 Bunn, Ronald F. The Ideology of the Federation of German Employers' Associations. American Journal of Economics and Sociology. 18:4 (July 1959), 369-379.

2287 Bunn, Ronald F. The Organization and Political Theory of the Postwar German Employers' Federation. Ph.D Thesis, Duke University, 1956.

2288 Carey, Jane Perry Clark. Political Organization of the Refugees and Expellees in West Germany. Political Science Quarterly. 66:2 (June 1951), 191-215.

2289 Celovsky, Boris. The Transferred Sudeten-Germans and Their Political Activity. Journal of Central European Affairs. 17:2 (July 1957), 127-149.

2290 Cole, R. Taylor. Functional Representation in the German Federal Republic. Midwest Journal of Political Science. 2:3 (August 1958), 256-277.

2291 Erdmann, Ernst-Gerhard. Organisation and Work of Employers' Associations in the Federal Republic of Germany. International Labour Review. 78:6 (December 1958), 533-551.

2292 Hartmann, Heinz. Cohesion and Commitment in Employers Organizations. World Politics. 2:3 (April 1959), 474-490.

2293 Hirsch-Weber, Wolfgang. Some Remarks on Interest Groups in the German Federal Republic. Interest Groups on Four Continents. Ed. Henry W. Ehrmann. Pittsburgh: University of Pittsburgh Press, 1958, Pp. 96-116.

2294 Hofmann, Wolfgang. The Public Interest Pressure Group: The Case of the Deutsche Staedtetag. Public Administration (London). 45:3 (Autumn 1967), 245-259.

2295 Holt, John B. Corporative Occupational Organization and Democracy in Germany. Public Administration Review. 8:1 (Winter 1948), 34-40.

2296 Macdonald, D. F. Employers' Associations in Western Germany. Berlin: Omgus, Manpower Division, Visiting Expert Series No. 9, August 1949, 29 P.

2297 Nordheim, Manfred Von. German State Legislators and the Representation of Interests. Ph.D. Thesis, University of California at Santa Barbara, 1972, 305 P.

2298 Przybylski, Peter. West Germany--Playground of Fascist Emigrant Organisations. German Foreign Policy (GDR). 3:6 (1964), 453-463.

2299 Schmidt, Manfred H. The East German Landsmannschaften in the German Federal Republic: Their Organization and Influence. Ph.D. Thesis, University of Michigan, 1959, 145 P.

2300 Schoonmaker, Donald O. The Politics of the Deutscher Beamtenbund: A Case of a Pressure Group, 1949-1963. Ph.D. Thesis, Princeton University, 1966, 250 P.

2301 Schumm, Siegfried. Interest Representation in France and Germany. Cahiers De Bruges. 8:3-4 (1958), 139-147.

2302 Szulc, H. German Refugee-Expellee Organizations. Poland and Germany. 2:4 (March 1958), 15-23.

2303 Vilmar, Fritz. The Military-Industrial Complex in West Germany and the Consequences for Peace Policy. Journal of Peace Research. 10:3 (1973), 251-258.

F.4. Political Parties (See Also E.2.1; F.1.3)

F.4.1. General

2304 Bolten, Seymour R. Military Government and the German Political Parties. Annals of the American Academy of Political and Social Science. 267 (January 1950), 55-67.

2305 Bonn, Moritz J. Germany Plays at Party Politics. Contemporary Review. 179:1022 (February 1951), 75-79.

2306 Bonn, Moritz J. Reunion in Germany: Party Leaders and Politics. Fortnightly. 172:1028 (August 1952), 75-79; and 172:1029 (September 1952), 155-159.

2307 Brookes, Marilyn. Party Organization and Electoral Response in West Germany: Activist Orientations. Ph.D. Thesis, University of California, Los Angeles, 1973, 441 P.

2308 Burkett, Tony. Parties and Elections in West Germany: The Search for Stability. New York: St. Martin's Press, 1975, 200 Pp.

2309 Conradt, David P. The West German Party System: An Ecological Analysis of Social Structure and Voting Behavior, 1961-1969. Sage Professional Papers, Comparative Politics Series, 01-028. Beverly Hills: Sage, 1972, 55 P.

2310 Diederich, Nils. Party Member and Local Party Branch. Party Systems, Party Organizations, and the Politics of New Masses. Ed. Otto Stammer. Berlin: Institut Fuer Politische

Wissenschaft an Der Freien Universitaet Berlin, 1968, Pp. 107-115.

2311 Dittberner, Juergen. The Role of the Party Congress in the Inner Party Process of Policy Making. German Political Studies, Vol. 1. Ed. Klaus Von Beyme. Beverly Hills: Sage Publications, 1974, Pp. 183-214.

2312 Duebber, Ulrich. Braunthal, Gerard. Comparative Studies in Political Finance: West Germany. Journal of Politics. 25:4 (November 1963), 774-789.

2313 Eliasberg, Vera Franke. Political Party Developments. The Struggle for Democracy in Germany. Ed. Gabriel A. Almond. Chapel Hill: University of North Carolina Press, 1949, Pp. 221-280.

2314 Eyck, Frank. Parties and Policies in West Germany. Contemporary Review. 187:1070 (February 1955), 79-82.

2315 Eyck, Frank. Parties in Western Germany. Contemporary Review. 182:1043 (November 1952), 272-276.

2316 Frye, Charles E. Parties and Pressure Groups in Weimar and Bonn. World Politics. 17:4 (July 1965), 635-655.

2317 Grieves, Forest L. Inter-Party Competition in the Federal Republic of Germany, 1945-1965: A Methodological Inquiry. Western Political Quarterly. 20:4 (December 1967), 910-918.

2318 Gunlicks, Arthur B. Intraparty Democracy in Germany: A Look at the Local Level. Comparative Politics. 2:2 (January 1970), 229-249.

2319 Gunlicks, Arthur B. Opposition in the Federal Republic of Germany. Political Opposition and Dissent. Ed. Barbara N. McLennan. New York: Dunellen, 1973, Pp. 185-227.

2320 Gunlicks, Arthur B. Representative and Party at the Local Level in Western Germany: The Case of Lower Saxony. Ph.D. Thesis, Georgetown University, 1967, 490 P.

2321 Gunlicks, Arthur B. Representative Role Perceptions Among Local Councilors in Western Germany. Journal of Politics. 31:2 (May 1969), 443-464.

2322 Heberle, Rudolf. Parliamentary Government and Political Parties in West Germany. Canadian Journal of Economics and Political Science. 28:3 (August 1962), 417-423.

2323 Heberle, Rudolf. Political Tendencies and Parties in Germany. Canadian Journal of Economics and Political Science. 25:4 (November 1959), 484-496.

2324 Heidenheimer, Arnold J. Comparative Party Finance: Notes on Practices and Toward a Theory. Journal of Politics. 25:4 (November 1963), 790-811.

2325 Heidenheimer, Arnold J. Federalism and the Party System: The Case of West Germany. American Political Science Review. 52:3 (September 1958), 809-828.

2326 Heidenheimer, Arnold J. Succession and Party Politics in West Germany. Journal of International Affairs. 18:1 (1964), 32-42.

2327 Heidenheimer, Arnold J. Langdon, Frank C. Business Associations and the Financing of Political Parties: A Comparative Study of the Evolution of Practices in Germany, Norway and Japan. The Hague: Nijhoff, 1968, 249 P., Esp. Pp. 43-88.

2328 Holtermann, Ursula. Political Parties in Western Germany. Ph.D. Thesis, University of Chicago, 1955.

2329 Johnson, Nevil. State Finance for Political Parties in Western Germany. Parliamentary Affairs. 18:3 (Summer 1965), 279-292.

2330 Kirchheimer, Otto. Germany: The Vanishing Opposition. Political Oppositions in Western Democracies. Ed. Robert A. Dahl. New Haven: Yale University Press, 1966, Pp. 237-259.

2331 Kommers, Donald P. Politics and Jurisprudence in West Germany: State Financing of Political Parties. American Journal of Jurisprudence. 16 (1971), 215-241.

2332 Lebovitz, Solomon. Military Government and the Revival of German Political Activity: Political Parties. Ph.D. Thesis, Harvard University, 1949.

2333 Leicht, Robert. Party Conferences in a Party-Political State. German Tribune Quarterly Review. No. 18 (8 June 1972), 13-16.

2334 Loewenberg, Gerhard. The Remaking of the German Party System: Political and Socioeconomic Factors. Polity. 1:1 (Fall 1968), 86-113.

2335 Merkl, Peter H. Party Government in the Bonn Republic. Lawmakers in a Changing World. Ed. Elke Frank. Englewood Cliffs: Prentice-Hall, 1966, Pp. 65-82.

2336 Meyer, Ernst W. Political Parties in Western Germany. Washington: Library of Congress, European Affairs Division, Reference Department, 1951, 52 P.

2337 Meyerhoff, Hans. Parties and Classes in Postwar Germany. South Atlantic Quarterly. 46:1 (January 1947), 12-26.

2338 Miller, Robert W. Recent Efforts Toward Legal Regulation of Political Parties in Western Germany. Papers of the Michigan Academy of Science, Arts, and Letters. 47 (1962), 299-310.

2339 Mookerjee, Girija K. A Study of German Political Parties. India Quarterly. 9:1 (January-March 1953), 35-59; and 9:3 (July-September 1953), 249-264.

2340 Moskowitz, Moses. The Political Reeducation of the Germans: The Emergence of Parties and Politics in Wuertemberg-Baden, May 1945-June 1946. Political Science Quarterly. 61:4 (December 1946), 535-561.

2341 Neumann, Robert G. The New Political Parties of Germany. American Political Science Review. 40:4 (August 1946), 749-759.

2342 Neumann, Sigmund. Germany: Changing Patterns and Lasting Problems. Modern Political Parties: Approaches to Comparative Politics. Ed. Sigmund Neumann. Chicago: University of Chicago Press, 1956, Pp. 354-392.

2343 Nix, Claire. Post-War German Parties: Allied Military Control Has Hampered German Political Development. Current History. 12:70 (June 1947), 573-579.

2344 Nyitray, Margot S. Political Parties in West Germany: The Effect of Political System and Party Variables on Party Organization. Ph.D. Thesis, Ohio State University, 1971, 388 P.

2345 Observer. Political Parties in the German Federal Republic. Poland and Germany. 1:2 (Summer 1957), 3-20.

2346 Pulzer, Peter G. J. The German Party System in the Sixties. Political Studies. 19:1 (March 1971), 1-17.

2347 Pulzer, Peter G. J. Western Germany and the Three Party System. Political Quarterly. 33:4 (October-December 1962), 414-426.

2348 Scammon, Richard M. Political Parties. Governing Postwar Germany. Ed. Edward H. Litchfield and Associates. Ithaca: Cornell University Press, 1953, Pp. 471-499.

2349 Schneider, Carl J. Political Parties and the German Basic Law of 1949. Western Political Quarterly. 10:3 (September 1957), 527-540.

2350 Sontheimer, Kurt. The Funding of Political Parties in West Germany. Political Quarterly. 45:3 (July-September 1974), 335-340.

2351 Sternberger, Dolf. Parties and Party Systems in Postwar Germany. Annals of the American Academy of Political and Social Science. 260 (November 1948), 10-31.

2352 US, Hicog, Office of Executive Secretary. Elections and Political Parties in Germany, 1945-1952. Bad Godesberg-Mehlem: Hicog, Office of Executive Secretary, Policy Reports Secretary, 1 June 1952, 93 P.

2353 US, Omgus, Civil Administration Division. Political Parties in Western Germany. Berlin: Omgus, Civil Administration Division, Political Activities Branch, 1949, 78 P.

2354 Valentin, Veit. Political Parties in Germany. Contemporary Review. 170:971 (November 1946), 263-268.

2355 Verkade, Willem. Democratic Parites in the Low Countries and Germany: Origins and Historical Developments. Leiden: Universitaire Pers Leiden, 1965, 331 P., Esp. Pp. 247-300.

2356 Wallach, Hans Gert Peter. Political Management and Party Democracy: Operational Patterns of Socialization, Recruitment, and Decision-Making in a West German State. Ph.D. Thesis, University of Connecticut, 1972, 269 P. CDU and SPD in North Rhine-Westfalia.

2357 Ziegler, David W. Opposition Politics in Germany. Ph.D. Thesis, Harvard University, 1969.

F.4.2. Christian Democractic Union (CDU)

2358 Baxter, Craig. Germany's Christian Democratic Party. Social Science. 30:1 (January 1955), 17-22.

2359 Bouscaren, Anthony T. The European Christian Democratic Parties. Ph.D. Thesis, University of California, Berkeley, 1951.

2360 Bouscaren, Anthony T. Origins of German Christian Democracy. Thought. 31:122 (Autumn 1956), 429-451.

2361 Christian Democratic Union. The Cologne Manifesto of the German Christian Democratic Union, 1961. European Political Institutions: A Comparative Government Reader. Ed. William G. Andrews. Princeton: Van Nostrand, 1962, Pp. 133-134.

2362 Christian Democratic Union. Duesseldorf Declaration, 1965. European Political Institutions: A Comparative Government Reader. 2D Ed. Ed. William G. Andrews. Princeton: Van Nostrand, 1966, Pp. 151-152.

2363 Christian Democratic Union, Federal Secretariat. The Christian Democratic Union of Germany: History, Idea, Program, Constitution. Bonn: Christian Democratic Union, Federal Secretariat, 1961, 64 P.

2364 Dowell, Jack D. Party, Caucus, and Chancellor: Authority in the CDU/Csu. Washington State University, Research Studies. 36:2 (June 1968), 131-142.

2365 Gohlert, Ernst W. The Christian Democratic Union: A Case Study in the Dynamics of Political Integration. Ph.D. Thesis, Washington State University, 1971, 184 P.

2366 Grace, Frank. The Majority Party. German Democracy at Work: A Selective Study. Ed. James K. Pollock. Ann Arbor: University of Michigan Press, 1955, Pp. 14-47.

2367 Heidenheimer, Arnold J. Adenauer and the CDU: The Rise of the Leader and the Integration of the Party. The Hague: Nijhoff, 1960, 259 P.

2368 Heidenheimer, Arnold J. Foreign Policy and Party Discipline in the CDU. Parliamentary Affairs. 13:1 (Winter 1959-60), 70-84.

2369 Heidenheimer, Arnold J. German Party Finance: The CDU. American Political Science Review. 51:2 (June 1957), 369-385.

2370 Herbst, Clarence A. The Founding of the New Center Party. Thought. 22:85 (June 1947), 269-282.

2371 Mayntz, Renate. Oligarchic Problems in a German Party District. Political Decision-Makers: Recruitment and Performance. Ed. Dwaine Marvick. New York: Free Press, 1961, Pp. 138-192.

2372 Pridham, Geoffrey. The CDU/Csu Opposition in West Germany, 1962-1972: A Party in Search of an Organisation. Parliamentary Affairs. 26:2 (Spring 1973), 201-217.

2373 Prittie, Terence C. F. German Christian Democracy. Occidente. 11:6 (December 1955), 509-518.

F.4.3. Social Democratic Party (SPD)

2374 Ahlers, Conrad. Living Democracy: Confidence and Doubts After the SPD's Nuremberg Conference. German Tribune Quarterly Review. No. 2 (20 July 1968), 1-2.

2375 Apel, Hans. The Social Democrats' Current Problems. German Tribune Quarterly Review. No. 13 (18 February 1971), 5-8.

2376 Ashkenasi, Abraham. The Berlin SPD's Differentiation From the Foreign Policy of The Federal German Social Democratic Party. Ph.D. Thesis, Columbia University, 1964, 363 P.

2377 Braje, Wilfried. The Foreign Policy of the German Social Democratic Party, 1949-1957. Ph.D. Thesis, Clark University, 1964, 439 P.

2378 Brand, Friedrich. Socialism Today--A Social Democratic Viewpoint. German Tribune Quarterly Review. No. 16 (December 1971).

2379 Bretton, Henry L. The German Social Democratic Party and the International Situation. American Political Science Review. 47:4 (December 1953), 980-996.

2380 Bretton, Henry L. The Opposition Party. German Democracy at Work: A Selective Study. Ed. James K. Pollock. Ann Arbor: University of Michigan Press, 1955, Pp. 48-78.

2381 Chalmers, Douglas A. The Social Democratic Party of Germany: From Working-Class Movement to Modern Political Party. New Haven: Yale University Press, 1964, 258 P.

2382 Chalmers, Douglas A. The Social Democratic Party of Germany: Movement or Cadre?. Ph.D. Thesis, Yale University, 1962.

2383 Childs, David. From Schumacher to Brandt: The Story of German Socialism 1945-1965. Oxford: Pergamon, 1966, 194 P.

2384 Childs, David. SPD at Dortmund: Ulbricht Sets the Pace. World Today. 22:7 (July 1966), 285-293.

2385 Christensen, Vagn A. C. The Godesberg Socialists and the German Catholic Community: an Appraisal of Their Relationship, 1959-1966. Ph.D. Thesis, University of California, Berkeley, 1968, 188 P.

2386 Cicłkosz, A. The German Social-Democrats and Polish-German Relations. Poland and Germany. 4:14 (October-December 1960), 19-28.

2387 Cornu, Auguste. German Utopianism: "True" Socialism. Science & Society. 12:1 (Winter 1948), 97-112.

2388 Dowell, Jack D. Social Democrats in West Germany's Grand Coalition. Political Science. 22:1 (July 1970), 52-65.

2389 Drummond, Gordon D. The Military Policy of the German Social Democratic Party, 1949-1960. Ph.D. Thesis, Stanford University, 1968, 332 P.

2390 Edinger, Lewis J. Chalmers, Douglas A. Overture or Swan Song: German Social Democracy Prepares for a New Decade. Antioch Review. 20:2 (Summer 1960), 163-175.

2391 Erler, Fritz. Socialism in Germany. Socialist Commentary. 19 (February 1955), 45-47.

2392 Fagan, H. Which Way Social Democracy?. Labour Monthly. 49:1 (January 1967), 26-31.

2393 Freund, Ludwig. The De-Marxification of the Social-Democratic Party of Germany. Modern Age. 5:3 (Summer 1961), 290-298.

2394 Glueckauf, Erich. West German Social Democracy and the Communists. World Marxist Review: Problems of Peace and Socialism. 7:4 (April 1964), 21-28.

2395 Glueckauf, Erich. Whither the Social Democratic Party of Germany?. World Marxist Review: Problems of Peace and Socialism. 4:8 (August 1961), 29-36.

2396 Goergey, Laszlo. The Influence of Foreign Policy on the Development of the Social Democratic Party of Germany. Ph.D. Thesis, University of Virginia, 1964, 381 P.

2397 Hahn, Walter F. The Socialist Left in West Germany. Orbis. 17:3 (Fall 1973), 912-929.

2398 Keller, John W. From the Kaiser to Willy Brandt: Social Democratic Policy From 1870 to 1972. New York: William Frederick, 1973.

2399 Krasomil, Dean Harold. The German Social Democratic Party After 1945: A Contribution to the Study of the SPD in the Period 1945-1952. Dr. Phil. Thesis, Frankfurt University, 1953, 182 P.

2400 Lens, Sidney. Social Democracy and Labor in Germany. New York: Foreign Policy Association, 1950, 152 P.

2401 Mander, John. Socialism in Germany. Socialist Commentary. (July 1958), 6-9.

2402 Maxwell, John Allen. Social Democracy in a Divided Germany: Kurt Schumacher and The German Question, 1945-1952. Ph.D. Thesis, West Virginia University, 1969, 532 P.

2403 Maynard, Peter. German Social Democracy. New Central European Observer. 2:3 (5 February 1949), 34.

2404 Niebuhr, Reinhold. The Anomaly of European Socialism. Yale Review. 42:2 (Winter 1952), 161-167. Deals with Inter Alia Berlin SPD Tactics.

2405 Ortlieb, Heinz-Dietrich. Loesch, Dieter. Young Socialists--The SPD of the Nineteen-Eighties. Central Europe Journal. 21:7 (July 1973), 184-188.

2406 Pachter, Henry M. A Left Turn Among German Socialists. Dissent. 20:3 (Summer 1973), 284-286.

2407 Paterson, William E. The SPD and European Integration. Lexington, Mass.: Lexington Books, 1974, 177 P.

2408 Prittie, Terence C. F. Socialist Dilemma in Germany. Socialist Commentary. (November 1957), 7-9.

2409 Schellenger, Harold K., Jr. The German Social Democratic Party After World War II: The Conservatism of Power. Western Political Quarterly. 19:2 (June 1966), 251-265.

2410 Schellenger, Harold K., Jr. The German Social Democratic Party After World War II: The Modernization of a European Socialist Party. Ph.D. Thesis, Cornell University, 1964, 421 P.

2411 Schellenger, Harold K., Jr. The SPD in the Bonn Republic: A Socialist Party Modernizes. The Hague: Nijhoff, 1968, 256 P.

2412 Shears, Ursula Hahn. The Social Democratic Party of Germany: Friend or Foe of European Unity. Ph.D. Thesis, Fletcher School of Law and Diplomacy, 1960.

2413 Skoug, Kenneth N., Jr. The Eastern Policy of the German Social Democratic Party in A Period of Party Reorganization and International Crisis. Ph.D. Thesis, George Washington University, 1964.

2414 Snell, John L. Schumacher's Successors: The Personal Factor in the Shaping of Contemporary German Social Democracy. Southwestern Social Science Quarterly. 36:4 (March 1956), 333-342.

2415 Social Democratic Party of Germany. Action Program: Adopted By the Party Conference at Dortmund. Bonn: Sozialdemokratische Partei Deutschlands, 1952, 39 P.

2416 Social Democratic Party of Germany. Basic Programme of the Social Democratic Party of Germany. Bonn: Sozialdemokratische Partei Deutschlands, 1959, 22 P. Bad Godesberg Program, November 1959.

2417 Social Democratic Party of Germany. "Government Team" Declaration, 1965. European Political Institutions: A Comparative Government Reader. 2D Ed. Ed. William G. Andrews. Princeton: Van Nostrand, 1966, Pp. 198-205.

2418 Social Democratic Party of Germany. The Social Democratic Party of Germany. Bonn: Sozialdemokratische Partei Deutschlands, 1953, 19 P.

2419 Thomas, Siegfried. On the Foreign-Political Opposition of Social Democracy (1949-1955). German Foreign Policy (GDR). 9:3 (1970), 187-205.

2420 Vardys, V. Stanley. Germany's Postwar Socialism: Nationalism and Kurt Schumacher (1945-1952). Review of Politics. 27:2 (April 1965), 220-244.

2421 Vrga, Djuro J. A Sociological Opinion and Prediction About Germans, and the German Social Democratic Party After World War II. Indian Sociological Bulletin. 7:3-4 (April-July 1970), 178-191. Disputes Talcott Parsons' 1945 Prediction About Germans.

2422 Wegener, Thomas. Apologetics of Capitalism: Apropos of the New Programme of The Social Democratic Party of Germany. World Marxist Review: Problems of Peace and Socialism. 3:1 (January 1960), 16-23.

2423 Winter, Herbert R. The Foreign Policy Position of the German Social Democratic Party. Ph.D. Thesis, State University of Iowa, 1961, 226 P.

2424 Winter, Herbert R. The German Social Democratic Party and European Integration. Rocky Mountain Review. 2:1 (Winter 1964-65), 17-27.

F.4.4. Minor Parties

2425 Fisher, Stephen L. The Minor Parties of the Federal Republic of Germany: Toward a Comparative Theory of Minor Parties. Ph.D. Thesis, Tulane University, 1972, 520 P.

2426 Fisher, Stephen L. The Minor Parties of the Federal Republic of Germany: Toward a Comparative Theory of Minor Parties. The Hague: Martinus Nijhoff, 1974, xiv and 218 pp.

2427 Tauber, Kurt P. Aspects of Nationalist-Communist Collaboration in Postwar Germany. Journal of Central European Affairs. 20:1 (April 1960), 51-68.

2428 Vogt, Siegfried A. The Bayernpartei: A Minor German Party in Transition. Ph.D. Thesis, Washington State University, 1972, 179 P.

F.4.5. Free Democratic Party (FDP)

2429 Bald, Richard H. The Free Democratic Party (FDP) and West German Foreign Policy, 1949-1959. Ph.D. Thesis, University of Michigan, 1963, 365 P.

2430 Braunthal, Gerard. The Free Democratic Party in West German Politics. Western Political Quarterly. 13:2 (June 1960), 332-348.

2431 Conradt, David P. The Role of Third Parties in Bipartite Systems: A Comparative Analysis of the British Liberals and West German Free Democrats. Ph.D. Thesis, Brown University, 1969, 369 P.

2432 Cromwell, Richard S. The Free Democratic Party in German Politics, 1945-1956: A Historical Study of a Contemporary Liberal Party. Ph.D. Thesis, Stanford University, 1961, 386 P.

2433 Free Democratic Party. Declaration of the German Free Democratic Party for the 1961 Bundestag Election. European Political Institutions: A Comparative Government Reader. Ed. William G. Andrews. Princeton: Van Nostrand, 1962, Pp. 117-122.

2434 Hoag, Wendy Jane. Party Incentives and Membership Participation: A Study of The Fdp in Cologne, West Germany. Ph.D. Thesis, University of Rochester, 1973, 232 P.

2435 Irving, R. E. M. The German Liberals: Changing Image of the Free Democratic Party. Parliamentary Affairs. 23:1 (Winter 1969-70), 46-64.

2436 Stoltz, Volker. The Policy of the German Free Democratic Party, 1965. European Political Institutions: A Comparative Government Reader. 2D Ed. Ed. William G. Andrews. Princeton: Van Nostrand, 1966, Pp. 135-139.

F.4.6. Communist Parties (KPD and DKP)

2437 Bergmann, Heinrich. The Conditions of the West German Peasantry and the Policy of the Communist Party. World Marxist Review: Problems of Peace and Socialism. 6:1 (January 1963), 25-31.

2438 Bergmann, Heinrich. Struggle of the Workers of West Germany. World Marxist Review: Problems of Peace and Socialism. 1:1 (September 1958), 59-62.

2439 Berry, Wallace W. A History and Case Study of the Communist Party of Germany (Kpd), 1945-1969. Ph.D. Thesis, Stanford University, 1971, 214 P.

2440 Douglas, William A. West German Communism as an Aid to Moscow. World Affairs (Washington). 132:4 (March 1970), 318-332.

2441 Geilinger, Eduard. West German Communism. Swiss Review of World Affairs. 1:3 (June 1951), 15-16.

2442 Horchem, Hans Josef. West Germany: "The Long March Through the Institutions". London: Institute for the Study of Conflict, Conflict Studies, No. 33, 1973, 20 P.

2443 K.B. New Programme of the Communist Party of Germany. World Marxist Review: Problems of Peace and Socialism. 11:4 (April 1968), 84-87

2444 Kapluck, Manfred. Fight to Legalize the Communist Party in Germany. World Marxist Review. 10:12 (December 1967), 23-26.

2445 Klemperer, Klemens Von. Toward a Fourth Reich? the History of National Bolshevism in Germany. Review of Politics. 13:2 (April 1951), 191-210.

2446 Mcinnes, Neil. The Communist Parties of Western Europe. London: Oxford University Press, 1975, xiv and 209 Pp.

2447 Mies, Herbert. German Communist Party: Third Year of Struggle. World Marxist Review: Problems of Peace and Socialism. 14:5 (May 1971), 52-63.

2448 Morris, Bernard S. Some Perspectives on the Nature and Role of the Western European Communist Parties. Review of Politics. 18:2 (April 1956), 157-169.

2449 Possony, Stefan T. Germany: Federal Republic of Germany. Yearbook on International Communist Affairs, 1973. Ed. Richard F. Staar. Stanford: Hoover Institution Press, 1973, Pp. 254-162.

2450 R.S. German Communist Party: Alive and Fighting. World Marxist Review: Problems of Peace and Socialism. 11:9 (September 1968), 81-82.

2451 Reimann, Max. The Communist Party of Germany in the Fight for Democracy. World Marxist Review: Problems of Peace and Socialism. 6:9 (September 1963), 16-23.

2452 Reimann, Max. Communist Party of Germany: Ten Years of Clandestine Struggle. World Marxist Review: Problems of Peace and Socialism. 9:7 (July 1966), 3-9.

2453 Reimann, Max. Fifty Years of the Communist Party in Germany. World Marxist Review: Problems of Peace and Socialism. 12:1 (January 1969), 21-27.

2454 Reimann, Max. Unity in the Fight for Peace. World Marxist Review: Problems of Peace and Socialism. 2:5 (May 1959), 2-9. Call for Kpd-SPD Unity.

2455 Schaefer, Max. The Communist Party and the Bundestag Elections. World Marxist Review: Problems of Peace and Socialism. 8:8 (August 1965), 69-71.

2456 Schmidt, Karl. Success for a "Non-Existent" Organization (Kpd). World Marxist Review: Problems of Peace and Socialism. 2:6 (June 1959), 8-16.

2457 Schultz, Heinrich. The German Communist Party Is at Its Post. World Marxist Review: Problems of Peace and Socialism. 1:4 (December 1958), 75-77.

2458 Starobin, Joseph R. Communism in Western Europe. Foreign Affairs. 44:1 (October 1965), 62-77.

2459 Steinkuehler, Manfred. Communist Parties' Conference Projects. Aussenpolitik. 26:2 (1975), 166-184.

2460 Ulbricht, Walter. Fiftieth

Anniversary of the Foundation of the Communist Party of Germany. Dresden: Zeit Im Bild, 1968, 42 P.

2461 Walbaum, O. Wissen Und Tat (Kpd Publication). World Marxist Review: Problems of Peace and Socialism. 2:5 (May 1959), 88-90.

F.4.7. Extreme Nationalism and Neo-Nazi Parties

2462 American Jewish Committee. Neo-Nazi and Nationalist Movements in West Germany. New York: American Jewish Committee, 1952, 37 P.

2463 American Jewish Committee. Neo-Nazi Strength and Strategy in West Germany. New York: American Jewish Committee, 1953, 38 P.

2464 American Jewish Committee. Recent Growth of Neo-Nazism in Europe. New York: American Jewish Committee, 1951, 30 P.

2465 Anglo-Jewish Association. Germany's New Nazis. New York: Philosophical Library, 1952, 76 P.

2466 Bartel, Walter. West German Rightist Bloc. German Foreign Policy (GDR). 10:2 (1971), 124-138.

2467 Berghahn, Volker. Right-Wing Radicalism in West Germany's Younger Generation. Journal of Central European Affairs. 22:3 (October 1962), 317-336.

2468 Bonn, Moritz J. Potential Dangers in Germany. Contemporary Review. 183:1047 (March 1953), 133-137.

2469 A Bonn Balance Sheet: The Resurrection of National Socialism. Round Table. 41:164 (September 1951), 344-350.

2470 Clarion, Nicolas. Does Democracy Need Nazi Partners? the Dangerous Course of Our German Reconstruction. Commentary. 7:4 (April 1949), 309-318.

2471 Cole, R. Taylor. Neo-Fascism in Western Germany and Italy. American Political Science Review. 49:1 (March 1955), 131-143.

2472 Coverley, Harvey M. Danger on the Right in Germany. Current History. 18:103 (March 1950), 138-143.

2473 Cromwell, Richard S. Rightist Extremism in Post-War West Germany. Western Political Quarterly. 17:2 (June 1964), 284-293.

2474 Davidson, Basil. Once Again: An Enquiry Into Certain Aspects of Reviving Nationalism in Germany. London: Union of Democratic Control, 1950, 25 P.

2475 Diggins, John P. The Search for a New Hitler. Social Studies. 56:4 (April 1965), 145-147.

2476 Emmet, Christopher. Muhlen, Norbert. The Vanishing Swastika: Facts and Figures on Nazism in West Germany. Chicago: Regnery, 1961, 66 P.

2477 Eyck, Frank. Neo-Nazism in Western Germany. Contemporary Review. 180:1031 (November 1951), 266-270.

2478 Institute of Jewish Affairs. January 30Th, 1933: Twenty Five Years After. New York: Institute of Jewish Affairs, 1958, 33 P. on Neo-Nazism in the FRG.

2479 Jaeger, Hans. The Reappearance of the Swastika: Neo-Nazism and Fascist International. London: Gamma Publications, 1960, 62 P.

2480 Jaeger, Hans. Second Edition of National Socialism. Contemporary Review. 175:998 (February 1949), 105-108.

2481 Joesten, Joachim. The Menace of Neo-Nazism. Great Barrington, Mass.: Joachim Joesten, New Germany Reports No. 15, September 1950.

2482 Lueth, Erich. Misconceptions of German Nationalism. German Tribune Quarterly Review. No. 1 (4 May 1968), 9-11.

2483 Luethy, Herbert. Behind Reawakened German Nationalism. Commentary. 13:2 (February 1952), 115-123.

2484 Marcuse, Herbert. Antidemocratic Popular Movements. Germany and the Future of Europe. Ed. Hans J. Morgenthau. Chicago: University of Chicago Press, 1951, Pp. 108-113.

2485 Meskil, Paul S. Hitler's Heirs. New York: Pyramid, 1961, 191 P.

2486 Middleton, Drew. Neo-Nazism: "A Cloud Like a Man's Hand". New York Times Magazine. (1 July 1951), 9+.

2487 Middleton, Drew. The Renazification of Germany. New York: Community Relations Service, 1949, 23 P.

2488 Miller, Alexander F., and Others. Mission to Germany. New York: B'Nai B'Rith, 1960, 42 P.

2489 Milyukova, Valentina. The "Brown Threat" in West Germany. International Affairs (Moscow). (April 1969), 95-98.

2490 Morgan, Edward P. Echoes of the Hitler Jugend in Germany. New York Times Magazine. (27 November 1949), 13+.

2491 National Front of Democratic Germany. Grey Book: Expansionist Policy and Neo-Nazism in West Germany: Backgrounds, Aims, Methods; a Documentation. Dresden: Zeit Im Bild, 1967, 230 P.

2492 Pirsch, Hans. Weiss, Martin. Bonn's Political Set-Up, the Root Cause of West Germany's Re-Nazification. German Foreign Policy (GDR). 7:6 (1968), 447-460.

2493 Polanyi, Ilona. Looming Ahead: A Nazi Underground Movement. London Quarterly of World Affairs. 11:1 (April 1945), 20-27.

2494 Reichmann, Eva G. Germany's New Nazis. London: Wiener Library, 1951, 8 P.

2495 Russell, Edward F. L., Lord of Liverpool. Return of the Swastika?. New York: Mckay, 1969, 144 P.

2496 Schaffer, Gordon. The Nazis Are Back. New World Review. 20:7 (July 1952), 10-14.

2497 Schaffer, Gordon. The Nazis Come Out Again. New Central European Observer. 5:23 (8 November 1952), 359.

2498 Sheppard, Alexander W. The Nazis Rise Again. Sydney: Gornall, 1950, 123 P.

2499 Snyder, Louis L. Nazism Resurgent: What Should Be Done About It?. Menorah Journal. 40:1 (Spring 1952), 37-54.

2500 Tauber, Kurt P. Beyond Eagle and Swastika: German Nationalism Since 1945. Middletown: Wesleyan University Press, 1967, 2 Vols., 1589 P.

2501 Tauber, Kurt P. Over Germany: Shadows From the Past. New York Times Magazine. (27 December 1959), 15+. Re-Emergence of Traditional Conservatism and Nationalism.

2502 Thompson, Elizabeth M. Neo-Nazism in Germany. Editorial Research Reports. (18 February 1953), 123-138.

2503 Tilton, Timothy Alan. Nazism, Democracy, and the Peasantry: Nazi Success and Neo-Nazi Failure in Rural

Schleswig-Holstein. Ph.D. Thesis, Harvard University, 1972.

2504 Tilton, Timothy Alan. Nazism, Neo-Nazism, and the Peasantry. Bloomington: Indiana University Press, 1975, 208 Pp.

2505 Trevor-Roper, Hugh R. The Danger of a Neo-Nazism. New York Times Magazine. (27 July 1947), 10+.

2506 Wiener Library. Survey of Leaders, Articles, and Letters to the Editor in British Newspapers and Periodicals Dealing With German Neo-Nazism and Nationalism. London: Wiener Library, 1952, 40 P.

F.4.8. National Democratic Party (NPD)

2507 An, Nack Young. NPD: Resurgence of Nazism or Innocuous Anomoly?. German Politics. Ed. Donald Schoonmaker. Lexington: Heath, 1971, Pp. 74-82.

2508 Aronsfeld, C. C. The New Nazis and the Old. Contemporary Review. 210:1214 (March 1967), 119-123.

2509 Bracher, Karl Dietrich. Democracy and Right Wing Extremism in West Germany. Current History. 54:321 (May 1968), 281-287.

2510 Brunner, Ronald D. Liepelt, Klaus. Data Analysis, Process Analysis, and System Change. Midwest Journal of Political Science. 16:4 (November 1972), 538-569.

2511 Cameron, James. A Shadow No Larger Than a Crooked Cross. New York Times Magazine. (11 September 1966), 94+.

2512 Childs, David. The Revival of the German Right. Contemporary Review. 209:1208 (September 1966), 127-136.

2513 Dittmer, Lowell. The German NPD: A Psycho-Sociological Analysis of "Neo-Nazism". Comparative Politics. 2:1 (October 1969), 79-110.

2514 Fichtner, Paula Sutter. NPD-Ndp, Europe's New Nationalism in Germany and Austria. Review of Politics. 30:3 (July 1968), 308-315.

2515 Fichtner, Paula Sutter. Protest on the Right: The NPD in Recent German Politics. Orbis. 12:1 (Spring 1968), 185-199.

2516 Galkin, A. Social Roots of Neo-Fascism. International Affairs (Moscow). (October 1968), 12-18.

2517 Hauptmann, Jerzy. The Reemergence of the German Radical Right: An Analysis in Political Theory. Central European Federalist. 15:2 (December 1967), 6-21.

2518 Heberle, Rudolf. Analysis of a Neo-Fascist Party: The NPD. Polity. 3:1 (Fall 1970), 126-134.

2519 Jones, William Treharne. Germany: Prospects for a Nationalist Revival. International Affairs (London). 46:2 (April 1970), 316-322.

2520 Kellermann, Erwin. Neo-Nazism--A Product of Bonn's Policy of Revenge. German Foreign Policy (GDR). 6:3 (1967), 227-237.

2521 Kuehnl, Reinhard. Neofascism on the Rise: An Analysis of the Structure and Programme of the National-Democratic Party in the German Federal Republic. Review of International Affairs (Belgrade). 18:405 (20 February 1967), 11-13; and 18:406 (5 March 1967), 8-11.

2522 Laqueur, Walter Z. "Bonn Is Not Weimar"--Reflections on the Radical Right in Germany. Commentary. 43:3 (March 1967), 33-42.

2523 Liepelt, Klaus. Supporters of the New Party of the Right: A Report and Disccussion of the German NPD's Sources of Support. Political Development and Change: A Policy Approach. Eds. Garry D. Brewer and Ronald D. Brunner. New York: Free Press, 1975, Pp. 128-157.

2524 Lomeiko, V. Right-Wing Radicalism in the F.R.G. International Affairs (Moscow). (June 1967), 17-22.

2525 Long, Wellington. The New Nazis of Germany. Philadelphia: Chilton, 1968, 254 P.

2526 Mander, John. The Neo-Nazis. Encounter. 28:2 (February 1967), 82-86.

2527 Nagle, John David. The National Democratic Party: Right Radicalism in the Federal Republic of Germany. Berkeley: University of California Press, 1970, 300 P.

2528 Nagle, John David. Right-Radicalism in the Federal Republic of Germany. Ph.D. Thesis, Harvard University, 1968.

2529 Peet, John. The Bonn Iceberg. Labour Monthly. 49 (March 1967), 113-115. Rise of NPD as "Facade" of Economic Miracle Crumbles?.

2530 Preece, Rodney J. C. Aspects of Totalitarianism: The Case of the NPD. Parliamentary Affairs. 21:3 (Summer 1968), 246-254.

2531 Preece, Rodney J. C. A Resurgence of Nazism in West Germany?. Contemporary Review. 210:1214 (March 1967), 132-136.

2532 Pritt, Denis N. Neo-Nazis and the Future of Europe. Labour Monthly. 48 (July 1966), 313-315.

2533 Pulzer, Peter G. J. Neo-Nazi Revival?. Socialist Commentary. (February 1967), 11-13.

2534 Rudolph, Karl. The NPD--Fears Abroad and Reality. German Tribune Quarterly Review. No. 4 (21 December 1968), 9-10.

2535 Savage, Paul L. Renascent German Nationalism and Political Culture: The Case of the "Nationaldemokratische Partei Deutschlands" (NPD). Ph.D. Thesis, University of Massachusetts, 1970, 401 P.

2536 Warnecke, Steven. The Future of Rightist Extremism in West Germany. Comparative Politics. 2:4 (July 1970), 629-652.

2537 Worsnop, Richard L. Neo-Nazism in West Germany. Editorial Research Reports. (12 April 1967), 263-280.

2538 Yefremov, A. The True Face of the West German National-Democrats. International Affairs (Moscow). (April 1967), 69-73.

F.5. General Political Surveys

F.5.1. 1949-53: 1st Legislative Period

2539 American Jewish Committee. The Status of Democracy in Western Germany. New York: American Jewish Committee, Foreign Affairs Department, 1951, 29 P.

2540 Arendt, Hannah. The Aftermath of Nazi Rule: Report From Germany. Commentary. 10:4 (October 1950), 342-353.

2541 Bidwell, Percy Wells. How Strong Is the New Germany. Yale Review. 42:4 (June 1953), 481-495.

2542 Bonn, Moritz J. The Beginning at Bonn. Contemporary Review. 177:1009 (January 1950), 5-10.

2543 Bonn, Moritz J. Compulsory Democracy in Germany. Fortnightly. 166:991 (July 1949), 1-8.

2544 Bonn, Moritz J. German Incertitudes. Bankers' Magazine (London). 168:1266 (September 1949), 182-187. Thoughts on '49 National Election.

2545 Bonn, Moritz J. Report on Germany. Contemporary Review. 180:1029 (September 1951), 133-138.

2546 Bonn, Moritz J. Whither Germany?. World Affairs (London). 5:1 (January 1951), 58-69.

2547 The Bonn Constitution and Its Chances: People and Parties in West Germany. Round Table. 39:156 (September 1949), 309-316.

2548 Burmeister, Werner. Germany--Conditions of Political Recovery. World Affairs (London). 5:4 (October 1951), 406-418.

2549 Burmeister, Werner. The Political Scene in Western Germany. World Affairs (London). 4:4 (October 1950), 438-448.

2550 Canine, Ralph J. Germany Builds for Its Future. Army Information Digest. 5:9 (September 1950), 49-52.

2551 Carleton, William G. Germany Seven Years After Defeat. Yale Review. 41:3 (Spring 1952), 321-335.

2552 Cohen, Elliot E. What Do the Germans Propose to Do?--An Address to the German People. Commentary. 10:3 (September 1950), 225-228.

2553 Davidson, Basil. Western Germany Today. Current Affairs (London). No. 106 (13 May 1950), 19 P.

2554 Eaton, Ken. Germany--An Ersatz Democracy. Contemporary Issues. 2:5 (Winter 1950), 68-71.

2555 Fay, Sidney B. Germany: A Progress Report. Current History. 21:21 (September 1951), 129-136.

2556 The Federal Republic of Germany. Current Notes on International Affairs. 23:8 (August 1952), 404-410.

2557 Fischer, Alfred Joachim. Germany of the Bonn Era. Contemporary Review. 176:1004 (August 1949), 69-75.

2558 Gibbs, Philip. Thine Enemy. New York: Medill McBride, 1950, 316 P.

2559 Greer, Leslie C. The New Regime in Western Germany. World Affairs (London). 3:4 (October 1949), 368-377.

2560 Greenwood, H. Powys. Germany Revisited. Contemporary Review. 181:1035 (March 1952), 140-145.

2561 Gumpert, Martin. Return to Europe. American Scholar. 19:3 (Summer 1950), 319-340.

2562 Gurland, Arcadius Rudolph Lang. Why Democracy Is Losing in Germany: Behind the Recent Elections. Commentary. 8:3 (September 1949), 227-237.

2563 H. G. I. Western Germany, June 1947 and Now. World Today. 5:9 (September 1949), 371-377.

2564 Hagelberg, Gerhard. Germany--Hope or Peril?. New York: German-American, March 1952, 32 P.

2565 Hagelberg, Gerhard. Germany--Promise or Menace?. New World Review. 20:6 (June 1952), 6-9.

2566 Hermens, Ferdinand A. The Bonn Republic. Current History. 17:96 (August 1949), 79-83.

2567 Howard, Elizabeth Fox. Barriers Down: Notes on Post-War Germany. London: Friends Home Service Committee, 1950, 111 P.

2568 Ickler, Albert. Germany, 1950. International House Quarterly. 15:2 (Spring 1951), 109-112.

2569 Joesten, Joachim. The West German State (Federal Republic of Germany). Great Barrington, Mass.: Joachim Joesten, New Germany Reports No. 13, May 1950, 19 P.

2570 Kahn, J. F. Germany Today: A Visitor's Observation. Political Science. 3:1 (March 1951), 43-52.

2571 Lower, Arthur R. M. Germany Revisited. International Journal. 5:2 (Spring 1950), 141-162.

2572 Mann, Thomas. Germany Today. New York Times Magazine. (25 September 1949), 14+.

2573 Mccloy, John J. Progress Report on Germany. Department of State Bulletin. 22:553 (6 February 1950), 195-197.

2574 Mccloy, John J. Report on Germany, September 21, 1949-July 31, 1952. Washington: Department of State, 1952, 299 P.

2575 Mcdougall, Ian. German Notebook. London: Elek, 1953, 162 P.

2576 Middleton, Drew. As Schierstein Goes to the Polls. New York Times Magazine. (14 August 1949), 11+.

2577 Middleton, Drew. Bonn Under Strain. New York Times Magazine. (24 February 1952), 49+.

2578 Middleton, Drew. Five Great Problems for West Germany. New York Times Magazine. (1 June 1952), 8+.

2579 Middleton, Drew. Vignettes of a Rudderless Germany. New York Times Magazine. (8 May 1949), 10+.

2580 Morgenthau, Hans J. Germany: The Political Problem. Germany and the Future of Europe. Ed. Hans J. Morgenthau. Chicago: University of Chicago Press, 1951, Pp. 76-88.

2581 Neumann, Franz L. German Democracy, 1950. International Conciliation. 461 (May 1950), 249-296.

2582 New Ideas Versus Old in Western Germany. World Today. 6:8 (August 1950), 331-340.

2583 The New Phase in Germany. Soundings. No. 27 (June 1949), 1-4.

2584 Newman, Bernard. Oberammergau Journey. London: Jenkins, 1951, 240 P.

2585 Pollock, James K. The First Year of the Bonn Government. Journal of Politics. 13:1 (February 1951), 19-34.

2586 Powell, Robert. The German Federal Republic. Fortnightly. 166:995 (November 1949), 302-306.

2587 Powell, Robert. The German Federal Republic. Fortnightly. 168:1006 (October 1950), 220-226.

2588 Prittie, Terence C. F. Western Germany on Trial. Toronto: Canadian Institute of International Affairs, Behind the Headlines Pamphlet No. 10:3, 1950, 20 P.

2589 Ritter, Gerhard. Prospects of a New Germany. Contemporary Review. 176:1006 (October 1949), 205-210.

2590 Roeper, Burkhardt. The Realization of Democratic Ideals in Germany. Confluence. 1:2 (June 1952), 14-22.

2591 Salin, Edgar. Social Forces in Germany Today. Foreign Affairs. 28:2 (January 1950), 265-277.

2592 Shirer, William L. Midcentury Journey: The Western World Through Its Years of Conflict. New York: Farrar, Straus & Young, 1952, 310 P., Esp. Pp. 113-171.

2593 Smith, Howard K. The State of Europe. New York: Knopf, 1949, 408 P., Esp. Pp. 101-134.

2594 Welles, Orson. Thoughts on Germany. Fortnightly. 169:1011 (March 1951), 141-151.

2595 West Germany Faces the Future. New Central European Observer. 2:20 (1 October 1949), 231.

2596 White, Theodore H. Germany: Year Six of the Peace. Reporter. 4:12 (12 June 1951), 12-16.

2597 Williams, J. Emlyn. The German Federal Republic Today. International Affairs (London). 28:4 (October 1952), 422-431.

2598 Williams, J. Emlyn. Tomorrow Is the New Moon. This Is Germany. Ed. Arthur Settel. New York: Sloane, 1950, Pp. 74-88.

F.5.2. 1953-57: 2nd Legislative Period

2599 Adenauer, Konrad. Adenauer Defines "The Mission of Germany". New York Times Magazine. (26 June 1955), 7+.

2600 Adenauer, Konrad. The Development of Parliamentary Institutions in Germany Since 1945. Parliamentary Affairs. 7:3 (Summer 1954), 279-286.

2601 Allemann, Fritz Rene. West Germany's Democratic Future. Commentary. 21:1 (January 1956), 53-58.

2602 Allemann, Fritz Rene. Will History Repeat Itself in Germany? Must the Bonn Republic Go the Way of Weimar?. Commentary. 19:3 (March 1955), 217-224.

2603 Alson, Jacob. Epstein, Benjamin R. Belth, Nathan C. Germany Nine Years Later. New York: Anti-Defamation League of B'Nai B'Rith, 1954, 30 P. Report of Anti-Defamation League of B'Nai B'Rith Study Tour Undertaken at FRG Invitation, July 1954.

2604 Arnold, G. L. Germany Yesterday and Tomorrow. Twentieth Century. 157:935 (January 1955), 32-41.

2605 Arnold, G. L. Germany's Post-Nazi Intellectual Climate. Commentary. 19:1 (January 1955), 78-82.

2606 Beer, Max. Germany Today. Chicago Jewish Forum. 14:2 (Winter 1955-56), 77-82.

2607 Bonn, Moritz J. Whither Sovereign Germany?. Contemporary Review. 187:1074 (June 1955), 369-373.

2608 Bonner, Thomas N. Europe Revisited. Journal of Higher Education. 28:3 (March 1957), 119-125. A Report on Conditions in Germany in 1955 and a Review of German Ideas Concerning Conditions in America.

2609 Bonner, Thomas N. Thoughts of a Fulbrighter on Today's Germany. Association of American Colleges Bulletin. 42:3 (October 1956), 374-380.

2610 Bretton, Henry L. Election Close-Up: Local Politics. German Democracy at Work: A Selective Study. Ed. James K. Pollock. Ann Arbor: University of Michigan Press, 1955, Pp. 103-138.

2611 Bretton, Henry L. Election Close-Up: Mirror of the Republic. German Democracy at Work: A Selective Study. Ed. James K. Pollock. Ann Arbor: University of Michigan Press, 1955, Pp. 139-149.

2612 Bretton, Henry L. Germany Today. German Democracy at Work: A Selective Study. Ed. James K. Pollock. Ann Arbor: University of Michigan Press, 1955, Pp. 1-13.

2613 Conant, James Bryant. The Foundations of a Democratic Future for Germany. Department of State Bulletin. 30:777 (17 May 1954), 750-755.

2614 Conant, James Bryant. The Future of Germany. University of Chicago Round Table. No. 875 (16 January 1955), 12-25.

2615 Connell, Brian. A Watcher on the Rhine: An Appraisal of Germany Today. New York: Morrow, 1957, 320 P.

2616 Dill, Marshall. Watch on the Rhine. Current History. 28:165 (May 1955), 269-274.

2617 Eyck, Frank. The Federal German Election. Contemporary Review. 184:1054 (October 1953), 197-202.

2618 Eyck, Frank. The German Situation. Contemporary Review. 186:1066 (October 1954), 196-199.

2619 Fay, Sidney B. Leadership at Bonn. Current History. 30:176 (April 1956), 217-224.

2620 Gardiner, Rolf. Centres of Hope in Western Germany. Contemporary Review. 191:1096 (April 1957), 215-217.

2621 Graham, Robert A. Germany's Next Four Years. Social Order. 3:9 (November 1953), 394-398.

2622 Grosser, Alfred. The Colossus Again: Western Germany From Defeat to Rearmanent. New York: Praeger, 1955, 249 P.

2623 Handler, M. S. Adenauer's Germany: Nation in Transition. New York Times Magazine. (10 June 1956), 12+.

2624 Hasan, K. Sarwar. The Challenge of Germany. Pakistan Horizon. 6:4 (December 1953), 139-148.

2625 Hirsch, Felix Edward. Adenauer or Schumacher. Current History. 22:126 (February 1952), 70-74.

2626 Hirsch, Felix Edward. Germany Ten Years After Defeat. Toronto: Institute of International Affairs, 1955, 16 P.

2627 Hiscocks, C. R. The Development of Democracy in Western Germany Since the Second World War. Canadian Journal of Economics and Political Science. 20:4 (November 1954), 493-503.

2628 Holborn, Hajo. Achievements and Prospects of German Democracy. Political Science Quarterly. 70:3 (September 1955), 421-434.

2629 Horne, Alistair. Return to Power: A Report on the New Germany. New York: Praeger, 1956, 415 P.

2630 Huberman, Leo. Sweezy, Paul M. Spotlight on West Germany. Monthly Review. 6:7 (November 1954), 225-237.

2631 Hughes, H. Stuart. Where Modern Germany Took the Wrong Turn. Commentary. 18:5 (November 1954), 470-474.

2632 Jackson, J. Hampden. The Post-War Decade: A Short History of the World, 1945-1955. London: Gollancz, 1955, 206 P., Esp. Ch. 1-3.

2633 Jacobi, Claus. German Paradoxes. Foreign Affairs. 35:3 (April 1957), 432-440.

2634 Jaspers, Karl. The Political Vacuum in Germany. Foreign Affairs. 32:4 (July 1954), 595-607.

2635 Kirchheimer, Otto. Notes on the Political Scene in Western Germany.

World Politics. 6:3 (April 1954), 306-321.

2636 Krause, Roland E. Whither Germany?. United States Naval Institute Proceedings. 80:7 (July 1954), 754-759.

2637 Loewenstein, Karl. The German Republic at Bonn. Current History. 28:164 (April 1955), 236-242.

2638 Luchsinger, Fred. A Survey of the West German Political Scene. Swiss Review of World Affairs. 6:7 (October 1956), 3-10.

2639 McInnis, Edgar. Adenauer's Germany: Some Post-Election Impressions. International Journal. 9:1 (Winter 1954), 1-7.

2640 Meyer, Henry Cord. Germany Renascent. Virginia Quarterly Review. 30:2 (Spring 1954), 229-245.

2641 Middleton, Drew. The Great Challenge of Germany. New York Times Magazine. (6 September 1953), 9+.

2642 Mueller, Albert. After the German Elections. Swiss Review of World Affairs. 3:7 (October 1953), 1-4.

2643 Muhler, Norbert. Democracy and Its Discontents: Germany. Encounter. 2:4 (April 1954), 27-31.

2644 Murray, John. Germany in Prospect: Recent Impressions. Studies. 43 (Winter 1954), 407-420.

2645 Nettl, John Peter. A Decade of Post-War Germany. Political Quarterly. 27:2 (April-June 1956), 162-175.

2646 Newman, Bernard. Berlin and Back. London: Jenkins, 1954, 218 P.

2647 Ollenhauer, Erich. German Politics at a Turning Point. Bonn: Social Democratic Party of Germany, 1956, 33 P.

2648 Ollenhauer, Erich. Our Common Concerns--A Social Democrat Speaks to Americans. Bonn: Sozialdemokratische Partei Deutschlands, 1953, 13 P.

2649 Pollock, James K. How the Voters Decide. German Democracy at Work: A Selective Study. Ed. James K. Pollock. Ann Arbor: University of Michigan Press, 1955, Pp. 79-102.

2650 Powell, Robert. West German Politics. Fortnightly. 174:1044 (December 1953), 381-386.

2651 Prittie, Terence C. F. How New Is the New Germany? Now That It Is a Partner of the West. Commentary. 19:6 (June 1955), 513-521.

2652 Roegele, Otto B. Adenauer's Electoral Victory, September 6, 1953. Review of Politics. 16:2 (April 1954), 212-234.

2653 Russell, Edward F. L., Lord of Liverpool. Germany--Yesterday, Today and Tomorrow. Midstream. 3:4 (Autumn 1957), 5-14.

2654 Samuel, Richard H. The General Elections in Germany. Australian Quarterly. 25:4 (December 1953), 69-78.

2655 Samuels, Gertrude. Germany's Mood: A Report on Two Cities. New York Times Magazine. (6 January 1957), 19+. Frankfurt and Berlin

2656 Schaffer, Gordon. Behind Adenauer's Victory. New World Review. 21:9 (October 1953), 29-32.

2657 Schaffer, Gordon. Germany: The Web of Lies. Labour Monthly. 36:11 (November 1954), 506-509.

2658 Schmid, Peter. The Germans' Present Conservatism: Its Roots. Commentary. 16:5 (November 1953), 419-427.

2659 Sprigge, Sylvia. The German Scene: Late Summer 1954. Encounter. 3:5 (November 1954), 27-33.

2660 Thayer, Charles Wheeler. The Unquiet Germans. New York: Harper and Row, 1957, 275 P.

2661 Thayer, James R. The Contribution of Public Opinion Polls to the Understanding of the 1953 Elections in Italy, West Germany, and Japan. Public Opinion Quarterly. 19:3 (Fall 1955), 259-278.

2662 Treuhaft, Gerd. Twilight Over Germany. Contemporary Review. 189:1082 (February 1956), 115-119.

2663 W. B. Changing Political Attitudes in the German Federal Republic. World Today. 13:1 (January 1957), 36-44.

2664 Wallenberg, Hans. Report on Democratic Institutions in Germany. New York: American Council on Germany, 1956, 91 P.

2665 Wolf, Simon. Germany Today. Contemporary Review. 188:1079 (November 1955), 296-299.

F.5.3. 1957-61: 3rd Legislative Period

2666 Adenauer the European: Aftermath of the German Election. Round Table. 48:189 (December 1957), 28-38.

2667 Allemann, Fritz Rene. Adenauer, and the Others. Encounter. 13:2 (August 1959), 65-67.

2668 Bentwich, Norman D. The Federal German Republic. Contemporary Review. 196 (October 1959), 155-158.

2669 Bolen, C. W. West Germany Elects a President. South Atlantic Quarterly. 59:3 (Summer 1960), 425-433.

2670 Bowie, Robert R. The World Watches as Germany Votes. New York Times Magazine. (15 September 1957), 17+.

2671 Boyle, Kay. Has Germany Changed?. Foreign Policy Bulletin. 39:15 (April 1960), 117-118.

2672 Braunthal, Gerard. The Succession Crisis of 1959. Cases in Comparative Politics. Ed. James B. Christoph. Boston and Toronto: Little, Brown, 1965, Pp. 209-240.

2673 Burmeister, Werner. The Consolidation of the German Federal Republic. Yearbook of World Affairs. 11 (1957), 138-155.

2674 Conant, James Bryant. Germany and Freedom: A Personal Appraisal. Cambridge: Harvard University Press, 1958, 117 P.

2675 Conly, Robert Leslie. Modern Miracle, Made in Germany. National Geographic Magazine. 115:6 (June 1959), 735-791.

2676 Davidson, Basil. Look Back in Anger: After Nine Years of Adenauer, What Kind of Peace?. London: Union of Democratic Control, 1959, 17 P.

2677 Dietze, Gottfried. The Federal Republic of Germany: An Evaluation After Ten Years. Journal of Politics. 22:1 (February 1960), 112-147.

2678 Donaldson, Gordon. Dossier on Germany. Toronto: The Telegramm, 1960, 15 P.

2679 Elections in the German Federal Republic. World Today. 13:9 (September 1957), 365-377.

2680 Eyck, Frank. Dr. Adenauer's Third Term. Contemporary Review. 192:1103 (November 1957), 251-253.

2681 Eyck, Frank. Tensions in Western Germany. Contemporary Review. 191:1098 (June 1957), 325-328.

2682 FRG, German Embassy. The Ten Years, 1949-1959: The Federal Republic of Germany. Washington: German Embassy, Press Office, 1959, 127 P.

2683 Forster, Arnold. Epstein, Benjamin R. Cross-Currents. Garden City: Doubleday, 1956, 389 P., Esp. Pp. 177-297.

2684 Fraenkel, Heinrich. Farewell to Germany. New York: Hanison, 1959, 142 P.

2685 Grabowski, K. German Cross-Currents. Poland and Germany. 2:5 (June 1958), 1-6.

2686 Grabowski, Z. A. The Mood of Germany. Quarterly Review. 297:621 (July 1959), 346-359.

2687 Hermens, Ferdinand A. Democracy at Bonn. Social Order. 9:5 (May 1959), 215-220.

2688 Heuss, Theodor. Elements of Democracy in Germany. Indo-German Intellectual Relations; Elements of Democracy in Germany; a Fragment of German Economic History. New Delhi: German Cultural Institute, 1961, 29 P.

2689 Hirsch, Felix Edward. Adenauer's Third Term. International Journal. 12:4 (Autumn 1957), 262-272.

2690 Hirsch, Felix Edward. Germany After Two World Wars. Current History. 38:221 (January 1960), 18-23.

2691 Hiscocks, Richard. Election Issues in Western Germany. International Journal. 12:3 (Summer 1957), 157-166.

2692 Joesten, Joachim. French Terrorism in Germany: The Truth About the Red Hand Murders. Great Barrington, Mass.: Joachim Joesten, New Germany Reports Nos. 47-48, March 1960, 40 P.

2693 Keller, John W. The Current German Political Scene. Current History. 38:221 (January 1960), 30-36.

2694 Kirchheimer, Otto. German Democracy in the 1950's. World Politics. 13:2 (January 1961), 254-266.

2695 Kirchheimer, Otto. The Political Scene in West Germany. World Politics. 9:3 (April 1957), 433-445.

2696 Kissinger, Henry A. The Search for Stability. Foreign Affairs. 37:4 (July 1959), 537-560.

2697 Kitzinger, Uwe W. German Electoral Politics: A Study of the 1957 Campaign. Oxford: Clarendon Press, 1960, 365 P.

2698 Kohn, Hans. Out of Castastrophe: Germany, 1945-1960. Review of Politics. 22:2 (April 1960), 163-174.

2699 Kohn, Hans. West Germany: New Era for German People. New York: Foreign Policy Association, Headline Series No. 131, September-October 1958, 62 P.

2700 Lerner, Max. After the Miracle--What?. Midstream. 3:4 (Autumn 1957), 15-25. Factors Contributing to Adenauer's Election Triumph.

2701 Lesser, Jonas. Opinions on the Germans. Contemporary Review. 195 (May 1959), 285-288.

2702 Lewis, Flora. West Germany Lives for the Moment. New York Times Magazine. (25 October 1959), 15+. Daily Lives and Concerns of Common People.

2703 Luchsinger, Fred. Germany and the Coming Elections. Swiss Review of World Affairs. 7:5 (August 1957), 9-10; and 7:6 (September 1957), 3-4.

2704 Mckee, Ilse. Tomorrow the World. London: Dent, 1960, 199 P.

2705 Menzel, Walter. Parliamentary Politics in the German Federal Republic From 1957-1960. Parliamentary Affairs. 13:4 (Autumn 1960), 509-519.

2706 Mueller, Albert. Chancellor Adenauer's Victory. Swiss Review of World Affairs. 7:7 (October 1957), 1-2.

2707 Mueller, Albert. A Third Term for Adenauer?. Swiss Review of World Affairs. 7:6 (September 1957), 1-2.

2708 Mueller, Albert. Will There Always Be a "Good" Germany?. Western World. 2:7 (July 1959), 12-15.

2709 Muhlen, Norbert. A Report on Germany Before the Elections. New York: American Council on Germany, 1957, 30 P.

2710 Murray, John. Western Germany After the Autumn Elections. Studies. 47 (Spring 1958), 39-52.

2711 Ollenhauer, Erich. Security for All. Bonn: Sozialdemokratische Partei Deutschlands, 1957, 16 P.

2712 Pachter, Henry M. Freedom and Democracy in Germany. World Politics. 11:2 (January 1959), 292-302.

2713 Packman, Martin. German Election, 1957. Editorial Research Reports. (21 August 1957), 605-621.

2714 Panter-Erick, Keith. Adenauer's Victory in Munich. Political Studies. 7:3 (October 1959), 246-268.

2715 Prittie, Terence C. F. Dr. Adenauer's New Government and Its Problems. Parliamentary Affairs. 11:1 (Winter 1957-58), 16-22.

2716 Pross, Harry. West Germany: Unfinished Democracy. Orbis. 2:3 (Fall 1958), 356-370.

2717 Sawer, G. Politics and the Constitution in West Germany. Australian Outlook. 14:2 (August 1960), 136-146.

2718 Schaffer, Gordon. Appeasing Adenauer. Labour Monthly. 42 (January 1960), 39-41.

2719 Schuschnigg, Kurt Von. on Revisiting Europe. Social Order. 8:1 (January 1958), 2-14.

2720 Shuster, George N. Has Germany Changed?. Foreign Policy Bulletin. 39:15 (April 1960), 116+.

2721 Szulc, H. Aftermath of the German Elections. Poland and Germany. 1:3 (Autumn 1957), 35-38.

2722 Western Germany. Planning (P.E.P.). 26:445 (17 October 1960), 292-298.

2723 Western Germany: A Financial Times Survey. London: Financial Times, 28 March 1960, 48 P.

2724 Williams, J. Emlyn. Western Germany Before the Summit. World Today. 16:2 (February 1960), 63-70.

F.5.4. 1961-65: 4th Legislative Period

2725 Abosch, Heinz. The Menace of the Miracle: Germany From Hitler to Adenauer. New York: Monthly Review, 1963, 277 P.

2726 Alexander, H. G. Germany Before the Elections. Political Quarterly. 32:2 (April-June 1961), 168-181.

2727 Allemann, Fritz Rene. The End of the Adenauer Era. Encounter. 20:2 (February 1963), 59-63.

2728 Anthon, Carl G. The End of the Adenauer Era. Current History. 44:260 (April 1963), 193-201.

2729 Aust, Hans Walter. West German

Reality 1964. German Foreign Policy (GDR). 4:1 (1965), 32-42.

2730 Berdes, George R. Up From Ashes: an American Journalist Reports From Germany. Milwaukee: Marquette University, Institute of German Affairs, 1964, 58 P.

2731 Berezowski, Z. Divergent Approaches. Poland and Germany. 8:1-2 (January-June 1964), 3-9. Adenauer and Erhard on the Future of Germany.

2732 Berezowski, Z. Dr. Adenauer's Record. Poland and Germany. 6:4 (October-December 1962), 1-12.

2733 Biswas, K. P. An Indian in Germany. Calcutta: Das Gupta, 1963, 212 P.

2734 Blumenfeld, F. Yorick. West German Election, 1961. Editorial Research Reports. (23 August 1961), 621-636.

2735 Born, Moritz J. The Demise of the Adenauer Era. Yearbook of World Affairs. 18 (1964), 41-55.

2736 Bracher, Karl Dietrich. Problems of a Parliamentary Democracy in Europe. A New Europe? Ed. Stephen R. Graubard. Cambridge: Riverside, 1963, Pp. 245-264.

2737 Chamberlin, William Henry. The German Phoenix. New York: Duell, Sloan and Pearce, 1963, 309 P.

2738 Eich, Hermann. The Unloved Germans. New York: Stein and Day, 1965, 255 P.

2739 Epstein, Klaus. Germany After Adenauer. New York: Foreign Policy Association, Headline Series No. 164, April 1964, 63 P.

2740 Erler, Fritz. Democracy in Germany. Cambridge: Harvard University Press, 1965, 139 P.

2741 FRG, Press and Information Office. Statement By Adenauer's Fourth Government. Bonn: Press and Information Office, 1961, 19 P. Given to Bundestag on 29 November 1961.

2742 Ford, Frederick. The Cold Terror in West Germany. Political Affairs. 41:7 (July 1962), 51-54.

2743 Freund, Gerald. Adenauer and the Future of Germany. International Journal. 18:4 (Autumn 1963), 458-467.

2744 Gellhorn, Martha. Is There a New Germany?. Atlantic. 213:2 (February 1964), 69-76.

2745 Germany and Berlin: Legacy of World Conflict. Moderator. 2:3 (Winter 1963-64), 30-39. A Symposium, with Johannes Borger, Peter C. M. S. Braun, Todd Gitlin, and Prince Huburtus Zu Loewenstein.

2746 Grabowski, K. Decline of the Adenauer Era. Poland and Germany. 6:3 (July-September 1962), 6-11.

2747 Grabowski, K. The Labyrinth of German Politics. Poland and Germany. 5:4 (October-December 1961), 7-16.

2748 Grabowski, K. West Germany Prepares for Elections. Poland and Germany. 5:2 (April-June 1961), 16-26.

2749 Grabowski, K. West Germany's Alternatives. Poland and Germany. 7:3 (July-September 1963), 3-10 as Adenauer Era Comes to an End.

2750 Hiscocks, Richard. The Adenauer Era. Philadelphia: Lippincott, 1966, 312 P.

2751 Jaspers, Karl. Our German Trouble. Encounter. 17:3 (September 1961), 21-24.

2752 Johnson, Nevil. The Era of Adenauer and After. Parliamentary Affairs. 17:1 (Winter 1963-64), 31-49.

2753 Kirchhoff, Werner. Has the "Adenauer Era" Really Ended?. German Foreign Policy (GDR). 3:1 (1964), 35-41.

2754 Kitzinger, Uwe W. West Germany: A Pre-Election Survey. World Today. 17:3 (March 1961), 110-122.

2755 Kitzinger, Uwe W. Will Willy Win?. Parliamentary Affairs. 14:3 (Summer 1961), 326-334.

2756 Kordt, Erich. Postwar Developments in Germany. Pakistan Horizon. 16:1 (1963), 22-32.

2757 Levi, Carlo. The Two-Fold Night: A Narrative of Travel in Germany. London: Cresset, 1962, 139 P.

2758 Lewis, Flora. Large Query About the New Germany. New York Times Magazine. (7 January 1962), 11+. Nationalism?

2759 Lewis, Flora. Six Big "If's" in Germany's Future. New York Times Magazine. (18 November 1962), 30+.

2760 Lichtheim, George. German Diary. Commentary. 38:3 (September 1964), 42-49.

2761 Lichtheim, George. West Germany Today. Commentary. 34:1 (July 1962), 28-38.

2762 Lueke, Rolf E. Germany After the Election. The Banker. 111:429 (November 1961), 738-741.

2763 Mader, Julius. Bonn and Lake Toplitz. German Foreign Policy (GDR). 4:2 (1965), 148-157. Search for Sunken Nazi Treasure.

2764 Mander, John. After the Apocalypse. Encounter. 22:4 (April 1964), 27-30.

2765 Mander, John. The Federal German Republic. Royal United Service Institution Journal. 110:637 (February 1965), 12-21.

2766 Menshikov, V. Election Campaign in West Germany. International Affairs (Moscow). (May 1961), 24-28.

2767 Morgenthau, Hans J. Germany Gives Rise to Vast Uncertainties. New York Times Magazine. (8 September 1963), 21+.

2768 Mueller, Albert. After the German Elections. Swiss Review of World Affairs. 11:7 (October 1961), 1-2.

2769 Mueller, Albert. Transition in Bonn. Swiss Review of World Affairs. 12:10 (January 1963), 1-2.

2770 An Octogenarian Chancellor: Prospects of the Adenauer Regime. Round Table. 53:210 (March 1963), 126-130.

2771 Perlmutter, Nathan. German Diary. Midstream. 10:1 (March 1964), 37-46. Random Thoughts Following a Month-Long Trip to Germany.

2772 Plischke, Elmer. The Adenauer Legacy. European Politics I: The Restless Search. Ed. William G. Andrews. Princeton: Van Nostrand, 1966, Pp. 139-192.

2773 Prittie, Terence C. F. Preview of the West German Election. International Journal. 16:3 (Summer 1961), 231-237.

2774 Pulzer, Peter G. J. The New Germany--After Adenauer. Socialist Commentary. (October 1963), 5-7.

2775 Rees, Goronwy. Diary: From Berlin to Munich. Encounter. 22:4 (April 1964), 3-12.

2776 Robertson, Brian, Lord of Oakridge. A Miracle? Potsdam 1945-Western Germany, 1965. International Affairs (London). 41:3 (July 1965), 401-410.

2777 Rothman, Stanley. The Future of German Politics: An Analysis. South Atlantic Quarterly. 60:4 (Autumn

1961), 447-454.

2778 Ruhm Von Oppen, Beate. The End of the Adenauer Era. World Today. 19:8 (August 1963), 343-352.

2779 Schoenbaum, David. The New Germany--A Changing Country. Socialist Commentary. (December 1964), 18-20.

2780 Spencer, Robert A. Germany in the "Erhard Era". International Journal. 19:4 (Autumn 1964), 458-473.

2781 Thorburn, H. G. Erhard's Germany. Queen's Quarterly. 71:1 (Spring 1964), 57-66.

2782 Toynbee, Arnold J. De Germania. Encounter. 22:4 (April 1964), 30-32.

2783 Vincent, Jean-Marie. West Germany: The Reactionary Democracy. The Socialist Register, 1964. Ed. Ralph Miliband and John Saville. New York: Monthly Review Press, 1964, Pp. 68-81.

2784 Wieser, Theodor. One Year of Erhard in Western Germany. Swiss Review of World Affairs. 14:9 (December 1964), 15-16.

2785 Williams, J. Emlyn. Federal Elections in West Germany. World Today. 17:12 (December 1961), 512-518.

2786 Williams, J. Emlyn. Recent West German Political Developments. World Today. 19:2 (February 1963), 70-77.

F.5.5. 1965-66: 5th Legislative Period

2787 Allemann, Fritz Rene. Election Year in West Germany. World Today. 21:5 (May 1965), 179-189.

2788 Andrews, William G. The Erhard Trusteeship. European Politics I: The Restless Search. Ed. William G. Andrews. Princeton: Van Nostrand, 1966, Pp. 192-205.

2789 Andrews, William G. The 1965 West German Election Campaign in Osnabrueck. European Political Institutions: A Comparative Government Reader. 2D Ed. Ed. William G. Andrews. Princeton: Van Nostrand, 1966, Pp. 303-313.

2790 Bailey, George. No Change in Germany. Reporter. 33:6 (7 October 1965), 32+.

2791 Childs, David. West Germany Decides to Stay With the Old Firm. Contemporary Review. 207:1198 (November 1965), 229-234.

2792 Clement, Alain. What Germany Has Become: Affluent, Yes, But Something Else Too. New Republic. 153:17 (23 October 1965), 12-14.

2793 Dowell, Jack D. Ludwig Erhard's "Structured Society". Washington State University, Research Studies. 35:1 (March 1967), 86-92.

2794 Elon, Amos. Journey Through a Haunted Land: The New Germany. New York: Holt, Rinehart and Winston, 1967, 259 P.

2795 Erhard, Ludwig. Counsel to the Whole Nation. European Political Institutions: A Comparative Government Reader. 2D Ed. Ed. William G. Andrews. Princeton: Van Nostrand, 1966, P. 512.

2796 Erhard, Ludwig. German Communitarian Democracy. European Political Institutions: A Comparative Government Reader. 2D Ed. Ed. William G. Andrews. Princeton: Van Nostrand, 1966, Pp. 70-77.

2797 Erhard, Ludwig. Spiegel Interview, 1965. German Politics. Ed. Donald O. Schoonmaker. Lexington: Heath, 1971, Pp. 120-132.

2798 Jaspers, Karl. The Future of Germany. Chicago: University of Chicago Press, 1967, 173 P.

2799 Kudlicki, S. After the West-German Elections. Poland and Germany. 9:4 (October-December 1965), 3-9.

2800 Kuebler, Jeanne. West German Election, September 19, 1965. Editorial Research Reports. (18 August 1965), 605-622.

2801 Luchsinger, Fred. Stable Federal Republic. Swiss Review of World Affairs. 15:7 (October 1965), 1-2.

2802 Mander, John. The German Dilemma. Encounter. 25:6 (December 1965), 48-51.

2803 Mikhailov, Vladimir Ivanovich. The Post-Election Scene in Bonn. International Affairs (Moscow). (January 1966), 31-38.

2804 Mueller, Gordon H. Germany's Emerging Nationalism: Trends Since the Berlin Wall. South Atlantic Quarterly. 67:4 (Autumn 1968), 659-671.

2805 Reimann, Max. After the Bundestag Elections: The Tasks of the Democratic Forces. World Marxist Review. 9:1 (January 1966), 11-17.

2806 Reinhold, Otto. FRG: The Fight for a Democratic Alternative and Its New Features. World Marxist Review: Problems of Peace and Socialism. 9:3 (March 1966), 28-34.

2807 Robson, Karl. The German Scene. Survey. No. 61 (October 1966), 4-13.

2808 Romoser, George K. Foster, Charles R. Safety First: The West German Election. Parliamentary Affairs. 19:1 (Winter 1965-66), 31-36.

2809 Smith, Gordon. The Future of West German Politics. Political Quarterly. 37:1 (January-March 1966), 86-95.

2810 Sontheimer, Kurt. Warning Signs for the Federal Republic. German Politics. Ed. Donald O. Schoonmaker. Lexington: Heath, 1971, Pp. 223-232. Review of Jaspers, the Future of Germany.

2811 Speier, Hans. Karl Jaspers on the Future of Germany. Santa Monica: Rand Corporation, P-3895, July 1968, 14 P.

2812 Ulbricht, Walter. Current Questions of Political Developments in West Germany. Dresden: Zeit Im Bild, 1966, 29 P.

2813 Walton, Henry. Germany. New York: Walker, 1969, 222 P.

2814 Wires, Richard. Postwar Germany--Nation of Uncertainties. Indiana Social Studies Quarterly. 20:1 (Spring 1967), 47-65.

F.5.6. 1966-69: Grand Coalition

2815 Allemann, Fritz Rene. Changing Scene in Germany. World Today. 23:2 (February 1967), 49-62.

2816 Childs, David. Bonn: Grand Coalition or Bunker Coalition?. Contemporary Review. 210:1214 (March 1967), 113-118.

2817 Childs, David. Bonn: The Grand Coalition, Year One. Contemporary Review. 212:1227 (April 1968), 190-198.

2818 Drummond, Stuart. West Germany: Land Elections, the Npd, and the Grand Coalition. World Today. 23:9 (September 1967), 385-395.

2819 Engelmann, Frederick C. Perceptions of the Great Coalition in West Germany, 1966-1969. Canadian Journal of Political Science. 5:1 (March 1972), 28-54.

2820 Epstein, Klaus. The Current West German Scene. Modern Age. 11:2 (Spring 1967), 161-175.

2821 Flannery, Harry W. Seger, Gerhart H. Which Way Germany?. New York: Hawthorne, 1968, 246 P.

2822 Grass, Guenter. Speak Out: Speeches, Open Letters, Commentaries. New York: Harcourt, Brace and World, 1969, 142 P.

2823 Hermens, Ferdinand A. Germany's Political Structure. United Asia. 19:6 (November-December 1967), 286-293.

2824 Herz, John H. The Formation of the Grand Coalition. Cases in Comparative Politics. 2D Ed. Ed. James B. Christoph and Bernard E. Brown. Boston: Little, Brown, 1969, Pp. 207-239.

2825 Kryukov, P. Bonn: New Stage, Old Play. International Affairs (Moscow). (March 1968), 14-21.

2826 Kudlicki, S. First Year of the Grand Coalition. Poland and Germany. 11:3-4 (July-December 1967), 3-20.

2827 Landauer, Carl. Germany: Illusions and Dilemmas. New York: Harcourt, Brace, and World, 1969, 360 P.

2828 Lehmbruch, Gerhard. The Ambiguous Coalition in West Germany. Government and Opposition. 3:2 (Spring 1968), 181-204.

2829 Lorenz, Jurgen. Germany After Erhard--An Analysis. Atlantic Community Quarterly. 5:1 (Spring 1967), 66-70.

2830 Luchsinger, Fred. End of an Era. Swiss Review of World Affairs. 16:9 (December 1966), 1-3.

2831 Mikhailov, Vladimir Ivanovich. Bonn Between Past and Present. International Affairs (Moscow). (October 1966), 20-26.

2832 Mikhailov, Vladimir Ivanovich. Bonn's Two Camps. International Affairs (Moscow). (August 1968), 70-76.

2833 Muller, Steven. Anxiety in Bonn: German Fears After Czechoslovakia. Bulletin of the Atomic Scientists. 25:3 (March 1969), 13-15.

2834 National Front of Democratic Germany. One Year of the Bonn Grand Coalition: The Result of an Unsuccessful Policy: Facts, Causes, Aims, Methods. Berlin (East): National Council of the National Front of Democratic Germany, 1967, 89 P.

2835 Pick, Otto. Tilford, Roger B. Gaullism Beyond the Rhine. International Journal. 23:2 (Spring 1968), 234-243.

2836 Pritt, Denis N. The Real Face of Bonn. Labour Monthly. 51 (January 1969), 27-32.

2837 Richardson, James L. West Germany Since Adenauer: Stresses and Strains of the Late 1960's. Australian Outlook. 24:1 (April 1970), 51-60.

2838 Rzhevsky, Yuri Sergeevich. A Year of the Big Coalition. International Affairs (Moscow). (October 1968), 9-15.

2839 Schaefer, Friedrich. Development of German Parliamentary System. United Asia. 19:6 (November-December 1967), 436-441.

2840 Shabecoff, Philip. The Fox and the Bear Are Curious Partners. New York Times Magazine. (5 February 1967), 20+. Kiesinger and Brandt.

2841 Shub, Anatole. Can Germany Ever Go Left?. Encounter. 28:2 (February 1967), 27-32.

2842 Spencer, Robert A. Germany After the Autumn Crisis. International Journal. 22:2 (Spring 1967), 210-230.

2843 Tilford, Roger B. The Coalition Discussion: Some European Experiences. Parliamentary Affairs. 21:1 (Winter 1967-68), 48-52.

2844 Tilford, Roger B. German Coalition Politics. Political Quarterly. 39:2 (April-June 1968), 169-180.

2845 Tilford, Roger B. Grand Coalition: Not So Grand for the Parliamentarians?. Parliamentary Affairs. 20:2 (Spring 1967), 136-143.

2846 Watt, Donald C. Manoeuverings in Bonn. World Today. 22:12 (December 1966), 508-511. Coalition Building.

2847 Wieser, Theodor. Kiesinger's First Hundred Days. Swiss Review of World Affairs. 17:2 (May 1967), 4-6.

2848 Zundel, Rolf. West Germany: The Grand Coalition and Its Consequences. World Today. 24:9 (September 1968), 367-375.

F.5.7. 1969-72: 6Th Legislative Period

2849 Allemann, Fritz Rene. Bonn Is Not Weimar. Encounter. 33:2 (August 1969), 86-91.

2850 Brandt, Willy. Germany's Prospects. Atlantic Community Quarterly. 8:1 (Spring 1970), 36-39. "State-of-Nation" Address, 14 January 1970; Comment By Oskar Fehrenbach, Pp. 40-42.

2851 Brandt, Willy. Report on the State of the Nation. Bonn: Press and Information Office, 1971, 78 P. Presented to Bundestag on 28 January 1971.

2852 Braunthal, Gerard. Politics in West Germany. Current History. 62:369 (May 1972), 244-248.

2853 Cattani, Alfred. Heinemann's Relapse. Swiss Review of World Affairs. 19:1 (April 1969), 6. Concern Over President's Partisan Comments After Election.

2854 Cattani, Alfred. Narrow Margin for Brandt. Swiss Review of World Affairs. 19:11 (February 1970), 2.

2855 Conradt, David P. Social Structure, Voting Behavior and Party Politics in West Germany: An Ecological Analysis of the 1969 Federal Election. Sozialwissenschaftliches Jahrbuch Fuer Politik, Vol 3. Ed. Rudolf Wildenmann. Munich and Vienna: Guenter Olzog Verlag, 1972, Pp. 175-230.

2856 Czechanowski, S. Changing the Guard in Bonn. Poland and Germany. 13:3-4 (July-December 1969), 3-7.

2857 Dahrendorf, Ralf. Bonn After Twenty Years: Are Germany's Problems Nearer Solution?. World Today. 25:4 (April 1969), 158-171.

2858 Edinger, Lewis J. Political Change in Germany: The Federal Republic After the 1969 Election. Comparative Politics. 2:4 (July 1970), 549-578.

2859 FRG, Federal Chancellor's Office. Report on the State of the Nation; the Basic Principles of The Federal Government's Policy; Statement to the Bundestag By Walter Scheel. Bonn: Press and Information Office, 1971, 78 P. Statement to Bundestag.

2860 FRG, Federal Chancellor's Office. The State of the Nation, 1971: Report By the Federal Chancellor and Summary of the Background Material. Bonn: Federal Ministry for Intra-German Relations, 1971, 119 P.

2861 Fisher, Joel M. Groennings, Sven.

German Electoral Politics in 1969. Government and Opposition. 5:2 (Spring 1970), 218-234.

2862 Graebner, Norman A. Germany Between East and West. Current History. 62:369 (May 1972), 225-228.

2863 Herz, John H., Editor. Special Issue on the West German Election of 1969. Comparative Politics. 2:4 (July 1970), 519-692.

2864 How the West Germans Voted (1969 Election). Poland and Germany. 13:3-4 (July-September 1969), 38-39.

2865 Kaltefleiter, Werner. The Impact of the Election of 1969 and the Formation of the New Government on the German Party System. Comparative Politics. 2:4 (July 1970), 593-604.

2866 Karanjia, Rustom Khurshedji. Round Germany With Hitler. New Delhi: People's Publishing House, 1970, 171 P.

2867 Klingemann, Hans D. Pappi, Franz Urban. The 1969 Bundestag Election in the Federal Republic of Germany: An Analysis of Voting Behavior. Comparative Politics. 2:4 (July 1970), 523-548.

2868 Luchsinger, Fred. The Paradoxical German Elections. Swiss Review of World Affairs. 19:8 (November 1969), 10-11.

2869 Mander, John. German Diary. Encounter. 35:4 (October 1970), 65-75.

2870 Mander, John. Must We Love the Germans?. Encounter. 33:6 (December 1969), 36-44.

2871 Mendershausen, Horst. Germany in 1970: A Summary of Political Developments. Santa Monica: Rand Corporation, P-4500, November 1970, 10 P.

2872 Merritt, Richard L. Merritt, Anna J. West Germany Enters the Seventies. New York: Foreign Policy Association, Headline Series No. 205, 1971, 64 P.

2873 Morgan, Roger P. The 1969 Election in West Germany. World Today. 25:11 (November 1969), 470-478.

2874 Morgan, Roger P. Political Prospects in Bonn. World Today. 28:8 (August 1972), 351-359.

2875 Pachter, Henry M. Willy Brandt Under Fire. Dissent. 18:3 (June 1971), 210-211.

2876 Robson, Karl. Radice, Jonathan. Hawkins, Irene. Willy Brandt's Inheritance: A Survey of Germany. Economist. 234:6594 (10 January 1970), 48-Page Section Following P. 42.

2877 Scheuner, Ulrich. The State as We Should Like to See It. German Tribune Quarterly Review. No. 7 (16 September 1969), 1-6.

2878 Schoenbaum, David. Elections in West Germany. Polity. 3:2 (Winter 1970), 265-271.

2879 Stein, Stanley. The Current West German Scene, National Elections 1969. Central European Federalist. 17:2 (December 1969), 7-12.

2880 Zholkver, A. F.R.G.: Pre-Election Carnival. International Affairs (Moscow). (May 1969), 33-42.

F.5.8. 1972-74: 7Th Legislative Period

2881 Conradt, David P. Lambert, Dwight. Party System, Social Structure, and Competitive Politics in West Germany: An Ecological Analysis of the 1972 Federal Election. Comparative Politics. 7:1 (October 1974), 61-86.

2882 Grosser, Alfred. Germany in Our Time. Upheaval and Continuity: A Century of German History. Ed. E. J. Feuchtwanger. Pittsburgh, Pa.: University of Pittsburgh Press, 1974, Pp. 183-188.

2883 Irving, R. E. M. Paterson, William E. The West German Parliamentary Election of November 1972. Parliamentary Affairs. 26:2 (Spring 1973), 218-239.

2884 Laux, William E. West German Political Parties and the 1972 Bundestag Elections. Western Political Quarterly. 26:3 (September 1973), 507-528.

2885 Luchsinger, Fred. The Failure of the Brandt Government. Swiss Review of World Affairs. 22:7 (October 1972), 2-3. Editorial on Background of Brandt's Request for Vote of No-Confidence.

2886 Mander, John. Willy Brandt's Victory. Encounter. 40:2 (February 1973), 68-75.

2887 Schuster, Hans. The Accepted Change of Roles. German Tribune Quarterly Review. No. 21 (22 March 1973), 10-16. SPD in Power, CDU in Opposition.

2888 Smith, Gordon. The New German Politics. Political Quarterly. 44:3 (July-September 1973), 283-293.

G. GDR: Government and Politics

G.1. Political Framework

G.1.1. Constitutional Developments

2889 Bothe, Michael. The 1968 Constitution of East Germany: A Codification of Marxist-Leninist Ideas on State and Government. American Journal of Comparative Law. 17:2 (1969), 268-291.

2890 Commission for the Drafting of a Socialist Constitution. Report on the Results of the Public Discussion of the New Socialist Constitution of the German Democratic Republic and the Amendments to the Draft Constitution. Law and Legislation in the German Democratic Republic. Ed. Association of German Democratic Lawyers. Berlin (East): Association of German Democratic Lawyers, C.1968, Pp. 69-88.

2891 FRG, Federal Ministry for All-German Affairs. Fiction and Fact: The Constitution of the German Democratic Republic in the Light of Its Application. Bonn: Bundesministerium Fuer Gesamtdeutsche Fragen, 1963, 34 P.

2892 GDR. Constitution of the German Democratic Republic. Berlin: Verlag "Die Wirtschaft," 1957, 47 P.

2893 GDR. Constitution of the German Democratic Republic. Berlin: Deutscher Zentralverlag, 1962, 72 P.

2894 GDR. The Constitution of the German Democratic Republic. Dresden: Staatsverlag and Zeit Im Bild, 3D Ed., 1970, 59 P.

2895 GDR. The Constitution of the Socialist State of the German Democratic Nation. Dresden: Zeit Im Bild, 1968, 107 P.

2896 GDR, Council of State. Charter of Freedom and Humanity: Draft Constitution of the Socialist State of the German Nation. Berlin: N.P., C.1967, 30 P. Presented to 7Th Session, People's Chamber.

2897 Hall, Martin. The GDR's Socialist Constitution. New World Review. 36:3 (Summer 1968), 76-82.

2898 Haupt, Lucie. Hafemann, Wilhelm. The People of the GDR Adopt a New

Constitution. German Foreign Policy (GDR). 7:2 (1968), 99-107.

2899 Kroeger, Herbert. The Class Character of State Sovereignty. German Foreign Policy (GDR). 11:4 (1972), 290-296. on GDR Constitution.

2900 Riemann, Tord. The GDR's Socialist Constitution. World Marxist Review: Problems of Peace and Socialism. 11:4 (April 1968), 20-24.

2901 Schoeneberg, Karl-Heinz. Constitution and Society: The GDR Constitution of 1949, Its Character and Operation. Law and Legislation in the German Democratic Republic. Ed. Association of German Democratic Lawyers. Berlin (East): Association of German Democratic Lawyers, C.1968, Pp. 19-34.

2902 Sharp, Samuel L. New Constitutions in the Soviet Sphere. Washington: Foundation for Foreign Affairs, 1950, 114 P.

2903 Sibirtsev, Yu. The G.D.R. at a New Stage of Its Development. International Affairs (Moscow). (October 1968), 29-34.

2904 US, Hicog, Foreign Relations Division. Constitutional Developments in the Soviet Zone. N.P.: Hicog, Foreign Relations Division, C.1951.

2905 US, Hicog, Office of Executive Secretary. Soviet Zone Constitution and Electoral Law. Berlin: Hicog, Office of Executive Secretary, Policy Reports Secretary, 1951, 107 P.

2906 Ultricht, Walter. The New Constitution of the GDR Will Be the Basic Law of Peace, Democracy, Socialism and Friendship Among Peoples. Dresden: Zeit Im Bild, 1967, 46 P.

2907 Ulbricht, Walter. New GDR Constitution: Guaranty for Further Advance of Socialism. German Foreign Policy (GDR). 7:4 (1968), 270-274.

2908 Wippold, Werner. The Legal Basis of People's Sovereignty in the German Democratic Republic. Law and Legislation in the German Democratic Republic. No. 2 (1969), 13-21.

G.1.2. Political Leadership

2909 Baylis, Thomas A. Communist Elites and Industrial Society: The Technical Intelligentsia in East German Politics. Ph.D. Thesis, University of California, Berkeley, 1968, 424 P.

2910 Baylis, Thomas A. The Technical Intelligentsia and the East German Elite: Legitimacy and Social Change in Mature Communism. Berkeley: University of California Press, 1974, Xx and 314 P.

2911 Childs, David. The East German Elite: Red Jesuits and Others. World Today. 22:1 (January 1966), 32-41.

2912 Croan, Melvin. Ulbricht: Will He Last?. East Europe. 10:12 (December 1961), 3-5.

2913 Directory of East German Officials. Washington: Biographic Reference Aid, Ba64-3, 1964, 221 P.

2914 GDR, Information Office. Wilhelm Pieck, President of the German Democratic Republic. Berlin: Information Office, C.1951, 45 P.

2915 Huizinga, J. H. Behind the Wall--The Success Story of Walter Ulbricht?. New York Times Magazine. (7 September 1969), 36+.

2916 International Committee for Information and Social Activity. Leading Men in the Soviet-Occupied Zone of Germany. Luxembourg: International Committee for Information and Social Activity, 1960, 31 P.

2917 Investigation Committee of Free Jurists. Ex-Nazis in the Services of the German Democratic Republic. Berlin-Zehlendorf-West: Untersuchungsausschuss Freiheitlicher Juristen, 1959, 64 P.

2918 Joesten, Joachim. Walter Ulbricht: East Germany's Strong Man and Chief of State. New York: Joachim Joesten, New Germany Reports No. 55, November 1961, 15 P.

2919 Joesten, Joachim. Who's Who in German Politics Today: Eastern Germany. Great Barrington, Mass.: Joachim Joesten, New Germany Reports No. 8, February 1949, 20 P.

2920 Leonhard, Wolfgang. Ulbricht and His Successor. East Europe. 20:10 (October 1971), 18-20. Discussion of Ulbricht and Honecker.

2921 Lewis, Flora. Moscow's No. 1 Man in Germany: Walter Ulbricht. New York Times Magazine. (1 February 1959), 15+.

2922 Lewis, Flora. Why Ulbricht Keeps His Job. New York Times Magazine. (25 March 1962), 27+.

2923 Luchsinger, Fred. The Unstoppable Walter Ulbricht. Swiss Review of World Affairs. 20:1 (April 1970), 2-3.

2924 Ludz, Peter Christian. The Changing Party Elite in East Germany. Cambridge: M.I.T. Press, 1972, 506 P.

2925 Ludz, Peter Christian. Experts and Critical Intellectuals in East Germany. Upheaval and Continuity: A Century of German History. Ed. E. J. Feuchtwanger. Pittsburgh, Pa.: University of Pittsburgh Press, 1974, Pp. 166-182.

2926 Ludz, Peter Christian. The Sed Leadership in Transition. Problems of Communism. 19:3 (May-June 1970), 23-31. The Choices Between Modernization and Stability.

2927 Olsen, Arthur J. Khrushchev's "Impossible" Man in Berlin: Walter Ulbricht. New York Times Magazine. (11 October 1964), 37+.

2928 Reiner, Conrad. Wilhelm Pieck: A Great German. New Masses. 58:1 (January 1946), 5-6.

2929 Richert, Ernst. Ulbricht and After. Survey. No. 61 (October 1966), 153-164.

2930 Schindzielorz, Hubert Ludwig. Patterns of Leadership Recruitment in the German Democratic Republic, 1950-1971. Ph.D. Thesis, University of Pittsburgh, 1972, 182 P.

2931 Stern, Carola. Ulbricht: A Political Biography. New York: Praeger, 1965, 231 P.

2932 Wilhelm, Bernhard. Willi Stoph: Ulbricht's Heir-Apparent?. Communist Affairs. 2:5 (September-October 1964), 21-22.

2933 Winzer, Otto. Pioneer of International Friendship: Walter Ulbricht. German Foreign Policy (GDR). 7:3 (1968), 179-185.

G.1.3. Ideological Developmments and Disputes

2934 Beyer, Heinz, Kanzig, Helga. Leninism and Its Application By the Socialist Unity Party of Germany. German Foreign Policy (GDR). 9:4 (1970), 282-296.

2935 Croan, Melvin. East German Revisionism: The Spectre and the Reality. Revisionism: Essays on the

History of Marxist Ideas. Ed. Leopold Labedz. New York: Praeger, 1962, Pp. 239-256.

2936 Fricke, Karl Wilhelm. Disunity of the Socialist Unity Party. Central Europe Journal. 14:6 (June 1966), 183-189.

2937 Haenisch, Werner. Krueger, Joachim. on the Dialectics of Home and Foreign Policy in the Strategy and Tactics of the Socialist Unity Party of Germany. German Foreign Policy (GDR). 10:4 (1971), 299-313.

2938 Harich, Wolfgang. The Testament of a Party Rebel. Bitter Harvest: The Intellectual Revolt Behind the Iron Curtain. Ed. Edmund O. Stillman. New York: Praeger, 1959, Pp. 290-298.

2939 Lamberg, Werner. Leninism and the Leading Role of the Working Class in the GDR. World Marxist Review: Problems of Peace and Socialism. 14:2 (February 1971), 59-70.

2940 Leonhard, Wolfgang. The Ideological Functionary. Soviet Affairs: St. Antony's Papers. 1 (1956), 69-84.

2941 Lippmann, Heinz. East Germany Today: The Limits of Reform Communism. Problems of Communism. 19:3 (May-June 1970), 15-22.

2942 Ludz, Peter Christian. Poverty of Philosophy. Survey. No. 34 (October-December 1960), 46-51.

2943 Mcinnes, Neil. Havemann and the Dialectic. Survey. No. 62 (January 1967), 25-37.

2944 Norden, Albert. The October Revolution and the German Working Class. International Affairs (Moscow). (August 1967), 8-16.

2945 Powik, Gerhard. The Dialectics of the Universal and the Particular in the Evolved Socialist Society. German Foreign Policy (GDR). 9:2 (1970), 99-104.

2946 Professor Havemann's Views. East Europe. 13:4 (April 1964), 21-22.

2947 Prof. Havemann and the East German Academy. Minerva. 4:3 (Spring 1966), 419-423.

2948 Raddatz, Fritz. The Case of Wolfgang Harich. Encounter. 24:2 (February 1965), 88-92. Prof. at Humboldt, Imprisoned in GDR in 1956.

2949 Redlow, Gotz. The Marxist-Leninist Ideology--The Intellectual Basis of Socialism. United Asia. 21:5 (September-October 1969), 272-281.

2950 Ruehle, Juergen. The Philosopher of Hope: Ernst Bloch. Revisionism: Essays on the History of Marxist Ideas. Ed. Leopold Labedz. New York: Praeger, 1962, 166-178.

2951 S. E. S. New Policy Trends in Eastern Germany: The S.E.D. Party's Third Conference and the "Back-to-Lenin" Line. World Today. 12:5 (May 1956), 173-181.

2952 Ulbricht, Walter. The October Revolution and the Transition to Socialism in Germany. World Marxist Review: Problems of Peace and Socialism. 10:11 (November 1967), 5-9.

2953 Weber, Bernd. Sed Ideology: Rapprochement and Demarcation. Aussenpolitik. 23:1 (1972), 41-48.

G.2. Political Structure and Processes (See Also H.2)

G.2.1. Institutions and Processes

2954 Arnold-Forster, Mark. The East German Parliament. Parliamentary Affairs. 5:2 (Spring 1952), 274-280.

2955 Correns, Erich. National Front of Democratic Germany in the Struggle for a Peace Treaty and Socialist Construction. World Marxist Review: Problems of Peace and Socialism. 5:3 (March 1962), 17-24.

2956 Croan, Melvin. Dependent Totalitarianism: The Political Process in East Germany. Ph.D. Thesis, Harvard University, 1960, 374 P.

2957 Egler, Gert. Hafemann, Wilhelm. Haupt, Lucie. Regarding the Structure and System of State Administration Within the Constitution of the German Democratic Republic. Law and Legislation in the German Democratic Republic. Ed. Association of German Democratic Lawyers. Berlin (East): Association of German Democratic Lawyers, C.1968, Pp. 5-18.

2958 Frei, Otto. Administrative Reforms in the Soviet Zone of Germany. Swiss Review of World Affairs. 4:1 (April 1954), 3-4.

2959 Fricke, Karl Wilhelm. Permament Changes in the Soviet Zone Administration. Central Europe Journal. 14:2 (February 1966), 51-56.

2960 Frigge, Peter. Citizen, State and Government in East Germany. Swiss Review of World Affairs. 17:3 (June 1967), 7-9.

2961 German Democratic Republic: Parties and Organizations. Dresden: Verlag Zeit Im Bild, 1970, 79 P.

2962 Matthes, Heinz. Towards a People's State: on the Establishment and Activities of the Workers' and Peasants' Inspection Office. Law and Legislation in the German Democratic Republic. No. 1 (1965), 46-52.

2963 Merritt, Richard L. Public Perspectives in Closed Societies. Foreign Policy Analysis. Ed. Richard L. Merritt. Lexington: D. C. Heath, 1975, Pp. 101-117.

2964 Sorgenicht, Klaus. The State and Parliament in the German Democratic Republic. United Asia. 21:5 (September-October 1969), 234-240.

2965 US, Department of State, Bureau of Intelligence & Research. A Guide to the Government, Political Parties and Organizations of the So-Called "German Democratic Republic". Washington: Department of State, Bureau of Intelligence and Research, Bd No. 277, 1961, 62 P.

2966 Weichelt, Wolfgang. The Right to Vote and the Electoral System of the German Democratic Republic. Law and Legislation in the German Democratic Republic. No. 2 (1964), 5-16.

G.2.2. SED and Other Political Parties

2967 Albin, Felix. The Socialist Unity Party of Germany. London: New Germany, 1946, 67 P.

2968 Axen, Hermann. The 25Th Anniversary of the Foundation of the Socialist Unity Party of Germany. German Foreign Policy (GDR). 10:3 (1971), 179-189.

2969 Childs, David. The Socialist Unity Party of East Germany. Political Studies. 15:3 (October 1967), 301-321.

2970 How the Multiparty System Functions in the GDR. World Marxist Review: Problems of Peace and Socialism. 9:8 (August 1966), 76-80.

2971 Kopp, Fritz. German History and the Sed. Survey. No. 34 (October-December 1960), 52-57.

2972 Krisch, Henry. German Politics Under Soviet Occupation: The Unification of the Communist and Social Democratic Parties in the Soviet Zone, April 1945 to May 1946. Ph.D. Thesis, Columbia University, 1968, 602 P.

2973 Ludz, Peter Christian. The Sed-- Organizational and Sociostructural Changes of a Mass Party. Party Systems, Party Organizations, and the Politics of New Masses. Ed. Otto Stammer. Berlin: Institut Fuer Politische Wissenschaft an Der Freien Universitaet Berlin, 1968, Pp. 180- 194.

2974 Matern, Hermann. The Multi-Party System in the German Democratic Republic. World Marxist Review: Problems of Peace and Socialism. 2:4 (April 1959), 26-33.

2975 Merritt, Richard L. Francisco, Ronald A. The SPD of East Berlin, 1945-1961. Comparative Politics. 5:1 (October 1972), 1-28.

2976 The Sed: Construction, Character, Situation. Cologne: Verlag Fuer Politik Und Wirtschaft, 1954, 28 P. Special Issue of Sbz-Archiv, January 1954.

2977 Seton-Watson, Hugh. Communist Parties in Eastern Europe. Occidente. 12:6 (November-December 1956), 473-491.

2978 US, Hicog. The Socialist Unity Party as the Soviet Instrument of Power in Eastern Germany. Frankfurt: Hicog, 1950, 13 P.

2979 US, Omgus, Military Governor. Kpd-SPD Merger in Berlin and the Soviet Zone. N.P.: Omgus, May 1946.

2980 Ulbricht, Walter. Lenin and the Socialist Unity Party of Germany. World Marxist Review: Problems of Peace and Socialism. 13:4 (April 1970), 42-48.

2981 Ulbricht, Walter. Some Aspects of the Ideological Work of the S.U.P.G. World Marxist Review: Problems of Peace and Socialism. 1:2 (October 1958), 16-24.

2982 Wagner, Helmut R. Loyalty and Commitment in a Totalitarian Party. Social Research. 26:3 (Autumn 1959), 272-282.

2983 Wolfe, James H. Minor Parties in the German Democratic Republic. East European Quarterly. 4:4 (January 1971), 457-478.

2984 Wortman, John August. The Minor Parties in the Soviet Zone of Germany: The Communist Preparation and Use of Transmission Belts to the East German Middle Class. Ph.D. Thesis, University of Minnesota, 1958, 401 P.

G.2.3. National People's Army

2985 Bader, Werner. Civil War in the Making: The Combat Groups of the Working Class in East Germany. London: Independent Information Center, 1964, 125 P.

2986 Childs, David. The "Nationale Volksarmee" of East Germany. German Life and Letters. 20:3 (April 1967), 195-204.

2987 Chopra, Maharaj K. East German Security. Military Review. 51:10 (October 1971), 12-20.

2988 Falk, Theodor. Militarism in the Soviet Zone. Bonn: Ruehmland, 1961, 47 P.

2989 Forster, Thomas Manfred. The East German Army: A Pattern of a Communist Military Establishment. South Brunswick: Barnes, 1968, 255 P.

2990 Frei, Otto. The Remilitarization of Eastern Germany. Swiss Review of World Affairs. 6:1 (April 1956), 9-11.

2991 GDR, Ministry of National Defense. The National People's Army of the German Democratic Republic. Dresden: Zeit Im Bild, 1968, 46 P.

2992 GDR, Ministry of National Defense. The National People's Army of the German Democratic Republic: An Army of a Peace-Loving Democratic State. Berlin: Ministerium Fuer Nationale Verteidigung, 1960, 99 P.

2993 GDR, Ministry of National Defense. Protection Against Weapons of Mass Destruction. New York: Joint Publications Research Service, Ny-454, 1958, 84 P.

2994 GDR, Ministry of National Defense. Soldiers of Peace. Dresden: Ministry of National Defense, Press Department, C.1970, 47 P.

2995 German Reports on East Bloc Activities: Central Planning for Atomic Protection in the East Bloc; and Ideological Training in the East German People's Army. Santa Monica: Rand Corporation, T-114, 1959, 10 P.

2996 Herspring, Dale Roy. East German Civil-Military Relations: The Impact of Technology, 1949-72. New York: Praeger, 1973, Xxxvii and 96 P.

2997 Herspring, Dale Roy. Totalitarianism, Groups, and Technology: A Case Study of Professionalism in the East German Military, 1949-1971. Ph.D. Thesis, University of Southern California, 1972, 420 P.

2998 Hinterhoff, Eugene. Ulbricht's Fighting Men. East Europe. 10:11 (November 1961), 14-16.

2999 Martin, Friedrich P. Know Your Enemy: The Background of the German Communist Army. London: Independent Information Centre, 1962, 160 P.

3000 Militarism in the Soviet Zone. Bonn: Ruehmland, 1961, 47 P.

3001 Political Control in the East German People's Army. Santa Monica: Rand Corporation, T-108, 1958, 10 P.

3002 Protest on the East German "Army". Current History. 19:107 (July 1950), 47-48. By U.S. to Soviet Foreign Minister Vishinsky, 23 May 1950.

3003 Ruehmland, Ullrich. The Total Militarisation of the Soviet Occupied Zone of Germany. Celle/Hanover: Pohl, C. 1959, 23 P.

3004 Smogorzewski, K. M. Soviet Satellite Armies in Europe. Fortnightly. 170:1018 (October 1951), 657-666.

3005 Van Den Berk, L. J. M. Military Developments in Poland, Czechoslovakia, and East Germany. Military Review. 46:12 (December 1966), 49-52.

3006 Van Den Berk, L. J. M. Military Propaganda in East Germany. Nato's Fifteen Nations. 10:4-5 (April-May 1965), 70-71.

3007 Wettig, Gerhard. The Soviet Decision to Rearm East Germany: A Case Study of The Early Cold War Period. Cologne: Bundesinstitut Fuer Ostwissenschaftliche Und Internationale Studien, 1968, 18 P.

G.2.4. Youth and Youth Movements

3008 Brown, James A. The Free German Youth: A Functional Analysis. Ph.D. Thesis, University of Virginia, 1972, 161 P.

3009 Clews, John. The Berlin Youth Festival. Twentieth Century. 150:896 (October 1951), 289-297.

3010 Fraenkel, Heinrich. The Boy Between.

London: Wingate, 1955, 221 P. East German Youth: Story of Karlheinz Schaeffer.

3011 GDR. Youth. Dresden: Zeit Im Bild, 1968, 61 P.

3012 GDR, Information Office. 3Rd World Festival of Youth and Students for Peace, Berlin, 1951. Berlin: Taegliche Rundschau, C.1953, 47 P.

3013 J. C. C. The Berlin Youth Festival. World Today. 7:7 (July 1951), 306-315.

3014 Mcclaskey, Beryl R. Erdmann, Elisabeth. The Free German Youth and the Deutschlandtreffen: A Case Study of Soviet Tactics. Bad Godesberg-Mehlem: Office of the U.S. High Commissioner for Germany, Office of the Executive Director, Historical Division, 1951, 171 P.

3015 US, Department of State, Office of Public Affairs. Communist Festival for Youth, East Berlin, August 1951: Background. Washington: Department of State Publication 4325, Government Printing Office, 1951, 8 P.

3016 US, Department of State, Office of Public Affairs. Two Weeks in August: East German Youth Strays West; Background. Washington: Department of State Publication 4363, Government Printing Office, 1951, 13 P.

3017 Ulbricht, Walter. Our Youth in the German Democratic Republic. New Central European Observer. 3:12 (10 June 1950), 132-133.

3018 Youth in the G.D.R. New Central European Observer. 5:17 (16 August 1952), 270-271.

G.3. Legal System (See Also H.3)

G.3.1. Codes and Procedures

3019 Benjamin, Hilde. The New Criminal Law of the GDR. Law and Legislation in the German Democratic Republic. No. 2 (1967), 5-10.

3020 Beyer, Karl-Heinz. On Some Aspects of the New Family Code. Law and Legislation in the German Democratic Republic. No. 1 (1966), 45-49.

3021 Buchholz, Erich. The Development of Economic Criminal Law. Law and Legislation in the German Democratic Republic. No. 1 (1967), 17-27.

3022 Buchholz, Erich. Seidel, Dietmar. Justified Economic Risk. Law and Legislation in the German Democratic Republic. No. 1 (1969), 27-39.

3023 Confederation of Free German Trade Unions. The Labour Code of the German Democratic Republic. Berlin (East): Tribuene, 1962, 223 P.

3024 Creuzburg, Harry. Conditions for Issuing an Arrest Warrant in the GDR. Law and Legislation in the German Democratic Republic. No. 2 (1964), 35-38.

3025 Eberhardt, Karl-Heinz. Property Provisions in the GDR Family Code. Law and Legislation in the German Democratic Republic. No. 1 (1969), 45-52.

3026 Einhorn, Hans. On the Draft Family Code. Law and Legislation in the German Democratic Republic. No. 2 (1965), 23-36.

3027 Frei, Otto. Ulbricht's New Labor Law. Swiss Review of World Affairs. 10:10 (January 1961), 7-8.

3028 GDR. The Labour Code of the German Democratic Republic. With Commentary By Roger Schlegel. Berlin: Tribune Trade Union Publishers, 1965, 207 P.

3029 GDR, People's Chamber. A Happy Family Life: The Concern of the Family Code of the GDR. Berlin: Ministry of Justice, 1966, 102 P.

3030 Grossfeld, Bernhard. Money Sanctions for Breach of Contract in a Communist Economy. Yale Law Journal. 72:7 (June 1963), 1326-1346.

3031 Grzybowski, Kazimierz. Protection of Personal Liberty in the Criminal Procedures of Eastern Europe. Journal of the International Commission of Jurists. 3:1 (Spring 1961), 69-86.

3032 Hartmann, Richard. GDR Criminal Law Relating to Juveniles. Law and Legislation in the German Democratic Republic. No. 1 (1965), 29-37.

3033 Hartmann, Richard. The Question of Guilt and Its Legal Regulation in the Criminal Code of the German Democratic Republic. Law and Legislation in the German Democratic Republic. No. 1 (1970), 52-62.

3034 Hegner, Manfred. The Development of Labour Jurisdiction Reflected in Statistics. Law and Legislation in the German Democratic Republic. No. 2 (1967), 17-20.

3035 Hemmerling, Joachim. The Position of the Innovator in the German Democratic Republic. Law and Legislation in the German Democratic Republic. No. 2 (1963), 13-21.

3036 Hiller, Rudolf. On Civil Jurisdiction in the GDR. Law and Legislation in the German Democratic Republic. No. 1 (1966), 51-55.

3037 Jescheck, Hans-Heinrich. Penal Law and Its Application in the Soviet-Occupied Zone of Germany. Tuebingen: Mohr, 1965, 29 P.

3038 Kachelmaier, Rolf. About the Legal Safeguards Governing the Protection of Environment in the GDR. Law and Legislation in the German Democratic Republic. No. 2 (1971), 24-41.

3039 Kirchheimer, Otto. The Administration of Justice and the Concept of Legality in East Germany. Yale Law Journal. 68:4 (March 1959), 705-749.

3040 Kunz, Frithjef. The Constitutional Basic Rights in the Field of Socialist Labour. Law and Legislation in the German Democratic Republic. Ed. Association of German Democratic Lawyers. Berlin (East): Association of German Democratic Lawyers, C.1968, Pp. 51-67.

3041 Luebchen, Gustav-Adolf. State Liability in GDR Legislation and Practice. Law and Legislation in the German Democratic Republic. No. 1 (1971), 5-15.

3042 Markovits, Inga S. Civil Law in East Germany--Its Development and Relation to Soviet Legal History and Ideology. Yale Law Journal. 78:1 (November 1968), 1-51.

3043 Nathan, Hans. The Position of the Family and Family Law in the German Democratic Republic. Law and Legislation in the German Democratic Republic. No. 1 (1960), 34-44.

3044 Nathan, Hans. Problems of Civil Legislation in the GDR. Law and Legislation in the German Democratic Republic. No. 1 (1962), 58-64.

3045 Poppe, Eberhard. The Basic Rights of Socialist Man in the GDR. German Foreign Policy (GDR). 6:5 (1967), 410-419.

3046 Przybylski, Peter. The Criminal Jurisdiction of the GDR Conforms to the Principle of Human Rights. Law and Legislation in the German Democratic Republic. No. 2 (1966), 23-28.

3047 Pueschel, Heinz. A New Copyright Code

in the GDR. Law and Legislation in the German Democratic Republic. No. 1 (1966), 31-43.

3048 Pueschel, Heinz. Work in Progress on New Civil Code of the German Democratic Republic. Law and Legislation in the German Democratic Republic. No. 1 (1962), 40-57.

3049 Ritter, Traudel. About the Decree on Petitions Procedure in the GDR. Law and Legislation in the German Democratic Republic. No. 2 (1971), 7-23.

3050 Rosenthal, Walther. The Powers of the Judiciary in East Germany. Journal of the International Commission of Jurists. 4:1 (Summer 1962), 134-149.

3051 Rudelt, Walter. The Second Law to Amend and Supplement the GDR Labour Code. Law and Legislation in the German Democratic Republic. No. 2 (1967), 11-16.

3052 Schlegel, Joachim. on the Question of Procedure Concerning Arrest Warrants in The German Democratic Republic. Law and Legislation in the German Democratic Republic. No. 1 (1971), 25-31.

3053 Schlegel, Roger. About the Labour Code of the German Democratic Republic. Law and Legislation in the German Democratic Republic. No. 1-2 (1961), 51-63.

3054 Schlegel, Roger. Liability for Damage in Industry. Law and Legislation in the German Democratic Republic. No. 2 (1963), 23-34.

3055 Toeplitz, Heinrich. The Code of Criminal Procedure of the German Democratic Republic. Law and Legislation in the German Democratic Republic. No. 2 (1970), 5-12. Followed By GDR Code of Criminal Procedure, Pp. 13-87.

3056 Toeplitz, Heinrich. The New Penal Code of the German Democratic Republic. Law and Legislation in the German Democratic Republic. No. 2 (1968), 5-13. Followed By 1968 Penal Code, Pp. 15-96.

3057 Toeplitz, Heinrich. Problems of Legality and Jurisdiction in the New Constitution of the German Democratic Republic. Law and Legislation in the German Democratic Republic. Ed. Association of German Democratic Lawyers. Berlin (East): Association of German Democratic Lawyers, C.1968, Pp. 35-50.

3058 Toeplitz, Heinrich. The Role of the GDR in Defence of Human Rights. Law and Legislation in the German Democratic Republic. No. 2 (1964), 63-65.

3059 Tomass, J. Two Aspects of East German Family Law. Manual of German Law, II. 2D Ed. Ed. Ernst J. Cohn. Dobbs Ferry: Cceana, 1971, Pp. 281-305.

3060 Wiemann, Horst. International Family Law of the GDR. Law and Legislation in the German Democratic Republic. No. 2 (1967), 29-39.

3061 Wuensche, Kurt. The New Socialist Penal Code in the German Democratic Republic and International Law. German Foreign Policy (GDR). 7:4 (1968), 251-259.

G.3.2. Structures

3062 Benjamin, Hilde. The Election of Judges in 1960 and the Further Development of the Administration of Justice in the German Democratic Republic. Law and Legislation in the German Democratic Republic. No. 1-2 (1969), 5-21.

3063 Benjamin, Hilde. The System of Law Courts in the German Democratic Republic. Law and Legislation in the German Democratic Republic. No. 1 (1960), 5-23.

3064 Benjamin, Michael. Review of the Activities of Arbitration Commissions. Law and Legislation in the German Democratic Republic. No. 1 (1967), 9-16.

3065 Benjamin, Michael. The Work of the Disputes Commissions in the Settling of Minor Breaches of Criminal Law. Law and Legislation in the German Democratic Republic. No. 2 (1962), 5-10.

3066 Biebl, Rudi. New Forms of Public Participation in Criminal Court Proceedings. Law and Legislation in the German Democratic Republic. No. 1 (1964), 11-16.

3067 Creuzburg, Harry. Competence of Disputes Commissions for Minor Criminal Matters. Law and Legislation in the German Democratic Republic. No. 1 (1965), 17-23.

3068 Friedman, Peter P. Social Courts in East Germany, as Instruments of Social and Political Control and "Re-Education". Ph.D. Thesis, Columbia University, 1971, 230 P.

3069 Hofmann, Manfred. The Activities of the Law Office for International Civil Law Matters. Law and Legislation in the German Democratic Republic. No. 1 (1969), 53-56.

3070 Kranke, Rudi. The Disputes Commission--Manifestation of Advancing Democracy in the Legislative Field in the German Democratic Republic. Law and Legislation in the German Democratic Republic. No. 2 (1962), 11-21.

3071 Krutzsch, Walter. The Arbitration Commission--A New Social Organ of the GDR Legal System. Law and Legislation in the German Democratic Republic. No. 2 (1964), 39-45.

3072 Schmidt, Wolfgang. The Hearing of Minor Civil Disputes. Law and Legislation in the German Democratic Republic. No. 1 (1965), 24-28.

3073 Semler, Hans-Joachim. Graf, Herbert. New Chapter in the Development of the Administration of Justice in the German Democratic Republic. Law and Legislation in the German Democratic Republic. No. 1 (1963), 5-18.

3074 Steiner, Helmut. Social Origin and Structural Pattern of the Body of Judges in the GDR. Law and Legislation in the German Democratic Republic. No. 1 (1967), 49-63.

3075 Streit, Josef. Character and Functions of the Procurator's Office of the German Democratic Republic. Law and Legislation in the German Democratic Republic. No. 1 (1964), 5-10.

3076 Toeplitz, Heinrich. The Functions of the Courts of the German Democratic Republic on the Basis of the State Council Decree. Law and Legislation in the German Democratic Republic. No. 1 (1963), 19-28.

3077 Toeplitz, Heinrich. Independence of the Courts--Myth or Reality?. Law and Legislation in the German Democratic Republic. No. 2 (1971), 42-59.

3078 Toeplitz, Heinrich. Baur, Walter. 20 Years of the Association of German Democratic Lawyers (Vdjd). Law and Legislation in the German Democratic Republic. No. 2 (1969), 23-33.

3079 Walter, Gerhard. Status and Terms of Reference of the State Arbitration Board of the GDR. Law and Legislation in the German Democratic Republic. No. 1 (1972), 75-87.

3080 Weiss, Edith Brown. The East German

Social Courts: Development and Comparison With China. American Journal of Comparative Law. 20:2 (Spring 1972), 266-289.

3081 Wolff, Friedrich. On the Office of Lawyers in the German Democratic Republic. Law and Legislation in the German Democratic Republic. No. 1 (1964), 17-24.

3082 Wuensche, Kurt. The Social Courts--Development and Legal Character. Law and Legislation in the German Democratic Republic. No. 2 (1969), 35-40.

G.3.3. Western Criticism

3083 Amnesty International. Prison Conditions in East Germany: Conditions for Political Prisoners. London: Amnesty International, 1966, 56 P.

3084 FRG, Federal Ministry for All-German Affairs. Injustice the Regime: Documentary Evidence of the Systematic Violation of Legal Rights in the Soviet Occupied Territory of Germany. Bonn: Bundesministerium Fuer Gesamtdeutsche Fragen, 1952, 229 P. Supplement for 1954-1959 Published in C. 1959.

3085 FRG, Federal Ministry for All-German Affairs. Memorandum: Violation of Human Rights in the Soviet-Occupied Zone of Germany. Bonn: Federal Ministry for All-German Affairs, 1966, 64 P.

3086 Frei, Otto. East German Justice Since June 17. Swiss Review of World Affairs. 3:9 (December 1953), 9-10.

3087 German National Union of Students. Names and Fates of Professors and Students Who, After 1945, Within the Soviet Occupied Zone of Germany Were Arrested, Displaced, or Kidnapped: Situation Up to February 1, 1954. Berlin-Dahlem: German National Union of Students, All-German Student Affairs Department, 1954, 44 P.

3088 Hill, Russell. The Underground Jurists of Communist Germany. Reporter. 4:12 (12 June 1951), 17-20.

3089 Hornstein, Erika Von. The Accused: Seven East Germans on Trial. London: Wolff, 1965, 224 P.

3090 Investigation Committee of Free Jurists. Catalogue of Injustice. Berlin-Zehlendorf-West: Investigation Committee of Free Jurists, 1956, 192 P.

3091 Juretzko, Werner I. Years Without Hope. Chicago: Krause, 1970, 127 P.

3092 Kelman, Steven. Behind the Berlin Wall: An Encounter in East Germany. Boston: Houghton Mifflin, 1972, 327 P.

3093 Klimov, Grigorii Petrovich. The Terror Machine: The Inside Story of the Soviet Administration in Germany. New York: Praeger, 1953, 400 P.

3094 Luchsinger, Fred. Justice in East Germany. Swiss Review of World Affairs. 1:4 (July 1951), 11-13.

3095 US, Hicog, Berlin Element. Use of Terror Tactics in Soviet Zone of Germany. Department of State Bulletin. 29:754 (7 December 1953), 786-788.

3096 US, Senate, Committee on the Judiciary. An American Prisoner in Communist East Germany. Washington: Government Printing Office, 1958, 36 P. Testimony of Walter Steinberg Before Subcommittee, 15 July 1958.

3097 US, Senate, Committee on the Judiciary. Soviet Terrorism in Free Germany. Washington: Government Printing Office, 1960, 39 P.

Testimony of Theodore Hans on GDR Abductions From West Berlin.

G.4. General Political Developments

G.4.1. Initial Phases, 1949-53

3098 Adler, Margrit. 20 Million Germans Rebuild. New World Review. 21:5 (May 1953), 28-33.

3099 Bolling, Landrum. Zone of Silence. This Is Germany. Ed. Arthur Settel. New York: Sloane, 1950, Pp. 370-413.

3100 Bondy, Francois. Berlin Congress for Freedom. Commentary. 10:3 (September 1950), 245-251.

3101 D. F. The Soviet Zone of Germany Today. World Today. 9:6 (June 1953), 238-249.

3102 Davidson, Basil. Contrast in Germany. Monthly Review. 2:5 (September 1950), 147-154. Economic and Social Changes in the GDR.

3103 FRG, Federal Ministry for All-German Affairs. The Soviet Occupation Zone of Germany, 1945-1953: A Chronological Review. Berlin: Federal Ministry for All-German Affairs, 1954, 71 P.

3104 Geilinger, Eduard. Sed Methods in Eastern Germany. Swiss Review of World Politics. 1:1 (April 1951), 16-17.

3105 Grossmann, Kurt R. The Political, Social and Economic Development of Eastern Germany During 1950. Political Science Quarterly. 67:1 (March 1952), 96-120.

3106 Ignotus. In Eastern Germany. Contemporary Review. 179:1021 (January 1951), 20-25.

3107 Jahn, Hans. A Look Behind the "Iron Curtain": Danger From the East. Frankfurt/Main: N.P., 1951, 60 P. Submitted to Delegates at 2D Congress of the International Federation of Free Trade Unions, Milan, 4-12 July 1951.

3108 Joesten, Joachim. The East German State (German Democratic Republic). Great Barrington, Mass.: Joachim Joesten, New Germany Reports No. 14, June 1950, 17 P.

3109 Kirchheimer, Otto. The Government of Eastern Germany. Germany and the Future of Europe. Ed. Hans J. Morgenthau. Chicago: University of Chicago Press, 1951, Pp. 131-141.

3110 Kuelz, H. R. The Soviet Zone of Germany: A Study of Developments and Policies. International Affairs (London). 27:2 (April 1951), 156-166.

3111 Loewenstein, Karl. Soviet Germany. Current History. 22:129 (May 1952), 278-284; and 22:130 (June 1952), 334-339.

3112 Moscow's German Satellite. Twentieth Century. 153:915 (May 1953), 335-339.

3113 Muhlen, Norbert. The New Nazis of Germany: The Totalitarians of the Eastern Zone. Commentary. 11:1 (January 1951), 1-10.

3114 Nettl, John Peter. The Eastern Zone and Soviet Policy in Germany, 1945-1950. London and New York: Oxford University Press, 1951, 324 P.

3115 Samuel, Richard H. The Eastern Zone of Germany. Australian Outlook. 6:4 (December 1952), 230-246; and 7:1 (March 1953), 36-39.

3116 Schaffer, Gordon. The Germany the West Ignores. New World Review. 20:10 (October 1952), 7-10.

3117 Schaffer, Gordon. The New Stage in Germany. New Central European

Observer. 2:23 (12 November 1949), 271-272. Creation of the GDR.

3118 Schaffer, Gordon. The West's Bad Guess on Eastern Germany. New World Review. 19:4 (June 1951), 37-41.

3119 The Soviet Zone of Germany. Current Notes on International Affairs. 23:12 (December 1952), 724-734.

3120 The Soviet Zone of Germany Today. World Today. 9:6 (June 1953), 238-249.

3121 Thomson, Stewart. Bialek, Robert. The Bialek Affair. London: Wingate, 1955, 203 P. Bialek's Postwar Role in Developing Freie Deutsche Jugend.

3122 US, Department of State, Office of Public Affairs. East Germany Under Soviet Control. Washington: Department of State Publication 4596, Government Printing Office, 1952, 94 P.

3123 Wheeler, George Shaw. Something to Write Home About. New World Review. 20:9 (September 1952), 38-42. Life in GDR as Fascist Shadows Recede.

3124 Young, Edgar P. The Soviet Zone Made Safe for Democracy. New Central European Observer. 2:21 (15 October 1949), 249-250.

G.4.2. Uprising in June 1953

3125 Baras, Victor. Berias Fall and Ulbrichts Survival. Soviet Studies 27:3 (July 1975), 381-395.

3126 Baring, Arnulf M. Uprising in East Germany: June 17, 1953. Ithaca: Cornell University Press, 1972, 194 P.

3127 Brant, Stefan (Pseud. for Klaus Harpprecht). The East German Rising, 17Th June, 1953. New York: Praeger, 1957, 202 P.

3128 Eastern Germany Since the Uprisings of June, 1953. World Today. 10:2 (February 1954), 58-69.

3129 FRG, Federal Ministry for All-German Affairs. It Happened in June 1953: Facts and Dates. Bonn and Berlin: Federal Ministry for All-German Affairs, 1966, 58 P.

3130 FRG, Federal Ministry for All-German Affairs. The People's Revolt of 17 June, 1953, in the Soviet Zone of Occupation and in East Berlin: A Cartographical Representation. Bonn: Federal Ministry for All-German Affairs, 1953.

3131 FRG, Federal Ministry for All-German Affairs. Revolt in June: Documents and Reports on the People's Uprising in East Berlin and in the Soviet Zone of Germany. Bonn: Federal Ministry for All-German Affairs, 1953, 64 P.

3132 FRG, Press and Information Office. for Humanity and Freedom: The Uprising of the People in the Soviet Sector of Berlin and in Soviet-Occupied Central Germany on June 16 and 17, 1953. Bonn: Press and Information Office, 1953.

3133 Fischer, Louis. Two Days That Shook the Soviet World; the Impossible Revolution in East Germany. Bombay: Popular Book Depot, 1954, 50 P.

3134 Gerhardt, Uta. The Uprising of June 17, 1953: Documentary Report. The Plebeians Rehearse the Uprising: A German Tragedy. New York: Harcourt, Brace & World, 1966, Pp. 113-122.

3135 Hildebrandt, Rainer. The Explosion: The Uprising Behind the Iron Curtain. New York: Duell, Sloan and Pearce, 1955, 198 P.

3136 Joesten, Joachim. Eastern Germany in Turmoil: A Comprehensive Account and Analysis of the Momentous Events of 1953. New York: Joachim Joesten, New Germany Reports Nos. 24-25, October-November 1953, 17 and 19 P.

3137 Kraus, Wolfgang H. Crisis and Revolt in a Satellite: The East German Case in Retrospect. Eastern Europe in Transition. Ed. Kurt London. Baltimore: Johns Hopkins University Press, 1966, Pp. 41-66.

3138 Krould, H. J. Soviet Zone of Germany. Tensions Within the Soviet Captive Countries. Washington: Library of Congress, Legislative Reference Service, Government Printing Office, 1954, Pt. 3.

3139 Lazar, Arpad Joseph Von. Limits and Problems of Decompression in the German Democratic Republic and Hungary. Ph.D. Thesis, University of North Carolina, Chapel Hill, 1963, 403 P.

3140 Lewis, Geoffrey W. Soviet Germany: The Unruly Satellite. Department of State Bulletin. 29:757 (28 December 1953), 883-891.

3141 Lohenbill, F. Berlin, 17Th June. Contemporary Issues. 5:18 (June-July 1954), 115-124.

3142 Luchsinger, Fred. Revolt in Berlin. Swiss Review of World Affairs. 3:4 (July 1953), 1-2. 17 June 1953.

3143 Mccormick, John. The Berlin Events: Cold War Turning Point?. Commentary. 16:2 (August 1953), 105-114.

3144 Muhlen, Norbert. Letter From Berlin: East Germany's Permanent Revolution. Encounter. 1:2 (November 1953), 69-71.

3145 Nessi, Serge. Change and Steadfastness: The New Course in East Germany, 1953-1954. Ph.D. Thesis, Columbia University, 1972, 566 P.

3146 Rutgers University, Department of Sociology. Soviet Reporting on the East German Uprisings of June, 1953: a Case Study of Soviet Propaganda. New Brunswick: Rutgers University, Department of Sociology, 1954, 48 P.

3147 Salomon, Ernst Von. The Silent Revolt. Confluence. 3:3 (September 1954), 295-306.

3148 Schaffer, Gordon. Behind the Events in Eastern Germany. New World Review. 21:7 (August 1953), 11-14.

3149 Sherman, George. East Germany: June Days, 1953. Oxford: St. Antony's College, 1955, 78 P.

3150 Sherman, George. The Russian and the East German Party: Prelude to June 17Th, 1953. Soviet Affairs: St. Antony's Papers. 1 (1956), 85-124.

3151 Socialist Unity Party of Germany, Central Committee. Recent Events and the Party's Immediate Tasks. Political Affairs. 32:7 (August 1953), 52-59.

3152 Warde, William F. The East German Uprising. Fourth International. 14:3 (May-June 1953), 68-70.

G.4.3. Consolidation, 1954-66

3153 Alden, Robert. Journey to the Silent Germany. New York Times Magazine. (8 April 1962), 36+.

3154 Allemann, Fritz Rene. Glimpses Through a Curtain: Some Observations on the Soviet Zone of Germany. Encounter. 5:1 (July 1955), 30-36.

3155 Anderson, Evelyn. East Germany. Polycentrism: The New Factor in International Communism. Ed. Walter Laqueur and Leopold Labedz. New York: Praeger, 1962, Pp. 96-106.

3156 Anderson, Evelyn. East Germany. Survey. No. 42 (June 1962), 96-106.

3157 Anthon, Carl G. East Germany. Current History. 30:176 (April 1956), 231-236.

3158 Anthon, Carl G. East Germany After the June Revolts. World Affairs Quarterly. 27:1 (April 1956), 27-47.

3159 Anthon, Carl G. Stalinist Rule in East Germany. Current History. 44:261 (May 1963), 265-272.

3160 Arzinger, Rudolf. Self-Determination in Germany. German Foreign Policy (GDR). 5:5 (1966), 327-337.

3161 Aust, Hans Walter. The Strength of Our State. German Foreign Policy (GDR). 2:6 (1963), 415-422.

3162 Balow, Erich (Pseud.). East Germany Today: Notes on a Somber Journey. Problems of Communism. 12:4 (July-August 1963), 8-14.

3163 Barkeley, Richard. The "German Democratic Republic". Contemporary Review. 196 (October 1959), 151-155.

3164 Bender, Peter. in Search of a New Policy. Survey. No. 61 (October 1966), 80-92.

3165 Blumenfeld, F. Yorick. Captive East Germany. Editorial Research Reports. (1 September 1961), 639-654.

3166 Brown, James F. Eastern Europe. Survey. No. 54 (January 1965), 65-88, Esp. Pp. 81-82.

3167 Brown, Michael Barratt. East Germany Revisited. Labour Monthly. 36:12 (December 1954), 546-551.

3168 Burns, Emile. The German Democratic Republic. Communist Review. 8:10 (October 1953), 291-298.

3169 Childs, David. Ulbricht Explains. Contemporary Review. 207:1195 (August 1965), 65-70.

3170 Conant, Grace Richards. The Cold War of the Mind: Regimentation in East Germany. Modern Age. 5:2 (Spring 1961), 117-124.

3171 Congress of East German Regional Representatives. The Road to Peace and Unification: Resolutions and Speeches. Leer, Ostfriesland: Kongress Der Ostdeutschen Landesvertretungen, 1964, 56 P.

3172 Croan, Melvin. East Germany: Lesson in Survival. Problems of Communism. 3:11 (May-June 1962), 7-12.

3173 Croan, Melvin. of Walls and Utopias. Survey. No. 51 (April 1964), 52-62.

3174 Croan, Melvin. Party Politics and the Wall. Survey. No. 61 (October 1966), 38-46.

3175 Croan, Melvin. Friedrich, Carl J. The East German Regime and Soviet Policy in Germany. Journal of Politics. 20:1 (February 1958), 44-63.

3176 Cumming, Hugh S. East Germany: Puppet Government. Department of State Bulletin. 40:1042 (15 June 1959), 868-871.

3177 Davidson, Eugene. A Look at East Germany. Modern Age. 4:4 (Fall 1960), 340-342.

3178 Dulles, Eleanor Lansing. The Soviet-Occupied Zone of Germany: A Case Study in Communist Control. Department of State Bulletin. 36:929 (15 April 1957), 605-610.

3179 Frankel, Max. You Can'T Go Home to Weissenfels. New York Times Magazine. (10 January 1965), 20+.

3180 Frei, Otto. A Little More Cultural Freedom in the Ddr. Swiss Review of World Affairs. 14:1 (April 1964), 3-4.

3181 Frei, Otto. Regime and People in the Ddr. Swiss Review of World Affairs. 7:10 (January 1958), 20-21.

3182 Frei, Otto. The Soviet-Communist Regime in East Germany. Swiss Review of World Affairs. 4:8 (November 1954), 6-11.

3183 GDR. Materials From 15Th GDR Anniversary Celebrations. Washington: Foreign Broadcast Information Service, 1964, 73 P.

3184 GDR, Council of State. to the Future Turned: on the Occasion of the Fifteenth Anniversary of the Founding of the German Democratic Republic. Berlin: Staatsverlag, 1965, 162 P.

3185 German Democratic Republic. Yearbook on International Communist Affairs. Stanford: Hoover Institution on War, Revolution and Peace, Annual, 1966+.

3186 Goetting, Gerald. The German Democratic Republic Is a Sovereign State. German Foreign Policy (GDR). 2:5 (1963), 325-328.

3187 Grotewohl, Otto. Towards a Peaceful Democratic and Socialist Germany. Berlin: Deutscher Zentralverlag, 1960, 119 P.

3188 Gyorgy, Andrew. East Germany. Eastern European Government and Politics. Ed. Vaclav Benes, Andrew Gyorgy, and George Stambuk. New York: Harper & Row, 1966, Pp. 100-139.

3189 Gyorgy, Andrew. East Germany--Profile of a Reluctant Satellite. United States Naval Institute Proceedings. 87:6 (June 1961), 50-62.

3190 Hager, Kurt. Some Aspects of Full-Scale Building of Socialism in the German Democratic Republic. World Marxist Review. 6:7 (July 1963), 2-9.

3191 Hall, Martin. The German Democratic Republic--Most Maligned of All the People's Republics of Eastern Europe. New World Review. 30:12 (December 1962), 13-19.

3192 Herz, John H. East Germany: Progress and Prospects. Social Research. 27:2 (Summer 1960), 139-156.

3193 Hirsch, Felix Edward. The Crisis of East Germany. International Journal. 9:1 (Winter 1954), 8-15.

3194 Hoover, Herbert C., Jr. The Record of Communist Imperialism in East Germany. Department of State Bulletin. 34:868 (13 February 1956), 242-246.

3195 Hornsby, Lex, Editor. Profile of East Germany. New York: Barnes, 1966, 120 P.

3196 Hornstein, Erika Von. Beyond the Berlin Wall. London: Wolff, 1962, 254 P.

3197 Horstmann, Lali Von S. We Chose to Stay. New York: Houghton, 1954, 206 P.

3198 Jaenicke, Martin. East Germany Today: The Persistence of Stalinism. Problems of Communism. 12:4 (July-August 1963), 1-8.

3199 Joesten, Joachim. Eastern Germany in 1958: The Political and Administrative Setup. Great Barrington, Mass.: Joachim Joesten, New Germany Reports No. 38, April 1958, 21 P.

3200 Joesten, Joachim. Eastern Germany in 1958: The Struggle for Power in the Ddr. Great Barrington, Mass.: Joachim Joesten, New Germany Reports No. 39, May 1958, 18 P.

3201 Joesten, Joachim. Eastern Germany

Revisited. New York: Joachim Joesten, New Germany Reports Nos. 52-54, August-October 1961, 3 Vols., 55 P.

3202 Koenigswald, Harald Von. in the Red Shadow: Everyday Life in Central Germany. Munich: Bechtle, 1964, 85 P.

3203 Leo, Walter. After the Wall. Atlas. 12:2 (August 1966), 33-36.

3204 Lewan, Kenneth M. Conversations in East Germany. East Europe. 12:12 (December 1963), 11-17.

3205 Lewis, Flora. Report From Khrushchev's Germany. New York Times Magazine. (20 March 1960), 25+.

3206 Lohr, George. Socialist Gains in East Germany. New World Review. 26:3 (March 1958), 29-32.

3207 Lohr, George. 10 Years of the German Democratic Republic. New World Review. 27:11 (December 1959), 18-22.

3208 Low, Alfred D. Recent Strains and Stresses in the German Democratic Republic. Journal of Human Relations. 9:2 (Winter 1961), 167-179.

3209 Ludz, Peter Christian. East Germany: The Old and the New. East Europe. 15:4 (April 1966), 23-27.

3210 Mander, John. Beyond the Wall: 1964. Encounter. 23:2 (August 1964), 40-47.

3211 The Middle Classes and Socialism. Dresden: Zeit Im Bild, 1966, 47 P.

3212 Military Control in East Germany. Current History. 26:154 (June 1954), 355-361.

3213 Milyukova, Valentina. The German Democratic Republic. International Affairs (Moscow). (September 1957), 109-116.

3214 Mohl, Kurt. Conference of the Communist Party of Germany: Impressions of a Delegate. World Marxist Review: Problems of Peace and Socialism. 3:5 (May 1960), 70-73.

3215 Nearing, Scott. Freedom Under Socialism--Public Discussion By Young Germans at Humboldt University, Berlin. New World Review. 32:2 (February 1964), 26-29.

3216 Nesselrode, Franz Von (Pseud. for Joachim Joesten). Germany's Other Half: A Journalist's Appraisal of East Germany. London and New York: Abelard-Schuman, 1963, 207 P.

3217 Newman, Bernard. Behind the Berlin Wall. London: R. Hale, 1964, 187 P.

3218 Ofodile, Gilbert. I Shall Never Return: Eight Months in Communist Germany, a Nigerian Student Reports. Munich: Becatle, 1967, 68 P.

3219 Ollssner, Fred. Laying the Foundations of Socialism in the GDR. International Affairs (Moscow). (October 1955), 17-30.

3220 Olsen, Arthur J. Since August 13, Everything's Different. New York Times Magazine. (19 September 1965), 36+.

3221 Pittman, Margrit. "Resurrected From the Ruins"--The German Democratic Republic Today. New World Review. 29:8 (August 1961), 7-11.

3222 Polak, Karl. The Development of the State in the German Democratic Republic in Connection With the Construction of Socialism. Law and Legislation in the German Democratic Republic. No. 1 (1960), 24-33.

3223 Prittie, Terence C. F. East Germany: Record of a Failure. Problems of Communism. 10:6 (November-December 1961), 1-7.

3224 Rau, Heinrich. Progress in Socialist Construction in the German Democratic Republic. World Marxist Review: Problems of Peace and Socialism. 2:10 (October 1959), 31-36.

3225 Rexin, Manfred. Recent Reforms in East Germany. World Today. 21:7 (July 1965), 300-307.

3226 Rogger, Hans. East Germany: Stable or Immobile?. Current History. 48:283 (March 1965), 135-141.

3227 Roucek, Joseph S. Lottich, Kenneth V. Behind the Iron Curtain. Caldwell, Idaho: Caxton, 1964, 631 P., Esp. Pp. 143-166.

3228 Ruehmland, Ullrich. Short Dictionary of Terms Used in the Soviet Zone of Occupation in Germany. Bonn-Roettgen: Bonner Druck and Verlagsgesellschaft, 1962, 23 P.

3229 Shell, Kurt L. Totalitarianism in Retreat: The Example of the Ddr. World Politics. 18:1 (October 1965), 105-116.

3230 Sloan, Pat. Life in East Germany: A Candid Look. New World Review. 31:9 (October 1963), 32-37.

3231 Stern, Carola. Between Oder and Elbe. Survey. No. 34 (October-December 1960), 30-34.

3232 Stern, Carola. East Germany. Communism in Europe. Ed. William E. Griffith. Cambridge: M.I.T. Press, 1966, Vol. 2, Pp. 41-154.

3233 Suri, Surindar. Tendencies in East Germany. Contemporary Review. 191:1094 (February 1957), 97-101.

3234 Thalheim, Karl C. East Germany. East Central Europe and the World: Developments in the Post-Stalin Era. Ed. Stephen D. Kertesz. Notre Dame: University of Notre Dame Press, 1962, Pp. 64-94.

3235 Thalheim, Karl C. Eastern Germany. The Fate of East Central Europe: Hopes and Failures of American Foreign Policy. Ed. Stephen D. Kertesz. Notre Dame: University of Notre Dame Press, 1956, Pp. 150-178.

3236 Thomas, Stefan. Beyond the Wall. Survey. No. 44-45 (October 1962), 54-65.

3237 Tortora, Vincent R. Communist Close-Up: A Roving Reporter Behind the Iron Curtain. New York: Exposition, 1954, 160 P.

3238 Ulbricht, Walter. Address, 18 August 1961. Berlin (East): N.P., 1961, 29 P.

3239 Ulbricht, Walter. The Historic Task of the German Democratic Republic and the Future of Germany. Berlin (East): League of the GDR for Friendship Among the Peoples, 1962, 63 P.

3240 Ulbricht, Walter. The Historical Task of the GDR and the Future of Germany. World Marxist Review: Problems of Peace and Socialism. 5:7 (July 1962), 2-7.

3241 Ulbricht, Walter. Programmatic Statement: A Reply to the Urgent Problems of Our Day and the Vital Questions of the German People. Berlin (East): N.P., C.1960, 23 P.

3242 Vincent, Jean-Marie. East Germany Between Past and Future. The Socialist Register, 1965. Ed. Ralph Miliband and John Saville. New York: Monthly Review Press, 1965, Pp. 45-61.

3243 Wechsberg, Joseph. Journey Through the Land of Eloquent Silence. Boston: Little, Brown, 1964, 146 P.

3244 Wiking, Paula. The Changing Germans. London: Lincolns-Prager, 1956, 138 P.

3245 Young, Edgar P. East Germany Revisited. Contemporary Review. 188:1075 (July 1955), 19-23.

G.4.4. Since 1967

3246 Axen, Hermann. 20 Years German Democratic Republic. German Foreign Policy (GDR). 9:1 (1970), 3-17.

3247 Baylis, Thomas A. East Germany--in Quest of Legitimacy. Problems of Communism. 21:2 (March-April 1972), 46-55.

3248 Bender, Peter. The Special Case of East Germany. Studies in Comparative Communism. 2:2 (April 1969), 14-33.

3249 Bittner, Horst. The German Democratic Republic--A State of Peace and Socialism. International Affairs (Moscow). (June 1970), 31-37.

3250 Black, Hilary. Honecker's First Year. World Today. 28:6 (June 1972), 235-239.

3251 Bleimann, Robert. Detente and the GDR: The Internal Implications. The World Today. 29:6 (June 1973), 257-265.

3252 Cattani, Alfred. The Cult of Tradition in the GDR. Swiss Review of World Affairs. 18:8 (November 1968), 5-7.

3253 Cattani, Alfred. The German Democratic Republic in Self-Isolation. Swiss Review of World Affairs. 18:7 (October 1968), 10-12.

3254 Childs, David. East Germany. New York: Praeger, 1969, 275 P.

3255 Childs, David. East Germany: Towards the Twentieth Anniversary. World Today. 25:10 (October 1969), 440-450.

3256 Croan, Melvin. After Ulbricht: The End of an Era?. Survey. 17:2 (Spring 1971), 74-92.

3257 Croan, Melvin. East Germany. The Communist States in Disarray, 1965-1971. Ed. Adam Bromke and Teresa Rakowska-Harmstone. Minneapolis: University of Minnesota Press, 1972, Pp. 73-94.

3258 Difficult Years Bear Fruit: The Birth and Development of The German Democratic Republic. Dresden: Zeit Im Bild, 1972, 189 P.

3259 Dornberg, John. The Other Germany. Garden City: Doubleday, 1968, 370 P.

3260 GDR. State and Society. Dresden: Zeit Im Bild, 1968, 63 P.

3261 GDR, State Secretariat for West German Affairs. Democracy in the GDR: Power Relations and Social Forms in The Socialist State of the German Nation. Dresden: Zeit Im Bild, 1968, 57 P.

3262 The GDR, an Anti-Fascist State. Dresden: Zeit Im Bild, 1969, 78 P.

3263 Hahn, Gerhard. Bollinger, Klaus. Viii. Congress of the Socialist Unity Party--Source of Further Progress. German Foreign Policy (GDR). 10:5 (1971), 371-377.

3264 Hanhardt, Arthur M., Jr. The German Democratic Republic. Baltimore: Johns Hopkins, 1968, 126 P.

3265 Hess, Peter. The East Germans and Their State. Swiss Review of World Affairs. 20:6 (September 1970), 4-5.

3266 Holm, Hans Axel. The Other Germans: Report From an East German Town. New York: Pantheon, 1970, 314 P.

3267 Homann, Heinrich. The 25Th Anniversary of May 8, 1945. German Foreign Policy (GDR). 9:4 (1970), 255-263.

3268 Inside East Germany: A Refugee's Report. New York Times Magazine. (22 August 1954), 10+.

3269 Institute for the Sciences of Society, Berlin. The Full-Scale Development of Socialism in the German Democratic Republic. Dresden: Zeit Im Bild, for Institut Fuer Gesellschaftswissenschaften, 1969, 91 P.

3270 Kanzig, Helga. Reissig, Karl. Prospects of Socialism in the GDR. German Foreign Policy (GDR). 8:5 (1969), 341-355.

3271 Karau, Guenter. Democracy in the GDR: Power Relations and Social Forms in The Socialist State of German Nation. Dresden: Zeit Im Bild, 1968, 57 P.

3272 Khvostov, V. M. Historic Significance of the German Democratic Republic. International Affairs (Moscow). (December 1966), 56-62.

3273 Kozlowski, E. The GDR--20 Years After. Poland and Germany. 14:1-2 (January-June 1970), 8-16.

3274 Lamberg, Werner. GDR on Threshold of 20Th Anniversary. World Marxist Review: Problems of Peace and Socialism. 12:5 (May 1969), 28-33.

3275 Ludz, Peter Christian. Continuity and Change Since Ulbricht. Problems of Communism. 21:2 (March-April 1972), 56-67.

3276 Ludz, Peter Christian. Discovery and "Recognition" of East Germany: Recent Literature on the GDR. Comparative Politics. 2:4 (July 1970), 681-692.

3277 Ludz, Peter Christian. The German Democratic Republic From the Sixties to the Seventies: A Sociopolitical Analysis. Cambridge: Harvard University, Center for International Affairs, 1970, 100 P.

3278 Lumer, Bob. A Culture of the People--The German Democratic Republic Builds for the Future. New World Review. 35:8 (August-September 1967), 34-37.

3279 Muhlberg, Dietrich. Humanist Traditions in Contemporary Socialist Society. United Asia. 21:5 (September-October 1969), 267-271.

3280 Possony, Stefan T. Germany: German Democratic Republic. Yearbook on International Communist Affairs, 1973. Ed. Richard F. Staar. Stanford: Hoover Institution Press, 1973, Pp. 22-35.

3281 Schmitt, Hans A. Men and Politics in East Germany. Current History. 52:308 (April 1967), 232-237.

3282 Schwarze, Hanns Werner. The GDR Today: Life in the "Other" Germany. London: Wolff, 1973, 128 P.

3283 Seifert, Karl Dieter. Twenty Years German Democratic Republic: The Achievement of the First German Workers and Farmers State. Dresden: Verlag Zeit Im Bild, 1969, 62 P.

3284 Shanor, Donald R. Soviet Europe. New York: Harper & Row, 1975, X and 252 P. Esp. Pp. 41-70.

3285 Smith, Jean Edward. Germany Beyond the Wall: People, Politics and Prosperity. Boston and Toronto: Little, Brown, 1969, 338 P.

3286 Smith, Jean Edward. Red Prussianism of the German Democratic Republic. Bulletin of the Atomic Scientists. 23:5 (May 1967), 24-30.

3287 Smith, Jean Edward. The Red Prussianism of the German Democratic Republic. Political Science Quarterly. 82:3 (September 1967), 368-385.

3288 Socialist Unity Party of Germany,

Central Committee. Report of the Central Committee to the Eighth Congress of The Sed. Dresden: Zeit Im Bild, 1971, 71 P.

3289 Socialist Unity Party of Germany, Central Committee. Report of the Central Committee to the 7Th Party Congress of the Socialist Unity Party of Germany, 1967. Dresden: Zeit Im Bild, 1967, 149 P.

3290 Spittmann, Ilse. East Germany: The Swinging Pendulum. Problems of Communism. 16:4 (July-August 1967), 14-20.

3291 Starrels, John Murry. Mallinckrodt, Anita M. Politics in the German Democratic Republic. New York: Praeger, 1975.

3292 Sylvester, Anthony. The Other Side of the Wall. East Europe. 16:6 (June 1967), 3-7.

3293 Ulbricht, Walter. 1968--Year of Important Decisions: New Year's Message. Dresden: Zeit Im Bild, 1968, 15 P.

3294 Ulbricht, Walter. on Questions of Socialist Construction in the GDR. Dresden: Zeit Im Bild, 1968, 708 P.

3295 Ulbricht, Walter. Opening Address. Dresden: Zeit Im Bild, 1971, 11 P. Before the 8Th Congress of the Sed.

3296 Ulbricht, Walter. The Role of the Socialist State in the Shaping of the Developed Social System of Socialism. Dresden: Zeit Im Bild, 1968, 28 P.

3297 Ulbricht, Walter. With Confidence, Optimism and Fresh Energy We Enter the Year of the 20Th Anniversary of the German Democratic Republic. Dresden: Zeit Im Bild, 1969, 22 P.

3298 Ulbricht, Walter. With Confidence and Optimism We Enter the 1970's: New Year's Message. Dresden: Zeit Im Bild, 1970, 15 P.

3299 Verner, Paul. Socialist Unity Party Congress. World Marxist Review: Problems of Peace and Socialism. 14:9 (September 1971), 14-21.

3300 Wiesenthal, Simon. The Same Language: First for Hitler, Now for Ulbricht. Born: Deutschland-Berichte, 1968, 65 P.

3301 Winnington, Alan. GDR--Twenty Years. Labour Monthly. 51 (October 1969), 471-473.

H. FRG-GDR: Political Comparisons

H.1. General

3302 Baerwald, Friedrich. Democracy German-Style--A Comparative Study. German Tribune Quarterly Review. No. 14 (29 April 1971), 5-8.

3303 Conant, James Bryant. Freedom and Slavery in a Divided Germany. Department of State Bulletin. 34:876 (9 April 1956), 583-588.

3304 Dahrendorf, Ralf. The New Germanies: Restoration, Revolution, Reconstruction. Encounter. 22:4 (April 1964), 50-52, 54-58.

3305 Dornberg, John. Schizophrenic Germany. New York: Macmillan, 1961, 302 P.

3306 Dornberg, John. The Two Germanys. New York: Dial Press, 1974, 215 P.

3307 Dowling, Walter C. Germany Divided: The Confrontation of Two Ways of Life. Department of State Bulletin. 44:1139 (24 April 1961), 588-591.

3308 F.A.V. The Two Germanies. British Survey. No. 43 (October 1952), 1-18.

3309 Hall, Martin. Germany, East and West--Danger at the Crossroads. New World Review. 35:5 (May 1967), 12-19.

3310 Hanley, Charles. The Two Germanies. Fourth International. 10:9 (October 1949), 270-274.

3311 Holbrook, Sabra. Germany: East and West. New York: Meredith, 1968, 241 P.

3312 Joesten, Joachim. Over the Great Divide. Antioch Review. 12:1 (March 1952), 47-56. on the Border Between East and West Germany.

3313 Lesser, Jonas. The Two Germanies Once Again. Contemporary Review. 184:1053 (September 1953), 155-157.

3314 Mcclellan, Grant S., Editor. The Two Germanies. New York: Wilson, Reference Shelf, Vol. 31, No. 1, 1959, 184 P.

3315 Neuse, Werner. Post-War Germany and the Teacher of German Today. German Quarterly. 28:4 (November 1955), 237-246.

3316 Newman, Bernard. The Three Germanies. London: Hale, 1957, 251 P.

3317 Payne, J. P. Germany Today: Introductory Studies. London: Methuen, 1971, 183 P.

3318 Pittman, Margrit. The Two Germanys Celebrate Their Twentieth Anniversary. New World Review. 37:3 (1969), 52-56.

3319 Roedel, Werner. From Germany to Germany; a Documentation. Dresden: Zeit Im Bild, 1965, 47 P.

3320 Schaffer, Gordon. Germany--The Threat and the Peaceful Alternative. London: British Peace Committee, 1954, 16 P.

3321 Schleck, Robert W. Germany's Political Future. Germany: Promise and Perils. Ed. Sigmund Neumann. New York: Foreign Policy Association, Headline Series No. 82, July-August 1950, Pp. 55-62.

3322 Taylor, Ronald. Germany--East and West. Contemporary Review. 212:1227 (April 1968), 199-202.

3323 Voigt, Fritz A. The Two Germanies. Quarterly Review. 291:595 (January 1953), 105-119.

3324 Wansbrough-Jones, Ll. Germany Today. Journal of the Royal United Service Institution. 96:581 (February 1951), 15-28.

3325 Werner, Max. Notes on a Divided Germany. Monthly Review. 1:7 (November 1949), 207-213.

3326 Wightman, Margaret. The Faces of Germany. London: Harrap, 1971, 288 P.

H.2. Political Structures and Processes

3327 Cruikshanks, Randal L. The Recruitment of Political Elites in West and East Germany: A Comparative Analysis. Ph.D. Thesis, University of Oregon, 1968, 183 P.

3328 GDR, Committee for German Unity. The Leaders of the Two German States: A Contrast. Berlin: Committee for German Unity, 1961, 52 P.

3329 Hancock, M. Donald. The Bundeswehr and the National Peoples Army: A Comparative Study of German Civil-Military Policy. Denver: University of Denver, Monograph Series in World Affairs No. 10:2, 1973, 44 P.

3330 Hanf, Kenneth I. Administrative Developments in East and West Germany: Stirrings of Reform. Political Studies. 21:1 (March 1973), 35-44.

3331 Hanhardt, Arthur M., Jr. Cruikshanks,

Randal L. Legislative Representatives and Social Change: Reichstag, Bundestag and Volkskammer. Political Science Review. 8:2 (April-June 1969), 245-254.

3332 Nelsor, Walter Henry. Germany Rearmed. New York: Simon and Schuster, 1972, 354 P. East and West.

3333 Reimann, Max. Socialism in the GDR and the Federal Republic. German Foreign Policy (GDR). 8:5 (1969), 356-366.

3334 UK, Foreign Office. Memorandum on Germany. London: H.M. Stationery Office, Cmd. 9213, 1954, 7 P. Comparative Strengths and Amounts of Police Forces in GDR and FRG; Preparatory Planning for FRG Membership in Edc.

3335 Wolfe, James H. Corporatism in German Political Life: Functional Representation in the GDR and Bavaria. Politics in Europe: Structures and Processes in Some Postindustrial Democracies. Ed. Martin C. Heisler. New York: David Mackay Company, 1974, Pp. 323-340.

H.3. Legal Systems

3336 Allison, Richard C. The Carl Zeiss Case. International Lawyer. 3:3 (April 1969), 525-535.

3337 Bernstein, Herbert L. Corporate Identity in International Business: The Zeiss Controversy. American Journal of Comparative Law. 20:2 (Spring 1972), 299-313.

3338 Cohn, Ernst J. German Legal Science Today. International and Comparative Law Quarterly. 2:2 (April 1953), 169-191.

3339 Contrasting Constitutions in Germany. World Today. 5:11 (November 1949), 486-495.

3340 Holborn, Louise W., Editor. Carter, Gwendolen M., Editor. Herz, John H., Editor. German Constitutional Documents Since 1871: Selected Texts and Commentary. New York: Praeger, 1970, 243 P.

3341 Hurter, Edwin. The Zeiss Story. Swiss Review of World Affairs. 7:1 (April 1957), 11-12.

3342 Janicki, Lech. The Territory and State Citizenship in the Legal Systems of The German Democratic Republic and the German Federal Republic. Polish Western Affairs. 12:1 (1971), 44-86.

3343 Kassube, Ruth. Women's Rights in Both German States. German Foreign Policy (GDR). 4:3 (1965), 198-208.

3344 Markovits, Inga S. Marriage and the State: A Comparative Look at East and West German Family Law. Stanford Law Review. 24:1 (November 1971), 116-199.

3345 Peck, Joachim. Two German States--Two German Constitutions. Dresden: Zeit Im Bild, 1968, 46 P.

3346 Schlesinger, Rudolf B. Western Germany: Recognition and Enforcement of Soviet Zone Criminal Judgments. American Journal of Comparative Law. 2:3 (Summer 1953), 392-399.

3347 Toeplitz, Heinrich. Two German States--Two Concepts of the Penal Code. German Foreign Policy (GDR). 2:2 (1963), 101-111.

I. FRG: Economic System

I.1. Data and Models

I.1.1. Economic Statistics

3348 Arndt, Klaus Dieter. Quarterly National Accounts in Western Germany. Income and Wealth, Series Xi: Studies in Short-Term National Accounts and Long-Term Economic Growth. Ed. Simon Goldberg and Phyllis Deane. London: Bowes & Bowes, 1965, Pp. 213-229.

3349 Bartels, H. Hanisch, G. Lackner, W. Input-Output Tables. Stuttgart: Kohlhammer, 1968, 26 P.

3350 Behrendt, Guenther. Ownership Policy in the Federal Republic of Germany. German Economic Review. 3:4 (1965), 281-289.

3351 Brechling, Frank R. P. Inflation in the United Kingdom and Western Germany (1950-1956): A Comparative Study of Prices, Wages, Labour Productivity, and Profits. Bankers Magazine. 184:1365 (December 1957), 442-451.

3352 Brems, Hans J. Wages, Prices, and Profits in a Macroeconomic Model, Illustrated by German Data. Weltwirtschaftliches Archiv. 89:2 (March 1962), 180-207.

3353 The Business Cycle in West Germany, 1950-1969. London: Econtel Research, 1970, 20 P.

3354 Dewhurst, J. Frederic, Et Al. Europe's Needs and Resources: Trends and Prospects in Eighteen Countries. New York: Twentieth Century Fund, 1961, 1198 P.

3355 Dolgilevich, R. Krasnopolsky, V. F.R.G.: Negative Economic Indicators. International Affairs (Moscow). (December 1967), 109-113.

3356 Economic Growth and Productivity in the U.S., Canada, United Kingdom, Germany and Japan in the Post-War Period. Review of Economic and Statistics. 46:1 (Febrary 1964), 33-40.

3357 FRG, Federal Ministry of Economics. Achievement in Figures. Bonn: Federal Ministry of Economics, Annual, 1949+.

3358 FRG, Federal Statistical Office. International Comparison of Consumer Prices. Stuttgart: Kohlhammer, 1970, 14 P.

3359 FRG, Federal Statistical Office. Seasonal and Other Recurrent Influences on Short-Term Economic Indicators. Stuttgart: Kohlhammer, 1958, 14 P.

3360 FRG, Federal Statistical Office. The Statistical Unit in Economic Statistics. Stuttgart: Kohlhammer, 1958, 34 P.

3361 German Industrial Institute. The West German Economy: A Handy Guide to Facts and Figures. Cologne: Deutsches Industrieinstitut, 2D Rev. Ed., C.1961, 826 P.

3362 Gilbert, Milton. Kravis, Irving B. An International Comparison of National Products and the Purchasing Power of Currencies: A Study of the United States, the United Kingdom, France, Germany and Italy. Paris: Organization for European Economic Cooperation, 1953, 204 P.

3363 Goeseke, Gerhard. The Effects of Redistribution on Size Distribution of Personal Income and Household Net Income in Germany in 1955 and 1959. Income and Wealth, Series X: Income Redistribution and the Statistical Foundations of Economic Policy. Ed. Colin Clark and Geer Stuvel. London: Bowes & Bowes, 1964, Pp. 220-247.

3364 Halbach, Guenter. Incentives to Personal Saving and Investment in the Federal Republic of Germany. International Labour Review. 87:2 (February 1963), 91-117.

3365 Helmstaedter, Ernst. The Trend of Income Distribution in the Federal

Republic of Germany, From the Standpoint of Distribution Theory. German Economic Review. 5:4 (1967), 278-292.

3366 Kuhlo, Karl Christian. Bases for Analysis of Growth. German Economic Review. 2:4 (1964), 289-297.

3367 Mendershausen, Horst. Prices, Money and the Distribution of Goods in Postwar Germany. American Economic Review. 39:3 (June 1949), 646-672.

3368 National Accounting Practice in the German Federal Republic: a Summary. Income and Wealth, Series X: Income Redistribution and the Statistical Foundations of Economic Planning. Ed. Colin Clark and Geer Stuvel. London: Bowes and Bowes, 1964, Pp. 337-345.

3369 Oecd. National Accounts of Oecd Countries, 1962-1973. Paris: Organization for Economic Cooperation and Development, April 1975, Vol. 1, 214 Pp.

3370 Roskamp, Karl W. Fiscal Policy and Effects of Government Purchases: An Input-Output Analysis. Public Finance. 24:1 (1969), 33-43.

3371 Schnitzer, Martin. Income Distribution: A Comparative Study of the U.S., Japan, Sweden, West Germany, the U.K. and East Germany. New York: Praeger, 1973.

3372 Schnitzer, Martin. Income Distribution: A Comparative Study of the United States, Sweden, West Germany, East Germany, the United Kingdom, and Japan. New York: Praeger, 1974, 254 P.

3373 Schreiber, Wilfrid. On Two Topical Questions of Distribution Theory and Policy. German Economic Review. 7:3 (1969), 199-215.

3374 US, Economic Cooperation Administration. Country Data Book: Germany (Fed. Rep.). Washington: Economic Cooperation Administration, Government Printing Office, March 1950, 78 P.

3375 US, Embassy. Handbook of Economic Statistics, Federal Republic of Germany and Western Sectors of Berlin. Bonn-Bad Godesberg: American Embassy, Quarterly, 1955+.

3376 US, Omgus, Manpower Division. Incomes and Expenditures of Workers' Families in Urban Areas of American-Occupied Germany. Berlin: Omgus, Manpower Division, Wages and Labor Standards Branch, 1946, 13 P.

I.1.2. Econometric Models

3377 Albach, Horst. Simulation Models of Firm Growth. German Economic Review. 5:1 (1967), 1-26.

3378 Gollnick, Heinz. Butter Demand and Inventories. Econometrica. 25:3 (July 1957), 393-422.

3379 Mintz, Ilse S. Dating Postwar Business Cycles: Methods and Their Application to Western Germany, 1950-1967. New York: Columbia University Press, 1969, 111 P.

3380 Muth, Wilfried Robert. An Econometric Model to Evaluate Monetary and Fiscal Policies in Germany. Ph.D. Thesis, Southern Methodist University, 1973, 475 P.

3381 Panic, M. Gross Fixed Capital Formation and Economic Growth in the United Kingdom and West Germany, 1954-1964. Bulletin of the Oxford Institute of Economics and Statistics. 29:4 (November 1967), 395-406.

3382 Van Der Werf, Dirk. The Economy of the Federal Republic of Germany in Fifteen Equations. German Economic Review. 10:3 (1972), 216-232.

I.1.3. Forecasting

3383 Balogh, Thomas. Productivity and Inflation. Oxford Economic Papers. 10:2 (June 1958), 220-245.

3384 The Economic Situation of the FRG. Intereconomics. No. 12 (December 1971), 389-390.

3385 Eppler, Erhard. Chance and Obligation for Germany. Intereconomics. No. 9 (September 1969), 276-280.

3386 FRG. Report on the Economic Situation and Its Possible Future Development Up to 1952-53. Bonn: N.P., 1951.

3387 FRG, Federal Ministry for the Marshall Plan. Western Germany's Special Situation at the Beginning of 1950: Survey and Forecast. Bonn: Federal Ministry for the Marshall Plan, 1950, 24 P.

3388 Federal Republic: in the Latter Phase of a Boom. Intereconomics. No. 6 (June 1970), 199-200.

3389 Moehring, Dieter. Business Prospects in Germany. Intereconomics. No. 9 (September 1971), 264-267.

3390 Oecd. Oecd Economic Surveys: Germany. Paris: Organisation for Economic Cooperation and Development, Annual, 1953+. Originally Published By Oeec With Title "Economic Conditions in the Federal Republic of Germany".

3391 Predoehl, Andreas. An Economic Crisis?--Stimulating Forces Still Strong Enough. Intereconomics. No. 10 (October 1966), 16-17.

3392 Sanderson, Fred H. Germany's Economic Situation and Prospects. The Struggle for Democracy in Germany. Ed. Gabriel A. Almond. Chapel Hill: University of North Carolina Press, 1949, Pp. 111-184.

3393 Schiller, Karl. Germany's Economic Requirements. Foreign Affairs. 43:4 (July 1965), 671-681.

3394 Schiller, Karl. An Optimistic Look at the Year 1968. Intereconomics. No. 1 (January 1968), 6-8.

3395 Schmahl, Hans-Juergen. German Economy Not Imperilled. Intereconomics. No. 12 (December 1969), 377-378.

3396 Stolper, Wolfgang F. The Long Term Economic Development of Germany. Weltwirtschaftliches Archiv. 103:2 (1969), 57-61.

I.2. Occupation Controls, 1945-48 (See Also D.3)

I.2.1. Allied Economic Policy

3397 Agranat, Leon. Price Control in Germany. Ph.D. Thesis, University of Nebraska, 1951.

3398 Backer, John H. Priming the German Economy: American Occupational Policies, 1945-1948. Durham: Duke University Press, 1971, 212 P.

3399 Backer, John H. Priming the German Economy: American Occupational Policies, 1945-1948. Ph.D. Thesis, Columbia University, 1972.

3400 Balabkins, Nicholas. Direct Controls in West Germany: 1945-1948. World Affairs Quarterly. 30:4 (January 1960), 314-331.

3401 Balabkins, Nicholas. Direct Controls of West German Economy From Surrender (1945) to Currency Reform (1948), With Special Reference to American Policies. Ph.D. Thesis, Rutgers University, 1957, 286 P.

3402 Balabkins, Nicholas. Germany Under

Direct Controls: Economic Aspects of Industrial Disarmament, 1945-1948. New Brunswick: Rutgers University Press, 1964, 265 P.

3403 Balabkins, Nicholas. The Interdependence of Industry and Agriculture: West Germany, 1945-1948. Zeitschrift Fuer Die Gesamte Staatswissenschaft. 119:1 (January 1963), 118-129.

3404 Balabkins, Nicholas. Repressed Inflation in West Germany From 1945 to 1948: Some Qualitative Observations. Kyklos. 15:4 (1962), 734-757.

3405 Bizonal Economic Area, Administrative Council. 1948-1949 Plan for Economic Reconstruction of the German Bizonal Area. Frankfurt: Hoechst, 1948, 160 P.

3406 Carr, Robert A. How German Experts Aid Our Research. Army Information Digest. 4:10 (October 1949), 15-19.

3407 Central Banking Laws for American Zone of Germany. Federal Reserve Bulletin. 33:2 (February 1947), 130-135.

3408 Control of Foreign Exchange and the Movement of Property: Law No. 53. Department of State Bulletin. 22:548 (2 January 1950), 17-20.

3409 Dean, Vera Micheles. Allies Tighten Economic Controls in Germany. Foreign Policy Bulletin. 25:3 (2 November 1945), 1-3.

3410 Dean, Vera Micheles. U.S. Proposes Industrial and Land Reforms in Germany. Foreign Policy Bulletin. 25:50 (27 September 1946), 2-3.

3411 Former German Consumers' Co-Operation and Allied Zones. Review of International Cooperation. 38:7 (July 1945), 105-107.

3412 Glickman, David Lloyd. The Big Four in Germany: The Treatment of Germany as an Economic Unit. Washington: National Planning Association, Planning Pamphlet Nos. 54-55, 1947, 79 P.

3413 Hermberg, Paul G. The Revival of German Economy and the American Impact. American Review. 2:4 (March 1963), 146-166.

3414 Hillhouse, A. M. Budget Management. Governing Postwar Germany. Ed. Edward H. Litchfield and Associates. Ithaca: Cornell University Press, 1953, Pp. 307-325.

3415 Hoover, Herbert. The President's Economic Mission to Germany and Austria. N.P.: N.P., 1947, 3 Vols., 51 P.

3416 Jones, Howard Palfrey. Currency, Banking, Domestic and Foreign Debt. Governing Postwar Germany. Ed. Edward H. Litchfield and Associates. Ithaca: Cornell University Press, 1953, Pp. 419-438.

3417 Kuklick, Bruce R. American Foreign Economic Policy and Germany, 1939-1946. Ph.D. Thesis, University of Pennsylvania, 1968, 413 P.

3418 Landauer, Carl. United States Economic Policy Toward Germany. Journal of Modern History. 19:3 (September 1947), 239-253. Review of Recent Literature.

3419 Maynard, Peter. The U.S. Rebuilds German War Economy. New Central European Observer. 1:16 (11 December 1948), 154.

3420 Mott, Rodney L. Public Finance. Governing Postwar Germany. Ed. Edward H. Litchfield and Associates. Ithaca: Cornell University Press, 1953, Pp. 326-358.

3421 New Central Bank for United States and British Zones of Germany. Federal Reserve Bulletin. 34:3 (March 1948), 279-283. Establishment of Bank Deutscher Laender.

3422 Pines, Jerome M. United States Economic Policy Toward Germany, 1945-1949. Ph.D. Thesis, Columbia University, 1958, 373 P.

3423 Schiffman, Edward Gottlieb. The Food and Agriculture Policies and Programs of U.S. Military Government in Post-War Germany: Beginning of Occupation to 30 June 1949. Ph.D. Thesis, Harvard University, 1953.

3424 Settel, Arthur, Editor. A Year of Potsdam: The German Economy Since the Surrender. Washington: Department of War, Civil Affairs Division, 1946, 217 P.

3425 Szymczak, M. S. Our Stake in German Economic Recovery. Federal Reserve Bulletin. 33:6 (June 1947), 681-688.

3426 Szymczak, M. S. American Economic Policy in Germany. Washington, D.C.: Board of Governors of the Federal Reserve System, M. S. Szymczak, 1947, 9 P.

3427 US, Department of Commerce, Office of International Trade. US, Omgus, Office of Economic Adviser. Trading With Post-War Germany. Washington: Department of Commerce, Office of International Trade, International Reference Service, 5:31 (May 1948), 34 P.

3428 US, Department of Commerce, Office of Technical Services. Reports Resulting From the Investigation of German Technology, 1945-1946, and Index of Personnel. Washington: Department of Commerce, Office of Technical Services, 1947, 306 P.

3429 US, Department of State. United States Economic Policy Toward Germany. Washington: Department of State Publication 2630, Government Printing Office, 1946, 149 P.

3430 US, Department of State, Division of Research for Europe. The Effect of a Financial Reform on German Production and Domestic and Foreign Trade. Washington: Department of State, Division of Research for Europe, Oir Report No. 4390, 1947, 7 P.

3431 US, Omgus. Economic Policies, Programs and Requirements on Occupied Germany: Answers to Questions Submitted By Members of the Select Committee on Foreign Aid, House of Representatives. N.P.: Omgus, 1947, 177 P.

3432 US, Omgus. Military Government Report on Industrial Aspects of the Occupation of Germany. Washington: War Department, Pacific Relations Division, News Branch, Publications Section, 1946, 126 P.

3433 US, Omgus, Economics Division. Bizonal Level of Industry Plan. N.P.: Omgus, November 1947.

3434 US, Omgus, Economics Division. Economic Unification. N.P.: Omgus, November 1947.

3435 US, Omgus, Finance Division. Financial and Economic Aspects of the Export-Import Program in the Event of Tri- or Quadripartitite Economic Fusion. N.P.: Omgus, November 1947.

3436 US, Omgus, Joint Export-Import Agency (Jeia). Monthly Report of the Jeia. N.P.: Omgus, January 1947 to September 1949. Supplementary Reports By Country and Commodity From September 1948 to September 1949.

3437 US, Omgus, Military Governor. Status of the Banks in the U.S. Zone. Berlin: Omgus, April 1946.

3438 US, Omgus, Omg Hesse, Economics Division. An Account of Economic Progress in Land Greater Hesse, June 1946. Wiesbaden: Omg Greater Hesse, Economics Division, 1946, 57 and 36 P.

3439 US, Omgus, Omg Hesse, Economics Division. The Economy of Hesse, Postwar Pattern. N.P.: Omg Greater Hesse, Economics Division, c.1946.

3440 United States Steel Corporation. Recommendations for Increasing German Steel Production in Bizonia. New York?: United States Steel Corporation, 1948, 155 P.

3441 Wennberg, Samuel G. Some Economic Problems of Allied Occupation Policy in Germany. American Journal of Economics and Sociology. 5:4 (July 1946), 425-447.

I.2.2. Economic Disarmament

3442 A. D. War Damage in Germany: Economic Consequences and Allied Policy. World Today. 2:5 (May 1946), 197-206.

3443 Alexandrov, Vladimir. The Dismantling of German Industry. Soviet Economic Policy in Postwar Germany. Ed. Robert Slusser. New York: Research Program on the Ussr, 1953, Pp. 14-17.

3444 Alexandrov, Vladimir. Soviet Dismantling of Equipment in Postwar Germany. New York: Research Program on the Ussr, 1953, 28 P.

3445 Allied Control Authority, Directorate of Economics. Activities of the Directorate of Economics, 1945-1948. N.P.: Omgus, Adjutant General, August 1949, 262 P.

3446 Allied Control Authority, Directorate of Economics. The Future Level of German Industry: Memorandum By the U.S. Representative. N.P.: Allied Control Authority, Directorate of Economics, Level of Industry Committee, 1946, 42 P.

3447 Baldwin, Charles C. Germany's Major Industrial Combines. N.P.: Omgus, Economics Division, Decartelization Branch, 1948, 334 P.

3448 Baldy, Francis H. Chronological Record: Reorganization of the West German Coal and Iron and Steel Industries Under Allied High Commission Law No. 27. Bad Godesberg-Mehlem: Office of the U.S. High Commissioner for Germany, Historical Division, 1952, 260 P.

3449 Bar-Zohar, Michel. The Hunt for German Scientists. New York: Hawthorn, 1967, 207 P.

3450 Bergo (Pseud.). Germany Dismantled. Soundings. No. 9 (December 1947), 38-44.

3451 Bizonal Economic Area, Administration for Economics. Report on the Effect of Envisaged Dismantling on Germany's Economic Situation and Her Role in European Reconstruction. Frankfurt: Verwaltung Fuer Wirtschaft, 1948, 20 P.

3452 Cloe, Carl W. The German Coal Industry, 1936-46. Ph.D. Thesis, University of Iowa, 1947.

3453 Decartelization Law for United States Zone in Germany. Department of State Bulletin. 16:401 (9 March 1947), 443-447.

3454 Frank, Isaiah. American Policy Concerning German Monopolies, Cartels and Combines in the Occupied Areas. Washington: Department of State Publication 2889, Government Printing Office, 1947, 13 P.

3455 Gareau, Frederick H. A Critical Examination of United States Policy Toward German Industrial Disarmament (1943-1955). Ph.D. Thesis, American University, 1957, 386 P.

3456 Gareau, Frederick H. Morgenthau's Plan for Industrial Disarmament in Germany. Western Political Quarterly. 14:2 (June 1961), 517-534.

3457 Gillen, J. F. J. Deconcentration and Decartelization in West Germany, 1945-1953. Bad Godesberg-Mehlem: Office of the U.S. High Commissioner for Germany, Historical Division, 1953, 126 P.

3458 Gross, Hermann. Facts and Figures Relating to the Disintegration of the I.G. Farbenindustrie Ag. Kiel: N.P., 1949.

3459 Gross, Hermann. Further Facts and Figures Relating to the Deconcentration of the I.G. Farbenindustrie Ag. Kiel: N.P., 1950.

3460 Hasenack, Wilhelm. Dismantling in the Ruhr Valley. Cologne: Westdeutscher, 1949, 100 P.

3461 Kilgore, Harley M. Germany Is Not Yet Defeated. New York Times Magazine. (12 August 1945), 10+.

3462 Lasby, Clarence G. Project Paperclip: German Scientists and the Cold War. New York: Atheneum, 1971, 338 P.

3463 Lasby, Clarence G. Project Paperclip: German Scientists Come to America. Virginia Quarterly Review. 42:3 (Summer 1966), 366-377.

3464 Mcgill, V. J. Cartels and the Settlement With Germany. Science and Society. 9:1 (Winter 1945), 23-54.

3465 Olsen, Arthur J. Trackdown of the German Scientist. New York Times Magazine. (22 September 1963), 30+.

3466 Parry, Albert. Russia's Rockets and Missiles. Garden City: Doubleday, 1960, 382 P., Esp. Pp. 111-130.

3467 Remmert, Wilhelm, Editor. Law No. 56: Prohibition of Excessive Concentraton of German Economic Power. Frankfurt: Klostermann, 1947.

3468 The Revised Plan for the Level of Industry in the United States-United Kingdom Zone in Germany (29 August 1947). Current History. 13:74 (October 1947), 232-234.

3469 Schneider, Wolfgang. The Marshall Plan and the Dismantling of Industries in Western Germany. Frankfurt: Allmayer, 1949, 32 P.

3470 Sokolov, Valentin. Soviet Use of German Sciences and Technology, 1945-1946. New York: Research Program on the Ussr, 1955, 31 P.

3471 Spectator. Dismantling in Western Germany. Fortnightly. 166:993 (September 1949), 145-151.

3472 US, Committee to Review Decartelization Program in Germany. Report to the Honorable Secretary of the Army. Washington: U.S. Army, Civil Affairs Division, Committee to Review the Decartelization Program in Germany, 1949, 129 P.

3473 US, Foreign Economic Administration. A Program for German Economic and Industrial Disarmament. Washington: Government Printing Office, 1946, 660 P. Study Submitted By Fea (Enemy Branch) to Senate Committee on Military Affairs, Subcommittee on War Mobilization.

3474 US, Omgus, Economics Division. Activities of the I.G. Farbenindustrie Ag. N.P.: Omgus, June 1946, 3 Vols. Volumes on Dyestuffs, Nitrogen, and Oils.

3475 US, Omgus, Economics Division. Industrial Demilitarization. N.P.: Omgus, November 1947, 8 P.

3476 US, Omgus, Finance Division. Dresdner and Deutsche Banks. N.P.: Omgus, Adjutant General, 1947, 34 P.

3477 US, Omgus, Military Governor. Control of I.G. Farben. N.P.: Omgus, October 1945.

3478 US, Omgus, Military Governor. Explosives Industry--U.S. Zone. Berlin: Omgus, January 1946, 28 P.

3479 US, Omgus, Omg Bavaria, Industry Branch. Industries in Bavaria. Munich: Omg Bavaria, Industry Branch, 1945, 83 P.

3480 Zvegintzov, Michael. Security Control of German Economy. Control of Germany. Ed. Louis F. Aubert Et Al. Paris: Riviere, 1949, Pp. 71-80.

I.2.3. Reparations

3481 Bonn, Moritz J. The Potsdam Reparation Plan. World Affairs (London). 3:1 (January 1949), 10-22.

3482 The Bonn Agreement (23 November 1949). Current History. 18:101 (January 1950), 43-44. Revising Capital Reparations Program; Giving FRG Right to Build Ships of Specific Tonnage.

3483 Carr, Albert Z. How Much in Plant Shall Germany Pay?. New York Times Magazine. (7 December 1947), 14+.

3484 Cohen, Benjamin J. Reparations in the Postwar Period: A Survey. Banca Nazionale Del Lavoro, Quarterly Review (Rome). 20:82 (September 1967), 268-281.

3485 Cole, G. D. H. Reparations and the Future of German Industry. London: Fabian Publications and Gollancz, Research Series No. 19, 1945, 19 P.

3486 Comstock, Alzada. German Reparations: The Potsdam Plan. Current History. 9:49 (September 1945), 193-198.

3487 Dobb, Maurice. How Germany Must Pay. New Masses. 55:11 (June 1945), 3-5.

3488 Evans, Joseph E. The Unpayable Debt. This Is Germany. Ed. Arthur Settel. New York: Sloane, 1950, Pp. 249-267. Reparations.

3489 France, French Embassy, Information Service. A French Study of the Best Use of German Plants for the Purposes of European Recovery. New York: French Embassy, Information Service, 1948, 4 P.

3490 German Reparation Program. Current History. 16:93 (May 1949), 295-297.

3491 Ginsburg, David. The Future of German Reparations; an International Committee Report. Washington: National Planning Association, Planning Pamphlets No. 57/58, 1947, 80 P.

3492 Gottlieb, Manuel. The Reparations Problem Again. Canadian Journal of Economic and Political Science. 16:1 (February 1950), 22-41.

3493 Howard, John B. The Paris Agreement on Reparation From Germany. Department of State Bulletin. 14:363 (16 June 1946), 1023-1027.

3494 Inter-Allied Reparations Agency. World Today. 5:6 (June 1949), 266-276.

3495 Inter-Allied Reparations Agency. Inter-Allied Reparations Agency: Report to Its Member Governments. Brussels: Inter-Allied Reparations Agency, June 1951, 30 and 77 P.

3496 Iyengar, H. V. R. Reparations From Germany. India Quarterly. 2:2 (May 1946), 124-129.

3497 Kuklick, Bruce R. American Policy and the Division of Germany: The Clash With Russia Over Reparations. Ithaca: Cornell University Press, 1972, 286 P.

3498 Kuklick, Bruce. The Division of Germany and American Policy on Reparations. Western Political Quarterly. 23:2 (June 1970), 276-293.

3499 Landauer, Carl. The German Reparations Problem. Journal of Political Economy. 56:4 (August 1946), 344-347.

3500 Lindholm, Richard W. Debt and Democracy in Germany. American Journal of Economics and Sociology. 6:1 (October 1946), 87-93.

3501 Mansfield, Don Lee. The Evolution of United States Policy Toward German Reparations: An Examination of Incremental Decision-Making. Ph.D. Thesis, University of Denver, 1973, 484 P.

3502 Mende, Tibor. German Reparations. Fortnightly. 162:971 (November 1947), 332-337.

3503 Moses, Fritz. Shall Foreigners and Nazi Victims Pay for German War Damages? Allied Policy in Germany and the Proposed Equalization of Burdens Law. New York: Axis Victims League, 1951, 30 P.

3504 Nettl, Peter. German Reparations in the Soviet Empire. Foreign Affairs. 29:2 (January 1951), 300-307.

3505 Price, Coy H. Prospects for German Industry Under the Reparation Plan. Ph.D. Thesis, University of Virginia, 1947.

3506 Quaestor. German Reparations. Labour Monthly. 29:5 (May 1947), 146-148.

3507 Ratchford, Benjamin Ulysses. Ross, William D. Berlin Reparations Assignment: Round One of the German Peace Settlement. Chapel Hill: University of North Carolina Press, 1947, 259 P.

3508 Reparation From Germany: Final Act and Annex of the Paris Conference on Reparations. International Conciliation. 420 (April 1946), 215-238.

3509 Rubinstein, Aryeh. German Reparations in Retrospect. Midstream. 8:1 (Winter 1962), 29-42.

3510 Schwarz, R. P. Reparations and Politics. Fortnightly. 159:954 (June 1946), 365-372.

3511 The Story of German Reparations. New Central European Observer. 1:10 (18 September 1948), 98-99.

3512 Sulzbach, Walter. German Reparations. South Atlantic Quarterly. 45:3 (July 1946), 286-296.

3513 UK, CCG. The Plan for Reparations and the Level of Post-War German Economy, in Accordance With the Berlin Protocol. Berlin: Control Commission for Germany (Be), 1946, 35 P. Report of Tripartite Conference of Berlin, 2 August 1945.

3514 US, Department of State, Office of Research & Intelligence. The German Standard of Living and Industrial Capacity Available for Reparations. Washington: Department of State, Office of Research and Intelligence, Oir Report No. 3383, 1946, 125 P.

3515 US, Omgus, Economics Division. Progress of German Reparations. N.P.: Omgus, Adjutant General, 1947, 11 P.

3516 US, Omgus, Property Division. Three Years of Reparations: Progress of Reparations From Germany in the Form of Capital Industrial Equipment. N.P.: Omgus, Property Division, November 1948, 7 P.

3517 US, Omgus, Public Relations Service. The Plan for Reparations and the Level of Post-War German Economy in Accordance With the Berlin Protocol. Berlin: Omgus, Public Relations Service, Allied Control Authority, 1946, 17 P.

3518 United States Requests Withdrawal of Soviet Reparation Mission From American Zone in Germany. Department of State Bulletin. 20:506 (13 March 1949), 320-322. Exchange of Notes Between Ussr and US

I.2.4. Overseas Assets and External Debts

3519 Cohn, Ernst J. German Enemy Property. International Law Quarterly. 3:3 (July 1950), 391-407; 3:4 (October 1950), 530-551; and 4:1 (January 1951), 60-77.

3520 Comstock, Alzada. German Assets in Switzerland. Current History. 11:60 (August 1946), 89-93.

3521 Dernburg, H. J. Some Basic Aspects of the German Debt Settlement. Journal of Finance. 8:3 (September 1953), 298-318.

3522 Devries, Henry P. The International Responsibility of the United States for Vested German Assets. American Journal of International Law. 51:1 (January 1957), 18-28.

3523 Ferencz, Benjamin B. Taxation of United Nations Nationals Under the German Equalization of Burdens Law. American Journal of Comparative Law. 9:2 (Spring 1960), 262-267; and 11:1 (Winter 1962), 96-102.

3524 Financial Relations With Germany: Agreement for Validation of Dollar Bonds. Department of State Bulletin. 28:315 (9 March 1953), 376-380.

3525 Financial Relations With Germany: External Debt Settlement. Department of State Bulletin. 28:715 (9 March 1953), 373-375.

3526 Harris, Charles W. International Legal and Political Factors in the United States' Disposition of Alien Enemy Assets Seized During the World War II: A Case Study on German Assets. Ph.D. Thesis, University of Wisconsin, 1959, 399 P.

3527 Harris, Charles W. International Relations and the Disposition of Alien Enemy Property Seized By the United States During World War II: A Case Study on German Properties. Journal of Politics. 23:4 (November 1961), 641-666.

3528 Intergov'Tal Group on Safeguarding Foreign Interests in Ger. The Protection of Foreign Interests in Germany. Department of State Bulletin. 21:537 (17 October 1949), 573-584.

3529 International Conference on German External Debts, London. Memorandum on the German Capacity to Pay in Deutsche Marks. Bonn: FRG, Delegation From the Federal Republic of Germany, 1951, 84 P.

3530 International Conference on German External Debts, London. Report. Washington: Department of State Publication No. 4746, Government Printing Office, 1952, 59 P.

3531 Johnson, D. H. N. Case No. 1, Between the Swiss Confederation and the Federal Republic of Germany, Under the Arbitration Tribunal for the Agreement on German External Debts. British Year Book of International Law. 34 (1958), 363-368.

3532 Mann, F. A. German External Assets. British Year Book of International Law. 24 (1947), 239-257.

3533 Maurer, Ely. Simsarian, James. Agreement to Resolve Conflicting Claims to German Enemy Assets Outside Germany. American Journal of International Law. 42:1 (January 1948), 157-164.

3534 Milroy, Nicholas R. German Economic Penetration of Switzerland. Washington: Department of State, 1946.

3535 Nadelmann, Kurt H. Local Enemy Assets and the Paris Agreement on Reparations. American Journal of International Law. 40:4 (October 1947), 813-817.

3536 Simpson, John L. The Agreement on German External Debts. International and Comparative Law Quarterly. 6:3 (July 1957), 472-486.

3537 Simpson, John L. The Liquidation of German Assets in Neutral Countries. British Yearbook of International Law. 34 (1958), 374-384.

3538 Sommerich, Otto C. Treatment By United States of World War I and II Enemy-Owned Patents and Copyrights. American Journal of Comparative Law. 4:4 (Autumn 1955), 587-600.

3539 Southworth, Constant. Shall Enemy Property Be Returned? a Long-Term View. American Political Science Review. 40:1 (February 1946), 101-112.

3540 Tripartite Commission on German Debts. Agreement on German External Debts, 27Th February, 1953. London: H. M. Stationery Office, 1953, 120 P.

3541 UK, Foreign Office. German External Debts: Report of Conference. London: H.M. Stationery Office, Cmd. 8653, September 1952, 71 P.

3542 UK, Foreign Office. Report and Recommendations of the Inter-Governmental Group on the Safeguarding of Foreign Interests in Germany, Paris, October 25Th-November 10Th, 1948. London: H.M. Stationery Office, Cmd. 7850, 1949.

3543 US, Senate, Committee on Foreign Relations. Debt Agreements With the Federal Republic of Germany. Washington: Government Printing Office, 1953, 15 P.

I.3. General Developments and Problems (See Also K.1)

I.3.1. Occupation Period, 1945-48

3544 Bell, G. K. A. If Thine Enemy Hunger. London: Gollancz, 1946, 8 P. Sermon By the Bishop of Chichester.

3545 Brown, Lewis H. A Report on Germany. New York: Farrar and Straus, 1947, 247 P. Rehabilitation of German Industry.

3546 Burchardt, F. A. Martin, Kingsley. Western Germany and Reconstruction. Bulletin of the Oxford University Institute of Statistics. 9:12 (December 1947), 405-416.

3547 Gollancz, Victor. Leaving Them to Their Fate: The Ethics of Starvation. London: Gollancz, 1946, 48 P.

3548 H. D. W. The Feeding of Western Germany. World Today. 4:1 (January 1948), 25-40.

3549 Hadsel, Winifred N. Unification Alone Will Not Solve German Economic Problem. Foreign Policy Bulletin. 26:13 (10 January 1947), 2-3.

3550 Harkort, Guenther. Some Data on the German Standard of Living. World Affairs (London). 2:3 (July 1948), 271-283.

3551 Hirsch, Felix Edward. What Future for Germany? Grim Outlook for the Coming Winter. Current History. 13:74

(October 1947), 204-209.

3552 Hoover, Calvin B. Future of the German Economy. American Economic Review. 36:2 (May 1946), 642-649.

3553 Hoover, Calvin B. Germany and European Economic Recovery. Yale Review. 37:3 (Spring 1948), 385-399.

3554 International Chamber of Commerce. The Economic Condition of Germany Today and Its International Repercussions. Paris: International Chamber of Commerce, Brochure No. 123, 1947, 46 P.

3555 Johnson, Alvin. Hamburger, Ernest. The Economic Problem of Germany. Social Research. 13:2 (June 1946), 135-182.

3556 Keeling, Ralph F. Gruesome Harvest. Chicago: Institute of American Economics, 1947, 140 P.

3557 Lauterbach, Albert. The Future of German Finance. Journal of Politics. 7:4 (November 1945), 378-410.

3558 M. Z. The British Zone in Germany: An Economic Stock-Taking. World Today. 2:12 (December 1946), 567-580.

3559 Noth, Ernst Erich (Pseud. for Paul Krantz). Bridges Over the Rhine. New York: Holt, 1947, 317 P.

3560 Saltzman, Charles E. The Problem of German Recovery. Annals of the American Academy of Political and Social Science. 258 (July 1948), 74-78.

3561 Sandulescu, Jacques. Hunger's Rogues: on the Black Market in Europe, 1948. New York: Harcourt Brace Jovanovich, 1974, 280 P.

3562 Stamp, Maxwell. Germany Without Incentive. Lloyds Bank Review. No. 5 (July 1947), 14-28.

3563 Sternberg, Fritz. The Coming Crisis. London: Gollancz, 1947, 221 P. Economic Reconstruction.

3564 US, Omgus, Economics Division. Economic Data on Potsdam Germany. N.P.: Omgus, Adjutant General, September 1947, 90 P.

3565 Wells, W. T. The German Prospect. Fortnightly. 162:967 (July 1947), 32-34. Prospect for Economic Recovery and Unitary Constitution.

I.3.2. Currency Reform and Aftermath

3566 Authorization of Bank of the German States to Issue Notes and Coins. Federal Reserve Bulletin. 34:9 (September 1948), 1101-1102.

3567 Bennett, Jack. German Currency Reform. Annals of the American Academy of Political and Social Science. 267 (January 1950), 43-54.

3568 Bergo (Pseud.). Currency Reform in Western Germany: Economic Background to The Berlin Crisis. Soundings. No. 17 (August 1948), 19-26.

3569 The Berlin Currency Issue. Current History. 16:89 (January 1949), 37-40.

3570 Bluecher, Franz. Financial Situation and Currency Reform in Germany. Annals of the American Academy of Political and Social Science. 260 (November 1948), 63-73.

3571 Bonn, Moritz J. Currency Reform in Germany: Can Planners Plan?. Bankers' Magazine (London). 166:1254 (September 1948), 166-171.

3572 Bonn, Moritz J. Germany's Second Revolution. Fortnightly. 164:981 (September 1948), 141-147. The Currency Reform.

3573 Chambers, S. P. Post-War German Finances. International Affairs (London). 24:3 (July 1948), 364-376.

3574 Eucken, Walter. Meyer, Fritz W. The Economic Situation in Germany. Annals of the American Academy of Political and Social Science. 260 (November 1948), 53-62.

3575 Germany Revisited, Autumn 1948. Bankers' Magazine (London). 167:1259 (February 1949), 108-112.

3576 Kelber, Magda. Bizonia After Currency Reform. World Affairs (London). 2:4 (October 1948), 366-372.

3577 Klopstock, Fred H. Monetary Reform in Western Germany. Journal of Political Economy. 57:4 (August 1949), 277-292.

3578 Lutz, Friedrich A. The German Currency Reform and the Revival of the German Economy. Economica. 16:62 (May 1949), 122-142.

3579 Rand, H. P. The Constabulary Delivers the Money--The Currency Reform. Army Information Digest. 4:6 (June 1949), 30-32.

3580 Reinsch, Ruth H. Currency Reform and Reconstruction of the West German Economy, 1948-1949. Ph.D. Thesis, University of Kentucky, 1951.

3581 Sauermann, Heinz. Consequences of the Currency Reform in Western Germany. Review of Politics. 12:2 (April 1950), 175-196.

3582 US, Department of the Army, Civil Affairs Division. Tripartite Currency Reform in Western Germany: Background Summary. N.P.: Department of the Army, Civil Affairs Division, 1948, 23 P.

3583 US, Department of the Army, Public Information Division. First Law of Currency Reform: Law No. 61 (Currency Law). N.P.: Department of the Army, Public Information Division, Press Section, 1948, 10 P.

3584 US, Omgus, Military Governor. Economic Developments Since Currency Reform. N.P.: Omgus, Adjutant General, November 1948, 23 P.

3585 W. H. Western Germany After Currency Reform. World Today. 5:7 (July 1949), 310-320.

3586 The West German Currency Reform. New Central European Observer. 1:7 (7 August 1948), 74-75.

I.3.3. Marshall Plan Assistance

3587 Allied High Commission. Longterm Program (1952-53) for the United States and United Kingdom Occupied Areas in Germany: European Recovery Program. Bonn: Hicog, 1949, 66 P.

3588 Anderson, Graydon K. Some Economic Inferences Drawn From the Record of the European Recovery Program. Ph.D. Thesis, University of Wisconsin, 1953,

3589 Bidwell, Percy Wells. The European Economic Recovery Program: Its Nature and Purposes. Germany's Contribution to Economic Life. Ed. Percy Wells Bidwell. Paris: Riviere, 1949, Pp. 19-67.

3590 Bluecher, Franz. The Marshall Plan: Germany. International Markets. 9:4 (April 1955), 18-19.

3591 Brown, Lewis H. American Economic Policy Relating to Germany and Western Europe. Proceedings of the Academy of Political Science. 22:4 (January 1948), 439-450.

3592 Carlson, Howard K. Woodley, W. John R. Role of the Eca Program in Imports of the Participating Countries and in U.S. Exports. Imf Staff Papers. 1:1 (February 1950), 71-113.

3593 FRG, Federal Ministry for the Marshall Plan. Report of the German Federal Government on the Progress of The Marshall Plan. Bonn: Federal Ministry for the Marshall Plan, 12 Quarterly Reports, 1 October 1949 to 30 June 1952. Continued By Federal Ministry for Economic Cooperation as "Report of the German Federal Government on the Continuation Of the American Economic Aid (Foa)".

3594 FRG, Federal Ministry for the Marshall Plan. What Happened in Germany: A Preliminary Balance. Bonn: Federal Ministry for the Marshall Plan, 1951, 22 P.

3595 Galbraith, John Kenneth. America and Western Europe. Can Europe Unite? New York: Foreign Policy Association, Headline Series No. 80, 1950, 62 P.

3596 Galbraith, John Kenneth. America and Western Europe. New York: Public Affairs Committee, Public Affairs Pamphlet No. 159, 1950, 32 P.

3597 Ganzert, Frederic W. The Erp and Western Germany's International Relations. World Affairs. 113:2 (Summer 1950), 42-45.

3598 Hickman, Warren L. Genesis of the European Recovery Program: A Study on the Trend of American Economic Policies. Geneva: Imprimeries Populaires, 1949, 297 P.

3599 Hillmann, H. C. American Aid and the Recovery of Germany. American Review. 2:4 (March 1963), 124-145.

3600 Hutcheson, Harold H. Bizonal Plan Designed to Bolster Western Germany Under Erp. Foreign Policy Bulletin. 27:15 (23 January 1948), 1-2.

3601 Jones, Joseph M. The Fifteen Weeks (February 21-June 5, 1947). New York: Viking Press, 1955, 296 P.

3602 Joseph, J. J. The Failure of the Marshall Plan. Science & Society. 14:1 (Winter 1949-50), 29-57.

3603 Joseph, J. J. Trends in the Marshall Plan, Germany. Science & Society. 13:1 (Winter 1948-49), 17-21.

3604 Krivine, J. D. The European Recovery Program. Year Book of World Affairs. 6 (1950), 234-236.

3605 Marjolin, Robert. The Erp--Halfway to Victory. United Nations World. 4:4 (April 1950), 59-62.

3606 Mathy, Leonard G. The European Recovery Program. Proceedings of the Institute of World Affairs. 25 (December 1948), 61-68.

3607 Mayer, Herbert C. German Recovery and the Marshall Plan, 1948-1952. Bonn: Edition Atlantic Forum, 1969, 125 P.

3608 US, Economic Cooperation Administration. Western Germany: Country Study, European Recovery Program. Washington: Economic Cooperation Administration, 1949, 103 P.

3609 US, Hicog, Office of Economic Affairs. UK, Hicog, Office of the Economic Adviser. The European Recovery Program: US-UK Occupied Areas of Germany. N.P.: Hicog, Office of Economic Affairs, Reports Office, 1949.

3610 US, House, Select Committee on Foreign Aid. Report on Germany. Washington: House of Representatives, Select Committee on Foreign Aid, Subcommittee on Germany, on H. Res. 296, Government Printing Office, 1948, 38 P.

3611 Wyman, Louis C. Dollar Shortages and Communism: How Much of an Answer Is Erp?. American Bar Association Journal. 36:6 (June 1950), 451-454.

I.3.4. Economic Recovery, 1949-55

3612 Acheson, Dean G. A Two-Year Record of Recovery. Department of State Bulletin. 22:563 (17 April 1950), 589-590.

3613 Alt, Peter. Schneider, Max. West Germany's Economic Miracle. Science & Society. 26:1 (Winter 1962), 46-57.

3614 Baade, Fritz. Germany and the Long Term Program for European Reconstruction. Economia Internazionale. 3:1 (1950), 1-15.

3615 Bentwich, Norman D. Light and Shade in Western Germany. Fortnightly. 175:1046 (February 1954), 93-96.

3616 Bentwich, Norman D. Recovery in Western Germany. Contemporary Review. 178:1020 (December 1950), 334-337.

3617 Boarman, Patrick M. Ludwig Erhard's Achievement. Social Order. 9:5 (May 1959), 221-233.

3618 Burns, Arthur R. European Economic Recovery: Progress and Problems. Proceedings of the Academy of Political Science. 23:4 (January 1950), 346-358.

3619 Cahan, J. Flint. Recovery of German Exports. International Affairs (London). 26:2 (April 1950), 172-179.

3620 Cairncross, A. K. The Economic Recovery of Western Germany. Lloyds Bank Review. No. 22 (October 1951), 19-34.

3621 Davenport, John. New Chance in Germany. Fortune. (October 1949), 72-76. New Hope on Economic Front, Especially in Ruhr.

3622 Davin, Louis E. The Basic Facts of the West German Economy. Banque De Bruxelles Quarterly Survey. 1 (1952), 3-12.

3623 Economic and Financial Developments in Western Germany. Federal Reserve Bank of New York, Monthly Review of Credit and Business Conditions. 35:1 (January 1953), 8-11.

3624 The Economic Position of West Germany. Institute of International Finance Bulletin. No. 178 (7 October 1952), 2-46.

3625 The Economy of Federal Germany. Statist. 158:3824 (23 June 1951), 856-857, and 64-Page Supplement.

3626 Erhard, Ludwig. Germany's Reconstruction. Current History. 30:176 (April 1956), 201-205.

3627 Erhard, Ludwig. Prosperity Through Competition. New York: Praeger, 1958, 260 P.

3628 Galbraith, John Kenneth. European Recovery: The Longer View. Review of Politics. 12:2 (April 1950), 165-174.

3629 The German Economy. Economist. 165:5695 (18 October 1952), 205-212.

3630 Germany at Work: Economic Recovery From Defeat. Round Table. 44:174 (March 1954), 153-160.

3631 Germany's New Year. Economist. 158:5550 (7 January 1950), 7-9.

3632 Glaeser, Ernst. The Shady Miracle. London: Secker & Warburg, 1963, 287 P.

3633 Gottlieb, Manuel. The German Economic Potential. Social Research. 17:1 (March 1950), 65-89.

3634 Granger, G. B. Occupation Feeding. Editorial Research Reports. (6 April 1949), 237-250.

3635 Gross, Herbert. Western Germany's Economic Recovery. International

Markets. 7:4 (April 1953), 32-34.

3636 Hart, Merwin K. Renaissance in Germany. Economic Council Letter. No. 250 (1 November 1950), 1-4.

3637 Heller, Walter W. The Role of Fiscal-Monetary Policy in German Economic Recovery. American Economic Review. 40:2 (May 1950), 522-578.

3638 Hennessy, Jossleyn. The German "Miracle". Economic "Miracles": Studies in the Resurgence of the French, German and Italian Economies Since the Second World War. Ed. Jossleyn Hennessy, Vera Lutz, and Giuseppe Scimone. London: Deutsch, 1964, Pp. 1-73.

3639 Higher Production and Living Standards for Europe Reported. Department of State Bulletin. 22:550 (16 January 1950), 99-102.

3640 Hirsch, Felix Edward. Germany: Road to Recovery. Current History. 18:102 (February 1950), 88-92.

3641 Hirsch, Felix Edward. Germany's Economic Struggle. Current History. 20:118 (June 1951), 335-339.

3642 Hirshleifer, Jack. Disaster and Recovery: A Historical Survey. Santa Monica: Rand Corporation, Rm-3079-Pr, April 1963, 146 P.

3643 Hoover, Calvin B. Germany: The Economic Problem. Germany and the Future of Europe. Ed. Hans J. Morgenthau. Chicago: University of Chicago Press, 1951, Pp. 40-50.

3644 Hovde, Bryn J. The Economic and Social Crisis of Europe. Social Research. 16:3 (September 1949), 271-288.

3645 Hurter, Edwin. West Germany's Economy in 1952. Swiss Review of World Affairs. 2:11 (February 1953), 13-15.

3646 Janossy, Ferenc. The Economic Miracle in the Federal Republic of Germany. Eastern European Economics. 10:1-2 (Fall-Winter 1971-72), 36-54.

3647 Joesten, Joachim. The Bonn "Economic Miracle": A Survey and Analysis of Western Germany's Prodigious Recovery Since the Currency Reform. New York: Joachim Joesten, New Germany Reports No. 22, June 1953, 18 P.

3648 Kiel University, Institute for International Economics. Viability and Full Employment: A Contribution to the Task of Economic Reconstruction of Western Germany. Bonn: 1950, 48 P.

3649 Kindleberger, Charles P. Germany and the Economic Recovery of Europe. Proceedings of the Academy of Political Science. 23:3 (May 1949), 288-301.

3650 Luedicke, Heinz E., Editor. The Truth About the German Recovery "Miracle"-- Postwar Progress and Unresolved Problems. New York: Journal of Commerce, 1954, 40 P.

3651 Malinkowski, Wladyslaw. The Economic Outlook for Europe. How Can We the People Achieve a Just Peace: Selected Speeches. South Hadley: Mount Holyoke College, Institute on the United Nations, 1949, Pp. 84-93.

3652 Margolies, Daniel F. Economic Conditions and Political Forces. Germany and the Future of Europe. Ed. Hans J. Morgenthau. Chicago: University of Chicago Press, 1951, Pp. 51-57.

3653 Mendershausen, Horst. Two Postwar Recoveries of the German Economy. Amsterdam: North-Holland, 1955, 130 P.

3654 Mercado, Perla N. The Economic Revival of West Germany. Economic Research Journal (Philippines). 10:2 (September 1963), 65-72.

3655 Midgley, John. Reconstruction in Germany. Progress. 43:237 (Winter 1952-53), 6-11.

3656 Morgan, D. J. The Economy of Europe. Economica. 16:63 (August 1949), 255-262.

3657 Myrdal, Gunnar. Economic Commission for Europe: Proposals for the Future Work Program. United Nations Bulletin. 8:10 (15 May 1950), 422-427.

3658 Myrdal, Gunnar. Prescription for Europe's Sick Economy. United Nations World. 4:6 (June 1950), 28-30.

3659 National Association of Manufacturers. Western Germany: An Economic Appraisal. New York: National Association of Manufacturers of the United States of America, Economic Policy Division, Spring 1952, 44 P.

3660 New York, Committee on Nuclear Attack Recovery. Digest of West German Economic Recovery Through Social Free Economy. Albany: State of New York, 1962, 23 P. Also Issued as App. 3 of Committee's "Planning to Recover From Nuclear Attack".

3661 Royal Institute of International Affairs. Documents on European Recovery and Defense: March, 1947-April, 1949. Oxford: Oxford University Press, 1949, 150 P.

3662 Seligman, Harold. Economic Recovery in Western Germany. Ph.D. Thesis, Harvard University, 1962.

3663 Soloveytchik, George. How Sound Is German Recovery?. Banker. 103:346 (November 1954), 289-296.

3664 Sternberg, Fritz. Living With Crisis: The Battle Against Depression and War. New York: Day, 1949, 184 P., Esp. Pp. 47-98.

3665 Stone, William T. West German Recovery. Editorial Research Reports. (19 January 1954), 43-59.

3666 Struve, Walter. West Germany's Economic Miracle. Current History. 44:260 (April 1963), 231-236, 245.

3667 Tuchtfeldt, Egon. The Development of the West German Economy Since 1945. Hamburg: Claassen, 1955, 168 P.

3668 US, Hicog, Office of Economic Affairs. Annual Economic Review, 1951. Bonn: Hicog, Office of Economic Affairs, Commercial Attache Division, Economic Reports Branch, April 1952, 152 P.

3669 Wallich, Henry C. The "German Miracle". Yale Review. 44:4 (June 1955), 501-519.

3670 Wallich, Henry C. Mainsprings of the German Revival. New Haven: Yale University Press, 1955, 401 P.

3671 Weir, Cecil. Economic Developments in Western Germany. International Affairs (London). 25:3 (July 1949), 249-256.

3672 Woischnik, Bernhard. Gateway to Germany. Bonn: Verlag Fuer Publizistik, for Federal Ministry for Economic Cooperation, Rev. Ed., 1954, 72 P.

3673 Wright, David M. Post-War West German and United Kingdom Recovery. Washington: American Enterprise Association, 1957, 27 P.

I.3.5. Prosperity, 1955-

3674 Bailey, George. West Germany's Economic Romantics. Reporter. 33:5 (23 September 1965), 37-41.

3675 Boenisch, Alfred. Topical Problems of Social and Economic Conceptions in Capitalism. German Foreign Policy (GDR). 10:2 (1971), 139-162. Especially SPD Views.

3676 Braunthal, Gerard. The Death of the German Economic Miracle. Current History. 54:321 (May 1968), 275-280.

3677 Business International S. A. Germany in the Seventies. Geneva: Business International S. A., Research Report No. 73-4, 1973, 141 P.

3678 Chester, T. E. West Germany--A Social Market Economy. Three Banks Review. No. 92 (December 1971), 33-46.

3679 Erhard, Ludwig. Building the Dynamic Society. Atlantic Community Quarterly. 3:3 (Fall 1965), 392-394.

3680 Erhard, Ludwig. The Economics of Success. Princeton: Van Nostrand, 1963, 412 P.

3681 Erhard, Ludwig. Germany's Economic Goals. Foreign Affairs. 36:4 (July 1958), 611-617.

3682 Falkenhausen, Bernhard Freiherr Von. Profitless Prosperity in Germany. World Banking. (December 1962), 83-85.

3683 Federal Republic of Germany. International Economic Survey (Chemical Corn Exchange Bank).No. 126 (April 1959), 1-11.

3684 Gerber, William. West German Prosperity. Editorial Research Reports. (29 January 1969), 65-82.

3685 The German Lesson. Economist. 221:6425 (15 October 1966) 32 P. (Following P. 270). Implications for UK of FRG's Recent Economic Experience.

3686 Groener, Helmut. Warnings of the Council of Experts on the Economic Situation in the Federal Republic of Germany. German Economic Review. 11:3 (1973), 261-272.

3687 Hallett, Graham. The Social Economy of West Germany. New York: St. Martin's Press, 1973, X and 150 P.

3688 Hallett, Graham. The West German Recession of 1966-1967 and Its Aftermath. Loughborough Journal of Social Studies. No. 5 (June 1968), 23-34.

3689 Kloten, Norbert. Vollmer, Rainer. Stability, Growth and Economic Policy. German Economic Review. 13:2 (1975), 97-116.

3690 Krengel, Rolf. Some Reasons for the Rapid Economic Growth of the German Federal Reupublic. Banca Nazionale Del Lavoro, Quarterly Review (Rome). 16:64 (March 1963), 121-144.

3691 Kroener, Arnold F. The Challenge of West Germany's Social Market Economy. Current History. 62:369 (May 1972), 250-253.

3692 Kurth, Edmund A. Ethical Aspects of Current West German Economic Policies. Review of Social Economy. 23:1 (March 1965), 17-50.

3693 Lewis, Flora. Inquiry Into German Prosperity. New York Times Magazine. (25 June 1961), 20+.

3694 Lutz, Friedrich A. Germany's Economic Resurgence. Lloyds' Bank Review. No. 39 (January 1956), 12-27.

3695 Macrae, Norman. The German Lesson. Economist. 221:6425 (15 October 1966), 32 P. Following P. 270.

3696 Mai, Ludwig H. Erhard's Social Market Economy. Southwestern Social Science Quarterly. 44:4 (March 1964), 329-334.

3697 Malik, Rex. Dr. Erhard on Economic Power. Contemporary Review. 197 (March 1960), 135-138.

3698 Melnikov, D. E. Economic Situation in the German Federal Republic Today. International Affairs (Moscow). (September 1955), 82-93.

3699 Miaudet, Francois. Germany's Economic Miracle 1970. Interplay. 3:8 (April 1970), 38-42.

3700 Moetteli, Carlo. The German Economy Between Yesterday and Tomorrow. Swiss Review of World Affairs. 17:2 (May 1967), 6-11.

3701 Moetteli, Carlo. 10 Years of Free Market Economy in West Germany. Koblenz: Rhenania, 1959, 15 P.

3702 Moetteli, Carlo. West Germans Debate Their Economy. Swiss Review of World Affairs. 12:2 (May 1962), 6-8.

3703 Moetteli, Carlo. West Germany's "Social Free-Market Economy"--An Interim Balance Sheet. Swiss Review of World Affairs. 8:12 (March 1959), 3-5.

3704 Moetteli, Carlo. West Germany's Social Market Economy After Erhard's Departure. Swiss Review of World Affairs. 16:10 (January 1967), 3-5.

3705 Nell-Breuning, Oswald Von. West Germany's Economic Revival. Social Order. 9:5 (May 1959), 201-214.

3706 Nickel, Herman. West Germany Minds Its Booming Business. New York Times Magazine. (27 March 1966), 54+.

3707 Opie, Redvers. West Germany's Economic Miracle. Three Banks Review. No. 53 (March 1962), 3-17.

3708 Radspieler, Anthony. The West Germany Economy. Current History. 50:297 (May 1966), 295-299.

3709 Richebaecher, Kurt. Germany--The End of the Miracle?. Banker. 112:436 (June 1962), 355-361.

3710 Richebaecher, Kurt. Germany on the Knife-Edge. The Banker. 111:423 (May 1961), 317-325.

3711 Richebaecher, Kurt. Germany--The Faltering Boom. The Banker. 116:484 (June 1966), 373-380.

3712 Richebaecher, Kurt. Germany's Fading Boom. The Banker. 113:443 (January 1963), 23-28.

3713 Richebaecher, Kurt. Tightening Squeeze in Germany. The Banker. 115:476 (October 1965), 664-671.

3714 Richebaecher, Kurt. Why Germany Missed Inflation (1964). Banker. 115:468 (February 1965), 90-96.

3715 Schmitt, Hans O. The West German "Miracle" Reconsidered. Challenge. 13:3 (February 1965), 4-6.

3716 Schneider, Erich. Economic Growth and Economic Order. German Economic Review. 7:2 (1969), 101-107.

3717 Sohmen, Egon. Competition and Growth: The Lesson of West Germany. American Economic Review. 49:5 (December 1959), 986-1003. Comments in 50:5 (December 1960), 1014-1031.

3718 Stolper, Gustav. German Realities. New York: Reynal and Hitchcock, 1948, 341 P.

3719 Stolper, Gustav. Haeuser, Karl. Borchardt, Knut. The German Economy: 1870 to the Present. New York: Harcourt, Brace & World, 1967, 353 P.

3720 Stolper, Wolfgang F. West German Development in an Expanding World Economy. World Politics. 9:1 (October 1956), 98-117.

3721 Tuchtfeldt, Egon. Social Market Economy and Demand Management--Two Experiments of Economic Policy. German Economic Review. 12:2 (1974), 111-133. 9:1 (October 1956), 98-117.

3722 UK, Hicog. The Federal Republic of Germany: Economic and Commercial Conditions in the Federal Republic of Germany and West Berlin. London: Board of Trade, Commercial Relations and Exports Department, H.M. Stationery Office, 1955, 404 P.

3723 West German Prosperity Surveyed. World Today. 14:4 (April 1958), 168-180.

3724 Woischnik, Bernhard. Germany, 1958. Bad Godesberg: Verlag Fuer Publizistik, for Federal Ministry for Federal Property, 1958, 64 P.

3725 Ziercke, Manfred. Effects of Post-War Inflation. Intereconomics. No. 6 (June 1971), 179-182.

I.4. Domestic Economy and Government

I.4.1. Money and Banking

3726 Abs, Hermann J. The German Capital Market--Problems and Prospects. The Banker. 116:488 (October 1966), 680-684.

3727 Abs, Hermann J. The Structure of the Western German Monetary System. Economic Journal. 60:239 (September 1950), 481-488.

3728 Achterberg, Erich. Structural Changes in German Bank Balance Sheets. Banca Nazionale Del Lavoro, Quarterly Review (Rome). 8:35 (December 1955), 200-214.

3729 Annual Report of the Bank Deutscher Laender. Federal Reserve Bulletin. 37:8 (August 1951), 942-951. Excerpts From Second Annual Report, General Economic Survey.

3730 Aufricht, Hans. Central Banking Legislation: A Collection of Central Bank, Monetary and Banking Laws. Washington: International Monetary Fund, 1967, Vol. 2, Pp. 249-300.

3731 Bank for International Settlements. European Central Banks: Organization and Activities. New York: Praeger, 1963, 336 P., Esp. Pp. 54-96 on Deutsche Bundesbank.

3732 Bank for International Settlements, Monetary & Econ. Dept. Germany: Monetary and Economic Developments, 1955-1964. Basle: Bank for International Settlements, Monetary and Economic Department, 1965, Unpaginated.

3733 The Banking System of the Federal Republic of Germany. Cologne: Bank-Verlag, 5Th Ed., 1969, 28 P.

3734 Blessing, Karl. The Situation as Regards Monetary Policy in the German Federal Republic. Revista Internazionale Di Scienze Economiche E Commerciali. 8:2 (Febuary 1961), 155-164.

3735 Brandt, Alfred. Central Banking in Western Germany From 1948 Through 1957. Ph.D. Thesis, New York University, 1961, 365 P.

3736 Currency and Banking in Western Germany. Institute of International Finance Bulletin. No. 173 (25 September 1951), 2-35.

3737 Deuss, Hanns. Capital Market Germany's Biggest Headache. World Banking. (December 1966), 119-126.

3738 Deuss, Hanns. Trends in Banking Policy. World Banking. (December 1963), 117-120.

3739 Economic Development and Central Bank Policies in Western Germany. Federal Reserve Bulletin. 36:10 (October 1950), 1293-1300. From First Annual Report of Bank Deutscher Laender.

3740 Eec, Monetary Committee. The Instruments of Monetary Policy in the Countries of the European Economic Community. N.P.: Publication Services of the European Communities, 1962, 268 P., Esp. Pp. 53-101.

3741 Eec, Monetary Committee. Monetary Policy in the Countries of the European Economic Community. N.P.: Publication Services of the European Communities, 1972; Supplement in 1974.

3742 Emmer, Robert E. Monetary and Fiscal Policy in Western Germany Since the End of World War II. Ph.D. Thesis, University of Chicago, 1954.

3743 Emmer, Robert E. West German Monetary Policy, 1948-1954. Journal of Political Economy. 63:1 (February 1955), 52-69.

3744 Farnell, Werner F. The Structure of the German Banking System With Some Comparisons With Banking in the United States. Munich: Bayerische Vereinsbank, 1965, 47 P.

3745 Federal Reserve Bank. Recent Financial Changes in Western Germany. Federal Reserve Bulletin. 40:10 (October 1954), 1041-1050.

3746 German Bankers' Association. Why German Banks Lend Long. The Banker. 104:349 (February 1955), 110-111.

3747 German Banking Since the War. Bankers' Magazine. 174:1304 (November 1952), 385-387.

3748 The German Bundesbank and Control of the Quantity of Central Bank Money. German Economic Review. 12:2 (1974), 186-192.

3749 German Federation of Trade Unions. The "Gemeinwirtschaftsbanken". Annals of Collective Economy. 26:3 (July 1955), 214-217.

3750 Gluck, Gustav. A Restrictive Credit Policy in Germany. World Banking. (December 1965), 123-130.

3751 Groseclose, E. The Decay of Money: A Survey of Western Currencies 1912-1962. Washington: Institute of Monetary Research, 1962, 32 P.

3752 Hein, John. The Mainsprings of German Monetary Policy. Economia Internazionale. 17:2 (May 1964), 317-324.

3753 Hein, John. Monetary Policy and External Convertibility: The German Experience, 1959-61. Economia Internazionale. 17:3 (August 1964), 509-531.

3754 Hein, John. Monetary Policy and External Surpluses: The German Experience, 1955-61. Ph.D. Thesis, Columbia University, 1963, 263 P.

3755 Hendrickson, Hildegard Roedig. The Deutsche Bundesbank and West German Monetary Policies, With Special Emphasis on 1955-1957. D.B.A. Thesis, University of Washington, 1966, 171 P.

3756 Heuser, Henry K. Recent Financial Changes in Western Germany. Federal Reserve Bulletin. 40:10 (October 1954), 1041-1050.

3757 Hodgman, Donald R. National Monetary Policies and International Monetary Cooperation. Boston: Little, Brown, 1974, X and 266 P., Esp. Pp. 53-84.

3758 Interview With Dr. Karl Klasen. The Banker. 121:539 (January 1971), 42-47.

3759 Joesten, Joachim. German Banks and Banking Today. Great Barrington,

Mass.: Joachim Joesten, New Germany Reports No. 4, August 1948, 17 P.

3760 Klaus, Joachim. Falk, Hans-Juergen. Monetary Policy and Overall Control. German Economic Review. 8:2 (1970), 97-114.

3761 Klein, John J. Price-Level and Money-Denomination Movements. Journal of Political Economy. 68:4 (August 1960), 369-378.

3762 Kohn, Donald L. West German Monetary Policy and Bank Portfolios, 1962-68. Ph.D. Thesis, University of Michigan, 1971, 162 P.

3763 Kolmin, Frank W. Monetary Policy in West Germany, 1948-1958. Ph.D. Thesis, Syracuse University, 1961, 326 P.

3764 Lanner, J. Changes in the Structure of the German Banking System. Economica. 18:70 (May 1951), 169-183.

3765 Loehr, Rodney C. The West German Banking System. Bad Godesberg-Mehlem: Office of the U.S. High Commissioner for Germany, Historical Division, 1952, 126 P.

3766 Lueke, Rolf E. Germany's Interest Rate Puzzle. Banker. 109:401 (June 1959), 374-377.

3767 Mirus, Karl Rolf. Monetary Policy and the Demand for Liquid Assets in Germany. Ph.D. Thesis, University of Minnesota, 1973, 140 P.

3768 Muthesius, Volkmar. West Germany's Capital Market Still Lagging. Bankers' Magazine. 178:1325 (August 1954), 129-132.

3769 Oecd. Monetary Policy in Germany. Paris: Organization for Economic Cooperation and Development, Monetary Studies Series No. 3, March 1974, 130 P.

3770 Panten, Hans-Joachim. The Come-Back of the German Big Three Banks. Bankers Magazine (London). 184:1363 (October 1957), 280-283.

3771 Panten, Hans-Joachim. The Growth and Activity of the West German Successor Banks. Bankers Magazine (London). 178:1325 (August 1954), 113-122.

3772 Peltzer, Martin. Carney, Brian. Germany Tries the Eardepot. The Banker. 122:554 (April 1972), 447-456.

3773 Pferdmenges, Robert. Banking in Germany. International Markets. 9:4 (April 1955), 40-45.

3774 Ponto, Juergen. Expansion and Competition in German Banking. The Banker. 121:539 (January 1971), 52-55.

3775 Pringle, Robin. New Freedom for German Banks. The Banker. 117:498 (August 1967), 684-690.

3776 Ray, Edward J. Finance in a Development Context: Lessons From West Germany. Ph.D. Thesis, Stanford University, 1971, 160 P.

3777 Recent Monetary Developments in Western Europe: Western Germany. Institute of International Finance Bulletin. No. 185 (4 March 1954), 22-27.

3778 Richebaecher, Kurt. X-Ray of German Interest Rates. Bankers Magazine (London). 185:1372 (July 1958), 14-21.

3779 Ringleb, Waldemar. German Banking Changes Back. Banker. 107:377 (June 1957), 388-392.

3780 Rittershausen, H. Banking in Western Germany. Comparative Banking. Ed. H. W. Auburn. London: Waterlow and Sons, 3D Ed., 1966, Pp. 63-71.

3781 Roskamp, Karl W. Laumas, Gurcharan S. The Rate of Interest and the Demand for Money. Weltwirtschaftliches Archiv. 102:1 (June 1969), 150-155.

3782 Roskamp, Karl W. Laumas, Gurcharan S. The Relative Importance of Autonomous Expenditures and Money in the West German Economy. Weltwirtschaftliches Archiv. 99:1 (1967), 127-137.

3783 Rozen, V. FRG Banks and Firms. International Affairs (Moscow). No. 9 (September 1973), 108-109.

3784 Schacht, Hjalmar Horace Greeley. The Magic of Money. London: Oldbourne, 1967, 230 P.

3785 Schlesinger, Helmut. Bockelmann, Horst. Monetary Policy in the Federal Republic of Germany. Monetary Policy in Twelve Industrial Countries. Ed. Karel Holbik. Boston: Federal Reserve Bank of Boston, 1973, Pp. 161-213.

3786 Schloenbach, Camilla. The Stabilization Programmes of the Federal Government in 1973. German Economic Review. 12:1 (1974), 78-83.

3787 Schmidt, Willi. Special Features of the West German Central Banking System. Bankers' Magazine. 178:1325 (August 1954) 123-129.

3788 Sherwin, Stephen F. Monetary Policy in Continental Western Europe, 1944-1952. Ph.D. Thesis, University of Wisconsin, 1956, 579 P.

3789 Snellings, Aubrey N. The Development of Monetary Policy in West Germany, 1948-1953. Ph.D. Thesis, University of Virginia, 1955, 261 P.

3790 Stuper, Rainer. An Empirical Analysis of the Debate Over Rules Versus Discretion With Special Reference to the Monetary Management of the German Bundesbank From 1958 to 1970. Ph.D. Thesis, Florida State University, 1973, 154 P.

3791 Trouvain, Franz-Josef. The German Capital Market. The Banker. 121:539 (January 1971), 57-63.

3792 Turroni, C. Bresciani. Some Recent Monetary Experience. Review of the Economic Conditions in Italy. 16:1 (January 1962), 5-10.

3793 Ulrich, Franz Heinrich. The Role of West German Banks in the Recent Recession and in the Present Phase of the Upturn. World Banking. (1967-68), 117-123.

3794 Veit, Otto. German Monetary Policy Under Strain. International Affairs (London). 27:4 (October 1951), 457-462.

3795 Voelling, Johannes. Development of the German Money Market. Intereconomics. No. 5 (May 1970), 151-154.

3796 Vosshall, Gerhard W. The West German Banking System. Ph.D. Thesis, New York University, 1964, 239 P.

3797 Woll, Artur. Monetary Aspects of a Stabilization Policy Geared to Growth. German Economic Review. 9:2 (1971), 105-121.

3798 Zencke, Hans-Henning. German Monetary Policy After Dm Revaluation. Bonn-Bad Godesberg: Inter Nationes, 1970, 28 P.

I.4.2. Fiscal Policy and Public Finance

3799 Andic, Suphan. Veverka, Jindrich. The Growth of Government Expenditure in Germany Since the Unification. Finanzarchiv. 23:2 (January 1964), 169-278.

3800 Biehl, Dieter. Hagemann, Guenter. Juettemeier, Karl-Heinz. Legler, Harald. on the Cyclical Effects of

Budgetary Policy From 1960 to 1970 in the Federal Republic of Germany. German Economic Review. 11:4 (1973), 273-291.

3801 Company Taxation: German Federal Republic. Company Taxation in Western Europe. Ed. Bank Mees & Hope Nv. Amsterdam: International Bureau of Fiscal Documentation, 1975, Pp. 38-50.

3802 Debatin, Helmut. Analysis of the German Tax System. Amsterdam: International Bureau of Fiscal Documentation, 1969, 297 P.

3803 Dieck, Margret. Collective-Economy Undertakings in the Federal Republic of Germany. Annals of Collective Economy. 39:2 (April-June 1968), 225-249; "Postscript" in 41:4 (October-December 1970), 369-394.

3804 FRG, Federal Ministry of Finance. A Report on German Fiscal Policy From 1949 to 1953. Bonn: Federal Ministry of Finance, 1953, 51 P. Report By Minister Schaeffer When Presenting 1953-54 Budget.

3805 Fantl, Irving L. A Study of the Influence of Different Methods of Corporate Taxation on the Dividend Policies of Publicly Held Corporations in France, the Federal Republic of Germany and The United Kingdom. Ph.D. Thesis, New York University, 1974, 287 P.

3806 Friedrich, Carl J. Baer, Theodore S. Public Finance in Six Contemporary Federations: A Comparative Constitutional Analysis. Public Policy. Vol. 4. Ed. Carl J. Friedrich and John Kenneth Galbraith. Cambridge: Graduate School of Public Administration, 1953, Pp. 180-227.

3807 Gerelli, Emilio. Intergovernmental Financial Relations: The Case of the German Federal Republic. Weltwirtschaftliches Archiv. 97:2 (1966), 273-301.

3808 Haller, Heinz. Changes in the Problems of Federative Public Economies. German Economic Review. 8:3 (1970), 177-201.

3809 Heidenheimer, Arnold J. Public Subsidization in West Germany and the U.S. Jahrbuch Des Oeffentlichen Rechts Der Gegenwart. Vol. 16. Ed. Gerhard Leibholz. Tuebingen: Mohr (Paul Siebeck), 1967, Pp. 367-378.

3810 Hensen, Bent. Fiscal Policy in Seven Countries, 1955-1965. Paris: Organisation for Economic Co-Operation and Development, March 1969, 548 P., Esp. Pp. 209-275.

3811 Joesten, Joachim. Germany's "People's Capitalism". Great Barrington, Mass.: Joachim Joesten, New Germany Reports No. 44, October 1959, 17 P.

3812 Kelly, Matthew A. The Socialization of German Industry. American Journal of Economics and Sociology. 9:2 (January 1950), 161-175.

3813 Keutgen, Rene. The Vereinigte Industrie-Unternehmen Ag: A German Public Enterprise. Annals of Collective Economy. 42:4 (October-December 1971), 303-346.

3814 Kullmer, L. Problems of the Financial Reform in the Federal Republic of Germany. German Economic Review. 7:1 (1969), 63-71.

3815 Markus, H. B. Local Taxation in Western Germany. Accounting Research (London). 8:1 (January 1957), 23-41; and 8:2 (April 1957), 125-144.

3816 Merkl, Peter H. The Financial Constitution (Finanzverfassung) of Western Germany. American Journal of Comparative Law. 6:2-3 (Spring-Summer 1957), 327-340.

3817 Neumark, Fritz. Some Recent Problems and Aspects of Fiscal Policy. German Economic Review. 4:3 (1966), 177-192.

3818 Oeftering, H. The Participation of the German Federal State in Economic Enterprise. Annals of Collective Economy. 24:3 (October-November 1953), 271-288.

3819 Oettle, Karl. Current Categories of Public Demand. German Economic Review. 9:4 (1971), 305-317.

3820 Pavlock, Ernest J. A Comparison of Periodic Income Reporting Among the United States, West Germany, the Netherlands, and Sweden. Ph.D. Thesis, University of Michigan, 1965, 402 P.

3821 Reuss, Frederick G. Fiscal Policy for Growth Without Inflation: The German Experiment. Baltimore: Johns Hopkins, 1963, 319 P.

3822 Roskamp, Karl W. The Distribution of Tax Burden in a Rapidly Growing Economy: West Germany in 1950. National Tax Journal. 16:1 (March 1963), 20-36.

3823 Rothweiler, Robert L. Revenue Sharing in the Federal Republic of Germany. Publius. 2:1 (Spring 1972), 4-25.

3824 Schmoelders, Guenter. Loan Policy of Public Authorities in Western Germany. Bankers' Magazine. 180:1339 (October 1955), 296-300.

3825 Schnitzer, Martin. "Soziale Marktwirtschaft" Revisited: West German Economic Policy, 1967-1971. Journal of Economic Issues. 6:4 (December 1972), 69-88.

3826 Tanzi, Vito. The Individual Income Tax and Economic Growth: An International Comparison. Baltimore: Johns Hopkins University Press, 1969, 136 P. France, FRG, Italy, Japan, UK, US.

3827 US, Department of State, Office of Intelligence Res. & Anal. Postwar Monetary and Fiscal Policies in Western Germany. Washington: Department of State, Office of Intelligence Research and Analysis, Oir Report No. 5171, 1951, 39 P.

3828 Van Hoorn, J., Jr. Post-War Changes in German Tax Legislation. Bulletin for International Fiscal Documentation. 1:4 (1946-47), 162-169.

3829 Wertheimer, Robert G. A Note on Incentive Taxation in West Germany, 1948-1955. Review of Economics and Statistics. 40:2 (May 1958), 183-185.

3830 Wiegand, G. Carl. Fiscal Developments in Postwar Germany and Their Economic, Political, and Monetary Background. Ph.D. Thesis, Northwestern University, 1950.

3831 Wiegand, G. Carl. Fiscal Developments in Post War Germany and Their Economic, Political, and Monetary Background. Journal of Finance. 8:3 (September 1953), 347-348.

3832 Zeitel, Gerhard. Government Loans as an Instrument of Financial and Economic Policy. German Economic Review. 6:3 (1968), 192-216.

3833 Zimmerman, Hans. De-Socialization in West Germany. Swiss Review of World Affairs. 9:6 (September 1959), 3-6.

I.4.3. Planning and Economic Policy

3834 Vente, Rolf E. Macro-Economic Planning, a Bibliography. Baden-Baden: Nomos, 1970, 292 P.

3835 Albach, Horst. New Trends in the Economic Policy of the Federal Republic of Germany. German Economic Review. 7:2 (1969), 108-128.

3836 Arndt, Hans-Joachim. West Germany: Politics of Non-Planning. Syracuse: Syracuse University Press, 1966, 162 P.

3837 Arndt, Klaus Dieter. Highlights of the Brandt Government's Economic Policy. Intereconomics. No. 3 (March 1970), 70-72.

3838 Balogh, Thomas. Germany: An Experiment in Planning By the "Free" Price Mechanism. Oxford: Blackwell, 1950, 72 P.

3839 Balogh, Thomas. Germany: An Experiment in Planning By the "Free" Price Mechanism. Banca Nazionale Del Lavoro, Quarterly Review (Rome). 3:13 (April-June 1950), 71-102.

3840 Baumgarten, Peter. Mueckl, Wolfgang J. on the Relationships Between Economic Targets in the Federal Republic of Germany, 1951-1969. German Economic Review. 9:1 (1971), 29-40.

3841 Besters, Hans. Economic Policy in Western Germany. Economic Policy in Our Time. Ed. E. S. Kirschen and Others. Amsterdam: North Holland, 1964, Vol. 3, Pp. 389-482.

3842 Denton, Geoffrey. Forsyth, Murray. Maclennan, Malcolm. Economic Planning and Policies in Britain, France and Germany. New York: Praeger, 1968, 424 P.

3843 Eucken, Walter. This Unsuccessful Age; or, the Pains of Economic Progress. New York: Oxford University Press, 1952, 96 P.

3844 Giersch, Herbert. Growth, Cycles, and Exchange Rates--The Experience of West Germany. Stockholm: Almqvist & Wiksell, 1970, 39 P.

3845 Heller, Walter W. Economic Policy and Political Equilibrium in Postwar Germany. Germany and the Future of Europe. Ed. Hans J. Morgenthau. Chicago: University of Chicago Press, 1951, Pp. 58-75.

3846 Hettlage, Karl M. The Problems of Medium-Term Financial Planning. Public Administration. 48:4 (Autumn 1970), 263-272.

3847 Juergensen, Harald. Private and Social Costs. German Economic Review. 2:4 (1964), 273-288.

3848 Kantzenbach, Erhard. Social Co-Ordination of Individual Economic Activities--Thoughts on Basic Economic Policy Decisions. German Economic Review. 7:3 (1969), 185-198.

3849 Keutgen, Rene. The Proposals for the Reorganisation of the Industrial Assets Owned By the Federal German Government. Annals of Collective Economy. 42:4 (October-December 1971), 347-368.

3850 Lueke, Rolf E. New Look in German Economic Policy. Banker. 107:383 (December 1957), 791-794.

3851 Oberhauser, Alois. Death Duties and Property Taxation as a Means of More Even Distribution of the Stock of Wealth. German Economic Review. 13:1 (1975), 1-15.

3852 Roskamp, Karl W. Capital Formation in West Germany. Detroit: Wayne State University Press, 1965, 287 P.

3853 Roskamp, Karl W. Economic Growth, Capital Formation, and Public Policy in West Germany, 1948 to 1957. Ph.D. Thesis, University of Michigan, 1960, 455 P.

3854 Schiller, Karl. Stability and Growth as Objectives of Economic Policy. German Economic Review. 5:3 (1967), 177-188.

3855 Tumlir, Jan. Investment Allocation as a Policy for Price Stability: West Germany, 1948-1959. Yale Economic Essays. 5:1 (Spring 1965), 255-277.

I.5. Agriculture and Natural Resources

I.5.1. Agricultural Sector

3856 US, Omgus, Economics Division. A Selected List of German Publications in the Fields of Agriculture and Agricultural Economics and Political Economy. Berlin: Omgus, Office of Economics Adviser, Food and Agriculture Group, 1949, 24 P.

3857 Agricultural and Home Economics Evaluation & Info. Service. Agricultural and Home Economics Advisory Services in the Federal Republic of Germany. Bad Godesberg: Land- Und Hauswirtschaftlicher Auswertungs- Und Informationsdienst, 1962, 56 P.

3858 Agricultural and Home Economics Evaluation & Info. Service. Agricultural Engineering in the Federal Republic of Germany. Bad Godesberg: Land- Und Hauswirtschaftlicher Auswertungs- Und Informationsdienst, 1961, 71 P.

3859 Agricultural and Home Economics Evaluation & Info. Service. Agricultural Organisations of the Federal Republic of Germany. Bad Godesberg: Land- Und Hauswirtschaftlicher Auswertungs- Und Informationsdienst, 6Th Ed., 1962, 47 P.

3860 Agricultural and Home Economics Evaluation & Info. Service. Agriculture of the Federal Republic of Germany. Bad Godesberg: Land- Und Hauswirtschaftlicher Auswertungs- Und Informationsdienst, 4Th Ed., 1958, 51 P.

3861 Agricultural and Home Economics Evaluation & Info. Service. Farm Construction in the Federal Republic of Germany. Bad Godesberg: Land- Und Hauswirtschaftlicher Auswertungs- Und Informationsdienst, 1963, 72 P.

3862 Agricultural and Home Economics Evaluation & Info. Service. Horticulture in the Federal Republic of Germany. Bad Godesberg: Land- Und Hauswirtschaftlicher Auswertungs- Und Informationsdienst, 1961, 76 P.

3863 Agricultural and Home Economics Evaluation & Info. Service. Livestock Breeding in the Federal Republic of Germany. Compiled By Arbeitsgemeinschaft Deutscher Tierzuechter E.V. Bad Godesberg: Land- Und Hauswirtschaftlicher Auswertungs- Und Informationsdienst, 1961, 120 P.

3864 Agricultural and Home Economics Evaluation & Info. Service. Seeds in the Federal Republic of Germany. Bad Godesberg: Land- Und Hauswirtschaftlicher Auswertungs- Und Informationsdienst, 1962, 136 P.

3865 Agricultural Employment Problems in the Federal Republic of Germany. International Labour Review. 71:6 (June 1955), 635-651.

3866 Agricultural Policy in the Federal Republic of Germany. International Labour Review. 77:2 (February 1958), 160-170.

3867 Alexander, D. J. Some Features of West German Policy for Improving the Agricultural Structure. Journal of Farm Economics. 46:4 (November 1964), 791-804.

3868 Behrendt, Guenther. The Agrarian Problem in the Federal Republic of Germany. German Economic Review. 2:2 (1964), 111-123.

3869 Bizonal Economic Area, Admin. for Food, Agric. & Forestry.

Possibilities of Increasing Agricultural Production in Germany. Frankfurt: Administration for Food, Agriculture and Forestry, 1948, 72 P.

3870 Breitenlohner, Cynthia A. The Agricultural Economy and Trade of the Federal Republic of Germany. Washington: Department of Agriculture, Economic Research Service, 1971, 27 P.

3871 Dietze, Constantin Von. The State of German Agriculture. Annals of the American Academy of Political and Social Science. 260 (November 1948), 74-79.

3872 Dobbins, Claude Edwin. The Livestock and Meat Industry of West Germany. Washington: Department of Agriculture, Foreign Agricultural Service, 1963, 20 P.

3873 FRG, Federal Ministry for Food, Agriculture and Forestry. Agriculture in the Federal Republic of Germany. Bonn: Federal Ministry for Food, Agriculture and Forestry, 1955, 49 P. Report to 8Th Session, Un-Fao Conference.

3874 FRG, Federal Statistical Office. Census of Agriculture, 1971. Stuttgart: Kohlhammer, Studies on Statistics No. 26, 1972, 1972, 12 P.

3875 Friedmann, Karen J. German Grain Policies and Prices, 1925-1964. Food Research Institute Studies (Stanford University). 5:1 (1965), 31-97.

3876 Friedmann, Karen J. Farnsworth, Helen C. Grains in German Farming: Past Developments and Prospects For 1970 and 1975. Stanford: Stanford University, Food Research Institute, 1966, 64 P.

3877 Gerschenkron, Alexander. Bread and Democracy in Germany. New York: Fertig, (1943) 1966, 238 P.

3878 Hallett, Graham. Agricultural Policy in West Germany. Journal of Agricultural Economics. 19:1 (January 1968), 87-95.

3879 Ifo Institute for Economic Research. Long-Term Development of Demand and Supply for Agricultural Products in the Federal Republic of Germany. Munich: Ifo-Institut Fuer Wirtschaftsforschung, 1967, 248 P.

3880 Klatt, Werner. Food and Farming in Germany. Weltwirtschaftliches Archiv. 64:1 (1950), 111-158.

3881 Klatt, Werner. Food and Farming in Germany. International Affairs (London). 26:1 (January 1950), 45-58; and 26:2 (April 1950), 195-207.

3882 Krause, Elfriede A. Structural Changes in West German Agriculture. Washington: U.S. Department of Agriculture, Economic Research Service, 1972, 66 P.

3883 Kuhnen, Frithjof. Non-Agricultural Income of Land-Cultivating Families in Germany. Journal of Farm Economics. 43:3 (August 1961), 659-662.

3884 Levy, Hermann J. Pattern for German Agriculture. Fortnightly. 161:964 (April 1947), 274-278.

3885 Malecky, J. M. German Agricultural Policy and the Green Plans. Quarterly Review of Agricultural Economics (Canberra). 15:1 (January 1962), 31-42.

3886 Mayhew, Alan. Structural Reform and the Future of West German Agriculture. Geographical Review. 60:1 (January 1970), 54-60.

3887 Mueller, Gerry G. Agricultural Problems in Western Germany. Agriculture Education Magazine. 26:2 (August 1953), 44.

3888 Oecd. Agricultural Policy in Germany. Paris: Organisation for Economic Cooperation and Development, Agricultural Policy Reports Series, January 1975, 60 P.

3889 Pritchard, Norris T. Steele, W. Scott. Huth, William P. Food Marketing in West Germany. Washington: Department of Agriculture, Economic Research Service, 1972, 50 P.

3890 Rossmiller, George E. The Grain-Livestock Economy of West Germany: With Projections to 1970 and 1975. East Lansing: Michigan State University, Institute of International Agriculture, 1968, 253 P.

3891 Schiller, Otto. Co-Operative Promotion of Agricultural Production in the Federal Republic of Germany: A New Approach to Co-Operative Farming Methods. German Economic Review. 3:1 (1965), 1-12.

3892 Schmidt, Hubert G. Hille, Hans G. Food and Agricultural Programs in West Germany, 1949-1951. Bad Godesberg-Mehlem: Office of the U.S. High Commissioner for Germany, Historical Division, 1952, 202 P.

3893 Schultz, Theodore W. Effects of Trade and Industrial Output of Western Germany Upon Agriculture. American Economic Review. 40:2 (May 1950), 522-530.

I.5.2. Land Tenure and Reform

3894 Erhart, Rainer R. Land Consolidation and Its Effects on the Agricultural Landscape of the Vogelsberg, Germany. Ph.D. Thesis, University of Illinois, 1967, 211 P.

3895 Kanaar, A. C. Land Reform in Germany. Twentieth Century. 139:832 (June 1946), 283-286.

3896 Macdonald, H. Malcolm. West German Succession to Farm Land. American Journal of Comparative Law. 2:2 (Spring 1953), 219-225.

3897 Mueller, Peter. Recent Developments in Land Tenure and Land Policies in Germany. Land Economics. 40:3 (August 1964), 267-275.

3898 Mende, Tibor. Land Reform in Germany. Fortnightly. 159:951 (March 1946), 170-176.

3899 US, Omgus, Economics Division. Land Reform. N.P.: Omgus, Adjutant General, 1947, 17 P.

3900 Ucker, Paul. Land Reform in Germany, U.S. Zone. American Journal of Economics and Sociology. 7:4 (July 1948), 461-468.

I.5.3. Fishing, Forestry, Natural Resources

3901 Agricultural and Home Economics Evaluation & Info. Service. The Fishing Industry in the Federal Republic of Germany. Bad Godesberg: Land- Und Hauswirtschaftlicher Auswertungs- Und Informationsdienst, 1961, 88 P.

3902 Agricultural and Home Economics Evaluation & Info. Service. Forestry and Wood Economy in the Federal Republic of Germany. Bad Godesberg: Land- Und Hauswirtschaftlicher Auswertungs- Und Informationsdienst, 5Th Ed., 1967, 151 P.

3903 Agricultural and Home Economics Evaluation & Info. Service. Forestry in the Federal Republic of Germany. Bad Godesberg: Land- Und Hauswirtschaftlicher Auswertungs- Und Informationsdienst, 4Th Ed., 1962, 79 P.

3904 Plochmann, Richard. Forestry in the Federal Republic of Germany. Corvallis: Oregon State University, School of Forestry, 1968, 52 P.

3905 Ryle, G. B. Forest Fire Protection in Germany: An Examination in Regierungs Bezirk Lueneburg. Forestry. 21:2 (1947), 141-145.

3906 US, Department of the Army, European Command. Water Resources, West Germany: Area File W-7. N.P.: Usareur Engineer Intelligence Center, 1960, 12 P.

3907 US, Department of the Interior. Natural Resources Mission to Germany: Special Report to the President. Washington: Government Printing Office, 1966, 32 P.

3908 US, Omgus, Economics Division. Non-Metallic Mineral Resources of Germany. N.P.: Omgus, Economics Division, Industry Branch, Coal & Non-Metallic Mining Section, 1945, 28 P.

3909 US, Omgus, Military Governor. Bizonal Area Forests: Their Condition and a Suggested Plan for Management. N.P.: Omgus, June 1949.

3910 US, Omgus, Military Governor. The German Forest Resources Survey. N.P.: Omgus, October 1948, 48 P.

I.6. Industry and Business

I.6.1. Industrial Organization and Production

3911 Arndt, Helmut. on Economic Concentration. Berlin: Duncker Und Humblot, 1971.

3912 Aust, Hans Walter. Crisis of the Krupp-Empire. German Foreign Policy (GDR). 6:3 (1967), 250-260.

3913 Barna, Tibor. Industrial Investment in Britain and Germany: A Clue to Export Performance. Banker. 108:384 (January 1958), 12-23.

3914 Barna, Tibor. Investment in Industry--Has Britain Lagged?. The Banker. 107:375 (April 1957), 219-230.

3915 Batty, Peter. The House of Krupp. London: Secker & Warburg, 1966, 333 P.

3916 British Productivity Council. The Chemical Industry in West Germany. London: British Productivity Council, 1961, 52 P.

3917 Center for Auto Safety. Small--on Safety: The Designed-in Dangers of the Volkswagen. New York: Grossman, 1972, 180 P.

3918 Cotton, Clare M. Chemicals in West Germany. New York: Schnell, 1971, 135 P.

3919 Eckert, Heinz. Salowsky, Heinz. Industry in the Federal Republic of Germany. Bonn: Press and Information Office, 3D Ed., 1967, 60 P.

3920 Erbe, Rene. Causes and Effects of Private Capital Movements in Germany, 1955-69. Kyklos. 23:4 (1970), 927-941.

3921 Felderer, Bernhard. Efficiency of Markets and Economic Growth--An Empirical Study. German Economic Review. 12:4 (1974), 302-318.

3922 Feldman, K. Frank. Is This the End of Krupps?. Contemporary Review. 183:1049 (May 1953), 269-274.

3923 Friedrich, Otto. Hamburg--The Industrial Center. International Markets. 9:4 (April 1955), 35+.

3924 Hoeping, Hubert. A Forward-Looking Industrial Project. Intereconomics. No. 8 (August 1969), 260-262.

3925 Hoffmann, Walther G. Prosperity Goods in the Growth Process. German Economic Review. 9:1 (1971), 1-10.

3926 Hopfinger, K. B. The Volkswagen Story. Cambridge: Bentley, 3D Ed., 1971, 215 P.

3927 India, National Productivity Council. Industrial Maintenance in West Germany, Britain and Usa. New Delhi: National Productivity Council, 1963, 76 P.

3928 India, National Productivity Council. Materials Handling in West Germany, Britain, and Usa. New Delhi: National Productivity Council, 1964, 92 P.

3929 Joesten, Joachim. Krupp Without Guns. Great Barrington, Mass.: Joachim Joesten, New Germany Reports No.S. 32-33, 1956, 29 P.

3930 Kain, Walter. Who Is Who in the German Chemical Industry. Baden-Baden: Kain, 1967, 79 P. Guide to Over 300 Companies; 12-Page Suppl. in January 1968.

3931 Kaldor, Mary. European Defence Industries--National and International Implications. Sussex, Eng.,: Institute for the Study of International Organisation, Isio Monograph No. 8, 1972, 79 P.

3932 Klass, Gert Von. Krupps: The Story of an Industrial Empire. London: Sidgwick and Jackson, 1954, 437 P.

3933 Kohler, Wilhelm F. The Cotton Textile Industry of Western Germany. Egyptian Cotton Gazette. 23:3 (September-October 1954), 49-51.

3934 Kolcum, Edward H. Miller, Barry. Fink, Donald E. Coleman, Herbert J. German Aerospace Industry. Aviation Week & Space Technology. 96:17 (24 April 1972), 32-119.

3935 Krengel, Rolf. Soviet, American, and West German Basic Industries: A Comparison. Soviet Studies. 12:2 (October 1960), 113-125.

3936 Krupp Today. Essen: Kruppscher Arbeitskreis, 1954, 54 P.

3937 The Krupp Works in Essen--History, Structure and Present Situation. Essen: Krupp, 1950, 48 P.

3938 Lasky, Melvin J. The Volkswagen: A Success Story. New York Times Magazine. (2 October 1955), 15+.

3939 Lellau, Willi. Hamburg's Industry. Hamburg: Holler, 1953, 45 P.

3940 Lochner, Louis Paul. Tycoons and Tyrant: German Industry From Hitler to Adenauer. Chicago: Regnery, 1954, 304 P.

3941 Manchester, William. The Arms of Krupp, 1587-1968. Boston: Little, Brown, 1968, 942 P., Esp. Pp. 569-833.

3942 Mccarthy, John J. Development of Supervisors in German Industry. Berlin: Omgus, Manpower Division, Visiting Expert Series No. 5, January 1949, 20 P.

3943 Muhlen, Norbert. The Incredible Krupps: The Rise, Fall and Comeback of Germany's Industrial Family. New York: Holt, 1959, 308 P.

3944 Nelson, Walter Henry. Small Wonder: The Amazing Story of the Volkswagen. Boston: Little, Brown, Rev. Ed., 1970, 311 P.

3945 Oecd. The Industrial Policies of 14 Member Countries. Paris: Organisation for Economic Cooperation and Development, 1971, 395 P., Esp. Pp. 9-48.

3946 Oecd. Industrial Research Associations in Germany. Industrial Research Associations in France, Belgium and Germany. Paris: Organisation for Economic Cooperation and Development, 1965, Pp. 1-26 (Pp. 92-117 Overall).

3947 Parker, William N. Entrepreneurship, Industrial Organization, and Economic Growth: A German Example. Journal of Economic History. 14:4 (December 1954), 380-400.

3948 Pritt, Denis N. Light on Krupp's. Labour Monthly. 39:9 (September 1957), 414-419.

3949 Rhodes, Edmund O. German High-Temperature Coal-Tar Industry. Washington: U.S. Bureau of Mines, Government Printing Office, September 1947, 117 P.

3950 Roux, Rene. Prospects and Problems of the Textile Industry in Western Germany. International Labour Review. 62:3-4 (September-October 1950), 264-290.

3951 Ruediger, Wilhelm. Index of the Net Value of Industrial Production. Stuttgart: Kohlhammer, 1957, 31 P.

3952 The Salzgitter Group of Industries. Salzgitter-Druette: Salzgitter Ag, 1970, 215 P.

3953 Schecker, Theodor. Hamburg--The Shipbuilding Center. International Markets. 9:4 (April 1955), 34+.

3954 Schmidt, Hubert G., Editor. Documents on the Reorganization of the West German Coal and Iron and Steel Industries Under the Allied High Commission for Germany, 1949-1952. Bad Godesberg-Mehlem: Office of the U.S. High Commissioner for Germany, Historical Division, 1952, 113 P.

3955 Steinberg, Jonathan. The Case of Herr Fritz Krupp. Midstream. 13:9 (November 1967), 10-19.

3956 Stern-Rubarth, Edgar. The Problem of German Industry. Contemporary Review. 169:964 (April 1946), 214-220.

3957 Stuchtey, Rolf. Competitiveness of German Steel Industry. Intereconomics. No. 2 (February 1967), 43-45.

3958 US, Business and Defense Services Administration. The Development of the West German Photographic Products Industry, 1954-1959. Washington: Business and Defense Services Administration, Scientific, Motion Picture and Photographic Products Division, 1960, 23 P.

3959 US, Hicog, Office of Economic Affairs. Annual Industries Report, 1952. Bonn: Hicog, Office of Economic Affairs, Commercial Attache Division, Economic Reports Branch, 1953, 9 Pts., C.800 P.

3960 US, Hicog, Office of Economic Affairs. Annual Report: Scientific and Industrial Research and Technological Advance, 1953. Bonn: Hicog, Office of Economic Affairs, Commercial Attache Division, Economic Reports Branch, 1954, 214 P.

3961 Van Riet, Joseph. Sandmann, Fritz. Prefabrication Makes Shipbuilding Competitive. Intereconomics. No. 3 (March 1967), 62-64.

3962 Vitger, Erhard. Automobile Industry Contributes to Germany's Recovery. International Markets. 9:4 (April 1955), 26+.

3963 The Weaving Industry in the Netherlands and Western Germany. London: British Productivity Council, 1963, 80 P. Report on October-November 1961 Visit By British Joint Management/Trade Union Team.

3964 The West German Coal and Steel Industries Since the War. World Today. 8:3 (March 1952), 111-122.

3965 Willey, Howard David. Growth of British and German Manufacturing, 1951-1962. Ph.D. Thesis, Columbia University, 1966, 300 P.

3966 Young, Gordon. The Fall and Rise of Alfried Krupp. London: Cassell, 1960, 178 P.

3967 Zelle, Arnold. Handicraft in Germany. Bonn: Presse- Und Informationsamt, 1963, 40 P.

3968 Zimmerman, Hans. German Chemicals--A Power on World Markets. Swiss Review of World Affairs. 20:7 (October 1970), 8-11.

I.6.2. Ruhr as an Industrial Area

3969 Agreement for Establishment of an International Authority for the Ruhr. American Journal of International Law. 43:3 (July 1949), 140-153. Draft Text, Signed at London, 28 April 1949.

3970 Bonn, Moritz J. End of the War Over the Ruhr?. Bankers' Magazine (London). 169:1275 (June 1950), 534-539.

3971 Daniell, Raymond. Danger Signs in the Ruhr. New York Times Magazine. (30 March 1947), 10+.

3972 Daniell, Raymond. What a Ruhr Miner Thinks About. New York Times Magazine. (17 August 1947), 5+.

3973 Diebold, William, Jr. A Special Regime for the Ruhr? an Essay in Clarification. Control of Germany. Ed. Louis F. Aubert Et Al. Paris: Riviere, 1949, Pp. 81-108.

3974 Europe and the Ruhr. Planning (P.E.P.). 13:256 (4 October 1946), 1-23.

3975 Freeman, Christopher. Economics of the Ruhr. London: Birch, Changing Epoch Series No. 3, Pp. 24-47.

3976 Friters, Gerard M. The International Authority for the Ruhr. World Affairs (London). 3:4 (October 1949), 378-389.

3977 Garbuny, Siegfried. The Ruhr--Valley of Decision. Current History. 13:71 (July 1947), 22-26.

3978 Greenwood, H. Powys. Peace and the Ruhr. Contemporary Review. 168:955 (July 1945), 17-22.

3979 Harris, Chauncy D. The Ruhr Coal-Mining District. Geographical Review. 36:2 (April 1946), 194-221.

3980 Joesten, Joachim. The Ruhr Industry Today. New York: Joachim Joesten, New Germany Reports No. 27, June 1954, 19 P.

3981 Koranyi, Karl H. Brickman, Myrtle. The Ruhr Area: Its Structure and Economic Importance. Washington: United States Office of International Trade, Government Printing Office, August 1949, 62 P.

3982 Lewis, Flora. Rebirth--and Challenge--of the Ruhr. New York Times Magazine. (29 March 1959), 7+.

3983 Pebworth, Robert. The German Ruhr Coal Industry Under the European Coal and Steel Community. Proceedings of the Indiana Academy of Social Sciences. 3 (1968), 76-84.

3984 Pounds, Norman J. G. The Ruhr: A Study in Historical and Economic Geography. London: Faber and Faber, 1952, 283 P.

3985 Prittie, Terence C. F. Eternal Triangle--The Ruhr. This Is Germany.

Ed. Arthur Settel. New York: Sloane, 1950, Pp. 268-292.

3986 Rogers, John M. The International Authority for the Ruhr. Ph.D. Thesis, American University, 1960, 382 P.

3987 Thumm, Garold Wesley. The Western European Powers and International Control of the Ruhr. Ph.D. Thesis, University of Pennsylvania, 1954, 344 P.

3988 US, Department of State, Interim Research & Intell. Service. Observations on the Ruhr Coal Situation in the Summer and Fall of 1945. Washington: Department of State, Interim Research and Intelligence Service, Research and Analysis Branch, Report No. 3370, 1945, 25 P.

3989 US, Omgus, Military Governor. Ownership and Control of the Ruhr Industries. N.P.: Omgus, November 1948, 49 P.

3990 Van Schaick, F. L. Rehabilitation of the Ruhr. Editorial Research Reports. (18 February 1948), 109-122.

3991 White, Theodore H. in the Valley of Europe's Destiny. New York Times Magazine. (10 August 1952), 12+. Ruhr Industry.

3992 Wolf, Simon. The Ruhr Today. Contemporary Review. 184:1052 (August 1953), 76-80.

3993 Yoder, Amos. The Ruhr Authority and the German Problem. Review of Politics. 17:3 (July 1955), 345-358.

I.6.3. Energy Production

3994 Boldt, Karl. Hamburg in Need of a Liberal Energy Policy. Intereconomics. No. 12 (December 1967), 329-331.

3995 FRG, Federal Ministry for Scientific Research. Atomic Energy Program of the Federal Republic of Germany, 1963-1967. Bonn: Hermes, 1963, 35 P.

3996 Gerwin, Robert. Atoms in Germany: A Report on the State and Development of Nuclear Research and Nuclear Technology in the Federal Republic of Germany. Duesseldorf: Econ-Verlag, in Cooperation With Federal Ministry for Scientific Research, 1964, 167 P.

3997 Groener, Helmut. Problems of the German Energy Policy. German Economic Review. 12:2 (1974), 173-185.

3998 Hurter, Edwin. Germany's Atomic Energy Program. Swiss Review of World Affairs. 7:11 (February 1958), 7-10.

3999 Joesten, Joachim. The German Oil Industry in 1955. Great Barrington, Mass.: Joachim Joesten, New Germany Reports No. 31, November 1955, 16 P.

4000 Mischaikow, Michael K. Post-War Variations in the Position of German Coal (and Their Effect Upon Importation of United States Coal). Ph.D. Thesis, Indiana University, 1961, 186 P.

4001 Un, Economic Commission for Europe. Coal Consumption Trends in the Western Zones of Germany. Geneva: United Nations, Economic and Social Council, Economic Commission for Europe, Industry Division, Coal Section, 1953, 177 P.

4002 Waller, Peter P. Swain, Harry S. Changing Patterns of Oil Transportation and Refining in West Germany. Economic Geography. 43:2 (April 1967), 143-156.

4003 Wessels, Theodor. Inquiry Into German Power Production. German Economic Review. 1:3 (1963), 222-230.

4004 Zimmerman, Hans. West Germany's Atom Energy Program. Swiss Review of World Affairs. 12:3 (June 1962), 16-17.

I.6.4. Business

4005 Abel, Rein. The German Experience With Uniform Accounting and Its Relevance to the U.S. Controversies on Uniformity. Ph.D. Thesis, Columbia University, 1967, 320 P.

4006 Agmon, Tamir. The Relations Among Equity Markets: A Study of Share Price Co-Movements in the United States, United Kingdom, Germany and Japan. Journal of Finance. 27:4 (September 1972), 839-855.

4007 Baker, James C. The German Stock Market: Its Operations, Problems, and Prospects. New York: Praeger, 1970, 204 P.

4008 Baker, James C. The Development of the German Securities Exchange System. Marquette Business Review. 12:3 (Fall 1968), 83-99.

4009 Baker, James C. The German Securities Exchanges: Their Development, Operations and Problems. D.B.A. Thesis, Indiana University, 1966, 302 P.

4010 Barton-Dobenin, Joseph. A Critical Analysis of Corporate Financial Reporting and Its Impact on Capital Flows in Post-World-War-II West Germany. Ph.D. Thesis, University of Nebraska, 1966, 249 P.

4011 Baudler, Paul G. Directory of American Business in Germany. Munich: Seibt, 4Th Ed., 1971, 533 P.

4012 Becker, Helmut. Consumer Information and the Image of Advertising in Germany With Signigicant Comparisons to America. D.B.A. Thesis, Indiana University, 1971, 462 P.

4013 Business Europe. Operating in and From the German Market. Geneva: Business International, C.1962, 55 P.

4014 Commerce Clearing House. Cch Business Guide to Germany. Frankfurt: Cch-Germany, 1972, 149 P.

4015 Conrad, Klaus. Juettner, D. Johannes. Recent Behaviour of Stock Market Prices in Germany and the Random Walk Hypothesis. Kyklos. 26:3 (1973), 576-599.

4016 Crespi, Leo P. America's Interest in German Survey Research. Empirische Sozialforschung: Meinungs- Und Marktforschung, Methoden Und Probleme. Frankfurt Am Main: Institut Zur Foerderung Oeffentlicher angelegenheiten E.V., 1952, Pp. 215-217.

4017 E. J. P. Publications. A "Pocket" Directory of Manufacturers and Exporters of Germany, Maidenhead: E. J. P. Publications, 1967, 71 P.

4018 Engelmann, Konrad. Outlook for the Accounting Profession in Postwar Germany. Journal of Accountancy. 86:2 (August 1948), 129-132.

4019 Ernst and Ernst. West Germany: Characteristics of Business Entities. New York: Ernst and Ernst, 1970, 49 P.

4020 Ernst and Ernst. West Germany: A National Profile. New York: Ernst and Ernst, 1969, 32 P.

4021 Federal Republic of Germany: A Survey for Businessmen. London: London Chamber of Commerce, 1970, 48 P.

4022 Gesellschaft Fuer Marktforschung, Hamburg. The Market for U.S. Electronic Components in Western Germany and Berlin. Washington: U.S. Department of Commerce, Business and Defense Services Administration, 1963, 39 P.

4023 Hammerbacher, Hans L. Chambers of Commerce in the United States, "Industrie- Und Handelskammern" in Germany--Similarities and Differences. International Markets. 9:7 (July 1955), 27-28.

4024 Herbst, Axel. The Commercial Counsellor's Field of Activity. Intereconomics. No. 10 (October 1969), 323-325.

4025 Holzer, H. Peter. Corporate Financial Reporting in West-Germany. Accounting Review. 34:3 (July 1959), 399-402.

4026 Holzer, H. Peter. Schoenfeld, Hanns-Martin. The German Solution of the Post-War Price Level Problem. Accounting Review. 38:2 (April 1963), 377-381.

4027 Hurter, Edwin. The Development of Industrial Investment in West Germany. Swiss Review of World Affairs. 3:2 (May 1953), 13-14.

4028 Jaeggi, Urs. Wiedemann, Herbert. Office Automation: The Impact on Managers and Clerks in West German Industry and Commerce. Office Automation: Administrative and Human Problems. Ed. William H. Scott. Paris: Organisation for Economic Co-Operation and Development, 1965, Pp. 69-88.

4029 Killius, Juergen. Steefel, Ernest C. Business Operations in West Germany. Washington: Tax Management, 1971.

4030 Motekat, Ula K. Company Acts and Income Accounting Theory: A Comparative Analysis of Great Britain and West Germany. D.B.A. Thesis, University of Colorado, 1971, 400 P.

4031 Mueller, Gerd. The German Life Insurance Business Since 1945. International Markets. 9:11 (December 1955), 12-17.

4032 Niehus, Rudolf J. Tax-Free Stock Dividends and the New Model Income Statement for German Corporations. Accounting Review. 36:2 (April 1961), 259-264.

4033 Plath, Werner. The German Insurance Industry Rebuilds. International Markets. 10:10 (October 1956), 23-27.

4034 Rademacher's Directory for Industry and Export Trade. Hamburg: Rademacher, 1953, 3 Vols.

4035 Raetsch, Herbert. The New Professional Code for Certified Accountants and Licensed Accountants in the Federal Republic of Germany. Accounting Review. 39:1 (January 1964), 140-144.

4036 Rolfe, Sidney E. Capital Markets in the Atlantic Economic Relationships. Boulogne-Sur-Seine: Atlantic Institute, 1967, 87 P.

4037 Schmidt, J. L. Antagonisms in the West German Monopolies. World Marxist Review: Problems of Peace and Socialism. 2:12 (December 1959), 70-76.

4038 Schmitt, Matthias. Hanover-Fair 1968--An Event of World-Wide Attraction. Intereconomics. No. 4 (April 1968), 120-121.

4039 Seibt, Arthur. Export Directory of German Industries. Munich: Seibt, 13Th Ed., 1954.

4040 Selling Consumer Goods to West Germany. London: British National Export Council, 1970, 84 P.

4041 Steefel, Ernest C. Trading Under the Laws of Germany. New York: German American Trade Promotion Office, 2D Ed., 1956, 231 P.

4042 Streit, M. E. Investment Reaction Patterns--The Case of American and West German Manufacturing Industry. Weltwirtschaftliches Archiv. 105:1 (January 1950), 66-86.

4043 Thorelli, Hans. Becker, Helmut. Engledow, Jack. The Information Seekers. Cambridge, Mass.: Ballinger Publishing Company, 1975, 288 P.

4044 US, Department of Commerce, Bureau of Foreign Commerce. World Trade Information Service. Washington: Department of Commerce, Bureau of Foreign Commerce, Government Printing Office, 1953-62. Numerous Reports on Economic Developments, Basic Data, Living Conditions, Foreign Trade, Marketing, Etc.; Superseded By "Overseas Business Reports," 1962 to Date.

4045 US, Economic Cooperation Administration. Guide and Directory for Trading With Germany. Frankfurt: Economic Cooperation Administration, Special Mission to Germany, 1950, 55 P.

4046 US, Economic Cooperation Administration. Western German Importers of U.S. Commodities for Industrial Use. Frankfurt: Economic Cooperation Administration, Special Mission to Germany, 1950, 82 P.

4047 Vagts, Detlev F. Reforming the "Modern" Corporation: Perspectives From the German. Harvard Law Review. 80:1 (November 1966), 23-89.

4048 Vogl, Frank. German Business After the Economic Miracle. London: The Macmillan Press Ltd., 1973, Vi and 264 P.

4049 Weis, George, Editor. On the Interpretation of "Fair Purchase Price" in the Meaning of Art. 3, Para. 2, Reao. Berlin: N.P., 1954, 24 P.

4050 Weismann, Arnold. Profit and Loss Accounts in the German Federal Republic. Journal of Common Market Studies. 2:3 (March 1964), 185-198.

4051 Werkman, Casper J. Trademarks: Their Creation, Psychology and Perception. New York: Barnes & Noble, 1974, Xviii and 496 P., Esp. Pp. 240-269.

4052 West German Manufacturers and Exporters of Electrical Goods. Hamburg: Schimmelpfeng, 1960, 38 P.

4053 Wilhelms, Christian. Boeck, Klaus. Market and Marketing in the Federal Republic of Germany: A Manual for Exporters From Developing Countries. Hamburg: Weltarchiv, 1971, 273 P.

I.6.5. Business Regulation (See Also E.3.4.4)

4054 Maier, Karl F. Has Western Germany a Liberal Market Economy?. Banca Nazionale Del Lavoro, Quarterly Review (Rome). 5:20 (January-March 1952), 37-43.

4055 Marburg, Theodore. Cartels, Competition and Public Policy in Germany. Marquette Business Review. 4:3 (June 1960), 18-31.

4056 Moetteli, Carlo. West Germany: Free Enterprise or Planned Economy?. Swiss Review of World Affairs. 1:12 (March 1952), 3-7.

4057 Oliver, Henry M. German Neoliberalism. Quarterly Journal of Economics. 74:1 (February 1960), 117-149.

4058 Stokes, William S. Economic Liberalism in Post-War Germany. New Individualist Review. 3:4 (Spring 1965), 30-38.

I.6.6. Management; Business Executives

4059 Bendix, Reinhard. Work and Authority in Industry: Ideologies of Management in the Course of Industrialization. New York: Wiley, 1956, Pp. 341-433.

4060 Copeman, George H. The Chief Executive and Business Growth: A Comparative Study in the United States, Britain and Germany. London and New York: Leviathan, 1971, 362 P.

4061 Detlefsen, J. A. Investigating German Personnel Management Techniques. Personnel Administration. 9:3 (January 1947), 9-11.

4062 Granick, David. The European Executive. Garden City: Doubleday, 1962, Esp. Pp. 49-59, 150-168, 212-221, 276-236.

4063 Haire, Mason. Ghiselli, Edwin E. Porter, Lyman W. Cultural Patterns in the Role of the Manager. Industrial Relations. 2:2 (February 1963), 95-118.

4064 Hartmann, Heinz. Authority and Organization in German Management. Princeton: Princeton University Press, 1959, 318 P.

4065 Hartmann, Heinz. Managers and Entrepreneurs: A Useful Distinction?. Administrative Science Quarterly. 3:4 (March 1959), 429-451.

4066 Klee, Josef. Wendt, Peter D. Physical Distribution in Modern Management. Munich: Moderne Industrie, 1972, 371 P.

4067 Lauterbach, Albert. Perceptions of Management: Case Materials From Western and Northern Europe. Administrative Science Quarterly. 2:1 (June 1957), 97-109.

4068 Lewis, Roy. Stewart, Rosemary. The Managers: A New Examination of the English, German, and American Executive. New York: New American Library, 1961, 256 P.

4069 P. S. J. C. Managerial Revolution in Western Germany. World Today. 7:6 (June 1951), 249-262.

4070 Swiridoff, Paul. Portraits From German Economic Life. Pfullingen: Neske, 1966, 218 P.

I.6.7. Cooperatives

4071 Agricultural and Home Economics Evaluation & Info. Service. Rural Cooperatives in the Federal Republic of Germany. Bad Godesberg: Land- Und Hauswirtschaftlicher Auswertungs- Und Informationsdienst, 1961, 35 P.

4072 Central Buying for Housing: A German Example. Review of International Cooperation. 45:6 (June 1952), 128-130.

4073 Evely, Richard. Patterns of Consumption and Cooperative Trade. Review of International Cooperation. 46:11 (November 1953), 272-275.

4074 Everling, H. Central Union of German Consumers' Societies 50 Years Old. Review of International Cooperation. 46:5 (May 1953), 100-105.

4075 Fluegge, Walter. Cooperative Mail Order Business. Review of International Cooperation. 52:7-8 (July-August 1959), 210-213.

4076 Gebauer, Werner. Aspects of the Cooperative Movement in the Federal Republic of Germany: Enterprise Co-Op. Review of International Cooperation. 62:5 (1969), 210-216.

4077 German Co-Operative Reconstruction. Review of International Cooperation. 40:1 (January 1947), 14-16.

4078 Gutmann, Rudolf. The Organization and Management of Co-Operative Societies: Manual for Co-Operative Officials. Berlin: Verband Deutscher Konsumgenossenschaften, 1967, 275 P.

4079 Hasselmann, Erwin. Consumer's Co-Operation in Germany. Hamburg: Verlagsgesellschaft Deutscher Konsumgenossenschaften M.B.H., 1953, 73 P.

4080 Hesselbach, Walter. Commonweal Enterprise: Essay of a Typology of Non-Capitalist Forms of Enterprise. Frankfurt: Bank Fuer Gemeinwirtschaft, 1970, 40 P.

4081 Hesselbach, Walter. The Importance of Commonweal Enterprise Within the German Ecconomy. Frankfurt: Bank Fuer Gemeinwirtschaft, 1970, 20 P.

4082 Infield, Henrik F. A German Cooperative Village. Review of International Cooperation. 47:3 (March 1954), 63-67.

4083 Kelly, Matthew A. The German Cooperative Movement in the Occupation. Sociology and Social Research. 33:4 (March-April 1949), 263-270.

4084 Pelster, H. The German Consumers' Movement in 1960. Review of International Cooperation. 54:6 (June 1961), 147-148.

4085 Pernica, Karel M. The German Problem and the Co-Operative Movement's Role. Prague: Central Co-Operative Council, 1961, 52 P.

4086 Peter, A. Industrial Cooperatives. Review of International Cooperation. 62:5 (1969), 221-224.

4087 Schumacher, Carl. A Ten Year Effort. Review of International Cooperation. 50:5 (May 1957), 129-135.

4088 Sierakowsky, Heinrich. Problems of the German Co-Operative Movement. Review of International Cooperation. 44:5 (May 1951), 120-124.

4089 Thiemeyer, Theo. Principles of a Theory of Commonweal Economy. Frankfurt: Bank Fuer Gemeinwirtschaft, 1970, 44 P.

4090 Watkins, W. P. The Co-Operative Sector in Western Germany. Review of International Cooperation. 43:9 (September 1950), 245-248.

4091 Weisser, Gerhard. Blume, O. Achievements of Self Help in the Federal Republic of Germany. Annals of Collective Economy. 28:1 (January-March 1957), 35-80.

4092 Weisser, Gerhard. Passnacht, Bertel. Co-Operatives as an Aid to Small Business in Germany. Law and Contemporary Problems. 24:1 (Winter 1959), 208-221.

4093 Winkler, Hans. Cooperatives and the North Atlantic Fisheries. Review of International Cooperation. 47:1 (January 1954), 18-23.

I.7. Labor Movements and Issues (See Also E.3.4.8)

I.7.1. Workers and Labor Market

4094 Beckner, Earl R. Unemployment and Underdevelopment in the Bizonal Area of Germany. Washington: War Department, Office of the Military Government, Civil Affairs Division, Manpower Division, 1949, 78 P.

4095 Bednarik, Karl. The Young Worker of to-Day, a New Type. London: Faber and Faber, 1955, 146 P.

4096 FRG, Federal Statistical Office. Statistics on Gainfully Active Persons and on Employment Cases. Stuttgart: Kohlhammer, 1959, 21 P.

4097 Hamilton, Richard F. Affluence and the Worker: The West German Case. American Journal of Sociology. 71:2 (September 1965), 144-152.

4098 Hurter, Edwin. West Germany's Unemployment Analyzed. Swiss Review of World Affairs. 2:9 (December 1952), 4-5.

4099 Kindleberger, Charles P. Europe's Postwar Growth: The Role of Labor Supply. Cambridge: Harvard University Press, 1967, Xi and 270 P.

4100 Klabunde, Hans. Meyer, Karl J. The Labour Market in the Federal Republic of Germany. Bonn: Federal Ministry of Labour and the Social Structure, Social Policy in Germany No. 2, 1965, 36 P.

4101 Kranz, Guenter. Hubbert, Bernd. Promotion of All-The-Year-Round Employment in the Building Industry. Bonn: Federal Ministry of Labour and the Social Structure, Social Policy in Germany No. 7, 1964, 28 P.

4102 Lutz, Burkhart. Weltz, Friedrich. Willener, Alfred. Technical Change and Manpower Planning: The Federal Republic of Germany. Technical Charge and Manpower Planning: Co-Ordination at The Enterprise Level. Ed. Solomon Barkin. Paris: Organisation for Economic Cooperation and Development, May 1967, Pp. 77-120.

4103 Manpower in Germany. International Labour Review. 57:3 (March 1948), 239-241.

4104 Neef, Arthur. International Unemployment Rates, 1960-64. Monthly Labour Review. 88:3 (March 1965), 256-259.

4105 Neuloh, Otto. The German Blue-Collar Worker. International Journal of Comparative Sociology. 10:1-2 (March-June 1969), 151-160.

4106 Oecd. Manpower Policy in Germany. Paris: Organization for Economic Cooperation and Development, May 1974, 163 P.

4107 Social Conditions of Transport Workers in Germany. International Labour Review. 56:5-6 (November-December 1947), 576-584.

4108 Sorrentino, Constance. Unemployment in Nine Industrialized Countries. Monthly Labor Review. 95:6 (June 1972), 29-33.

4109 US, Hicog, Office of Administration. Unemployment in Western Germany: A Graphic Study. Frankfurt: Hicog, Office of Administration, 1950, 62 P.

4110 US, Omgus, Manpower Division. Labor. N.P.: Omgus, November 1947.

4111 US, Omgus, Manpower Division. Registration, Employment and Unemployment, U.S. Zone. N.P.: Omgus, Manpower Division, Periodically From March 1946 to November 1948.

4112 US, Omgus, Manpower Division. Unemployment, Vacant Positions, Placements--Bizonal Area and French Zone, May 1949. N.P.: Omgus, July 1949.

4113 Wagner, Helmut R. A New Generation of German Labor. Social Research. 23:2 (Summer 1956), 151-170.

4114 Wedderburn, Dorothy. Enterprise Planning for Change: Co-Ordination of Manpower and Technical Planning. Paris: Organisation for Economic Cooperation and Development, April 1968, 140 P.

4115 Wittich, Guenter J. The German Road to Full Employment. Ph.D. Thesis, University of California, Berkeley, 1966, 289 P.

4116 Working Conditions in Germany. International Labour Review. 56:5-6 (November-December 1947), 611-613.

4117 Wuelker, Gabriele. Demographic Structure and the Labour Market. United Asia. 19:6 (November-December 1967), 339-342.

I.7.2. Trade Unions

4118 Behrendt, Albert. The W.F.T.U. and the German Trade Unions. Berlin (East): Tribuene, 1965, 291 P.

4119 Brickman, Harry. Freedom of Association in Eight European Countries. Monthly Labour Review. 86:9 (September 1963), 1020-1025.

4120 Carey, James B. Trade Unions and Democracy; a Comparative Study of United States, French, Italian and West German Unions. Washington: National Planning Association, 1957, 90 P.

4121 Cook, Alice Hanson. Bavarian Trade Union Youth. Frankfurt: Hicog, Office of Labor Affairs, Visiting Expert Series No. 17, July 1950, 38 P.

4122 Davis, Melton S. The New German Trade Unions. Fortnightly. 161:963 (March 1947), 198-203.

4123 Dietrich, George Philipp. The Trade Union Role in the Reconstruction of Germany. Berlin: Omgus, Manpower Division, Visiting Expert Series No. 6, March 1949, 26 P.

4124 Dobell, Peter. Trade Unionism in West Germany. International Journal. 6:4 (Autumn 1951), 308-318.

4125 Erhard, Ludwig. Labor and German Prosperity. Current History. 37:216 (August 1959), 65-67.

4126 Esser, F. K. Some Aspects of the Trade Union Movement in Western Germany. Occidente. 11:4 (1955), 300-310.

4127 Field, Peter. Germany. Labour Monthly. 27:11 (November 1945), 349-352.

4128 Fikentscher, Wolfgang. Political Strikes Under German Law. American Journal of Comparative Law. 2:1 (Winter 1953), 72-78.

4129 Friedmann, Wolfgang G. The Aim of German's Trade Unions. Fortnightly. 172:1031 (November 1952), 291-295.

4130 Geilinger, Eduard. West German Trade Union Policy. Swiss Review of World Affairs. 3:9 (December 1953), 11+.

4131 Gerns, Willi. Incomes Policy and Trade Unions in the FRG. World Marxist Review. 14:2 (February 1971), 96-103.

4132 Gottfurcht, Hans. Trade Unions in Germany. Socialist Commentary. 12 (September 1948), 271-273.

4133 Grebing, Helga. The History of the German Labour Movement--A Survey. London: Wolff, 1969, 227 P.

4134 Hartfiel, Guenter. White-Collar Trade Unions: Germany. White-Collar Trade Unions: Contemporary Developments in Industrialized Societies. Ed. Adolf Sturmthal. Urbana: University of Illinois Press, 1966, Pp. 127-164.

4135 Heidenheimer, Arnold J. Trade Unions, Benefit Systems and Party Mobilization Styles: "Horizontal" Influences on the British Labour and German Social Democratic Parties. Comparative Politics. 1:3 (April 1969), 313-342.

4136 Heimburger, Artur. The Decisive Step--Recollections of a Veteran Trade Unionist of the First Post-War Years of Trade Union Activity in Germany. Berlin (East): Tribuene, 1966, 31 P.

4137 Hesselbach, Walter. Co-Operative Enterprises in West Germany: The Contribution of the Trade Unions to a

Consumer-Oriented Economic Policy. Frankfurt: Europaeische Verlagsanstalt, 1967, 127 P.

4138 Huddleston, Joan. Trade Unions in the German Federal Republic. Political Quarterly. 38:2 (April-June 1967), 165-176.

4139 Joensson, Algot. Organized Labor and Democracy in Germany. Frankfurt: Omgus, Manpower Division, Visiting Expert Series No. 15, October 1949, 15 P.

4140 Joesten, Joachim. German Trade Unions, 1945-1949. Great Barrington, Mass.: Joachim Joesten, New Germany Reports No. 10, May 1949, 20 P.

4141 Kelly, Matthew A. Communists in German Labor Organizations. Journal of Political Economy. 57:3 (June 1949), 213-226.

4142 Kelly, Matthew A. The Reconstitution of the German Trade Union Movement. Political Science Quarterly. 64:1 (March 1949), 24-49.

4143 Kendall, Walter. The Labour Movement in Europe. London: Allen Lane, 1974, 448 P. France, FRG, Italy, UK, Belgium, Netherlands.

4144 Kerr, Clark. The Trade Union Movement and the Redistribution of Power in Postwar Germany. Quarterly Journal of Economics. 68:4 (November 1954), 535-564.

4145 Kirchheimer, Otto. West German Trade Unions. World Politics. 8:4 (July 1956), 484-514.

4146 Kirchheimer, Otto. West German Trade Unions: Their Domestic and Foreign Policies. Santa Monica: Rand Corporation, RM-1673-Rc, 1956, 168 P.

4147 Kirchheimer, Otto. West German Trade-Unions: Their Domestic and Foreign Policies. West German Leadership and Foreign Policy. Ed. Hans Speier and W. Phillips Davison. Evanston, White Plains: Row, Peterson, 1957, Pp. 136-194.

4148 Kirkwood, Thomas W. Contemporary Leadership Dilemmas in the German Trade Union Movement: An External Cross-Pressure Analysis. Ph.D. Thesis, University of Colorado, 1974.

4149 Kuenzli, Irvin R. Trade Unions and Public Education in Western Germany. Frankfurt: Omgus, Manpower Division, Visiting Expert Series No. 11, September 1949, 16 P.

4150 Ledwohn, Josef. The Fight for the Trade Unions in Federal Germany. World Marxist Review: Problems of Peace and Socialism. 5:9 (September 1962), 42-48.

4151 Lepinski, Franz. The German Trade Union Movement. International Labour Review. 79:1 (January 1959), 57-78.

4152 Liss, Samuel. Revival of Free Labor Organizations in the United States Occupation Zone in Germany: A Preview. Southern Economic Journal. 13:3 (January 1947), 247-256.

4153 Loesche, Peter. Stages in the Evolution of the German Labor Movement. The International Labor Movement in Transition. Ed. Adolf Sturmthal and James G. Scoville. Urbana: University of Illinois Press, 1973, Pp. 101-122.

4154 Marahrens, Friedhelm. Cooperative Trade Union Banking. Review of International Cooperation. 46:2 (February 1953), 30-34.

4155 Meijer, Hendricus Johannes. Koppens, Hendrikus Wilhelmus. Laan, Reint, Jr. A Message From Dutch Trade Unionists to German Labor. Berlin: Omgus, Manpower Division, Visiting Expert Series No. 7, March 1949, 12 P.

4156 Mende, Tibor. Europe and German Labour Unity. Fortnightly. 159:953 (May 1946), 299-306.

4157 Mire, Joseph. Labor Organization in German Public Administration and Services. Berlin: Omgus, Manpower Division, Visiting Expert Series No. 8, May 1949, 33 P.

4158 Neumann, Franz L. The Labor Movement in Germany. Germany and the Future of Europe. Ed. Hans J. Morgenthau. Chicago: University of Chicago Press, 1951, Pp. 100-107.

4159 Phillips, Paul. German Trade Union Movement Under American Occupation, 1945-1949. Science & Society. 14:4 (Fall 1950), 289-306.

4160 Reich, Nathan. The Political "Dilemma" of German Trade Unionism. American Journal of Economics and Sociology. 20:4 (July 1961), 411-424.

4161 Reich, Nathan. Germany's Labor and Economic Recovery. Proceedings of the Academy of Political Science. 26:2 (January 1955), 47-64.

4162 Rimlinger, Gaston V. International Differences in the Strike Propensity of Coal Miners: Experience in Four Countries. Industrial and Labor Relations Review. 12:2 (April 1959), 389-405. Usa, UK, France, FRG.

4163 Rosenberg, Ludwig. Trade Unions in a Social Constitutional State. Berlin: German Trade Union Federation, 1966, 32 P. Address at 7Th Ordinary Congress of Dgb.

4164 Saposs, David J. Current Trade-Union Movements of Western Europe. Social Research. 21:3 (Autumn 1954), 297-313.

4165 Saposs, David J. Recent Labor Political Action in Western Europe. Social Research. 21:4 (Winter 1954), 451-466.

4166 Schuyler, Joseph B. Germany's Dgb. Social Order. 4:6 (June 1954), 257-262.

4167 Sturmthal, Adolf. Comparative Labor Movements: Ideological Roots and Institutional Development. Belmont: Wadsworth, 1972, 176 P.

4168 Taft, Philip. Germany. Comparative Labor Movements. Ed. Walter Galenson. New York: Russell & Russell, 1968, Pp. 243-312.

4169 Tarnow, Fritz. Labor and Trade Unionism in Germany. Annals of the American Academy of Political and Social Science. 260 (November 1948), 90-98.

4170 Trade Union Membership in Germany. International Labour Review. 57:4 (April 1948), 400-401.

4171 US, Department of State, Office of Research & Intelligence. Status and Prospects of German Trade-Unions and Works Councils. Washington: Department of State, Office of Research and Intelligence, Oir Report No. 3381, 1946, 63 P.

4172 US, Omgus, Manpower Division. Union Membership, Trade Union and Economic Group, Three Western Zones, 31 December 1949-Western Sectors of Berlin, 6 April 1949. N.P.: Omgus, Statistical Bulletin No. 2, May 1949.

4173 US, Omgus, Military Governor. Labor Organization in the U.S. Zone of Germany. N.P.: Omgus, April 1946, 20 P.

4174 Wagenfuehr, Rolf. Unions in Western Germany. Socialist Commentary. 14 (August 1950), 188-190.

4175 Wells, Roger Hewes. The Revival of German Unions of Local Authorities After World War II. American

Political Science Review. 41:6 (December 1947), 1182-1187.

4176 Willey, Richard James. Democracy in the West German Trade Unions: A Reappraisal of the "Iron Law". Sage Professional Papers in Comparative Politics. 2:23 (1971), 703-755.

4177 Willey, Richard James. Labor and Politics in West Germany: The Deutscher Gewerkschaftsbund, 1949-1963. Ph.D. Thesis, Princeton University, 1964, 346 P.

4178 Willey, Richard James. Trade Unions and Political Parties in the Federal Republic Of Germany. Industrial and Labor Relations Review. 28:1 (October 1974), 38-59.

4179 Wohlgemuth, Ernest. The Revival of Trade Unionism in Western Germany. Ph.D. Thesis, University of Chicago, 1957, 232 P.

4180 World Federation of Trade Unions. Report of the Commission to Investigate Conditions in Germany. Moscow: World Federation of Trade Unions, June 1946, 64 P.

I.7.3. Law and Policymaking

4181 Earl, Lewis H. Linton, John H. Mullady, Philomena. Manpower Policy and Programs in Five Western European Countries: France, Great Britain, the Netherlands, Sweden, and West Germany. Washington: Department of Labor, Manpower Administration, 1966, 59 P.

4182 Edelman, Murray. Fleming, Robben W. The Politics of Wage-Price Decisions: A Four-Country Analysis. Urbana: University of Illinois Press, 1965, 331 P. Italy, West Germany, United Kingdom, Netherlands.

4183 Handsaker, Morrison. Labor Courts in Germany. Arbitration Journal. 8:3 (1953), 131-133.

4184 Kelly, Matthew A. Allied Policy on Wages in Occupied Germany. International Labour Review. 55:5 (May 1947), 351-371.

4185 Nipperdey, Hans Carl. Development of Labour Law in the Federal Republic of Germany Since 1945. Geneva: International Labour Office, 1954, 39 P.

4186 Nipperdey, Hans Carl. The Development of Labour Law in the Federal Republic of Germany Since 1945. International Labour Review. 70:1 (July 1954), 26-43; and 70:2 (August 1954), 148-167.

4187 Ostwald, Walter. West German Labour Legislation. Contemporary Review. 190:1089 (September 1956), 168-170.

4188 Roberts, Benjamin C. National Wages Policy in War and Peace. New York: Macmillan, 1958, 180 P.

4189 Sahmer, Heinz. The Labour Courts. Bonn: Federal Ministry of Labour and the Social Structure, Social Policy in Germany No. 24, 1965, 17 P.

4190 Ulman, Lloyd. Flanagan, Robert J. Wage Restraint: A Study of Incomes Policies in Western Europe. Berkeley: University of California Press, 1971, 257 P., Esp. Pp. 171-199.

4191 Weigert, Oscar. Labor Legislation in Western Germany During the Occupation. Monthly Labor Review. 71:6 (December 1950), 668-672.

I.7.4. Labor-Management Relations; Codetermination

4192 Altmar, Wilfred. German Labour Relations. Contemporary Review. 193:1108 (April 1958), 212-216.

4193 Balke, Siegfried. Erdmann, Ernst-Gerhard. Expansion of Co-Determination in the Federal Republic of Germany: The Myth of Codetermination. Cologne: Bundesvereinigung Der Deutschen Arbeitgeberverbaende, 1966, 54 P.

4194 Beal, Edwin F. Origins of Codetermination in Western Germany. Ph.D. Thesis, Cornell University, 1953.

4195 Beal, Edwin F. Origins of Codetermination. Industrial and Labor Relations Review. 8:4 (July 1955), 483-498.

4196 Blumenthal, Werner Michael. Codetermination in the German Steel Industry: A Report of Experience. Princeton: Princeton University, Department of Economics and Sociology, Industrial Relations Section, 1956, 116 P.

4197 Blumenthal, Werner Michael. Labor-Management Relations in the German Steel Industry, 1947-54. Ph.D. Thesis, Princeton University, 1956, 338 P.

4198 Cole, R. Taylor. Labor Relations. Governing Postwar Germany. Ed. Edward H. Litchfield and Associates. Ithaca: Cornell University Press, 1953, Pp. 361-380.

4199 Cole, R. Taylor Labor Relations in Western Germany. Berlin: Omgus, Manpower Division, Visiting Expert Series No. 2, October 1948, 35 P.

4200 Crossman, George R. Codetermination and the West German Trade Unions. Ph.D. Thesis, Columbia University, 1961, 305 P.

4201 De Schweinitz, Dorothea. Labor-Management Consultation in the Factory: The Experience in Sweden, England, and the Federal Republic of Germany. Honolulu: University of Hawaii, Industrial Relations Center, Occasional Publication No. 55, 1966, 128 P.

4202 Dowell, Jack D. The Legislative Process in the West German Bundestag: The Codetermination Law of May, 1951. Ph.D. Thesis, Stanford University, 1958, 217 P.

4203 Dowell, Jack D. The Legislative Process in the West German Bundestag: The Struggle for Codetermination in the Basic Industries. Washington State University, Research Studies. 33:3 (September 1965), 79-144.

4204 FRG. German Works Council Act of 1972. Chicago: Commerce Clearing House, 1972, 123 P.

4205 Fischer, Guido. Problems Arising From Workers' Co-Determination in the Federal German Republic. Transactions of the Third World Congress of Sociology. London: International Sociological Association, 1956, Vol. 2, Pp. 204-212.

4206 Fisher, Paul. Labor Codetermination in Germany. Social Research. 18:4 (December 1951), 449-485.

4207 Fisher, Paul. Works Councils in Germany. Frankfurt: Hicog, Office of Labor Affairs, Visiting Expert Series No. 18, March 1951, 43 P.

4208 Friedrich, Otto. German Co-Determination: Parity Is the Goal. Columbia Journal of World Business. 5:1 (January-February 1970), 49-55.

4209 Fuerstenberg, Friedrich. Workers' Participation in Management in the Federal Republic of Germany. Bulletin of the International Institute for Labour Studies (Geneva). No. 6 (June 1969), 94-148.

4210 German Federation of Trade Unions. Co-Determination: A Contemporary Demand. Duesseldorf: Deutscher

Gewerkschaftsbund, 1966, 37 P.

4211 Hartmann, Heinz. Codetermination in West Germany. Industrial Relations. 9:2 (February 1970), 137-147.

4212 Herbst, Fritz. Notice of Dismissal and Protection Against Dismissal. Bonn: Federal Ministry of Labour and the Social Structure, Social Policy in Germany No. 13, 1963, 18 P.

4213 Herding, Richard. Job Control and Union Structure: A Study on Plant-Level Industrial Conflict in the United States with a Comparative Perspective on West Germany. Rotterdam: Rotterdam University Press, 1972, 401 P.

4214 Herschel, Wilhelm. Employee Representation in the Federal Republic of Germany. International Labour Review. 64:2-3 (August-September 1951), 207-215.

4215 Hurter, Edwin. West Germany's Codetermination Law. Swiss Review of World Affairs. 2:6 (September 1952), 13-14.

4216 Jungbluth, Adolf. The Role of the Labour Manager in Undertakings Under Co-Management in the Federal Republic of Germany. International Labour Review. 78:4 (October 1958), 368-387.

4217 Kerr, Clark. Collective Bargaining in Post-War Germany. Industrial Labor Relations Review. 5:3 (April 1952), 377-382.

4218 Kerr, Clark. Collective Bargaining in Postwar Germany. Contemporary Collective Bargaining in Seven Countries. Ed. Adolf F. Sturmthal. Ithaca: Cornell University, Institute of International Industrial and Labor Relations, 1957, Pp. 168-209.

4219 King, Charles D. Participative Industrial Relations: A Study of the Systems of Worker's Participation in Great Britain, West Germany and Yugoslavia. Ph.D. Thesis, State University of New York at Buffalo, 1969, 356 P.

4220 Kitano, Tosinobu G. F. A Genetic Study of German Managerial Policy of Works Community. Ph.D. Thesis, St. Louis University, 1960, 241 P.

4221 Klein, Alfons. Co-Determination and the Law Governing Works Councils and Staff Representation in the Public Services. Bonn: Federal Ministry of Labour and the Social Structure, Social Policy in Germany No. 23, 1963, 60 P.

4222 Kronstein, Heinrich. Collective Bargaining in Germany: Before 1933 and After 1945. American Journal of Comparative Law. 1:3 (Summer 1952), 199-214.

4223 Kurth, Edmund A. Codetermination in Germany--Peace at Last?. Social Order. 4:1 (January 1954), 19-28.

4224 Kurth, Edmund A. Codetermination in West Germany. Review of Social Economy. 11:1 (March 1953), 54-69.

4225 Kurth, Edmund A. German Catholic Thought on Codetermination. Ph.D. Thesis, Loras College, 1953.

4226 Lauer, Quentin. Co-Management in Germany. Social Order. 1:1 (January 1951), 11-22.

4227 Ledwohn, Josef. Federal Republic of Germany: The Workers Want a Share in Management. World Marxist Review: Problems of Peace and Socialism. 9:11 (November 1966), 18-24.

4228 Mcpherson, William H. Codetermination: Germany's Move Toward a New Economy. Industrial and Labor Relations Review. 5:1 (October 1951), 20-32.

4229 Mcpherson, William H. Codetermination in Practice. Industrial and Labor Relations Review. 8:4 (July 1955), 499-519.

4230 Mcpherson, William H. European Variations on the Mediation Theme. Labor Law Journal. 6:8 (August 1955), 525-536.

4231 Mcpherson, William H. Labor Relations in Postwar Germany. Annals of the American Academy of Political and Social Science. 310 (March 1957), 55-65.

4232 Mcpherson, William H. Public Employee Relations in West Germany. Ann Arbor: University of Michigan and Wayne State University, Institute of Labor and Industrial Relations, 1971, 251 P.

4233 Mcpherson, William H. Blumenthal, Werner Michael. Keller, Peter. Kerr, Clark. Spiro, Herbert J. Weigert, Oscar. German Experience With Codetermination. Proceedings of the Eighth Annual Meeting, New York City, 28-30 December 1955, Industrial Relations Research Association. Ed. L. Reed Tripp. Madison: Industrial Relations Research Association, 1956, Pp. 118-149. A Panel Discussion With Audience Participation.

4234 Neuloh, Otto. Changes in German Industrial Organization: A Systematic and Historical Introduction to Co-Determination. Transactions of the Third World Congress of Sociology. London: International Sociological Association, 1956, Vol. 2, Pp. 41-48.

4235 The New West German Co-Determination Law. World Today. 8:10 (October 1952), 409-411.

4236 Rachocki, Janusz. The Doctrine of Social Partnership ("Soziale Partnerschaft") and Relations Between Labour and Capital in the German Federal Republic. Polish Western Affairs. 12:2 (1971), 207-225.

4237 Reichel, Hans. Recent Trends in Collective Bargaining in the Federal Republic of Germany. International Labour Review. 104:6 (Decmeber 1971), 469-487.

4238 Reichel, Hans. Ringer, Franz. Freedom of Association and the Relationship Betwwen the Two Sides of Industry. Bonn: Federal Ministry of Labour and the Social Structure, Social Policy in Germany No. 18, 1964, 34 P.

4239 Reichel, Hans. Wlotzke, Otfried. Collective Bargaining and the Law Governing Collective Agreements. Bonn: Federal Ministry of Labour and the Social Structure, Social Policy in Germany No. 19, 1963, 30 P.

4240 Reichel, Hans. Zschocher, Hanns. Conciliation and Arbitration and the Law as Applied to Labour Disputes. Bonn: Federal Ministry of Labour and the Social Structure, Social Policy in Germany No. 20, 1963, 22 P.

4241 Rosenberg, Ludwig. Co-Determination Rights of Workers in Germany. Duesseldorf: German Trade Union Federation, N.D., 31 P.

4242 Ross, Arthur M. Prosperity and Labor Relations in Europe: The Case of West Germany. Quarterly Journal of Economics. 76:3 (August 1962), 331-359.

4243 Scharff, Monroe B. Human Relations in a West German Plant. Personnel. 29:1 (July 1952), 44-49.

4244 Shuchman, Abraham. Codetermination in West Germany. Ph.D. Thesis, University of Pennsylvania, 1955, 623 P.

4245 Shuchman, Abraham. Codetermination: Labor's Middle Way in Germany. Washington: Public Affairs Press,

1957, 247 p.

4246 Shuchman, Abraham. Economic Rationale of Codetermination. Industrial and Labor Relations Review. 10:2 (January 1957), 270-283.

4247 Spiro, Herbert J. Co-Determination in Germany. American Political Science Review. 48:4 (December 1954), 1114-1127.

4248 Spiro, Herbert J. The Politics of German Codetermination. Cambridge: Harvard University Press, 1958, 180 p.

4249 Sturmthal, Adolf. Workers Councils: A Study of Workplace Organization on Both Sides of the Iron Curtain. Cambridge: Harvard University Press, 1964, 217 p., Esp. pp. 53-85.

4250 UK, Foreign Office. Industrial Relations in Germany, 1945-1949: An Account of The Post-War Growth of Employers' and Workers' Organisations in the British Zone of Germany. London: H.M. Stationery Office, Cmd 7923, 1950, 25 p.

4251 Wachenheim, Hedwig. German Labor Asks Co-Management. Foreign Affairs. 31:2 (January 1953), 310-320.

4252 Weigert, Oscar. Co-Determination in Western Germany. Monthly Labor Review. 73:6 (December 1951), 649-656.

4253 Wunderlich, Frieda. Co-Determination in German Industry. Social Research. 20:1 (Spring 1953), 75-90.

I.7.5. Foreign Workers

4254 Bain, Trevor. Pauga, Alvis. Foreign Workers and the Intraindustry Wage Structure in West Germany. Kyklos. 25:4 (1972), 820-824.

4255 Boehning, W. R. The Migration of Workers in the United Kingdom and the European Community. London: Oxford University Press, 1972, xvi and 167 p.

4256 Boehning, W. R. Maillat, D. The Effects of the Employment of Foreign Workers. Paris: Organization for Economic Cooperation and Development, July 1974, 189 p.

4257 Botsas, Eleutherios N. Some Economic Aspects of Short-Run Greek Labor Emigration to Germany. Weltwirtschaftliches Archiv. 105:1 (January 1970), 163-173.

4258 Castles, Stephen. Kosack, Godula. Immigrant Workers and Class Structure in Western Europe. New York: Oxford University Press, for Institute of Race Relations, 1973, 514 p.

4259 Dreyer, Heinrich M. Immigration of Foreign Workers Into the Federal Republic of Germany. International Labour Review. 84:1-2 (July-August 1961), 1-25.

4260 Elsner, Lothar. Facts and Fictions About "Guest Workers". German Foreign Policy (GDR). 1:4 (1962), 406-415.

4261 Kuehlewind, Gerhard. The Employment of Foreign Workers in the Federal Republic of Germany and Their Family and Living Conditions. German Economic Review. 12:4 (1974), 356-364. 1972 Sample Survey By Federal Institution of Labor.

4262 Lehmann-Grube, Hinrich. The City and the Foreign Workers: The German Experience. Local Government Throughout the World. 2:4 (October 1963), 60-64.

4263 Narpati, B. Immigrant Workers in Western Germany. Contemporary Review. 208:1203 (April 1966), 182-186.

4264 Un, Economic and Social Council. The Welfare of Migrant Workers and Their Families. New York: United Nations, Economic and Social Council, Commission for Social Development, E/Cn.5/515, 14 October 1974, 45 p.

4265 US, Department of State, Bureau of Intelligence & Research. Use of Foreign Labor in West Germany. Washington: Department of State, Bureau of Intelligence and Research, Report No. 8359, 1960, 6 p.

4266 Voelker, Gottfried E. Impact of Turkish Labour Migration on the Economy of the Federal Republic of Germany. German Economic Review. 11:1 (1973), 61-77.

I.7.6. Other Labor Questions

4267 Balke, Siegfried. Occupational Safety in Industry. International Social Security Association Bulletin. 23:3 (1970), 461-468.

4268 Becker, Hermann-Josef. The Employment of Seriously Disabled Persons. Bonn: Federal Ministry of Labour and the Social Structure, Social Policy in Germany No. 4, 1965, 27 p.

4269 Becker, Hermann-Josef. Labor Placing. Bonn: Federal Ministry of Labour and the Social Structure, Social Policy in Germany No. 3, 1963, 22 p.

4270 Bolton, J. Harvey. Flexible Working Hours. Wembley: Anbar, 1971, 55 p.

4271 Dismissal Procedures in the Federal Republic of Germany. International Labour Review. 80:3 (September 1959), 262-278.

4272 Gillen, J. F. J. Labor Problems in West Germany--With Special Reference to The Policies and Programs of the Office of Labor Affairs of The Office of the United States High Commissioner for Germany. Bad Godesberg-Mehlem: Office of the U.S. High Commissioner for Germany, Historical Division, 1952, 119 p.

4273 Grieschmann, Guenther. The Merchant-Shipping Law and the Law as Applied to Dock Workers. Bonn: Federal Ministry of Labour and the Social Structure, Social Policy in Germany No. 16, 1964.

4274 Halbach, Guenter. Workers' Inventions and the Recompense. Bonn: Federal Ministry of Labour and the Social Structure, Social Policy in Germany No. 15, 1963, 14 p.

4275 Herbst, Fritz. Annual Holidays. Bonn: Federal Ministry of Labour and the Social Structure, Social Policy in Germany No. 14, 2D Ed., 1965, 27 p.

4276 Hoenekopp, Joseph. The Raiffeisen Movement. Review of International Cooperation. 62:5 (1969), 217-221.

4277 Hoffmann, Walther G. The Industrial Wage Structure. German Economic Review. 4:1 (1966), 25-29.

4278 Koetzing, Kurt. Safety and Health Protection at Work. Bonn: Federal Ministry of Labour and Social Structure, 1965, 25 p.

4279 Latten, Friedrich. Koetzing, Kurt. Safety and Health Protection at Work. Bonn: Federal Ministry of Labour and the Social Structure, Social Policy in Germany No. 25, 1965, 25 p.

4280 Leber, Georg. Accumulation of Assets for the Worker: Programme, Response, Result. Frankfurt: Industriegewerkschaft Bau-Steine-Erden, 1964, 187 p.

4281 Libbert, Werner. The Protection of Home-Workers. Bonn: Federal Ministry of Labour and the Social Structure, Social Policy in Germany No. 22, 1967, 32 p.

4282 Neu, Axel. Elstermann, Gert. Flexibility of Retirement Age in the Federal Republic of Germany. Flexibility of Retirement Age. Paris: Organisation for Economic Cooperation and Development, 1971, Pp. 143-224.

4283 Sahmer, Heinz. Compulsory Military Service and the Right of Re-Instatement. Bonn: Federal Ministry of Labour and the Social Structure, Social Policy in Germany No. 17, 1963.

4284 Schelp, Guenther. The Contract of Services. Bonn: Federal Ministry of Labour and the Social Structure, Social Policy in Germany No. 12, 1965, 43 P.

4285 Schulz, Guenter. Occupational Noise and Vibration Protection in the Federal Republic of Germany. International Labour Review. 105:5 (May 1972), 451-462.

4286 Scott, William H. Automation and the Non-Manual Worker: An Interim Report on An International Comparative Study. Transactions of the Fifth World Congress of Sociology. Louvain: International Sociological Association, 1962, Vol. 4, Pp. 255-264.

4287 Scott, William H. Office Automation and the Non-Manual Worker. Paris: Organisation for Economic Co-Operation and Development, 1962.

4288 Shaw, Charles E. Human Relations in Industry. Berlin: Omgus, Manpower Division, Visiting Expert Series No. 4, December 1948, 13 P.

4289 Stets, Walter. Vocational Guidance in the Federal Republic of Germany. International Labour Review. 75:4 (April 1957), 319-334.

4290 Vergin, Heinz. Determinants of Money Wage Changes in German Industry: An Analysis of German Wage Behavior From 1953 to 1960. Ph.D. Thesis, University of Minnesota, 1963, 131 P.

4291 Wacke, Gerhard. Legal Forms of State Employment. International Review of Administrative Sciences. 25:2 (1959), 155-159.

I.8. Transportation and Shipping

4292 Bischof, Alfons. The White Fleet: With the Koeln-Duesseldorfer on the Rhine and Mosel. Cologne: Bachem, 1972, 77 P.

4293 Bradley, Jack A. Rehabilitation of Transportation in Western Germany. Economic Geography. 25:3 (July 1949), 180-189.

4294 Braunthal, Gerard. The West German Legislative Process: A Case Study of Two Transportation Bills. Ithaca: Cornell University Press, 1972, 290 P.

4295 Busch, Fritz. Transportation in Postwar Germany. Annals of the American Academy of Political and Social Science. 260 (November 1948), 80-89.

4296 Carter, John P. The German Railways: An Analysis of Economic Adaptation. Land Economics. 28:4 (November 1952), 307-317.

4297 Coverdale and Colpitts, Consulting Engineers. Report on the Deutsche Bundesbahn, July 12, 1950. New York: Coverdale and Colpitts, 12 July 1950, 223 P.

4298 FRG, Federal Railway. The German Federal Railway. Darmstadt: Roehrig, 1962, 184 and 150 P.

4299 G. G. W. The Revival of Western Germany's Ocean Shipping. World Today. 7:9 (September 1951), 393-404.

4300 Gragt, Frits Van Der. Europe's Greatest Tramways Network: Tramways in the Rhein-Ruhr Area of Germany. Leiden: Brill, 1968, 140 P.

4301 Guenther, Arno. The German Railways and the Collective Economy. Annals of Collective Economy. 31:1 (January-March 1960), 24-90.

4302 Hoeping, Hubertus. Container Via Hamburg. Intereconomics. No. 10 (October 1968), 316-318. Container Transport System.

4303 Joesten, Joachim. The Coming Crisis of German Shipping. New York: Joachim Joesten, New Germany Reports No. 59, November 1962, 14 P.

4304 Joesten, Joachim. German Shipbuilding and Shipping in 1952. New York: Joachim Joesten, New Germany Reports No. 19, September 1952, 17 P.

4305 Leber, Georg. The Government's Transport Policy Programme. Intereconomics. No. 7 (July 1968), 216-218.

4306 Marquardt, Paul. Hamburg Commerce and Shipping. Hamburg: Holler, 1951, 22 P.

4307 Michel, Aloys A. The Canalization of the Moselle and West European Integration. Geographical Review. 52:4 (October 1962), 475-491.

4308 Ridley, F. F. The German Federal Railways--A State Administered System. Parliamentary Affairs. 17:2 (Spring 1964), 182-194.

4309 Rinck, Gerd. The International Factors in German Air Transport. Journal of Air Law and Commerce. 33:1 (Winter 1967), 102-116.

4310 Sauer, Wolfgang. German Air Tourism in the Next Ten Years. Paris: Institut Du Transport Aerien, 1970, 36 P.

4311 Schnitzer, Ewald W. Some Developments in German Aviation. Santa Monica: Rand Corporation, Rm-1056, 1953, 41 P.

4312 Schweda, R. Truestedt, H. The Programme of the Census of the Transport Industry, 1962. Stuttgart: Kohlhammer, 1965, 17 P.

4313 Schwenk, Walter. Transportation Administration in the Federal Republic--With Emphasis on Aviation. Journal of Air Law and Commerce. 33:2 (Spring 1967), 269-287.

4314 Swoboda, Richard A. Socio-Economic Implications of Urban Transportation. a Systems Analysis: Case Study, Stuttgart. Stuttgart: Institut Fuer Staedtebau Und Raumordnung, 1968, 113 P.

4315 Taplin, Michael Redvers. Tramways of Eastern Germany. London: Light Railway Transport League, 1973, 57 P.

4316 US, Omgus, Armed Forces Division. Aviation in Germany Other Than By German Nationals. N.P.: Omgus, 1947, 8 P.

4317 US, Omgus, Transport Division. Transport. N.P.: Omgus, 1947.

I.9. International Economics

I.9.1. International Trade

4318 Abs, Hermann J. West German Foreign Trade Policy. Bankers' Magazine (London). 182:1350 (September 1956), 191-194.

4319 Adebahr, Hubertus. Basic Foreign Trade Characteristics. Intereconomics. No. 9 (September 1970), 275-276.

4320 Audouard, Rolf. A Practical View of

the German Export Situation. Intereconomics. No. 1 (1966), 4-9.

4321 Baer, Werner. The Postwar German Foreign Trade Recovery. Ph.D. Thesis, Harvard University, 1958.

4322 Baker, Russell. Bohlig, Robert. The Control of Exports--A Comparison of the Laws of the United States, Canada, Japan, and the Federal Republic of Germany. International Lawyer. 1:2 (January 1967), 163-191.

4323 Bellstedt, Christoph, Editor. International Transactions Tax Reform Act. Cologne: Verlag Dr. Otto Schmidt, 1972, 88 P.

4324 Biedermann, C. Export-Import. Hamburg: Biedermann, 1949+.

4325 Boden, Hans. Germany's International Trade. International Markets. 9:4 (April 1955), 20-33+.

4326 Brechling, Frank R. P. Anglo-German Export Competition. Three Banks Review. No. 41 (March 1959), 3-20.

4327 Bruecher, Horst. West Germany's Trade and Commerce. Journal of World Trade Law. 1:5 (September-October 1967), 511-539.

4328 Burchard, Hans-Joachim. Trends on the World Energy Market. Aussenpolitik. 22:4 (1971), 377-388.

4329 Committee for Economic Development. The International Trade Organization and the Reconstruction of World Trade: A Statement on National Policy. N.P.: Committee for Economic Development, Research and Policy Commission, 1949, 43 P.

4330 Competition From Germany. Planning (P.E.P.). 20:366 (21 June 1954), 133-148.

4331 Contimart. The West German Market. London: Contimart, 1969, 79 P.

4332 Daven, Angela. Changes in Hamburg's Foreign Trade. Intereconomics. No. 7 (July 1971), 222-224.

4333 Dean, Robert W. West German Trade With the East: The Political Dimension. New York: Praeger, 1974.

4334 Dernburg, H. J. Germany's External Economic Position. American Economic Review. 44:4 (September 1954), 530-558.

4335 Erhard, Ludwig. German-American Economic Relations. International Markets. 9:6 (June 1955), 24-25.

4336 Erhard, Ludwig. Maltzan, Baron Von. Germany's Comeback in the World Market. New York: Macmillan, 1954, 276 P.

4337 FRG, Foreign Trade Information Office. The German Customs Regulations. Cologne: Foreign Trade Information Office, 1967, 90 P.

4338 Flanders, June. Development of Intra-European Trade After World War II, With Reference to the Postwar Recovery of Western Germany. Ph.D. Thesis, University of Chicago, 1952.

4339 Friedrich, Klaus. West Germany's Trade: An Enviable Dilemma. Current History. 62:369 (May 1972), 254-258.

4340 Friedrich, Klaus. West Germany's Trade Policies. Current History. 54:321 (May 1968), 288-292.

4341 Gemmill, Robert Fleming. Western Germany's Postwar Trade and Payments. Ph.D. Thesis, Harvard University, 1954.

4342 Germany Review. International Markets. 8:4 (April 1954), 19-56.

4343 Germany Supplies. Darmstadt: Gemeinschaftsverlag, 14Th Ed., 1972, 672, 320 P.

4344 Germany's Economic Situation. International Markets. 9:4 (April 1955), 16-34.

4345 Gross, Herbert. German Production and Foreign Trade. Pakistan Horizon. 4:4 (December 1951), 209-216.

4346 Hesse, Helmut. Determinants for Variations in Export Growth. Intereconomics. No. 2 (February 1968), 47-50.

4347 Holthus, Manfred. The State of the Nation's External Economy. Intereconomics. No. 4 (April 1971), 124-126.

4348 India, Directorate of Commercial Publicity. Importers of Indian Products: West Germany. Delhi: Manager of Publications, 1964, 39 P.

4349 India's Trade With U.K. and West Germany: Increased Trade in 1955. Journal of Industry and Trade. 6:7 (July 1956), 968-970.

4350 Indo-German Chamber of Commerce. Indian Goods Having a Market in Germany: Guidelines for Export. Bombay: Indo-German Chamber of Commerce, 1971, Iv and 21 P.

4351 Jensen, Wiebke. Grober, Guenter. Change in the German Foreign Trade Climate. Intereconomics. No. 1 (January 1971), 15-18.

4352 Joesten, Joachim. German Industry Conquers the World. Great Barrington, Mass.: Joachim Joesten, New Germany Reports No. 37, October 1957, 17 P.

4353 Joesten, Joachim. Germany's Bid for World Markets: The German Automobile Industry in 1952. New York: Joachim Joesten, New Germany Reports No. 21, December 1952, 18 P.

4354 Joesten, Joachim. Germany's Foreign Trade Boom. New York: Joachim Joesten, New Germany Reports No. 26, May 1954, 17 P.

4355 Kern, Helmuth. Topical Problems of German-Indonesian Trade. Intereconomics. No. 6 (June 1966), 6-7.

4356 Kilachand, Arvind. Indo-German Collaborations: Great Potentiality of Establishment of Export-Based Industries. Major Industries of India Annual. 16 (1967-68), 141-145.

4357 Kindleberger, Charles P. German Terms of Trade By Commodity Classes and Areas. Review of Economic and Statistics. 36:2 (May 1954), 167-174.

4358 Klopfer, Karl E. Egyptian Cotton in Western Germany. Egyptian Cotton Gazette. 41:3 (September 1960), 1-8.

4359 Liesner, Hans Hubertus. The Import Dependence of Britain and Western Germany: A Comparative Study. Princeton: Princeton University, Department of Economics and Sociology, International Finance Section, 1957, 83 P.

4360 Lilly, Claude Clifford. Government Export Credit Insurance in the United States, the United Kingdom, Japan, and the Federal Republic of Germany. Ph.D. Thesis, Georgia State University, 1973, 381 P.

4361 Lutz, Friedrich A. Obstacles to Multilateral Trade in Europe. Proceedings of the Academy of Political Science. 23:4 (January 1950), 359-368.

4362 Maltzan, Baron Von. Five Years of German Trade Policy, 1950-1954. Economics and Finance in Indonesia. 8:1 (November 1955), 688-695.

4363 Markus, Joseph. Some Observations on the West German Trade Surplus. Oxford

Economic Papers. 17:1 (March 1965), 136-145.

4364 Mckinnor, Thomas Ray. The Effects of Changes in National Income on Exports for the Federal Republic of Germany, Japan, and Canada. Ph.D. Thesis, University of Mississippi, 1972, 153 P.

4365 Mendershausen, Horst. Anglo-German Export Competition. Review of Economics and Statistics. 34:3 (August 1952), 262-269.

4366 Mendershausen, Horst. Fitting Germany Into a Network of World Trade. American Economic Review. 40:2 (May 1950), 548-567.

4367 Mendershausen, Horst. The Impact of Germany's Economic Recovery on World Markets. Proceedings of the Academy of Political Science. 26:2 (January 1955), 65-85.

4368 Michaelis, Alfred. The German Trade Position in the Middle East. Middle Eastern Affairs. 3:11 (November 1952), 309-314.

4369 Muenchmeyer, Alwin H. International Rivalry in Export Conditions--The German System of Export Financing. Intereconomics. No. 4 (April 1967), 90-92.

4370 Nathan, Paul. Resurgent German Exports to Latin America. Current Economic Comment. 15:4 (November 1953), 38-46.

4371 Note on European Trade Agreements for 1949. Economic Bulletin for Europe. 1:1 (July 1949), 22-23.

4372 Olsen, Erling. German Protectionism and Western Europe. International Journal. 10:3 (Summer 1955), 210-217.

4373 Reisener, Wolfgang. How to Face Growing Competition. Intereconomics. No. 9 (September 1967), 241-244. Port of Hamburg.

4374 Roskamp, Karl W. Factor Proportions and Foreign Trade: The Case of West Germany. Weltwirtschaftliches Archiv. 91:1 (1963), 319-326.

4375 Roskamp, Karl W. Mcmeekin, Gordon C. Factor Proportions, Human Capital, and Foreign Trade: The Case of West Germany Reconsidered. Quarterly Journal of Economics. 82:1 (February 1968), 152-160.

4376 Sammet, Rolf. German Chemicals in the World's Markets. Intereconomics. No. 6 (June 1970), 177-179.

4377 Schaffer, Gordon. The Problem of German Exports. New Central European Observer. 2:4 (19 February 1949), 40-41.

4378 Schmidt, Helmut. The Struggle for the World Product. Foreign Affairs. 52:3 (April 1974), 437-451.

4379 Schmidt, Helmut. The Washington Energy Conference: A German View. Atlantic Community Quarterly. 12:1 (Spring 1974), 37-42.

4380 Schmidt, Hubert G. Erdmann, Elisabeth. The Liberalization of West German Foreign Trade, 1949-1951. Bad Godesberg-Mehlem: Office of the U.S. High Commissioner for Germany, Historical Division, 1952, 124 P.

4381 Thwaites, J. B. International Development and Trade. Public Affairs. 12:3 (Spring 1950), 82-88.

4382 US, Department of Commerce, Bureau of Int'L Commerce. Report of the 1964 Trade Mission to Germany. Washington: Department of Commerce, Government Printing Office, 1964, 24 P. From "International Commerce" of 13 and 20 April 1964.

4383 US, Federal Reserve Bank. Recent Changes in Germany's Foreign Trade Balance. Federal Reserve Bulletin. 38:3 (March 1952), 237-243.

4384 Ungerer, Werner. Consequences of the Oil Crisis. Aussenpolitik. 25:2 (1974), 213-226.

4385 West Germany's Rising Competition With British Exports. Board of Trade Journal (London). 171:3104 (July 1956), 173-181.

4386 What Challenge From Germany?. The Banker. 105:354 (July 1955), 25-30.

4387 Williams, Ewart. German Competition: A Balanced Assessment of the Effect Upon British Exports of the German Trade Revival. Scope. (December 1952), 44-53, 96.

I.9.2. Trade With USSR and Soviet Bloc (See Also K.2)

4388 Amerongen, Otto Wolff Von. Aspects of German Trade With the East. Aussenpolitik. 21:1 (1970), 83-89.

4389 Aust, Hans Walter. The Tube Embargo and Its Consequences. German Foreign Policy (GDR). 2:4 (1963), 245-253. FRG Embargo of Shipments to Ussr.

4390 Brown, Michael Barratt, and Others. East-West Trade. London: National Peace Council, Peace Aims Pamphlet No. 48, 1950, 24 P.

4391 Darby, Joseph J. Soviet Trade With a Member of the Common Market: A Survey With Special Reference to the Commercial Aspects of Private International Law. Ph.D. Thesis, Columbia University, 1966, 324 P.

4392 Dean, Robert W. The Politics of West German Trade With the Soviet Bloc, 1954-1968. Ph.D. Thesis, University of Denver, 1970, 535 P.

4393 Joesten, Joachim. German-Soviet Trade Today and Tomorrow. Great Barrington, Mass.: Joachim Joesten, New Germany Reports No. 42, July 1959, 17 P.

4394 Mcgoldrick, Frederick Ford. The Politics of West German Foreign Economic Policy Toward The Communist States of Eastern Europe, 1955-1968. Ph.D. Thesis, American University, 1973, 567 P.

4395 Marx, Daniel, Jr. Economic and Political Factors Affecting Trade Between Eastern and Western Europe. Political Science Quarterly. 66:2 (June 1951), 161-190.

4396 Peukert, Werner. West Germany's "Red Trade". German Foreign Policy (GDR). 6:2 (1967), 138-147.

4397 Schaffer, Gordon. Germany Needs East-West Trade. New Central European Observer. 2:14 (9 July 1949), 162.

4398 Schildmann, Gerhard. Revised Embargo Policy Towards the Ussr. Intereconomics. No. 1 (January 1967), 19-20.

4399 Schmitt, Matthias. East-West Cooperation Through Co-Production. Aussenpolitik. 24:2 (1973), 137-146.

4400 US, Hicog, Information Services Division. Press Reaction to Illegal West/East Trade. Frankfurt: Hicog, Office of Public Affairs, Information Services Division, Press and Publications Branch, 1951, 4 P.

4401 Wangemann, Karl. Tube for Gas: The Contract With Moscow. Aussenpolitik. 21:2 (1970), 179-186.

I.9.3. Exchange Rates

4402 Artus, Jacques R. The Effect of Revaluation on the Foreign Travel Balance of Germany. Imf Staff Papers. 17:3 (November 1970), 602-619.

4403 Barrett, Charles E. Imported Inflation and the German Experience, 1950-1960. Ph.D. Thesis, University of Maryland, 1961, 185 P.

4404 Bonn, Moritz J. Devaluation, 1931 and 1949. Bankers' Magazine (London). 168:1269 (December 1949), 410-417.

4405 Brechling, Frank R. E. The Recession and Western Germany. Bankers Magazine. 185:1377 (December 1958), 439-445.

4406 Brehmer, Ekhard. Official Forward Exchange Operations: The German Experience. Imf Staff Papers. 11:3 (November 1964), 389-411.

4407 Child, Frank C. The Theory and Practice of Exchange Control in Germany: A Study of Monopolistic Exploitation in International Markets. The Hague: Nijhoff, 1958, 241 P.

4408 Emminger, Otmar. Stability Through Revaluation. Intereconomics. No. 11 (November 1969), 341-342.

4409 Europe's Dangerous Discord. The Banker. 108:386 (March 1958), 143-148.

4410 Europe's Problem Currencies. The Banker. 107:378 (July 1957), 425-429.

4411 Evitt, H. E. Should Germany Import Inflation?. Bankers' Magazine (London). 183:1354 (January 1957), 26-29.

4412 FRG, Council of Experts on Overall Economic Development. Toward a New Basis for International Monetary Policy. Princeton: Princeton University, International Finance Section, 1972, 45 P. Trans. of Portions of Annual Report of Sachverstaendigenrat Zur Begutachtung Der Gesamtwirtschaftlichen Entwicklung.

4413 Fedorov, V. Revaluation of the Mark: Underlying Causes. International Affairs (Moscow). (April 1970), 98-102.

4414 The German Approach to Convertibility. World Today. 10:10 (October 1954), 430-439.

4415 Gramann, Ernst-August. Negative Impact Upon Hamburg's Economy. Intereconomics. No. 12 (December 1969), 379-380.

4416 Guarnieri, Robert Louis. Currency Revaluation: The German Cases in the 1960's. Ph.D. Thesis, New York University, 1973, 235 P.

4417 Hanmer, Udo. A Latent Currency Crisis. Intereconomics. No. 9 (September 1969), 281-284.

4418 Hankel, Wilhelm. Speculations About a Dm-Devaluation. Intereconomics. No. 10 (October 1968), 290-295.

4419 Hesselbach, Walter. Facing Reality at Last. World Banking. (1969-1970), 131-136.

4420 Kaufmann, Hugo M. A Debate Over Germany's Revaluation, 1961. Weltwirtschaftliches Archiv. 103:2 (1969), 181-212.

4421 Kaufmann, Hugo M. The German Revaluation Debate, 1959-1961: A Chapter in Political Economy. Ph.D. Thesis, Columbia University, 1968, 243 P.

4422 Kebschull, Dietrich. A German-American Problem. Intereconomics. No. 1 (January 1969), 3-4.

4423 Kebschull, Dietrich. Little Solution--No Solution. Intereconomics. No. 6 (June 1969), 171-172. Devaluing the Mark Not Sufficient.

4424 Kebschull, Dietrich. "Tranquiliser"--Revaluation. Intereconomics. No. 11 (November 1969), 340-341.

4425 Krivine, J. D. The Little Marshall Plan. World Affairs (London). 3:4 (October 1949), 337-345. The Intra-European Payment Scheme.

4426 Layton, C. W. The Coming Test of the D-Mark. Banker. 106:363 (April 1956), 207-214.

4427 Linder, Willy. After the Dm Storm. Swiss Review of World Affairs. 19:3 (June 1969), 11-12.

4428 Lueke, Rolf E. Dearer Money and the Deutschemark. The Banker. 110:408 (February 1960), 81-85.

4429 Lueke, Rolf E. Europe's Currency Cauldron: The German View. Banker. 107:380 (September 1957), 571-576.

4430 Measures Taken By the Federal Government to Stabilise the International Monetary System. German Economic Review. 7:1 (1969), 77-94.

4431 The New Currency System in Europe. The Banker. 109:397 (February 1959), 82-88.

4432 Oppenheimer, P. M. The Deutschmark. World Today. 25:1 (January 1969), 3-10.

4433 Richebaecher, Kurt. International Pressures on German Monetary Policy. The Banker. 121:539 (January 1971), 65-68.

4434 Richebaecher, Kurt. View From Frankfurt: Germany After the Revaluation. Banker. 119:525 (November 1969), 1162-1167.

4435 Scammell, W. M. The Deutschemark Problem. Bankers' Magazine (London). 188:1389 (December 1959), 431-437.

4436 Scharrer, Hans-Eckart. Effects of the Dm-Devaluation. Intereconomics. No. 12 (December 1969), 374-376.

4437 Schiller, Karl. The International Monetary Situation After the Bonn Conference of the Group of Ten. German Tribune Quarterly Review. No. 5 (March 1969).

4438 Schmahl, Hans-Juergen. Has the Federal Government an Alternative?. Intereconomics. No. 10 (October 1968), 295-297. Alternative to Dm-Revaluation.

4439 Sherman, Heidemarie C. The Effect of Revaluation on the International Competitiveness of West Germany. Ph.D. Thesis, Wayne State University, 1970, 287 P.

4440 Sherman, Heidemarie C. The Effect of the Revaluation on Germany's Exports. Economia Internazionale. 17:4 (November 1964), 721-740.

4441 What Danger From the Deutschemark?--for Germany and the World. The Banker. 110:414 (August 1960), 507-513.

4442 Wolff, Salomon. Germany, Europe and the West: The Mark Gap. Western World. No. 3 (July 1957), 58-62; and No. 4 (August 1957), 55-59.

I.9.4. Balance of Payments

4443 Agreement on Principles of Intra-European Payments System for 1949-50. Department of State Bulletin. 21:525 (25 July 1949), 115-117.

4444 Boarman, Patrick M. Germany's Economic Dilemma: Inflation and the Balance of Payments. New Haven: Yale University Press, 1964, 344 P.

4445 Eschenberg, Horst Hermann Heinz. German Balance of Payments Problems Since 1950. Ph.D. Thesis, Purdue

University, 1960, 245 P.

4446 Grimwood, Gordon B. Recent Changes in Germany's Foreign Trade Balance. Federal Reserve Bulletin. 38:3 (March 1952), 237-243.

4447 Iwanska, George M. Postwar German Balance of Payments, 1946-1952. Ph.D. Thesis, University of Wisconsin, 1955.

4448 Kahn, R. F. A Possible Intra-European Payments Scheme. Economica. 16:64 (November 1949), 293-304.

4449 Kindleberger, Charles P. Europe and the Dollar. Cambridge: M.I.T. Press, 1966, 297 P.

4450 Kresl, Peter K. The Responsibilities of Surplus Countries in Balance of Payments Adjustment: West Germany, a Case Study. Ph.D. Thesis, University of Texas at Austin, 1970, 287 P.

4451 Lindemann, Jens Richard. West German Demand for Foreign Exchange Reserves. Ph.D. Thesis, University of Kentucky, 1972, 189 P.

4452 Michaely, Michael. Balance-of-Payments Adjustment Policies: Japan, Germany and the Netherlands. New York: Columbia University Press, 1968, 112 P.

4453 Recent Trends in West Germany's Balance of Payments. Federal Reserve Bank of New York, Monthly Review of Credit and Business Conditions. 35:12 (December 1953), 181-185.

4454 Richebaecher, Kurt. Germany's Unsought Surplus. The Banker. 114:458 (April 1964), 219-226.

4455 Robertson, W. The Finance of West Germany's Export Surplus, 1952-1958. Economia Internazionale. 13:3 (August 1960), 529-539.

4456 Stodieck, Helmut. The Balance of Goods and Services. Intereconomics. No. 4 (April 1968), 121-122.

4457 Wadbrook, William P. West German Balance-of-Payments Policy: The Prelude to European Monetary Integration. New York: Praeger, 1972, 340 P.

4458 Winckler, Heino. Some Thoughts on the German Balance of Payments. Public Policy, Vol. 11. Ed. Carl J. Friedrich and Seymour E. Harris. Cambridge: Graduate School of Public Administration, 1961, Pp. 262-278.

I.9.5. International Capital Movements

4459 Abs, Hermann J. Banks Step Up Capital Exports. World Banking. (1968-1969), 119-126.

4460 Awni-Al-Ani. German Investment in Developing Countries. Intereconomics. No. 7 (July 1969), 219-221.

4461 Boetticher, Dietrich Von. A New Approach to Taxation of Investments in Less Developed Countries: A Comparison of Tax Laws in the United States and Germany. American Journal of Comparative Law. 17:4 (1969), 529-558.

4462 Brems, Hans J. The Profitability of Direct Investment, National and International. Swedish Journal of Economics. 72:4 (December 1970), 278-300.

4463 Bruecher, Horst, Editor. Pulch, Dieter, Editor. The German Law Concerning the Distribution of Foreign Investment Shares. Frankfurt: Knapp, 1970, 123 P.

4464 Calder, Donald B. American Business in Germany. International Markets. 10:10 (October 1956), 28.

4465 Carroll, Mitchell B. Germany, Japan and Sweden Show the United States How to Reach Tax Treaties With South American Countries. George Washington Law Review. 38:2 (December 1969), 199-214.

4466 Dagon, Roger. Regulation of Capital Influx: Recent Developments in France, Germany, and Switzerland. American Journal of Comparative Law. 14:1 (Winter 1965), 38-67.

4467 Divo-Institut. American Subsidiaries in the Federal Republic of Germany: An Analysis and Critical Evaluation. Chicago: Commerce Clearing House, 1969, 271 P.

4468 Dorrance, Graemes. Brehmer, Ekhard. Controls on Capital Inflow: Recent Experience of Germany and Switzerland. Imf Staff Papers. 8:3 (December 1961), 427-438.

4469 Duckwitz, Georg Ferdinand. Indo-German Relations: Collaborations in Private Industry. Major Industries of India Annual. 13 (1964-65), 233-239.

4470 Fry, Richard. German Banks Look Outward. The Banker. 121:539 (January 1971), 42-47.

4471 Germany and Asia: A Special Survey. Far Eastern Economic Review. 44:9 (28 May 1964), 425-469.

4472 Germany in Asia. Far Eastern Economic Review. 69:28 (9 July 1970), 21-68. Symposium.

4473 Hoffman, Michael L. Capital Movements and International Payments in Postwar Europe. Review of Economics and Statistics. 31:4 (November 1949), 261-265.

4474 Issing, Otmar. Foreign Assets and the Investment Income Balance of the Federal Republic of Germany in the Years 1950-1970. German Economic Review. 12:1 (1974), 16-37.

4475 Kapferer, Clodwig. How to Extend German Private Investment in Developing Countries. Intereconomics. No. 10 (October 1966), 13-15.

4476 Kraemer, M. Economic Relations With West Africa. Germany. 5:17 (March 1960), 44-46.

4477 Krasnov, Y. Ussr-FRG: Business Cooperation. International Affairs (Moscow). No. 10 (October 1973), 74-79.

4478 Leopold, G. Vernon. American Business and the Common Market: Methods of Operation in Germany. Boston College Industrial and Commercial Law Review. 6:3 (Spring 1965), 487-499.

4479 Lueke, Rolf E. Lending Germany's Surplus. The Banker. 108:393 (October 1958), 648-652.

4480 Mittendorf, Herbert. Deg--Promoter of German Investment. Intereconomics. No. 9 (September 1969), 272-275.

4481 Mittendorf, Herbert. Hendus, Heinrich. Sohn, Karl-Heinz. Private Investment in Africa--Perspectives of German Business Activities. Intereconomics. No. 10 (October 1967), 254-256.

4482 Murphy, Michael E. Investment in an Offshore Subsidiary; A West German Prototype. International Lawyer. 5:4 (October 1971), 690-708.

4483 Oecd, Committee for Invisible Transactions. The Capital Market, International Capital Movements, Restrictions on Capital Operations in Germany. Paris: Organisation for Economic Cooperation and Development, 1969, 43 P.

4484 Ost, Friedhelm. International Activities of German Banks. Intereconomics. No. 7 (July 1970), 212-214.

4485 Qu, C. Chau-Fei. German Banks' Demand for Short-Term Foreign Assets and the Monetary Dependence of the German Economy, 1960-1967. Ph.D. Thesis, University of North Carolina, 1969, 238 P.

4486 Philipps, Eugene A. American Direct Investment in West German Manufacturing Industries, 1945-1959. Current Economic Comment. 22:2 (May 1960), 29-44.

4487 Pohle, Wolfgang. Direct Investment as Seen By German Industry. Intereconomics. No. 10 (October 1971), 314-317.

4488 Pohle, Wolfgang. Germany Copes With Foreign Investment. Columbia Journal of World Business. 5:5 (September-October 1970), 33-38.

4489 Stieber, Hans R., Editor. The Joint Enterprise: Philippine-German Cooperation. Manila: Regal, 1967, 79 P.

I.9.6. Development Assistance (See Also O.3)

4490 Abs, Hermann J. Some Aspects of German Development Aid. Intereconomics. No. 1 (January 1967), 10-12.

4491 Bahr, Egon. The Gymnich Theses: Development Policy of the Federal Republic of Germany. Aussenpolitik. 26:3 (1975), 319-325.

4492 Bauer, Leo. Eppler, Erhard. Development Aid--A Policy of Change. German Tribune Supplement. No. 1 (24 February 1972), 1-6. Interview With Eppler, FRG Minister for Economic Cooperation.

4493 Billerbeck, Klaus. Europeanization of Development Aid. Berlin: German Development Institute, Occasional Papers Nos. 10-12, 1972, 40, 45, and 117 P.

4494 Bluecher, Franz. Germany and the Development of Asian Countries. Pakistan Horizon. 10:1 (March 1957), 3-12.

4495 Bosse, Hans. The Function of Research Into Developing Countries as a Part of the Policy for Peace. German Tribune Supplement. No. 1 (24 February 1972), 6-11.

4496 Bryson, Phillip J. The International Cost-Sharing Role of West German Development Assistance. Ph.D. Thesis, Ohio State University, 1967, 308 P.

4497 Burisch, M. Aid Administration: The Case of the Federal Republic of Germany. International Problems (Tel-Aviv). 7:1-2 (May 1969), 70-76.

4498 Cisar, Mary Ann. Patterns of West German Development Aid Policy. Ph.D. Thesis, Ohio State University, 1965, 197 P.

4499 Combination of Practice and Theory. Intereconomics. No. 2 (February 1967), 36-37. Interview With German Foundation for Developing Countries, Bonn.

4500 Credit Institute for Reconstruction. German Loans to Developing Countries. Frankfurt: Kreditanstalt Fuer Wiederaufbau, 1969, 71 P.

4501 Divo-Institut. West German Attitudes Toward Economic Aid for Underdeveloped Areas. Santa Monica: Rand Corporation, T-136, 1961, 8 P.

4502 Editors of German International. Twelve Years of German Development Assistance: Industry's and Government's Contribution Toward Advancing Economic and Technical Standards in the Developing Nations. Bonn: Moeller, 1964, 104 P.

4503 Eppler, Erhard. Progress in German Development Assistance. Intereconomics. No. 1 (January 1969), 6-10.

4504 Eppler, Erhard. Kiep, Walther Leisler. Development Policy in the Conflict of Opinions. Intereconomics. No. 7 (July 1971), 200-203.

4505 FRG, Press and Information Office. The Development Assistance Policy of the Federal Republic of Germany in 1968. Bonn: Press and Information Office, 1969, 36 P.

4506 FRG, Federal Ministry for Economic Cooperation. Development Policy Concept of the Federal Republic of Germany for the Second Development Decade. Bonn: Federal Ministry for Economic Cooperation, 1971, 31 P.

4507 FRG, Federal Ministry for Economic Cooperation. German Development Assistance Policies. Bonn: Bundesministerium Fuer Wirtschaftliche Zusammenarbeit, Annual, 1967+.

4508 FRG, Press and Information Office. German Development Assistance Policies in 1969. Bonn: Press and Information Office, 1970, 47 P.

4509 FRG, Press and Information Office. Twelve Years of German Development Assistance. Bonn: Heinz Moeller, 1964, 104 P.

4510 Fasbender, Karl. Critical Notes on German Development Strategy. Intereconomics. No. 8 (August 1971), 249-252.

4511 Friedmann, Wolfgang G. Methods and Policies of Principal Donor Countries in Public International Development Financing: A Preliminary Appraisal. New York: Columbia University Press, 1962, 49 P.

4512 German-Pak Friendship; Being an Account of German Contribution to Pakistan's Growth and Development. Lahore: Ferozsons, 1967, 80 P.

4513 Hankel, Wilhelm. New Proposals for Development Aid. Intereconomics. No. 6-7 (June-July 1967), 153-156.

4514 Haubenreisser, Johannes. Brussels: Unctad-Preferences and Association. Aussenpolitik. 23:1 (1972), 82-91.

4515 Havemann, Hans A., Editor. Kraus, Willy, Editor. A Handbook of Development Aid. Baden-Baden: Nomos Verlagsgesellschaft, 13Th Yr., 1973, Looseleaf With Continuing Supplements.

4516 Holbik, Karel. West German Development Aid--The Means and Ends. Quarterly Review of Economics and Business. 5:4 (Winter 1965), 5-20.

4517 Holbik, Karel. Myers, Henry Allen. West German Foreign Aid, 1956-1966: Its Economic and Political Aspects. Boston: Boston University Press, 1968, 158 P.

4518 Hunck, Josef M. India's Silent Revolution: A Survey of Indo-German Cooperation. Duesseldorf: Handelsblatt, 1958, 172 P.

4519 Knusel, Jack L. An Analysis of German Development Aid. Ph.D. Thesis, University of Colorado, 1965, 316 P.

4520 Knusel, Jack L. West German Aid to Developing Nations. New York: Praeger, 1968, 214 P.

4521 Lamby, Werner. German Development Aid in 1963. Germany. 9:38 (1964), 13-16.

4522 Megnin, Donald F. German Economic Assistance to India: An Analysis of Its Principles and Effects on Indo-German Relations. Ph.D. Thesis, Syracuse University, 1968, 530 P.

4523 Meyer, Ernst W. Indo-German Economic Relations--Greater Co-Operation Urged. Major Industries of India. 5 (1955-56), 219-223.

4524 Mirbach, Baron D. Von. Germany's Contribution to India's Industrial Development. Major Industries of India Annual. 15 (1966-67), 227-231.

4525 Petersmann, Ernst U. A Common Development Policy for the Eec. German Tribune Quarterly Review. No. 19 (28 September 1972), 12-16.

4526 Roeh, Klaus. Rourkela--An Example of Co-Operative Development Aid. Intereconomics. No. 6 (June 1966), 17-21. Test Case of German Development Aid in Steelworks in India.

4527 Scheel, Walter. Technology as an Element of Foreign Policy. Aussenpolitik. 23:3 (1972), 243-251.

4528 Schrokel, Wolfe W. German Aid to Africa. Current History. 44:260 (April 1963), 219-225.

4529 Schulz, Heinz-Friedrich. German View on Unctad II. Intereconomics. No. 3 (March 1968), 66-70.

4530 Sohn, Karl-Heinz. Prejudice and Revolutionary Dreams. German Tribune Supplement. No. 3 (18 January 1973), 14-16. FRG's Development Aid Policy.

4531 Sohn, Karl-Heinz. Reshaping German Development Aid. Intereconomics. No. 9 (September 1970), 270-274.

4532 Stahn, Eberhard. Development Aid--A New Form of Colonialism?. German Tribune Quarterly Review. No. 8 (16 December 1969), 7-13.

4533 Stahn, Eberhard. A Search for a Strategy for the Second Decade of Development Aid. German Tribune Quarterly Review. No. 12 (10 December 1970), 8-13.

4534 Uhlig, Christian. German Development Aid: 1.23 Per Cent. Intereconomics. No. 9 (September 1969), 291-293.

4535 White, John. German Aid. London: Ministry of Overseas Development, 1965, 217 P.

4536 White, John. West German Aid to Developing Countries. International Affairs (London). 41:1 (January 1965), 74-88.

4537 Wischnewski, Hans-Juergen. Reforms--Not Revolutionary Changes. Intereconomics. No. 6-7 (June-July 1967), 150-152. Clarification of FRG's Development Aid Program.

4538 Wittkopf, Eugene R. Western Aid Allocations: A Comparative Study of Recipient State Attributes and Aid Received. Sage Professional Papers in International Studies. 1:5 (1972), 1-62. Donor Countries Are FRG, UK, US, France.

4539 Zimmerman, Hans. West Germany's Contribution to International Development Aid. Swiss Review of World Affairs. 12:5 (August 1962), 14-15.

I.9.7. Eastern Charges of Neo-Imperialism

4540 Ardakyev, N. West German Neo-Colonialism in Asia. International Affairs (Moscow). (April 1963), 76-82.

4541 Afro-Asian Solidarity Committee in the GDR. The Neo-Colonialism of the West German Federal Republic: A Documentation. Dresden: Zeit Im Bild, 1965, 255 and 32 P.

4542 Erusalemskii, Arkadii S. German Imperialism: Its Past and Present. Moscow: Progress Publishing, 1969, 522 P.

4543 Etinger, Y. Bonn Makes a Bid for Africa. International Affairs (Moscow). (December 1965), 53-57.

4544 Etinger, Y. West German Monopolies in Africa. International Affairs (Moscow). (December 1960), 25-30.

4545 Fenzlein, Volkmar. on Problems of Bonn's Neo-Colonialism. German Foreign Policy (GDR). 2:5 (1963), 365-373.

4546 Friedlander, Paul. German Neo-Colonialism in Action. World Marxist Review: Problems of Peace and Socialism. 3:2 (February 1960), 48-54.

4547 Friedlander, Paul. Schilling, Hartmut. West German Imperialism--Bulwark of Colonialism. World Marxist Review: Problems of Peace and Socialism. 5:4 (April 1962), 16-23.

4548 GDR, Committee for German Unity. Bonn, Enemy of the Peoples of Africa and Asia; Documentation on the Colonial Policy of the Adenauer Government. Berlin: Committee for German Unity, 1961, 72 P.

4549 GDR, Committee for German Unity. Colonialism in Action: Documentary Report. Berlin: Committee for German Unity, C.1960, 87 P.

4550 Halpap, Paul. West Germany's Technical Aid to Latin America and Its Background. German Foreign Policy (GDR). 2:5 (1963), 358-365.

4551 Hutschenreuter, Klaus. Kunze, Juergen. West German Bourgeois Theories on the Social Structure and The Social Processes in the Developing Countries. German Foreign Policy (GDR). 10:6 (1971), 469-492.

4552 Kalandarov, S. West German Neo-Colonialism in Asia. German Foreign Policy (GDR). 5:3 (1966), 202-214.

4553 Lyubsky, M. West German Aid in Action. International Affairs (Moscow). (September 1962), 84-91.

4554 Markow, W. West German Neo-Colonialism Is the Enemy of Freedom-Loving Peoples. World Marxist Review: Problems of Peace and Socialism. 2:9 (September 1959), 79-80.

4555 Pichugin, B. Economic Expansion of West German Monopolies. International Affairs (Moscow). (July 1956), 58-68.

4556 Schirmer, Gregor. West German Neo-Colonialism--A Grave Danger to the Free Peoples of Africa and Asia. German Foreign Policy (GDR). 4:3 (1965), 185-197.

4557 Shenayev, V. West Germany and Its Place in the System of World Imperialism. Modern Capitalism: Its Nature and National Features. Moscow: Novosty Press Agency, 1971.

J. GDR: Economic System

J.1. General, 1948-63 (See Also K.1)

4558 Apel, Erich. The Basic Economic Task of the German Democratic Republic. World Marxist Review: Problems of Peace and Socialism. 3:6 (June 1960), 52-57.

4559 Central Bank for Soviet Zone of Germany. Federal Reserve Bulletin. 35:1 (January 1949), 16-20. Smg Order No. 122/1948 on German Bank of Issue.

4560 Crosfield and Sons, Ltd. Eastern Germany. Warrington: Joseph Crosfield and Sons, Ltd., East European Chemical Industry Report No. 3, 1959, 145 P.

4561 East European Fund. Soviet Economic Conditions in Postwar Germany. New York: East European Fund, 1952, 36 P.

4562 East German Economic Development Trends. Swiss Review of World Affairs. 5:12 (March 1956), 16-17.

4563 Eastern Germany's Economic Development. Economia Internazionale. 9:2 (May 1956), 279-308.

4564 Fraser, R. A. Rich, Fern. Economic Progress in East Germany: Impressions of a Recent Visit. World Today. 15:9 (September 1959), 341-351.

4565 GDR, Information Office. The Five Year Plan for the Development of the Economy of the German Democratic Republic (1951-1955). Berlin: Information Office, 1952, 83 P.

4566 GDR, Information Office. Law on the Second Five-Year Plan for the Development of the People's Economy in the German Democratic Republic for the Years 1956-1960. New York: U.S. Joint Publications Research Service, Dc-50, 1958, 38 P.

4567 GDR, People's Chamber. Law on the Seven Year Plan for the Development of the National Economy of the German Democratic Republic From 1959 to 1965. Berlin: People's Chamber, C.1960, 80 P. Law Adopted 1 October 1959.

4568 German Democratic Republic in Construction. Berlin (East): Verlag Volk Und Welt, Bimonthly, January-February 1953+.

4569 Germanicus. The East German Economy. Survey. No. 37 (July-September 1961), 110-112.

4570 Heinrichs, Wolfgang. The Economics of Domestic Trade in the GDR. Washington: Department of Commerce, Joint Publications Research Service, 2 May 1962.

4571 Huiskamp, J. C. L. Taxation in the Eastern Zone of Germany. Law in Eastern Europe, No. 2. Ed. Z. Szirmai. Leyden: Sijthoff, 1958, Pp. 102-131. Supplement in No. 7 (1963), Pp. 257-260.

4572 Joesten, Joachim. Eastern Germany in 1958: Economy in the Crucible. Great Barrington, Mass.: Joachim Joesten, New Germany Reports No. 40, August 1958, 18 P.

4573 Joesten, Joachim. Eastern Germany's Maritime Challenge. Great Barrington, Mass.: Joachim Joesten, New Germany Reports No. 46, February 1960, 16 P.

4574 Joesten, Joachim. Soviet Rule in Eastern Germany: The Economic System of the Soviet Zone. Great Barrington, Mass.: Joachim Joesten, New Germany Reports No. 5, September 1948, 21 P.

4575 Kartun, Derek. The Revival in Eastern Germany. New Central European Observer. 4:14 (7 July 1951), 211.

4576 Koziolek, Helmut. on the Economic Development of the German Democratic Republic. German Foreign Policy (GDR). 1:6 (1962), 605-613.

4577 Mueller, Eva. The Input-Output Table of Fixed Capital (GDR). Eastern European Economics. 3:2 (Winter 1964-65), 57-68.

4578 Russia's German Base. Economist. 159:5580 (5 August 1950), 271-272.

4579 Schattmann, Stephan. Banking in the Soviet Zone: An Instrument of Economic Discipline. Banker. 88:273 (October 1948), 26-32.

4580 Schattmann, Stephan. Banking Strait-Jacket on East Germany. Banker. 100:326 (March 1953), 134-139.

4581 Schenk, Fritz. East Germany's Rudderless Economy. East Europe. 11:5 (May 1962), 32-34.

4582 Schmidt, Heinz A. F. Civil Aviation in the German Democratic Republic. German Foreign Policy (GDR). 2:6 (1963), 438-445.

4583 Sergeyev, V. Some Problems of the Development of Domestic Trade in the GDR. Problems of Economics. 2:5 (September 1959), 87-90.

4584 Society for Cultural Relations With Foreign Countries. Development of the Economic Foundations. Berlin (East): Gesellschaft Fuer Kulturelle Verbindungen Mit Dem Ausland, 1957, 64 P.

4585 Stolper, Wolfgang F. The National Product of East Germany. Kyklos. 12:2 (1959), 131-166.

4586 Stolper, Wolfgang F. The Structure of the East German Economy. Cambridge: Harvard University Press, 1960, 478 P.

4587 Such, Heinz. The Economic Contracts of Socialist Firms. Law and Legislation in the German Democratic Republic. No. 2 (1964), 17-26.

4588 Taborsky, Eduard. The "Old" and the "New" Course in Satellite Economy. Journal of Central European Affairs. 17:4 (January 1958), 378-403.

4589 Turgeon, Lynn. Germany's Real Economic Miracle. Monthly Review. 19:9 (February 1968), 42-50.

4590 Ulbricht, Walter. The Five Year Plan of Peaceful Construction. Berlin (East): Office of Information of the German Democratic Republic, 1951, 47 P.

4591 W. U. K. Backs to the Wall: East Germany's Economy in 1962. World Today. 18:6 (June 1962), 242-248.

4592 Wiegand, G. Carl. Business and Finance in Communist Germany. Illinois Law Review. 46:6 (January-February 1952), 851-885.

4593 Young, Edgar P. Industrial Progress in East Germany. New World Review. 24:10 (October 1956), 22-26.

J.2. New Economic System

4594 Apel, Hans. Income and Its Distribution in East Germany. Challenge. 13:3 (February 1965), 7-11.

4595 Bartl, Wilhelm. Luck, Herbert. Optimum Proportions Among National Income, Accumulation and Consumption (GDR). Eastern European Economics. 3:2 (Winter 1964-65), 7-25.

4596 Baylis, Thomas A. Economic Reform as Ideology: East Germany's New Economic System. Comparative Politics. 3:2 (January 1971), 211-230.

4597 Baylis, Thomas A. The New Economic System: The Role of Technocrats in the Ddr. Survey. No. 61 (October 1966), 139-152.

4598 Berger, Wolfgang. The New Economic System in the GDR--Its Essence and Problems. World Marxist Review: Problems of Peace and Socialism. 8:2 (February 1965), 9-14.

4599 Boehme, Hans. East German Price Formation Under the New Economic System. Soviet Studies. 19:3 (January 1968), 340-358.

4600 Boettcher, Manfred. Where Do We Stand With Planning in the New Economic System--German Democratic Republic. Eastern European Economics. 6:3 (Spring 1968), 50-54.

4601 Bryson, Phillip J. Liberal Socialism "Ohne Markt": Price Reform in the German Democratic Republic. East European Quarterly. 5:3 (September 1971), 393-405.

4602 Directives for the New Economic System of Planning and Managing the Economy in the GDR. Eastern European Economics. 3:3 (Spring 1965), 3-27.

4603 Elliott, James R. Scaperlanda, Anthony E. East Germany's Liberman-Type Reforms in Perspective. Quarterly Review of Economics and Business. 6:3 (Autumn 1966), 39-52.

4604 Fahrenkrog, Heinz. Consumers' Co-Operative Societies in the German Democratic Republic. Review of International Cooperation. 64:6 (1971), 192-197.

4605 GDR, Central Statistical Office. The GDR's National Economic Plan and How It Was Fulfilled in 1972. Dresden: Verlag Zeit Im Bild, 1973, 19 P.

4606 GDR, People's Chamber. for the Well-Being of US All: The People's Chamber of the GDR Adopts the Law on the 1971-1975 Five-Year Plan. Dresden: Zeit Im Bild, 1971, 45 P.

4607 GDR, State Central Administration for Statistics. Results of Good Work and a Good Policy: Report on the Development of the National Economy of the GDR in the First Half of 1968. Dresden: Zeit Im Bild, c.1969, 15 P.

4608 Goettner, Reinhard. Central State Planning and Management of the National Economy and Self-Responsible Activity of Enterprises in the GDR. German Foreign Policy (GDR). 8:4 (1969), 279-290.

4609 Goettner, Reinhard. Economic System of Socialism in the GDR. German Foreign Policy (GDR). 8:3 (1969), 169-176.

4610 Herlitzius, Erwin. National Economic Planning in the GDR. Teaching Postwar Germany in America: Papers and Discussions.Ed. Louis F. Helbig and Eberhard Reichmann. Bloomington: Indiana Univeristy, Institute of German Studies, 1972.

4611 Heuer, Klaus. Basic Features of the Movement and Laws Concerning GDR Cooperatives. Law and Legislation in the German Democratic Republic. No. 2 (1966), 43-50.

4612 Heuer, Uwe-Jens. Klinger, Guenter. Foundations of Socialist Economic Law. Law and Legislation in the German Democratic Republic. No. 1 (1972), 5-73.

4613 Kahrs, Karl H. East Germany's New Economic System From the Point of View of Cybernetics. East European Quarterly. 6:3 (September 1972), 287-300.

4614 Kahrs, Karl H. The "Economic System of Socialism" in East Germany. Ph.D. Thesis, University of California, Santa Barbara, 1970, 524 P.

4615 Keren, Michael. Central Allocation of Resources Under Uncertainty. Ph.D. Thesis, Yale University, 1968, 311 P.

4616 Keren, Michael. The New Economic System in the GDR: An Obituary. Soviet Studies. 24:4 (April 1973), 554-587. Responses By Henry W. Schaefer, 25:2 (October 1973), 274-275; and Jacob Naor, 276-282.

4617 Klatt, Werner. The Politics of Economic Reforms. Survey. No. 70-71 (Winter-Spring 1969), 154-168.

4618 Koehler, Gerhard. Steeger, Horst. Steinitz, Klaus. Criteria for Determining the Economic Effectiveness of the Development of the Whole Economy and of Its Several Branches in the Perspective Plan-- GDR. Eastern European Economics. 5:4 (Summer 1967), 23-39.

4619 Krueger, Werner. Commitment to Progress: Consumer Cooperative Societies in The Twentieth Year of the German Democratic Republic. Berlin (East): Verband Deutscher Konsumgenossenschaften, 1969, 60 P.

4620 Leptin, Gerd. The German Democratic Republic. The New Economic Systems of Eastern Europe. Ed. Hans-Hermann Hoehmann, Michael Kaser, and Karl C. Thalheim. Berkeley: University of California Press, 1975, Pp. 43-77.

4621 Leptin, Gerd. Income Distribution and Economic Reforms in East Germany. Il Politico. 39:3 (1974), 369-403.

4622 Mesa-Lago, Carmelo, Editor. Beck, Carl, Editor. Comparative Socialist Systems: Essays on Politics and Economics. Pittsburgh: University of Pittsburgh Center for International Studies, 1975, Xvi and 450 Pp.

4623 Mieczkowski, Bogdan. Personal and Social Consumption in Eastern Europe: Poland, Czechoslovakia, Hungary, and East Germany. New York: Praeger, 1975, 368 P.

4624 Miller, Dorothy. Trend, Harry G. Economic Reforms in East Germany. Problems of Communism. 15:2 (March-April 1966), 29-36.

4625 Mittag, Guenter. Aspects of Party Economic Policy. World Marxist Review. 15:4 (April 1972), 19-26.

4626 The Next Steps in the National Economy of the GDR on the Road to the Completion of Socialism. Dresden: Zeit Im Bild, c.1969, 70 P.

4627 Reiher, Klaus. Schierz, Erich. The Relation Between Prices and Production-Financial Planning in the New Economic System. Eastern European Economics. 5:4 (Summer 1967), 40-51.

4628 Sach, Kurt. Some Basic Ideas of an Appropriate Market System in Socialism. L'Egypte Contemporaine. 56:321 (July 1965), 23-41.

4629 Schurer, Gerhard. The Role of the Socialist State in the Economic Sphere. United Asia. 21:5 (September-October 1969), 241-251.

4630 Strohbach, Heinz. Commercial Arbitrage in the GDR. Law and Legislation in the German Democratic Republic. No. 1 (1966), 57-65.

4631 Uckert, Gerhart. Educational Work of the Consumer Co-Operatives of the German Democratic Republic. Berlin: Verband Deutscher Konsumgenossenschaften, 1970, 71 P.

4632 Ulbricht, Walter. Excerpts From Walter Ulbricht's 24 June 1963 Speech to the Berlin Economic Conference. Washington: Federal Broadcast Information Service, Daily Report, Suppl.: Ussr & East Europe No. 18, 1963, 53 P.

4633 Wolf, Herbert. Problems of the Lines of Development of Scientific Planning in the Comprehensive Building of Socialism in the G.D.R. Eastern European Economics. 5:4 (Summer 1967), 3-22.

J.3. Agriculture

4634 Bernitz, Alexander. The Agricultural Situation in East Germany. Washington: Department of Agriculture, Economic Research Service, Regional Analysis Division, 1961, 24 P.

4635 Diamond, Dorothy M. Farmers in East Germany. New Central European Observer. 5:3 (2 February 1952), 45.

4636 Dovring, Karen. Land Reform as a Propaganda Theme. Land and Labor in Europe, 1900-1950: A Comparative Study of Recent Agrarian History. Ed. Folke Dovring. The Hague: Nijhoff, 1956, Pp. 261-348, 432-438.

4637 FRG, Federal Ministry for All-German Affairs. The Compulsory Collectivization of Independent Farms in the Soviet Zone of Occupation in Germany. Bonn: Federal Ministry for All-German Affairs, Rev. Ed., 1960, 121 P.

4638 GDR. Government Declaration on the Development of Agricultural Production Co-Operatives. N.P.: N.P., 1960, 30 P. Delivered in People's Chamber By Ulbricht, 25 April 1960.

4639 GDR, Ministry for Agriculture and Forestry. Agriculture in the German Democratic Republic. Berlin: Ministerium Fuer Land Und Forstwirtschaft, 1959, 121 P.

4640 German Democratic Republic: Agriculture. Dresden: Verlag Zeit Im Bild, 1972, 62 P.

4641 Harris, Lement. A New Germany--Notes of a Farm Survey in the German Democratic Republic. New World Review. 33:1 (January 1965), 41-48.

4642 Heuer, Klaus. Cooperation Relations-- A New Phase in the Development of Agricultural Producers' Cooperatives in the GDR. Law and Legislation in the German Democratic Republic. No. 2 (1967), 21-27.

4643 Heuer, Klaus. Principles of the Law of Agricultural Producers' Cooperatives (Lpg) of the German Democratic Republic. Law and Legislation in the German Democratic Republic. No. 1-2 (1961), 64-77.

4644 Johnson, Alvin. The Communist Farmer. Social Research. 25:2 (Summer 1958), 228-233.

4645 Koenig, Ernest. The Agricultural Situation in East Germany. Washington: U.S. Department of Agriculture, Foreign Agricultural Service, Fas-M-31, February 1958, 16 P.

4646 Lazarcik, Gregor. East German Agricultural Expenses, Gross and Net Product, and Productivity, 1934-38 and 1950-1970. New York: Riverside Research Institute, Occasional Papers Of the Research Project on National Income in East Central Europe, No. Op-36, 1972, Iv and 76 P.

4647 Lohr, George. Modern Farming Comes to East Germany. New World Review. 27:7 (July 1959), 30-33.

4648 Mendershausen, Horst. Agriculture in Communist Germany. Santa Monica: Rand Corporation, Rm-2175, 1958, 73 P.

4649 Raup, Philip M. Land Reform in Post-War Germany: The Soviet Zone Experiment. Ph.D. Thesis, University of Wisconsin, 1949.

4650 Scarlett, Dora. Farming in the Soviet Zone. New Central European Observer. 2:19 (17 September 1949), 226-227.

4651 Seidel, Gerhard, and Others. Agriculture in the German Democratic Republic. Leipzig: Veb Edition, 1962, 218 P.

4652 Stoeckigt, Rolf. Democratic Land Reform in the GDR. German Foreign Policy (GDR). 4:2 (1965), 110-121.

4653 Ulbricht, Walter. The Development of the Agriculture in the German Democratic Republic. Berlin (East): N.P., 1960, 30 P.

4654 Ulbricht, Walter. Government Declaration on the Development of Agricultural Production Co-Operatives. Berlin (East): Staatsverlag, 1960, 30 P. Delivered in Volkskammer, 25 April 1960.

4655 Wunderlich, Frieda. Agriculture and Farm Labor in the Soviet Zone of Germany. Social Research. 19:2 (June 1952), 198-219.

4656 Wunderlich, Frieda. Farmer and Farm Labor in the Soviet Zone of Germany. New York: Twayne, 1958, 162 P.

J.4. Industrial Organization and Production

4657 Boettcher, Manfred. Industry. Dresden: Zeit Im Bild, 1968, 62 P.

4658 Czirjak, Laszlo. Growth of East German Industrial Output, 1936, 1946, 1948, and 1950-1967. New York: Riverside Research Institute, Occasional Papers Of the Research Project on National Income in East Central Europe, No. Op-35, 1972, Iv and 74 P.

4659 The First Stage of Industrial Price Reform Goes Into Effect: New Prices for Important Basic Materials Starting April 1, 1964 (in the GDR). Eastern European Economics. 3:3 (Spring 1965), 41-46.

4660 Friedrich, Gerd. Problems of Economic Direction in the Vvb's and Factories as Posed By Differentiated Conditions of Reproduction. Eastern European Economics. 6:2 (Winter 1967-68), 39-54.

4661 GDR, Office for Inventions and Patents. Contributions on Current Questions of the Protection of Industrial Property. Berlin: Amt Fuer Erfindungs- Und Patentwesen, 1968, 70 P.

4662 The GDR--A Modern Industrial State. Dresden: Zeit Im Bild, 1966, 47 P.

4663 Goettner, Reinhard. Commodity Production, Plan and Market in the Economic System of Socialism in the German Democratic Republic. German Foreign Policy (GDR). 8:5 (1969), 377-389.

4664 Goettner, Reinhard. The Enterprise in the Economic System of Socialism in the GDR. German Foreign Policy (GDR). 8:6 (1969), 449-458.

4665 Grabley, Peter. Buechel, Hans Joachim. Chemical Industry of the GDR and Cmea. German Foreign Policy (GDR). 3:5 (1964), 376-382.

4666 Grimes, Warren S. The Changing Structure of East German Industrial Enterprises. American Journal of Comparative Law. 17:1 (1969), 61-76.

4667 Grishin, Nikolai. The Saxony Uranium Mining Operations ("Vismut"). Soviet Economic Policy in Postwar Germany. Ed. Robert Slusser. New York: Research Program on the Ussr, 1953, Pp. 127-155.

4668 Industry. Dresden: Zeit Im Bild, 1972, 63 P.

4669 Jaeger, Martin. Karbstein, Werner. Rudick, Georg. Some Findings Based on the Input-Output Table of Aggregate Production of the GDR. Eastern European Economics. 3:2 (Winter 1964-65), 26-48.

4670 Linsel, H. Some Ideas Concerning Role and Function of Socialist Credit in Industry. L'Egypte Contemporaine. 56:321 (July 1965), 5-21.

4671 Mab, Mikhail. The Administration of Fuel Enterprises and Power. Soviet Economic Policy in Postwar Germany. Ed. Robert Slusser. New York: Research Program on the Ussr, 1953, Pp. 77-86.

4672 Roskamp, Karl W. East German Industrial Production, 1958-1965. Weltwirtschaftliches Archiv. 100:2 (1968), 306-319.

4673 Streich, Rudolf. Legal Problems of Enterprises With State Participation. Law and Legislation in the German Democratic Republic. No. 1 (1967), 39-48.

4674 Streich, Rudolf. The Legal Status of Nationally-Owned Industries in the GDR. Law and Legislation in the German Democratic Republic. No. 1 (1968), 35-46.

4675 Supranowitz, Stephan. The Law of State-Owned Enterprises in a Socialist State. Law and Contemporary Problems. 26:4 (Autumn 1961), 794-801.

4676 Young, Edgar P. A Real "People's Shipyard". Labour Monthly. 40:5 (May 1958), 239-240.

4677 Zauberman, Alfred. Industrial Progress in Poland, Czechoslovakia and East Germany, 1937-1962. London and New York: Oxford University Press, 1964, 338 P.

J.5. Labor

4678 Baum, Samuel. Combs, Jerry W. The Labor Force of the Soviet Zone of Germany and the Soviet Sector of Berlin. Washington, D.C.: Bureau of the Census, International Population Statistics Reports, Series P-90, No. 11, Government Printing Office, 1959, 30 P.

4679 Dulles, Eleanor Lansing. Labor Rejects Communism--East Germany Department of State Bulletin. 38:981 (14 April 1958), 615-620.

4680 Fejtoe, Francois. Trade Unionism in Eastern Europe. International Affairs (London). 33:4 (October 1957), 427-441.

4681 Kiss, Sandor. Hungary's "Gastarbeiter" in East Germany. East Europe. 18:10 (October 1969), 8-10.

4682 Scharf, Carl Bradley. Labor Organizations in East Germany Today. Ph.D. Thesis, Stanford University, 1974, 341 P.

4683 Stolper, Wolfgang F. The Labor Force and Industrial Development in Soviet Germany. Quarterly Journal of Economics. 71:4 (November 1957), 518-545.

J.6. Foreign Trade (See Also K.2)

4684 Brass, Heinz. Schulmeister, Dieter. Input-Output Analysis as an Instrument for Coordinating Production and Foreign Trade. American Review of Soviet and Eastern European Foreign Trade. 2:3 (May-June 1966), 25-49.

4685 Domdey, K.-H. Economic Aspects of the Foreign Policy of the G.D.R. Co-Existence. 8:2 (July 1971), 161-167.

4686 Domdey, K.-H. The Efforts of the GDR to Establish Normal Economic Relations With Capitalist States: A Case of Peaceful Co-Existence. Co-Existence. 9:1 (March 1972), 58-76.

4687 Drobnig, Ulrich. Waehler, Jan F. Legal Aspects of Foreign Trade in East Germany. Journal of World Trade Law. 2:1 (January-February 1968), 28-46.

4688 Faude, E. Maier, W. The New Economic System of Planning and Managing the Economy and Foreign Trade Profitability. American Review of Soviet and Eastern European Foreign Trade. 2:2 (March-April 1966), 27-68.

4689 Faulwetter, Helmut. Foreign Trade Relations of the GDR. United Asia. 21:5 (September-October 1969), 252-259.

4690 Frei, Otto. at the Leipzig Trade Fair. Swiss Review of World Affairs. 15:1 (April 1965), 9-10.

4691 GDR. The Labour Code of the German Democratic Republic. Berlin (East): Tribuene Trade Union Publishing House, 1968, 188 P.

4692 Grote, Gerhard. Problems of Realizing the New Economic System of Planning and Managing the Economy in the Area of Foreign Trade. American Review of Soviet and Eastern Europe Foreign Trade. 2:2 (March-April 1966), 3-26.

4693 Koehler, Heinz. East Germany's Terms of Trade: 1950-1961. Kyklos. 16:2 (1963), 286-302.

4694 Koehler, Heinz. on East Germany's Foreign Economic Relations. Social Research. 29:2 (Summer 1962), 225-237.

4695 Kohlmey, Guenther. Economic Growth and Foreign Trade. American Review of Soviet and Eastern Europe Foreign Trade. 2:3 (May-June 1966), 3-24.

4696 Kohlmey, Guenther. Special Features of the Development of Industry and Foreign Economic Ties of the German Democratic Republic. Problems of Economics. 1:7 (November 1958), 40-45.

4697 Natarajan, B. Economic and Trade Relations Between India and the GDR. United Asia. 21:5 (September-October 1969), 260-266.

4698 Otto, G. Problems of Linear Optimization in Foreign Trade Practice. American Review of Soviet and Eastern European Foreign Trade. 2:3 (June 1966), 50-64.

4699 Senger, W. Experience of the GDR State Planning Commission With Complex Planning of Production and Foreign Trade By Mathematical Methods. Soviet and Eastern European Foreign Trade. 5:1-2 (Spring-Summer 1969), 88-94.

4700 Stolper, Wolfgang F. Roskamp, Karl W. An Input-Output Table for East Germany With Applications to Foreign Trade. Bulletin of the Oxford University Institute of Statistics. 23:4 (November 1961), 379-392.

4701 Strohbach, Heinz. The Election of Arbitrators for Proceedings Before the Arbitration Court of the Chamber of Foreign Trade. Law and Legislation in the German Democratic Republic. No. 1 (1969), 40-44.

4702 Weiss, Gerhard. World Trade Conference and the German Democratic Republic. German Foreign Policy (GDR). 2:1 (1963), 5-11.

J.7. Comecon; Soviet Bloc Trade

4703 A. N. Trade Between Poland and East Germany. Poland and Germany. 5:2 (April-June 1961), 27-30.

4704 Albert, Lothar. Ries, Wolfgang. Foreign Trade Between East Germany and the Soviet Union. Joint Publications Research Service. 43,453 (27 November 1967), 1-9.

4705 Alexandrowicz, C. Comecon: The Soviet Retort to the Marshall Plan. World Affairs (London). 4:1 (January 1950), 35-47.

4706 Ames, Kenneth. Suicide in East Germany: A Casualty of Russian Colonialism. New Leader. 49:1 (3 January 1966), 7-10.

4707 Boerner, Manfred. United for European Security. German Foreign Policy (GDR). 7:3 (1968), 189-194. Cmea.

4708 Dietrich, Helmut. Bank of Cooperation of the Socialist Camp. German Foreign Policy (GDR). 4:2 (1965), 140-147.

4709 Drobnig, Ulrich. Soviet Corporations in Eastern Germany. Journal of Central European Affairs. 17:2 (July 1957), 150-166.

4710 Jeschonnek, Emil. Successful Economic

Co-Operation Between the G.D.R. and Socialist Czechoslovakia. German Foreign Policy (GDR). 2:3 (1963), 200-209.

4711 Koehler, Heinz. East Germany's Economic Integration Into the Communist Bloc. Ph.D. Thesis, University of Michigan, 1961, 522 P.

4712 Koehler, Heinz. Economic Integration in the Soviet Bloc, With an East German Case Study. New York: Praeger, 1965, 402 P.

4713 Korbonski, Andrzej. Comecon. International Conciliation. No. 549 (September 1964), 62 P.

4714 Krause, Heinz. Economic Structure of East Germany and Its Position Within The Soviet Bloc. Washington: Council for Economic and Industry Research, 1955, 2 Vols.

4715 Pryor, Frederic L. The Communist Foreign Trade System. Cambridge: M.I.T. Press, 1963, 296 P.

4716 Richter, Hans. The Economic Community Between the German Democratic Republic and Poland. German Foreign Policy (GDR). 2:5 (1963), 348-353.

4717 Rutgaizer, V. Structural Changes in the Economies of the European Members of Comecon. Problems of Economics. 8:5 (September 1965), 41-51.

4718 Schaefer, Henry W. Comecon and the Politics of Integration. New York: Praeger, 1972, 200 P.

4719 Spulber, Nicolas. Soviet Undertakings and Soviet Mixed Companies in Eastern Europe. Journal of Central European Affairs. 14:2 (July 1954), 154-173.

4720 Stolper, Wolfgang F. Planning and International Integration in Soviet Germany. Banca Nazionale Del Lavoro, Quarterly Review (Rome). 14:57 (June 1961), 184-196.

4721 Thalheim, Karl C. The Development of the East German Economy in the Framework of the Soviet Bloc. Eastern Europe in Transition. Ed. Kurt London. Baltimore: Johns Hopkins University Press, 1966, Pp. 145-172.

4722 Vinogradov, K. Collaboration of Socialist Countries in the Development of Machine Building. Problems of Economics. 3:2 (June 1960), 51-55.

4723 Weiss, Gerhard. The German Democratic Republic and Socialist Economic Integration. International Affairs (Moscow). (June 1971), 24-28.

4724 Wilke, Werner. G.D.R.-U.S.S.R. Economic Community. German Foreign Policy (GDR). 1:3 (1962), 249-255.

4725 Winston, Victor. The Soviet Satellites: Economic Liability?. Problems of Communism. 7:1 (January-February 1958), 14-20.

4726 Wszelaki, Jan. Communist Economic Strategy: The Role of East-Central Europe. Washington: National Planning Association, 1959, 132 P.

4727 Wyschka, Gerhard. Economic Relations of the GDR With the Socialist Countries. German Foreign Policy (GDR). 7:6 (1968), 442-447.

4728 Wyschka, Gerhard. Koenig, Helmut. The GDR Within the Council for Mutual Economic Assistance--Prospects, Problems and Tasks of the Foreign Economy. German Foreign Policy (GDR). 8:2 (1969), 83-91.

K. FRG-GDR Economic Comparisons and Transactions

K.1. General

4729 Busch, E. Economic Competition of the Two German States. International Affairs (Moscow). (July 1961), 80-81.

4730 Cash, Webster C. A Comparison of the Effects of Government Policies on Industrial Recovery in West and East Germany, 1945-1955. Ph.D. Thesis, University of Chicago, 1957, 263 P.

4731 Economic Commission for Europe. Structure Adaptation in Eastern and Western Germany. Economic Bulletin for Western Germany. 8:3 (November 1956), 45-86.

4732 GDR, Ministry of Foreign Affairs. GDR, Ministry of Agriculture. Where the Past Has Been Finally Overcome: Greenbook on the Two Roads Taken to Change the Conditions in Agriculture in The Two German States. Berlin: Ministries of Foreign Affairs and Agriculture, 1960, 31 P.

4733 Gregory, Paul R. Normal Comparisons of Industrial Structures in East and West Germany. Weltwirtschaftliches Archiv. 104:2 (February 1970), 325-332.

4734 Haeuser, Karl. The Partition of Germany. The German Economy: 1870 to the Present. Ed. Gustav Stolper, Karl Haeuser, and Knut Borchardt. New York: Harcourt, Brace & World, 1967, Pp. 175-217.

4735 Lit, Theodore. Unions in Democratic and Soviet Germany. Monthly Labour Review. 76:1 (January 1953), 1-7.

4736 Meimberg, Rudolf. The Economic Development in West Berlin and in the Soviet Zone. Berlin: Duncker and Humblot, 2D Ed., 1952, 120 P.

4737 Mendershausen, Horst. East and West German Agriculture. Santa Monica: Rand Corporation, P-3209, August 1965, 6 P.

4738 Petterson, Harold. The Two Germanies, 1948-1958: A Challenge to Britain. National Provincial Bank Review. No. 43 (August 1958), 13-20.

4739 Pryor, Frederic L. East and West German Governmental Expenditures. Public Finance. 20:3-4 (1965), 300-365.

4740 Pryor, Frederic L. Public Expenditures in Communist and Capitalist Nations. Homewood: Irwin, 1968, 543 P.

4741 Renning, H. Dieter. Competition in "Miracles"?--How to Study the Postwar Development of the German Economies. Teaching Postwar Germany in America: Papers and Discussions. Ed. Louis F. Helbig and Eberhard Reichmann. Bloomington: Indiana University, Institute of German Studies, 1972.

4742 Roskamp, Karl W. The East German Economy: Who Did Better in the 1950's, East or West Germany?. Social Research. 29:2 (Summer 1962), 221-225.

4743 Scherpenberg, Albert H. Van. German Economy Today. Pakistan Horizon. 3:4 (December 1950), 192-201. Effect of Division Into Eastern and Western Zones.

4744 Schnitzer, Martin. East and West Germany: A Comparative Economic Analysis. New York: Praeger, 1972, 446 P.

4745 Snell, Edwin M. Comparison of the National Products of East and West Germany. Washington: Central Intelligence Agency, June 1960, 57 P.

4746 Stolper, Wolfgang F. Germany Between East and West: The Economics of Competitive Co-Existence. Washington: National Planning Association, 1960, 80 P.

4747 Structural Adaptation in Eastern and Western Germany. Economic Bulletin for Europe. 8:3 (November 1956), 45-86; and 9:1 (May 1957), 109.

4748 Unions in Democratic and Soviet Germany. Monthly Labour Review. 76:1 (January 1953), 1-7.

4749 Weber, Alfred. Agricultural Modernization in Market and Planned Economies: the German Experience. Studies in Comparative Communism. 6:3 (Autumn 1973), 280-300.

K.2. Intra-German Trade

4750 Dean, Robert W. West German Trade With the East: The Political Dimension. New York: Praeger, 1974, 288 P.

4751 Holbik, Karel. German Interzonal Trade, 1946-61. Quarterly Review of Economics and Business. 3:1 (Spring 1963), 77-35.

4752 Holbik, Karel. Myers, Henry Allen. Postwar Trade in Divided Germany: The Internal and International Issues. Baltimore: Johns Hopkins University Press, 1964, 138 P.

4753 Joetze, Guenter. The Legal Nature of the Trade Agreements Between West and East Germany. Yearbook of World Affairs. 16 (1962), 172-196.

4754 Mendershausen, Horst. Interzonal Trade in Germany: Interaction with Early Berlin Conflicts. Santa Monica: Rand Corporation, Rm-3686-Pr, November 1963, 69 P.

4755 Mendershausen, Horst. Interzonal Trade in Germany: The Trade and the Contractual Relations. Santa Monica: Rand Corporation, Rm-3686-Pr, July 1963, 45 P.

4756 Ollig, Gerhard. Economic Relations With the GDR. Aussenpolitik. 26:2 (1975), 185-200.

4757 Ollig, Gerhard. The Future of Intra-German Trade. Aussenpolitik. 25:1 (1974), 50-60.

4758 Pre-War Regional Interdependence and Post-War Interzonal Trade in Germany. Economic Bulletin for Europe. 1:3 (1949), 25-62.

L. Social Structure and Policy

L.1. FRG: Social Structure

L.1.1. General

4759 Allwood, Martin S. The Changing Role of the Handwerk in Germany's Middletown: A Study in Connections Between Personality and a Social Institution. Mullsjo, Sweden: Institute of Social Research, 1955, 42 P.

4760 Becker, Howard. Changes in the Social Stratification of Contemporary Germany. American Sociological Review. 15:3 (June 1950), 333-342.

4761 Becker, Howard. Field Work Among Scottish Shepherds and German Peasants: "Wholes" and Their Handicaps. Social Forces. 35:1 (October 1956), 10-15.

4762 Berkowitz, William R. A Cross-National Comparison of Some Social Patterns of Urban Pedestrians. Journal of Cross-Cultural Psychology. 2:2 (June 1971), 129-144. FRG, UK, US, Sweden, Italy, Turkey, Iran, Afghanistan.

4763 Bolte, Karl Martin. Some Aspects of Social Mobility in Western Germany. Transactions of the Third World Congress of Sociology. London: International Sociological Association, 1956, Vol. 3, Pp. 183-190.

4764 Dahrendorf, Ralf. Recent Changes in the Class Structure of European Societies. A New Europe? Ed. Stephen R. Graubard. Cambridge: Riverside, 1963, Pp. 291-337.

4765 Hirsch, Felix Edward. The End of the Junker Class. Current History. 10:54 (February 1946), 146-151.

4766 Janowitz, Morris. Social Stratification and Mobility in West Germany. American Journal of Sociology. 64:1 (July 1958), 6-24.

4767 Kaupen-Haas, Heidrun. Socio-Cultural Variables in the Doctor-Patient Relationship. Transactions of the Sixth World Congress of Sociology. Geneva: International Sociological Association, 1966, Vol. 4, Pp. 213-225.

4768 Kunde, Thelma A. Dawis, Rene V. Comparative Study of Occupational Prestige in Three Western Cultures. Personnel and Guidance Journal. 37:5 (January 1959), 350-352.

4769 Markiewicz, Wladyslaw. Social Transformations in the German Federal Republic. Polish Western Affairs. 5:2 (1964), 275-310.

4770 Mayer, Karl Ulrich. Dimensions of Mobility Space: Some Subjective Aspects of Career Mobility. Social Science Information. 11:5 (October 1972), 87-115.

4771 Mayer, Karl Ulrich. Mueller, Walter. Roles, Status and Careers: Some Comments on Mobility Analysis and New Data on Intergenerational Mobility in West Germany. Transactions of the Seventh World Congress of Sociology. Sofia: International Sociological Association, 1973, Vol. 5, Pp.. 335-348.

4772 Mueller, Walter. Family Background, Education and Career Mobility. Social Science Information. 11:5 (October 1972), 223-255.

4773 Scheuch, Erwin K. An Instrument to Measure Social Stratification in Western Germany. Transactions of the Third World Congress of Sociology. London: International Sociological Association, 1956, Vol. 8, Pp. 185-189.

4774 Scheuch, Erwin K. Rueschemeyer, Dietrich. Scaling Social Status in Western Germany. British Journal of Sociology. 11:2 (June 1960), 151-168.

4775 Schulze, Rolf H. K. An Analytical Comparison of Selected German Associations in Reference to Their Belief Systems, Membership Alienation and Related Social Characteristics. Ph.D. Thesis, Michigan State University, 1966, 362 P.

4776 Schwartz, Harry. Rural Conditions in Postwar Germany. Rural Sociology. 11:4 (December 1946), 330-339.

4777 Wilkening, Eugene A. Van Es, Johannes C. Aspirations and Attainments Among German Farm Families. Rural Sociology. 32:4 (December 1967), 446-455.

L.1.2. Community Studies

4778 Anderson, Nels. A Community Survey of Darmstadt, Germany. Transactions of the Second World Congress of Sociology. London: International Sociological Association, 1954, Vol. 1, Pp. 79-82.

4779 Elmer, Frank L. German Village; a Case Study in Privately Financed Restoration. N.P.: 1970, 72 P.

4780 Loomis, Charles. Political and Occupational Cleavages in a Hanoverian Village, Germany. Sociometry. 9:4 (November 1946), 316-333.

4781 Meyer, Henry J. Weeks, H. Ashley. Darmstadt Community Survey: Development of Local Community Research in Germany. Frankfurt: Omgus, Manpower Division, Visiting Expert Series No. 13, October 1949, 34 p.

4782 Pilgert, Henry P. Community and Group Life in West Germany, With Special Reference to the Policies and Programs of the Office of the U.S. High Commissioner for Germany. Bad Godesberg-Mehlem: Office of the U.S. High Commissioner for Germany, Historical Division, 1952, 91 P.

4783 Wurzbacher, Gerhard. Pilot Study of a Rural Community in Western Germany. Transactions of the Second World Congress of Sociology. London: International Sociological Association, 1954, Vol. 1, Pp. 132-140.

L.1.3. Family (See Also E.3.4.6)

4784 Baumert, Gerhard. Changes in the Family and the Position of Older Persons in Germany. International Journal of Comparative Sociology. 1:2 (September 1960), 202-210.

4785 Baumert, Gerhard. Some Observations on Current Trends in the German Family. Transactions of the Third World Congress of Sociology. London: International Sociological Association, 1956, Vol. 4, Pp. 161-168.

4786 Becker, Howard. German Families Today. Germany and the Future of Europe. Ed. Hans J. Morgenthau. Chicago: University of Chicago Press, 1951, Pp. 12-24.

4787 Brandes, O. Jean. The Effect of War on the German Family. Social Forces. 29:2 (December 1950), 164-173.

4788 Devereux, Edward C., Jr. Family Authority and Child Behavior in West Germany and the United States: Some Problems and Strategies in a Cross-National Validation Study. Transactions of the Fifth World Congress of Sociology. Louvain, Belgium: International Sociological Association, 1964, Vol. 4, Pp. 303-312.

4789 Devereux, Edward C., Jr. Bronfenbrenner, Urie. Suci, George J. Patterns of Parent Behavior in the United States of America and the Federal Reupublic of Germany: A Cross-National Comparison. International Social Science Journal 14:3 (1962), 488-506.

4790 Elder, Glen H., Jr. Democratic Parent-Youth Relations in Cross-National Perspective. Social Science Quarterly. 49:2 (September 1968), 216-228.

4791 Elder, Glen H., Jr. Family Structure and Educational Attainment: A Cross-National Analysis. American Sociological Review. 30:1 (January 1965), 81-96.

4792 Elder, Glen H., Jr. Role Relations, Sociocultural Environments and Autocratic Family Ideology. Sociometry. 28:2 (June 1965), 173-196.

4793 Freedman, Ronald. Baumert, Gerhard. Bolte, Karl Martin. Expected Family Size and Family Size Values in West Germany. Population Studies. 13:2 (November 1959), 136-150.

4794 Karr, Chadwick. Wesley, Frank. Comparison of German and U.S. Child-Rearing Practices. Child Development. 37:3 (September 1966), 715-723.

4795 Koenig, Rene. Family and Authority: The German Father in 1955. Sociological Review. 5:1 (July 1957), 107-127.

4796 Kooy, Gerrit A. Koetter, Herbert. Some Problems Encountered in an Investigation Concerning the European Rural Family. Transactions of the Fifth World Congress of Sociology. Louvain: International Sociological Association, 1962, Vol. 4, Pp. 319-332.

4797 Lamouse, Annette. Family Roles of Women: A German Example. Journal of Marriage and the Family. 31:1 (February 1969), 145-152.

4798 Litwak, Eugene. Group Pressure and Family Breakup: A Study of German Communities. American Journal of Sociology. 61:4 (January 1956), 345-354.

4799 Lueschen, Guenther. Staikof, Zaharj. Heiskanen, Veronica Stolte. Ward, Conor. Family, Ritual and Secularization--A Cross-National Study Conducted in Bulgaria, Finland, Germany and Ireland. Social Compass. 19:4 (1972), 519-536.

4800 Lupri, Eugen. Contemporary Authority Patterns in the West German Family: A Study in Cross-National Validation. Journal of Marriage and the Family. 31:1 (February 1969), 134-144.

4801 Lupri, Eugen. The West German Family Today and Yesterday: A Study in Changing Family Authority Patterns. Ph.D. Thesis, University of Wisconsin, 1967, 293 P.

4802 Metraux, Rhoda Bubendey. Parents and Children: An Analysis of Contemporary German Child Care and Youth-Guidance Literature. Childhood in Contemporary Cultures. Eds. Margaret Mead and Martha Wolfenstein. Chicago: University of Chicago Press, 1956, Pp. 204-228.

4803 Metraux, Rhoda Bubendey. A Portrait of the Family in German Juvenile Literature. Childhood in Contemporary Cultures. Eds. Margaret Mead and Martha Wolfenstein. Chicago: University of Chicago Press, 1956, Pp. 253-276.

4804 Rainwater, Lee. Social Status Differences in the Family Relationships of German Men. Marriage and Family Living. 24:1 (February 1962), 12-17.

4805 Rapp, Don W. Child Rearing Attitudes of Mothers in Germany and in the United States. Ph.D. Thesis, Florida State University, 1960, 81 P. R

4806 Schelsky, Helmut. The Family in Germany. Marriage and Family Living. 16:4 (November 1954), 331-335.

4807 Scheuch, Erwin K. Family Cohesion in Leisure Time. Sociological Review. 8:1 (July 1960), 37-61.

4808 Taylor, Donald L. The Changing German Family. International Journal of Comparative Sociology. 10:3-4 (September-December 1969), 299-302.

L.1.4. Women: Roles and Status

4809 Barden, Judy. Candy-Bar Romance--Women of Germany. This Is Germany. Ed. Arthur Settel. New York: Sloane, 1950, Pp. 161-176.

4810 Daniel, Anita. It's Still the Three K's in Germany. New York Times Magazine. (28 March 1954), 19+.

4811 Deneke, Helena. Norris, Betty. The Women of Germany. London: National Council of Social Service, for the Women's Group on Public Welfare, 1947, 31 P.

4812 Duverger, Maurice. The Political Role of Women. Paris: Unesco, 1955, 221 P. Political Practice in FRG, Norway, France, Yugoslavia.

4813 Employment of Women in the Federal

Republic of Germany. International Labour Review. 95:5 (May 1967), 482-487.

4814 Hartmann, Heinz. The Enterprising Woman: A German Model. Columbia Journal of World Business. 5:2 (March-April 1970), 61-66.

4815 Hirkson, Pamela. The Women of Germany. Fortnightly. 163:875 (March 1948), 176-181.

4816 Long, Tania. They Long for a New Fuehrer. New York Times Magazine. (9 December 1945), 8+.

4817 Maxson, Rhea F. The Woman Worker in Germany. Bad Godesberg-Mehlem: Office of the U.S. High Commissioner for Germany, Office of Labor Affairs, 1952.

4818 Mosheim, Berthold. The Legal Effects of Equal Marital Rights for Women in Germany. International and Comparative Law Quarterly. 2:3 (July 1953), 430-442.

4819 Pilgert, Henry P. Waschke, Hildegard. Women in West Germany, With Special Reference to the Policies and Programs of the Women's Affairs Branch, Office of Public Affairs, Office of the U.S. High Commissioner for Germany. Bad Godesberg-Mehlem: Office of the U.S. High Commissioner for Germany, Historical Division, 1952, 72 P.

4820 Southall, Sara. Newman, Pauline M. Women in German Industry. Frankfurt: Omgus, Manpower Division, Visiting Expert Series No. 14, October 1949, 31 P.

4821 Tritz, Maria. The Employment of Women in the Federal Republic of Germany. Bonn: Federal Ministry of Labour and the Social Structure, Social Policy in Germany No. 5, 1965, 25 P.

4822 Welzel, Karl. The Protection of Working Mothers. Bonn: Federal Ministry of Labour and the Social Structure, Social Policy in Germany No. 29, 1963, 15 P.

L.1.5. Youth and Youth Movements (See Also F.1.1)

4823 Allerbeck, Klaus R. Some Structural Conditions for Youth and Student Movements. International Social Science Journal. 24:2 (1972), 257-270.

4824 Baker, Kendall L. The Young Germans: A Study in Political Culture. Ph.D. Thesis, Georgetown University, 1969, 446 P.

4825 Baker, Kendall L. Political Alienation and the German Youth. Comparative Political Studies. 3:1 (April 1970), 117-130.

4826 Becker, Howard. German Youth: Bond or Free. London: Kegan Paul, Trench, Trubner, 1946, 286 P.

4827 Blumenthal, Ralph. A Berlin Commune Is a Big Happy Family (Sometimes). New York Times Magazine. (1 December 1968), 52+.

4828 Divo-Institut. Basic Orientation and Political Thinking of West German Youth and Their Leaders, 1956. Frankfurt and Bad Godesberg: Divo-Institut, 1956, 231 and 173 P.

4829 Domandi, Mario. The Youth Movement and Its Place in German Culture. Ph.D. Thesis, Columbia University, 1952, 91 P.

4830 Fried, Edrita G. Lissance, Marjorie Fiske. The Dilemmas of German Youth. Journal of Abnormal and Social Psychology. 44:1 (January 1949), 50-60.

4831 German National Committee for International Youth Work. This Young Generation. Bonn-Venusberg: German National Committee for International Youth Work, C.1971, 50 P.

4832 Heck, Bruno. Youth Work and Youth Policy in Germany. United Asia. 19:6 (November-December 1967), 335-338.

4833 Josephson, Eric. Political Youth Organization in Europe, 1900-1950: A Comparative Study of Six Radical Parties and Their Youth Auxiliaries. Ph.D. Thesis, Columbia University, 1959, 335 P.

4834 Kellermann, Henry J. The Present Status of German Youth. Department of State Bulletin. 15:367 (14 July 1946), 49-55, 63; 15:368 (21 July 1946), 83-88.

4835 Kellermann, Henry J. The Present Status of German Youth. Washington: Department of State Publication No. 2583, Government Printing Office, 1946, 25 P.

4836 Lane, Robert E. Adolescent Influence, Rebellion and Submission in the United States and Germany: Patterns of Political Maturation. Paris: International Political Science Association, 1964, 31 P.

4837 Laqueur, Walter Z. Young Germany: A History of the German Youth Movement. New York: Basic Books, 1962, 253 P., Esp. Pp. 216-237.

4838 Lasky, Melvin J. Germany's Greatest Unknown Quantity. New York Times Magazine. (16 January 1955), 12+. Deals With the Young People of Germany.

4839 Limbert, Paul M. Youth Activities in Germany. Educational Record. 28:1 (January 1947), 33-44.

4840 Long, Tania. Spawn of the Nazi Code. New York Times Magazine. (25 November 1945), 8+. German Youth Has Lost Roots, Visibly Grows More Demoralized.

4841 Luchsinger, Fred. German Youth Today. Swiss Review of World Affairs. 5:6 (September 1955), 7-10.

4842 Mcgranahan, Donald V. Janowitz, Morris. Studies of German Youth. Journal of Abnormal and Social Psychology. 41:1 (January 1946), 3-14.

4843 Middleton, Drew. German Youth: Skeptical, Cynical But Bold. New York Times Magazine. (21 May 1950), 13+.

4844 Middleton, Drew. The Hitler Youth Eight Years After. New York Times Magazine. (3 May 1953), 17+.

4845 Muhlen, Norbert. German Youth in a Vacuum: The Threat of a New Lost Generation. Commentary. 9:5 (May 1950), 426-434.

4846 Naumann, Theodor. Problems of German Youth Since World War I. Ph.D. Thesis, Oregon State College, 1954, 107 P.

4847 Norris, Grace. Young Germany: Children of Germany at Work and Play. New York: Dodd, Mead, 1969, 64 P.

4848 Oppe, Hubert W. The German Youth Movement: A Sociological Analysis. Ph.D. Thesis, University of California, Berkeley, 1957, 116 P.

4849 Planck, Ulrich. The Rural Youth in Western Germany. Rural Sociology. 25:4 (December 1960), 442-446.

4850 Porter, Rose Albert. Youth in the West Zone. Survey. 87:2 (February 1951), 76-78.

4851 Remmers, H. H. Cross-Cultural Studies of Teenagers' Problems. Journal of Educational Psychology. 53:6 (December 1962), 254-261. U.S.,

Puerto Rico, FRG, India.

4852 Rimlinger, Gaston V. Welfare Policy and Industrialization in Europe, America, and Russia. New York: John Wiley & Sons, 1971, Xi and 362 P., Esp. Pp. 89-192.

4853 Samuels, Gertrude. Can German Youth Teach Its Elders?. New York Times Magazine. (22 July 1951), 18+.

4854 Schwarzweller, Harry K. Community of Residence and Career Choices of German Rural Youth. Rural Sociology. 33:1 (March 1968), 46-63.

4855 Some Characteristics of the Younger Generation in Germany. World Today. 10:9 (September 1954), 406-412.

4856 UK, CCG. Report of Survey on Voluntary Youth Councils in the British Zone. Bielefeld?: CCG (Be), 1949, 41 P.

4857 US, Department of State, Office of Public Affairs. Young Germany: Apprentice to Democracy. Washington: Department of State Publication 4251, Government Printing Office, 1951, 78 P. on US-Sponsored Programs for German Youth.

4858 US, Department of the Army, European Command, Headquarters. US, Omgus, Internal Affairs and Communications Division. German Youth Activities Guide: Army Assistance Program. N.P.: Eucom Headquarters, Opot Division, Training and Education Branch, in Collaboration With Omgus, Internal Affairs and Communications Division, Education and Religious Affairs Branch, 1948, 135 P.

4859 US, Omgus, Education and Cultural Relations Division. German Youth Between Yesterday and Tomorrow, 1 April 1947-30 April 1948. Berlin: Omgus, Education and Cultural Relations Division, 1948, 36 P.

4860 US, Omgus, Education and Cultural Relations Division. Giving Youth New Goals. N.P.: Omgus, August 1946.

4861 Waln, Nora. Children in Germany. Atlantic Monthly. 176:6 (December 1945), 52-54.

L.2. GDR: Social Structure

4862 Apteker, Bettina. A New City Is Born in the GDR. Political Affairs. 48:11 (November 1969), 42-46.

4863 Dohnke, Dieter. The Analysis of Conditions Applying to Society as a Whole--A Prerequisite for the Sociological Understanding of Small Social Units. Transactions of the Seventh World Congress of Sociology. Sofia: International Sociological Association, 1972, Vol. 3, Pp. 332-336.

4864 Friedman, Peter. Women, Peace, and Socialism: Equal Opportunity in East Germany. Dalhousie Review. 44:3 (Autumn 1964), 299-311.

4865 Hahn, Erich. Sociological System Conception and Social Prognosis. Transactions of the Seventh World Congress of Sociology. Sofia: International Sociological Association, 1970, Vol. 1, Pp. 69-82.

4866 Hardin, William Russell. Emigration, Occupational Mobility, and Institutionalization: the German Democratic Republic. Ph.D. Thesis, Massachusetts Institute of Technology, 1971.

4867 Kubitschek, Helga. Women's Rights in the GDR. German Foreign Policy (GDR). 7:2 (1968), 135-141.

4868 Lockwood, W. B. Lusatian in the German Democratic Republic Today. Slavonic and East European Review. 35:85 (June 1957), 462-472.

4869 Marriage and Family Under Communism. East Europe. 6:3 (March 1957), 22-31.

4870 Raede, John W. De-Germanization of the Upper Lusatian Language. Slavic and East European Journal. 11:2 (Summer 1967), 185-190.

4871 Stone, Gerald C. The Smallest Slavonic Nation: The Sorbs of Lusatia. London: Athlone, 1972, 201 P.

L.3. FRG-GDR: Social Structure

4872 Cate, Donald Francis. Democracy as Exemplified By Western Powers and the Soviet Union in the Reorientation of Youth in Occupied Germany. Ph.D. Thesis, Oregon State College, 1951, 185 P.

4873 Sommerkorn, Ingrid N. Women's Careers: Experience From East and West Germany. Planning (P.E.P.). 36:521 (October 1970), 1-132.

L.4. Religion

L.4.1. FRG: General (See Also N.2.7)

4874 Amery, Carl (Pseud. for Christian Mayer). Capitulation: The Lesson of German Catholicism. New York: Herder & Herder, 1967, 231 P., Esp. Pp. 104-224.

4875 Baerwald, Friedrich. German Catholics and Labor. Social Order. 8:4 (April 1958), 163-167.

4876 Bieri, Ernst. Flight From Responsibility, or Pastor Niemoeller in No Man's Land. Swiss Review of World Affairs. 2:11 (February 1953), 15-17. Can a Christian Really Remain "Uninvolved"?.

4877 C. C. W. The Protestant Church in Germany. World Today. 7:10 (October 1951), 439-449.

4878 Cox, Harvey. German Ecumenism: Politics and Dialogue. Commonweal. 77:25 (March 1963), 635-638.

4879 Dibelius, Otto. Day Is Dawning: The Story of Bishop Otto Dibelius, Based on His Proclamations and Authentic Documents. Philadelphia: Christian Education, 1956, 222 P.

4880 Dibelius, Otto. in the Service of the Lord: Autobiography. New York: Holt, Rinehart and Winston, 1964, 280 P.

4881 Dowell, Jack D. The Politics of Accommodation: German Social Democracy and The Catholic Church. Journal of Church and State. 7:1 (Winter 1965), 78-90.

4882 Dowell, Jack D. Uneasy Allies: Catholics and Christian Democrats in West Germany. Australian Journal of Politics and History. 18:3 (December 1972), 360-366.

4883 Gable, Lee J. Church and World Encounter: The Evangelical Academies in Germany and Their Meaning for the Ecumenical Church. Philadelphia: United Church Press, 1964, 111 P.

4884 Gable, Lee J. Evangelical Academy and Parish in West Germany, 1945-1961. Ph.D. Thesis, University of Pennsylvania, 1962, 242 P.

4885 Gable, Lee J. Evangelical Academy and Parish in West Germany, 1945-1961. Lancaster: Lancaster Theological Seminary, 1962, 234 P.

4886 German-Polish Dialogue: Letters of the Polish and German Bishops and International Statements. Bonn: Atlantik-Forum, 1966, 127 P.

4887 Golde, Guenter. Catholics and Protestants: Agricultural Modernization in Two German Villages. New York: Academic Press, Inc., 1975, xiii and 198 p.

4888 Gollwitzer, Helmut. The Christian Faith and the Marxist Criticism of Religion. Edinburgh: St. Andrew Place, 1970, 173 p.

4889 Gollwitzer, Helmut. The Demands of Freedom: Papers By a Christian in West Germany. New York and Evanston: Harper & Row, 1965, 176 p.

4890 Greinacher, Norbert. The Development of Applications to Leave the Church and the Transfer From One Church to Another, and Its Causes. Social Compass. 8:1 (1961), 61-72.

4891 Grimm, Hans. Answer of a German: An Open Letter to the Archbishop of Canterbury. Dublin: Euphorion, 1952, 237 p.

4892 Groner, Franz. The Social Standing of Catholics in the Federal Republic of Germany. Social Compass. 9:5-6 (1962), 539-553.

4893 Kisielewski, Stefan. Civilization in West Germany: A Dissenting Polish View. East Europe. 11:9 (September 1962), 24-27. Excerpts From a Catholic Weekly Published in Cracow.

4894 Kleine, Erwin. The Catholic Church Today: Germany. The Catholic Church Today: Western Europe. Ed. Matthew A. Fitzsimons. Notre Dame: University of Notre Dame Press, 1969, Pp. 29-60.

4895 Littell, Franklin H. Church and Sect. Ecumenical Review. 6:3 (April 1954), 262-276.

4896 Littell, Franklin H. The German Phoenix: Men and Movements in the Church in Germany. Garden City: Doubleday, 1960, 226 p.

4897 Luckman, Thomas. Four Protestant Parishes in Germany: A Study in the Sociology of Religion. Social Research. 26:4 (Winter 1959), 423-448.

4898 Mcclaskey, Beryl R. Forstmeier, Friedrich. The History of U.S. Policy and Program in the Field of Religious Affairs Under the Office of the U.S. High Commissioner for Germany. Bad Godesberg-Mehlem: Office of the U.S. High Commissioner for Germany, Office of the Executive Director, Historical Divisior, 1951, 107 p.

4899 Matthes, Joachim. Preconceptions and Institutionalisation. Social Compass. 10:5 (1963), 377-386. Crucial Problem for Research in Sociology of Religion.

4900 Matthijssen, M. A. J. M. Catholic Intellectual Emancipation in the Western Countries of Mixed Religion. Social Compass. 6:3 (1958-59), 91-113, Esp. Pp. 97-100.

4901 Memorandum of the Eight Evangelical Churchmen. Poland and Germany. 6:3 (July-September 1962), 21-26.

4902 Memorandum of the German Evangelical Church (Excerpt). Poland and Germany. 10:1 (January-March 1966), 41-44.

4903 Northcott, Cecil. Martin Niemoeller. Contemporary Review. 201 (May 1962), 253-255.

4904 Rubin, Henry B. The Anatomy of a "Good German"--Martin Niemoeller. Chicago Jewish Forum. 5:4 (Fall 1946), 238-243.

4905 Scharffs, Gilbert W. Mormonism in Germany: A History of the Church of Jesus Christ of Latter-Day Saints in Germany Between 1840 and 1970. Salt Lake City: Deseret, 1970, 256 p.

4906 Schreuder, Osmund. Religious Attitudes, Group Consciousness, Liturgy and Education. Social Compass. 10:1 (1963), 29-52.

4907 Spotts, Frederic. The Churches and Politics in Germany. Middletown: Wesleyan University Press, 1973, xii and 419 p.

4908 Wentzel, Fred D. Day Is Dawning: The Story of Bishop Otto Dibelius, Based on His Proclamations and Authentic Documents. Philadelphia: Christian Education Press, 1956, 222 p.

4909 Werner, Philipp. General Studies in Germany Today. Christian Scholar. 37:2 (June 1954), 101-105.

4910 Wilder, Amos N. Moral Aspects of German Recovery. Religion in Life. 22:4 (Autumn 1953), 527-537.

4911 Worries of a German Protestant. Swiss Review of World Affairs. 2:5 (August 1952), 15-17.

4912 US, Hicog. Religion in Public Life. Wiesbaden: Hicog, 1951.

4913 US, Omgus, Education and Cultural Relations Division. Religious Affairs. N.P.: Omgus, Education and Cultural Relations Division, 1946, 36 p.

4914 US, Omgus, Education and Cultural Relations Division. US, Hicog, Education and Cultural Relations Division. Reports on Mass Media in German Religious Life. N.P.: Omgus-Hicog, Education and Cultural Relations Division, Religious Affairs Branch, 1949-51.

4915 US, Omgus, Education and Cultural Relations Division. US, Hicog, Education and Cultural Relations Division. Reports on Religious Life in Germany: Reports of U.S. and Eropean Consultants in Social Action to Evangelical Affairs. N.P.: Omgus-Hicog, Education and Cultural Relations Division, Religious Affairs Branch, 1949-51.

4916 US, Omgus, Education and Cultural Relations Division. US, Hicog, Education and Cultural Relations Division. Reports on Religious Youth and Women's Groups in Germany. N.P.: Omgus-Hicog, Education and Cultural Relations Division, Religious Affairs Branch, 1949-51.

4917 US, Omgus, Education and Cultural Relations Division. US, Hicog, Education and Cultural Relations Division. Reports on Social Action and International Religious Groups in Germany. N.P.: Omgus-Hicog, Education and Cultural Relations Division, Religious Affairs Branch, 1949-51.

4918 US, Omgus, Education and Cultural Relations Division. US, Hicog, Education and Cultural Relations Division. Reports on the Church and Labor in Germany. N.P.: Omgus-Hicog, Education and Cultural Relations Division, Religious Affairs Branch, 1949-51.

4919 US, Omgus, Internal Affairs and Communications Division. Historical Report, Education and Religious Affairs, Winter 1941-Spring 1946. N.P.: Omgus, Adjutant General, 1948, 21 p.

L.4.2. FRG: Judaism; Attitudes to Jews (See Also D.3.3; O.3.2.)

4920 Wiener Library. Post-War Publications on German Jewry: Books and Articles, 1945-1955. Yearbook of the Leo Baeck Institute of Jews From Germany. London: Leo Baeck Institute, 1956, Vol. 1, Pp. 393-446. Bibliographies Also Appear in Subsequent Yearbooks.

4921 Allen, Robert. Arnold Frank of Hamburg. London: Clarke, 1966, 224 p.

4922 American Institute of International Information. Report on a Remnant of Nazi Victims: The Jews of Germany. New York: American Institute of

International Information, 1948, 29 P. Supplement: Germany's Nazi Legacies, By Fred M. Hechinger.

4923 American Jewish Committee. Anti-Semitism in Western Europe Today. Paris: American Jewish Committee, European Office, June 1956, 20 P.

4924 American Jewish Committee. The Position of the Jews in the Post-War World. New York: Research Institute on Peace and Post-War Problems of the American Jewish Committee, 1943, 64 P.

4925 American Jewish Committee. Program for Postwar Jewish Reconstruction. New York: American Jewish Committee, 1945, 16 P.

4926 American Jewish Congress. The German Dilemma: An Appraisal of Anti-Semitism, Ultra-Nationalism and Democracy in West Germany. New York: Commission on International Affairs, World Jewish Congress, 1959, 63 P.

4927 Association of Jewish Communities in the GDR. Anti-Semitism in West Germany: Enemies and Murderers of Jews in the Ruling Apparatus of the Federal Republic. Berlin (East): Association of Jewish Communities in the German Democratic Republic, 1967, 117 P.

4928 Balabkins, Nicholas. West Germany and the Jews: Bonn's Moral Comeback. Orbis 11:3 (Fall 1967), 897-902.

4929 Baron, Salo W. Jews and Germans: A Millenial Heritage. Midstream. 13:1 (January 1967), 3-13.

4930 Bentwich, Norman D. The Jewish Remnant in Germany. Contemporary Review. 183:1046 (February 1953), 73-77.

4931 Bentwich, Norman D. The Jewish Remnant in Germany. Quarterly Review. 298:624 (April 1960), 214-220.

4932 Bentwich, Norman D. The Jews in Germany: 1945-1956. Contemporary Review. 190:1091 (November 1956), 268-273.

4933 Bieber, Hugo. Anti-Semitism in the First Years of the German Republic. Yivo Annual of Jewish Social Science. 4 (1949), 123-145.

4934 Board of Deputies of British Jews. The Jews in Europe: Their Martyrdom and Their Future. London: Board of Deputies of British Jews, 1945, 64 P.

4935 Davis, Robert Gorham. Passion at Oberammergau. Commentary. 29:3 (March 1960), 198-204.

4936 Deutsch, Martin. The 1960 Swastika Smearings: Analysis of the Apprehended Youth. Merrill-Palmer Quarterly of Behavior and Development. 8:2 (April 1962), 99-120. Under Auspices of Anti-Defamation League, B'Nai B'Rith.

4937 Donaldson, Gordon. The Jews in Germany Today: A Report on Their New Wounds and Fresh Fears. Toronto: The Telegram, July 1959, 8 P.

4938 FRG. White Paper on the Anti-Semitic and Nazi Incidents From 25 December 1959 Until 28 January 1960. Bonn: N.P., 1960, 79 P.

4939 FRG, Press and Information Office. Germany and the Jews Since 1945. Washington: German Embassy, Press and Information Office, 195-, 18 P.

4940 Fleischner, Eva Maria. The View of Judaism in German Christian Theology Since 1945: the Relationship of Christianity and Israel Considered in Terms of Mission. Ph.D. Thesis, Marquette University, 1972, 286 P.

4941 GDR, Committee for German Unity. Witch Hunt Against Jews: The West German Government Encourages Anti-Semitism: A Documentation. Berlin: Committee for German Unity, 1959, 15 P.

4942 Gershon, Karen, Editor. Postscript: A Collective Account of the Lives of Jews in West Germany Since the Second World War. London: Gollancz, 1969, 191 P.

4943 Goldschmidt, Hermann Levin. Jewish Reconstruction in Germany Since 1945. Jewish Journal of Sociology. 4:1 (June 1962), 127-129. Review of Harry Maor, "Ueber Den Wiederaufbau Der Juedischen Gemeinden in Deutschland Seit 1945".

4944 Gottschalk, Max. Duker, Abraham G. Jews in the Post-War World. New York: Dryden, 1945, 224 P.

4945 Grossmann, Kurt R. The Jews and Germany: A Re-Appraisal. Chicago Jewish Forum. 9:3 (Spring 1951), 199-203.

4946 Hain, Jack. Status of Jewish Workers and Employers in Post-War Germany. Berlin: Omgus, Manpower Division, Visiting Expert Series No. 10, August 1949, 11 P.

4947 Hilberg, Raul. The Destruction of the European Jews. Chicago: Quadrangle Books, 1961, 788 P., Esp. Ch. 9.

4948 Jacoby, Gerhard. Anti-Democratic Trends and the Jewish Position in Western Germany. New York: Institute of Jewish Affairs, 1951, 38 P.

4949 Jacoby, Gerhard. West Germany--1953. New York: Institute of Jewish Affairs, 1953, 45 P.

4950 Jewish Travel Guide. Jewish Life in Germany. Stuttgart: Paneuropaeische Edition, 1954, 128 P.

4951 Katcher, Leo. Post-Mortem: The Jews in Germany Today. New York: Delacorte, 1968, 267 P.

4952 Lehrman, Hal. The New Germany and Her Remaining Jews. Commentary. 16:6 (December 1953), 513-524.

4953 Lesser, Jonas. Germany: The Symbol and the Deed. New York: Yoseloff, 1965, 601 P., Esp. Pp. 512-565.

4954 Levy, Lillian. West Germany and Anti-Semitism. Chicago Jewish Forum. 18:3 (Spring 1960), 211-215.

4955 Liepman, Heinz. Lights and Shadows in West Germany. Menorah Journal. 47:1-2 (Autumn-Winter 1959), 86-103. A Jew's Impression of the Jewish Condition in FRG.

4956 Lueth, Erich. The German Jews: A Problem in Political Morality. Confluence. 3:1 (March 1954), 82-92.

4957 Lynx, J. J., Editor. The Future of the Jews: A Symposium. London: Drummond, 1945, 195 P.

4958 Muhlen, Norbert. The Survivors: A Report on the Jews in Germany. New York: Crowell, 1962, 228 P.

4959 Nadich, Judah. Eisenhower and the Jews. New York: Twayne, 1953, 271 P.

4960 Prinz, Joachim. Germans and Jews--Is There a Bridge?. Jubilee Volume Dedicated to Curt C. Silberman. Ed. Herbert A. Strauss and Hanns G. Reissner. New York: American Federation of Jews From Central Europe, Inc., 1969, Pp. 48-59.

4961 Schalk, Adolph. The Jews in Germany--Do They Have Any Future?. Commonweal. 79:7 (8 November 1963), 185-187.

4962 Schalk, Adolph. The Jews in Germany Today. U.S. Catholic. 33:5 (September 1967), 38-44.

4963 Schwab, Hermann. Jewish Rural

Communities in Germany. London: Cooper, 1957, 93 P.

4964 Schwarz, Leo Walder. The Redeemers: A Saga of the Years 1945-1952. New York: Farrar, Straus & Young, 1953, 385 P.

4965 Seydewitz, Ruth. Seydewitz, Max. Anti-Semitism in West Germany. Berlin (East): Committee for German Unity, 1956, 80 P.

4966 Streit, Josef. Neo-Fascism and Anti-Semitism in West Germany. Law and Legislation in the German Democratic Republic. No. 1 (1960), 45-56.

4967 Turner, Joel. A Corner in Hamburg. Chicago Jewish Forum. 16:1 (Fall 1957), 47-49.

4968 Walter, Hilde. German Students Seek "Peace with the Jews"--Behind the Fight Against Nazi Movie-Makers. Commentary. 14:2 (August 1952), 124-130.

4969 Wise, James Waterman. A Jew Revisits Germany. New York: Daily Compass, 1950, 31 P.

4970 Zimmels, Hirsch Jacob. The Echo of the Nazi Holocaust in the Rabbinic Literature. Dublin: Irish University Press, 1974, 400 P.

L.4.3. GDR: General

4971 Adler, Elizabeth, Editor. Here for a Reason: Christian Voices in a Communist State. New York: Macmillan, 1964, 136 P.

4972 Althausen, Johannes. East German Perspectives on Evangelism. Ecumenical Review. 20:2 (April 1968), 156-158.

4973 Barth, Karl. Hamel, Johannes. How to Serve God in a Marxist Land. New York: Association, 1959, 126 P.

4974 Barth, Markus. Church and Communism in East Germany. Christian Century. 83:47 (23 November 1966), 1440-1443; and 83:48 (30 November 1966), 1469-1472.

4975 Beigel, Greta. Recent Events in Eastern Germany. New York: Institute of Jewish Affairs, 1953, 19 P. Jews in Germany.

4976 Brand, George H. Accomodation and Resistance: A Study of Church-State Relations in the German Democratic Republic. Ph.D. Thesis, Columbia University, 1974.

4977 Conrad, Richard. Communist Control of Religion: A Sociological Case Study of the Protestant Church in East Germany. Maxwell Air Force Base, Ala.: Air Research and Development Command, Human Resources Research Institute, 1954, 28 P.

4978 Croan, Melvin. Kirchenkampf in East Germany. Survey. No. 31 (January-March 1960), 81-87.

4979 The Evangelical Church in Berlin and the Soviet Zone of Germany. Witten: Eckart, 1959, 51 P.

4980 Goetting, Gerald. Christians and Politics in the German Democratic Republic. Berlin (East): Union, 1966, 150 P.

4981 Gust, Kurt. East German Protestantism Under Communist Rule, 1945-1961. Ph.D. Thesis, University of Kansas, 1966, 362 P.

4982 Hamel, Johannes. A Christian in East Germany. New York: Association Press, 1960, 126 P.

4983 Harrington, Eugene C. Religious Liberty in East Germany. London: Sword of the Spirit Pamphlet No. 11, 1958, 24 P.

4984 Lee, Robert E. A. Question 7: Based on the Motion Picture Screenplay By Allan Sloane. Grand Rapids: Eerdmans, 1962, 133 P.

4985 Maceoin, Gary. The Communist War on Religion. New York: Devin-Adair, 1951, 264 P.

4986 Moennich, Martha L. Europe Behind the Iron Curtain. Grand Rapids: Zondervan, 1948, 153 P., Esp. Pp. 89-100. Views on Religious Freedom, Based on Personal Tour.

4987 Niebuhr, Reinhold. Barth's East German Letter. Christian Century. 76:6 (11 February 1959), 167-169.

4988 Robertson, Edwin Hanton. The Bible in East Germany. New York: Association Press, 1961, 93 P.

4989 The Roman Catholic Church in Berlin and in the Soviet Zone of Germany. Berlin: Morus, 1959, 63 P.

4990 Shuster, George N. Religion Behind the Iron Curtain. New York: Macmillan, 1954, 281 P., Esp. Pp. 32-60.

4991 Solberg, Richard W. God and Caesar in East Germany: The Conflicts of Church and State in East Germany Since 1945. New York: Macmillan, 1961, 294 P.

4992 Strong, Kendrick. A Sunday in East Berlin. Christian Century. 81:49 (2 December 1964), 1500-1504.

4993 West, Charles C. The Christian, the University, and a Communist Land. Christian Scholar. 37:2 (June 1954), 106-113.

L.4.4. FRG-GDR Comparisons

4994 Alexander, Edgar. Church and Society in Germany. Church and Society: Catholic Social and Political Thought and Movements, 1789-1950. Ed. Joseph N. Moody. New York: Arts, 1953, Pp. 325-583.

4995 Brunotte, Heinz. The Evangelical Church in Germany. Hanover: Verlag Des Amtsblattes Der Evangelischen Kirche in Deutschland, 1955, 16 P.

4996 Drummond, Andrew Landale. German Protestantism Since Luther. London: Epworth, 1951, 282 P.

4997 Frei, Otto. Evangelical Church Leaders and All-German Discussions at Leipzig. Swiss Review of World Affairs. 4:5 (August 1954), 11-12.

4998 Herman, Stewart Winfield. The Rebirth of the German Church. London: S.C.M. Press, 1946, 276 P.

4999 Howard, Wilbert Francis. Continental Theology After the War. London Quarterly and Holborn Review. 171:1 (January 1946), 1-4.

5000 Jackson, Joseph Harrison. Stars in the Night; Report on a Visit to Germany. Philadelphia: Christian Education, 1950, 72 P.

5001 Knappen, Marshall M. Allied Military Government Policy and the Religious Situation in Germany. Church History. 16 (June 1947), 92-103.

5002 Kuehnelt-Leddihn, Erik R. Von. Catholicism of the Germanies. Dublin Review. 227:460 (Summer 1953), 122-139.

5003 Leiper, Henry Smith. Ecumenical Trends in Present Day Germany: A Statement Based on an Interview With Martin Niemoeller. Christendom. 12:2 (Winter 1947), 230-233.

5004 Thielicke, Helmut. Religion in Germany. Annals of the American Academy of Political and Social Science. 260 (November 1948), 144-154.

5005 Thielicke, Helmut. Religion in Germany. Contemporary Review. 175:1001 (May 1949), 273-277.

5006 Vermehren, E. M. Political Catholicism in Germany. Dublin Review. 218:436 (January 1946), 90-96.

L.5. FRG: Social Policy

L.5.1. General

5007 Braun, Heinrich. Industrialization and Social Policy in Germany. Cologne: Heymann, 1956, 381 P.

5008 Heidenheimer, Arnold J. The Politics of Public Education, Health and Welfare in the U.S.A. and Western Europe: How Growth and Reform Potentials Have Differed. British Journal of Political Science. 3:3 (July 1973), 315-340.

5009 Koellermann, Hans Werner. Social Policy in Germany: A Systematic and Historical Introduction. Bonn: Federal Ministry of Labour and the Social Structure, Social Policy in Germany No. 1, 1967, 56 P.

5010 Rimlinger, Gaston V. The Economics of Postwar German Social Policy. Industrial Relations. 6:2 (February 1967), 184-205.

5011 Zoellner, Detlev. Social Legislation in the Federal Republic of Germany. Bonn: Asgard, 1970, 61 P.

L.5.2. Social Security, Pensions

5012 An Actuarial Analysis of the Pension Schemes in the Federal Republic of Germany and the Land Berlin. International Labour Review. 72:6 (December 1955), 535-540.

5013 Blank, Theodor. Situation and Problems of Social Security in the Federal Republic of Germany. International Social Security Association Bulletin. 13:6 (June 1960), 261-269. Address Given at Opening of Congress of the International Social Security Association at Munich on 2 May 1960.

5014 Bloch, Max. Social Insurance in Post-War Germany. International Labour Review. 58:3 (September 1948), 306-344.

5015 Burkus, John. Some Aspects of Income Redistribution Through Social Security in Four Western European Countries. International Labour Review. 97:2 (February 1968), 167-190.

5016 Claussen, Wilhelm. Provision for Old Age in Germany. Progress. 53:298 (1968-69), 55-59.

5017 Elsholz, Konrad. The Cost of Social Security in the Federal Republic of Germany. International Social Security Association Bulletin. 9:9-10 (September-October 1956), 363-366.

5018 Fisher, Paul. Old-Age and Sickness Insurance in West Germany in 1965. Washington: Department of Health, Education, and Welfare, Social Security Administration, Office of Research and Statistics, 1966, 56 P.

5019 Horlick, Max, Skolnik, Alfred M. Private Pension Plans in West Germany and France. Washington: U.S. Social Security Administration, Office of Research and Statistics, 1971, 78 P.

5020 Jantz, Kurt. Pension Reform in the Federal Republic of Germany. International Labour Review. 83:2 (February 1961), 136-155.

5021 Kaim-Caudle, P. R. Comparative Social Policy and Social Security: A Ten Country Study. New York: Dunellen, 1973, viii and 357 P.

5022 Kaufmann, Francois Xavier. Psychological Aspects of Social Security in the Federal Republic of Germany. International Social Security Association Bulletin. 19:7-8 (July-August 1966), 298-301.

5023 Kuebler, Ulrich. Data Storage in Pensions Insurance Records in the Federal Republic of Germany. International Social Security Association Bulletin. 18:11-12 (November-December 1965), 514-524.

5024 Noell, Kurt. The Federal Agricultural Old-Age Assistance in the Federal Republic of Germany. International Social Security Association Bulletin. 13:1-2 (January-February 1960), 11-18.

5025 Pascholt, Eduard. Social Security for Persons Working on the Land in Germany. International Social Security Association Bulletin. 8:5-6 (May-June 1955), 196-198.

5026 Recent Developments in Social Security Legislation in the Federal Republic of Germany. International Labour Review. 88:6 (December 1963), 629-634.

5027 Rimlinger, Gaston V. Social Change and Social Security in Germany. Journal of Human Resources. 3:4 (Fall 1968), 409-421.

5028 Schewe, Dieter. Nordhorn, Karlhugo. Schenke, Klaus. Survey of Social Security in the Federal Republic of Germany. Bonn: Federal Ministry for Labour and Social Affairs, 1972, 270 P.

5029 Social Security Developments in the Federal Republic of Germany Since 1949. International Labour Review. 66:5-6 (November-December 1952), 485-501.

5030 US, Omgus. An Analysis of Social Insurance Experience. N.P.: Omgus, 1946, 7 P.

5031 Wissell, Rudolf. Social Insurance in Germany. Annals of the American Academy of Political and Social Science. 260 (November 1948), 118-130.

5032 Zoellner, Detlev. Old Age Pensions for Farmers. Bonn: Federal Ministry of Labour and the Social Structure, Social Policy in Germany No. 35, 1965, 18 P.

I.5.3. Social Benefits for Workers

5033 Braun, Heinrich. Rehabilitation of the Disabled in Germany. Frankfurt: Deutscher Verein Fuer Oeffentliche Und Private Fuersorge, 1966, 73 P.

5034 International Society for Rehabilitation of the Disabled. Industrial Society and Rehabilitation--Problems and Solutions. Heidelberg-Schlierbach: Deutsche Vereinigung Fuer Die Rehabilitation Behinderter, 1967, 400 P.

5035 Lauterbach, Herbert. Compulsory Industrial Accident Insurance in the Federal Republic of Germany. International Social Security Association Bulletin. 13:10-11 (October-November 1960), 498-521.

5036 Leder, Herbert. Unemployment Benefit and Unemployment Assistance. Bonn: Federal Ministry of Labour and the Social Structure, Social Policy in Germany No. 11, 1963, 32 P.

5037 Linthe, Hans. Compulsory Industrial Accident Insurance. Bonn: Federal Ministry of Labour and the Social Structure, Social Policy in Germany No. 38, 2D Ed., 1966, 40 P.

5038 Scharmann, Theodor. Rehabilitation of Disabled Persons in the Federal

Republic of Germany. International Labour Review. 88:5 (November 1963), 458-475.

5039 Schmidt, Friedrich. History and Evolution of Unemployment Insurance in the German Federal Republic. International Social Security Association Bulletin. 16:10-11 (October-November 1963), 319-330.

L.5.4. Social Services and Welfare

5040 Boylan, Marguerite T. Rebuilding for Social Services. Survey. 83:10 (October 1947), 278-280.

5041 Caseworker's Diary. Survey. 84:2 (February 1948), 45-46. From a Social Worker in Berlin.

5042 Cormack, Una. German Visit: Social Work in Present-Day Germany. Social Work. 5:3 (July 1948), 196-201.

5043 Evangelical Churches in Germany. Living Conditions in Germany, 1947: A Survey By the Hilfswerk. Stuttgart: Evangelical Churches in Germany, 1947, 74 P.

5044 Gangloff, Perry J. The Public Welfare Program in Berlin Military Government: A Way of Interpreting Democracy. Social Service Review. 24:2 (June 1950), 198-212.

5045 Houlihan, Jack. Community Service Through Voluntary Councils in German Cities. N.P.: Hicog, Community Activities Branch, 1951, 48 P.

5046 Hunter, David R. Studd, Howard R. Postwar Social Service in Berlin. Social Services Review. 22:2 (June 1948), 141-159.

5047 Kelber, Magda. Germany-British Zone-- From a Relief Worker's Diary. World Affairs (London). 1:2 (April 1947), 155-162.

5048 Polligkeit, Wilhelm. German Social Welfare After the Currency Reform. Annals of the American Academy of Political and Social Science. 260 (November 1948), 115-117.

5049 US, Hicog, Education and Cultural Relations Division. One Out of Each Million: Report of Eleven Dependent Families, Germany 1950. N.P.: Hicog, Education and Cultural Relations Division, 1950, 25 P.

L.5.5. Public Health; Health Insurance

5050 Altenstetter, Christa. Health Policy- Making and Administration in West Germany and The United States. Beverly Hills: Sage Professional Papers in Administrative and Policy Studies, No. 03-013, 1974, 96 P.

5051 Bauer, William Waldo. Public Health Practices in Germany. N.P.: Omgus, C.1949.

5052 Bauer, William Waldo. Public Health Practices in Germany. American Journal of Public Health. 40:9 (September 1950), 1077-1083.

5053 Deforest, Walter R. Public Health Practices in Germany Under U.S. Occupation, 1945-1949. American Journal of Public Health. 40:9 (September 1950), 1072-1076.

5054 FRG, Federal Statistical Office. Statistical Atlas on Public Health in the Federal Republic of Germany. Stuttgart and Mainz: Kohlhammer, for the Federal Ministry For Public Health, 1963.

5055 Field, Mark G. Former Soviet Citizens' Attitudes Toward the Soviet, the German, and the American Medical Systems. American Sociological Review. 20:6 (December 1955), 674-679.

5056 Harmsen, Hans. Notes on Abortion and Birth Control in Germany. Population Studies. 3:4 (March 1950), 402-405.

5057 Health and Human Relations in Germany. New York: Josiah Macy, Jr., Foundation, 1950, 207 P. Report of a Conference, Princeton, N.J., 26-30 June 1950.

5058 Health and Human Relations in Germany. New York: Josiah Macy, Jr. Foundation, 1951, 30 P. Report of Conference, Williamsburg, Va., 1950.

5059 Health and Human Relations in Germany. New York: Blakiston, 1953, 192 P. Report of a Conference Sponsored By the Josiah Macy, Jr., Foundation, Hiddesen Near Detmold, Germany, 2-7 August 1951.

5060 Kraus, Hertha. Health and Welfare. Governing Postwar Germany. Ed. Edward H. Litchfield and Associates. Ithaca: Cornell University Press, 1953, Pp. 381-402

5061 Leutz, G. Teirich, Hildebrand R. Group Psychotherapy in Germany. Group Psychotherapy. 11:3 (September 1958), 177-185.

5062 Medical Research Council. Studies of Undernutrition, Wuppertal 1946-9. London: H.M. Stationery Office, 1951, 404 P. Conducted By Members of the Department of Experimental Medicine, Cambridge, and Associated Workers.

5063 Mueller, Wilhelm Johann. Re-Use of Waste Water in Germany. Paris: Organisation for Economic Cooperation and Development, 1969, 29 P.

5064 Murphy, L. E. Report on Progress in Sanitary Engineering in Western Germany. Frankfurt: Hicog, 1951, 40 P.

5065 Oecd. Treatment of Mixed Domestic Sewage and Industrial Waste Waters in Germany. Paris: Organisation for Economic Cooperation and Development, 1966, 113 P.

5066 Price, Arnold H. Health Insurance in West Germany. Current History. 44:262 (June 1963), 345-350.

5067 Safran, William. Health Insurance in West Germany: A Case Study in Interest Group Politics. Ph.D. Thesis, Columbia University, 1964, 329 P.

5068 Safran, William. Veto-Group Politics: The Case of Health-Insurance Reform in West Germany. San Francisco: Chandler, 1967, 320 P.

5069 Toens, Hans. Sickness Insurance Benefits in the Federal Republic of Germany. International Social Security Association Bulletin. 19:9-10 (September-October 1966), 339-354.

5070 Umrath, Oscar. Sickness Insurance Schemes in the Federal Republic of Germany. Bulletin of the International Social Security Association. 14:3 (March 1961), 117-130.

5071 UK, Foreign Office. Tuberculosis in the British Zone of Germany, With a Section on Berlin. London: H.M. Stationery Office, 59-108, 1948. Report on Enquiry in September-October 1947.

5072 US, Omgus, Civil Administration Division. Tuberculosis--U.S. Zone of Germany. N.P. Omgus, Adjutant General, May 1948, 26 P.

5073 US, Spec. Commission to Study Nutrition in Bizonal Germany. Report. Wiesbaden: Special Commission to Study Nutrition in Bizonal Germany, 1948, 9 P.

L.5.6. Children and Child-Care

5074 Brosse, Therese. War-Handicapped Children: Report on the European Situation. New York: Columbia University Press, 1950, 142 P.

5075 Dybwad, Gunnar. Child Care in Germany. Survey. 87:3 (March 1951), 110-114.

5076 Eliot, Martha M., and Others. Mission on Maternal and Child Health and Welfare. Washington: N.P., 1949, 30 P.

5077 Lauterbach, Herbert. The German Child Allowances Law. International Social Security Association Bulletin. 8:5-6 (May-June 1955), 184-195.

5078 Pfaffenberger, Hans. Planning for German Children of Mixed Racial Background. Social Service Review. 30:1 (March 1956), 33-37.

5079 Reinemann, John O. The Mulatto Children in Germany. Mental Hygiene. 37:3 (July 1953), 365-376.

5080 Stone, Vernon W. German Baby Crop Left By Negro Gi's. Survey. 85:11 (November 1949), 579-583.

L.5.7. Housing

5081 Ambrosius, Wolfgang. Housing Cooperatives. Review of International Cooperation. 62:5 (1969), 225-231.

5082 Brauer, Anna E. Washke, Hildegard. Erdmann, Elisabeth. The German Housing Program and U.S. Aid. Bad Godesberg-Mehlem: Office of the U.S. High Commissioner for Germany, Historical Division, 1953, 292 P.

5083 FRG, Federal Ministry for Housing. From the Building of Houses to the Development of Towns: The Period From 1949 to 1959 Passed in Review. Bad Godesberg: Federal Ministry for Housing, C.1960, 18 P.

5084 FRG, Federal Ministry for Housing. Housebuilding and Finance of Housing in the Federal Republic of Germany. Bad Godesberg: Federal Ministry of Housing, 1955-56, 2 Vols.

5085 FRG, Federal Ministry for Housing and Urban Construction. Private Housing and Urban Development: Model Housing Projects of the Federal Ministry for Housing and Urban Construction. Berlin: Bundesministerium Fuer Wohnungswesen Und Staedtebau, 1968.

5086 German Federation of Housing, Town- and Regional Planning. Urban Renewal in the Federal Republic of Germany. Cologne-Muellheim: German Federation of Housing, Town- and Regional Planning, 1966, 51 P.

5087 Hallett, Graham. Housing Policy in West Germany. Loughborough Journal of Social Studies. No. 6 (November 1968), 5-15.

5088 Heigert, Hans. Wirsing, Werner. Houses for Young People. Munich: Juventa, 1960, 183 P.

5089 Howes, Eric G. Housing in Germany. Planning (P.E.P.). 31:490 (August 1965), 250-263.

5090 Lubowski, Herbert. Mortgage Bank's Contribution to Housing. World Banking. (December 1962), 86-90.

5091 The Nonprofit Housing Enterprises in the Federal Republic of Germany. Hamburg: Hammonia, 1969, 56 P.

5092 The Solution of the Housing Problem in the Federal Republic of Germany. International Labour Review. 72:2-3 (August-September 1955), 187-202.

5093 Wendt, Paul F. Housing Policy--The Search for Solutions: A Comparison of The United Kingdom, Sweden, West Germany, and the United States Since World War II. Berkeley: University of California Press, 1962, Xii and 283 P., Esp. Pp. 111-144.

5094 Wertheimer, Robert G. The Miracle of German Housing in the Postwar Period. Land Economics. 34:4 (November 1958), 338-345.

L.5.8. Criminology and Rehabilitation (See Also E.3.4.5)

5095 Abbott, Edith. Juvenile Delinquency in Germany. Social Service Review. 20:4 (December 1946), 569-573.

5096 Alt, Herschel. Observations on Juvenile Delinquency in Germany. Social Service Review. 23:2 (June 1949), 184-203.

5097 Holzschuh, Karl. Creative Restitution: Ambulatory Treatment of Youthful Offenders in Germany. Journal of Social Therapy. 5:2 (1959), 120-127.

5098 Kite, St. Alban. Parole Goes to Germany. Yearbook of the National Probation and Parole Association. Advances in Understanding the Offender. Ed. Marjorie Bell. New York: National Probation and Parole Association, 1950, Pp. 218-230.

5099 Schepses, Erwin. Juvenile Vagrancy in Germany. Social Service Review. 22:1 (March 1948), 40-45.

5100 Willner, Dorothy K. An Area Study of Delinquency and Related Socio-Economic Factors in a European City (Frankfurt Am Main, Germany). Ph.D. Thesis, University of Pennsylvania, 1958, 189 P.

5101 Wuertenberger, Thomas. German Criminology and Anglo-American Research. Criminology in Transition. Ed. Tadeusz Grygier. London: Tavistock, 1965, Pp. 197-209.

L.5.9. Environmental Control

5102 Eppler, Erhard. Ecology More Vital Than Economy. German Tribune Supplement. No. 2 (17 August 1972), 1-5.

5103 Fair, Gordon M. Pollution Abatement in the Ruhr District. Comparisons in Resource Management. Henry Jarrett, Editor. Baltimore: Johns Hopkins Press, 1961, Pp. 142-171.

5104 FRG, Federal Ministry of the Interior. Report of the Federal Republic of Germany on the Human Environment. Bonn: Federal Ministry of the Interior, 1972, 160 P.

5105 Klevorick, Alvin K. Kramer, Gerald H. Social Choice on Pollution Management: The Genossenschaften. Journal of Public Economics. 2:2 (April 1973), 101-146.

5106 Kneese, Allen V. Water Quality Management By Regional Authorities in the Ruhr Area. Papers and Proceedings of the Regional Science Association. 11 (1963), 229-250.

5107 Kneese, Allen V. Bower, Blair T. Managing Water Quality: Economics, Technology, Institutions. Baltimore: Johns Hopkins University Press, 1973, X and 328 Pp., Esp. Pp. 237-253 on the Ruhr.

5108 Mueller, Paul. Protection of the Environment in Agriculture and Forestry. German Economic Review. 11:1 (1973), 77-88.

5109 Oecd. Monitoring of Radioactive Effluents. Paris: Organization for Economic Cooperation and Development, September 1974, 446 P. Proceedings of the N.E.A. Seminar, Karlsruhe 1974, in Collaboration With the German Ministry for Research and Technology and the Karlsruhe Nuclear Research Centre.

5110 Oels, Heinrich. Noise Abatement and Measures to Combat Pollution of the Atmosphere. Bonn: Federal Ministry of Labour and the Social Structure, Social Policy in Germany No. 26, 1964, 24 P.

5111 Picht, Georg. Effective Protection of the Environment Means Going Without Material Wealth. German Tribune Supplement. No. 2 (17 August 1972), 6-8.

5112 Schweinfurth, Ulrich. Environment and the Tasks for Foreign Policy. Aussenpolitik. 22:2 (1971), 142-155.

5113 Timmler, Markus. Stockholm Conference on the Human Environment. Aussenpolitik. 23:4 (1972), 450-460.

5114 Tugendhat, Georg. Facing the Cost of Pollution Control. The Banker. 121: 548 (October 1971), 1177-1182.

L.6. GDR: Social Policy

L.6.1. General

5115 Mampel, Siegfried. Hauck, Karl. Social Policy in the Soviet Occupied Zone of Germany. Bonn: Federal Ministry of Labour and the Social Structure, Social Policy in Germany No. 48, 2D Ed., 1966, 104 P.

5116 Recent Developments in Social Insurance Legislation in the German Democratic Republic. International Labour Review. 87:3 (March 1963), 272-274.

5117 Recent Developments in Social Insurance Legislation in the German Democratic Republic. International Labour Review. 89:3 (March 1964), 287-288.

5118 Social Insurance Developments in the German Democratic Republic Since 1949. International Labour Review. 72:5 (November 1955), 437-447.

5119 Social Insurance in the German Democratic Republic. Dresden: Zeit Im Bild, 1971, 120 P.

5120 Thude, Guenther. The Workers and Their Social Insurance: The Social Insurance for Workers and Employees in the G.D.R. and Its Prospects in the Seven-Year Plan. Ed. National Executive Committee of the Confederation of Free German Trade Unions (Fdgb). Berlin (East): Tribuene, 1961, 134 P.

5121 Titel, Werner. Problems of Protection of the Environment. German Foreign Policy (GDR). 10:4 (1971), 323-337.

L.6.2. Public Health

5122 GDR, Institute for Planning and Organization of Pub. Health. Some Aspects of Socialist Public Health in the German Democratic Republic. Berlin: Institut Fuer Planung Und Organisation Des Gesundheitsschutzes, 1964, 23P.

5123 Gebhard, Bruno. Public Health in East Germany. American Journal of Public Health and the Nation's Health. 54:6 (June 1964), 928-931.

5124 Gehring, Michael. Health and Social System. Dresden: Zeit Im Bild, 1968, 62 P.

5125 Health and Social System: German Democratic Republic. Dresden: Zeit Im Bild, 1969, 61 P.

5126 May, Jacques M. The Ecology of Malnutrition in Five Countries of Eastern and Central Europe: East Germany, Poland, Yugoslavia, Albania, Greece. New York: Hafner, 1963, 292 P.

5127 Winter, K., Et Al. Public Health in the German Democratic Republic. Berlin (East): Postgraduate Medical School of the German Democratic Republic on Behalf of the Ministry of Health, 1972, 32 P.

L.6.3. Criminology and Rehabilitation

5128 Buchholz, Erich. Szkibik, Heinz. Principles of the Penal System of the GDR and the Standard Minimum Rules of the Un. Law and Legislation in the German Democratic Republic. No. 1 (1970), 5-15.

5129 Harrland, Harri. Criminality and Its Control in the GDR. Law and Legislation in the German Democratic Republic. No. 1 (1973), 35-51.

5130 Harrland, Harri. From the GDR Statistics on Criminality for 1964. Law and Legislation in the German Democratic Republic. No. 2 (1965), 39-46.

5131 Harrland, Harri. Trends and Control of Crime in the GDR. Law and Legislation in the German Democratic Republic. No. 1 (1967), 29-38.

5132 Hinderer, Hans. The Fight Against Criminality as a Social Responsibility. Law and Legislation in the German Democratic Republic. No. 2 (1966), 9-21.

5133 Hugot, Heinz. Mettin, Harry. Society and the Reintegration of Former Criminal Offenders. Law and Legislation in the German Democratic Republic. No. 2 (1969), 41-55.

5134 Kunze, Kurt. The Penal System of the German Democratic Republic. Law and Legislation in the German Democratic Republic. No. 1 (1965), 38-45.

5135 Lehmann, Guenter. Renneberg, Joachim. The Development of a Complex System of Crime Control and Prevention in the German Democratic Republic. Law and Legislation in the German Democratic Republic. No. 1 (1970), 16-34.

5136 Lekschas, John. On Some Aspects of Criminality in Socialist Society. Law and Legislation in the German Democratic Republic. No. 1 (1971), 16-24.

5137 Lekschas, John. Hartmann, Richard. Basic Problems of Socialist Criminology. Law and Legislation in the German Democratic Republic. No. 1 (1966), 17-21.

5138 Renneberg, Joachim. Buchholz, Erich. Hennig, Walter. Hinderer, Hans. Krutzsch, Walter. Social Foundations and Forms of Organisation of the Fight for the Gradual Suppression of Criminality in the GDR. Law and Legislation in the German Democratic Republic. No. 1 (1966), 5-16.

5139 Wesner, Charlotte. The Court Censure in the Fight Against Criminality. Law and Legislation in the German Democratic Republic. No. 1 (1966), 23-29.

L.7. FRG-GDR Comparisons

5140 Dasbach, Fernando Louis. Child Welfare: An East and West German Perspective on the Adoption of Children and Illegitimacy Statutes From 1949 to 1970. D.S.W. Thesis, Catholic University, 1972, 346 P.

5141 Harrland, Harri. On the Question of Crime in Both German States. Law and Legislation in the German Democratic Republic. No. 2 (1964), 27-33.

5142 Ludz, Peter Christian. Social Change in the FRG and the GDR. Teaching Postwar Germany in America: Papers and Discussions. Ed. Louis F. Helbig and Eberhard Reichmann. Bloomington: Indiana University, Institute of German Studies, 1972.

M. Communications

M.1. FRG

M.1.1. General

5143 Bohlen, Adolf. The History and Theory of Mass Media in Germany. Year Book of Education, 1960: Communication Media and the School. Yonkers-on-Hudson: World, 1960, Pp. 377-393.

5144 Breitenkamp, Edward C. The U.S. Information Control Division and Its Effect on German Publishers and Writers, 1945 to 1949. Grand Forks, N.D.: Edward C. Breitenkamp, 1953, 101 P.

5145 Davison, W. Phillips. The Mass Media in West German Political Life. West German Leadership and Foreign Policy. Ed. Hans Speier and W. Phillips Davison. Evanston: Row, Peterson, 1957, Pp. 242-281.

5146 Davison, W. Phillips. Political Significance of Recognition Via Mass Media: An Illustration From the Berlin Blockade. Public Opinion Quarterly. 20:1 (Spring 1956), 327-333.

5147 Davison, W. Phillips. The Role of Mass Communications During the Berlin Blockade. Santa Monica: Rand Corporation, 1955, 12 P.

5148 Hellack, Georg. Mass Media in the Federal Republic of Germany. Bonn-Bad Godesberg: Inter Nationes, 1971, 36 P.

5149 Lang, Kurt. Images of Society: Media Research in Germany. Public Opinion Quarterly. 38:3 (Fall 1974), 335-351.

5150 Lerg, Winfried. A Decade of German Books on Mass Communications. Journalism Quarterly. 40:3 (Summer 1963), 354-361, 415.

5151 McClure, Robert A. Textor, Gordon E. Rebuilding Germany's Information Media. Army Information Digest. 3:6 (June 1948), 7-20.

5152 Mahle, Walter A. Richter, Rolf. Communication Policies in the Federal Republic of Germany. Paris: Unesco Press, 1974, 86 P.

5153 Pilgert, Henry P. Dobbert, Helga. Press, Radio and Film in West Germany, 1945-1953. Bad Godesberg-Mehlem: Office of the U.S. High Commissioner for Germany, Historical Division, 1953, 123 P.

5154 Spahn, Raymond J. Foste, Lester I. Germans Hail America: Some Aspects of Communication Media in Occupied Germany. Modern Language Journal. 33:6 (October 1949), 417-426.

5155 Tijmstra, L. F. The Challenge of Tv to the Press: The Impact of Television on Advertising Revenues and Circulations of Newspapers. Gazette. 5:3 (1959), 293-315.

5156 Ungerer, Werner. Satellite Problems and Intelsat Negotiations. Aussenpolitik. 21:2 (1970), 155-169.

5157 US, Omgus, Economics Division. International Communications. N.P.: Omgus, November 1947.

5158 US, Omgus, Information Control Division. Books, Pamphlets and Periodicals Produced By Licensed German Publishers in the United States Zone of Germany, Including Berlin Sector and Bremen. N.P.: Omgus, Information Control Divison, Publications Control Branch, 1947, 72 P.

5159 US, Omgus, Information Control Division. Information Control in Germany. Munich: Omgus, Information Control Division, 1946, 28 P.

5160 US, Omgus, Information Services Division. Control of Press and Radio. N.P.: Omgus, November 1947.

5161 US, Omgus, Information Services Division. German Book Publishing and Allied Subjects. Munich and New York: N.P., December 1948, 171 P. Report By Visiting Committee of American Book Publishers.

5162 Vogel, Rudolf. Press and Radio in Germany. Confluence. 1:4 (December 1952), 15-23.

M.1.2. Newspapers and Periodicals

5163 Beck, Elmer A. Trade Union Press in the U.S.-Occupied Area (Germany). Berlin: Omgus, Manpower Division, Visiting Expert Series No. 3, October 1948, 18 P.

5164 Bennion, Sherilyn C. Mass Magazine Phenomenon: The German Illustrierte. Journalism Quarterly. 38:3 (Summer 1961), 360-362.

5165 Bieri, Ernst. A German Study of the German Press. Swiss Review of World Affairs. 4:4 (July 1954), 15-16.

5166 Blumenthal, Henry. The Image of the United States in the Zeitschrift Fuer Geopolitik, 1924-1965. Southwestern Social Science Quarterly. 48:1 (June 1967), 44-52.

5167 Brandt, Joseph A. Testing Time for the West German Press. Journalism Quarterly. 34:2 (Spring 1957), 239-246.

5168 Dalcher, Laurence P. The Effect of Currency Reform on German Publishing. Public Opinion Quarterly. 13:3 (Fall 1949), 513-517.

5169 Dovifat, Emil. The German Press Council. Gazette. 5:1 (1959), 117-122.

5170 Duesenberg, Albert. The Press in Germany. Bonn: Scholl, 1960, 64 P.

5171 Eser, Wolfgang. The Farmer as Reader. Gazette. 5:1 (1959), 110-113.

5172 Hermens, Ferdinand A. The Danger of Stereotypes in Viewing Gemany. Public Opinion Quarterly. 9:4 (Winter 1945-46), 418-427. Part Played By Newspaper Correspondents.

5173 Hirsch, Felix Edward. The German Press, Yesterday and Tomorrow. Current History. 9:48 (August 1945), 104-111.

5174 Iben, Icko. The Germanic Press of Europe: An Aid to Research. Muenster: Fahle, 1965, 146 P.

5175 Jacobi, Claus. The New German Press. Foreign Affairs. 32:2 (January 1954), 323-330.

5176 Joesten, Joachim. German Periodicals in 1947. New York: Joachim Joesten, New Germany Reports No. 2, October 1947, 19 P.

5177 Joesten, Joachim. The German Press in 1947. New York: Joachim Joesten, New Germany Reports No. 1, September 1947, 20 P.

5178 Koszyk, Kurt. German Newspapers With Socialist Tendency, Since 1945. Gazette. 5:1 (1959), 41-53.

5179 Krane, Jay B. Polls, Press and Occupation Policy. Columbia Journal of International Affairs. 2:1 (Winter 1948), 71-75.

5180 Liebes, Peter. The Post-Licensed German Press. Journalism Quarterly. 33:1 (Winter 1956), 61-73.

5181 Loeffler, Martin. The Present Legal Position of the Press in West Germany. Gazette. 5:1 (1959), 13-29.

5182 Man and the Press. Munich: Hueber, 1970, 151 P.

5183 Marigold, W. G. Some Notes on the Cultural Periodicals of Post-War Germany. German Quarterly. 29:1 (January 1956), 38-42.

5184 Meier, Ernest. The Licensed Press in the U.S. Occupation Zone of Germany. Journalism Quarterly. 31:2 (Spring 1954), 223-231.

5185 Nelson, Kenneth H. United States Occupation Policy and the Establishment of a Democratic Newspaper Press in Bavaria, 1945-1949. Ph.D. Thesis, University of Virginia, 1966, 260 P.

5186 Schalk, Adolph. Putting the Starch in the German Press. Saturday Review of the Arts. (25 March 1972), 80-82.

5187 Schwarz, Urs. Press Law for Our Times: The Example of the German Legislation. Zurich: International Press Institute, 1966, 116 P.

5188 Seymour-Ure, Colin. Editorial Policy-Making in the Press. Government and Opposition. 4:4 (Autumn 1969), 427-525. Worldwide, Including Sueddeutsche Zeitung.

5189 Straus, Richard. Postwar Development of the German Press. Department of State Bulletin. 28:713 (23 February 1953), 294-301.

5190 US, Hicog, Information Services Division. The Effect of the Swiss Press on West German Newspapers, March 1951. Frankfurt: Hicog, Office of Public Affairs, Information Services Division, Press and Publications Branch, 1951, 5 P.

5191 US, Hicog, Information Services Division. List of Publishers and Periodicals in the U.S. Zone of Germany. Bad Nauheim: Hicog, Office of Public Affairs, Information Services Division, Press and Publications Branch, C.1949, 44 P.

5192 US, Omgus. Fair Practice Guide for German Journalists. N.P.: Omgus, 1947, 22 P. (Pp. 1-10 in English).

5193 US, Omgus, Information Control Division. List of Periodicals Appearing in the U.S. Occupied Zone of Germany (Including U.S. Sector of Berlin) as of 1 March 1948. Berlin: Omgus, Information Control Division, Publications Control Branch, 1948, 27 P.

5194 US, Omgus, Information Control Division. A Study of Newspapers in the American Zone. Berlin: Omgus, Information Control Division, Intelligence Branch, 1947.

5195 US, Omgus, Information Services Division. The German Press in the U.S. Occupied Area, 1945-1948. N.P.: Omgus, 1949, 39 P.

5196 Viedebantt, Joachim. The Periodical Press in the Federal Republic. Gazette. 5:1 (1959), 125-131.

5197 Willenz, Eric. German Press Reaction to the Air War in Korea. Santa Monica: Rand Corporation, Rm-515, 1951, 25 P.

5198 Williams, J. Emlyn. The West German Press. Gazette. 5:1 (1959), 1-10, 338.

5199 Zander, Ernst. Interim Balance Sheet: The Bankruptcy of Power Politics. Contemporary Issues. 1:4 (Autumn 1949), 252-293. Negative View of Allied Policy in Germany and German Newspapers' Role in It.

M.1.3. Conservative Press

5200 Hofmann, Josef. The CDU Press of the German Federal Republic. Gazette. 5:1 (1959), 31-36.

5201 Joesten, Joachim. Axel C. Springer: Germany's New Press Lord. New York: Joachim Joesten, New Germany Reports No. 57, February 1962, 16 P.

5202 Klotzbach, Kurt. Profile of a Paper: The Deutsche National-Zeitung. Bulletin of the Wiener Library. 21:4 (Autumn 1967), 17-21.

5203 Knipping, Franz. Mass Media Dominated By the West German Monopolies. German Foreign Policy (GDR). 5:5 (1966), 363-372.

5204 Kohl, Heribert. Profile of a Paper: The Deutsche Nachrichten. Bulletin of the Wiener Library. 22:1 (Winter 1967-68), 28-36.

5205 Mueller, Hans Dieter. Press Power: A Study of Axel Springer. London: Macdonald, 1969, 200 P.

5206 Springer, Axel Caesar. Much Ado About a Newspaper Publishing House. Berlin: Springer, 1967, 26 P.

5207 Van Voorst, L. Bruce. Press Lord Axel Springer Is a German Problem. New York Times Magazine. (17 March 1968), 34+.

5208 Will the Press Octopus Grab Tv?. Atlas. 9:4 (April 1965), 218-221. Article From "Der Spiegel" About Axel Caesar Springer.

M.1.4. Press Freedom; Spiegel Affair

5209 Bernstein, Herbert L. Free Press and National Security: Reflections on the Spiegel Case. American Journal of Comparative Law. 15:3 (1966-67), 547-561.

5210 Bunn, Ronald F. German Politics and the Spiegel Affair: A Case Study of the Bonn System. Baton Rouge: Louisiana State University Press, 1968, 230 P.

5211 Bunn, Ronald F. The Spiegel Affair and the West German Press: The Initial Phase. Public Opinion Quarterly. 30:1 (Spring 1966), 54-68.

5212 Bunn, Ronald F. West Germany: The Spiegel Affair. Politics and Civil Liberties in Europe: Four Case Studies. Ed. Ronald F. Bunn and William G. Andrews. Princeton: Van Nostrand, 1967, Pp. 93-166.

5213 Fliess, Peter J. Freedom of the Press in the Bonn Republic. Journal of Politics. 16:4 (November 1954), 664-684.

5214 Gimbel, John. The "Spiegel Affair" in Perspective. Midwest Journal of Political Science. 9:3 (August 1965), 282-297.

5215 Gross, Franz B. Freedom of the Press Under Military Government in Western Germany, 1945-49. Ph.D. Thesis, Harvard University, 1952.

5216 Hirsch, Felix Edward. How Free Is the German Press?. Current History. 44:260 (April 1963), 226-230, 244-245.

5217 Jordan, Wayne. Germany's Cultural Heritage Impedes Free Press Program. Journalism Quarterly. 25:2 (June 1948), 163-169.

5218 Kirchheimer, Otto. Menges, Constantine. A Free Press in a Democratic State? the Spiegel Case. Politics in Europe: 5 Cases in European Government. Ed. Gwendolen M. Carter and Alan F. Westin. New York: Harcourt, Brace & World, 1965, Pp. 87-138.

5219 Kirkpatrick, William S. Showing German Editors a Free Press at Work. Journalism Quarterly. 26:1 (March 1949), 29-35.

5220 Kommers, Donald P. The Spiegel Affair: A Case Study in Judicial Politics. Political Trials. Ed. Theodore L. Becker. Indianapolis: Bobbs-Merrill, 1971, Pp. 5-33.

5221 Luchsinger, Fred. The Spiegel Affair. Swiss Review of World Affairs. 12:12 (March 1963), 3-5.

5222 Olsen, Arthur J. The Man Who Holds the Mirror to Germany: Rudolf Augstein. New York Times Magazine. (7 February 1965), 30+.

5223 Schoenbaum, David. The Spiegel Affair. Garden City: Doubleday, 1968, 239 P.

5224 The Spiegel Affair Debate (in Parliament). German Politics. Ed. Donald C. Schoonmaker. Lexington: Heath, 1971, Pp. 195-205.

5225 The "Spiegel" Case in the Bundestag. European Political Institutions: A Comparative Government Reader. 2D Ed. Ed. William G. Andrews. Princeton: Van Nostrand, 1966, Pp. 409-410.

5226 Storette, Ronald Frank. Freedom of the Press: The "Spiegel" Case. Harvard International Law Journal. 8:2 (Spring 1967), 364-372.

M.1.5. Radio and Television

5227 Bettiza, Enzo. German Tv: Too Good to Last?. Atlas. 9:4 (April 1965), 216-218.

5228 Brack, Hans. German Radio and Television: Organization and Economic Basis. Geneva: European Broadcasting Union, 1968, 68 P.

5229 Braunthal, Gerard. Federalism in Germany: The Broadcasting Controversy. Journal of Politics. 24:3 (August 1962), 545-561.

5230 Doeker, Guenther. Television Competence. American Journal of Comparative Law. 10:3 (Summer 1961), 277-281. Legal Aspects.

5231 Eckert, Gerhard. Television in Germany. Gazette. 5:1 (1959), 135-148.

5232 Emery, Walter B. National and International Systems of Broadcasting: Their History, Operation and Control. East Lansing: Michigan State University Press, 1969, Xxxi and 752 P., Esp. Pp. 295-308.

5233 Freed, Paul E. A Study of the Extent to Which the Indicated Objectives of American-Produced Religious Radio Programs Prepared for Broadcasting to Europe Would Be Achieved According to French, German, and Spanish Religious Leaders. Ph.D. Thesis, New York University, 1960, 455 P.

5234 Gong, Walter, Editor. Your Reporter in Germany: A Cross-Section of the Deutsche Welle Program Beamed to North America. Cologne: Deutsche Welle, 1965, 227 P.

5235 Holt, Robert T. The Munich Operation of Radio Free Europe. Ph.D. Thesis, Princeton University, 1957, 528 P.

5236 Holt, Robert T. Radio Free Europe. Minneapolis: University of Minnesota Press, 1958, 249 P.

5237 International Public Opinion Research, Inc. Frankfurt University, Institute for Social Research. The Effectiveness of Candor in Voa Broadcasts to West Germany. New York: International Public Opinion Research, Inc., 1953.

5238 Knauth, Percy. The Voice of Free Berlin: Rias. Reporter. 6:7 (1 April 1952), 17-21.

5239 Maletzke, Gerhard. The Development of Broadcasting Research in Germany. International Studies of Broadcasting, With Special Reference to the Japanese Studies. Ed. H. Eguchi and H. Ichinohe. Tokyo: Nhk Radio & Tv Culture Research Institute, 1971, Pp. 201-218.

5240 Parson, Ruby A. Radio in the U.S. Zone of Germany: Stations Achieving Independence. Department of State Bulletin. 21:525 (25 July 1949), 83-85.

5241 Paulu, Burton. Radio and Television Broadcasting on the European Continent. Minneapolis: University of Minnesota Press, 1967, 290 P.

5242 Rias Berlin. Rias: A Free Voice of the Free World. Berlin: Rias Berlin, 1962, 27 P.

5243 Robinson, John P. Converse, Philip E. The Impact of Television on Mass Media Usage: A Cross-National Comparison. Transactions of the Sixth World Congress of Sociology. Geneva: International Sociological Association, 1966, Vol. 3, Pp. 415-432.

5244 Rugh, William A. The Politics of Broadcasting in West Germany After World War Ii. Ph.D. Thesis, Columbia University, 1967, 375 P.

5245 Russi, Bernard A., Jr. The History and Development of German Broadcasting as an Instrument of Social Control. Ph.D. Thesis, Wayne State University, 1963, 298 P.

5246 US, Hicog, Information Services Division. Eighteen Months of Religious Radio, July 1949-December 1950: a Radio Scrutiny Report. N.P.: Hicog, Office of Public Affairs, Information Services Division, Radio Branch, 1951, 25 P.

5247 US, Hicog, Office of Public Affairs. One Year of Cultural Radio, July 1949-June 1950: A Radio Scrutiny Report. N.P.: Hicog, Office of Public Affairs, 1951, 33 P.

5248 US, Hicog, Office of Public Affairs. One Year of German Radio: Radio Bremen, April 1949-April 1950, South German Radio, Stuttgart, July 1949-July 1950. N.P.: Hicog, Office of Public Affairs, C.1951, 43 P.

5249 US, Omgus, Information Services Division. Suggestions for the New German Radio. N.P.: Omgus, July 1949.

M.2. GDR

5250 Bluecher, Viggo Graf. Content Analysis of the Press in the East German Republic. Gazette. 5:1 (1959), 89-106.

5251 Dasbach, Anita Mallinckrodt. Propaganda Behind the Wall: A Case Study of the Use of Propaganda as a Tool of Foreign Policy By Communist Governments. Ph.D. Thesis, George Washington University, 1968, 263 P.

5252 Davison, W. Phillips. An Analysis of the Soviet-Controlled Press. Public Opinion Quarterly. 11:1 Spring 1947), 40-57. Content Analysis Indicates That News Is Carefully Chosen According to Predetermined Themes.

5253 GDR. Regulations for the Postal and Telecommunications System of The German Democratic Republic. New York: Joint Publications Research Service, 958-D, 1959, 137 P.

5254 Grothe, Peter. to Win the Minds of Men: The Story of the Communist Propaganda War in East Germany. Palo Alto: Pacific Books, 1958, 241 P.

5255 Kahler, Franz. Mass Media and Publishing in the GDR. United Asia. 21:5 (September-October 1969), 302-309.

5256 Paul, H. W. Propaganda in the East-German Democratic Republic. Gazette. 5:1 (1959), 57-82.

M.3. FRG-GDR Comparisons

5257 Bazillion, Richard. "Zeitungswissenschaft" in the Two Germanies. Canadian Slavic Studies. 5:4 (Winter 1971), 551-553.

5258 Conrad, Richard. Newspaper Images in Communist East Germany and in Democratic West Germany: A Comparative Study of Social Images. Maxwell Air Force Base, Ala.: Air Research and Development Command, Human Resources Research Institute, 1953, 11 P.

5259 Conrad, Richard. Social Images in East and West Germany: A Comparative Study of Matched Newspapers in Two Social Systems. Social Forces. 33:3 (March 1955), 281-285. Based on Berlin Newspapers.

5260 GDR, Ministry of Postal and Telecommunications Services. Two German States, Two Postal Areas. Berlin and Dresden: Zeit Im Bild, 1967, 57 P.

N. Education and Culture

N.1. FRG: Education

N.1.1. General

5261 Henderson, James L. Some Sources for the Study of German Education. British Journal of Educational Studies. 9:1 (November 1960), 48-56.

5262 Oecd. Educational Statistics Yearbook. Paris: Organization for Economic Cooperation and Development, May 1975, Vol. 2, 436 Pp.

5263 Price, Arnold H. West German Education: A Survey. Quarterly Journal of the Library of Congress. 25:1 (January 1968), 40-49.

5264 Wenke, Hans. Education in Western Germany: A Post-War Survey. Washington: Library of Congress, Reference Department, European Affairs Division, 1953, 102 P.

5265 Armytage, Walter H. The German Influence on English Education. London: Routledge, 1969, 131 P.

5266 Delong, Vaughn R. German Education in Transition. Department of State Bulletin. 27:686 (18 August 1952), 246-251.

5267 Driscoll, Justin A. Education in West Germany. Catholic Education Review. 59:2 (February 1961), 108-112.

5268 Flitner, Wilhelm. Germany. Year Book of Education, 1950. London: Evans Brothers, 1950, Pp. 546-552.

5269 Friedeburg, Ludwig Von. Education in West Germany. Review of Educational Research. 32:3 (June 1962), 308-319.

5270 Grace, Alonzo G. Islands of Democratic Ferment in Germany. American Scholar. 19:3 (Summer 1950), 341-352.

5271 Haley, Harold. Germany: Eight Years After the War. Institute of International Education News Bulletin. 30:5 (February 1955), 8-11, 64.

5272 Henderson, James L. Education in Modern Germany: An Appraisal. Education Forum. 21:3 (March 1957), 315-326.

5273 Hilker, Franz. Educational Progress in 1958-1959. International Yearbook of Education. 21 (1959), 195-204.

5274 Hilker, Franz. Educational Progress in 1961-1962. International Yearbook of Education. 24 (1962), 142-149.

5275 Hirlekar, Yamunabai. Education in Germany: Personal Impressions and Experiences. Bombay: Hirlekar, 1955, 152 P.

5276 Huebener, Theodore. The Schools of West Germany. Journal of Educational Sociology. 35:6 (February 1962), 264-267.

5277 Huebener, Theodore. The Schools of West Germany: A Study of German Elementary and Secondary Schools. New York: New York University Press, 1962, 181 P.

5278 Hylla, Erich J. Recent Developments in Education in the Federal Republic of Germany. Comparative Education Review. 2:1 (June 1958), 12-16.

5279 Hylla, Erich J. Kegel, Friedrich O. Education in Germany. Frankfurt: Hochschule Fuer Internationale Paedagogische Forschung, 1958, 2D Ed., 79 P.

5280 Jarman, T. L. German Education and the German Problem. Journal of Education (London). 83:986 (September 1951), 477-478.

5281 Knoll, Joachim H. The German Educational System. Bad Godesberg: Inter Nationes, 1967, 72 P.

5282 Lawson, Robert Frederic. The Political Foundations of German Education. Comparative Education Review. 6:1 (March 1970), 193-204.

5283 Lindegren, Alina Marie. Germany Revisited: Education in the Federal Republic. Washington: Department of Health, Education, and Welfare, Office of Education, 1957, 107 P.

5284 Loeffler, E. Educational Developments in 1951-1952. International Yearbook of Education. 14 (1952), 128-139.

5285 Loeffler, E. Educational Progress in 1952-1953. International Yearbook of Education. 15 (1953), 158-168.

5286 Loeffler, E. Educational Progress in 1953-1954. International Yearbook of Education. 16 (1954), 171-182.

5287 Mallinson, Vernon. Education in Western Germany Today. Journal of Education (London). 86:1025 (December 1954), 541-544.

5288 Mayer, Herbert C. German Education Can Be Saved. School and Society. 74:1907 (July 1951), 1-3.

5289 Mcclure, Worth. The Educational Battle in Germany. Phi Delta Kappan. 32:5 (January 1951), 207-208.

5290 Mckay, Llewelyn R. The "New Look" in West German Schools. History of Education Journal. 7:4 (Summer 1956), 144-151.

5291 Minssen, Frederic. Educational Progress in 1959-1960. International Yearbook of Education. 22 (1960), 180-189.

5292 Minssen, Frederic. Educational Progress in 1960-1961. International Yearbook of Education. 23 (1961), 149-155.

5293 Nothardt, Fritz. Educational Progress in 1962-1963. International Yearbook of Education. 25 (1963), 143-151.

5294 Nothardt, Fritz. Educational Progress in 1964-1965. International Yearbook of Education. 27 (1965), 146-153.

5295 Nothardt, Fritz. Educational Progress in 1965-1966. International Yearbook of Education. 28 (1966), 138-144.

5296 Nothardt, Fritz. Educational Progress in 1966-1967. International Yearbook of Education. 29 (1967), 169-176.

5297 Nothardt, Fritz. Educational Progress in 1967-1968. International Yearbook of Education. 30 (1968), 185-195.

5298 Reimers, H. Educational Progress in 1954-1955. International Yearbook of Education. 17 (1955),167-180.

5299 Reimers, H. Educational Progress in 1955-1956. International Yearbook of Education. 18 (1956), 168-178.

5300 Reimers, H. Educational Progress in 1956-1957. International Yearbook of Education. 19 (1957), 175-183.

5301 Reimers, H. Educational Progress in 1957-1958. International Yearbook of Education. 20 (1958), 145-155.

5302 Ringwald, Siegfried C. Some Observations on German Schools. Phi Delta Kappan. 36:9 (June 1955), 377-380.

5303 Samuel, Richard H. Thomas, R. Hinton. Education and Society in Modern Germany. London: Routledge and Kegan Paul, 1949, 191 P.

5304 Schueler, Herbert. Education in West Germany. Education. 76:6 (February 1956), 384-389.

5305 Schultze, Walter. Fuehr, Christoph. Schools in the Federal Republic of Germany. Weinheim: Beltz, 1967, 180 P.

5306 Schuppe, Erwin. The State, Problems and Trends in the Development of the West German Education System. Comparative Education. 5:2 (June 1969), 125-138.

5307 Specht, Minna. Education in Post-War Germany. London: International Publishing Company, 1944, 40 P.

5308 Spranger, Eduard. Reflections on Education (Germany). Confluence. 6:2 (Summer 1957), 158-168.

5309 Stahl, Walter, Editor. Education for Democracy in West Germany: Achievements--Shortcomings--Prospects. New York: Praeger for Atlantik-Bruecke, 1961, 356 P.

5310 Wenke, Hans. Germany. Year Book of Education, 1951. London: Evans Brothers, 1951, Pp. 515-540.

5311 Wenke, Hans. Germany. Year Book of Education, 1952. London: Evans Brothers, 1952, Pp. 352-385.

5312 Zuckerman, Stanley B. Education in Germany Today: An American Appraisal. Progressive Education. 32:6 (November 1955), 173-175.

N.1.2. Comparative Perspective

5313 Beck, Robert H. Change and Harmonization in European Education. Minneapolis: University of Minnesota Press, 1971, 206 P., Esp. Pp. 142-163.

5314 Belding, Robert E. European Classrooms: Schools of Four Nations. Iowa City: Sernoll, 1966, 120 P., Esp. Pp. 57-81.

5315 Chapline, Allen. European Education--Pro and Con. Clearing House. 33:7 (March 1959), 393-396.

5316 Cogan, Morris. Some Comparisons of American and European Programs. Nea Journal. 48:4 (April 1959), 28.

5317 Cramer, John F. Browne, George S. Contemporary Education: A Comparative Study of National Systems. New York: Harcourt, Brace, 1956, 637 P., Esp. Pp. 432-473.

5318 Duggan, Stephen. Education in Europe Today. Journal of Higher Education. 18:2 (February 1947), 57-62. Critique By William F. Amann, 18:6 (June 1947), 317-319.

5319 Franzen, Carl G. F. Educational Systems of Major Foreign Countries and Their Cultural Functions and Outcomes. North Central Association Quarterly. 34:4 (April 1960), 273-283.

5320 International Conference on Comparative Education, Chiemsee, 25-29 April 1949. Frankfurt: Omgus, Education and Cultural Relations Division, 1949, 148 P.

5321 Mallinson, Vernon. An Introduction to the Study of Comparative Education. London: Heinemann, 3D Ed., 1966, 249 P.

5322 Oecd. Classification of Educational Systems: Finland, Germany, Japan. Paris: Organisation for Economic Cooperation and Development, May 1972, 77 P.

5323 Scanlon, David G. Some Comparative Reflections on German and Italian School Reforms. Comparative Education Review. 4:1 (June 1960), 31-34.

5324 Scarangello, Anthony. Europe's Schools. Clearing House. 32:6 (February 1958), 323-332.

5325 Shafer, Susanne M. Germany. Perspectives on World Education. Ed. Carlton E. Beck. Dubuque, Iowa: Brown, 1970, Pp. 45-53.

5326 Thut, I. N. Adams, Don. Educational Patterns in Contemporary Societies. New York: Mcgraw-Hill, 1964, 494 P., Esp. Pp. 76-109.

5327 Ulich, Robert. The Education of Nations: A Comparison in Historical Perspective. Cambridge: Harvard Universtiy Press, 1961, 325 P., Esp. Pp. 175-224.

N.1.3. Reconstruction Under Allied Occupation (See Also D.3.4)

5328 Banks, Richard G. The Development of Education in Wuerttemberg-Baden Under United States Military Government. Ph.D. Thesis, University of Virginia, 1949, 293 P.

5329 Barth, Pius J. German Education and the Social Order. Catholic Educational Review 46:4 (April 1948), 204-213; and 46:5 (May 1948), 275-282.

5330 Benton, William. The United States Mission Reports on Education in Germany. American Teacher. 31:5 (February 1947), 15-17.

5331 Birley, Robert. Education in the British Zone of Germany. International Affairs (London). 26:1 (January 1950), 32-44.

5332 Borinski, Fritz. German Educational Reconstruction. Erziehung Und Politik: Minna Specht Zu Ihrem 80. Geburtstag. Ed. Hellmut Becker, Willi Eichler, and Gustav Heckmann. Frankfurt: Oeffentliches Leben, 1960, Pp. 77-89.

5333 Brickman, William W. Education Under Totalitarianism and Reconstruction. School and Society. 66:1722 (27 December 1947), 511-519.

5334 Brueckner, Leo J. Educational Change in Germany. Journal of Educational Research. 42:6 (February 1949), 471-473.

5335 Christofferson, H. C. Educational Reconstruction in Land Hesse, Germany. Educational Forum. 13:3 (March 1949), 313-319.

5336 Costrell, Edward S. Reforming the German People: German Education and the American Occupation, 1945-1949. Ph.D. Thesis, Clark University, 1950, 353 P.

5337 Council for a Democratic Germany. A

Plan for the Reconstruction of the German Educational System. School and Society. 62:1618 (December 1945), 435-436.

5338 Delong, Vaughn R. School Reform in Land Hesse. American School Board Journal. 117:4 (October 1948), 39-40; 17:5 (November 1948), 32-34; and 117:6 (December 1948), 35-37.

5339 Delong, Vaughn R. United States Educational Activities in Germany. School and Society. 74:1924 (November 1951), 281-283.

5340 De Young, Chris A. The Educational Situation in Germany. School and Society. 67:1740 (May 1948), 329-332.

5341 Elliott, A. Randle. Education in Germany: The American Zone of Occupation. Year Book of Education, 1948. London: Evans Brothers, 1948, Pp. 525-534.

5342 Engelmann, Susanne Charlotte. German Education and Re-Education. New York: International Universities Press, 1945, 147 P.

5343 English, Mildred. Rebuilding the German Educational System. Educational Leadership. 6:1 (October 1948), 3-7.

5344 Ferguson, Elva Claire. Education of German Youth Under the American Occupation. Ph.D. Thesis, Stanford University, 1949, 160 P.

5345 Frost, Norman. Some Post-War Problems of German Schools. Peabody Journal of Education. 26:6 (May 1949), 338-342.

5346 Germany: The British Zone of Occupation. Year Book of Education, 1948. London: Evans Brothers, 1948, Pp. 513-524.

5347 Goetzinger, Hermann. Problems of School Reform in the United States Zone in Germany. Ph.D. Thesis, Claremont Graduate School, 1951, 119 P.

5348 Grace, Alonzo G. Basic Elements of Educational Reconstruction in Germany. Washington: American Council on Education, 1949, 14 P.

5349 Grace, Alonzo G. Education. Governing Postwar Germany. Ed. Edward H. Litchfield and Associates. Ithaca: Cornell University Press, 1953, Pp. 439-468.

5350 Grace, Alonzo G. Education in Occupied Germany. Phi Delta Kappan. 31:7 (March 1950), 305-309.

5351 Hall, Robert King. The Battle of the Mind: American Educational Policy in Germany. Columbia Journal of International Affairs. 2:1 (Winter 1948), 59-70.

5352 Hawes, Vincent L. The Reconstruction of German Education in the United States Zone of Occupation, 1945-1949. Ph.D. Thesis, Boston College, 1952, 100 P.

5353 Hopkins, L. Thomas. Educational Progress in Germany. Teachers College Record (Columbia University). 51:1 (October 1949), 14-21.

5354 Kapp, William K. The Future of German Education. Journal of Higher Education. 19:8 (November 1948), 394-396.

5355 Keller, Franklin J. Germany: Clinical Case, High Points. 30:4 (April 1948), 22-43.

5356 Kelty, Mary G. Specific Advances in Germany's New Task of Social Education. Social Education. 13:1 (January 1949), 15-21.

5357 Lawson, Robert Frederic. The English Approach to Educational Reorientation in Postwar Germany. Comparative Education Review. 8:1 (June 1964), 58-64.

5358 Lewison, Robert. Education--for What?. This Is Germany. Ed. Arthur Settel. New York: Sloane, 1950, Pp. 89-115.

5359 Liddell, Helen. Education in Occupied Germany: A Field Study. International Affairs (London). 24:1 (January 1948), 30-62.

5360 Liddell, Helen, Editor. Education in Occupied Germany. Paris: Riviere, 1949, 148 P.

5361 Lightfoot, Georgia. Teaching German Youth to Take Hold. Army Information Digest. 2:4 (April 1947), 24-29.

5362 Loeffler, E. Educational Developments From 1946 to 1951. International Yearbook of Education. 13 (1951), 120-129.

5363 Meister, Charles W. A Year in Berlin Education. Harvard Educational Review. 16:4 (Fall 1946), 255-272.

5364 Melby, Ernest O. Our Responsibility in Germany. Journal of Educational Sociology. 23:2 (October 1949), 68-77.

5365 Morgan, Edward P. A Formula for German Youth. New York Times Magazine. (2 April 1950), 12+. French Zone Educational Plan, Being Brought Into U.S. Zone.

5366 Newman, James R. The Second Phase of De-Nazifying German Schools in Greater Hessen. American School Board Journal. 113:2 (August 1946), 32-33+.

5367 Phillips, Burr W. The Redirection of German Education. Social Education. 11:8 (December 1947), 340-342.

5368 Pilgert, Henry P. The West German Educational System, With Special Reference to the Policies and Programs of the Office of the U.S. High Commissioner for Germany. Bad Godesberg-Mehlem: Office of the U.S. High Commissioner for Germany, Historical Division, 1953, 136 P.

5369 Pitt, Felix N. Education Mission to Germany. America. 76:16 (18 January 1947), 429-432.

5370 Prakken, Lawrence W. American Educational Policy in Germany. Education Digest. 13:2 (October 1947), 1-6.

5371 Report of the Education Mission to Germany. Department of State Bulletin. 15:382 (27 October 1946), 764-771.

5372 Rogin, Lawrence The Caste System in German Education. American Teacher. 31:8 (May 1947), 18-19.

5373 Santelli, Cesar. Germany: The French Zone of Occupation. Yearbook of Education, 1948. London: Evans Brothers, 1948, Pp. 535-547.

5374 Schatz, Frederick C. A Study of the Reconstruction of Education in the United States Zone of Germany With Emphasis on the Social Studies. Ed.D. Thesis, University of Tennessee, 1960, 249 P.

5375 Shuster, George N. American Occupation and German Education. Proceedings of the American Philosophical Society. 97:2 (1953), 159-162.

5376 Simmons, M. M. Education in the British Zone of Germany. Educational Record. 29:4 (October 1948), 423-427.

5377 Smith, Thomas V. Personal Impressions of Current Education in Italy, Germany, and Japan. Educational Record. 28:1 (January 1947), 21-32.

5378 Stadler, K. R. Education for

Democracy in Germany. Adult Education. 20:1 (September 1947), 17-24.

5379 Strevell, Wallace H. School Fiscal Policy Study, U.S. Zone of Germany. (Berlin?): Office of the U.S. High Commissioner for Germany, Education and Cultural Relations Division, 1950, 88 P.

5380 Trial, George. Goldsmith, M. K. Rebuilding Germany's Schools. Current History. 11:60 (August 1946), 101-108.

5381 US, Department of State. Report of the U.S. Education Mission to Germany. Washington: Department of State Publication 2664, Government Printing Office, 1946, 50 P.

5382 US, Hicog, Education and Cultural Relations Division. Education Service Centers. N.P.: Hicog, Education and Cultural Relations Division, Education Branch, 1951, 134 P.

5383 US, Hicog, Education and Cultural Relations Division. A Guide to Education and Cultural Relations. Bad Nauheim: Hicog, Education and Cultural Relations Division, 1950, 72 P.

5384 US, Hicog, Education and Cultural Relations Division. Postwar Changes in German Education: US Zone and US Sector Berlin. Frankfurt: Hicog, Education and Cultural Relations Division, Education Branch, 1951, 294 P.

5385 US, Hicog, Education and Cultural Relations Division. Second Handbook of Basic Education Statistics, U.S. Occupied Area of Germany. N.P.: Hicog, Education and Cultural Relations Division, 1950, 88 P.

5386 US, Hicog, Education and Cultural Relations Division. Supplementary Material for the Educational Reorientation Program for Fy 1950. N.P.: Hicog, Education and Cultural Relations Division, Education Branch, 1950, 58 P.

5387 US, Omgus, Education and Cultural Relations Division. Educational Reconstruction in Germany. Berchtesgaden: Omgus, Education and Cultural Relations Division, 1948, 51 P. Proceedings, Berchtesgaden Conference, 7-12 October 1948.

5388 US, Omgus, Education and Cultural Relations Division. Democratization of Education in Germany. N.P.: Omgus, November 1947.

5389 US, Omgus, Education and Cultural Relations Division. Handbook of Education Statistics, U.S. Occupied Area of Germany. N.P.: Omgus, Adjutant General, 1949, 67 P.

5390 Wells, Herman B. Our Educational Stake in Germany. Official Report, 74Th Annual Convention of the American Association of School Administrators. Washington: American Association of School Administrators, 1948, Pp. 62-72.

5391 Wirth, Fremont P. Wells, Guy. Frost, Norman. Report From Germany. Peabody Journal of Education. 26:1 (July 1948), 10-18.

5392 Wooton, Richard C. A Co-Operative Approach to School Reform: The Story of Schloss Wallenberg. School and Society. 69:1801 (June 1949), 450-452.

5393 Zucker, A. E. Educational Conditions in Germany. News Bulletin of the Institute of International Education. 21:8 (May 1946), 23.

5394 Zucker, F. The Present Intellectual Situation and Tasks of Education in Germany. Bulletin of the Association of American Colleges. 31:3 (October 1945), 377-383.

N.1.4. Planning and Policymaking

5395 Assmann, Ingeborg. West German Education in Transition. Ph.D. Thesis, University of Southern California, 1966, 293 P.

5396 Aurin, Kurt. The Role of Empirical Research in Educational Planning and Policy-Making. Western European Education. 1:4 (Winter 1969-70), 74-92.

5397 Becker, Hellmut. Research and Planning in Education. Western European Education. 1:4 (Winter 1969-1970), 23-41.

5398 Cornell, Francis G. Administration and German School Reform. School Executive. 69:4 (December 1949), 35-36.

5399 Cullity, John P. The Growth of Educational Employment in Three Countries, 1895-1964. Journal of Human Resources. 4:1 (1969), 84-92. Germany, the United Kingdom, and the United States.

5400 Ellinger, Thomas R. Democratization of Educational Administration in Four Selected States of West Germany, 1949-1969. Ph.D. Thesis, Miami University, 1970, 143 P.

5401 FRG, Federal Government. Report of the Federal Government on Education 1970: The Federal Government's Concept for Educational Policy. Bonn: Bundesministerium Fuer Bildung Und Wissenschaft, 1970, 227 P.

5402 Friemond, Hans. Educational Planning in the Federal Republic. German Tribune Quarterly Review. No. 15 (26 August 1971), 8-12.

5403 Oecd. Educational Policy and Planning: Germany. Paris: Organisation for Economic Cooperation and Development, January 1973, 294 P.

5404 Oecd. Reviews of National Policies for Education: Germany. Paris: Organisation for Economic Cooperation and Development, January 1972, 151 P.

5405 Oecd, Directorate for Scientific Affairs. Educational Policy and Planning: Germany. Paris: Organisation for Economic Co-Operation and Development, 1972, II and 294 P.

5406 Springer, Ursula K. West Germany's Turn to "Bildungspolitik" in Educational Planning. Comparative Education Review. 9:1 (February 1965), 11-17.

5407 Wernecke, Hanns B. Interprovincial Cooperation in Education in West Germany and Canada, 1945-1969: The West German Conference of Ministers of Education and the Council of Ministers of Education (Canada). Ph.D. Thesis, University of Pennsylvania, 1971, 654 P.

N.1.5. Educational Reform

5408 Dahrendorf, Ralf. The Crisis in German Education. Journal of Contemporary History. 2:3 (July 1967), 139-147.

5409 Enderwitz, Herbert. Two German Education Reform Schemes: The "Rahmenplan" and The Bremerplan. Comparative Education Review. 7:1 (June 1963), 47-50.

5410 Fuehr, Christoph, Editor. Educational Reform in the Federal Republic of Germany. Hamburg: Unesco Institute for Education, 1970, 182 P.

5411 Greenberg, D. S. West Germany: Educational Reform Is the Major Domestic Issue. Science. 167:3921 (20

February 1970), 1108-1110.

5412 Hahn, Walter F. Changing School Patterns in West Germany. Clearing House. 45:5 (January 1971), 300-304.

5413 Heidenheimer, Arnold J. The Politics of Educational Reform: Explaining Different Outcomes of School Comprehensivization Attempts in Sweden and West Germany. Comparative Education Review. 18:3 (October 1974), 388-410.

5414 Huebener, Theodore. Proposed Reforms in the German Schools. Comparative Education Review. 6:1 (June 1962), 44-47.

5415 Huebener, Theodore. Reform of German Education. German Quarterly. 26:3 (May 1953), 150-153.

5416 Kirkpatrick, Ursula. The "Rahmenplan" for West German School Reform. Comparative Education Review. 4:1 (June 1960), 18-25.

5417 Kohr, Leopold. Educational Reform Plans in Germany and Austria. Education Forum. 12:3 (March 1948), 261-266.

5418 Lawson, Robert Frederic. Reform of the West German School System, 1945-1962. Ann Arbor: University of Michigan, School of Education, 1965, 230 P.

5419 Lawson, Robert Frederic. Reform of the West German School System, 1945-1962. Ph.D. Thesis, University of Michigan, 1963, 297 P.

5420 Lawson, Robert Frederic. Selection and Reform in West German Education. Journal of Educational Thought. 1:2 (August 1967), 100-111.

5421 Leonhardt, Rudolf Walter. in Lieu of Robbins. Encounter. 22:4 (April 1964), 80-82.

5422 Merritt, Richard L. Flerlage, Ellen P. Merritt, Anna J. Democratizing West German Education. Comparative Education. 7:3 (December 1971), 121-136.

5423 Merritt, Richard L. Flerlage, Ellen P. Merritt, Anna J. Political Man in Postwar West German Education. Comparative Education Review. 15:3 (October 1971), 346-361.

5424 Nixdorff, Peter W. The Pace of West German Educational Reform as Affected By Land Politics. Ph.D. Thesis, University of Florida, 1969.

5425 Raiser, Ludwig. A German View of the Robbins Committee's Report. Minerva. 2:3 (Spring 1964), 336-342.

5426 Randall, Earle S. Things Are Happening in Bremen Schools. German Quarterly. 28:3 (May 1955), 168-174.

5427 Robinsohn, Saul B. Kuhlmann, J. Caspar. Two Decades of Non-Reform in West German Education. Comparative Education Review. 11:3 (October 1967), 311-330.

5428 Sommerkorn, Ingrid N. The Campaign for Education in Berlin. Western European Education. 1:2-3 (Summer-Fall 1969), 117-124.

5429 Springer, Ursula K. West German School Reform in Social-Political Context. Ph.D. Thesis, Columbia University, 1964, 335 P.

5430 Thomas, Helga. Innovation in Education--Germany. Paris: Organisation for Economic Cooperation and Development, Centre for Educational Research and Innovation, June 1971, 58 P.

5431 Tone, Fred H. Warninghoff, Hans. The Bremen School Reform. Educational Forum. 14:3 (March 1950), 331-345.

N.1.6. Teachers and Teacher Training

5432 Aubert, Vilhelm. Fisher, Burton R. Rokkan, Stein. A Comparative Study of Teachers' Attitudes to International Problems and Policies: Preliminary Review of Relationsships in Interview Data From Seven Western European Countries. Journal of Social Issues. 10:4 (1954), 25-39.

5433 Blaettner, Fritz. Western Germany. Year Book of Education, 1953: Status and Position of Teachers. Yonkers-on-Hudson: World, 1953, 324-342.

5434 Fine, Benjamin. The New German Teacher and Student. Educational Forum. 26:3 (March 1962), 261-280.

5435 Fuehr, Christoph. Teacher Training in the Federal Republic of Germany. Western European Education. 2:2-3 (Summer-Fall 1970), 109-125.

5436 Fuhrig, Wolf D. Teachers Unions and Associations: West Germany. Teachers Unions and Associations. Ed. Albert A. Blum. Urbana: University of Illinois Press, 1969, Pp. 83-118.

5437 Hahn, Walter F. West Germany's Secondary-School Teachers Preparation. Comparative Education Review. 9:3 (October 1965), 346-355.

5438 Hilker, Franz. Organization and Structure of Teacher Education in the German Federal Republic. Year Book of Education, 1963: The Education and Training of Teachers. New York: Harcourt, Brace & World, 1963, Pp. 256-273.

5439 Hilker, Franz. Religion and the Control of Teachers: The Case of Germany. World Year Book of Education, 1966: Church and State in Education. New York: Harcourt, Brace & World, 1966, Pp. 293-314.

5440 Kaldegg, A. A Study of German and English Teacher-Training Students By Means of Projective Techniques. British Journal of Psychology. 42:1-2 (March-May 1951), 56-113.

5441 Kisiel, Chester A. Some Perspectives on the Role of the German Teacher. School Review. 74:3 (Autumn 1966), 292-318.

5442 Lynch, James. The Birth of a Profession: German Grammar School Teachers and New Humanism. Comparative Education Review. 16:1 (February 1972), 85-97.

5443 Lynch, James. A Problem of Status--Teacher Training in West Germany. Comparative Education. 3:3 (June 1967), 219-224.

5444 Mitter, Wolfgang. Social Studies in Teacher Education: An Experiment in Germany. Indiana Social Studies Quarterly. 23:3 (Winter 1970-71), 81-90.

5445 Northrhine-Westphalia Planning Council for Higher Education. Teacher Education for the School of the Future. Western European Education. 2:2-3 (Summer-Fall 1970), 126-132.

5446 Oecd. Training, Recruitment and Utilization of Teachers in Primary and Secondary Education. Paris: Organisation for Economic Cooperation and Development, 1971, 471 P.

5447 Oecd, Directorate for Scientific Affairs. Study on Teachers: Germany, Belgium, United Kingdom. Paris: Organisation for Economic Cooperation and Development, 1969, 312 P.

5448 Perryman, J. Nelson. German Teachers Visit America. Social Education. 14:1 (January 1950), 14-15, 30.

5449 Rust, Val Dean. Teacher Control in Pre-Schools of Los Angeles, London, and Frankfurt. Comparative Education

Review. 17:1 (February 1973), 11-25.

5450 Ryter, Eva. Germany. Germany, Belgique, United Kingdom: Training, Recruitment and Utilisation of Teachers: Country Case Studies: Primary and Secondary Education. Ed. Oecd, Directorate for Scientific Affairs. Paris: Organisation for Economic Cooperation and Development, 1969, Pp. 1-132.

5451 Schultze, Walter. The German Institute's Contribution to the Advanced Scientific Training of Teachers. Western European Education. 2:2-3 (Summer-Fall 1970), 247-254.

5452 Shaver, James P. Hofmann, Helmut P. Richards, Hyrum E. The Authoritarianism of American and German Teacher Education Students. Journal of Social Psychology. 84:2 (August 1971), 303-304.

5453 Siemsen, Hans. New Teachers for Germany. School and Society. 65:1672 (11 January 1947), 28-30.

5454 Teacher Education for Wuerttemberg-Baden: Report of Workshop at Esslingen. Stuttgart: Klett, 1949, 136 P.

5455 US, Omgus, Education and Cultural Relations Division. Teacher Education in Germany, American Zone. N.P.: Omgus, August 1946.

5456 World Confederation of Organizations of Teaching Profession. Report of the Wcotp Inquiry Commission on Berlin, December 1961. Washington: World Confederation of Organizations of the Teaching Profession, Inquiry Commission on Berlin, 1961, 20 P.

N.1.7. Other Developments

5457 Auer, Howard J. M., Jr. Self-Concept of Academic Ability of West German Eighth-Grade Students. Ph.D. Thesis, Michigan State University, 1971, 155 P.

5458 Beck, Earl Ray. New Schools in Hamburg, Germany. Peabody Journal of Education. 40:1 (July 1962), 44-48.

5459 Bremen, Senator for Schools and Education. The Economic, Social and Domestic Conditions of the Schoolchildren in Postwar Bremen. Bremen: Senator for Schools and Education, 1947, 20 P.

5460 Education and Child Care Institute in Germany. Hanover: Arbeiter-Wohlfahrt, 1950, 86 P.

5461 Hausmann, G. A Megapolis: The Ruhr/Rhein Complex. World Year Book of Education, 1970: Education in Cities. New York: Harcourt, Brace & World, 1970, Pp. 251-265.

5462 Ingenkamp, Karlheinz. Educational Organization and Structure in West Germany. World Year Book of Education, 1969: Examinations. New York: Harcourt, Brace & World, 1969, Pp. 140-145.

5463 International Workshop on Guidance. Proceedings, Findings and Recommendations for the German Schools. Frankfurt: Office of the U.S. High Commissioner for Germany, Office of Public Affairs, Educational and Cultural Affairs Division, Education Branch, 1951, 171 P. Report of a Workshop in Weilburg, Germany, 15 July-17 August 1951.

5464 Koelle, Willi. Selection Procedures in the Schools of the Federal Republic of Germany. Year Book of Education, 1962: The Gifted Child. New York: Harcourt, Brace & World, 1962, Pp. 259-270.

5465 Linn, Rolf N. Selective Service for German Education. School and Society. 62:1609 (October 1945), 259-260.

5466 Mackey, William Francis. Bilingual Education in a Binational School: A Study of Equal Language Maintenance Through Free Alternation. Rowley, Mass: Newbury House Publishers, 1972, Xviii and 185P.

5467 Preston, Ralph C. Reading Achievement of German and American Children. School and Society. 90:2214 (20 October 1962), 350-354.

5468 Preston, Ralph C. Issues Raised By the Philadelphia-Wiesbaden Reading Study. Comparative Education Review. 7:1 (June 1963), 61-65.

5469 Schwarzweller, Harry K. Educational Aspirations and Life Chances of German Young People. Comparative Education. 4:1 (November 1967), 35-50.

5470 Shafer, Susanne M. Germany's European Children. Teachers College Record. 65:4 (January 1964), 361-371.

5471 Specht, Minna. Rosenberg, Alfons. Experimental Schools in Germany. London: Westminster Press, German Educational Reconstruction (G.E.R.) Pamphlet No. 1, 1945, 24 P. Specht, "Private Boarding Schools"; and Rosenberg, "Day Schools."

5472 Warren, Richard L. Education in a German Village: A Study of Cultural Transmission. Ph.D. Thesis, Stanford University, 1966, 276 P.

5473 Warren, Richard L. Education in Rebhausen: A German Village. New York: Holt, Rinehart and Winston, 1967, 114 P.

N.2. FRG: Schools and Curricula

N.2.1. Preschools and Elementary Schools

5474 Clay, Dorothy N. The Reconstruction of Elementary Education in the U.S. Zone of Western Germany, 1945-1955. Ph.D. Thesis, University of Southern California, 1957, 182 P.

5475 Ritter, Annelies J. New Paths for Preschool Education: Preliminary Guidelines and Experiments in the Federal Republic of Germany. Western European Education. 1:2-3 (Summer-Fall 1969), 157-164.

5476 Shafer, Susanne M. Persistence of Post-War American Proposals for the Study of Contemporary Affairs in the West German Volksschule. Ph.D. Thesis, University of Michigan, 1962, 368 P.

5477 Shafer, Susanne M. Postwar American Influence on the West German Volksschule. Ann Arbor: University of Michigan, School of Education, 1965, 281 P.

5478 Snyder, Agnes. Elementary Education in Occupied Germany. National Elementary Principal. 26:6 (June 1947), 2-8.

5479 US, Omgus, Education and Cultural Relations Division. Elementary Education in Germany. N.P.: Omgus, August 1946.

N.2.2. Lower and Upper Secondary Schools

5480 Buckley, Dennis La Vern. The German Gymnasium in Flux: A Case Study. Ph.D. Thesis, University of California, Los Angeles, 1971, 328 P.

5481 Dewitt, Charles M. The German Abiturial System. Phi Delta Kappan. 36:9 (June 1955), 353-356.

5482 Friedland, Diepold K. Social Studies in Secondary Schools in Western Germany After World War II. Ph.D. Thesis, Boston University, 1957, 39 P.

5483 Fries, Guenter. Methods of History

Teaching in the Ninth School Year. Western European Education. 3:2-3 (Summer-Fall 1971), 145-153.

5484 Hahn, Walter F. German Secondary Education, With Emphasis on the Problem of The Postwar Period. Ph.D. Thesis, University of Utah, 1950, 264 P.

5485 Hall, J. P. E. An Alternative Way to Tertiary Education: West Germany's Fachoberschule. Comparative Education. 10:2 (June 1974), 121-129.

5486 Klafki, Wolfgang. Pedagogical and Didactic Aspects of the New "Hauptschule". Western European Education. 1:1 (Spring 1969), 112-123.

5487 Klasek, Charles Bernard. Reconstruction of the German Public Secondary School Under British and American Occupation, 1945-1948. Ph.D. Thesis, University of Nebraska, 1948, 190 P.

5488 Oecd. Development of Secondary Education: Trends and Implications. Paris: Organisation for Economic Cooperation and Development, 1969, 183 P.

5489 O'Connor, Roger Day. Education for Real Life: A Study of the Curriculum of the German Mittelschule. Ed.D. Thesis, Wayne State University, 1967, 448 P.

5490 Schultze, Walter. Recent Changes in the Secondary Schools, Federal Republic of Germany. Phi Delta Kappan. 43:2 (November 1961), 64-68.

5491 Spolton, Lewis. The Upper Secondary School: A Comparative Survey. Oxford: Pergamon, 1967, 291 P., Esp. Pp. 223-236.

5492 Thomas, Basil E. The Abitur Examination in Germany. Trends in Education. 2 (April 1966), 31-37.

5493 US, Omgus, Education and Cultural Relations Division. Secondary Schools in Germany, American Zone. N.P.: Omgus, Adjutant General, 1946, 14 P.

5494 Van De Graaff, John H. West Germany's Abitur Quota and School Reform. Comparative Education Review. 11:1 (February 1967), 75-86.

N.2.3. Vocational Training; Industrial Education

5495 Abraham, Karl. The System of German Technical Schools. Year Book of Education, 1958: The Secondary School Curriculum. Yonkers-on-Hudson: World, 1958, Pp. 191-197.

5496 Agricultural and Home Economics Evaluation & Info. Service. Vocational Education in Agriculture. Bad Godesberg: Land- Und Hauswirtschaftlicher Auswertungs- Und Informationsdienst, 1963, 71 P.

5497 Albach, Horst. Towards a Levy-Grant System of Vocational Training in Germany? German Economic Review. 12:3 (1974), 258-263.

5498 Arlt, Fritz. Wilms, Dorothee. From Apprenticeship to Leadership: The Structure and Organization of Aids to the Training and Advancement of Industrial Manpower in the Federal Republic of Germany. Cologne: Deutsche Industrieverlagsgesellschaft, 1969, 73 P.

5499 Armbruster, Wolfgang. Winterhager, Wolfgang D. Education and Industrial Training: The Educational Viewpoint. World Year Book of Education, 1968: Education Within Industry. New York: Harcourt, Brace & World, 1968, Pp. 32-36.

5500 Belding, Robert E. Perennial Model Revisited. Journal of Secondary Education. 40:3 (March 1965), 120-125. Compulsory Continuation Schools (Berufsschulen).

5501 Coit, Eleanor G. Labor Education in Germany. Frankfurt: Hicog, Office of Labor Affairs, Visiting Expert Series No. 16, June 1950, 57 P.

5502 Cook, Alice Hanson. Workers Education in the U.S. Zone (Germany). Berlin: Omgus, Manpower Division, Visiting Expert Series No. 1, June 1947, 33 P.

5503 Edenhofner, Siegfried A. Training in the Retail Trades in the German Federal Republic. World Year Book of Education, 1968: Education Within Industry. New York: Harcourt, Brace & World, 1968, Pp. 256-257.

5504 Fahle, Walter. Vocational Education in the Federal Republic of Germany. Western European Education. 5:1 (Spring 1973), 6-22.

5505 Federation of German Trade Unions. The Educational Activities Within the German Federation of Trade Unions (Dgb). Duesseldorf: Federation of German Trade Unions, 1967, 63 P.

5506 Hirlekar, Yamunabai. Vocational Education in Germany. Bombay: Hirlekar, 1962, 175 P.

5507 Huddleston, John. Trade Union Education in the Federal Republic of Germany. International Review of Education. 14 (1968), 24-41.

5508 Keller, Franklin J. Vocational Guidance in Germany. Occupations. 26:7 (April 1948), 403-405.

5509 Krause, Erwin. Improving in-Plant Training in the Federal Republic of Germany. International Labour Review. 83:6 (June 1961), 547-553.

5510 Krause, Erwin. Vocational Training in the Federal Republic of Germany. International Labour Review. 77:3 (March 1958), 209-219.

5511 Kuhn, Charles G. A Comparison of the Training Programs for Business Education in the System of Education of the Federal Republic of Germany With That of the Public School System of the United States. Ph.D. Thesis, State University of Iowa, 1962, 329 P.

5512 Lorig, Arthur N. Training Accountants in Holland and West Germany. Accounting Review. 36:2 (April 1961), 232-238.

5513 Niens, Walter. The Historical and Social Background to Education Within Industry in West Germany. World Year Book of Education, 1968: Education Within Industry. New York: Harcourt, Brace & World, 1968, Pp. 108-119.

5514 Patterns and Reforms in West German Vocational Education. Western European Education. 3:1 (Spring 1971), 19-33.

5515 Pommernelle, Lothar. Grants for Vocational Training. Bonn: Federal Ministry of Labour and the Social Structure, Social Policy in Germany No. 9, 1964, 24 P.

5516 Pommernelle, Lothar. Vocational Guidance and Placing in Apprenticeship and Trainee Occupations. Bonn: Federal Ministry of Labour and the Social Structure, Social Policy in Germany No. 8, 1964, 23 P.

5517 Rauschenplat, Helmut Von. Vocational Training in Germany. London: German Educational Reconstruction Pamphlet No. 2, 1945, 32 P.

5518 Robinson, Harold. Education for Citizenship in Vocational Schools. Stuttgart: Mueller, 1951, 63 P. Based on the Reports of the Second

International Conference Vocational Education, Maulbronn, Germany, 1951.

5519 Robinson, Harold, Editor. Problems of Vocational Education. Stuttgart: Mueller, 1952, 149 P.

5520 Ware, George Whitaker. Vocational Education and Apprenticeship Training in Germany. (Bad Godesberg?): Office of the U.S. High Commissioner for Germany, Office of Public Affairs, 1952, 73 P.

N.2.4. Adult and Permanent Education

5521 Becker, Hellmut. Education for Adults and Workers Today. Comparative Education. 5:1 (February 1969), 9-16.

5522 Cook, Alice Hanson. Adult Education in Citizenship in Postwar Germany. Pasadena, Calif.: Fund for Adult Education, 1954, 73 P.

5523 Deming, Robert C. Adult Education in the U.S. Zone of Germany. Adult Education Bulletin. 12:2 (December 1947), 37-43.

5524 Dickerman, Watson. Adult Education in the German Universitites. Journal of Higher Education. 24:5 (May 1953), 241-248.

5525 Dolff, Helmuth. Can the Volkshochschulen of Today Answer the Requirements of Adult Education for Tomorrow?. Convergence. 5:3 (1972), 31-36.

5526 Hopman, A. N. Adult Education in Occupied Germany--U.S. Zone. School and Society. 66:1722 (December 1947), 505-507.

5527 Huddleston, John. Adult Education and German Democracy. Contemporary Review. 210:1214 (March 1967), 124-131.

5528 Huddleston, John. German Universities and Adult Education. British Journal of Educational Studies. 18:1 (February 1970), 42-55.

5529 Huebener, Theodore. Adult Education in Germany. High Points. 32:11 (November 1950), 5-9.

5530 Kaplan, Abbott. Adult Education in Germany. Adult Education. 5:1 (1954), 22-29.

5531 Knoll, Joachim H. Adult Education with or Without the Universities. Convergence. 5:1 (1972), 71-87.

5532 Rebel, Karlheinz. The Necessity of Further Education in the Professions and Home Study as a Means of Realization. Convergence. 3:4 (1970), 66-75.

5533 Schadt, Armin L. Adult Education in Germany: Bibliography. Syracuse: Eric Clearinghouse on Adult Education, 1969, 40 P.

5534 Schadt, Armin L. The Volkshochschule: A Comparative Study of Adult Education in the Federal Republic of Germany and the German Democratic Republic. Ph.D. Thesis, Ohio State University, 1969.

5535 Simpson, J. A. Today and Tomorrow in European Adult Education: A Study of The Present Situation and Future Developments. Strasbourg: Council of Europe, 1972, 223 P.

5536 Tietgens, Hans. Restructuring Education. Permanent Education: A Compendium of Studies Commissioned By the Council for Cultural Co-Operation. Strasbourg: Council of Europe, 1970, Pp. 305-339.

5537 US, Omgus, Education and Cultural Relations Division. Adult Education: A Manual. N.P.: Omgus, August 1946.

N.2.5. Curriculum and Textbooks

5538 Arndt, Christian O. Teaching the Nazi Period in the German Gymnasium. School and Society. 88:2181 (November 1960), 442-444.

5539 Bunn, Ronald F. Treatment of Hitler's Rise to Power in West German School Textbooks. Comparative Education Review. 6:1 (June 1962), 34-43.

5540 Chiout, Herbert. Significant Experiments in the German Federal Republic. Year Book of Education, 1958: The Secondary School Curriculum. Yonkers-on-Hudson: World, 1958, Pp. 515-527.

5541 Davis, Kathleen S. Nationalism in German Schools. Educational Forum. 18:4 (May 1954), 443-450.

5542 Deethardt, John Fred, Jr. A History of Speech Education in the Volksschulen, Mittelschulen and Gymnasien of the West German State of Hessen, 1945-1965. Ph.D. Thesis, Northwestern University, 1967, 386 P.

5543 Farnen, Russell F. German, Daniel Bernard. Youth, Politics, and Education: England, Italy, Sweden, the United States, and West Germany. Political Youth, Traditional Schools: National and International Perspectives. Ed. Byron G. Massialas. Englewood Cliffs: Prentice-Hall, 1972, Pp. 161-177.

5544 Foreign Languages in Germany. School and Society. 97:2319 (October 1969), 389-390.

5545 Hahn, Walter F. Textbooks in European High Schools. Clearing House. 33:7 (March 1959), 396-400.

5546 Holtzclaw, Katharine. Germany Plans Home Economics Education. Journal of Home Economics. 40:10 (December 1948), 559-561.

5547 Huebener, Theodore. What Is German Youth Taught About the Nazis?. German Quarterly. 35:2 (March 1962), 171-178.

5548 International Workshop on Social Studies, Heidelberg, 1950. Proceedings and Suggestions for the Formation of Social Studies in the Public Schools of Germany. Frankfurt: Hicog, Education and Cultural Relations Division, Education Branch, 1951, 154 P.

5549 Konieczny, Jozef. The Problem of Political Education in the German Federal Republic. Polish Western Affairs. 12:2 (1971), 226-246.

5550 Ladd, Edward T. Germany: Present Day Case Study in Citizenship Education. Proceedings of the Middle States Council for the Social Studies. 50 (1953), 51-55.

5551 Lawson, Robert Frederic. Developing Democratic Attitudes in German Schools. Journal of Education of the Faculty of Education (Vancouver). No. 13 (May 1967), 71-77.

5552 Lynch, James. West German Curriculum Construction. Trends in Education. 18 (April 1970), 18-21.

5553 Multhoff, Robert. The Work of the Brunswick International Schoolbook Institute in Revising History Textbooks. Western European Education. 2:1 (Spring 1970), 71-85.

5554 Neumeister, Hermann. Education for International Understanding in the Federal Republic of Germany. Phi Delta Kappan. 51:5 (January 1970), 259-263.

5555 Pillsbury, Kent. International Cooperation in Textbook Evaluation: The Braunschweig Institute. Comparative Education Review. 10:1 (February 1966), 48-52.

5556 Robinsohn, Saul B. Educational Reform Through Curriculum Revision. Western European Education. 1:1 (Spring 1969), 20-29.

5557 Roemer, Joseph. The German Textbook in the U.S. Zone of Germany. Peabody Journal of Education. 28:6 (May 1951), 346-352.

5558 Seif, N. S. The Teaching of Modern Languages in Belgium, England, Holland and Germany. Comparative Education Review. 9:2 (June 1965), 163-169.

5559 Shafer, Suzanne M. American Social Studies in West German Schools. Comparative Education Review. 8:2 (October 1964), 146-152.

5560 Sobanski, Waclaw. School Textbooks in the German Federal Republic. Warsaw: Zachodnia Agencja Prasowa, 1962, 254 p.

5561 Torney, Judith. Oppenheim, A. N. Farnen, Russell F. Civic Education in Ten Nations: An Empirical Study. New York: John Wiley, Halsted Press, 1975.

5562 US, Hicog, Education and Cultural Relations Division. Report on Textbook Evaluation, 1945-1948. N.P.: Hicog, Education and Cultural Relations Division, Education Branch, 1950.

5563 US, Omgus, Internal Affairs and Communications Division. Textbooks in Germany, American Zone. N.P.: Omgus, Internal Affairs and Communications Division, Education and Religious Affairs Branch, 1946, 30 P.

5564 Wolff, Kurt H. German Attempts at Picturing Germany: Texts. Columbus: Ohio State University, Department of Sociology and Anthropology, 1955, 136 p.

N.2.6. Educational Technology

5565 Dohmen, Guenther. Multi-Media Systems, Home Study Courses, and Continued Training. Western European Education. 2:2-3 (Summer-Fall 1970), 209-221.

5566 Gutschow, Harald. Educational Technology in the German Federal Republic: Tradition and Innovation. Education Technology. 9:11 (November 1969), 20-21.

5567 Keilhacker, Martin. The Organization of Film and Television in the Schools of The German Federal Republic. Year Book of Education, 1960: Communication Media and the School. Yonkers-on-Hudson: World, 1960, Pp. 547-552.

5568 Loughary, John W. Technology in German Education. Journal of Educational Data Processing. 6:5 (December 1969), 318-322.

5569 Rueckriem, Georg. The Radio Course "Science of Education". Western European Education. 2:2-3 (Summer-Fall 1970), 176-191.

5570 US, Omgus, Education and Cultural Relations Division. Education By Radio in the U.S. Area of Occupation. N.P.: Omgus, Adjutant General, September 1948, 27 P.

5571 US, Omgus, Education and Cultural Relations Division. Visual Aids in German Education, American Zone. N.P.: Omgus, August 1946.

5572 Wasem, Erich. Audiovisual Media—Unused Potential. Western European Education. 3:2-3 (Summer-Fall 1971), 158-160.

N.2.7. Religion and Education

5573 Delfiner, Henry. Church-State Relations and Religious Instruction in the Public Elementary Schools of Switzerland, West Germany and The United States. Ph.D. Thesis, Fletcher School of Law and Diplomacy, 1965.

5574 Helmreich, Ernst Christian. Religious Education in German Schools: An Historical Approach. Cambridge: Harvard University Press, 1959, 365 P.

5575 Helmreich, Ernst Christian. Religious Education in Germany: Post-War Measures. Current History. 19:110 (October 1950), 210-216.

5576 Hunt, Chester L. Religious Instruction Versus Secularization: The German Experience. Journal of Educational Sociology. 22:4 (December 1948), 304-310.

5577 Obermayer, Klaus. Religious Schools and Religious Freedom: Proposals for Reform of the German Public School System. American Journal of Comparative Law. 16:4 (1968), 552-562.

N.3. FRG: Universities

N.3.1. Universities: General

5578 Abrahams, Frederick F. Sommerkorn, Ingrid N. The Planning Process for the University of Bremen. Participatory Planning in Education. Paris: Organisation for Economic Co-Operation and Development, 1974, Pp. 195-213.

5579 Altbach, Philip G. Comparative Higher Education Abroad: Bibliography and Analysis. New York: Praeger, 1976.

5580 Anthon, Carl G. The Birth of the Free University. American Scholar. 24:1 (Winter 1954-55), 49-64.

5581 Assmann, Ingeborg. Social Mobility and Education in the Federal Republic of Germany. New Era. 51:1 (January 1970), 3-8.

5582 Boening, Eberhard. Roeloffs, K. Three German Universitites: Aachen, Bochum, and Konstanz. Paris: Organisation for Economic Co-Operation and Development, 1970, 168 P.

5583 Burn, Barbara B. Higher Education in the Federal Republic of Germany. Higher Education in Nine Countries: A Comparative Study of Colleges and Universities Abroad. Ed. Barbara B. Burn. New York: McGraw-Hill, 1971, Pp. 165-195.

5584 Buschbeck, Malte. The Politicization of the University. Western European Education. 3:4 (Winter 1971-1972), 329-348.

5585 Cerf, Walter. A Field Trip to German Universities. Journal of Higher Education. 26:3 (March 1955), 134-140.

5586 Chettiar, L. Some Aspects of Higher Ecuation in Germany. Journal of Annamalai University. 20 (1956), 163-166.

5587 Cole, R. Taylor. Federalism and Universities in West Germany: Recent Trends. American Journal of Comparative Law. 21:1 (Winter 1973), 45-68.

5588 Cottrell, Donald P. Higher Education and the Problem of Germany Today. Education Forum. 12:3 (March 1948), 267-275.

5589 Cottrell, Donald P. University in Germany Today. School and Society. 66:1722 (27 December 1947), 481-484.

5590 Cumming, William P. What Is Happening in the German Universities. South Atlantic Quarterly. 46:2 (April 1947), 167-181.

5591 Davis, Paul Ford. National Goals and Higher Education in West Germany and West Berlin. Ed.D. Thesis, Indiana Univeristy, 1962, 168 P.

5592 Detwiler, Donald S. The Climate of Higher Education in West Germany. Institute of International Education News Bulletin. 35:9 (May 1960), 11-15.

5593 Donors Association for German Science. The Scientific and Academic World. Essen-Bredeney: Stifterverband Fuer Die Deutsche Wissenschaft, Rev. Ed., 1962, 243 P.

5594 Donors Association for German Science. Scientific and Academic Life in the Federal Republic of Germany: A Handbook. Essen-Bredeney: Stifterverband Fuer Die Deutsche Wissenschaft, Rev. Ed., 1963, 174 P.

5595 Donovan, Herman Lee. Observations of German Universities in the American Zone. Peabody Journal of Education. 26:2 (September 1948), 70-75.

5596 Edding, Friedrich. The Planning of Higher Education in the Federal Republic of Germany. Economic Aspects of Higher Education. Ed. Seymour E. Harris. Paris: Organisation for Economic Cooperation and Development, 1964, Pp. 153-176.

5597 Edding, Friedrich. The University Enrollment in West Germany. Comparative Education Review. 9:1 (February 1965), 5-10.

5598 Eilsberger, Rupert. The Comprehensive University in International Perspective. Western European Education. 4:4 (Winter 1972-1973), 307-329.

5599 Eith, Wolfgang. The State of European University Cooperation: The International and Supranational Situation. Western European Education. 5:4 (Winter 1973-74), 56-70.

5600 Engelhardt, Werner. The Institute for Cooperative Studies at the University of Cologne. Review of International Cooperation. 54:12 (December 1961), 325-327.

5601 Fischer, Andreas. American University Planning and Its Relevance to German Educational Policy. International Review of Education. 20:2 (1974), 138-154.

5602 Free German Youth, Central Council, Student Section. Militarism and Neofascism at the West German Universities and Colleges: A Documentation. Berlin (East): Junge Welt, 1960, 55 P.

5603 Fuhrig, Wolf D. A Quasi-Union: West German University Association. Industrial Relations. 5:1 (October 1965), 116-127.

5604 Fuhrig, Wolf D. State and University in the Federal Reupublic of Germany. Ph.D. Thesis, Columbia University, 1966, 256 P.

5605 Grace, Alonzo G. "Freie Universitaet"-Berlin. School and Society. 70:1817 (October 1949), 241-244.

5606 Gray, J. Glenn. Munich University: Class of '50--A Case Study in German Re-Education. Commentary. 5:5 (May 1948), 440-448.

5607 Hahn, Walter F. Patterns and Trends in West German Universities. Journal of Higher Education. 36:5 (May 1965), 245-253.

5608 Hallstein, Walter. The Universities. Annals of the American Academy of Political and Social Science. 260 (November 1948), 155-167.

5609 Havighurst, Robert J. Higher Education in Germany. Journal of Higher Education. 19:1 (January 1948), 13-20.

5610 Helde, Thomas T. Academic Freedom and German Politics: The Goettingen Incident. Yale Review. 47:1 (September 1957), 76-92.

5611 Herz, Otto. Plans for Comprehensive Higher Institutions. Western European Education. 2:4 (Winter 1970-1971), 351-365.

5612 Hess, Gerhard. Universities in Germany, 1930-1970. Bad Godesberg: Inter Nationes, 1968, 51 P.

5613 Hesse, M. Harry. Aachen's Technische Hochschule. Institute of International Education News Bulletin. 31:6 (March 1956), 34-37.

5614 Hirlekar, Yamunabai. University Education in Western Germany: A Brief Survey. Bombay: Popular Book Depot, 1956, 212 P.

5615 Joesten, Joachim. German Universities in 1948. Great Barrington, Mass.: Joachim Joesten, New Germany Reports No. 6, 1948, 16 P.

5616 Kerr, Anthony. Universities of Europe. Westminster: Canterbury, 1962, 235 P.

5617 Kiehn, Ludwig. Alternative Paths to the University--Germany. Year Book of Education, 1959: Higher Education. Yonkers-on-Hudson: World, 1959, Pp. 475-483.

5618 King, Edmund J. Education and Development in Western Europe. Reading: Addison-Wesley, 1969, 187 P., Esp. Pp. 87-131.

5619 Kloss, G. The Growth of Federal Power in the West German University System. Minerva. 9:4 (October 1971), 510-527.

5620 Knight, Rose. Trends in University Entry: An Inter-Country Comparison. Social Objectives in Educational Planning. Paris: Organisation for Economic Cooperation and Development, 1967, Pp. 149-212.

5621 Kraushaar, Otto F. New Stirrings in German Universities. Scientific Monthly. 78:4 (April 1954), 201-207.

5622 Luchsinger, Fred. in the German Federal Republic--Higher Learning and Research as a Political Issue. Swiss Review of World Affairs. 6:11 (February 1957), 9-10.

5623 May, Arthur J. Austrian and German Universities in 1948. Journal of Central European Affairs. 9:3 (October 1949), 315-320.

5624 Mayer, Lyle V. A Study of German Universities in the American Zone of Occupation, 1945 to 1953. Ph.D. Thesis, University of Maryland, 1954, 233 P.

5625 Mckay, Llewelyn R. Higher Education in Germany. School and Society. 83:2082 (31 March 1956), 113-115.

5626 Phillip, Werner. General Studies in Germany Today. Christian Scholar. 37:2 (June 1954), 101-105.

5627 Read, James M. German Universities. Yale Review. 42:1 (September 1952), 83-94.

5628 Recommendations of the Science Council for the Development of Scientific Institutions in Western Germany. Minerva. 1:1 (Autumn 1962), 87-105.

5629 Recommendations of the Science Council for the Development of Scientific Institutions in Western Germany. Minerva. 5:3 (Spring 1967), 413-428.

5630 Recommendations of the Science

Council on the Reorganisation of University Teaching Staffs in Western Germany. Minerva. 4:2 (Winter 1966), 246-253.

5631 Regnery, Henry. The Malaise of the German University. Modern Age. 18:2 (Spring 1974), 121-132.

5632 Sauer, Ernst. Catholic Higher Education: The Experience in Germany. Dublin Review. 233:479 (Spring 1959), 17-19.

5633 Shuster, George N. The Free University of Berlin. Institute of International Education News Bulletin. 32:3 (December 1956), 12-14.

5634 Snell, Bruno, and Others. Goettingen Versus Schlueter. Manchester: Bulletin of the Committee on Science and Freedom No. 3, 1955, 31 P.

5635 Suggestions of the Science Council on the Pattern of New Universities in Western Germany. Minerva. 1:2 (Winter 1963), 217-225.

5636 Will, Frederic. Tuebingen: 1957. Antioch Review. 18:2 (Summer 1958), 146-158.

5637 Wuliger, Robert. West German Universities. New Republic. 166:3 (15 January 1972), 28, 32, 34.

5638 Zook, George F. German Universities. Institute of International Education News Bulletin. 22:5 (February 1947), 4-7.

N.3.2. University Reform

5639 Bodenman, Paul S. Academic Reforms in Selected Universities of the Federal Republic of Germany. Ph.D. Thesis, University of Maryland, 1973, 329 P.

5640 Bretton, Henry L. Reforming a German University. Journal of Education. 129:6 (September 1946), 198-200.

5641 Brezinka, Wolfgang. German Universities--Crisis and Reform. Educational Record. 49:4 (Fall 1968), 419-428.

5642 Council of Europe, Council for Cultural Co-Operation. Higher Education in the Federal Republic of Germany: Problems and Trends. Reform and Expansion of Higher Education in Europe: National Reports, 1962-1967. Strasbourg: Council of Europe, Council for Cultural Co-Operation, 1967, Pp. 63-100.

5643 Hahn, Walter F. Departure From Tradition in West German Universities. Educational Record. 55:3 (Summer 1972), 250-255.

5644 Hahn, Walter F. Higher Education in West Germany: Reform Movements and Trends. Comparative Education Review. 7:1 (June 1963), 51-60.

5645 Halting Movements Towards University Reform. Minerva. 7:3 (Spring 1969), 527-533.

5646 Havighurst, Robert J. German Proposals for University Reform. School and Society. 69:1801 (June 1949), 441-443.

5647 Heald, David. Reform and Tradition in German Universities Today. Universities Quarterly. 21:4 (September 1967), 453-461.

5648 Heald, David. The Transformation of the German Universities. Universities Quarterly. 23:4 (Autumn 1969), 408-419.

5649 Kloss, G. University Reform in West Germany: The Burden of Tradition. Minerva. 6:3 (Spring 1968), 323-353. Includes Extensive Bibliography.

5650 Kress, Guenther Gerhard. German Universities in Transition: The Innovative Capabilities of University Authorities of Bavaria and Hesse. Ph.D. Thesis, University of California, Davis, 1972, 253 P.

5651 Krueger, Marlis. Wallisch-Prinz, Baerbel. University Reform in West Germany. Comparative Education Review. 16:2 (June 1972), 340-351.

5652 Mason, Henry L. Reflections on a Politicized University: The Academic Crisis in the Federal Republic of Germany. Aaup Bulletin. 60:3 (September 1974), 299-312. Response By Charles R. Foster, 61:2 (August 1975), 221-223.

5653 The Reform of Courses of Study in West German Universities. Minerva. 8:2 (April 1970), 250-267.

5654 Teichler, Ulrich. University Reform and Skeleton Legislation on Higher Education in the Federal Republic of Germany. Western European Education. 4:3 (Fall 1972), 224-238; and 5:4 (Winter 1973-74), 34-55.

5655 UK, CCG, University Commission. UK, Foreign Office. University Reform in Germany: Report By a German Commission. London: H.M. Stationery Office, 1949, 67 P.

5656 Van De Graaff, John H. The Politics of German University Reform, 1810-1970. Ph.D. Thesis, Columbia University, 1973, 408 P.

N.3.3. Teaching and Administrative Personnel

5657 Busch, Alexander. The Vicissitudes of the Privatdozent: Breakdown and Adaptation in the Recruitment of the German University Teacher. Minerva. 1:3 (Spring 1963), 319-341.

5658 Ferber, Christian Von. The Social Background of German University and College Professors Since 1864. Transactions of the Third World Congress of Sociology. London: International Sociological Association, 1956, Vol. 3, Pp. 239-244.

5659 Fitzpatrick, Edward A. His Magnificence: The Rector of the German University. School and Society. 75:1943 (March 1952), 161-164.

5660 Kloeckner, Alfred J. Teaching Assistant in Germany. Institute of International Education News Bulletin. 31:5 (February 1956), 34-36.

5661 Loewenstein, Karl. American Scholars and German Universities. Institute of International Education News Bulletin. 22:7 (April 1947), 5-8.

5662 Thieme, Werner. Controversy in Public Administration--The University President in Germany. Midwest Review of Public Administration. 3:2 (August 1969), 153-156.

N.3.4. University Students

5663 Anderson, C. Arnold. The Social Status of University Students in Relation to Type of Economy: An International Comparison. Transactions of the Third World Congress of Sociology. London: International Sociological Association, 1956, Vol. 5, Pp. 51-63.

5664 Daniel, Vera. German Snapshots. Contemporary Review. 172:983 (November 1947), 277-280. Problems of German Students.

5665 Frykholm, Yngve. The Situation of German Students. Christian Education. 29:5 (September 1946), 335-339.

5666 Lewis, Flora. German Youth Duels With

the Past. New York Times Magazine. (17 June 1962), 31+. Revival of Student Tradition of Ritual Saber Fights.

5667 Olsen, Arthur J. The Dueling Scar Reappears in Germany. New York Times Magazine. (18 August 1957), 12+.

5668 Schmidt, George P. The University Student in Germany. Journal of Higher Education. 24:2 (February 1953), 64-69.

5669 Tauber, Kurt P. Nationalism and Social Restoration: Fraternities in Postwar Germany. Political Science Quarterly. 78:1 (March 1963), 66-85.

N.3.5. Student Protest

5670 Adel-Czlowiekowski, Ignatius J. The European Student Revolt. Dalhousie Review. 49:3 (Autumn 1969), 305-318.

5671 Allerbeck, Klaus R. Structural Conditions of Student Movements: The Student Community and the Student Role. Transactions of the Seventh World Congress of Sociology. Sofia: International Sociological Association, 1972, Vol. 3, Pp. 157-168.

5672 Blumenfeld, Erik. Student Unrest and the Future of Europe. German Tribune Quarterly Review. No. 4 (21 December 1968), 1-4.

5673 Deepening Radicalism: The Aftermath of the Shah's Visit and the Death of Benno Ohnesorg. Minerva. 6:2 (Winter 1968), 283-287.

5674 Dovifat, Emil. From Gandhi to Marcuse: The Degeneration of Demonstrations to the Use of Force. German Tribune Quarterly Review. No. 6 (24 June 1969), 13-16.

5675 Fest, Joachim. The Romantic Counter-Revolution of Our Time. Encounter. 36:6 (June 1971), 58-61.

5676 Flerlage, Ellen P. Organizational Dynamics of the Berlin New Left. Ph.D. Thesis, University of Illinois at Urbana-Champaign, 1971, 501 P.

5677 Friedeburg, Ludwig Von. Youth and Politics in the Federal Republic of Germany. Youth & Society. 1:1 (September 1969), 91-109.

5678 Friedlander, Albert H. The Student Revolt: Berlin--1968. Midstream. 14:6 (June-July 1968), 32-40.

5679 Geck, Wilhelm Karl. Student Power in West Germany. American Journal of Comparative Law. 17:3 (1969), 337-358.

5680 German, Daniel Bernard. Student Political Orientations Toward Legitimacy, Efficacy, and Dissent/Opposition in the United States, England, Sweden, and West Germany. Ph.D. Thesis, Georgetown University, 1970, 291 P.

5681 German Information Center. Germany's Student Revolt. School and Society. 96:2310 (October 1968), 373-376.

5682 Goldschmidt, Dietrich. Psychological Stress: A German Case Study. Student Power. Ed. Julian Nagel. London: Merlin, 1969, Pp. 59-72.

5683 Habermas, Juergen. Toward a Rational Society: Student Protest, Science, and Politics. Boston: Beacon, 1970, 132 P., Esp. Pp. 1-49.

5684 Heer, Friedrich. Challenge of Youth. University: University of Alabama Press, 1974.

5685 Heigert, Hans. Germany's Restive Students. Interplay. 3:7 (March 1970), 35-41.

5686 Hermann, Kai. End of the Revolt?. Encounter. 31:3 (September 1968), 57-60.

5687 Hermann, Kai. Germany's Young Left. Encounter. 30:4 (April 1968), 67-72.

5688 Hollander, Arie N. J. Den. Contagious Conflict: The Impact of American Dissent on European Life. Leiden: E. J. Brill, 1973, Iv and 263 P.

5689 Hunnius, F. C. The New Left in West Germany. Our Generation Against Nuclear War. 6:1-2 (May-July 1968), 29-65.

5690 Hunnius, F. C. Student Revolts: The New Left in West Germany. London: Housmans, War Resisters' International Publication, 1968, 40 P.

5691 Hurwitz, Harold. Germany Today: Student Revolt. Survey. No. 67 (April 1968), 90-99.

5692 Hurwitz, Harold. Germany's New Left Revolt. New Leader. 51:10 (6 May 1968), 9-12.

5693 Hurwitz, Harold. Notes on Germany's Ambivalent Student Revolt. Party Systems, Party Organizations, and the Politics of New Masses. Ed. Otto Stammer. Berlin: Institut Fuer Politische Wissenschaft an Der Freien Universitaet Berlin, 1968, Pp. 451-477.

5694 Irreconcilables and Fumbling Reformers. Minerva. 7:1-2 (Autumn-Winter 1968-69), 153-176. University Revolt and Reform.

5695 Karl, Willibald. Students and the Youth Movement in Germany: Attempt at a Structural Comparison. Journal of Contemporary History. 5:1 (1970), 113-127.

5696 Klein, Richard D. A Comparative Study of Student Political Activism: The Free University of Berlin, the London School of Economics, the University of Paris at Nanterre. Ph.D. Thesis, Columbia University, 1970, 282 P.

5697 The Krippendorff Case. Minerva. 6:2 (Winter 1968), 274-281.

5698 Lasky, Melvin J. Ulrike & Andreas. New York Times Magazine. (11 May 1975), 14+. Baader-Meinhof Group as Radical Subculture.

5699 Lindemann, Helmut. The Dilemma of Liberal Fathers. German Tribune Quarterly Review. No. 3 (5 October 1968), 13-16.

5700 Luchsinger, Fred. Violence and the German Intellectuals. Swiss Review of World Affairs. 22:4 (July 1972), 18-19.

5701 Mayntz, Renate. Germany: Radicals and Reformers. Public Interest. No. 13 (Fall 1968), 160-172.

5702 Mehnert, Klaus. The Weather Makers. The Intellectual in Politics. Ed. H. Malcolm Macdonald. Austin: University of Texas Press, 1966, Pp. 90-102.

5703 Merritt, Richard L. The Student Protest Movement in West Berlin. Comparative Politics. 1:4 (July 1969), 516-533.

5704 Nellessen, Bernd. The Corpse of the Free University. Encounter. 32:4 (April 1969), 61-64.

5705 The New Left in the United States of America, Britain, the Federal Republic of Germany. The Hague: International Documentation and Information Centre, C.1972, 81 P. Interdoc Conference.

5706 Ortlieb, Heinz-Dietrich. Student Revolt--A Hope for Social Policy in the Future?. German Tribune Quarterly Review. No. 4 (21 December 1968), 4-8.

5707 Pinner, Frank A. Tradition and Transgression: Western European Students in The Postwar World. Daedalus. 97:1 (Winter 1968), 137-155.

5708 Relentless Revolutionaries: Reluctant Reformers. Minerva. 6:4 (Summer 1968), 690-736.

5709 Scheuch, Erwin K. The Liberation From Right Reason. Encounter. 32:4 (April 1969), 56-61. Student Protest Movement.

5710 Shabecoff, Philip. The Followers of Red Rudi Shake Up Germany. New York Times Magazine. (28 April 1968), 26+.

5711 Shell, Kurt L. The American Impact on the German New Left. Contagious Conflict: The Impact of American Dissent on European Life. Ed. A. N. J. Den Hollander. Leiden: E. J. Brill, 1973, Pp. 30-49.

5712 Shell, Kurt L. Extraparliamentary Opposition in Postwar Germany. Comparative Politics. 2:4 (July 1970), 653-680.

5713 Shell, Kurt L. Students and Politics in Germany. Party Systems, Party Organizations, and the Politics of New Masses. Ed. Otto Stammer. Berlin: Institut Fuer Politische Wissenschaft an Der Freien Universitaet Berlin, 1968, Pp. 478-483.

5714 Skirmishes: Student Protest at the Free University of Berlin. Minerva. 6:2(Winter 1968), 281-283.

5715 Sontheimer, Kurt. Anti-Democratic Tendencies in Contemporary German Thought. Political Quarterly. 40:3 (July-September 1969), 268-282.

5716 Sontheimer, Kurt. Student Opposition in Western Germany. Government and Opposition. 3:1 (Winter 1968), 49-67.

5717 Spender, Stephen. The Year of the Young Rebels. New York: Random House, 1969, 186 P., Esp. Pp. 81-95.

5718 A Steady State of Disorder: The Sds at Work. Minerva. 7:3 (Spring 1969), 533-542.

5719 Students as an Anti-Parliamentary Opposition. Minerva. 6:3 (Spring 1968), 448-457.

5720 Weller, Eva. Will, Wilfried Van Der. Protest in Western Germany. Student Power. Ed. Julian Nagel. London: Merlin, 1969, Pp. 45-58.

5721 Wieser, Theodor. German Students Between Protest and Power Struggle. Swiss Review of World Affairs. 17:12 (March 1968), 4-6.

5722 Winegarten, Renee. The Middle East Conflict and the European Left. Midstream. 13:7 (August-September 1967), 21-26.

5723 Wolff, Karl-Dietrich. Reichling, Heidi. West Germany. Students in Revolt. Ed. Janet Harris. New York: Mcgraw Hill, 1970, 43-60.

N.3.6. Educational and Cultural Exchange

5724 Aich, Prodosh. The Problems of Coloured Students in Germany. Social Sciences Information. 1:4 (December 1962), 37-49.

5725 Aich, Prodosh. Asian and African Students in West German Universities. Minerva. 1:4 (Summer 1963), 439-452.

5726 Barker, Ernest. G.E.R.--A Society for Promoting Anglo-German Educational Relations. Institute of International Education News Bulletin. 25:8 (May 1950), 3-5.

5727 Bateman, Kenneth E. A Casebook Recording the Cooperative Effort of Educators of Germany and the United States in Establishing an Experimental School in Hessen, Germany. Ed.D. Thesis, Wayne State University, 1962, 750 P.

5728 Bell, Frank E. German Students in Cambridge. Fortnightly. 165:986 (February 1949), 103-109.

5729 Clarke, Eric T. Colleges' and Military Government's Program for Cultural Exchange. Association of American Colleges Bulletin. 35:1 (March 1949), 82-87.

5730 Etzkorn, Peter K. Wolff, Kurt H. Hans Vogel: The Case Study of a German Farmer on a Visit to the United States. Columbus: Ohio State University, Department of Sociology and Anthropology, 1954, 31 P.

5731 Grubel, Herbert G. Mcalpin, Michelle Burge. Austrian, German and Swiss Economists in the United States. Kyklos. 21:2 (1968), 299-312.

5732 Gruen, Walter. Attitudes of German Exchange Students During a Year in the United States. Public Opinion Quarterly. 23:1 (Spring 1959), 43-54.

5733 Hall, Robert D. Army Schools Make Friends in Germany. Social Education. 20:3 (March 1956), 123-124.

5734 Institute for Research in Human Relations. Change of Attitudes in German Exchangees. Philadelphia: Institute for Research in Human Relations, 1950.

5735 International Public Opinion Research, Inc. Cooperative Action Terms: A Study of Effectiveness. New York: International Public Opinion Research, Inc., 1954. US-FRG Exchange of Persons Program.

5736 International Research Associates. A Follow-Up Study of German Teenager Exchangees. New York: International Research Associates, 1954, Various Pagings.

5737 International Research Associates. German Exchangees: A Study in Attitude Change. New York: International Research Associates, 1953, Various Pagings.

5738 Kline, James D. German Exchanges, Before and After Fulbright. Institute of International Education News Bulletin. 28:5 (February 1953), 23-27.

5739 Lippitt, Ronald. Watson, Jeanne. Some Special Problems of Learning and Teaching Process in Cross-Cultural Education. International Social Science Bulletin. 7:1 (1955), 59-65.

5740 Martin, Robert Lee, Jr. An Investigation of Selected Student Variables and Their Associations in Participants of Summer Study Abroad Programs in Germany. Ed.D. Thesis, University of Georgia, 1971, 175 P.

5741 Mischel, Walter. German Exchange Students at Ohio State University: An Analysis of Responses to an Incomplete Sentences Test. Columbus: Ohio State University, Department of Sociology and Anthropology, 1957, 54 P.

5742 Muehlenberg, Friedrich. Foreign Students in Germany. Interecomomics. No. 12 (December 1967), 324-328.

5743 Pabsch, Wiegand. Foreign Student Exchanges: Germany. Governmental Policy and International Education. Ed. Stewart Fraser. New York: Wiley, 1965, Pp. 251-267.

5744 Pfeffer, Karl Heinz. Foreign Training for Pakistanis: A Study of Pakistanis Returned From Training in Germany. Lahore: University of the Panjab, Social Sciences Research Centre, 1961, 64 P.

5745 Pilgert, Henry P. Forstmeier, Friedrich. The Exchange of Persons Program in Western Germany. Bad Godesberg-Mehlem: Office of the U.S. High Commissioner for Germany, Historical Division, 1951, 89 P.

5746 Preparation for Tomorrow: A German Boy's Year in America. Washington: State Department, Office of Public Affairs, Publication 4138, 1951, 53 P. Photographs From the Lantz Family Album.

5747 Rust, Val Dean. German Interest in Foreign Education Since World War I. Ann Arbor: University of Michigan, School of Education, 1965, 251 P., Esp. Pp. 135-220.

5748 Rust, Val Dean. German Interest in Foreign Education Since World War I. Ph.D. Thesis, University of Michigan, 1967, 258 P.

5749 Schneider, Dieter. The Daad: Its History and Its Tasks. Bonn: Deutsche Akademische Austauschdienst, 1962, 27 P.

5750 Snyder, Harold E. Educational and Cultural Relations With the Occupied Countries. Association of American Colleges Bulletin. 35:1 (March 1949), 74-81.

5751 Snyder, Harold E., Editor. Austin, Margretta S., Editor. Cultural Relations with Occupied Countries. Washington: American Council on Education, 1951, 107 P.

5752 Snyder, Harold E., Editor. Beauchamp, George E., Editor. An Experiment in International Cultural Relations. Washington: American Council on Education, 1951, 112 P.

5753 US, Hicog, Land Commission for Bavaria. Ambassadors in Overalls: Letters From German Farm Youth in The United States Under the Department of State's Cultural Exchange Program. Munich: Hicog, Office of Land Commissioner for Bavaria, 1951, 22 P.

5754 US, Hicog, Office of Public Affairs. Exchanges Reorientation Program, Fiscal Year 1951. N.P.: Hicog, Office of Public Affairs, 1950, 2 Vols.

5755 US, Omgus, Civil Administration Division. The Governmental Affairs Cultural Exchange Program. Berlin: Omgus, Civil Administration Division, 1949, 73 P. for Period 1 July 1948 to 30 June 1949.

5756 US, Omgus, Interdivisional Reorientation Committee. Cultural Exchange Program. N.P.: Omgus, Interdivisional Reorientation Committee, February 1949, 80 P.

5757 Van Riper, Paul P. The Cultural Exchange Program. Annals of the American Academy of Political and Social Science. 267 (January 1950), 98-105.

5758 Watson, Jeanne. Lippitt, Ronald. Cross-Culture Learning. Institute of International Education News Bulletin. 30:9 (June 1955), 2-5, 19.

5759 Watson, Jeanne. Lippitt, Ronald. Learning Across Cultures: A Study of Germans Visiting America. Ann Arbor: Institute for Social Research, 1955, 205 P.

5760 Wells, Herman B. Cultural Exchange With Germany. Institute of International Education News Bulletin. 23:7 (May 1948), 3-6.

5761 Wolff, Kurt H. Etzkorn, Peter K. Hans Vogel: The Case Study of a German Farmer on a Visit to the United States. Columbus: Ohio State University, Department of Sociology and Anthropology, 1954, 31 P. Appendix: A Visit to Hans Vogel's Hometown, July 1957, 9 P.

N.4. FRG: University Programs and Research

N.4.1. Humanities, Area Studies, Education

5762 Anderson, Eugene N. The Humanities in German and Austrian Universities. Washington: American Council of Learned Societies, 1950, 101 P.

5763 Anweiler, Oskar. The Study of Soviet and East European Education in West Germany. Comparative Education Review. 9:3 (October 1965), 341-345.

5764 Barnstorff, Hermann. A New German Educational Journal. School and Society. 70:1809 (Ausust 1949), 121-122.

5765 Fetscher, Iring. Germany: Marxismus-Studien. Revisionism: Essays on the History of Marxist Ideas. Ed. Leopold Labedz. New York: Praeger, 1962, Pp. 337-350.

5766 Fetscher, Iring. Marxismusstudien: Rediscovery of a Native Son. Survey. No. 33 (July-September 1960), 84-92.

5767 Foshay, Arthur W. The Use of Empirical Methods in Comparative Education: A Pilot Study to Extend the Scope. International Review of Education. 9:3 (1963-64), 257-267.

5768 George, D. E. R. The American Study Center in Germany. Comparative Education Review. 13:1 (February 1969), 104-118.

5769 Grossmann, Bernhard. China Research in Germany. Aussenpolitik. 23:2 (1972), 225-233.

5770 Hacker, Jens. Soviet Studies in Western Europe: Germany. Survey. No. 50 (January 1964), 107-118.

5771 Hammerschmidt, Ernst. Ethiopian Studies at German Universities. Wiesbaden: Steiner, 1970, 75 P.

5772 Hilker, Franz. Comparative Education in the Documentation and Information Center in Bonn. Comparative Education Review. 3:3 (February 1960), 13-15.

5773 Huber, Ludwig. Research-Oriented Study. Western European Education. 3:3-4 (Summer-Fall 1971), 230-236.

5774 Kursanov, G. Institute of Marxist Studies (Frankfurt-Am-Main, FRG). World Marxist Review. 13:8 (August 1970), 35-38.

5775 Meier, P. J. The Work of the Hamburg Research Center in Entrepreneurial History. Journal of Economic History. 21:3 (September 1961), 364-371.

5776 Offenberg, Maria. Promise for a Better Future. Survey. 84:11 (November 1948), 338-339. Director's Account of Life in School of Social Work, Aachen.

5777 Robinsohn, Saul B. The Newly Founded Institute for Educational Research Within The Max-Planck-Gesellschaft. Comparative Education. 2:1 (November 1965), 31-36.

5778 Schairer, Reinhold. The German Institute of Talent Study in Cologne. Year Book of Education, 1962: The Gifted Child. New York: Harcourt, Brace & World, 1962, Pp. 271-274.

5779 Schultze, Walter. Educational Research in the Federal Republic of Germany. School Review. 66:3 (Autumn 1958), 298-312.

5780 Steger, Hanns-Albert. Schrader, Achim. Graebener, Juergen. Research on Latin America in the Federal Republic of Germany and West Berlin. Latin American Research Review. 2:3 (Summer 1967), 99-118.

N.4.2. Law

5781 Dahrendorf, Ralf. The Education of an Elite: Law Faculties and the German Upper Class. Transactions of the Fifth World Congress of Sociology. Louvain: International Sociological Association, 1962, Vol. 3, Pp. 259-274.

5782 Kronstein, Heinrich. Reflections on the Case Method--in Teaching Civil Law. Journal of Legal Education. 3:2 (Winter 1950), 265-272.

5783 Rheinstein, Max. The German Referendar Training Program at the University of Chicago Law School. Journal of Legal Education. 3:2 (Winter 1950), 273-281.

5784 Riegert, Robert A. The Max-Planck-Institute for Foreign and International Criminal Law. American Journal of Comparative Law. 16:1-2 (1968), 247-257.

5785 Riegert, Robert A. The Max Planck Institute for Foreign Public Law and International Law. International Lawyer. 3:3 (April 1969), 506-524.

5786 Riegert, Robert A. The Max Planck Institute for Foreign and International Patent, Copyright, and Unfair Competition Law. International Lawyer. 3:4 (July 1969), 797-809.

5787 Shartel, Burke. Report on German Legal Education. Journal of Legal Education. 14:4 (1962), 425-483.

5788 Wengler, Wilhelm. Law Studies in Western Germany. Journal of Legal Education. 18:2 (1966), 176-183.

N.4.3. Social Sciences

5789 Adorno, Theodor W. Contemporary German Sociology. Transactions of the Fourth World Congress of Sociology. London: International Sociological Association, 1959, Vol. 1, Pp. 33-56.

5790 Beyme, Klaus Von. Bibliographical Essay on the State of Research in Political Science in the Federal Republic of Germany. German Political Studies, Vol. 1. Ed. Klaus Von Beyme. Beverly Hills: Sage Publications, 1974, Pp. 253-284.

5791 Bondy, Curt. Social Psychology in Western Germany. Washington: Library of Congress, 1956, 84 P.

5792 Conradt, David P. The Development of Empirical Political Science Research in West Germany. Comparative Political Studies. 6:3 (October 1973), 380-391.

5793 Czempiel, Ernst-Otto. Research and Teaching Programmes on International Organization and European Integration in the Federal Republic of Germany. Journal of Common Market Studies. 3:2 (February 1965), 169-179.

5794 Frankfurt Institute for Social Research. Aspects of Sociology. Boston: Beacon, 1972, 210 P.

5795 Glaser, Kurt. Report on the Anthropological-Sociological Conference at the University of Mainz. American Sociological Review. 14:6 (December 1949), 801-802.

5796 Goldschmidt, Dietrich. Jenne, Michael. Educational Sociology in the Federal Republic of Germany. Social Science Information. 8:4 (August 1969), 19-29.

5797 Gurland, Arcadius Rudolph Lang. Political Science in Western Germany: Thoughts and Writings 1950-1952. Washington: Library of Congress, Reference Department, European Affairs Division, 1952, 118 P.

5798 Hartenstein, Wolfgang. Liepelt, Klaus. Archives for Ecological Research in West Germany. Quantitative Ecological Analysis in the Social Sciences. Ed. Mattei Dogan and Stein Rokkan. Cambridge: M.I.T. Press, 1969, Pp. 555-566.

5799 Heidenheimer, Arnold J. Nixdorff, Peter W. "Import" Interest in American and German Political Science as Reflected in Library Holdings. Journal of Politics. 29:1 (February 1967), 167-173.

5800 Heinze, A. Higher Education as a Subject of Sociological Research. Education in Europe. Ed. M. A. Matthijssen and C. E. Vervoort. The Hague: Mouton, 1969, Pp. 269-278.

5801 Hirsch, Joachim. Scientific-Technical Progress and the Political System. German Political Studies, Vol. 1. Ed. Klaus Von Beyme. Beverly Hills: Sage Publications, 1974, Pp. 107-139.

5802 Horkheimer, Max. Survey of the Social Sciences in Western Germany. Washington: Library of Congress, Reference Department, European Affairs Division, 1952, 225 P., 350 Items.

5803 Horn, Klaus. Approaches to Social Psychology Relevant to Peace Research as Developed in the FRG. Journal of Peace Research. 10:3 (1973), 305-315.

5804 Jay, Martin. The Dialectical Imagination: A History of the Frankfurt School and the Institute of Social Research, 1923-1950. Boston: Little, Brown, 1973, 382 P., Esp. Pp. 219-299.

5805 Klima, Rolf. Theoretical Pluralism, Methodological Dissension and the Role of the Sociologist: The West German Case. Social Science Information. 11:3-4 (June-August 1972), 69-108.

5806 Koenig, Rene. Report on Some Experiences in Social Research Techniques in Switzerland and Germany. Transactions of the Second World Congress of Sociology. London: International Sociological Association, 1954, Vol. 1, Pp. 58-73.

5807 Meyer, Ernst W. Political Science and Economics in Western Germany: A Postwar Survey. Washington: Library of Congress, European Affairs Division, 1950, 23 P.

5808 Muehlmann, W. E. Sociology in Germany: Shift in Alignment. Modern Sociological Theory in Continuity and Change. Ed. Howard Becker and Alvin Boskoff. New York: Dryden, 1957, Pp. 658-694.

5809 Murphy, John George. The Culture of Cities as a Type: A Comparative Analysis of Type Construction in the German and Chicago Schools of Urban Sociology. Ph.D. Thesis, Fordham University, 1973, 421 P.

5810 Pfotenhauer, David. Conceptions of Political Science in West Germany and the United States, 1960-1969. Journal of Politics. 34:2 (May 1972), 554-591.

5811 Robson, Charles B. Arensberg, C. M. The Present Position of Social Sciences in Germany. International Social Science Bulletin. 3:1 (1951), 101-105.

5812 Rothschild, K. W. The Old and the New: Some Recent Trends in the Literature of German Economics. American Economic Review. 54:2 (March 1964), 1-33.

5813 Roucek, Joseph S. The American and the German Sociologist. Indian Journal of Social Research. 3:1 (January 1962), 150-158.

5814 Roucek, Joseph S. The American and the German Sociologist: a Study in Comparative Sociology. Kansas Journal of Sociology. 2:4 (Fall 1966), 118-126. Comment By Bartholomew Landheer,

Pp. 127-128.

5815 Rueschemeyer, Dietrich. Sociology of Law in Germany. Law & Society Review. 5:2 (November 1970), 225-237.

5816 Schmidt, Gert. The Industrial Enterprise, History and Society: The Dilemma of German "Industrie-Und Betriebssoziologie". Social Science Information. 8:6 (December 1969), 117-133.

5817 Schmoelders, Guenter. Socio-Economic Behavior Research. German Economic Review. 1:1 (1963), 6-16.

5818 Schnitzer, Ewald W. German Geopolitics Revived: A Survey of Geopolitical Writing in Germany Today. Santa Monica: Rand Corporation, RM-1210, 1954, 97 P.

5819 Schnitzer, Ewald W. German Geopolitics Revived. Journal of Politics. 17:3 (August 1955), 407-423.

5820 Senghaas, Dieter, Editor. Peace Research in the Federal Republic of Germany. Journal of Peace Research (Special Issue). 10:3 (1973), 159-315.

5821 Sheehan, James J. Quantification in the Study of Modern German Social and Political History. The Dimensions of the Past: Materials, Problems, and Opportunities for Quantitative Work in History. Ed. Val R. Lorwin and Jacob M. Price. New Haven: Yale University Press, 1972, Pp. 301-331.

5822 Silberman, L. Some Recent Social Investigations in Germany. British Journal of Sociology. 5:2 (June 1954), 163-167. Review Article.

5823 Sodhi, Kripal S. Research on Racial Relations: Federal Republic of Germany. International Social Science Bulletin. 10:3 (1958), 387-403.

5824 Stehr, Nikolaus. Evaluations of the Consequences of Science and Technology By the German Public: A Study in the Sociology of Science. Ph.D. Thesis, University of Oregon, 1970, 147 P.

5825 Stendenbach, Franz Josef. Sociology in Germany Since 1945. Social Sciences Information. 3:3 (September 1964), 7-51.

5826 Sternberger, Dolf. Research in Germany on Pressing Social Problems: A Social Science Survey of German Social Issues. Washington: Library of Congress, Reference Department, European Affairs Division, 1951, 31 P.

5827 Voigt, Fritz A. The Organization of Research in the Social Sciences: The Federal Republic of Germany. Social Sciences Information. 2:1 (January 1963), 35-55; and 2:2 (July 1963), 113-126.

5828 Westphal-Hellbusch, Sigrid. The Present Situation of Ethnological Research in Germany. American Anthropologist. 61:5 (October 1959), 848-865.

5829 Wiese, Leopold Von. The Place of Social Science in Germany Today. American Journal of Sociology. 57:1 (July 1951), 1-6.

N.4.4. Sciences and Technical Education

5830 Agricultural and Home Economics Evaluation & Info. Service. Agricultural Science in Germany: A Guide. Bad Godesberg: Land- Und Hauswirtschaftlicher Auswertungs- Und Informationsdienst, 1962, 174 P.

5831 Agricultural and Home Economics Evaluation & Info. Service. Studying Agriculture, Horticulture, and Forestry in the Universities of the Federal Republic of Germany: A Guide. Bad Godesberg: Land- Und Hauswirtschaftlicher Auswertungs- Und Informationsdienst, 1959, 69 P.

5832 Audrieth, Ludwig F. Chinn, Herman I. The Organization of Science in Germany. Washington: National Science Foundation, Office of International Science Activities, 1963, 121 P. Natural Sciences and Technology.

5833 Bierfelder, W. H. The Pool of Talent and Recruitment for Management in the German Federal Republic. Year Book of Education, 1962: The Gifted Child. New York: Harcourt, Brace & World, 1962, Pp. 458-471.

5834 Boeckenheuer, Jessie M. A Report of American Visiting Consultant in Home Economics. Bad Godesberg: Hicog, 1952, 43 P.

5835 FRG, Federal Ministry for Food, Agriculture and Forestry. Catalogue of Technical Schools, Colleges and Other Educational Institutes for Agriculture, Wine Growing, Horticulture, and Forestry. Bad Godesberg: Bundesministerium Fuer Ernaehrung, Landwirtschaft Und Forsten, 1959, 184 P.

5836 Fassbender, Siegfried. in-Career Training in Management Education. Management Education. Ed. Baron Carl Henrik Von Platen. Paris: Organisation for Economic Cooperation and Development, 1972, Pp. 41-50.

5837 German Academic Exchange Service. Study of Medicine, Dentistry, Veterinary Science in Germany. Bonn: Madel, for Deutsche Akademische Austauschdienst, 1962, 33 P.

5838 German Academic Exchange Service. Technical Studies and Technical Training in Germany. Bonn: Madel, for Deutsche Akademische Austauschdienst, 1961, 42 P.

5839 Krause, Erwin. The Training of Technicians and Engineers in the Federal Republic of Germany. International Labour Review. 89:2 (February 1964), 156-165.

5840 Schiffgen, Werner. Training of Cooperative Experts for Developing Countries. Review of International Cooperation. 62:4 (1969), 186-191.

5841 Schmitt-Ott, Dietrich, Editor. Physics and Chemical Sciences in Western Germany: A Symposium on Current Research. Washington: Library of Congress, European Affairs Division, 1954, 123 P.

5842 Schmitz-Esser, Winfried, Editor. Gareis, Herbert, Editor. German Science Re-Emerges. Bonn-Langsdorf: Heinz Moeller, 1967, 131 P.

5843 US, Omgus, Economics Division. Agricultural Education, Research, and Extension Institutions and Activities in Germany. N.P.: Omgus, Economics Division, Food and Agriculture Branch, Land and Institution Section, 1948.

5844 US, Omgus, Education and Cultural Relations Division. Statistical Report on Agricultural Education and Research Institutions, and the Rural Population in the U.S. Zone of Germany. N.P.: Omgus, July 1948.

5845 Ueberreiter, Kurt, Editor. The Natural Sciences in Western Germany: A Symposium on Current Research. Washington: Library of Congress, Reference Department, European Affairs Division, 1951, 127 P.

5846 Ueberreiter, Kurt. A Statistical Postwar Survey on the Natural Sciences and German Universities. Washington: Library of Congress, European Affairs Division, 1950, 31 P.

5847 Vossschmidt, Theo. Training of Cooperative Advisors for Developing Countries in the Federal Republic of Germany. Review of International Cooperation. 58:2 (March 1965), 72-74.

5848 Ware, George Whitaker. Summary Report on Agricultural Schools and Agricultural Research Institutions in Bavaria. Munich: Omg Bavaria, 1946, 18 P.

N.4.5. Research Organization, Archives, Libraries

5849 Ben-David, Joseph. The Universities and the Growth of Science in Germany and The United States. Minerva. 7:1-2 (Autumn-Winter 1968-69), 1-35.

5850 Born, Lester K. The Archives and Libraries of Postwar Germany. American Historical Review. 56:1 (October 1950), 34-57.

5851 Busse, Gisela Von. West German Library Developments Since 1945, With Special Emphasis on the Rebuilding of Research Libraries. Washington: Library of Congress, 1962, 82 P.

5852 Danton, J. Periam. Book Selection and Collections: A Comparison of German and American University Libraries. New York: Columbia University Press, 1963, 188 P.

5853 Forssmann, Werner. Experiments on Myself: Memoirs of a Surgeon in Germany. New York: St. Martin's Press, 1974, 352 P. Nobel Laureate Discusses Early Research, Service Under the Nazi Regime, and Reconstruction of Medical Establishment in Frg.

5854 FRG, German Research Association. German Research Association: Structure and Functions. Wiesbaden: Steiner, 1961, 96 P.

5855 FRG, Federal Ministry of Economics. Report on Research Activities in the Federal Republic of Germany. Bonn: Federal Ministry of Economics, 1952, 42 P.

5856 FRG, Federal Ministry for Scientific Research. State, Science and Economy as Partners. Berlin: Koska, 1967, 244 P.

5857 Geimer, Reinhold. Geimer, Hildegard. Science in the Federal Republic of Germany: Organization and Promotion. Born-Bad Godesberg: Deutscher Akademischer Austauschdienst, 3 Ed., 1974, 108 P.

5858 Heuser, Frederick W. J. German University and Technical Libraries: Their Organization, Condition, Activities and Needs. New York: Germanistic Society of America, 1951, 51 P.

5859 Jaspers, Karl. Re-Dedication of German Scholarship. American Scholar. 15:2 (April 1946), 180-188.

5860 Mommsen, Hans. Historical Scholarship in Transition: The Situation in the Federal Republic of Germany. Daedalus. 100:2 (Spring 1971), 485-508.

5861 Mueller-Wieland, Marcel. Educational Research in German-Speaking Countries: Austria, the German Federal Republic and German-Speaking Switzerland. Review of Educational Research. 27:1 (February 1957), 57-74.

5862 Salomon, Jean-Jacques. Ferne, Georges. Caty, Gilbert. Wald, Salomon. The Research System: Comparative Survey of the Organisation and Financing of Fundamental Research. Paris: Organisation for Economic Cooperation and Development, Vol. 1 (France, Germany, United Kingdom), June 1972, 258 P.

5863 Sandgreter, John. German Science Reemerges. Interplay. 3:4 (November 1969), 22-27.

5864 Science Policy and Organization of Research in the Federal Republic of Germany. Paris: Unesco, 1969, 95 P.

5865 Stevenson, Henry G. The Classified Catalogs of German University Libraries, in Theory and Practice, Between 1900 and 1970. Ph.D. Thesis, Indiana University, 1970, 208 P.

5866 Thompson, Lawrence S. The Effect of the War on German Research Libraries. German Quarterly. 21:2 (March 1948), 77-82.

5867 US, Hiccg, Commercial Attache Division. Scientific and Industrial Research and Technical Advance, Federal Republic of Germany and Western Berlin. Bonn: Hicog, Commercial Attache Division, Economic Reports Branch, Annual.

5868 US, Hicog, Office of Public Affairs. An Appraisal of the America Houses in Germany; a Program Guidance Study on Effectiveness of the U.S. Information Centers. Bonn: Hicog, Office of Public Affairs, Research Staff, 1955, 362 P.

5869 US, Omgus, Omg Bavaria, Monuments, Fine Arts & Archives Sec. Post-War Status of Chief Archival Institutions in Bavaria. N.P.: Omg Bavaria, Monuments, Fine Arts & Archives Section, 1948, 37 P.

5870 Welsch, Erwin K. Libraries and Archives in Germany. Pittsburgh: Council for European Studies, 1975, 275 Pp.

N.5. GDR: Education

N.5.1. General

5871 Arndt, Edward J. An Administrative History of the Educational System of the German Democratic Republic From 1945 to 1964. Ph.D. Thesis, American University, 1966, 352 P.

5872 Berndt, Siegfried. Training in the Karl Liebknecht Transformer Works, East Germany. World Year Book of Education, 1968: Education Within Industry. New York: Harcourt, Brace & World, 1968, Pp. 286-293.

5873 Bodenman, Paul S. The Educational System of East Germany. Washington: Office of Education Publ. No. 75-19116, Government Printing Office, 1975.

5874 Bodenman, Paul S. Education in the Soviet Zone of Germany. School Life. 41:3 (December 1958), 14-17.

5875 Bodenman, Paul S. Education in the Soviet Zone of Germany. Washington: Department of Health, Education and Welfare, office of Education, 1959, 162 P.

5876 Brickman, William W. Academic Adventures in East Germany. Educational Forum. 35:4 (May 1971), 461-469.

5877 Cerf, Jay H. Political Indoctrination and Control of Students in East Germany. Ph.D. Thesis, Yale University, 1958.

5878 Dorpalen, Andreas. The Unification of Germany in East German Perspective. American Historical Review. 73:4 (April 1968), 1069-1083. Marxist Interpretation of 1866.

5879 Education in the German Democratic Republic. Leipzig: Veb Edition, 1962, 182 P.

5880 Erickson, Harold B. An Analysis of Some Aspects of Secondary Education in East Germany. Ph.D. Thesis, University of California, Berkeley, 1954, 376 P.

5881 GDR. Education and Training in the German Democratic Republic. Berlin: Staatsverlag, 1966, 123 P.

5882 GDR, Council of Ministers, State Office for Voc. Training. Modern Vocational Training. Dresden: Zeit Im Bild, 1970, 48 P.

5883 GDR, Council of Ministers, State Office for Voc. Training. Vocational Training in the German Democratic Republic. Dresden: Verlag Zeit Im Bild, 1971, 63 P.

5884 GDR, German Central Pedagogical Institute. The System of Public Instruction in the German Democratic Republic. Berlin: German Central Pedagogical Institute on Behalf of Ministry of Education, C.1963, 15 P.

5885 GDR, German Institute for Occupational Training. Occupational Training in the German Democratic Republic. Berlin: German Institute for Occupational Training, 1961, 104 P.

5886 GDR, Ministry of Education. Act on the Integrated Socialist Educational System of the German Democratic Republic. Berlin (East): Staatsverlag Der Deutschen Demokratischen Republik, 1972, 77 P.

5887 Gehrig, Hans. The School System of the GDR. Swiss Review of World Affairs. 18:6 (September 1968), 11-12.

5888 German Democratic Republic: Education. Dresden: Verlag Zeit Im Bild, 1971, 60 P.

5889 Halsall, Thomas. Marxist Socialism and Art Education: A Descriptive Study of Art Education in Grades One Through Twelve in the German Democratic Republic. Ed.D Thesis, Columbia University, 1973, 208 P.

5890 Hanhardt, Arthur M., Jr. Political Socialization in the German Democratic Republic. Societas. 1:2 (Spring 1971), 101-121.

5891 Hofmann, Erich. The Changing School in East Germany. Comparative Education Review. 6:1 (June 1962), 48-57.

5892 Huebener, Theodore. History as Taught Through East German Textbooks. School and Society. 99:2330 (January 1971), 56-59.

5893 King, Edmund J. Communist Education. London: Methuen, 1963, 309 P.

5894 Kohn, Erwin. Postler, Fred. Polytechnical Training and Education in the German Democratic Republic. Dresden: Zeit Im Bild, for Ministry of Education, 1965, 58 P.

5895 Lightfoot, Claude. Education Against Racism in the GDR. Political Affairs. 51:2 (February 1972), 32-43.

5896 Lilge, Frederic. German Educational Reforms in Soviet Zone of Occupation. Harvard Educational Review. 18:1 (Winter 1948), 35-46.

5897 Lottich, Kenneth V. Extracurricular Indoctrination in East Germany. Comparative Education Review. 6:3 (February 1963), 209-211.

5898 Moehle, Horst. Educational Organization and Structure in the German Democratic Republic. World Year Book of Education, 1969: Examinations. New York: Harcourt, Brace & World, 1969, Pp. 146-151.

5899 Moore-Rinvolucri, Mina J. Education in East Germany. Newton Abbott: David & Charles; and Hamden, Conn.: Archon Books, 1973, 141 P.

5900 Postler, Fred. Polytechnical Instruction and Education in the German Democratic Republic. Berlin: Volk and Wissen, 1962, 111 P.

5901 Reischock, Wolfgang. Pioneers of Education. German Foreign Policy (GDR). 4:6 (1965), 422-429. Educational Reform in GDR.

5902 Schaul, Hans. Vorholzer, Jorg. The Socialist Education of the Working Class in the German Democratic Republic. World Marxist Review: Problems of Peace and Socialism. 4:5 (May 1961), 37-45.

5903 Schlesinger, G. Wills, S. Germany: The Russian Zone of Occupation. Year Book of Education, 1948. London: Evans Brothers, 1948, Pp. 548-553.

5904 Schmitt, Karl. Education and Politics in the German Democratic Republic. Comparative Education Review. 19:1 (February 1975), 31-50.

5905 Smart, K. F. Education in East Germany. Educational Forum. 25:4 (May 1961), 463-471.

5906 Stadler, K. R. "Volksbildung" in the Russian Zone of Germany. Adult Education. 20:2 (December 1947), 54-60.

5907 Starrels, John Murry. Political Learning in East Germany: The Primary School. Ph.D. Thesis, University of California, Santa Barbara, 1972.

5908 Suri, Surindar. Education in Eastern Germany. Contemporary Review. 192:1100 (August 1957), 96-98.

5909 US, Hicog. Sovietization of the Public School System in East Germany. N.P.: Hicog, 1951, 22 P.

5910 Wilke, Alfred. Industrial Training in the German Democratic Republic. World Year Book of Education, 1968: Education Within Industry. New York: Harcourt, Brace & World, 1968, Pp. 129-135.

5911 Williams, A. An Investigation of the Education System of the Ddr. German Life and Letters. 24:3 (April 1971), 262-271.

5912 Winterhager, J. W. The Challenge of Totalitarian Youth Training. Educational Forum. 21:4 (May 1957), 437-442.

N.5.2. Higher Education and Research

5913 Ajao, Aderogba. on the Tiger's Back. Cleveland: World, 1962, 149 P. Hungarian, Spent 1952-58 in GDR Communist Training School.

5914 Anthon, Carl G. The East German Universities. American-German Review. 20:4 (April-May 1954), 8-12+; and 20:5 (June-July 1954), 28-31.

5915 Bohring, Guenther, Editor. Taubert, Horst, Editor. Sociological Research in the German Democratic Republic. Berlin (East): Verlag Der Wissenschaften, for the Scientific Council for Sociological Research in the GDR, 1970, 129 P.

5916 Carsten, Francis L. History Under Ulbricht: Facts and Standards. Survey. No. 37 (July-September 1961), 90-98.

5917 Chatterjee, Subrata. An Indian Student in the German Democratic Republic. German Foreign Policy (GDR). 3:6 (1964), 434-438.

5918 GDR, State Secretariat for West German Questions. How Does the GDR Solve the Problem of Higher Education?. Dresden: Zeit Im Bild, C.1970, 84 P.

5919 Gagliardo, John. Archives in East Germany. American Archivist. 20:3

5920 Hannardt, Arthur M., Jr. The Deutsche Akademie Der Wissenschaften Zu Berlin and the Organization of Research in East Germany. Ph.D. Thesis, Northwestern University, 1963.

5921 Kruger, Horst. Indology in the German Democratic Republic. United Asia. 21:5 (September-October 1969), 282-287.

5922 Liljegren, S. B. A Visiting Professor in Eastern Germany. South Atlantic Quarterly. 58:1 (Winter 1959), 13-19.

5923 Ludz, Peter Christian. East Germany. Problems of Communism. 14:1 (January-February 1965), 66-70. Rediscovery of Social Sciences in Communist Germany.

5924 Moehle, Horst. Progressive Changes in the Content and Methods of Extramural Studies at the Karl Marx University, Leipzig. Convergence. 5:2 (1972), 37-42.

5925 Mork, Gordon R. Archives in the GDR: Opportunities and Problems. Newsletter on Comparative Studies of Communism. 6:1 (November 1972), 42-45.

5926 Mork, Gordon R. The Archives of the German Democratic Republic. Central European History. 2:3 (September 1969), 273-284.

5927 N. M. Some Student Problems in East German Universities. World Today. 13:11 (November 1957), 481-489.

5928 Petrashik, A. GDR Institute of Marxism-Leninism. World Marxist Review. 14:6 (June 1971), 76-81.

5929 Pryor, Frederic L. Koehler, Heinz. Doing Research on East Germany. Eastern European Economics. 3:2 (Winter 1964-65), 3-6.

5930 Reinhardt, Rudolf. The Universities in East Germany. Survey. No. 40 (January 1962), 68-76.

5931 Schaefer, Hans-Dieter. The Contribution of Higher Education to the Construction of The Developed Socialist Society in the GDR. Teaching Postwar Germany in America: Papers and Discussions. Ed. Louis F. Helbig and Eberhard Reichmann. Bloomington: Indiana Univeristy, Institute of German Studies, 1972.

5932 Silveston, Peter. A Visit to the University of Leipzig. Institute of International Education News Bulletin. 31:1 (October 1955), 25-29.

5933 Slamecka, Vladimir. Science in East Germany. New York: Columbia University Press, 1963, 124 P.

5934 Slamecka, Vladimir. The Semi-Centralized System of Technical Documentation and Information of the Czechoslovak Socialist Republic and East Germany. D.L.S. Thesis, Columbia University, 1962, 216 P.

5935 The University in East Germany. Confluence. 6:1 (Spring 1957), 58-67.

5936 Winter, K. Instruction and Education at the Medical Faculty (Charite) Of the Humboldt University, Berlin, in the Process of Changing. Education in Europe. Eds. M. A. Matthijssen and C. E. Vervoort. The Hague: Mouton, 1969, Pp. 247-253.

5937 Wirzberger, Professor. Socialist Education in the Light of Three University Reforms. United Asia. 21:5 (September-October 1969), 288-293.

5938 Woeltge, Herbert. Student in the German Democratic Republic. Dresden: Zeit Im Bild, C.1966, 112 P.

5939 Yerofeyev, T. Kiselyov, A. Rzheshevsky, O. GDR Scientists on the Economic Laws of Socialism. World Marxist Review. 13:2 (March 1970), 99-105.

5940 Young, Edgar P. Training Center for Scientists: The Dresden College of Technology. New World Review. 32:8 (September 1955), 34-36.

N.6. FRG-GDR: Comparative Education

5941 Hahn, Walter F. Education in East and West Germany--A Study of Similarities and Contrasts. Studies in Comparative Communism. 5:1 (Spring 1972), 47-116.

5942 Hanhardt, Arthur M., Jr. Political Socialization in Divided Germany. Journal of International Affairs. 27:2 (1973), 187-203.

5943 Hearnden, Arthur. Individual Freedom and State Intervention in East and West German Education. Comparative Education. 10:2 (June 1974), 131-135.

5944 Hearnden, Arthur. Inter-German Relations and Educational Policy. Comparative Education. 9:1 (March 1973), 3-16.

5945 Krug, Mark M. The Teaching of History at the Center of the Cold War--History Textbooks in East and West Germany. School Review. 69:4 (Winter 1961), 461-487.

5946 Lawson, Robert Frederic. Education as Change Agent and Change Object in the Two Germanies. Teaching Postwar Germany in America: Papers and Discussions. Ed. Louis F. Helbig and Eberhard Reichmann. Bloomington: Indiana Univeristy, Institute of German Studies, 1972.

5947 Merritt, Richard L. Perspectives on History in Divided Germany. Public Opinion and Historians: Interdisciplinary Perspectives. Ed. Melvin Small. Detroit: Wayne State University Press, 1970, Pp. 139-174.

N.7. FRG: Cultural Developments

N.7.1. General Culture and the Arts

5948 Beck, Earl Ray. Germany Rediscovers America. Tallahassee: Florida State University Press, 1968, 333 P., Esp. Pp. 225-279.

5949 Beer, R. R. Social Aspects of Local Authority Cultural Activity. Studies in Comparative Local Government. 3:1 (Summer 1969), 5-15.

5950 Birnbaum, Norman. Stirrings in West Germany. Commentary. 37:4 (April 1964), 53-58. Intellectual Life.

5951 Ernestus, Horst. Developing Public Library Services: A German Outlook. Toronto: University of Toronto, School of Library Science, 1969, 26 P.

5952 Frankel, Theodore. Letter From Munich. Yale Review. 48:4 (Summer 1959), 541-558.

5953 Grabowski, Z. A. Cultural Life in Western Germany. Contemporary Review. 195 (April 1959), 212-216.

5954 Gregor, Ulrich. The German Film in 1964: Stuck at Zero. Film Quarterly. 18:2 (Winter 1964), 7-21.

5955 Hafter, Rudolph P. A German Film and the Defense of the West. Swiss Review of World Affairs. 1:7 (October 1951), 17-18. "The Wives of Mr. S." Draws Parallels Between Occupation of Ancient Athens and Modern Germany.

5956 Helm, Everett. "and This From Wagner's Grandson!": WIELAND WAGNER. New York Times Magazine. (5 June 1966), 68+.

5957 Hirsch, Felix Edward. Changing Culture in Germany. Current History. 50:297 (May 1966), 289-294+.

5958 Joesten, Joachim. The German Film Industry, 1945-1948. Great Barrington, Mass.: Joachim Joesten, New Germany Reports No. 3, May 1948, 16 P.

5959 Joesten, Joachim. German Libraries in 1951. Great Barrington, Mass.: Joachim Joesten, New Germany Reports No. 16, September 1951, 17 P.

5960 Joll, James. Intellectuals and German Politics. Occidente. 10:1 (January-February 1954), 28-38.

5961 Kaufmann, Walter A. German Thought Today. Kenyon Review. 19:1 (Winter 1957), 15-30.

5962 Krauss, Paul G. Continuing Anglo-American Influence on German. American Speech. 41:1 (February 1966), 28-38.

5963 Marcuse, Ludwig. German Intellectuals Five Years After the War. Books Abroad. 24:4 (Autumn 1950), 346-351.

5964 Mcelheny, Victor K. West Germany Debates a "Cultural Crisis". Science. 147:3658 (5 February 1965), 589-591.

5965 Melchinger, Siegfried. The Opulent Culture: Does the "German System" Really Work?. Encounter. 22:4 (April 1964), 67-71.

5966 Muhlen, Norbert. The Return of Goebbel's Film-Makers. Commentary. 11:3 (March 1951), 245-250.

5967 Saal, Hubert. Who Ever Heard of a German Ballet Company?. New York Times Magazine. (18 July 1971), 10+.

5968 Schalluck, Paul, Editor. Germany: Cultural Developments Since 1945. Munich: Hueber, 1971, 216 P.

5969 Scheuch, Erwin K. Sport and Politics. German Tribune Quarterly Review. No. 20 (16 November 1972), 1-7.

5970 Sievers, W. David. The Subsidized Theatre of West Germany. Educational Theatre Journal. 12:1 (March 1960), 1-8.

5971 Sutton, Horace, Editor. Munich, the Olympics, and the German World. Saturday Review of the Arts. (25 March 1972), 39-82.

5972 Swiridoff, Paul. German Intellectual Life. Pfullingen: Neske, 1966, 192 P.

5973 UK, CCG, Information Services Division. Catalogue of Forbidden German Feature and Short Film Productions, Held in Zonal Film Archives. Hamburg: Control Commission for Germany (Be), Information Services Division, Film Section, C.1951, 161 P.

5974 US, Hicog, Office of Public Affairs. Educational and Cultural Activities in Germany Today. Frankfurt: Hicog, Office of Public Affairs, 1950, 93 P.

5975 Walbruck, H. A. German Culture. Germany: Comparative Culture and Government. Ed. William O. Westervelt. Skokie: National Textbook, 1970, Pp. 36-49.

5976 Werner, Alfred. The Miracle of Postwar German Art. Antioch Review. 17:3 (September 1957), 366-373.

5977 Wieser, Theodor. Sex Wave Over Germany. Swiss Review of World Affairs. 18:10 (January 1969), 10-11.

5978 Wolf, Gotthard. The Scientific Film in Germany. Wuppertal: Lucas, C.1957, 80 P.

5979 Zoeller, Josef Othmar. Sport, Society and Politics. German Tribune Quarterly Review. No. 20 (16 November 1972), 12-16.

N.7.2. Literature

5980 Abrams, Susan Diane. Communication and Narrative Structure in Two Contemporary German Novels: Uwe Johnson's Das Dritte Buch Ueber Achim and Franz Tumler's Aufschreibung Aus Trient. Ph.D. Thesis, Yale University, 1969, 300 P.

5981 Bauer, Edward F. Voices Crying in the Wilderness: Thematic Development in Post-War German Prose. Ph.D. Thesis, Princeton University, 1966, 184 P.

5982 Baumgart, Reinhard. Six Theses on Literature and Politics. Mosaic. 3:1 (Fall 1969), 80-86.

5983 Botsford, Keith. Guenter Grass Is a Different Drummer. New York Times Magazine. (8 May 1966), 28+.

5984 Cunliffe, W. Gordon. Guenter Grass. New York: Twayne, 1969, 146 P.

5985 Demetz, Peter. Uwe Johnson: A Critical Portrait. Ventures. 10:1 (Spring 1970), 48-53.

5986 Forster, Leonard. German Poetry, 1944-1948. Cambridge: Bowes and Bowes, 1949, 72 P.

5987 Ghurye, Charlotte W. The Movement Toward a New Social and Political Consciousness in Postwar German Prose. Ph.D. Thesis, Northwestern University, 1967, 241 P.

5988 Govier, Robert A. Heinrich Boell as a Critic of Contemporary German Society. Ph.D. Thesis, University of Iowa, 1967, 146 P.

5989 Hamburger, Michael. An Embattled Playground: The German Literary Scene. Encounter. 26:4 (April 1966), 55-64.

5990 Helmke, Henry C. The Image of the School in Contemporary German Literature. Ph.D. Thesis, Ohio State University, 1971, 175 P.

5991 Holthusen, Hans Egon. Crossing the Zero Point: German Literature Since the Second World War. International Literary Annual. Ed. Arthur Boyars and Pamela Lyon. London: Calder, Vol. 3, 1961, Pp. 87-109.

5992 Holthusen, Hans Egon. The Zero Point: The Literary and Cultural Situation of Postwar Germany. Confluence. 2:3 (September 1953), 25-41.

5993 Horst, Karl August. The Quest of 20th Century German Literature. New York: Ungar, 1971, 159 P.

5994 Joesten, Joachim. German Writers and Writing Today. Antioch Review. 8:3 (September 1948), 359-367.

5995 Joesten, Joachim. Who's Who in German Letters Today: Western Germany. Great Barrington, Mass.: Joachim Joesten, New Germany Reports No. 11, September 1949, 18 P.

5996 Keith-Smith, Brian, Editor. Essays on Contemporary German Literature. Philadelphia: Dufour, 1966, 280 P.

5997 Kopp, William L. The Currency of German Literature in the United States, 1945-1960. Ph.D. Thesis, Pennsylvania State University, 1965, 383 P.

5998 Lauckner, Nancy Ann. The Image of the Jew in the Postwar German Novel. Ph.D. Thesis, University of Wisconsin, 1971, 420 P.

5999 Leonard, Irene. Guenter Grass. New York: Barnes and Noble, 1974.

6000 Maier, Kurt S. Images of the Jew in Postwar German Fiction and Drama (1945-1965). Ph.D. Thesis, Columbia University, 1969, 284 P.

6001 Primeau, John King. The Non-Political Man in the Modern German Novel. Ph.D. Thesis, Boston College, 1973, 212 P.

6002 Reich-Ranicki, Marcel. The Writer in Divided Germany. to Find Something New: Studies in Contemporary Literature. Ed. Henry Grosshans. Pullman: Washington State University Press, 1969, Pp. 136-145.

6003 Reichmar, Felix. The Reorganization of the Book Trade in Germany. Library Quarterly. 17:3 (July 1947), 165-200.

6004 Steiner, George. The Hollow Miracle: Notes on the German Language. Reporter. 22:4 (18 February 1960), 36-41. Has Stopped Growing; No Longer Vessel for Myth.

6005 Steiner, George. The Nerve of Guenter Grass. Commentary. 37:5 (May 1964), 77-80.

6006 Szewczyk, Wilhelm. The Revanchist Trend in West German Fiction. Polish Western Affairs. 4:1 (1963), 120-143.

6007 Tank, Kurt L. Guenter Grass. New York: Unger, 1969, 127 P.

6008 Thomas, R. Hinton. Bullivan, Keith. Literature in Upheaval: West German Writers and the Challenge of the 1960's. New York: Barnes & Noble, 1974.

6009 Thomas, R. Hinton. Will, Wilfried Van Der. The German Novel and the Affluent Society. Toronto: University of Toronto Press, 1968, 167 P.

6010 Todd, Gaylord H. The New Novel in France and Germany: Convergence and Divergence. Ph.D. Thesis, University of Minnesota, 1970, 274 P.

6011 Van Abbe, Derek Maurice. Image of a People: The Germans and Their Creative Writing Under and Since Bismarck. New York: Barnes and Noble, 1964, 246 P.

6012 Waidson, Herbert M. The Modern German Novel: A Mid-Twentieth Century Survey. London and New York: Oxford University Press, 1959, 130 P.

6013 Zehm, Guenter. A Poet in Berlin. Encounter. 25:1 (July 1965), 89-91. Autobiographical; Former Political Prisoner Meets Informer at Poetry Reading.

N.7.3. Drama and Theater

6014 Bahn, Eugene H. Report From Western Germany: The Theatre in the U.S. Zone, 1945-48. Educational Theatre Journal. 5:3 (October 1953), 207-214; and 5:4 (December 1953), 313-321.

6015 Bond, Martyn A. German Radio Drama Between 1951 and 1965. Gazette. 17:1-2 (1971), 75-93.

6016 Brooks, Alfred Glenn. The Subsidized Theatre in Western Germany, 1945-1960. Ph.D. Thesis, University of Illinois, 1962, 329 P.

6017 Carmichael, Joel. Peter Weiss' Infantile Leftism. Midstream. 12:9 (November 1966), 20-26.

6018 Clausen, Oliver. Weiss/Propagandist and Weiss/Playwright. New York Times Magazine. (2 October 1966), 28+.

6019 Esslin, Martin J. A Playwright Who Drops Political Blockbusters: Rolf Hochhuth. New York Times Magazine. (19 November 1967), 48+.

6020 Garten, Hugh F. Modern German Drama. Fair Lawn: Essential Books, 1959, 272 P., Esp. Pp. 239-252.

6021 Hayman, Ronald, Editor. The German Theatre: A Symposium. London: Wolff, 1975, 287 P.

6022 Hilton, Ian. The Theatre of Fact in Germany. Forum for Modern Language Studies. 4:3 (July 1968), 260-268.

6023 Lewis, Flora. Germany's Cabarets Laugh at Politics. New York Times Magazine. (14 June 1959), 15+.

6024 Mcgranahan, Donald V. Wayne, Ivor. German and American Traits Reflected in Popular Drama. Human Relations. 1:4 (November 1948), 429-455. Content Analysis of Plays of 1927.

6025 Michalski, John. German Drama and Theater in 1965. Books Abroad. 40:2 (Spring 1966), 137-140.

6026 Milfull, John. From Kafka to Brecht: Peter Weiss's Development Towards Marxism. German Life and Letters. 20:1 (October 1966), 61-71.

6027 Read, Ralph R., Iii. The Politization of Modern German Historical Drama. Ph.D. Thesis, University of California, Berkeley, 1968, 286 P.

6028 Talbot, Joanne Hines. The Theme of "The Scientist's Responsibility in the Nuclear Age" in Contemporary German Drama. Ph.D. Thesis, Boston University, 1968, 246 P.

N.7.4. Recent History in Literature and Drama (See Also A.4;D.3.5)

6029 Alley, Gary Lee. History on the German Stage, 1960-1970: a Survey of Themes and Methods. Ph.D. Thesis, University of Wisconsin, 1971, 282 P.

6030 Bays, Robert Alexander, Jr. Modern German Drama: The Aesthetics of Guilt. Ph.D. Thesis, University of Minnesota, 1972, 235 P.

6031 Burkhart, Sylvia Davis. World War II in German Drama: The Individual Versus War. Ph.D Thesis, University of Cincinnati, 1969, 217 P.

6032 Dawson, John S. Interpretations of Dictatorship in the Works of Certain Modern German Authors. Ph.D. Thesis, Univeristy of Toronto, 1963, 202 P.

6033 Frankel, Theodore. German Fiction and Purification. Commentary. 6:30 (December 1960), 524-527.

6034 Loram, Ian C. The Resistance Movement in the Recent German Drama. German Quarterly. 33:1 (January 1960), 7-13.

6035 Lydon, Roger M. Some Reactions to Nazism and the War in Postwar German Drama and Lyric Poetry. Ph.D. Thesis, University of Southern California, 1954.

6036 Nahrgang, Wilbur Lee. Attitudes Toward War in German Prose Literature of the Second World War: 1945-1960. Ph.D. Thesis, University of Kansas, 1966, 221 P.

6037 Olsen, Arthur J. Anne Frank Speaks to the Germans. New York Times Magazine. (17 February 1957), 15+.

6038 Reddick, John. The "Danzig Trilogy" of Guenter Grass: A Study of "The Tin Drum," "Cat and Mouse" and "Dog Years." New York: Harcourt Brace Jovanovich, 1975, 289 P.

6039 Soper, Vera. The German Postwar Novel--The Reflection of the Years 1933-1945. Ph.D. Thesis, University of Southern California, 1953.

6040 Werner, Alfred. A German Explains. Journal of Central European Affairs. 9:2 (July 1949), 159-166.

6041 Werner, Alfred. Germany's New Flagellants. American Scholar. 27:2 (Spring 1958), 169-181. Collective Guilt Question.

N.8. GDR: Cultural Developments

N.8.1. General Culture and the Arts

6042 Brasch, Horst. Cultural Policy for the Victory of Socialism. German Foreign Policy (GDR). 6:5 (1967),

378-381.

6043 Carsten, Francis L. East Germany's Intellectuals: A Note. Problems of Communism. 6:6 (November 1957), 49-50.

6044 Carter, Frank T. C. The Influence of Political Change on Language in East Germany. Loughborough Journal of Social Studies. No. 7 (June 1969), 25-38.

6045 Croan, Melvin. Intellectuals Under Ulbricht. Survey. No. 34 (October-December 1960), 35-45.

6046 Fiebelkorn, Joachim. A New Chapter in the History of German Sport. Dresden: Zeit Im Bild, 1965, 63 P.

6047 Fiebelkorn, Joachim. 1966, a Year of World Sports, a Year of GDR Triumphs. German Foreign Policy (GDR). 6:1 (1967), 74-81.

6048 GDR, Ministry of Culture. Society for Cultural Relations With Foreign Countries. Babelsberg: Film Capital of the German Democratic Republic. Berlin: Ministry of Culture and Society for Cultural Relations With Foreign Countries, 1958, 56 P.

6049 Hanwehr, Wolfram Von. A Critical Analysis of the Structure of the East German Film "Berlin Wall". Ph.D. Thesis, University of Southern California, 1970, 454 P.

6050 Heym, Stefan. Letter From East Germany. New York Times Magazine. (23 March 1975), 34+. GDR Writer's Comments on General Conditions and Art.

6051 Hildebrandt, Rainer, Editor. 2 X 2 = 8: The Story of a Group of Young Men in the Soviet Zone of Germany. Bonn: Federal Ministry for All-German Affairs, 1961, 64 P.

6052 Hoepcke, Klaus. Power for the Intellect: Cultural and Intellectual Life in The German Democratic Republic. Dresden: Zeit Im Bild, 1969, 34 P.

6053 Kersten, Heinz. The Intellectual Scene in East Germany. Survey. No. 19 (September 1957), 4-9.

6054 Kersten, Heinz. Letter From Berlin. Survey. No. 34 (October-December 1960), 66-73.

6055 Kersten, Heinz. Repercussions in East Germany. Survey. No. 48 (July 1963), 36-46. Impact of Soviet Cultural Policies on the GDR.

6056 Kersten, Heinz. Ulbricht and the Intellectuals: Zhdanovism Resurrected. Survey. No. 25 (July-September 1958), 47-52.

6057 Lehmann-Haupt, Hellmut. Art Under a Dictatorship. New York: Oxford University Press, 1954, 277 P., Esp. Pp. 200-215.

6058 National Sport and Olympic Medals: Physical Culture and Sport in the GDR. Dresden: Zeit Im Bild, 1972, 28 P.

6059 Schmidt, Jutta. The Fine Arts in the German Democratic Republic. United Asia. 21:5 (September-October 1969), 294-301.

6060 Society for Cultural Relations With Foreign Countries. Cultural Activities. Berlin (East): Gesellschaft Fuer Kulturelle Verbindungen Mit Dem Ausland, 1957, 64 P.

6061 Wagner, Helmut R. The Cultural Sovietization of East Germany. Social Research. 24:4 (Winter 1957), 395-426.

N.8.2. Literature

6062 Bentley, Eric. In Bahnhof Friedrichstrasse. Partisan Review. 33:1 (Winter 1966), 97-109.

6063 Brandt, Sabine. Production of Literature. Survey. No. 34 (October-December 1960), 58-65.

6064 Demetz, Peter. Literature in Ulbricht's Germany. Problems of Communism. 11:4 (July-August 1962), 15-21.

6065 Eifler, Margret. GDR Literature--A Literature of Conflict and Dissent. Teaching Postwar Germany in America: Papers and Discussions. Ed. Louis F. Helbig and Eberhard Reichmann. Bloomington: Indiana Univeristy, Institute of German Studies, 1972.

6066 Flores, John M. Adjustments and Visions: Poetry in the German Democratic Republic (1945-1969). Ph.D. Thesis, Yale University, 1969, 508 P.

6067 Flores, John M. Poetry in East Germany: Adjustments, Visions, and Provocations, 1945-1970. New Haven: Yale University Press, 1971, 354 P.

6068 Frey, John R. Socialist Realism in East Germany. German Quarterly. 26:4 (November 1953), 272-278.

6069 Huebener, Theodore. The Literary Scene in East Germany. Modern Language Journal. 50:4 (April 1966), 208-213.

6070 Huebener, Theodore. The Literature of East Germany. New York: Ungar, 1970, 134 P.

6071 Joesten, Joachim. Who's Who in German Letters Today: Eastern Germany. Great Barrington, Mass.: Joachim Joesten, New Germany Reports No. 12, March 1950, 17 P.

6072 Marcuse, Ludwig. German Ideology--1946: A Berlin Literary Manifesto. Books Abroad. 21:3 (Summer 1947), 274-278. East Zone Literature.

6073 Paul, Wolfgang. Proceeding Against Readers. Frankfurt: Boersenverein Des Deutschen Buchhandels, 1961, 123 P. on the Book Trade in the GDR.

6074 Reich-Ranicki, Marcel. The Writer in East Germany. Survey. No. 61 (October 1966), 188-195.

6075 Shorris, Earl. Expatriate Chess on the Other Side of the Wall. New York Times Magazine. (23 May 1971), 30+. Writers in the GDR; "Das Magazin"; Stefan Heym.

6076 Vallance, Margaret. Wolf Biermann. Survey. No.61 (October 1966), 177-187.

6077 Wieser, Theodor. A Writers' Congress in East Berlin. Swiss Review of World Affairs. 5:12 (March 1956), 13-15.

6078 Wunderlich, Eva C. Literature in Soviet-Occupied Germany. Thought. 32:126 (Autumn 1957), 338-366.

N.8.3. Drama and Theater; Brecht

6079 Brown, Thomas K. Brecht and the 17Th of June, 1953. Monatshefte. 63:1 (Spring 1971), 48-55.

6080 Demetz, Peter. Galileo in East Berlin: Notes on the Drama in the Ddr. German Quarterly. 37:3 (May 1964), 239-245.

6081 Esslin, Martin J. Bert Brecht: The Last Years. Survey. No. 27 (January-March 1959), 40-48.

6082 Esslin, Martin J. Bert Brecht's Difficulties. Encounter. 11:6 (December 1958), 73-74.

6083 Esslin, Martin J. Brecht: The Man and His Work. Garden City: Doubleday,

1960, 360 P.

6084 Esslin, Martin J. New Light on Brecht. Encounter. 14:6 (June 1960), 65-66.

6085 Ewen, Frederic. Bertolt Brecht: His Life, His Art and His Times. New York: Citadel, 1967, 573 P.

6086 Glade, Henry. Death of Mother Courage. Drama Review. 12:1 (Fall 1967), 69-87.

6087 Huettich, H. G. Theater in the Planned Society: The Contemporary Topical Drama of the German Democratic Republic. Ph.D. Thesis, University of Wisconsin, 1972, 376 P.

6088 Krispyn, Egbert. The Radioplay in the German Democratic Republic. German Life and Letters. 21:1 (October 1967), 45-57.

6089 Luethy, Herbert. "Of Poor Bert Brecht". Encounter. 7:1 (July 1956), 33-53.

6090 Noessig, Manfred. East Germany. World Theatre. 14:5 (September-October 1965), 506-508.

6091 Rippley, Lavern J. Brecht the Communist and America's Drift From Capitalism. Twentieth Century Literature. 14:3 (October 1968), 143-148.

6092 Szczesny, Gerhard. The Case Against Bertolt Brecht: With Arguments Drawn From His Life of Galileo. New York: Ungar, 1969, 126 P.

6093 Willett, John. The Theatre of Bertolt Brecht: A Study From Eight Aspects. London: Methuen, 1967, 243 P.

N.9. FRG-GDR: Cultural Comparisons

6094 Demetz, Peter. Postwar German Literature: A Critical Introduction. New York: Pegasus, 1970, 264 P.

6095 Mcclelland, Charles E. Scher, Steven P. Postwar German Culture: An Anthology. New York: E. P. Dutton & Co., Inc., 1974, Xx and 444 P.

O. FRG: Foreign Policy

O.1. General (See Also E.3.4.7; F.1.4; I.9)

O.1.1. Allied High Commission

6096 Charter of the Allied High Commission for Germany. Current History. 17:97 (September 1949), 163-167.

6097 Conley, Samuel Glenn. Exercise Harvest: A Test of Teamwork. Army Information Digest. 5:1 (January 1950), 18-27. US Military Maneuvers, September 1949.

6098 Dunham, Chadbourne. The Amerika Haeuser in Germany. Institute of International Education News Bulletin. 27:8 (May 1952), 7-10.

6099 Engler, Robert. Individual Soldier and the Occupation. Annals of the American Academy of Political and Social Science. 267 (January 1950), 77-86.

6100 Gillen, J. F. J. The Special Projects Program of the U.S. High Commissioner for Germany. Bad Godesberg-Mehlem: Office of the U.S. High Commissioner for Germany, Historical Division, 1952, 76 P.

6101 Gillen, J. F. J. Forstmeier, Friedrich. The Employment of German Nationals By the Office of the U.S. High Commissioner for Germany. Bad Godesberg-Mehlem: Office of the U.S. High Commissioner for Germany, Historical Division, 1952, 118 P.

6102 Jones, Edgar M. Front Lines in the Cold War. Army Information Digest. 7:9 (September 1952), 49-54. US Military Police Customs Unit.

6103 Kirkpatrick, Ivone. The Inner Circle: Memoirs. London: Macmillan, 1959, 275 P. Former British High Commissioner in West Germany.

6104 Lee, Guy A. Field Organization of the Office of the U.S. High Commissioner for Germany, 1949-1951. Bad Godesberg-Mehlem: Office of the U.S. High Commissioner for Germany, Historical Division, 1952, 138 P.

6105 Lee, Guy A. Guide to Studies of the Historical Division Office of the U.S. High Commissioner for Germany. Bad Godesberg-Mehlem: Office of the U.S. High Commissioner for Germany, Office of the Executive Director, Management and Budget Division, 1953, 131 P.

6106 Lee, Guy A. The Organization of the Office of the U.S. High Commissioner for Germany, 1949-1952, With Special Reference to Planning for Embassy Status. Bad Godesberg-Mehlem: Office of the U.S. High Commissioner for Germany, Historical Division, 1953, 215 P.

6107 Lee, Guy A. Loehr, Rodney C. The Establishment of the Office of the U.S. High Commissioner for Germany. Bad Godesberg-Mehlem: Office of the U.S. High Commissioner for Germany, Historical Division, 1951, 92 P.

6108 Lee, Guy A., Editor. Documents on Field Organization of the Office of the U.S. High Commissioner for Germany, 1949-1951. Bad Godesberg-Mehlem: Office of the U.S. High Commissioner for Germany, Historical Division, 1952, 70 P.

6109 Lockett, Edward B. High Commissioner for Germany: John J. Mccloy. New York Times Magazine. (29 May 1949), 8+.

6110 Nobleman, Eli E. American Military Government Courts in Germany: With Special Reference to Historic Practice and Their Role in the Democratization of the German People. Fort Gordon, Ga.: U.S. Army, Civil Affairs School, Rev. Ed., 1961, 261 P.

6111 Olsen, Arthur J. Touchy Coexistence: G.I. and German. New York Times Magazine. (9 September 1956), 15+.

6112 Pilgert, Henry P. The History of the Development of Information Services Through Information Centers and Documentary Films. Bad Godesberg-Mehlem: Office of the U.S. High Commissioner for Germany, Historical Division, 1951, 86 P.

6113 Plischke, Elmer. The Allied High Commission for Germany. Bad Godesberg-Mehlem: Office of the U.S. High Commissioner for Germany, Historical Division, 1953, 215 P.

6114 Plischke, Elmer. Allied High Commission Relations With the West German Government. Bad Godesberg-Mehlem: Office of the U.S. High Commissioner for Germany, Historical Division, 1952, 209 P.

6115 Plischke, Elmer. Hille, Hans J. History of the Allied High Commission for Germany: Its Establishment, Structure and Procedures. Washington: Office of the U.S. High Commissioner for Germany, Historical Division, 1951, 122 P.

6116 Plischke, Elmer. Pilgert, Henry P. Erdmann, Elisabeth. U.S. Information Programs in Berlin. Bad Godesberg-Mehlem: Office of the U.S. High Commissioner for Germany, Historical Division, 1953, 108 P.

6117 UK, Foreign Office. Charter of the Allied High Commission for Germany, Paris, 20Th June, 1949. London: H.M.

Stationery Office, Cmd. 7727, 1949, 8 p.

6118 US, Hicog. Hicog Construction Program: Bonn-Bad Godesberg Area. Bonn: Hicog, 1953, 295 P.

6119 US, Hicog, Division of Internal Political and Gov. Affairs. A Program to Foster Citizen Participation in Government and Politics in Germany. Frankfurt: Hicog, Division of Internal Political and Governmental Affairs, 1951, 32 P.

6120 US, Hicog, Management and Budget Division. The America Houses: A Study of the U.S. Information Center in Germany. N.P.: Hicog, Management and Budget Division and Office of Public Affairs, 1953, 144 P.

6121 US, Hicog, Office of General Counsel. Cumulative Index of Legislation of the Control Council for Germany, U.S. Military Government for Germany, Allied High Commission, Office of the U.S. High Commissioner for Germany. Frankfurt: Hicog, Office of General Counsel, 1951+.

6122 US, Hicog, Public Relations Division. The Resident Officer: Hicog's Ambassador in the Field. Frankfurt: Hicog, Public Relations Division, 1951, 40 P.

6123 Wilken, David. Rimestad, Idar. Blackmar, C. F. The Kreis Resident Officer. N.P.: Hicog, 1950, 28 P.

0.1.2. Policymaking Processes

6124 Baring, Arnulf M. The Institutions of German Foreign Policy. Britain and West Germany: Changing Societies and the Future of Foreign Policy. Ed. Karl Kaiser and Roger Morgan. London: Oxford University Press, 1971, Pp. 151-170.

6125 Berkley, Eliot S. The Establishment of Foreign Relations By the German Federal Republic. Ph.D. Thesis, Princeton University, 1952, 581 P.

6126 Besson, Waldemar. The Conflict of Traditions: The Historical Basis of West German Foreign Policy. Britain and West Germany: Changing Societies and the Future of Foreign Policy. Ed. Karl Kaiser and Roger Morgan. London: Oxford University Press, 1971, Pp. 61-80.

6127 Besson, Waldemar. The Federal Republic's National Interest. Aussenpolitik. 21:2 (1970), 123-135.

6128 Blishchenkov, I. P. The Foreign Office of the German Federal Republic. German Foreign Policy (GDR). 1:6 (1962), 641-649.

6129 Brunner, Guido. Why a Foreign Policy Planning Staff?. Aussenpolitik. 23:4 (1972), 418-423.

6130 Craig, Gordon A. From Bismarck to Adenauer: Aspects of German Statecraft. New York: Harper & Row, Rev. Ed., 1965, 138 P.

6131 Deutsch, Karl W. Edinger, Lewis J. Foreign Policy of the German Federal Republic. Foreign Policy in World Politics. 3D Ed. Ed. Roy C. Macridis. Englewood Cliffs: Prentice-Hall, 1967, Pp. 102-155.

6132 Deutsch, Karl W. Edinger, Lewis J. Germany Rejoins the Powers. Yale Review. 49:1 (Autumn 1959), 20-42.

6133 Deutsch, Karl W. Edinger, Lewis J. Germany Rejoins the Powers: Mass Opinion, Interest Groups, and Elites in Contemporary German Foreign Policy. Stanford: Stanford University Press, 1959, 320 P.

6134 Frank, Paul. Problems of Foreign Service Reform. Aussenpolitik. 23:2 (1972), 175-182.

6135 Frank, Paul. Reorganization in the German Foreign Office. Aussenpolitik. 24:2 (1973), 147-153.

6136 GDR, Ministry of Foreign Affairs. From Ribbentrop to Adenauer: A Documentation on the West German Foreign Office. Berlin: Ministry of Foreign Affairs, 1961, 67 P.

6137 Hafter, Rudolph P. Germany's New Foreign Service. Swiss Review of World Affairs. 1:6 (September 1951), 17-19.

6138 Hanrieder, Wolfram F. International System and Foreign Policy: The Foreign Policy Goals of the Federal Republic of Germany. Ph.D. Thesis, University of California, Berkeley, 1963, 409 P.

6139 Hanrieder, Wolfram F. West German Foreign Policy, 1949-1963: International Pressure and Domestic Response. Stanford: Stanford University Press, 1967, 275 P.

6140 Hartman, F. L. Federalism as a Limitation on the Treaty Power of the United States, West Germany, and India. Western Reserve Law Review. 18:1 (November 1966), 134-156.

6141 Joesten, Joachim. The New "Wilhelmstrasse": Western Germany's Foreign Office, 1949-1952. New York: Joachim Joesten, New Germany Reports No. 18, May 1952, 19 P.

6142 Joffee, Josef. Society and Foreign Policy in the Federal Republic, 1949-1962. Ph.D. Thesis, Harvard University, 1975.

6143 Keller, John W. From the Kaiser to Willy Brandt: Social Democratic Foreign Policy, 1870-1974. New York: William Frederick Press, 1974.

6144 Kellermann, Henry J. Party Leaders and Foreign Policy. West German Leadership and Foreign Policy. Ed. Hans Speier and W. Phillips Davison. Evanston and White Plains: Row, Peterson, 1957, Pp. 57-95.

6145 Lewin, Daniel M. The Decline of Tradition in the German Foreign Service. Western Political Quarterly. 19:4 (December 1966), 653-662.

6146 Lewin, Daniel M. The West German Foreign Service: A Study of German Diplomats Under Adenauer. Ph.D. Thesis, Princeton University, 1961, 346 P.

6147 Merkl, Peter H. Politico-Cultural Restraints on West German Foreign Policy: Sense of Trust, Identity, and Agency. Comparative Political Studies. 3:4 (January 1971), 443-468.

6148 Narr, Wolf-Dieter. Social Factors Affecting the Making of Foreign Policy. Britain and West Germany: Changing Societies and the Future of Foreign Policy. Ed. Karl Kaiser and Roger Morgan. London: Oxford University Press, 1971, Pp. 105-126.

6149 Relations With the Federal Republic of Germany: The New Zealand Embassy in Bonn. New Zealand Foreign Affairs Review. 22:1 (January 1972), 3-10.

6150 Sasse, Christoph, Editor. Domestic Determinants of Foreign Policy. Washington, D.C.: Georgetown University, School of Foreign Service, C. 1975, vi and 34 P. Speeches and Discussion of the Third German-American Forum at Georgetown University, 6-8 October 1974.

6151 Sigrist, Helmut. Roding, Horst. Selection and Training for the German Foreign Service. India Quarterly. 12:3 (July-September 1956), 290-297.

6152 Speier, Hans, Editor. Davison, W. Phillips, Editor. West German Leadership and Foreign Policy. Evanston and White Plains: Row,

Peterson, 1957, 323 P.

6153 Wahrhaftig, Samuel L. The Development of German Foreign Policy Institutions. West German Leadership and Foreign Policy. Ed. Hans Speier and W. Phillips Davison. Evanston and White Plains: Row, Peterson, 1957, Pp. 7-56.

6154 Watt, Donald C. The Reform of the German Foreign Service. World Today. 26:8 (August 1970), 352-358.

0.1.3. Cultural Policy

6155 Arnold, Hans. Foreign Cultural Policy 1973 to 1976. Aussenpolitik. 24:2 (1973), 165-175.

6156 Arnold, Hans. The German-Speaking Cultural Region. Aussenpolitik. 25:4 (1974), 401-417.

6157 Breitenstein, Rolf. New Departures in Cultural Relations Abroad. German Tribune Quarterly Review. No. 15 (26 August 1971), 13-16.

6158 Dill, Richard W. Broadcasting and Foreign Culture Policy. Aussenpolitik. 24:2 (1973), 176-188.

6159 Etinger, Y. Peace Corps a La Bonn. International Affairs (Moscow). (June 1964), 82-84.

6160 Eyck, F. Gunther. External Information and Cultural Relations Programs of the Federal Republic of Germany. Washington: United States Information Agency, Research Service, 1973, Iii and 94 P.

6161 Herrmann, H. C. Bonn Schools Abroad. German Foreign Policy (GDR). 2:1 (1963), 37-47.

6162 Heuss, Theodor. Indo-German Intellectual Relations. Indo-German Intellectual Relations; Elements of Democracy in Germany; a Fragment of German Economic History. New Delhi: German Cultural Institute, 1961, 29 P.

6163 Lupescu, Amando. The Goethe Institute, Instrument of West German Imperialism. German Foreign Policy (GDR). 7:1 (1968), 58-67.

6164 Moennig, Richard. Cultural Dialogue. United Asia. 19:6 (November-December 1967), 470-473.

6165 Schlagintweit, Reinhard. Foreign Cultural Policy and Foreign Policy. Aussenpolitik. 25:3 (1974), 255-271.

6166 Schmid, Walter. German Cultural Relations With Eastern Europe. Aussenpolitik. 23:3 (1972), 290-298.

6167 Schmidt, Joachim. West German Cultural Policy Towards the German-Speaking Population of South and South West Africa. German Foreign Policy (GDR). 7:2 (1968), 126-135.

6168 Steltzer, Hans Georg. Foreign Cultural Policy as Peace Policy. Aussenpolitik. 22:3 (1971), 243-255.

6169 Stoltenberg, Gerhard. Scientific Policy as an Element of Foreign Policy. German Tribune Quarterly Review. No. 1 (4 May 1968), 12-16.

6170 Witte, Barthold. German--A World Language? Aussenpolitik. 23:4 (1973), 406-415.

6171 Wulf, Amandus. West German Cultural Policy Abroad. German Foreign Policy (GDR). 8:6 (1969), 436-448.

0.1.4. Foreign Policy, 1949-55; Sovereignty and Rearmament

6172 Abs, Hermann J. Germany and the London and Paris Agreements. International Affairs (London). 31:2 (April 1955), 167-173.

6173 Act of the London 9-Power Conference on Freeing and Re-Arming West Germany. Current History. 27:160 (December 1954), 372-378.

6174 Adenauer, Konrad. Germany and the Problems of Our Time. International Affairs (London). 28:2 (April 1952), 156-161.

6175 Adenauer, Konrad. World Indivisible: With Liberty and Justice for All. New York: Harper, 1955, 128 P.

6176 Agreements Relating to Germany, 1952 and 1954. American Journal of International Law. 49:3 (July 1955), 55-148.

6177 Allied Council Communique on Germany and Nato. Current History. 20:114 (February 1951), 109.

6178 Berlin Conference and After. Political Quarterly. 25:2 (April 1954), 101-104.

6179 The Berlin Conference: From Cold War to Frozen Peace. Round Table. 44:174 (March 1954), 115-117.

6180 Bishop, Joseph W., Jr. The Contractual Agreements With the Federal Republic of Germany. American Journal of International Law. 49:2 (April 1955), 125-147.

6181 Bonn, Moritz J. The London Conference. Contemporary Review. 186:1067 (November 1954), 260-264.

6182 Boothby, Robert. The Turning Point in Europe. Twentieth Century. 152:905 (July 1952) 13-20.

6183 Boothby, Robert. Frederick, Pierre. Hastings, Lewis. Mosely, Philip E. Shuster, George N. Younger, Kenneth. The Berlin Conference. University of Chicago Round Table. No. 822 (10 January 1954), 1-10. Radio Discussion.

6184 Brailsford, H. N. Brailsford, Evamaria. Germany's Influence on War or Peace. Contemporary Review. 176:1005 (September 1949), 133-138.

6185 Brandt, Karl. Germany: Key to Peace in Europe. Claremont: Associated Colleges at Claremont, 1949, 109 P.

6186 Briggs, Herbert W. The Final Act of the London Conference on Germany: A Study in the Law of International Engagements. American Journal of International Law. 49:2 (April 1955), 148-165.

6187 British Note to Soviet on German Rearmament. Current History. 20:115 (March 1951), 173-174.

6188 Clay, Lucius D. Germany and the Fight for Freedom. Cambridge: Harvard University Press, 1950, 83 P.

6189 Constantine of Bavaria, Prince. After the Flood. London: Weidenfeld and Nicolson, 1954, 215 P.

6190 Cross-Currents in Western German Opinion. World Today. 10:7 (July 1954), 283-293.

6191 Crossman, Richard H. S. No German Rearming Without Atlantic Union. Commentary. 10:6 (December 1950), 507-517.

6192 Eilers, Rudolph M. Postwar Western Germany: Aspects and Problems of Foreign Policy, 1945-1955. Ph.D. Thesis, American University, 1956.

6193 Fertig, Norman. The Berlin Conference. World Affairs Interpreter. 25:2 (July 1954), 140-151.

6194 Flenley, Ralph. Post-War Germany: An Account of How the German People Are Being Restored to the Community of Nations. Current Affairs for the Canadian Forces. 6:5 (1 March 1954),

1-38.

6195 Germany and World Peace: A German Social Democrat View. World Today. 9:4 (April 1953), 153-161.

6196 Germany in Europe: Politics and Strategy of Western Defence. Round Table. 40:159 (June 1950), 208-214.

6197 Goldstein, Israel. Statement of American Jewish Congress in Reference to the Proposed Convention Establishing Relations Between the Three Powers and the Federal Republic of Germany. Washington: American Jewish Congress, 1952, 13 P.

6198 H. G. L. German Opinion and the Berlin Conference. World Today. 10:3 (March 1954), 105-113.

6199 Harris, Wilson. The World Outlook: Berlin to Geneva. Contemporary Review. 185:1060 (April 1954), 193-196.

6200 Healey, Denis. The Turning Point in Germany. Twentieth Century. 151:904 (June 1952), 479-483.

6201 Hiscocks, C. R. Germany Goes West: The Re-Education of a People. Queens Quarterly. 61:4 (Winter 1955), 434-443.

6202 Hoffman, Paul G. Peace Can Be Won. Garden City: Doubleday, 1951, 188 P.

6203 How Germany Can Aid Peace: An Interview with Konrad Adenauer. U.S. News and World Report. 28:20 (19 May 1950), 24-26.

6204 Hudson, G. F. From Berlin to Geneva. Twentieth Century. 155:927 (May 1954), 399-406.

6205 Joint Declaration on Germany: Text Issued at London on May 14, (1950) By Foreign Ministers Bevin, Schuman, and Acheson. Department of State Bulletin. 22:568 (22 May 1950), 787-788.

6206 Kellermann, Henry J. Germany Today and Tomorrow. Department of State Bulletin. 26:674 (26 May 1952), 807-813; and 26:675 (2 June 1952), 851-857.

6207 Kunz, Josef L. Contractual Agreements With the Federal Reupublic of Germany. American Journal of International Law. 47:1 (January 1953), 106-114.

6208 Kunz, Josef L. Ending the War With Germany. American Journal of International Law. 46:1 (January 1952), 114-119.

6209 Kunz, Josef L. The London and Paris Agreements on West Germany. American Journal of International Law. 49:2 (April 1955), 210-216.

6210 Kunz, Josef L. The Status of Occupied Germany Under International Law: A Legal Dilemma. Western Political Quarterly. 3:4 (December 1950), 538-565.

6211 Laun, Kurt Von. The Legal Status of Germany. American Journal of International Law. 45:2 (April 1951), 267-285.

6212 Litchfield, Edward H. The Hour of Crisis Nears in Germany. New York Times Magazine. (14 May 1950), 9+.

6213 Mcinnis, Edgar. The German "Peace Contract": A Brief Analysis. International Journal. 7:3 (Summer 1952), 184-188.

6214 Menczer, Bela. Coal and Steel or Blood and Iron. Contemporary Review. 184:1051 (July 1953), 41-45.

6215 Molotov, Viacheslav Mikhailovich. Results of the Berlin Conference. Moscow: Foreign Languages Publishing House, 1954, 28 P.

6216 Molotov, Viacheslav Mikhailovich. Statements at Berlin Conference of Foreign Ministers of U.S.S.R., France, Great Britain and U.S.A. (January 25-February 18, 1954). Moscow: Foreign Languages Publishing House, 1954, 142 P.

6217 Nettl, John Peter. The End of Military Government in Germany. Contemporary Review. 177:1013 (May 1950), 265-270.

6218 Neumann, Franz L. Germany and World Politics. Toronto: Canadian Institute of International Affairs, Behind the Headlines Series, Vol. 14, No. 2, 1954, 16 P.

6219 Niebuhr, Reinhold. Germany and Western Civilization. Germany and the Future of Europe. Ed. Hans J. Morgenthau. Chicago: University of Chicago Press, 1951, Pp. 1-11.

6220 A Peace Contract With Germany. Current History. 23:131 (July 1952), 28-38. Contract of 26 May 1952 Between FRG and Western Allies.

6221 Peace With Germany. Current History. 21:124 (December 1951), 366-367.

6222 Plischke, Elmer. Contractual Agreements and Changing Allied-West German Relations. Political Science Quarterly. 69:2 (June 1954), 241-265.

6223 Plischke, Elmer. Revision of the Occupation Statute for Germany. Bad Godesberg-Mehlem: Office of the U.S. High Commissioner for Germany, Historical Division, 1952, 95 P.

6224 Polyzoides, Adamantios Th. America Signs a German Alliance. World Affairs Interpreter. 23:2 (Summer 1952), 195-209.

6225 Price, M. Philips. The German Treaties. Contemporary Review. 182:1041 (September 1952), 129-133.

6226 Schnitzer, Ewald W. Bundestag Debates on Allied-German Relations: Allied-German Relations as Reflected in Selected Debates of the Bundestag, January to April 1952. Santa Monica: Rand Corporation, Rm-967, 1952, 26 P.

6227 The Soviet Harassment Campaign in Germany: Correspondence Between Allied and Soviet Representatives. Department of State Bulletin. 27:688 (1 September 1952), 311-320.

6228 Soviet Note on Rearming Germany. Current History. 20:114 (February 1951), 107-108.

6229 Soviet Note to Western Big Three on Remilitarization of Western Germany. Current History. 20:114 (February 1951), 109-110.

6230 Szaz, Zoltan Michael. Principal Foreign Policy Problems of the Federal Republic of Germany, 1949-1954. Ph.D. Thesis, Catholic University, 1959, 470 P.

6231 UK, Central Office of Information. The West and Germany. London: Central Office of Information, April 1952 and October 1952, 8 and 18 P.

6232 UK, Central Office of Information. Western Germany Since 1947. London: Central Office of Information, 1951-52, 23 P.

6233 UK, Foreign Office. Correspondence Between Her Majesty's Government in the United Kingdom and the Soviet Government About the Future of Germany. London: H.M. Stationery Office, Cmd. 8501, 1952, 5 P. Further Correspondence: Cmd. 8551, 1952, 7 P.; Cmd. 8610, 7 P.; Cmd. 8663, 1952, 7 P.; Cmd. 8945, 1953, 15 P.; and Cmd. 9037, 1954, 3 P.

6234 UK, Foreign Office. Documents Relating to the Termination of the Occupation Regime in the Federal

Republic of Germany, Bonn, 1952, Paris, 1954. London: H.M. Stationery Office, Cmd. 9368, 1955, 171 P.

6235 UK, Foreign Office. Germany: The Three Power Meeting in Paris on 9Th and 10Th November, 1949, and Subsequent Events, With Annex. London: H.M. Stationery Office, Cmd. 7849, 1949, 9 P.

6236 UK, Foreign Office. Instrument of Revision of the Charter of the Allied High Commission for Germany, London, 6Th March, 1951. London: H.M. Stationery Office, Cmd. 8251, 1951, 11 P.

6237 UK, Foreign Office. Memorandum on Relations Between the Three Powers and the Federal Republic of Germany, May 26, 1952. London: H.M. Stationery Office, Cmd. 8563, 1952, 9 P.

6238 UK, Foreign Office. Revision of the Occupation Controls in Germany: Bonn, 6Th March, 1951. London: H.M. Stationery Office, Cmd. 8252, 1951, 15 P.

6239 UK, Foreign Office. Statements Issued By the Foreign Ministers of the United Kingdom, the United States and France in Washington on September 14, 1951, on the Subject of Germany. London: H.M. Stationery Office, Cmd. 8626, 1952.

6240 UK, Foreign Office. Supplementary Documents to the Conventions Signed at Bonn, 27 March-27 May 1952. London: H.M. Stationery Office, Cmd. 8576, 1952, 12 P.

6241 UK, Foreign Office. UK, Central Office of Information. Germany's Place in the New Europe: Her Military Position, Her Financial Contribution, Her International Obligations. London: H.M. Stationery Office, 1952, 15 P.

6242 US, Department of State. Foreign Ministers Meeting; Berlin Discussions, January 25-February 28, 1954. Washington: Department of State Publication 5399, Government Printing Office, 1954, 241 P.

6243 US, Department of State. London and Paris Agreements, September-October 1954. Washington: Department of State Publication 5659, Government Printing Office, 1954, 128 P.

6244 US, Department of State. Nine-Power Conference, London, September 28-October 3, 1954. Washington: Department of State Publication 5635, Government Printing Office, 1954, Pp. 515-530. Reprint From Department of State Bulletin, 11 October 1954.

6245 US, Department of State. Summaries of Contractual Agreements With Germany and Supporting Documents. Washington: Library of Congress, Legislative Reference Service, Foreign Affairs Section, 1952, 32 P.

6246 US, Department of State, Office of Public Affairs. Current Problems in the Occupation of Germany: A Fact Sheet. Washington: Department of State Publication 3871, Government Printing Office, 1950, 8 P.

6247 US, Hicog. Report on Germany. Washington: Government Printing Office, 11 Quarterly Reports From 21 September-31 December 1949 to 31 July 1952.

6248 US, House, Committee on Foreign Affairs. Report on Germany. Washington: Government Printing Office, 1952, 48 P.

6249 US, Senate, Committee on Foreign Relations. Agreements With the Federal Republic of Germany. Washington: Government Printing Office, 1953, 243 P.

6250 US, Senate, Committee on Foreign Relations. Convention on Relations With the Federal Republic of Germany and a Protocol to the North Atlantic Treaty: Hearings. Washington: Government Printing Office, 1952, 267 P.

6251 Warburg, James P. Germany and World Peace. Germany and the Future of Europe. Ed. Hans J. Morgenthau. Chicago: University of Chicago Press, 1951, Pp. 142-162.

6252 Warburg, James P. Germany, Key to Peace. Cambridge: Harvard University Press, 1953, 344 P.

6253 Warburg, James P. Last Call for Common Sense. New York: Harcourt, Brace, 1949, 311 P.

6254 Warburg, James P. Our Last Chance in Germany: Stop, Look, and Negotiate. New York: Current Affairs Press, 1952, 25 P.

6255 Ward, Barbara. Is Germany Still a Menace to Peace?. New York Times Magazine. (2 October 1949), 13+.

6256 West Germany Becomes a Sovereign State. Current History. 29:167 (July 1955), 54.

6257 White, Theodore H. Germany as Seen By Her Neighbors. This Is Germany. Ed. Arthur Settel. New York: Sloane, 1950, Pp. 359-369.

6258 White, Theodore H. Germany: The Allies' Great Gamble. Reporter. 6:13 (24 June 1952), 9-14.

6259 White, Theodore H. The Ring of Hate Around Germany: Poles, French, Belgians, Czechs Never Forget. United Nations World. 3:10 (October 1949), 17-20.

6260 Wright, Quincy. The Status of Germany and the Peace Proclamation. American Journal of International Law. 46:2 (April 1952), 299-308.

C.1.5. Foreign Policy, 1955-

6261 Auburn, F. M. The North Sea Continental Shelf Boundary Settlement. Archiv Des Voelkerrechts. 16:1 (1973), 28-36.

6262 Barclay, G. St. J. Third Time Lucky, Germany's Return to World Power. World Review. 5:1 (March 1966), 14-20.

6263 Birnbaum, Immanuel. Peace as the Basic Concept of German Foreign Policy. Pakistan Horizon. 21:3 (1968), 224-228.

6264 Bonn, Moritz J. Will There Be a Peace Conference?. Bankers' Magazine (London). 187:1380 (March 1959), 218-221.

6265 Borch, Herbert Von. The Chances for Negotiation: What Can Still Be Done?. Confluence. 6:3 (Autumn 1957), 245-254.

6266 Bracher, Karl Dietrich. Foreign Policy of the Federal Republic of Germany. Foreign Policies in a World of Change. Ed. Joseph E. Black and Kenneth W. Thompson. New York: Harper & Row, 1963, Pp. 115-147.

6267 Brandt, Willy. East-West Problem as Seen From Berlin. International Affairs (London). 34:3 (July 1958), 297-304.

6268 Brandt, Willy. The Means Short of War. Foreign Affairs. 39:2 (January 1961), 196-207.

6269 Brandt, Willy. A Peace Policy for Europe. New York: Holt, Rinehart and Winston, 1969, 225 P.

6270 Braunthal, Gerard. West German Foreign Policy in Ferment. Current History. 58:345 (May 1970), 292-297.

6271 Braunthal, Gerard. West Germany's Foreign Policy. Current History. 64:380 (April 1973), 150-153.

6272 Chamberlin, William Henry. The Revival of Anti-Germanism. Modern Age. 6:3 (Summer 1962), 277-283.

6273 Conference of Foreign Ministers Geneva, 1959: Principal Documents. London: H. M. Stationery Office, 1959, 43 P.

6274 Connors, Michael F. Dealing in Hate: The Development of Anti-German Propaganda. London: Britons, 1966, 85 P.

6275 Connors, Michael F. Rising Germanophobia: The Chief Obstacle to Current World War II Revisionism. Rampart Journal. 2:1 (Spring 1966), 75-90.

6276 Czempiel, Ernst-Otto. Foreign Policy Issues in the West German Federal Election of 1969. Comparative Politics. 2:4 (July 1970), 605-628.

6277 Dehio, Ludwig. Germany and World Politics in the Twentieth Century. New York: Knopf, 1959, 141 P.

6278 Deutsch, Karl W. Arms Control and the Atlantic Alliance: Europe Faces Coming Policy Decisions. New York: Wiley, 1967, 167 P.

6279 Deutsch, Karl W. Integration and Arms Control in the European Political Environment: A Summary Report. American Political Science Review. 60:2 (June 1966), 354-365.

6280 Deutsch, Karl W. Edinger, Lewis J. Macridis, Roy C. Merritt, Richard L. France, Germany and the Western Alliance: A Study of Elite Attitudes on European Integration and World Politics. New York: Scribner's, 1967, 324 P.

6281 Deutsch, Karl W. Edinger, Lewis J. Macridis, Roy C. Merritt, Richard L. Voss-Eckermann, Helga. French and German Elite Responses, 1964: Code Book and Data. New Haven: Yale University, Political Science Research Library, 1966, 267 P.

6282 Dick, Royer. Our Allies: Their Problems and Outlook: The Federal German Republic. Royal United Service Institution Journal. 110:637 (February 1965), 12-21.

6283 Dutt, Vidya Prakash. The "Summit" Conference at Geneva. Foreign Affairs Reports (New Delhi). 4:10 (October 1955) 125-138.

6284 Erhard, Ludwig. German Policy Today. Atlantic Community Quarterly. 1:4 (Winter 1963-64), 501-511.

6285 FRG, Press and Information Office. for Peace and Relaxation of Tensions: Documents on German Efforts for Peace and Relaxation of Tensions, 1949 Up to August 1968. Bonn: Press and Information Office, 1968, 29 P.

6286 FRG, Press and Information Office. Prerequisites of a Peace Treaty with Germany. Bonn: Press and Information Office, 1959, 15 P.

6287 Feilchenfeld, Ernst H., and Others. Status of Germany. World Polity: A Yearbook of Studies in International Law an D Organization. 1 (1957), 177-227.

6288 Fritz, Friedrich (Pseud.). Once Again: Germany's Legal Status. World Polity: A Yearbook of Studies in International D Organization. 1 (1957), 229-247.

6289 Gauthier, David F. The Problem of Germany. Queen's Quarterly. 71:1 (Spring 1964), 44-56.

6290 Genscher, Hans-Dietrich. Dimensions of German Foreign Policy. Aussenpolitik. 25:4 (1974), 363-374.

6291 Gottlieb, Manuel. The German Peace Settlement and the Berlin Crisis. New York: Paine-Whitman, 1960, 275 P.

6292 Grewe, Wilhelm G. A Peace Treaty With Germany? an Analysis. Washington: German Embassy, Press and Information Off 959, 22 P.

6293 Hanrieder, Wolfram F. The Stable Crisis: Two Decades of German Foreign Poli New York: Harper & Row, 1970, 221 P.

6294 Hanrieder, Wolfram F. West German Foreign Policy: Background to Current Iss Orbis. 13:4 (Winter 1970), 1029-1049.

6295 Hermens, Ferdinand A. Bonn's Foreign Policy. Current History. 30:176 (April 1956), 193-200.

6296 International Association of Democratic Lawyers. International Conference on the Legal Aspects of a Tre Peace With Germany, Berlin, 1961. Brussels: International Association of Democratic Law C.1961, 53 P.

6297 Kaiser, Karl. German Foreign Policy in Transition: Bonn Between Eas West. London: Oxford University Press, 1968, 153 P.

6298 Kaiser, Karl. Prospects for West Germany After the Berlin Agreement. World Today. 28:1 (January 1972), 30-35.

6299 Kohn, Hans. Germany in World Politics. Current History. 44:260 (April 1963), 202-207, 243.

6300 Kuby, Heinz. German Foreign, Defence and European Policy. Journal of Common Market Studies. 6:2 (December 1967), 156-178.

6301 Lahr, Rolf. Some Problems of German Foreign Policy. Pakistan Horizon. 20:4 (1967), 350-357.

6302 Lasky, Melvin J. Germany's Mood on the Eve of Moscow. New York Times Magazine. (4 September 1955), 18+.

6303 Ludz, Peter Christian. Germany's Multi-Dimensional Policy. Aussenpolitik. 25:3 (1974), 247-254.

6304 Mann, F. A. Germany's Present Legal Status Revisited. International and Comparative Law Quarterly. 16:3 (July 1967), 760-799.

6305 Melnikov, D. E. The German Peace Treaty and the Interests of European Security. International Affairs (Moscow). (May 1959), 18-23.

6306 Melnikov, D. E. The West and a German Peace Treaty. International Affairs (Moscow). 5:11 (November 1959), 28-33.

6307 Middleton, Drew. Germany: British Doubts Vs. French Logic. New York Times Magazine. (13 March 1960), 23+.

6308 Mookerjee, Girija K. Federal Republic of Germany and Its Foreign Policy. Political Science Review. 5:1 (April 1966), 72-81.

6309 Morgan, Roger P. The Scope of German Foreign Policy. Yearbook of World Affairs. 20 (1966), 78-105.

6310 Paterson, William E. Foreign Policy and Stability in West Germany. International Affairs (London). 49:3 (July 1973), 413-430.

6311 Rutherford, Malcolm. A Prospect of Germany. Round Table. No. 255 (July 1974), 277-286.

6312 Scheel, Walter. An Interim Report on German Foreign Policy. Aussenpolitik. 22:2 (1971), 123-131.

6313 Scheel, Walter. Main Features of

German Foreign Policy. Foreign Affairs Reports. 20:4 (April 1970), 33-37.

6314 Scheuner, Ulrich. Aims and Limitations of Federal Republic Foreign Polic German Tribune Quarterly Review. No. 9 (March 1970).

6315 Schmidt, Helmut. The Balance of Power: Germany's Peace Policy and the Powers. London: Kimber, 1971, 301 P.

6316 Schmidt, Helmut. Germany in the Era of Negotiations. Foreign Affairs. 49:1 (October 1970), 40-50.

6317 Schmitt, Hans A. Germany's Search for Identity. Current History. 47:280 (December 1964), 326-331.

6318 Schroeder, Gerhard. German Responsibility--German Interests. Bonn: Bundesdruckerei, 1964, 22 P.

6319 Schroeder, Gerhard. Germany, Europe, and the Free World. Bonn: Koellen, 1962, 16 P.

6320 Schroeder, Gerhard. The Main Problems of German Policy. Bonn: N.P., 1962, 7 P.

6321 Schroeder, Gerhard. Peace, Freedom, Order: The Basic Principles of German Foreign Policy. Bonn: Koellen, 1962, 16 P. Speech, 10Th Federal Conference of CDU/Csu Protestant G Group, Wiesbaden, 5 October 1962.

6322 Schuetz, Wilhelm Wolfgang. German Foreign Policy: Foundation in the West--Aims I East. International Affairs (London). 35:3 (July 1959), 310-315.

6323 Schulz, Eberhard. Reflections on a European Peace Settlement. German Tribune Quarterly Review. No. 8 (16 December 1969), 1-5.

6324 Schwarz, Hans-Peter. The Roles of the Federal Republic in the Community of States. Britain and West Germany: Changing Societies and the of Foreign Policy. Ed. Karl Kaiser and Roger Morgan. London: Oxford University Press, 1971, Pp. 219-259.

6325 Treadmill at Geneva: A Steep Climb to the Summit. Round Table. 49:195 (June 1959), 215-217.

6326 UK, Foreign Office. Documents About the Future of Germany (Including Berli London: H.M. Stationery Office, Cmd. 634, 1959, 27 P. 670, 1959, 19 P.; Cmd. 719, 1959, 11 P.; and Cmd. 145 Y 1961, 16 P.

6327 UK, Foreign Office. Documents Relating to the Meeting of Foreign Ministers Geneva, 27 October-16 November 1955. London: H.M. Stationery Office, November 1955, 185 P.

6328 UK, Foreign Office. Documents Relating to the Meeting of Heads of Governme France, the United Kingdom, the Soviet Union and the States of America, Geneva, July 18-23, 1955. London: H.M. Stationery Office, 1955, 31 P.

6329 UK, Foreign Office. Selected Documents on Germany and the Question of Berl 1944-1961. London: H.M. Stationery Office, Cmd. 1552, 1961, 483

6330 US, Department of State. The Geneva Meeting of Foreign Ministers, October 27- November 16, 1955. Washington: Department of State Publication 6156, Government Printing Office, 1955, 307 P.

6331 US, Department of State, Bureau of Intelligence & Research. Chronology of Events Bearing on West German Foreign Affairs, December 1958. Washington: Department of State, Bureau of Intelligence and Research, Report Iib-7.4, 1959, 17 P.

6332 US, Department of State, Division of Research for W. Europe. Chronology of Events Bearing on West German Foreign Affairs, May 5, 1955 to April 30, 1956. Washington: Department of State, Office of Intelligence Research, OIR Report No. 7270.1, 1956, 20 P.

6333 US, Department of State, Historical Division. Foreign Ministers Meeting, May-August 1959, Geneva: Documentary Publication. Washington: Department of State Publication 6882, Government Printing Office, 1959, 603 P.

6334 US, Department of State, Historical Division. US, Senate, Committee on Foreign Relations. Documents on Germany, 1944-1959: Background Documents on Germany, 1944-1959, and a Chronology of Political Developments Affecting Berlin, 1945-1956. Washington: Government Printing Office, 1959, 491 P.

6335 US, Department of State, Historical Division. US, Senate, Committee on Foreign Relations. Documents on Germany, 1944-1961. Washington: Government Printing Office, 1961, 833 P.

6336 US, Department of State, Historical Office. US, Senate, Committee on Foreign Relations. Documents on Germany, 1944-1970. Washington: Government Printing Office, 1971, 897 P. Combines and Updates Volumes for 1944-59 and 1944-61.

6337 U.S. Proposes Foreign Ministers Meeting to Consider Problem of Germany. Department of State Bulletin. 40:1028 (9 March 1959), 333-343. US-Ussr Exchange of Notes in Early 1959.

6338 Vali, Ferenc A. Legal-Constitutional Doctrines on Germany's Post-World II Status. North Dakota Law Review. 42:1 (November 1965), 20-45.

6339 Voigt, Johannes H. The Foreign Policy of the SPD/FDP Coalition Government in West Germany. Australian Outlook. 24:1 (April 1970), 61-69.

6340 Warburg, James P. The German Dilemma: Agenda for the Conference of the Foreign Ministers. Western Political Quarterly. 8:3 (September 1955), 341-353.

6341 Weissberg, Robert. Nationalism, Integration, and French and German Elites. International Organizations. 23:2 (Spring 1969), 337-347.

6342 Wengler, Wilhelm. International Law Problems of the Situation of Germany. Revue Egyptienne De Droit International. 15 (1959), 1-18.

6343 The Western Package Plan for a German Settlement. Current History. 37:218 (October 1959), 239-243.

6344 The Western Principles for a German Settlement. Current History. 37:218 (October 1959), 243-244.

6345 Windsor, Philip. West Germany in Divided Europe. The Foreign Policies of the Powers. Ed. F. S. Northedge. New York: Free Press, 1974, Pp. 237-268.

6346 Ziock, Hermann. The German Image in the World. United Asia. 19:6 (November-December 1967), 424-433.

O.1.6. Eastern and Socialist Views: Militarism

6347 Adler, Margrit. Strait Jacket for Germans, Threat to World Peace. New World Review. 20:7 (July 1952), 15-21.

6348 Alexandrov, V. The International Political Development of Federal Germany and Her Foreign Problems. International Affairs (Moscow).

1:12(December 1956), 49-55;
2:1(January 1957), 60-68;
2:2(February 1957), 29-37.

6349 Arzinger, Rudolf. The Potsdam Agreement and European Security. German Foreign Policy (GDR). 4:5 (1965), 368-379.

6350 Bartel, Walter. Psychological Weapons of the Bonn Militarists. International Affairs (Moscow). 7:3(March 1961), 26-31.

6351 Bartel, Walter. West German Revanchism Threatens the Peace in Europe. International Affairs (Moscow). (July 1961), 49-51.

6352 Barth, Herbert. Nuclear Dance Macabre of the Imperialists. German Foreign Policy (GDR). 2:2 (1963), 94-100. Militarism in Bonn.

6353 Baumann, Otto. German Militarism and How to Curb It. World Marxist Review: Problems of Peace and Socialism 2:6 (June 1959), 8-16.

6354 Busch, E. Bonn in Search of New Tactics. International Affairs (Moscow). (January 1967), 37-41.

6355 Commentator. Bonn's "Frontal Assault" on Peace. International Affairs (Moscow). (November 1962), 50-52.

6356 Dieckmann, Johannes. Reason and Good Will Better Than the Bomb. German Foreign Policy (GDR). 3:1 (1964), 1-4.

6357 Dluski, O. German Militarism: A Threat to Peace. World Marxist Review: Problems of Peace and Socialism 1:1 (September 1958), 43-49.

6358 Dobias, F. Koutek, J. Marvan, M. The Bonn Military: Opponents of a Peaceful Settlement. International Affairs (Moscow). (September 1963), 46-51.

6359 Drang Nach Osten: Some Notes on German Revisionism. New Central European Observer. 2:10 (14 May 1949), 114-115.

6360 Dubrovin, Vi. Federal Germany Steps Up Arms Drive. International Affairs (Moscow). (November 1964), 55-60.

6361 Dubrovin, Vi. U.S. Role in the Revival of West German Militarism. International Affairs (Moscow). (May 1965), 84-87.

6362 Ersil, Wilhelm. An Appraisal of West German Foreign Policy. German Foreign Policy (GDR). 8:6 (1969), 422-435.

6363 Ersil, Wilhelm. From Restoration to Expansion. German Foreign Policy (GDR). 6:3 (1967), 238-250.

6364 Fenzlein, Volkmar. West German Policy Against Peaceful Coexistence. German Foreign Policy (GDR). 3:3 (1964), 213-218.

6365 Florin, Peter. Stop West German Militarism!. World Marxist Review: Problems of Peace and Socialism 4:9 (September 1961), 22-29.

6366 Fyodorov, T. The West German Economy Serves Plans for Aggression. International Affairs (Moscow). (January 1962), 39-46.

6367 GDR, Committee for German Unity. Conspiracy Against Europe: The Paris Agreements--A War Plot. Berlin: Committee for German Unity, 1955, 155 P.

6368 GDR, Committee for German Unity. Memorandum on the Threat to Peace Represented By the Armament Policy of West Germany. Berlin: Committee for German Unity, 1958, 29 P.

6369 GDR, Committee for German Unity. West Germany Prepares War of Revenge: Facts on the Rebirth of German Militarism in the Bonn State. Berlin: Committee for German Unity, C.1954, 119 P.

6370 GDR, Information Office. White Book on the Bonn War Treaty. Berlin: Information Office, 1952, 228 P.

6371 GDR, Ministry of Foreign Affairs. The Atomic Arming of the West German Federal Republic: Imminent Danger to World Peace. Berlin: Ministry of Foreign Affairs, 2D Ed., 1965, 70

6372 GDR, Ministry of Foreign Affairs. White Book on the Aggressive Policy of the West German Federal Republic. Berlin: Ministry of Foreign Affairs, 1958, 160 P.

6373 Galkin, A. Expansion of the West German Monopolies in Europe. International Affairs (Moscow). No.5(May 1958), 48-55.

6374 German Revisionism. New Central European Observer. 1:14 (13 November 1948), 134-135.

6375 Glazunov, N. Militaristic Fever in Federal Germany. International Affairs (Moscow). (February 1969), 20-26.

6376 Grabska, Wirginia. Economic Integration and the Post-War Re-Emergence of German Imperialism. International Affairs (Moscow). (July 1961), 73-75.

6377 Huberman, Leo. Sweezy, Paul M. Turning Point in Germany?. Monthly Review. 4:1 (May 1952), 6-11.

6378 Institute for International Politics and Economics. Beware: German Revenge-Seekers Threaten Peace. Prague: Orbis, 1959, 78 P.

6379 Jahn, Wolfgang. Bonn's Fight Against a Detente. German Foreign Policy (GDR). 2:6 (1963), 405-414.

6380 Jeske, Reinhold. The Eastern Expansion of the German Monopoly Bourgeoisie and the Concept for Europe of Franz Josef Strauss. German Foreign Policy (GDR). 8:4 (1969), 265-278.

6381 Kahn, Siegbert. West Germany's Policy of Rearmament and Revanche. International Affairs (Moscow). No.5(May 1960), 47-51.

6382 Krolikowski, Herbert. Bonn's Plans for Denmark. German Foreign Policy (GDR). 4:6 (1965), 415-421.

6383 Kruczkowski, Adam, Editor. Ort, Alexandr, Editor. Razmerov, V. V., Editor. European Security and the Menace of West German Militarism. Prague: Orbis, 1962, 495 P.

6384 Krusche, Heinz. Bonn's Forward Strategy in the Baltic. German Foreign Policy (GDR). 6:4 (1967), 314-321.

6385 Krusche, Heinz. West German Aggressive Course in Nato. German Foreign Policy (GDR). 4:5 (1965), 344-356.

6386 Kryukov, P. Bonn's Aggressive Foreign Policy. International Affairs (Moscow). (June 1966), 13-19.

6387 Kryukov, P. Mulin, V. Bonn: Enemy of Peaceful Co-Existence. International Affairs (Moscow). (December 1962), 57-61.

6388 Kryukov, P. Mulin, V. Bonn: Policy of Blackmail and Aggression. International Affairs (Moscow). (May 1963), 11-16.

6389 Kurchatov, A. Aggressive Policy of West German Imperialism. International Affairs (Moscow). (December 1966), 45-55.

6390 Lambilliotte, Maurice. German Militarism and West Germany's Neighbours. International Affairs (Moscow). (September 1966), 14-17.

6391 Langbein, Thomas. Schrader, Erich. On the Imperialist Foreign Policy of the Kiesinger-Strauss Government. German Foreign Policy (GDR). 7:5 (1968), 376-390.

6392 Lavergne, Bernard. Threat to European Nations. International Affairs (Moscow). (January 1960), 30-33.

6393 Maier, Lutz. New Trends in Development of West German Imperialism. World Marxist Review. 13:7 (July 1970), 62-67.

6394 Martin, Alexander. West German Revanchism and International Law. German Foreign Policy (GDR). Spec. Ed. 1 (October 1961), 75-95.

6395 Melnikov, D. E. West German Imperialism Today. German Foreign Policy (GDR). 1:4 (1962), 416-425.

6396 Melnikov, D. E. West Germany and European Peace. International Affairs (Moscow). (March 1960), 50-56.

6397 Mikhailov, Vladimir Ivanovich. Bonn: The Old Road. International Affairs (Moscow). (August 1967), 38-45.

6398 National Front of Democratic Germany. Strauss and Brandt Are Mobilizing the SS: Instigators of 1962, Revanchist Sentiment in West Berlin. Berlin (East): National Front of Democratic Germany, 47 P.

6399 National Front of Democratic Germany. Where Is the Federal Republic Heading? Falling Into Line for the Third Try: Documentation on Causes, Aims and Methods of the Peace-Endangering Policy of the West German State. Berlin (East): National Council of the National Front Democratic Germany, 1966, 76 P.

6400 National Front of Democratic Germany. Where Is the Federal Republic Heading? Ten Questions on the Policies of the West German State. Dresden: Zeit Im Bild, 1966, 29 P.

6401 National Front of Democratic Germany. White Book on the American and British Policy of Intervention in West Germany and the Revival of German Imperialism. Berlin (East): National Council of the National Front of Democratic Germany, 1951, 199 P.

6402 Nikolsky, F. Shevchenko, N. West Germany's Military Preparations at the New Stage. International Affairs (Moscow). (May 1965), 80-84.

6403 Norden, Albert. German Imperialism Prepares for War. World Marxist Review: Problems of Peace and Socialism 8:9 (September 1965), 8-21.

6404 Novoseltsev, Y. Bonn's Excessive Ambitions. International Affairs (Moscow). (February 1966), 29-36.

6405 Novoseltsev, Y. Ideological Principles of West German Foreign Policy. International Affairs (Moscow). (January 1967), 71-78.

6406 Novoseltsev, Y. Ideologists of Revanchism--Enemies of Peaceful Co-Existence. International Affairs (Moscow). (July 1961), 75-76.

6407 Ostoya, M. Germany's Instability. Poland and Germany. 4:11 (January 1960), 1-5. Which Direction Will Germany Take in Years Ahead?--Renewed Aggressiveness or Cooperation?.

6408 Pen (International Writers Organization). From Potsdam to Mlf--The Rearming of West Germany. New World Review. 32:11 (December 1964), 27-32.

6409 Panfilov, Y. West Germany's Foreign Policy Impasse and the Big Coalition. International Affairs (Moscow). (May 1967), 9-14.

6410 Pastusiak, Longin. Dangerous Bonn-Washington Deal. International Affairs (Moscow). (July 1966), 45-48.

6411 Pavlov, A. Bonn's Foreign Policy: "Philosophy and Reality". International Affairs (Moscow). (May 1964), 79-84.

6412 Pelius, P. German Militarism and West-European Security. World Marxist Review: Problems of Peace and Socialism 3:6 (June 1960), 12-17.

6413 Perlo, Victor. Partners in Plunder. International Affairs (Moscow). (November 1961), 48-57.

6414 Perlo, Victor. West German and U.S. Imperialism. Political Affairs. 39:8 (August 1960), 48-59.

6415 Peters, P. German Militarism and West-European Security. World Marxist Review. 3:6 (June 1960), 12-17.

6416 Pogodin, A. Bonn's Strategic Plans in the Baltic. International Affairs (Moscow). (September 1961), 33-37.

6417 Pritt, Denis N. Danger-Signal in West Germany. Labour Monthly. 50 (June 1968), 279-280.

6418 Pritt, Denis N. Unrepentant Aggressors: An Examination of West German Policies. Berlin (East): Seven Seas, 1969, 235 P.

6419 Prokop, Siegfried. New Aspects of Bonn's Counter-Revolutionary Strategy. German Foreign Policy (GDR). 5:2 (1966), 146-154.

6420 Quaestor. The Crime at Bonn. Labour Monthly. 34:7 (July 1952), 307-314. Establishment of FRG.

6421 Quaestor. The War Programme of German Imperialism. Labour Monthly. 50 (January 1968), 32-35.

6422 Quaestor. West German Focus of War. Labour Monthly. 34:10 (October 1952), 460-464.

6423 Questions Which Were Not Asked in the Adenauer Television. Interview on February 8, 1963. German Foreign Policy (GDR). 2:2 (1963), 133-137.

6424 Roberts, Holland. West Germany Threatens the Peace. New World Review. 33:6 (June 1965), 26-32.

6425 Rzhevsky, Yuri Sergeevich. F.R.G. in the System of Western Alliances. International Affairs (Moscow). (December 1968), 24-29.

6426 Sanakoyev, Sh. The Threat of West German Militarism: Its Forms and Contents at the Present Stage. International Affairs (Moscow). (July 1961), 68-70.

6427 Schaffer, Gordon. Formula for War--West German Finance Minister Strauss Proposes a United States of Europe. New World Review. 35:3 (March 1967), 12-14.

6428 Schaffer, Gordon. Menace of Adenauer Germany. Labour Monthly. 35:10 (October 1953), 450-454.

6429 Schaffer, Gordon. Who Wrecked Potsdam?. New World Review. 19:3 (May 1951), 11-15.

6430 Schleifstein, Josef. Bonn Foreign Policy--Legend and Reality. World Marxist Review: Problems of Peace and Socialism 10:5 (May 1967), 21-28.

6431 Schliebe, Heinz Dieter. Bonn's Naval "Forward Strategy". German Foreign Policy (GDR). 4:4 (1965), 283-288.

6432 Schumann, Wolfgang. Bednareck, Horst.

The Expansionist Policy of German Imperialism. German Foreign Policy (GDR). 9:2 (1970), 132-137.

6433 Smith, Jessica. The Berlin Conference--and After. New World Review. 22:3 (March 1954), 3-7.

6434 Smith, Jessica. The Choice Before US. New World Review. 20:4 (April 1952), 47-50. Lisbon Road to War, or Four-Power Conference on German Treaty?.

6435 Smith, Jessica. Germany--Tool for War, or Force for Peace?. New World Review. 20:5 (May 1952), 51-56.

6436 Soviet Efforts for Peace in Europe and Against German Re-Armament. London: Soviet News, Booklet No. 4, January 1955, 160 P.

6437 Stadler, Heinz. Berlin, Bonn and European Security. German Foreign Policy (GDR). 5:5 (1966), 338-341.

6438 Streit, Josef. Revanchism in the German Federal Republic. Law and Legislation in the German Democratic Republic. No. 1-2 (1961), 22-36.

6439 Thomas, Siegfried. The Expansionist Policy of German Imperialism. German Foreign Policy (GDR). 9:2 (1970), 137-150.

6440 West Germany Prepares War of Revenge: Facts on the Rebirth of German Militarism in the Bonn State. Berlin (East): N.P., 1954, 120 P.

6441 Wilke, Willi. Bonn Demands Atomic Weapons. German Foreign Policy (GDR). 3:2 (1964), 100-116.

6442 Winzer, Otto. Some Features of West German Foreign Policy. International Affairs (Moscow). (August 1956), 50-60.

6443 Yuryev, N. The Atomic-Missile Rush in West Germany. International Affairs (Moscow). (April 1964), 42-47.

6444 Yuryev, N. European Security and the German Question. International Affairs (Moscow). (October 1965), 56-60.

6445 Zboralski, Dietrich. The "Ultimate Aim" of West German Foreign Policy. German Foreign Policy (GDR). 8:2 (1969), 101-108.

O.2. United States and West Europe (See Also O.5)

O.2.1. North Atlantic Area

6446 Anthon, Carl G. Germany's Westpolitik. Current History. 62:369 (May 1972), 234-238.

6447 Aubrey, Henry G. Atlantic Economic Cooperation: The Case of the Oecd. New York: Praeger, 1967, 214 P.

6448 Birrenbach, Kurt. The Future of the Atlantic Community: Toward European-American Partnership. New York: Praeger, 1963, 94 P.

6449 Brandt, Willy. Europe, Germany, America. Journal of International Affairs. 15:2 (1961), 125-133.

6450 Brandt, Willy. Germany's "Westpolitik". Foreign Affairs. 50:3 (April 1972), 416-426.

6451 Dillard, Hardy C. Western Germany and the West. Virginia Quarterly Review. 27:3 (Summer 1951), 334-351.

6452 Fay, Sidney B. Germany and North Atlantic Community: The Issue of Reunification. Current History. 24:138 (February 1953), 84-90.

6453 Geiger, Theodore. The Fortunes of the West: The Future of the Atlantic Nations. Bloomington: Indiana University Press, 1972, 320 P.

6454 Germany and the West. Soundings. No. 23 (February 1949), 1-6.

6455 Goodman, Elliot R. The Fate of the Atlantic Community. New York: Praeger, 1975, Xxii and 583 P.

6456 Hahn, Walter F. The Germans and the West. Orbis. 1:2 (Summer 1957), 184-198.

6457 Hallstein, Walter. Atlantic Partnership Needs European Community. Atlantic Community Quarterly. 1:2 (Summer 1963), 143-149.

6458 Lower, Arthur R. M. The West and Western Germany. International Journal. 6:4 (Autumn 1951), 300-307.

6459 Ludz, Peter Christian. Dreyer, H. Peter. Pentland, Charles. Ruhl, Lothar. Dilemmas of the Atlantic Alliance: Two Germanys, Scandinavia, Canada, Nato and the EEC. New York: Praeger, 1975.

6460 Mally, Gerhard, Editor. The New Europe and the United States: Partners or Rivals. Lexington, Mass.: Lexington-Heath, 1974, Xxii and 462 P.

6461 Mann, Golo. Germany and the West. Encounter. 17:6 (December 1961), 54-57.

6462 Mayne, Richard, Editor. The New Atlantic Challenge. New York: Halsted Press, 1975, 375 P.

6463 Mendershausen, Horst. Atlantica, Europa, Germania: 1966. Santa Monica: Rand Corporation, Rm-5170-Pr, October 1966, 74 P.

6464 Roberts, Frank. The German-Soviet Treaty and Its Effects on European and Atlantic Policies: A British View. Atlantic Community Quarterly. 9:2 (Summer 1971), 184-195.

6465 Sommer, Theo. for an Atlantic Future. Foreign Affairs. 43:1 (October 1964), 112-125.

6466 Strauss, Franz-Josef. An Alliance of Continents. International Affairs (London). 41:2 (April 1965), 191-203.

O.2.2. United States

6467 Acheson, Dean G. Present at the Creation: My Years in the State Department. New York: Norton, 1969, 798 P.

6468 Adenauer, Konrad. Journey to America. Washington: German Diplomatic Mission, 1953, 192 P. Collected Speeches, Statements, Radio and Tv Interviews, 6-18 April 1953.

6469 Alexander, Thomas L. The Relationship Between United States Foreign Policy Aims Respecting the Federal Republic of Germany and the Information Center Service (Usia) Support of These Objectives. Ph.D. Thesis, American University, 1964, 247 P.

6470 American Policy as Regards Germany. Proceedings of the Institute of World Affairs. 24:5 (December 1947), 50-56.

6471 Aptheker, Herbert. Ideas in Our Time--The United States and Germany. Political Affairs. 38:4 (April 1959), 11-29; and 38:5 (May 1959), 41-57.

6472 Besson, Waldemar. Europe Needs America More Than Ever. German Tribune Quarterly Review. No. 14 (29 April 1971), 8-11.

6473 Boehm, Anton. Vietnam and US. German Tribune Quarterly Review. No. 2 (20 July 1968), 3-6.

6474 Bowie, Robert R. Shaping the Future--Foreign Policy in an Age of Transition. New York: Columbia University Press, 1964, 118 P.

6475 Brandt, Edward R. Confidence and Crises of Confidence in International Relations: A Case Study of West German Political Attitudes Toward the United States During the Postwar Period. Ph.D. Thesis, University of Minnesota, 1970, 432 P.

6476 Brandt, Willy. Germany Says "Thank You" for the Marshall Plan. Atlantic Community Quarterly. 10:3 (Fall 1972), 351-356.

6477 Bretton, Henry L. United States Foreign Policy and the Election. German Democracy at Work: A Selective Study. Ed. James K. Pollock. Ann Arbor: University of Michigan Press, 1955, Pp. 150-173.

6478 Brown, Ralph A. Some Problems of American-German Communications. Interkulturelle Kommunikation Zwischen Industrielaendern und Entwicklungslaendern. Ed. Gerhard Maletzke. Berlin: Deutsches Institut Fuer Entwicklungspolitik, Pp. 282-294.

6479 Brzezinski, Zbigniew K. Alternative to Partition: for a Broader Conception of America's Role in Europe. New York: Mcgraw-Hill, 1965, 208 P., Esp. Pp. 88-104.

6480 Bundy, Mcgeorge, Editor. The Pattern of Responsibility: From the Record of Secretary of State Dean Acheson. Boston: Houghton Mifflin, 1952, 309 P., Esp. Pp. 101-122.

6481 Butz, Otto. Germany: Dilemma for American Foreign Policy. Garden City: Doubleday, 1954, 69 P.

6482 Byroade, Henry A. Our German Problem Today. Washington: Department of State, Office of Public Affairs, 1949, 706 P.

6483 Campbell, Angus. German Embassy Study. Ann Arbor: University of Micaigan, Survey Research Center, SRC Study 706, May 1962, 85 P. US Public Opinion on FRG.

6484 Campbell, John C. Europe, East and West. The United States and Eastern Europe. Ed. Robert F. Byrnes. Englewood Cliffs: Prentice-Hall, 1967, Pp. 125-150.

6485 Common Council for American Unity. European Beliefs Regarding the United States: A Study. New York: Common Council for American Unity, 1949, 135 P.

6486 Conant, James Bryant. The Federal Republic of Germany, Our New Ally. Minneapolis: University of Minnesota, 1957, 20 P.

6487 Conant, James Bryant. Our New Partner--The Federal Republic of Germany. Washington: Department of State, Public Services Division, Series S, No. 36, 1955, 17 P. Address Before Union League Club, Chicago, 20 June 1955.

6488 Dean, Vera Micheles. Europe and the United States. New York: Knopf, 1950, 349 P.

6489 Deutsch, Harold C. Our Changing German Problems. Chicago: Science Research Associates, Rev. Ed., 1956, 64 P.

6490 Deutsch, Harold C. A Problem Paper on Present and Future United States Policy Toward Germany. Itasca Park, Minn.: Midwest Seminar on United States Foreign Policy, 12-16 September 1955, 71 P.

6491 Dulles, John Foster. Our Policy for Germany. Washington: Department of State, Pub. 5408, March 1954, 28 P. Remarks at Berlin Foreign Ministers Conference, 25 January-18 February 1954.

6492 Dworkin, Martin S. Clean Germans and Dirty Politics. Dalhousie Review. 41:4 (Autumn 1961), 522-530. WW II Germans as Portrayed in American Films of the 1950's.

6493 Earle, Edward Mead. A Half-Century of American Foreign Policy: Our Stake in Europe, 1898-1948. Political Science Quarterly. 64:2 (June 1949), 168-188.

6494 Ehrhardt, Carl A. Disenchantment Between Europe and America. Aussenpolitik. 24:4 (1973), 377-392.

6495 Eisenhower, Dwight D. The White House Years: Mandate for Change, 1953-1956. Garden City: Doubleday, 1963, 650 P., Esp. Pp. 395-427.

6496 Eisenhower, Dwight D. The White House Years: Waging Peace, 1956-1961. Garden City: Doubleday, 1965, 741 P., Esp. Pp. 329-360, 397-449.

6497 Epstein, Fritz Theodor. Germany and the United States: Basic Patterns of Conflict and Understanding. Lawrence: University of Kansas Press, 1959, 314 P.

6498 Erler, Fritz. The Basis of Partnership. Foreign Affairs. 42:1 (October 1963), 84-95.

6499 FRG, German Information Center. The Marshall Plan and the Future of U.S.-European Relations. New York: German Information Center, 1972, 55 P. Contains Speeches By George C. Marshall (1947) and Willy Brandt (1972) as Well as Information on the Marshall Plan and the German Marshall Fund.

6500 Fulbright, J. William. Old Myths and New Realities. New York: Random House, 1964, 147 P., Esp. Pp. 79-108.

6501 Fyodorov, T. Washington and Bonn-Alliance Against Peace. International Affairs (Moscow). (April 1965), 12-19.

6502 Gatzke, Hans W. The United States and Germany. Current History. 38:221 (January 1960), 6-10.

6503 Gerson, Louis L. John Foster Dulles. New York: Cooper Square, 1967, 372 P.

6504 Goold-Adams, Richard. The Time of Power: A Reappraisal of John Foster Dulles. London: Weidenfeld and Nicolson, 1962, 320 P.

6505 Graper, Elmer D. American Influence on the Attitudes of Western Europe. Annals of the American Academy of Political and Social Science. 278 (November 1951), 12-22.

6506 Griffith, William E. The German Problem and American Policy. Survey. No. 61 (October 1966), 105-117.

6507 Habe, Hans (Pseud. for Jean Bekessy). Our Love Affair With Germany. New York: Putnam, 1953, 247 P.

6508 Handler, M. S. What U.S. Policy for Europe--and Germany?. Decisions. . . 1957. New York: Foreign Policy Association, Headline Series No. 121, January-February 1957, Pp. 19-31.

6509 Hester, Hugh B. The Tragedy of United States German Policies. Our Generation Against Nuclear War. 1:2 (Winter 1962), 35-43.

6510 Holborn, Hajo. The United States and Germany in World Politics. Germany and Europe: Historical Essays By Hajo Holborn. Garden City: Doubleday, 1970, Pp. 283-298.

6511 Howley, Frank L. Your War for Peace. New York: Holt, 1953, 166 P.

6512 Johnk, James P. Development of United States Policy Toward a United Germany. Towson State Journal of International Affairs. 5:2 (Spring 1971), 73-86.

6513 Kaiser, Karl. Europe and America: A Critical Phase. Foreign Affairs. 52:4 (July 1974), 725-741.

6514 Kaltefleiter, Werner. Europe and the Nixon Doctrine: A German Point of View. National Strategy in a Decade of Change: An Emerging U.S. Policy.. Ed. William B. Kintner and Richard B. Foster. Lexington, Mass.: Lexington-Heath, 1973, 37-56 P.

6515 Kaltefleiter, Werner. Europe and the Nixon Doctrine: A German Point of View. Orbis. 17:1 (Spring 1973), 75-94.

6516 Kennan, George F. Memoirs, 1925-1950. Boston: Little, Brown, 1967, 583 P., Esp. Pp. 415-448.

6517 Kennedy, John F. The Strategy of Peace. Ed. Allan Nevins. New York: Harper, 1960, 233 P.

6518 Kissinger, Henry A. The Necessity for Choice: Prospects of American Foreign Policy. New York: Harper, 1961, 370 P.

6519 Kissinger, Henry A. Nuclear Weapons and Foreign Policy. New York: Harper, 1957, 463 P.

6520 Kohn, Hans. West Germany and the United States. Current History. 50:297 (May 1966), 277-280+.

6521 Lengyel, Emil. Should the U.S. Change Its German Policy?. Foreign Policy Bulletin. 31:23 (15 August 1952), 5-6.

6522 Loch, Theo M. Estrangement Between America and Europe. German Tribune Quarterly Review. No. 1 (4 May 1968), 5-8.

6523 Mally, Gerhard. The European Community in Perspective: The New Europe, the United States, and the World. Lexington, Mass.: Lexington Books, 1973, XXVI and 349 P.

6524 Mccloy, John J. The Challenge to American Foreign Policy. Cambridge: Harvard University Press, 1953, 81 P.

6525 Mcgeehan, Robert J. The German Rearmament Question: American Diplomacy and European Defense After World War II. Urbana: University of Illinois Press, 1971, 280 P.

6526 Mensonides, Louis J. United States Foreign Policy: Germany, 1945-1959, With Emphasis on the Eisenhower Administration. Ph.D. Thesis, University of Kentucky, 1964, 258 P.

6527 Metcalfe, John C. Our Stake in Germany. Washington: Washington College Press, 1961, 96 P.

6528 Morgan, Roger P. The United States and West Germany, 1945-1973: A Study in Alliance Politics. London: Oxford University Press, 1974, Xii and 282 P.

6529 Morgan, Roger P. Washington and Bonn: A Case Study in Alliance Politics. International Affairs (London). 47:3 (July 1971), 489-502.

6530 Morgenthau, Hans J. Conquest of the United States By Germany. Politics in the Twentieth Century: Impasse of American Foreign Policy. Ed. Hans J. Morgenthau. Chicago: University of Chicago Press, 1962, Pp. 152-167.

6531 Norman, Albert. Our German Policy: Propaganda and Culture. New York: Vantage, 1951, 85 P.

6532 Pastusiak, Longin. The Role of the Usa in the Remilitarisation of West Germany. German Foreign Policy (GDR). 3:3 (1964), 231-237; and 3:4 (1964), 305-311.

6533 Pauls, Rolf Friedemann. on German-American Relations. Aussenpolitik. 24:1 (1973), 3-11.

6534 Peel, Doris. The Inward Journey. Boston: Houghton Mifflin, 1953, 241 P.

6535 Pollock, James K. Should the U.S. Change Its German Policy?. Foreign Policy Bulletin. 31:23 (15 August 1952), 5-6.

6536 Pollock, James K. Mason, Edward S. American Policy Toward Germany. New York: Foreign Policy Association, 1947, 212 P.

6537 Riesenfeld, Stefan. German Reconstruction and American Foreign Policy. International House Quarterly. 17:2 (Spring 1953), 82-85.

6538 Rostow, Walt Whitman. The Diffusion of Power: An Essay in Recent History. New York: Macmillan, 1972, 739 P., Esp. Pp. 222-234.

6539 Schlamm, William S. Germany and the East-West Crisis: The Decisive Challenge to American Policy. New York: Mckay, 1959, 237 P.

6540 Schlesinger, Arthur M., Jr. A Thousand Days: John F. Kennedy in the White House. Boston: Houghton Mifflin, 1965, 1087 P., Esp. Pp. 379-405, 842-923.

6541 Schoenthal, Klaus. Bonn-Washington: The Maturing Alliance. Aussenpolitik. 21:1 (1970), 42-52.

6542 Smith, Gaddis. Dean Acheson. New York: Cooper Square, 1972, 473 P.

6543 Speier, Hans. Germany in American Foreign Policy. Santa Monica: Rand Corporation, P-3321, March 1966, 47 P.

6544 Speier, Hans. Germany in American Foreign Policy. Force and Folly: Essays on Foreign Affairs and the History of Ideas. Cambridge: M.I.T. Press, 1969, Pp. 100-134.

6545 Spencer, Frank. The United States and Germany in the Aftermath of War: The Second World War. International Affairs (London). 44:1 (January 1968), 48-62.

6546 Stanley, Timothy W. Whitt, Darnell M. Detente Diplomacy: United States and European Security in The 1970's. New York: Dunellen, 1970, 170 P.

6547 Straus, Richard. America's Changing Relationship With Germany. Department of State Bulletin. 29:732 (6 July 1953), 10-12.

6548 Teplinsky, B. Pentagon-Bonn Axis. International Affairs (Moscow). (February 1962), 22-28.

6549 Treick, Edward L. The United States Dependents Schools in Germany. Ph.D. Thesis, Central Washington College of Education, 1958.

6550 Truman, Harry S. Memoirs. Garden City: Doubleday, 1955-56, 2 Vols., 596 and 594 P.

6551 US, Department of State. The United States and Germany, 1945-1955. Washington: Department of State Publication 5827, Government Printing Office, 1955, 56 P.

6552 US, Department of State, Historical Division. American Foreign Policy, 1950-1955: Basic Documents. Washington: State Department Publication 6446, Government Printing Office, 1957, 2 Vols., 3244 P.

6553 US, Senate, Committee on Armed Services. Staff Report on Drug and Alcohol Abuse Among U.S. Military Personnel and Dependents in Germany. Washington: Senate, Committee on Armed Services, Subcommittee on Drug Abuse in the Military, 1972, 11 P.

6554 United States Policy and Germany. Proceedings of the Institute of World

Affairs. 23:5 (December 1946), 43-45.

6555 Vladimirov, N. West German "Mafia" in Washington. International Affairs (Moscow). (September 1965), 35-44.

6556 Walker, Richard. Germany and Our National Interest. Political Affairs. 33:12 (December 1954), 14-31.

6557 Westerfield, H. Bradford. The Instruments of America's Foreign Policy. New York: Crowell, 1963, 538 P.

6558 Wolfers, Arnold. Germany: Protectorate or Ally?. New Haven: Yale University, Institute of International Studies, 1950, 49 P.

6559 Wolfers, Arnold. United States Policy Toward Germany. New Haven: Yale University, Institute of International Studies, Memorandum No. 20, 1947, 29 P.

6560 Wolfers, Arnold. West Germany: Protectorate or Ally?. Yale Review. 40:2 (December 1950), 223-244.

6561 Yahraes, Richard A. The Germans as Partners?. Antioch Review. 13:4 (December 1953), 468-484.

6562 Zahn, Peter Von. From Germany. As Others See US: The United States Through Foreign Eyes. Ed. Franz M. Joseph. Princeton: Princeton University Press, 1959, Pp. 95-117.

0.2.3. West Europe

6563 Adenauer, Konrad. Germany and Europe. Foreign Affairs. 31:3 (April 1953), 361-366.

6564 Anthon, Carl G. West Germany and Europe. Current History. 50:297 (May 1966), 270-276+.

6565 Barman, Thomas. Britain, France and West Germany: The Changing Pattern of Their Relationship in Europe. International Affairs (London). 46:2 (April 1970), 269-279.

6566 Bergo (Pseud.). France and Germany-- and Britain. Soundings. No. 34 (January 1950), 17-21.

6567 Brentano, Heinrich Von. Germany and Europe: Reflections on German Foreign Policy. New York: Praeger, 1964, 224 P.

6568 Buchan, Alastair, Editor. Europe's Futures, Europe's Choices: Models of Western Europe in the 1970S. New York: Columbia University Press, 1969, 167 P.

6569 Bullock, Alan. Germany and the Future of Europe. University of Chicago Round Table. No. 822 (10 January 1954), 11-15.

6570 Burmeister, Werner. Western Germany and Western Europe. World Affairs (London). 3:2 (April 1949), 164-174.

6571 De Menil, Lois A. F. Germany in De Gaulle's Europe. Ph.D. Thesis, Harvard University, 1972.

6572 Dichgans, Hans. Europe From Spain to Poland. German Tribune Quarterly Review. No. 2 (20 July 1968), 13-16.

6573 Dulles, Eleanor Lansing. Germany in Europe. How Can We the People Achieve a Just Peace? Selected Speeches. South Hadley: Mount Holyoke College, Institute on the United Nations, 1949, Pp. 57-59.

6574 Erhard, Ludwig. European Policy of the German Federal Government. Atlantic Community Quarterly. 2:3 (Fall 1964), 377-388.

6575 FRG, German Information Center. Germany in Europe. New York: German Information Center, C.1965, 40 P.

6576 Gasteyger, Curt. Kewenig, Wilhelm A. Kohlhase, Norbert. Europe--The Shape of Things to Come. German Tribune Quarterly Review. No. 11 (15 October 1970), 1-8.

6577 Grazynski, Michal. Dangerous Illusions. Eastern Quarterly. 5:3-4 (August-October 1952), 30-35.

6578 Haffner, Sebastian. Germany and European Unity. Twentieth Century. 152:907 (September 1952), 240-249.

6579 Hermens, Ferdinand A. Europe Between Democracy and Anarchy. Notre Dame: University of Notre Dame Press, 1951, 291 Esp. Ch. 9.

6580 Hermens, Ferdinand A. Germany, Europe and the World. Review of Politics. 7:3 (July 1945), 325-342.

6581 Kayser, Elmer Louis. Western Germany and Europe. World Affairs. 116:4 (Winter 1953), 106-108.

6582 King, David Burnett. Diplomacy and Power: Germany, Europe and the Future. South Atlantic Quarterly. 70:4 (Autumn 1971), 439-448.

6583 Kohn, Hans. Germany in the New Europe. Current History. 31:183 (November 1956), 257-261.

6584 Kohn, Hans. Germany in the New Europe. Contemporary Review. 190:1091 (November 1956), 261-265.

6585 Kwilecki, Andrzej. The Substance and Functions of the "European" Ideology in th G.F.R. (1945-1968). Polish Western Affairs. 10:2 (1969), 263-285.

6586 Luchsinger, Fred. Adenauer's Aim and Work--The Europeanization of Germany. Swiss Review of World Affairs. 17:2 (May 1967), 3-4.

6587 Luchsinger, Fred. Bonn and Europe. Swiss Review of World Affairs. 10:3 (June 1960), 5-6+.

6588 Mansfield, Michael J. Germany and the Future of Europe. Proceedings of the Academy of Political Science. 26:2 (January 1955), 113-122.

6589 Mckenzie, R. T. Germany and Europe. Canadium Forum. 27:319 (August 1947), 104-106.

6590 Mehnert, Klaus. Germany in Europe Today. Pakistan Horizon. 8:1 (March 1955), 260-269.

6591 Milyukova, Valentina. Political Integration in Bonn's Interest. International Affairs (Moscow). (July 1963), 20-25.

6592 Morgenthau, Hans J. Germany and Europe. Politics in the Twentieth Century: Impasse of American Foreign Policy. Ed. Hans J. Morgenthau. Chicago: University of Chicago Press, 1962, Pp. 195-246.

6593 Morgenthau, Hans J., Editor. Germany and the Future of Europe. Chicago: University of Chicago Press, 1951, 180 P.

6594 Nanes, Allan S. West German Policy in West Europe. Current History. 44:260 (April 1963), 214-218, 243-244.

6595 Polyanov, N. Bonn's Challenge to Europe. International Affairs (Moscow). (January 1969), 21-28.

6596 Reyman, K. How European Are the German Socialists?. Central European Federalist. 3:2-3 (November 1955), 4-8.

6597 Scherpenberg, Albert H. Van Germany and European Co-Operation. Pakistan Horizon. 5:4 (December 1952), 162-170.

6598 Schmid, Carlo. Germany and Europe. International Affairs. 27:3 (July

6599 Schmid, Carlo. Germany and Europe: The German Social Democratic Program. Foreign Affairs. 30:4 (July 1952), 531-544.

6600 Stern-Rubarth, Edgar. Is German Youth Ready for Europe?. Contemporary Review. 178:1019 (November 1950), 285-289.

6601 Stettner, Edward A., Editor. Perspectives on Europe. Cambridge: Schenkman, 1970, 191 P.

6602 Strauss, Franz-Josef. Challenge and Response: A Program for Europe. New York: Atheneum, 1970, 175 P.

6603 Walser, Martin. A German Mosaic. Encounter. 22:4 (April 1964), 33-38.

6604 Wirth, Joseph. Germany and Europe. Labour Monthly. 36:9 (September 1954), 399-404.

6605 Younger, Kenneth. Europe in the New World Power System. Aussenpolitik. 24:1 (1973), 25-38.

0.2.4. United Kingdom

6606 Albert, Ernst. Britain--Interpreter Between Europe and the Usa. Aussenpolitik. 23:4 (1972), 383-393.

6607 Beglov, S. Bonn--London: New Axis?. International Affairs (Moscow). (June 1969), 65-70.

6608 Britain and Europe: The Future. London: Times, 1967, 74 P. British and German View of Political and Economic Prospects.

6609 Donelan, Michael. West Germany and Britain: The New International Environment. Britain and West Germany: Changing Societies and the Future of Foreign Policy. Ed. Karl Kaiser and Roger Morgan. London: Oxford University Press, 1971, Pp. 41-60.

6610 Eden, Anthony. Full Circle: Memoirs. Boston: Houghton Mifflin, 1960, 676 P.

6611 Foster, John G., Editor. Britain in Western Europe: Weu and the Atlantic Alliance. London: Oxford University Press, 1956, 121 P. Report By a Chatham House Study Group.

6612 Gooch, George P. A Backward Glance. Encounter. 22:4 (April 1964), 13-16. Anglo-German Relations.

6613 Hallett, Graham. Britain and the Future of Germany. Political Quarterly. 39:3 (July-September 1968), 283-300.

6614 Henderson, James L. The G.E.R. Vale Lecture: A Contribution to Anglo-German Understanding, 1942-1958. London: Board of Anglo-German Educational Relations, 46 P.

6615 Herwarth, Hans Von. Anglo-German Relations: A German View. International Affairs (London). 39:4 (October 1963), 511-520.

6616 Hinterhoff, Eugene. The Koenigswinter Conference. Poland and Germany. 6:2 (April-June 1962), 5-10. Anglo-German Conference.

6617 Hinterhoff, Eugene. Koenigswinter in Oxford. Poland and Germany. 8:1-2 (January-June 1964), 10-17. 15Th Annual Anglo-German Conference Held in Oxford.

6618 Kaiser, Karl. Interdependence and Autonomy: Britain and the Federal Republic in Their Multinational Environment. Britain and West Germany: Changing Societies and the Future of Foreign Policy. Ed. Karl Kaiser and Roger Morgan. London: Oxford University Press, 1971, Pp. 17-40.

6619 Kaiser, Karl, Editor. Morgan, Roger P., Editor. Britain and West Germany: Changing Societies and the Future of Foreign Policy. London: Oxford University Press, 1971, 294 P.

6620 Lesser, Jonas. Germans and British. Contemporary Review. 197 (June 1960), 331-334.

6621 Levy, Hermann J. England and Germany: Affinity and Contrast. Leigh-on-Sea, Essex: Thames Bank, 1949, 167 P.

6622 Macmillan, Harold. Pointing the Way, 1959-1961. New York: Harper & Row, 1972, 504 P.

6623 Macmillan, Harold. Riding the Storm, 1956-1959. New York: Harper & Row, 1971, 786 P.

6624 Macmillan, Harold. Tides of Fortune, 1945-1955. New York: Harper & Row, 1969, 729 P.

6625 Morgan, Roger P. The New Germany: Implications for British Policy. Round Table. 60:239 (July 1970), 249-255.

6626 Norden, Albert. Britain and German Competition. New Central European Observer. 5:7 (29 March 1952), 107-108.

6627 Northedge, F. S. British Foreign Policy: The Process of Readjustment, 1945-1961. London: Allen and Unwin, 1962, 336 P., Esp. Ch. 3.

6628 Prittie, Terence C. F. The Germans and the English: Who Is Being Beastly to Whom?. Encounter. 13:6 (December 1959), 23-38. Response By Francis Williams in 14:2 (February 1960), 60-62.

6629 Prittie, Terence C. F. Still Beastly to the Germans?. Encounter. 27:1 (July 1966), 42-43.

6630 Proebst, Herman. German-British Relations Since the War: A German View. Britain and West Germany: Changing Societies and the Future of Foreign Policy. Ed. Karl Kaiser and Roger Morgan. London: Oxford University Press, 1971, Pp. 191-202.

6631 Public Opinion: Attitudes to the German People. Political Quarterly. 19:2 (April-June 1948), 160-166. British Attitudes Toward Germans.

6632 Quaestor. Britain, the Ussr and Germany. Labour Monthly. 49 (February 1967), 68-75.

6633 Quaestor. Wilson's Bonn Visit. Labour Monthly. 51 (March 1969), 122-125.

6634 Richner, Edmund. Wilton Park--A Bridge Between Two Nations. Swiss Review of World Affairs. 2:7 (October 1952), 20-22. German-British Discussions Among Leaders of Public Opinion.

6635 Rose, Saul. The Labour Party and German Rearmament: A View From Transport House. Political Studies. 14:2 (June 1966), 133-144.

6636 Schaffer, Gordon. The British People and German Militarism. German Foreign Policy (GDR). 1:3 (1962), 272-278.

6637 Schaffer, Gordon. British Policy Towards Germany. German Foreign Policy (GDR). 3:6 (1964), 431-434.

6638 Steel, Sir Christopher. Anglo-German Relations. International Affairs (London). 39:4 (October 1963), 521-532.

6639 Strauss, Emil. Common Sense About the Common Market: Germany and Britain in Post-War Europe. London: Allen and Unwin, 1958, 168 P.

6640 UK, Foreign Office. Documents

Relating to the Further Support of the United Kingdom Forces Stationed in the Territory of the Federal Republic of Germany for 1956-57. London: H.M. Stationery Office, Cmd. 9802, 1956, 3 P.

6641 Watt, Donald C. Anglo-German Relations Today and Tomorrow. Britain and West Germany: Changing Societies and the Future of Foreign Policy. Ed. Karl Kaiser and Roger Morgan. London: Oxford University Press, 1971, Pp. 203-218.

6642 Watt, Donald C. Britain and Germany: The Last Three Years. International Journal. 23:4 (Autumn 1968), 560-569.

6643 Watt, Donald C. Britain Looks to Germany: British Opinion and Policy Towards Germany Since 1945. London: Wolff, 1965, 164 P.

6644 Watt, Donald C. Koenigswinter, 1965. Quarterly Review. 303:646 (October 1965), 433-443.

6645 Wilmot, Chester. Britain's Strategic Relationship to Europe. International Affairs (London). 29:4 (October 1953), 409-417.

6646 Wilson, Harold. The Labour Government, 1964-1970: A Personal Record. London: Weidenfeld and Nicolson, and Michael Joseph, 1971, 836 P.

6647 Zilliacus, K. Britain and the Menace of German Militarism. International Affairs (Moscow). (March 1959), 38-45.

0.2.5. France

6648 Bechtoldt, Heinrich. German-French Friendship. Aussenpolitik. 24:1 (1973), 52-62.

6649 Billoux, Francois. The German Peace Treaty and De Gaulle's Policy. World Marxist Review. 4:12 (December 1961), 9-14.

6650 Brogan, Denis W. Still Europe's Riddle: France and Germany. New York Times Magazine. (26 September 1954), 9+.

6651 Chopra, H. S. Willy Brandt's "Ostpolitik" and Its Impact on Franco-German Relations. India Quarterly. 28:3 (July-September 1972), 227-235.

6652 Claude, Henri. Economic Aspects of the Paris-Bonn Axis. World Marxist Review: Problems of Peace and Socialism 6:12 (December 1963), 28-35.

6653 Delarue, Maurice. France--for a European Future. Aussenpolitik. 25:2 (1974), 134-145.

6654 Deutsch, Harold C. The Impact of the Franco-German Entente. Annals of the American Academy of Political and Social Science. 348 (July 1963), 82-94.

6655 Dolinin, V. Economic Foundation of Paris-Bonn Axis. International Affairs (Moscow). (November 1962), 19-24.

6656 Dubrovin, Vi. Military and Economic Collaboration Between France and Germany. International Affairs (Moscow). (January 1963), 80-85.

6657 Duroselle, J. B. German-Franco Relations Since 1945. Review of Politics. 14:4 (October 1952), 501-519.

6658 Dziewanowski, M. K. France and the Problem of Security in Germany. Current History. 15:85 (September 1948), 144-148.

6659 Fackler, Maxim. The Franco-German Treaty: The End of Hereditary Enmity.

World Today. 21:1 (January 1965), 24-33.

6660 Farquharson, John E. Holt, Stephen C. Europe From Below: An Assessment of Franco-German Popular Contacts. London: Allen and Unwin, 1975, Xi and 218 Pp.

6661 Fiedler, Horst. The War Pact Between West Germany and France. German Foreign Policy (GDR). 2:3 (1963), 191-199.

6662 Franco-German Treaty of Reconciliation. Current History. 44:260 (April 1963), 237-239, 245.

6663 Gandillac, Maurice De. France Faces Germany. Review of Politics. 9:2 (April 1947), 173-182.

6664 Gooch, George P. Franco-German Coexistence at Last?. Foreign Affairs. 37:3 (April 1959), 432-442.

6665 Grosser, Alfred. France and Germany: Divergent Outlooks. Foreign Affairs. 44:1 (October 1965), 26-36.

6666 Grosser, Alfred. France and Germany in the Atlantic Community. International Organization. 17:3 (Summer 1963), 550-573.

6667 Grosser, Alfred. France and Germany: Less Divergent Outlooks?. Foreign Affairs. 48:2 (January 1970), 235-244.

6668 Grosser, Alfred. Franco-Soviet Relations Today. Santa Monica: Rand Corporation, Rm-5382-Pr, August 1967, 103 P.

6669 Grosser, Alfred. Germany and France: A Confrontation. France Defeats Edc. Ed. Daniel Lerner and Raymond Aron. New York: Praeger, 1957, Pp. 54-70.

6670 Hart, Adrian Liddell. Strange Company. London: Weidenfeld & Nicolson, 1953, 211 P. Germans in French Foreign Legion.

6671 Kairouz, Akl. Franco-German Relations Between 1958-1968. Ph.D. Thesis, University of Utah, 1968, 269 P.

6672 Knapton, Ernest J. France and Germany: France Has Lost Her Voice in Europe. Current History. 15:87 (November 1948), 264-268.

6673 Koch, Susan J. The Local Impact of the European Economic Community: Economic and Social Ties of Alsace With West Germany. International Organization. 28:2 (Spring 1974), 153-178.

6674 Lauret, Rene. France and Germany: The Legacy of Charlemagne. Chicago: Regnery, 1964, 272 P.

6675 Lavergne, Bernard. Deep Differences Between Paris and Bonn. International Affairs (Moscow). (December 1960), 65-67.

6676 Lerner, Daniel. Franco-German Relations: Politics, Public and the Press Journal of International Affairs. 10:2 (1956), 138-152.

6677 Lewis, Flora. Franco-German "Twins"-- A Startling Fact. New York Times Magazine. (29 May 1960), 14+. Twin Cities.

6678 Lewis, Flora. From Deadly Hatred to Solemn Accord: France and Germany. New York Times Magazine. (8 July 1962), 6-7.

6679 Lewis, Flora. The Hard Thing Is the German Uniform. New York Times Magazine. (20 November 1960), 14+. German Nato Troops in France.

6680 Luchsinger, Fred. After De Gaulle's Visit to West Germany. Swiss Review of World Affairs. 12:7 (October 1962), 5-6.

6681 Luchsinger, Fred. De Gaulle's Germany Policy. Swiss Review of World Affairs. 14:12 (March 1965), 9-12.

6682 Luchsinger, Fred. Estrangement Between Paris and Bonn. Swiss Review of World Affairs. 14:7 (October 1964), 1-2.

6683 Lutz, Hermann. German-French Relations: Basis for European Peace. Chicago: Regnery, 1957, 257 P.

6684 Lvov, M. Mishin, A. France and West Germany. International Affairs (Moscow). (April 1959), 21-29.

6685 Macridis, Roy C. Conflicts Muted By Hegemony: France and Germany. Conflict in World Politics. Ed. Steven L. Spiegel and Kenneth N. Waltz. Cambridge: Winthrop, 1971, Pp. 139-154.

6686 Observer. The Bonn-Paris Axis. World Marxist Review: Problems of Peace and Socialism 2:4 (April 1959), 18-26.

6687 O'Donnell, James P. Beauty and the Beast--France Takes a Slow New Look at Germany. This Is Germany. Ed. Arthur Settel. New York: Sloane, 1950, Pp. 346-358.

6688 Parias, Louis-Henri. Franco-German Reconciliation and European Unity. Western Integration and the Future of Eastern Europe. Ed. David S. Collier and Kurt Glaser. Chicago: Regnery, 1964, Pp. 162-174.

6689 Paris-Bonn Axis--Conspiracy Against Peace. International Affairs (Moscow). (March 1963), 46-56. Panel Discussion.

6690 Puchala, Donald J. Integration and Disintegration in Franco-German Relations 1954-1965. International Organization. 24:2 (Spring 1970), 183-208.

6691 Schlagintweit, Reinhard. Bonn-Paris: Models for Cultureurope. Aussenpolitik. 23:3 (1972), 252-262.

6692 Schmitt, Hans A. Germany, France and "Europe". Current History. 54:321 (May 1968), 257-262.

6693 Schuman, Robert. French Policy Towards Germany Since the War. London: Oxford University Press, 1954, 24 P. Stevenson Memorial Lecture, No. 4.

6694 Schumann, Maurice. France and Germany in the New Europe. Foreign Affairs. 41:1 (October 1962), 66-77.

6695 Slotta, Peter L. France, Germany, and European Unification: A Formal Analysis. Ph.D. Thesis, University of Pennsylvania, 1968, 312 P.

6696 Townroe, B. S. Post-War Alsace. Contemporary Review. 169:965 (May 1946), 284-288.

6697 White, Theodore H. France and Germany--Fear and Hatred. New York Times Magazine. (1 February 1953), 7+

6698 Willis, F. Roy. France, Germany and the New Europe, 1945-1967. Stanford: Stanford University Press, 1968, 431 P.

6699 Yuryev, N. Bonn-Paris Axis: Murky Prospects. International Affairs (Moscow). (November 1964), 16-22.

6700 Zhukov, Yuri. Paris-Bonn Alliance: Who Stands to Gain?. International Affairs (Moscow). (August 1963), 60-70.

O.2.6. France: Saar Question

6701 Blow, Jonathan. Quiet Flows the Saar. Quarterly Review. 288:585 (July 1950), 318-328.

6702 Boeckman, M. June. Halpern, Manfred. Price, Arnold H. The Present Status of the Saar. Documents and State Papers, Vol. 1, October 1948. Washington: Department of State, Office of Public Affairs, October 1948, Pp. 435-450.

6703 Burtenshaw, D. Regional Renovation in the Saarland. Geographical Review. 62:1 (January 1972), 1-12.

6704 Colby, Reginald. The Saar Past and Present. Quarterly Review. 292:602 (October 1954), 497-509.

6705 Collins, Ellen. The Saarland: Key to European Unity. World Affairs. 116:2 (Summer 1953), 42-43.

6706 Council of Europe, Consultative Assembly. The Future Position of the Saar: Basic Documents. Strasbourg: Council of Europe, Consultative Assembly, 5th Session, 1953, 285 P.

6707 Cowan, Laing Gray. France and the Saar, 1680-1948. New York: Columbia University Press, 1950, 247 P., Esp. pp. 179-232.

6708 Craddock, Walter R. United States Diplomacy and the Saar Dispute, 1949-195 Orbis. 12:1 (Spring 1968), 247-267.

6709 E. W. The Return of the Saar to Germany. World Today. 13:1 (January 1957), 27-36.

6710 Fay, Sidney B. The Saar Problem: France and Germany in Conflict. Current History. 18:105 (May 1950), 257-262.

6711 Freymond, Jacques. The Saar Conflict, 1945-1955. New York: Praeger, 1960, 395 P.

6712 Held, Colbert C. The New Saarland. Geographical Review. 41:4 (October 1951), 590-605.

6713 John, I. G. France, Germany, and the Saar. World Affairs (London). 43:3 (July 1950), 277-293.

6714 Kitzinger, Uwe W. The Economics of the Saar Question. Oxford: N.P., 1958, 160 P.

6715 Laubach, John H. The Franco-German Saar Statute: Some Factors Contributing to Its Rejection in the 1955 Referendum. Ph.D. Thesis, Harvard University, 1958.

6716 Rawlings, E. H. The Saar Problem. Contemporary Review. 183:1046 (February 1953), 77-80.

6717 Reischer, O. R. Saar Coal After Two World Wars. Political Science Quarterly. 64:1 (March 1949), 50-64.

6718 Roegele, Otto B. Aspects of the Saar Problem. Review of Politics. 14:4 (October 1952), 484-500.

6719 The Saar as an International Problem. World Today. 8:7 (July 1952), 299-307.

6720 Schneider, Heinrich. Voices of the German Saar Opposition. Wiesbaden: Deutscher Saarbund, 1952, 22 P.

6721 Stern-Rubarth, Edgar. The Saar. Contemporary Review. 177:1011 (March 1950), 136-139.

6722 Taylor, A. J. P. France, Germany, and the Saar. International Journal. 8:1 (Winter 1952-53), 27-31.

6723 Thumm, Garold Wesley. The Saar. Current History. 30:176 (April 1956), 225-230.

6724 US, Hicog, Office of Political Affairs. Saar Constitution. N.P.: Hicog, Office of Political Affairs, 1950, 24 P.

6725 Van Hoek, Kees. The Saar. Contemporary Review. 180:1032

(December 1951), 329-333.

6726 White, Theodore H. Europe's Aching Trouble Spot--The Saar. New York Times Magazine. (23 November 1952), 11+.

6727 Wiskemann, Elizabeth. The Saar Moves Toward Germany. Foreign Affairs. 34:2 (January 1956), 287-296.

O.2.7. Other European Countries

6728 A. H. H. Some Problems Facing Denmark. World Today. 8:10 (October 1952), 420-429.

6729 Berghes, Ingeborg Von. Spain En Route to Europe. Aussenpolitik. 21:2 (1970), 229-236.

6730 Debrouwere, Jan. Belgium's Position and the German Question. German Foreign Policy (GDR). 1:1 (1962), 58-62.

6731 Gruben, Baron De. Belgian Views on the German Treaty. International Affairs. 23:3 (July 1947), 326-335.

6732 Hynd, John B. Germany and Austria. British Speeches of the Day. 4:5 (June 1946), 348-359. Extracts of Addresses, House of Commons, 10 May 1946.

6733 Katzenstein, Peter J. Displaced Partners: Austria and Germany Since 1815. Ph.D. Thesis, Harvard University, 1973.

6734 Klein, Peter. Austria Between E.E.C. and Neutrality. German Foreign Policy (GDR). 1:5 (1962), 497-504.

6735 Sabelnikov, L. West German Economic Penetration of Austria. International Affairs (Moscow). (February 1960), 75-80.

6736 Seidl-Hohenveldern, Ignaz. The Austrian-German Arbitral Tribunal. Syracuse: Syracuse University Press, 1972, 261 P. Established By Property Treaty, 15 June 1957.

O.3. Other Regions and Organizations (see Also I.9.6; I.9.7)

O.3.1. Middle East

6737 Geiss, Imanuel. The Germans and the Middle East Crisis. Midstream. 13:9 (November 1967), 3-9.

6738 Gerlach, Frederick H. The Tragic Triangle: Israel, Divided Germany, and the Arabs, 1956-1965. Ph.D. Thesis, Columbia University, 1968, 415 P.

6739 Germany and the Uar. Egyptian Economic and Political Review. 6:7 (July-August 1960), 30-Page Suppl. Following P. 18

6740 Hauenstein, Fritz. West Germany and the Middle East. Middle Eastern Affairs. 7:1 (January 1956), 11-19.

6741 Hoeppner, Rolf-Roger. Iran - Germany - European Community. Aussenpolitik. 26:3 (1975), 338-353.

6742 Imhoff, Christoph Von. Germans and Arabs--Prospects and Limitations of Bonn's Middle Eastern Policies. Bulletin of the Wiener Library. 25:22-23 (1971), 17-23.

6743 Ivens, Hans. Bonn's "Hallstein Doctrine" Is Also Retreating in Iraq. German Foreign Policy (GDR). 1:6 (1962), 635-640.

6744 Joesten, Joachim. Germany and the Suez Crisis. Great Barrington, Mass.: Joachim Joesten, New Germany Reports No. 34, January 1957, 16 P.

6745 Joesten, Joachim. Hjalmar Schacht's Greatest Coup: How He Masterminded Plot Designed to End American Influence in Saudi Arabia. New York: Joachim Joesten, New Germany Reports No. 30 January 1955, 22 P.

6746 Joesten, Joachim. Those German Rocketeers in Egypt. New York: Joachim Joesten, New Germany Reports No. 62, November 1963-May 1964, 17 and 14 P.

6747 Koroljov, W. Bonn, Algeria, O.A.S.... German Foreign Policy (GDR). 1:5 (1962), 482-490.

6748 Laqueur, Walter Z. Bonn, Cairo, Jerusalem: The Triple Crisis. Commentary. 39:5 (May 1965), 29-38.

6749 Malone, Joseph J. Germany and the Suez Crisis. Middle East Journal. 20:1 (Winter 1966), 20-30.

6750 Natorp, Klaus. Germany and the Arab World. United Asia. 19:6 (November-December 1967), 434-435.

6751 Sedar, Irving. Greenberg, Harold J. Behind the Egyptian Sphinx: Nasser's Strange Bedfellows. Philadelphia: Chilton, 1960, 171 P., Esp. Pt. 1, Ch. 3.

6752 Speier, Hans. Crisis and Catharsis in the Middle East, 1965: A Chapter of German Foreign Policy. Santa Monica: Rand Corporation, P-3615, June 1967, 80 P.

O.3.2. Israel (See Also D.3.3; L.4.2)

6753 Astakhov, S. Bonn-Tel Aviv Axis. International Affairs (Moscow). (November 1968), 41-45.

6754 Balabkins, Nicholas. West German Reparations to Israel. New Brunswick: Rutgers University Press, 1970, 416 P.

6755 Brecher, Michael. Decisions in Israel's Foreign Policy. New Haven: Yale University Press, 1974, 675 P.

6756 Brecher, Michael. Images, Process and Feedback in Foreign Policy: Israel's Decisions on German Reparations. American Political Science Review. 67:1 (March 1973), 73-102.

6757 Deutschkron, Inge. Bonn and Jerusalem: The Strange Coalition. Philadelphia: Chilton, 1970, 357 P.

6758 Feron, James. A German Ambassador to Israel: Rolf F. Pauls. New York Times Magazine. (31 October 1965), 102+.

6759 Fischer, Alfred Joachim. Israel and the German Federal Republic. Contemporary Review. 192:1100 (August 1957), 98-101.

6760 German Reparations to Israel. World Today. 10:6 (June 1954), 258-274.

6761 Giniewski, Paul. Germany and Israel. India Quarterly. 11:1 (January 1955), 15-30. German-Israeli Reparation Treaty, 10 September 1952.

6762 Giniewski, Paul. Germany and Israel: The Reparations Treaty of September 10, 1952. World Affairs Quarterly. 30:2 (July 1959), 169-185.

6763 Grossmann, Kurt R. The German-Israeli Agreement. Chicago Jewish Forum. 12:2 (Winter 1953-54), 73-79.

6764 Grossmann, Kurt R. The German-Israeli Agreement. South Atlantic Quarterly. 53:4 (October 1954), 464-476.

6765 Grossmann, Kurt R. Germany and Israel: Six Years Luxemburg Agreement. New York: Herzl Institute Pamphlet No. 11, 1958, 31 P.

6766 Grossmann, Kurt R. Germany's Moral Debt: The German-Israel Agreement. Washington: Public Affairs Press, 1954, 71 P.

6767 Groussard, Serge. The Blood of Israel: The Massacre of the Israeli Athletes, The Olympics, 1972. New York: William Morrow, 1975, 464 P.

6768 Honig, Frederick. The Reparations Agreement Between Israel and the Federal Republic of Germany. American Journal of International Law. 48:4 (October 1954), 564-578.

6769 Shabecoff, Philip. Action Atonement. New York Times Magazine. (7 November 1965), 149+.

6770 Society for Christian and Jewish Cooperation. Agreement Between the Federal Republic of Germany and State of Israel, September 10, 1952-September 10, 1962. Duesseldorf: Kalima, 1962, 15 P.

6771 Vogel, Rolf. The German Path to Israel: A Documentation. Chester Springs, Pa.: Dufour, 1969, 325 P.

6772 Walichnowski, Tadeusz. Israel and the German Federal Republic. Warsaw: Interpress, 1968, 199 P.

O.3.3. Africa

6773 Afro-Asian Solidarity Committee in the GDR. Memorandum on Cooperation Between the West German Federal Republic and the Republic of South Africa in the Military and Atomic Fields. Berlin: Afro-Asian Solidarity Committee in the GDR, 1964, 29 P.

6774 Afro-Asian Solidarity Committee in the GDR. The Bonn-Pretoria Alliance: The Expansionist Policy of the Federal Republic of (West) Germany in Southern Africa and Its Basis in the Republic of South Africa. Dresden: Zeit Im Bild, 1967, 96 P.

6775 Czaya, Eberhard. The New Colonial Policy of German Imperialism With Regard to Tanganyika. German Foreign Policy (GDR). 1:2 (1962), 166-174.

6776 Czaya, Eberhard. Apartheid Propaganda in West Germany. German Foreign Policy (GDR). 3:4 (1964), 299-304.

6777 Eze, Onyeabo. Germany as I See It. Bad Godesberg: Inter Nationes, 1968, 87 P.

6778 FRG, German Embassy in Malawi. Fruitful Years: The Story of Malawian-German Friendsh 1964-67. Limbe, Malawi: German Embassy, C.1968, 23 P.

6779 Fischer, Per. German Policy in Africa. Aussenpolitik. 21:2 (1971), 187-199.

6780 Kirchner, Wolfram. A Major Setback for Bonn's Foreign Policy. German Foreign Policy (GDR). 4:5 (1965), 380-385. FRG-Tanzanian Relations.

6781 Schmokel, Wolfe W. Germany in the Underdeveloped World. Current History. 50:297 (May 1966), 281-288+.

6782 Wetzel, Gerhard. How the Press of the German Imperialists Writes About Africans. German Foreign Policy (GDR). 3:4 (1964), 291-298.

O.3.4. Asia; Oceania

6783 Abduction of South Korean Students and Teachers From West Germany. Minerva. 6:1 (Autumn 1967), 144-146.

6784 Afro-Asian Solidarity Committee in the GDR. The West German Government Involved in Vietnam. Dresden: Afro-Asian Solidarity Committee in the GDR, Vietnam Committee, 1966, 38 P.

6785 Bechtoldt, Heinrich. Federal Republic of Germany and China: Problems of Trade and Diplomacy. Policies Towards China: Views From Six Continents. Ed. Abraham M. Halpern. New York: Mcgraw-Hill, 1965, Pp. 77-102.

6786 Cattani, Alfred. Bonn's Relations With Peking. Swiss Review of World Affairs. 22:8 (November 1972), 7.

6787 Fitt, A. B. A Study of Racial Attitudes During and After the War by the Thurstone Technique. British Journal of Psychology. 46:4 (November 1955), 306-309. Australian Attitudes Toward Germans and Japanese, 1940-1953.

6788 Frank, Paul. German Policy Towards Asia. Aussenpolitik. 22:1 (1971), 3-8.

6789 Henle, Guenter. Germany and India. Foreign Affairs Reports (New Delhi). 7:4 (April 1958), 42-46.

6790 Leifer, Walter. India and the Germans: 500 Years of Indo-German Contacts. Bombay: Shakuntala Publishing House, 1971, VII and 350 P.

6791 Martin, Bernd. Kiesinger's Unpeaceful Mission in Asia. German Foreign Policy (GDR). 7:2 (1968), 118-122.

6792 Mookerjee, Girija K. Indo-German Relations Today. United Asia. 19:6 (November-December 1967), 275-283.

6793 Rennhack, Horst. Bonn Engaged in the Barbarous War in Vietnam. German Foreign Policy (GDR). 5:5 (1966), 342-354.

6794 Sommer, Theo. Germany and the Commonwealth: A Wobbly Bridge Between Races. Round Table. 61:244 (October 1971), 503-505.

6795 Wirsing, Giselher. Germany and Asia. United Asia. 19:6 (November-December 1967), 457-461.

O.3.5. Latin America

6796 Arnold, Hans. Cultural Cooperation With Latin America. Aussenpolitik. 25:1 (1974), 73-79.

6797 Dorn, Herbert. Germany in Latin America. Current History. 28:163 (March 1955), 168-176.

6798 Gleich, Albrecht Von. Germany and Latin America. Santa Monica: Rand Corporation, Rm-5523-Rc, June 1968, 124 P.

6799 Grigoryan, Y. Bonn Leaps Into South America. International Affairs (Moscow). (February 1964), 73-77.

6800 Hampe, Karl-Alexander. Latin America Enters World Politics. Aussenpolitik. 25:2 (1974), 227-241.

6801 Heilman, John Greene. Ideological Conflict and Institutional Differentiation In West German Relations With Latin America. Ph.D. Thesis, New York University, 1973, 287 P.

6802 Uschner, Manfred. West Germany and Latin America. German Foreign Policy (GDR). 8:3 (1969), 195-205.

6803 Westphalen, Juergen. A German-Latin American Economic Congress?. Intereconomics. No. 11 (November 1970), 338-340.

O.3.6. International Organizations (See Also E.3.4.7)

6804 Beer, Max. Germany and the United Nations. Swiss Review of World Affairs. 6:7 (October 1956), 11-13.

6805 Beloff, Max. National Government and International Government. International Organization. 13:4 (Autumn 1959), 538-549.

6806 Chaumont, Charles. A French View on Security Through International Organization. International Organization. 4:2 (May 1950), 236-

246.

6807 Droege, Heinz. Muench, Fritz. Puttkamer, Ellinor Von. The Federal Republic of Germany and the United Nations. New York: Carnegie Endowment for International Peace, 1967, 206 P.

6808 Gehlhoff, Walter. The Federal Republic of Germany in the Un. Aussenpolitik. 25:1 (1974), 3-12.

6809 George, Manfred. West Germany Sends a Liberal to the Un: A Portrait of Felix Von Eckardt. New Leader. 38:10 (7 March 1955), 7.

6810 Hay, John. Germany in International Organization. Governing Postwar Germany. Ed. Edward H. Litchfield and Associates. Ithaca: Cornell University Press, 1953, Pp. 184-203.

6811 Hoehnel, Gerd. The West German Federal Republic and the United Nations. German Foreign Policy (GDR). 6:2 (1967), 177-183.

6812 Plehwe, F.-K. Von. The International Organizations. Aussenpolitik. 22:2 (1971), 156-165.

6813 Rapp, J. The United Nations and Germany. International and Comparative Law Quarterly. 1:3 (July 1952), 354-358.

6814 Ungerer, Werner. The United Nations Revisited. Aussenpolitik. 24:3 (1973), 307-317.

0.4. Defense and Detente

0.4.1. National Security Policy (See Also 0.1.6)

6815 FRG, Federal Ministry of Defense. White Paper 1969 on the Defense Policy of the Government of The Federal Republic of Germany. Bonn: Press and Information Office, 1969, 83 P.

6816 Geffer, William. The Role of the Military in West German Defense Policy Making. Ph.D. Thesis, University of Denver, 1971, 592 P.

6817 Gerlach, Hans. The West German Contribution to Nato and European Security. Orbis. 13:1 (Spring 1969), 199-209.

6818 Gohlert, Ernst W. An Organizational Perspective on German National Security Policy. Comparative Defense Policy. Ed. Frank B. Horton III. Baltimore: Johns Hopkins University Press, 1974, Pp. 146-155.

6819 Hahn, Walter F. Between Westpolitik and Ostpolitik: Changing West German Security Views. Beverly Hills: Sage Publications, 1975.

6820 Jensen, Lloyd. Postwar Democratic Polities: National-International Linkages in the Defense Policy of the Defeated States. Linkage Politics: Essays on the Convergence of National and International Systems. Ed. James N. Rosenau. New York: Free Press, 1969, Pp. 304-323.

6821 Lough, Thomas S. The Military Liaison Missions in Germany. Journal of Conflict Resolution. 11:2 (June 1967), 258-261.

6822 Mackintosh, Malcolm. Three Detentes: 1955-1964. Detente: Cold War Strategies in Transition. Ed. Eleanor Lansing Dulles and Robert Dickson Crane. New York: Praeger, 1965, Pp. 103-120.

6823 Magathan, Wallace C. Some Bases of West German Military Policy. Journal of Conflict Resolution. 4:1 (March 1960), 123-137.

6824 Magathan, Wallace C. West German Defense Policy. Orbis. 8:2 (Summer 1964), 292-315.

6825 Mendershausen, Horst. Defense Policies and Developments in the Federal Republic of Germany. Santa Monica: Rand Corporation, P-3792, February 1968, 19 P.

6826 Mendershausen, Horst. West Germany's Defense Policies. Current History. 54:321 (May 1968), 268-274.

6827 Nanes, Allan S. German Rearmament and the European Balance. Current History. 38:221 (January 1960), 24-29.

6828 Plischke, Elmer. West German Foreign and Defense Policy. Orbis. 12:4 (Winter 1969), 1098-1136.

6829 Schmidt, Helmut. Defense or Retaliation: A German View. New York: Praeger, 1962, 264 P.

6830 Schrader, Rudolf. International Research for Defence. Aussenpolitik. 23:2 (1972), 197-204.

6831 Steinhaus, Rolf. Defence and European Unification. Aussenpolitik. 24:3 (1973), 298-306.

6832 Strauss, Franz-Josef. Maritime Deterrence in the Baltic Sea. Free World Forum. 1:1 (January 1959), 44-46.

6833 Wieck, Hans-Georg. Defence Policy and Force Structure. Aussenpolitik. 24:2 (1973), 154-164.

6834 Ziemke, Earl F. West Germany's Security Policy. Current History. 62:369 (May 1972), 239-243.

0.4.2. Rearmament Within Edc, 1949-54 (See Also E.4)

6835 Agreement on Rearming Western Germany. Current History. 20:114 (February 1951), 106-107.

6836 Amery, Julian. German Rearmament: The Hour of Decision. Twentieth Century. 152:907 (September 1952), 233-239.

6837 Arms for Germans. Round Table. 41:161 (December), 22-23.

6838 Baldwin, Hanson W. Strategy for Two Atomic Worlds. Foreign Affairs. 28:3 (April 1950), 386-397.

6839 Bevan, Aneurin, and Others. It Need Not Happen: The Alternative to German Rearmament. London: Tribune, 1954, 32 P.

6840 Birch, Lionel. Germany and Western Union. Current Affairs. No. 107 (27 May 1950), 1-14.

6841 Brandt, Gerhard. Socio-Economic Aspects of German Rearmament. Archives Europeennes De Sociologie. 6:2 (1965), 294-308.

6842 Bussche, Axel Von Dem. German Rearmament: Hopes and Fears. Foreign Affairs. 32:1 (October 1953), 68-79.

6843 Clark, Delbert. Again the Goose Step: The Lost Fruits of Victory. Indianapolis: Bobbs-Merrill, 1949, 297 P.

6844 Davidson, Basil. Edc--The Shadow of a Gunman. London: Union of Democratic Control, 1954, 11 P.

6845 Davidson, Basil. Guns for the Germans? the Arguments for and Against German Rearmament. London: Peace News, 1950, 13 P.

6846 Davidson, Basil. The Road to Hell. London: Union of Democratic Control, 1952, 18 P. Rearmament.

6847 De Mendelssohn, Peter. Germany's Generals Stage a Comeback. Commentary. 12:4 (October 1951), 314-323.

6848 Dobrich, Joseph J. R. The European

Defense Treaty in France and Germany. Ph.D. Thesis, New School for Social Research, 1958.

6849 The European Defence Community: Germany and the Western Alliance. Round Table. 43:172 (September 1953), 335-342.

6850 Fliess, Walter. Germany's Contribution to Defence. Socialist Commentary. 14 (October 1950), 224-226.

6851 Fliess, Walter. Re-Armament of Germany--Now or Later?. Socialist Commentary. 15 (March 1951), 52-54.

6852 Geilinger, Eduard. Spotlight on the New German Army. Swiss Review of World Affairs. 2:9 (December 1952), 3-4.

6853 Geilinger, Eduard. West Germany Will Contribute--at a Price. Swiss Review of World Affairs. 1:10 (January 1952), 3-5.

6854 The German Ally: Prospects of European Defence. Round Table. 42:168 (September 1952), 312-318.

6855 Gerst, Wilhelm Karl. The Remilitarisation of West Germany. New Central European Observer. 4:2 (20 January 1951), 295-296.

6856 H. G. L. German Rearmament. World Today. 7:2 (February 1951), 69-76.

6857 Harsch, Joseph C. Can Germany Contain Russia Safely?. Annals of the American Academy of Political and Social Science. 282 (July 1952), 36-40.

6858 Holborn, Hajo. Germany's Role in the Defense of Western Europe. Proceedings of the Academy of Political Science. 26:2 (January 1955), 86-100.

6859 Huberman, Leo. Sweezy, Paul M. Eisenhower, German Rearmament, and World Peace. Monthly Review. 2:11 (March 1951), 479-486.

6860 Joesten, Joachim. The Challenge of German Neutralism. New York: Joachim Joesten, New Germany Reports No. 17, 1952, 21 P.

6861 Kennan, George F. For the Defense of Europe: A New Approach. New York Times Magazine. (12 September 1954), 7+.

6862 Kimche, Jon. Can Germany Be Defended?. Twentieth Century. 148:884 (October 1950), 207-216.

6863 Kimche, Jon. Is a German Army Necessary?. Twentieth Century. 147:880 (June 1950), 347-355.

6864 Klugmann, James. Uncle Sam's New Recruits. Labour Monthly. 32:4 (April 1950), 181-186. German Rearmament.

6865 Kuehnelt-Leddihn, Erik R. Von. German Rearmament. Catholic World. 172:1031 (February 1951), 365-371.

6866 Kunz, Josef L. Treaty Establishing the European Defense Community. American Journal of International Law. 47:2 (April 1953), 275-281.

6867 Lania, Leo. Guns for Germans: But Which Germans?. United Nations World. 4:12 (December 1950), 13-16.

6868 Leites, Nathan C. De La Malene, Christian. Paris From Edc to Weu. Santa Monica: Rand Corporation, Rm-1668-Rc, 1956, 210 P. French Parliamentarians' Attitudes Toward German Rearmament.

6869 Lerner, Daniel, Editor. Aron, Raymond, Editor. France Defeats Edc. New York: Praeger, 1957, 225 P.

6870 Lincoln, G. A. Germany's Place in the Search for Security. How Can We the People Achieve a Just Peace? Selected Speeches. South Hadley: Mount Holyoke College, Institute on the United Nations, 1949, Pp. 60-67.

6871 Loewenstein, Karl. The Bonn Constitution and the European Defense Community Treaties: A Study in Judicial Frustration. Yale Law Journal. 64:6 (May 1955), 805-839.

6872 Luethy, Herbert. The First Step Toward "One Europe". Commentary. 15:1 (January 1953), 19-28.

6873 Martel, Giffard. The Defence of the West: Regular Armies and German Man-Power. Commonwealth and Empire Review. 84:534 (October 1950), 11-14.

6874 Martin, Laurence W. The American Decision to Rearm Germany. American Civil-Military Decisions: A Book of Case Studies. Ed. Harold Stein. Birmingham: University of Alabama Press, 1963, Pp. 643-665.

6875 Max, Alan. Nazi Army; or, Peaceful German?. New York: New Century, 1952, 15 P.

6876 Mcgeehan, Robert J. American Diplomacy and the German Rearmament Question, 1950-1953. Ph.D. Thesis, Columbia University, 1969, 542 P.

6877 Middleton, Drew. Ghosts of the Old Wehrmacht. New York Times Magazine. (29 January 1950), 13+.

6878 Morris, Stuart. Neutrality: Germany's Way to Peace. London: Peace News, 1953, 12 P.

6879 Neumann, Franz L. Germany and Western Union. Proceedings of the Academy of Political Science. 23:3 (May 1949), 35-45.

6880 Onslow, C. G. D. West German Rearmament. World Politics. 3:4 (July 1951), 450-485.

6881 Parkin, Ben. Security--or Nazis Re-Armed?. Labour Monthly. 36:10 (October 1954), 447-450.

6882 Pollitt, Harry. In Defence of Peace: The Case Against Rearming the Nazis. London: Communist Party, 1954, 16 P.

6883 Polyzoides, Adamantios Th. Germany: Our Major Problem. World Affairs Interpreter. 22:1 (Spring 1951), 57-71.

6884 The Remilitarisation of Germany. Contemporary Issues. 2:8 (Spring 1951), 312-320.

6885 Riemeck, Renate. Rearmament and Democracy in Germany. Fortnightly. 168:1008 (December 1950), 357-362.

6886 Schaffer, Gordon. The Plot to Re-Arm Germany. New Central European Observer. 2:26 (24 December 1949), 310.

6887 Schnitzer, Ewald W. Public Discussion in Western Germany of the Defense of Europe, March to June 1952. Santa Monica: Rand Corporation, Rm-981, 1952, 95 P.

6888 Schnitzer, Ewald W. Some German Press Views on the Defense of Europe; A Survey of West German Press Opinion on Military Aspects of The Defense of Europe. Santa Monica: Rand Corporation, Rm-1372, 1954, 80 P.

6889 Shuster, George N. Will Germany Rearm?. Foreign Policy Bulletin. 31:12 (1 March 1952), 1-2.

6890 Smith, Jessica. Review and Comment on German Rearmament. New World Review. 19:1 (March 1951), 33-36.

6891 Stone, William T. German Rearmament. Editorial Research Reports. (19 October 1954), 755-772.

6892 Stop the Remilitarisation of Germany.

Berlin (East): Tribuene, 1951, 80 P.

6893 Thompson, Elizabeth M. France and Germany in West European Defense. Editorial Research Reports. (15 November 1952), 783-800.

6894 UK, Foreign Office. German Defence Contribution and the European Defence Community. London: H.M. Stationery Office, Cmd. 8492, 1952, 27 P.

6895 Walton, Clarence C. Background for the European Defense Community. Political Science Quarterly. 68:1 (March 1953), 42-69.

6896 Willenz, Eric. Early Discussions Regarding a Defense Contribution in Germany (1948-1950). Santa Monica: Rand Corporation, Rm-968, 1952, 23 P.

6897 Younger, Kenneth. Germany and Western Defence. Socialist Commentary. 16 (May 1952), 100-103.

0.4.3. NATO (See Also 0.2.1)

6898 Acheson, Dean G. Withdrawal From Europe? an Illusion. New York Times Magazine. (15 December 1963), 7+.

6899 Adenauer, Konrad. Germany, the New Partner. Foreign Affairs. 33:2 (January 1955), 177-183.

6900 Adenauer, Konrad. Germany and the Western Alliance. Journal of International Affairs. 12:1 (1958), 82-89.

6901 After E.D.C.: German Co-Operation With the West. Round Table. 45:177 (December 1954), 26-35.

6902 Andreyev, N. West Germany--Nato Spearhead in Europe. International Affairs (Moscow). (February 1965), 23-28.

6903 Atkinsor, James T. Western Germany, Nato and World Peace. Free World Forum. 1:1 (January 1959), 35, 54.

6904 Bahr, Egon. Renunciation of Force and the Alliance. Aussenpolitik. 24:3 (1973), 243-254.

6905 Barth, Herbert. On the History of Mlf. German Foreign Policy (GDR). 4:2 (1965), 127-134.

6906 Barzel, Rainer. The Nuclear Defense of Western Europe. Round Table. 62:246 (April 1972), 165-174.

6907 Bathurst, Maurice E. Simpson, John L. Germany and the North Atlantic Community: A Legal Survey. New York: Praeger, 1956, 217 P.

6908 Baudissin, Wolf Graf Von. Confines and Possibilities of Military Alliance Systems. German Tribune Quarterly Review. No. 9 (March 1970).

6909 Beer, Francis A. Integration and Disintegration in Nato: Processes of Alliance Cohesion and Prospects for Atlantic Community. Columbus: Ohio State University Press, 1969, 330 P.

6910 Birrenbach, Kurt. Europe's Security in the Changed World. Aussenpolitik. 24:3 (1973), 285-297.

6911 Birrenbach, Kurt. Partnership and Consultation in Nato. Atlantic Community Quarterly. 2:1 (Spring 1964), 62-71.

6912 Bowie, Robert R. Tensions Within the Alliance. Foreign Affairs. 42:1 (October 1963), 49-69.

6913 Brodie, Bernard. Strategic Implications of the North Atlantic Pact. Yale Review. 39:4 (December 1949), 193-208.

6914 Brzezinski, Zbigniew K. Moscow and the M.L.F.: Hostility and Ambivalence. Foreign Affairs. 43:1 (October 1964), 126-134.

6915 Calleo, David. The Atlantic Fantasy: The U.S., Nato, and Europe. Baltimore: Johns Hopkins University Press, 1970, 182 P.

6916 Charisius, Albrecht. Zeimer, Siegfried. Nato and the Aggressive Programme of West German Imperialism. German Foreign Policy (GDR). 6:3 (1967), 207-219.

6917 Cleveland, Harlan. Nato: The Transatlantic Bargain. New York: Harper & Row, 1970, 204 P.

6918 Craig, Gordon A. Germany and Nato: The Rearmament Debate, 1950-1958. Nato and American Security. Ed. Klaus Knorr. Princeton: Princeton University Press, 1959, Pp. 236-259.

6919 Craig, Gordon A. Nato and the New German Army. Princeton: Princeton University, Center of International Studies, Memorandum No. 8, 1955, 30 P.

6920 Edinger, Lewis J. West German Armament. Maxwell Air Force Base, Ala.: Air University, Research Studies Institute, Documentary Research Division, 1955, 154 P.

6921 Erler, Fritz. The Alliance and the Future of Germany. Foreign Affairs. 43:3 (April 1965), 436-446.

6922 Erler, Fritz. Partners in Strategy. Atlantic Community Quarterly. 2:2 (Summer 1964), 292-302.

6923 Finer, Herman. Halperin, S. William. Mowat, Charles L. West Germany: Our New Ally. University of Chicago Round Table. No. 875 (16 January 1955), 1-11. Radio Discussion.

6924 Fyodorov, T. A German Peace Treaty and Nato. International Affairs (Moscow). (June 1962), 18-22.

6925 Garnett, John. Baor and Nato. International Affairs (London). 46:4 (October 1970), 670-681.

6926 Gelb, Leslie H. Halperin, Morton H. Why West Europe Needs 300,000 G.I.S. Atlantic Community Quarterly. 9:1 (Spring 1971), 56-60.

6927 Gelber, Lionel. A Marriage of Inconvenience. Foreign Affairs. 41:2 (January 1963), 310-322.

6928 Germany, Nato and West European Union. Current Affairs for the Canadian Forces. 9:8 (15 October 1955), 1-30.

6929 Goodman, Elliot R. Nato and German Reunification. Survey. No. 76 (Summer 1970), 30-40.

6930 Hallstein, Walter. Nato and the European Economic Community. Orbis. 6:4 (Winter 1963), 564-574.

6931 Hartmann, Ruediger. The European Nuclear Option. Aussenpolitik. 25:3 (1974), 282-292.

6932 Hassel, Kai-Uwe Von. Organizing Western Defense: The Search for Consensus. Foreign Affairs. 43:2 (January 1965), 209-216.

6933 Hassner, Pierre. The Implications of Change in Eastern Europe for the Atlantic Alliance. Orbis. 13:1 (Spring 1969), 237-255.

6934 Heusinger, Adolf Ernst. Vietman and the U.S. Role in Europe. Atlantic Community Quarterly. 3:4 (Winter 1966), 486-495. Interview in "U.S. News and World Report," 23 August 1965.

6935 Jenkins, Clive. Germany's Balance of Influence: The Changing Situation in Nato. London: Union of Democratic Control, 1961, 21 P.

6936 Kaplan, Lawrence S. Nato and Adenauer's Germany: Uneasy

Partnership. International Organization. 15:4 (Autumn 1961), 618-629.

6937 Kielmansegg, Johann Adolf Graf. What's to Become of Nato?. Aussenpolitik. 21:1 (1970), 25-41.

6938 Kissinger, Henry A. Coalition Diplomacy in a Nuclear Age. Foreign Affairs. 42:4 (July 1964), 525-545.

6939 Kissinger, Henry A. Strains on the Alliance. Foreign Affairs. 41:2 (January 1963), 261-285.

6940 Kissinger, Henry A. The Troubled Partnership: A Re-Appraisal of the Atlantic Alliance. New York: Mcgraw-Hill, 1965, 266 P.

6941 Krekeler, Heinz L. German Defense Contribution. Annals of the American Academy of Political and Social Science. 312 (July 1957), 84-88.

6942 Kressler, Diane A. Germany, Nato and Europe. Orbis. 10:1 (Spring 1966), 223-239.

6943 Legault, Albert. Atomic Weapons for Germany?. International Journal. 21:4 (Autumn 1966), 447-469.

6944 Lider, Julian. West Germany in Nato. Warsaw: Zachodnia Agencja Prasowa, 1965, 270 P.

6945 Loewenstein, Prince Hubertus Zu. Zuehlsdorff, Volkmar Von. Nato and the Defense of the West. New York: Praeger, 1963, 383 P.

6946 Melnikov, D. E. West Germany and Nato. International Affairs (Moscow). (July 1961), 70-72.

6947 Melnikov, D. E. West German and Nato Policy. International Affairs (Moscow). (November 1960), 29-40.

6948 Mendershausen, Horst. Troop Stationing in Germany: Value and Cost. Santa Monica: Rand Corporation, Rm-5881-Pr, December 1968, 144 P.

6949 Mendershausen, Horst. Unrest and Cohesion in the Atlantic Alliance: Nato and the German Question. Santa Monica: Rand Corporation, Rm-4936-Pr, April 1966, 46 P.

6950 Mettler, Eric. British Dragoons in the Teutoburger Forest. Swiss Review of World Affairs. 15:5 (August 1965), 3-5.

6951 Miksche, Ferdinand O. The Atlantic Pact and Germany. Military Review. 29:12 (March 1950), 23-28.

6952 Monckton of Brenchley, Major-General the Viscount. Forward Strategy in Germany. Royal United Service Institution Journal. 113:649 (February 1968), 27-33.

6953 Newhouse, John. Croan, Melvin. Fried, Edward R. Stanley, Timothy W. U.S. Troops in Europe: Issues, Costs, and Choices. Washington: Brookings, 1971, 177 P., Esp. Pp. 78-101.

6954 Nerlich, Uwe. The Federal Republic's Nuclear Dilemma. International Affairs (Moscow). (March 1966), 62-66.

6955 Norder, Albert. Multilateral Atomic Force--Torpedo Against the Reunification of Germany. German Foreign Policy (GDR). 3:2 (1964), 87-99.

6956 Osgood, Robert Endicott. Nato: The Entangling Alliance. Chicago: University of Chicago Press, 1962, 416 P.

6957 Poltorak, Arkadii I. Zaitsev, Evgenii. Remember Nuremberg. Moscow: Foreign Languages Publishing House, 1961, 296 P. Attack on West German Rearmament.

6958 Raven, Wolfram Von. Nato's Biggest North Atlantic Manoeuvres. Aussenpolitik. 23:4 (1972), 406-417.

6959 Richardson, James L. Germany and the Atlantic Alliance: The Interaction of Strategy and Politics. Cambridge: Harvard University Press, 1966, 403 P.

6960 Ruge, Friedrich. Mlf: A German Point of View. United States Naval Institute Proceedings. 92:9 (September 1966), 42-51.

6961 Sawicki, Jerzy. From Nuremberg to the New Wehrmacht. Warsaw: Polonia Publishing House, 1957, 459 P.

6962 Schirmer, Gregor. International Law and the Mlf. German Foreign Policy (GDR). 3:2 (1964), 124-127.

6963 Schnitzer, Ewald W. A German Discussion of Atomic Weapons and the Law. Santa Monica: Rand Corporation, P-1106, 1957, 9 P.

6964 Schrader, Rudolf. Agard--Model for International Cooperation. Aussenpolitik. 22:1 (1971), 102-114.

6965 Schroeder, Gerhard. Integrated Defense. Atlantic Community Quarterly. 4:2 (Summer 1966), 226-228.

6966 Schwarz, Siegfried. West Germany's Particular Role in Nato. German Foreign Policy (GDR). 8:2 (1969), 91-101.

6967 Schwarz, Urs. The Rearmament of Germany. Swiss Review of World Affairs. 4:10 (January 1955), 1-7.

6968 Sharfman, Peter J. The International Negotiations Preceding West German Rearmament, 1949-1955. Ph.D. Thesis, the University of Chicago, 1972.

6969 Spaak, Paul-Henri. New Tests for Nato. Foreign Affairs. 37:3 (April 1959), 357-365.

6970 Sperker, Heinrich. Nato Crisis. German Foreign Policy (GDR). 3:5 (1964), 342-350.

6971 Thomas, Stephan G. Germany and a Nato Policy Toward the East. Orbis. 13:1 (Spring 1969), 256-260.

6972 Vandevanter, E., Jr. Nuclear Forces and the Future of Nato. Santa Monica: Rand Corporation, P-2739, April 1963, 18 P.

6973 Yochelson, John. The American Military Presence in Europe: Current Debate the United States. Orbis. 25:3 (Fall 1971), 784-807.

6974 Zedler, John N. The Multilateral Force: A Misreading of German Aspirations. Los Angeles: University of California, Security Studies Paper No. 14, 1968, 29 P.

O.4.4. Arms Limitation

6975 Afheldt, Horst. Political Conclusions of the Study "The Consequences of War and the Prevention of War". Journal of Peace Research. 10:3 (1973), 259-263.

6976 Bechtoldt, Heinrich. The Federal Republic and the Non-Proliferation Treaty. German Tribune Quarterly Review. No. 2 (20 July 1968), 11-13.

6977 Becker, Egon. Germany--Obstacles to Disarmament. Our Generation Against Nuclear War. 3:3 (April 1965), 50-53.

6978 Einhorn, Claere. Non-Proliferation of Nuclear Weapons. German Foreign Policy (GDR). 7:4 (1968), 275-282.

6979 FRG, Press and Information Office. Treaty on the Non-Proliferation of Nuclear Weapons: German Attitude and Contribution, Documentation. Bonn:

Press and Information Office, December 1969, 64 P.

6980 GDR, Ministry of Foreign Affairs. Barrage-Fire Against Treaty on the Non-Proliferation of Nuclear Weapons. Dresden: N.P., 1967, 31 P.

6981 Gaitskell, Hugh. Disengagement: Why? How?. Foreign Affairs. 36:4 (July 1958), 539-556.

6982 Gorden, Morton. Lerner, Daniel. The Setting for European Arms Controls: Political and Strategic Choices of European Elites. Journal of Conflict Resolution. 9:4 (December 1965), 419-433.

6983 Hall, Martin. West Germans for Peace--Demonstrations Along the Rhine For Peace in Europe. New World Review. 32:9 (October 1964), 31-36.

6984 Healey, Denis. A Neutral Belt in Europe?. London: Fabian Society, 1958, 16 P.

6985 Hinterhoff, Eugene. Disengagement. London: Stevens, 1959, 445 P.

6986 Howard, Michael. Disengagement in Europe. Baltimore: Penguin, 1958, 92 P.

6987 Kernan, George F. Disengagement Revisited. Foreign Affairs. 37:2 (January 1959), 187-210.

6988 Klein, Peter. Topical Issues of Disarmament. German Foreign Policy (GDR). 9:2 (1970), 87-99.

6989 Lawrence, R. M. Nth Country Threat Analysis: West Germany, Sweden, Canada, Israel, and Selected Other Nations. Menlo Park: Stanford Research Institute, Technical Report No. 5205-32, May 1968, 427 P.

6990 Merritt, Richard L. Pirro, Ellen B. Press Attitudes to Arms Control in Four Countries, 1946-1963. New Haven: Yale University, Political Science Research Library, January 1966, 212 P.

6991 Murphy, Patrick W. The Response of the Federal Republic of Germany to the Challenge of the Nuclear Non-Proliferation Treaty. Ph.D. Thesis, Columbia University, 1974.

6992 Nerlich, Uwe. The Federal Republic of Germany: Constraining the Inactive. Nuclear Proliferation, Phase II. Ed. Robert M. Lawrence and Joel Larus. Lawrence: University Press of Kansas, for the National Security Education Program, 1974, Pp. 86-111.

6993 Petri, Alexander. Germany's Part in the Nonproliferation Treaty. Aussenpolitik. 21:1 (1970), 14-24.

6994 Polikeit, George. The Peace Movement in the German Federal Republic. Political Affairs. 46:3 (March 1967), 9-21.

6995 Ponomarev, G. Bonn: Enemy of Disarmament. International Affairs (Moscow). (January 1963), 52-55.

6996 Russett, Bruce M. Cooper, Carolyn C. Arms Control in Europe: Proposals and Political Constraints. Denver: University of Denver, Social Science Foundation and Graduate School of International Studies, Monograph Series in World Affairs No. 2, 1967, 85 P.

6997 Salvin, Marina. Neutralism in Germany. International Conciliation. No. 472 (June 1951), 304-318.

6998 Schmidt, Helmut. Military Disengagement in Central Europe. Santa Monica: Rand Corporation, T-122, 1960, 16 P.

6999 Schulz, Joachim. Non-Proliferation of Nuclear Weapons and International Law. German Foreign Policy (GDR). 5:3 (1966), 187-197.

7000 Talensky, N. Anti-Missile Systems and Disarmament. International Affairs (Moscow). (October 1964), 15-19.

7001 Ungerer, Werner. Non-Proliferation Treaty and Controls. Aussenpolitik. 22:4 (1971), 363-376.

7002 Waskow, Arthur I. Keeping the World Disarmed. Santa Barbara: Center for the Study of Democratic Institutions, 1965, 88 P.

7003 Wettig, Gerhard. Soviet Non-Proliferation Policy: An Analysis of Soviet Public Statements From November 1966 to January 1968. Cologne: Bundesinstitut Fuer Ostwissenschaftliche Und Internationale Studien, 1968, 44 P.

C.4.5. European Security

7004 Bertram, Christoph. West German Perspectives on European Security: Continuity and Change. World Today. 27:3 (March 1971), 115-123.

7005 Brandt, Willy. Detente Over the Long Haul. Survival. 9:10 (October 1967), 310-312, 326.

7006 Bressensdorf, Erwin B. Von. Security and Economics in Europe. Aussenpolitik. 24:2 (1973), 130-136.

7007 Duckwitz, Georg Ferdinand. Security Policy and European Security. Aussenpolitik. 21:1 (1970), 5-13.

7008 Groll, Goetz Von. The Csce Bundestag Debate. Aussenpolitik. 25:4 (1974), 375-384.

7009 Groll, Goetz Von. The Foreign Ministers in Helsinki. Aussenpolitik. 24:3 (1973), 255-274.

7010 Groll, Goetz Von. The Geneva Csce Negotiations. Aussenpolitik. 25:2 (1974), 158-165.

7011 Groll, Goetz Von. The Geneva Final Act of the Csce. Aussenpolitik. 26:3 (1975), 247-269.

7012 Groll, Goetz Von. The Helsinki Consultations. Aussenpolitik. 24:2 (1973), 123-129.

7013 Hadik, Laszlo. The Process of Detente in Europe. Orbis. 13:4 (Winter 1970), 1008-1028.

7014 Hassel, Kai-Uwe Von. Detente Through Firmness. Foreign Affairs. 42:2 (January 1964), 184-194.

7015 Hunter, Robert E. Security in Europe. Bloomington: Indiana University Press, 2D Ed., 1972, 281 P.

7016 Klefisch, Johannes W. The Art of Securing Peace Today--Reflections on a European Security Conference. German Tribune Quarterly Review. No. 17 (23 March 1972), 1-6.

7017 Kogon, Eugen. Peace and Security in Europe. German Tribune Quarterly Review. No. 11 (15 October 1970), 8-11.

7018 Kollatz, Udo, Editor. German and American Detente Policies. Washington, D.C.: Georgetown University, School of Foreign Service, C. 1974, Xvii and 104 P. Speeches and Discussions of the Second German-American Forum at Georgetown Univeristy, 21-23 October 1973.

7019 Korbel, Josef. Detente in Europe: Real or Imaginary?. Princeton: Princeton University Press, 1972, 302 P., Esp. Pp. 141-251.

7020 Legvold, Robert. European Security Conference. Survey. No. 76 (Summer 1970), 41-52.

7021 Quilitzsch, Siegmar. Aspects of Soviet Struggle for European Security. German Foreign Policy (GDR). 10:3 (1971), 200-223.

7022 Rumpf, Helmut. European Security and Alliance Policy. Aussenpolitik. 22:1 (1971), 70-84.

7023 Sommer, Theo. Detente and Security: The Options. Atlantic Community Quarterly. 9:1 (Spring 1971), 34-49.

7024 Sommer, Theo. Germany's Strategic Position in the European Power Balance. Upheaval and Continuity: A Century of German History. Ed. E. J. Feuchtwanger. Pittsburgh, Pa.: University of Pittsburgh Press, 1974, Pp. 152-165.

7025 Speidel, Hans. The Essential Basis of Detente. Atlantic Community Quarterly. 7:4 (Winter 1969-70), 506-509.

7026 Wieck, Hans-Georg. Perspectives of Mbfr in Europe. Aussenpolitik. 23:1 (1972), 36-40.

7027 Wieck, Hans-Georg. Thoughts on Security in Europe. Aussenpolitik. 23:3 (1972), 263-270.

7028 Williams, Geoffrey Lee. Williams, Alan Lee. Crisis in European Defence: The Next Ten Years. London: Charles Knight, 1974, Xviii and 334 P., Esp. Pp. 185-198.

7029 Windsor, Philip. Germany and the Management of Detente. New York: Praeger, 1971, 207 P.

7030 Woller, Rudolf. Red Army in the Rhineland: How It Could Happen. Atlas. 17:1 (January 1969), 30-32.

0.5. Western European Integration

0.5.1. General Trends

7031 Acheson, Dean G. Europe: Decision or Drift. Foreign Affairs. 44:2 (January 1966), 198-205.

7032 Albrecht, Karl. Patterns of Economic Integration. Bonn: Bonner Universitaet Buchdruckerei, 1951, 23 P.

7033 American Committee on United Europe. The Union of Europe: Declarations of European Statesmen. New York: American Committee on United Europe, 1949, 75 P.

7034 Anthon, Carl G. Germany in the European Community. Current History. 38:221 (January 1960), 11-17, 23.

7035 Anthon, Carl G. Germany's Role in Western Europe. Current History. 40:233 (January 1961), 17-23.

7036 Berkowitz, Morton. Co-Existence in West Europe. Current History. 43:254 (October 1962), 211-217.

7037 Bloemer, Klaus. Germany and a European Europe. Orbis. 10:1 (Spring 1966), 240-246.

7038 Bonn, Moritz J. Whither Europe--Union or Partnership?. London: Cohen & West, 1952, 207 P.

7039 Brandt, Willy. European Union Is Germany's Hope. Atlantic Community Quarterly. 12:1 (Spring 1974), 76-80.

7040 Churchill, Winston S. Europe United: Speeches, 1947-1948. Ed. Randolph S. Churchill. Boston: Houghton Mifflin, 1950, 506 P.

7041 Clough, Shepard B. Toward European Economic Organization. Proceedings of the Academy of Political Science. 23:4 (January 1950), 369-380.

7042 Control of Western Germany: Political Union and the Marshall Plan. Round Table. 39:154 (March 1949), 118-124.

7043 Dean, Vera Micheles. Europe's Effort to Unite. Can Europe Unite?. New York: Foreign Policy Association, Headline Series No. 80, 1950, 62 P.

7044 "Deutschland, Deutschland Ueber Alles!" a Topical Reflection on the West German Striving for Hegemony in Western Europe. Dresden: Zeit Im Bild, 1969, 38 P.

7045 Ellis, Howard S. Obst, Maxwell. The Prospects of European Viability By 1952-53. Columbia Journal of International Affairs. 4:1 (Winter 1950), 5-15.

7046 FRG, Federal Ministry of Economics. The Economic Integration of Europe. Frankfurt: Klostermann, for Federal Ministry of Economics, Scientific Advisory Council, 1953, 28 P.

7047 Friedrich, Carl J. Europe: An Emergent Nation?. New York: Harper & Row, 1969, 269 P.

7048 Fromm, Ernst Ulrich. President De Gaulle's Vision of Europe. Atlantic Community Quarterly. 4:2 (Summer 1966), 224-226.

7049 Grosser, Alfred. The Evolution of European Parliaments. A New Europe? Ed. Stephen R. Graubard. Cambridge: Riverside, 1963, Pp. 219-244.

7050 Grosser, Alfred. Germany and Europe. European Integration. Ed. C. Grove Haines. Baltimore: Johns Hopkins University Press, 1957, Pp. 177-195.

7051 Haberler, Gottfried. Economic Aspects of a European Union. World Politics. 1:4 (July 1949), 431-441.

7052 Hall, Martin. A United Europe--Led By Bonn?. New World Review. 30:1 (January 1962), 12-15.

7053 Hassner, Pierre. German and European Reunification. Survey. No. 61 (October 1966), 14-37.

7054 Hawtrey, Sir Ralph George. Germany's Part in European Economic Life. Germany's Contribution to European Economic Life. Ed. Percy Wells Bidwell. Paris: Riviere, 1949, Pp. 131-147.

7055 Healey, Denis. The Crisis in Europe. International Affairs (London). 38:2 (April 1962), 145-155.

7056 Healey, Denis. Western Europe: The Challenge of Unity. Toronto: Canadian Association for Adult Education, 1950, 24 P.

7057 Heineman, Leopold. Germany's Dream--A United States of Europe. New Europe. 5:4-5 (April-May 1945), 29-31.

7058 Helms, Andrea. Nation-Building in the European Community: Regional Post-National Political Development in Western Europe. Ph.D. Thesis, University of Connecticut, 1969.

7059 Hennessy, Jossleyn. The Free Trade Area Through German Eyes. Lloyds Bank Review. No. 47 (January 1958), 29-42.

7060 Huang, R. Chu-Kua. Toward European Union. Ph.D. Thesis, University of Kentucky, 1953, 192 P.

7061 International Chamber of Commerce. European Union and Cooperation. New York: International Chamber of Commerce, U.S. Council, Commission on European Affairs, 1950, 9 P. Statement on Economic Union and Cooperation Approved By Icc-Cea at Paris Meeting, 10 March 1950.

7062 Kiep, Walther Leisler. A New Challenge for Western Europe: A View From Bonn. New York: Mason & Lipscomb Publishers, 1974, Xvi and 217 P.

7063 Knappstein, K. Heinrich. The Projected European Union and the Question of German Unity. Annals of the American Academy of Political and Social Science. 348 (July 1963), 73-81.

7064 Koever, J. P. The Integration of Western Europe. Political Science Quarterly. 69:3 (September 1954), 354-373.

7065 Kohl, Helmut. Europe's Unification as a World Factor. Central Europe Journal. 21:12 (December 1973), 297-300.

7066 Kohn, Hans. The Future of Political Unity in Western Europe. Annals of the American Academy of Political and Social Science. 348 (July 1963), 95-101.

7067 Koppe, Karlheinz. An Eminent German Federalist Answers Questions. Central European Federalist. 16:2 (December 1968), 20-23.

7068 Kreinin, Mordechai E. The Outer Seven and European Integration. American Economic Review. 50:3 (June 1960), 370-386.

7069 Lange, Halvard M. European Union: False Hopes and Realities. Foreign Affairs. 28:3 (April 1950), 441-450.

7070 Loveday, A. The European Movement. International Organization. 3:4 (November 1949), 620-632.

7071 Mehnert, Klaus. European Unity: A German View. Detente: Cold War Strategies in Transition. Ed. Eleanor Lansing Dulles and Robert Dickson Crane. New York: Praeger, 1965, Pp. 203-214.

7072 Middleton, Drew. Germany in a Time of Transition. New York Times Magazine. (21 October 1951), 12+.

7073 Milyukova, Valentina. Why Is Adenauer Forcing the Political Union of Western Europe Now?. German Foreign Policy (GDR). 1:5 (1962), 516-528.

7074 Mosley, Oswald. The European Situation: The Third Force. Ramsbury, Wilts: Mosley, 1950, 18 P.

7075 Motives and Methods of European Integration: A German Government View. World Today. 9:4 (April 1953), 145-152.

7076 Murray, John. Western Europe in the Summer of 1959: Further Reflections Upon Union and Unity in Western Europe. Studies. 48 (Summer 1959), 206-217.

7077 Patterson, William E. The German Social Democratic Party and European Integration in Emigration and Occupation. European Studies Review. 5:4 (October 1975), 429-441.

7078 Plehwe, F.-K. Von. Weu and the European Institutions. Aussenpolitik. 22:4 (1971), 419-426.

7079 Plehwe, F.-K. Von. W.E.U.'s Part in European Cooperation. Aussenpolitik. 21:2 (1970), 150-154.

7080 Powell, George L. The Council of Europe. International Law Quarterly. 3:2 (April 1950), 164-196.

7081 Puchala, Donald J. International Transactions and Regional Integration. International Organization. 24:4 (Autumn 1970), 732-763.

7082 Puchala, Donald J. Patterns in West European Integration. Journal of Common Market Studies. 9:2 (December 1970), 117-142.

7083 Rabier, Jacques-Rene. Europeans and the Unification of Europe. Government and Opposition. 6:4 (Autumn 1971), 477-501.

7084 Reynaud, Paul. The Unifying Force for Europe. Foreign Affairs. 28:2 (January 1950), 255-264.

7085 Sauvant, Karl P. Multinational Corporations and Western European Integration. Lexington, Mass.: Lexington Books, 1974.

7086 Schack, Alard Von. Modern Nationalism. German Tribune Quarterly Review. No. 3 (5 October 1968), 10-12. Need for Europe-Consciousness.

7087 Scheel, Walter. Europe at the Crossroads. Aussenpolitik. 25:2 (1974), 123-133.

7088 Schmitt, Hans A. European Union: From Hitler to De Gaulle. New York: Van Nostrand Reinhold, 1969, 159 P.

7089 Schroeder, Gerhard. Decision for Europe. London: Thames and Hudson, 1964, 248 P.

7090 Schwamm, Henri. German Business Attitudes to Europe. Journal of World Trade Law. 5:5 (September-October 1971), 567-573.

7091 Schwarz, George M. Integration of Western European Nations. Columbia Journal of International Affairs. 4 (Winter 1950), 19-21.

7092 Schwarz, Siegfried. Bonn and the Political Integration of Western Europe. German Foreign Policy (GDR). 7:4 (1968), 260-269.

7093 Sommer, Theo. Will Europe Unite?. Atlantic Community Quarterly. 5:4 (Winter 1967-68), 551-558.

7094 Sonnenhol, G. A. The Difficult Path to a Europe of the Fatherlands. Aussenpolitik. 23:1 (1972), 49-56.

7095 Spaak, Paul-Henri. Europe in a Western Community. Annals of the American Academy of Political and Social Science. 282 (July 1952), 45-52.

7096 Spaak, Paul-Henri. The Search for Consensus: A New Effort to Build Europe. Foreign Affairs. 43:2 (January 1962), 199-209.

7097 Strauss, Franz-Josef. How Can Progress in European Integration Be Achieved?. Atlantic Community Quarterly. 2:3 (Fall 1964), 389-395.

7098 Tauber, Kurt P. German Nationalists and European Union. Political Science Quarterly. 74:4 (December 1959), 564-589.

7099 Toussaint, Donald Ray. French Policy Toward the Political Unification of Europe: 1944-1954. Ph.D. Thesis, Stanford University, 1956, 433 P.

7100 Wallich, Henry C. Loud, Frederick V. Intra-European Trade and European Integration. Columbia Journal of International Affairs. 4:1 (Winter 1950), 33-46.

7101 Zaunitzer-Haase, Ingeborg. at the Intersection of Markets: Efta Investments in the Area of Hamburg/Schleswig-Holstein. Intereconomics. No. 5 (1966), 14-17.

7102 Zellentin, Gerda. Survey of German Literature on the Problems of European Integration. Journal of Common Market Studies. 2:3 (March 1964), 263-272.

7103 Zimmerman, Hans. European Economic Integration as Seen in West Germany. Swiss Review of World Affairs. 14:1 (April 1964), 5-6.

0.5.2. Schuman Plan (Ecsc)

7104 Bonn, Moritz J. The Schuman Pact. Fortnightly. 169:1014 (June 1951), 357-363.

7105 Bonnet, Henri. The Schuman Plan. World Affairs. 114:4 (Winter 1951),

99-102.

7106 Callender, Harold. Can There Be Peace Across the Rhine?. New York Times Magazine. (18 June 1950), 15+. Franco-German Negotiations on Steel Plan.

7107 Coker, J. A. Steel and the Schuman Plan. Economic Geography. 28:4 (October 1952), 283-294.

7108 Diebold, William, Jr. Imponderables of the Schuman Plan. Foreign Affairs. 29:1 (October 1950), 114-129.

7109 Diebold, William, Jr. The Schuman Plan: A Study in Economic Cooperation, 1950-1959. New York: Praeger, 1959, 750 P.

7110 Gelber, Lionel. The Schuman Plan and German Revival. International Journal. 6:3 (Summer 1951), 180-188.

7111 Kriesberg, Louis. German Businessmen and the Union Leaders and the Schuman Plan. Social Science. 35:2 (April 1960), 114-121.

7112 Lister, Louis. Europe's Coal and Steel Community. New York: Twentieth Century Fund, 1960, 495 P.

7113 Mckesson, John A. The Schuman Plan. Political Science Quarterly. 57:1 (March 1952), 18-35.

7114 Mendershausen, Horst. First Tests of the Schuman Plan. Review of Economics and Statistics. 35:4 (November 1953), 269-288.

7115 P. V. Z. German View on the Schuman Plan. World Today. 7:7 (July 1951), 292-298.

7116 Sethur, Frederick. The Schuman Plan and Ruhr Coal. Political Science Quarterly. 67:4 (December 1952), 503-520.

7117 Sommer, Louise. The Franco-German Steel and Coal Pact. World Affairs. 113:3 (Fall 1950), 80-82.

7118 A Special Correspondent. The Coal-Steel Example. The Banker. 106:370 (November 1956), 669-673.

7119 Townsley, W. A. The Schuman Plan: An Experiment in Union. Australian Outlook. 7:1 (March 1953), 22-35.

7120 Utley, T. E. The Schuman Plan. Fortnightly. 168:1003 (July 1950), 1-5.

7121 Vernon, Raymond. The Schuman Plan: Sovereign Powers of the European Coal and Steel Community. American Journal of International Law. 47:2 (April 1953), 183-202.

7122 Warburg, James P. How to Rescue the Schuman Plan. Common Cause. 4:3 (October 1950), 128-132.

0.5.3. European Community (EEC)

7123 Aust, Hans Walter. Common Market Crisis. German Foreign Policy (GDR). 4:5 (1965), 331-343.

7124 Aust, Hans Walter. Integration Contrasts. German Foreign Policy (GDR). 1:1 (1962), 5-30. Efta and Eec.

7125 Bartlett, John L. American Bond Issues in the European Economic Community. Stanford Law Review. 19:6 (June 1967), 1337-1357.

7126 Bauer, Leo. Haferkamp, Wilhelm. The Way Ahead for the Community. German Tribune Quarterly Review. No. 19 (28 September 1972), 5-8.

7127 Baumann, Otto. European "Integration" and Strengthening of German Imperialism. World Marxist Review: Problems of Peace and Socialism. 2:10 (October 1959), 74-79.

7128 Bechtoldt, Heinrich. Germany and the Common Market. India Quarterly. 16:3 (July-September 1960), 249-258.

7129 Biggs-Davison, John. Mitteleuropa and the Common Market. Quarterly Review. 297:620 (April 1959), 123-129.

7130 Bolles, Blair. The Common Market and the Future of Germany. Western World. 2:3 (March 1959), 35-38.

7131 Braun, Sigismund Freiherr Von. Progress in the Work of the Community. Aussenpolitik. 22:2 (1971), 132-141.

7132 Brems, Hans J. West German Problems: Price Discipline and Economic Integration. Quarterly Review of Economics and Business. 4:4 (Winter 1964), 51-58.

7133 Burchard, Hans-Joachim. Towards a Common European Energy Policy. Aussenpolitik. 21:1 (1970), 76-82.

7134 Dahrendorf, Ralf. Possibilities and Limits of a European Community Foreign Policy. The European Community in the 1970's. Ed. Steven J. Warnecke. New York: Praeger, 1972, Pp. 111-126.

7135 Dale, Edwin L., Jr. Hallstein Runs an Uncommon Experiment. New York Times Magazine. (15 July 1962), 8+.

7136 Dohnanyi, Klaus Von. Europe Now: Some Reflections on European Technology Policy. German Tribune Quarterly Review. No. 11 (15 October 1970), 12-16.

7137 Ehrhardt, Carl A. The Dimensions of Eec Extension. Aussenpolitik. 23:4 (1972), 394-405.

7138 Ehrhardt, Carl A. Eec and the Mediterranean. Aussenpolitik. 22:1 (1971), 20-30.

7139 Ehrhardt, Carl A. Europe After the Paris Summit Conference. Aussenpolitik. 24:1 (1973), 63-85.

7140 Ehrhardt, Carl A. New Dynamics in European Politics. Aussenpolitik. 21:1 (1970), 53-64.

7141 Ehrhardt, Carl A. The Structure of the Extended Community. Aussenpolitik. 22:4 (1971), 404-418.

7142 FRG, Press and Information Office. The European Community: From the Summit Conference at the Hague to the Europe of the Ten. Bonn: Press and Information Office, 1972, 136 P.

7143 Findorff, W. B. China and the European Community. Aussenpolitik. 24:2 (1973), 210-216.

7144 Focke, Katharina. European Policy Developments After the Hague Conference. German Tribune Quarterly Review. No. 10 (16 July 1970), 1-7.

7145 Hallstein, Walter. Eec After Nine and a Half Years. Atlantic Community Quarterly. 5:3 (Fall 1967), 336-343.

7146 Hallstein, Walter. European Economy and European Policy. Atlantic Community Quarterly. 3:3 (Fall 1965), 364-368.

7147 Hallstein, Walter. Politics and Economics. Atlantic Community Quarterly. 3:4 (Winter 1966), 522-527.

7148 Hallstein, Walter. United Europe: Challenge and Opportunity. Cambridge: Harvard University Press, 1962, 109 P.

7149 Hay, Peter. Four Lectures on the Common Market: Trade Provisions--German and French Company Law--Establishment. University of Pittsburgh Law Review. 24:4 (June 1963), 685-770.

7150 Hohnstein, Willard E. West Germany's Role in the Common Market. Ph.D. Thesis, University of Oklahoma, 1966, 128 P.

7151 Hughes, Barry B. Schwarz, John E. Dimensions of Political Integration and the Experience of The European Community. International Studies Quarterly. 16:3 (September 1972), 263-294.

7152 Jensen, Finn B. Walter, Ingo. The Common Market: Economic Integration in Europe. Philadelphia: Lippincott, 1965, 278 P.

7153 Joesten, Joachim. Germany and the Common Market: The Struggle for a Common Farm Policy. New York: Joachim Joesten, New Germany Reports No. 56, January 1962, 17 P.

7154 Kebschull, Dietrich. Germany in the Enlarged Common Market. Intereconomics. No. 10 (October 1971), 299-300.

7155 Kroebel, Gerhard. European Integration: From the European Idea to the European Economic Community. Duesseldorf: German Trade Union Federation, Federal Committee, Department of Economic Policy, 3D Ed., 1963, 84 P.

7156 Lerner, Daniel. Will European Union Bring About Merged National Goals?. Annals of the American Academy of Political and Social Science. 348 (July 1963), 34-45.

7157 Lindberg, Leon N. The Political Dynamics of European Economic Integration. Ph.D. Thesis, University of California, 1962.

7158 Lindberg, Leon N. The Political Dynamics of European Economic Integration. Stanford: Stanford University Press, 1963, 367 P.

7159 Merkl, Peter H. European Assembly Parties and National Delegations. Journal of Conflict Resolution. 8:1 (March 1964), 50-64.

7160 Meyer, Klaus. Integration and Its Institutions. Aussenpolitik. 23:1 (1972), 68-81.

7161 Nowak, Zdzislaw. The German Federal Republic and the Economic Integration of Western Europe. Polish Western Affairs. 6:1 (1965), 59-84.

7162 Oberdoerfer, Conrad W. Gleiss, Alfred. Hirsch, Martin. Common Market Cartel Law. New York: Commerce Clearing House, 2D Ed., 1971, 302 P.

7163 Parfitt, Trevor. The Eec: Mansholt in Transition. World Today. 26:8 (August 1970), 344-351.

7164 Pouyat, Anna-Juliette. Freedom of Movement Within the Common Market. Journal of the International Commission of Jurists. 9:2 (December 1968), 45-59.

7165 Reinhold, Otto. West Germany Monopoly Capital and the Common Market. World Marxist Review: Problems of Peace and Socialism. 7:2 (February 1964), 36-42.

7166 Richter, Kurt. Eec and Political Union. German Foreign Policy (GDR). 4:3 (1965), 209-216.

7167 Riggs-Davidson, John. Mitteleuropa and the Common Market. Quarterly Review. 297:2 (April 1959), 123-129.

7168 Scheingold, Stuart A. Law and Politics in Western European Integration. Ph.D. Thesis, University of California, Berkeley, 1963.

7169 Schmidt, Gerold. Completion of the Common Commercial Policy. Aussenpolitik. 24:4 (1973), 393-405.

7170 Schroeder, Gerhard. Bonn Calls for an Outward-Looking Common Market Policy. Atlantic Community Quarterly. 1:2 (Summer 1963), 150-156.

7171 Staden, Berndt Von. The Identity of the European Community. Aussenpolitik. 23:4 (1972), 363-370.

7172 Staden, Berndt Von. Political Cooperation in the European Community. Aussenpolitik. 23:2 (1972), 123-133.

7173 Terfloth, Klaus. Foreign Policy of the Nine-Nation Community. Aussenpolitik. 24:1 (1973), 12-24.

7174 Tietmeyer, Hans. European Economic and Currency Union--A Political Challenge. German Tribune Quarterly Review. No. 15 (26 August 1971), 1-5.

7175 Ungerer, Werner. The Verification Agreement Euratom/Iaea. Aussenpolitik. 24:2 (1973), 189-199.

7176 Valkenburg, S. Van. Land Use Within the European Common Market. Economic Geography. 35:1 (January 1959), 1-24.

7177 Wagner, Wolfgang. The Future of the European Community After Expansion. German Tribune Quarterly Review. No. 19 (28 September 1972), 1-5.

7178 Warren, Kenneth. The Changing Steel Industry of the European Common Market. Economic Geography. 43:4 (October 1967), 314-332.

7179 Weil, Gordon Lee, Editor. A Hand-Book on the European Economic Community. New York: Praeger, 1965, 480 P.

7180 Woischnik, Bernhard. The European Economic Communities: Different Ways Towards The Same End. Bad Godesberg: Verlag Fuer Publizistik, 1964, 64 P.

7181 Yondorf, Walter. Europe of the Six: Dynamics of Integration. Ph.D. Thesis, University of Chicago, 1962.

O.6. FRG and Soviet Bloc (See Also I.9.2; Q.1)

O.6.1. Eastern Policy to 1966

7182 Allemann, Fritz Rene. Adenauer's Eastern Policy. Survey. No. 44-45 (October 1962), 29-36.

7183 Berezowski, Z. Germany's Eastern Policies. Poland and Germany. 2:4 (March 1958), 1-4.

7184 Berezowski, Z. Policy for a New Order. Poland and Germany. 5:3 (July-September 1961), 1-8. Germany and Eastern Europe.

7185 Bergo (Pseud.). Germany, Russia and China; A Century Ago and Now. Soundings. No. 27 (June 1949), 20-24.

7186 Birnbaum, Immanuel. German Eastern Policy: Yesterday and Tomorrow. International Affairs (London). 31:4 (October 1955), 427-434.

7187 Bonn's Dialogue With Eastern Europe. East Europe. 15:5 (May 1966), 2-9.

7188 Bregman, Alexander. German Illusions and Fallacies. Central European Federalist. 13:1 (June 1965), 9-14.

7189 Bregman, Alexander. Germany's Search for an Eastern Policy. East Europe. 15:3 (March 1966), 2-7.

7190 Brzezinski, Zbigniew K. Griffith, William E. Peaceful Engagement in Eastern Europe. Foreign Affairs. 39:4 (July 1961), 642-654.

7191 Byrnes, Robert F., Editor. The United States and Eastern Europe. Englewood Cliffs: Prentice-Hall, 1967, 176 P.

7192 Collier, David S., Editor. Glaser, Kurt, Editor. Western Policy and Eastern Europe. Chicago: Regnery, 1966, 245 P.

7193 Czechanowski, S. West Germany's Eastern Policy Moves. Poland and Germany. 10:3 (July-September 1966), 3-6.

7194 Dobriansky, Lev E. Germany, Eastern Europe and the Free World. Ukranian Quarterly. 19:4 (Winter 1963), 315-323.

7195 Dowell, Jack D. Not Paris, Not Bonn, But Moscow. Washington State University, Research Studies. 34:3 (September 1966), 150-155.

7196 Dushnyck, Walter. New Germany and Eastern Europe. Ukrainian Quarterly. 17:4 (Winter 1961), 301-310.

7197 Dziewancwski, M. K. West Germany and East Europe. Current History. 44:260 (April 1963), 208-213, 243.

7198 Friedlaender, Ernst. Germany and Eastern Europe. Western World. No. 7 (November 1957), 14-17.

7199 Goergey, Laszlo. Emerging Patterns in West German-East European Relations. Orbis. 10:3 (Fall 1966), 911-929.

7200 Grossman, Vladimir. The Pan-Germanic Web: Remaking Europe. London: Macmillan, 1944, 179 P.

7201 Grote, Manfred W. H. A New West German Policy Toward Eastern Europe. Ph.D. Thesis, University of Maryland, 1967, 216 P.

7202 Halasz, Nicholas. Germany's Danubian Neighbors. New Europe. 5:4-5 (April-May 1945), 26-29.

7203 Hinterhoff, Eugene. Germany's Eastern Policy. Poland and Germany. 6:3 (July-September 1962), 12-20.

7204 Hinterhoff, Eugene. Some American Views on Germany and Eastern Europe. Poland and Germany. 9:4 (October-December 1965), 13-21.

7205 Hrabyk, Klaudiusz. Germany and the Central-Eastern European Zone. Eastern Quarterly. 2:2 (September 1949), 3-6.

7206 Jaksch, Wenzel. Germany and Eastern Europe: Two Documents of the Third German Bundestag, 1961. Bonn: Edition Atlantic-Forum, 1962, 56 P.

7207 Krippendorff, Ekkehart. Bonn's Ostpolitik. Survey. No. 61 (October 1966), 47-55.

7208 Kudlicki, S. West German's Eastern European Policy. Poland and Germany. 10:4 (October-December 1966), 3-9.

7209 Lemberg, Eugen. The German Image of East European Peoples. Western Policy and Eastern Europe. Ed. David S. Collier and Kurt Glaser. Chicago: Regnery, 1966, Pp. 110-126.

7210 Loir, Raymond. The New German Drive to the East. Contemporary Review. 189:1083 (March 1956), 167-169.

7211 Luchsinger, Fred. Fata Morgana in Germany. Swiss Review of World Affairs. 16:3 (June 1966), 4-5. Hopes for East-West Accords.

7212 Luethy, Herbert. Bonn Joins the Co-Existence Game Again: Whither Germany?. Commentary. 20:5 (November 1955), 413-420.

7213 Nakashidze, Niko. The Truth About A.B.N.: An Answer to the Provocations of Moscow's Fifth Column in the West. Munich: A.B.N. Press and Information Bureau, 1960, 62 P. Anti-Bolshevik Bloc of Nations.

7214 Jakropin, O. Strognanov, A. The Cardinal Solution of the German Problem. International Affairs (Moscow). (March 1959), 24-28.

7215 Nowak, Zdzislaw. Some Economic Aspects of the Eastern Policy of the German Federal Republic. Polish Western Affairs. 2:2 (1961), 235-259.

7216 Poznanski, V. J. Contradictions in German Policy. Poland and Germany. 7:4 (October-December 1963), 29-33.

7217 Rhode, Gotthold. The Image of Germany in Eastern Europe. Western Policy and Eastern Europe. Ed. David S. Collier and Kurt Glaser. Chicago: Regnery, 1966, Pp. 89-109.

7218 Rubinstein, Alvin Z. The Soviet Image of Western Europe. Current History. 47:279 (November 1964), 280-285.

7219 Schneider, Horst. Phony Self-Determination. German Foreign Policy (GDR). 4:6 (1965), 439-442. Oder-Neisse and Sudetenland Territories.

7220 Schreiber, Hermann. Teuton and Slav: The Struggle for Central Europe. London: Constable, 1965, 392 P., Esp. Pp. 352-371.

7221 Schroeder, Gerhard. Germany Looks at Eastern Europe. Foreign Affairs. 44:1 (October 1965), 15-25.

7222 Stehle, Hansjakob. The Federal Republic and Eastern Europe. Survey. No. 61 (October 1966), 70-79.

7223 Voslensky, M. A Peaceful Settlement With Germany and the Court Opposition. International Affairs (Moscow). (March 1962), 39-45.

7224 Wiewiora, Boleslaw. The Aims of the Present Eastern Policy of the German Federal Republic. Polish Western Affairs. 4:1 (1963), 3-19.

7225 Wiskemann, Elizabeth. Germany's Eastern Neighbours. Survey. No. 44-45 (October 1962), 45-53.

7226 Wiskemann, Elizabeth. Germany's Eastern Neighbors: Problems Relating to the Oder-Neisse Line and the Czech Frontier Regions. London: Oxford University Press, 1956, 309 P.

7227 Yefimov, D. Bonn, Outpost of Anti-Communism. International Affairs (Moscow). (October 1962), 24-28.

O.6.2. Eastern Policy, 1966-

7228 Allemann, Fritz Rene. The Right to Change One's Mind. German Tribune Quarterly Review. No. 10 (16 July 1970), 13-16. Eastern Policy Under Brandt.

7229 Becker, Frederick A. The Development of an Eastern Policy in West Germany's Foreign Relations. Ph.D. Thesis, Claremont Graduate School, 1972, 386 P.

7230 Beyme, Klaus Von. The Ostpolitik in the West German 1969 Elections. Government and Opposition. 5:1 (Spring 1970), 193-217.

7231 Billington, James H. Force and Counterforce in Eastern Europe. Foreign Affairs. 47:1 (October 1968), 26-35.

7232 Birnbaum, Karl E. Peace in Europe: East-West Relations 1966-1968 and the Prospects for a European Settlement. London and New York: Oxford University Press, 1970, 172 P.

7233 Birrenbach, Kurt. The West and German Ostpolitik—The German Opposition View. Atlantic Community Quarterly. 9:2 (Summer 1971), 196-204.

7234 Bleimann, Robert. Ostpolitik and the GDR. Survey. 18:3 (Summer 1972), 36-53.

7235 Bonn's Position on the Eastern Treaties. Poland and Germany. 16:1 (January-March 1972), 40-42.

7236 Brandt, Willy. German Policy Toward

the East. Foreign Affairs. 46:3 (April 1968), 476-486.

7237 Brzezinski, Zbigniew K., Moderator. Normalization of Relations Between the Federal Republic of Germany and Eastern Europe. Eastern Europe in the 1970S. Ed. Sylva Sinanian, Istvan Deak, and Peter C. Ludz. New York: Praeger, 1972, Pp. 228-241.

7238 Bundestag Votes on Ostpolitik. Poland and Germany. 16:2-3 (April-September 1972), 32-34.

7239 Burmeister, Werner. Brandt's Opening to the East. The Year Book of World Affairs, 1973. New York: Praeger, for the London Institute of World Affairs, 1973, Pp. 24-38.

7240 Carstens, Karl. Point of View of the Opposition in Bonn. Central Europe Journal. 21:8-9 (August-September 1973), 209-212. Ostpolitik.

7241 Czechanowski, S. Eastern European Policy Unchanged. Poland and Germany. 11:1-2 (January-June 1967), 3-6.

7242 Czechanowski, S. Eastern Policy in a Quagmire. Poland and Germany. 12:3-4 (July-December 1968), 3-6.

7243 Dirks, Walter. German Spring?. German Tribune Quarterly Review. No. 17 (23 March 1972), 14-16.

7244 Doenhoff, Marion Graefin. Bonn Looks Eastward. Interplay. 3:10 (July 1970), 13-15.

7245 Domes, Alfred, Editor. Hauptmann, Jerzy, Editor. United Europe Faces the East. Kansas City: Park College, Governmental Research Bureau, East Europe Monographs No. 3, 1972, 92 P.

7246 Duchene, Francois. Salt, the Ostpolitik, and the Post-Cold War Context. World Today. 26:12 (December 1970), 500-511.

7247 Duckwitz, Georg Ferdinand. The Turning Point in the East. Aussenpolitik. 21:4 (1970), 363-379.

7248 Ermarth, Fritz. The German Case for Ostpolitik. Santa Monica: Rand Corporation, Paper P-4242, November 1969, 8 P.

7249 Fann, Willerd R. Germany and East Europe: Problems of Detente. Current History. 54:321 (May 1968), 263-267.

7250 Frank, Paul. German Ostpolitik in a Changing World. Aussenpolitik. 23:1 (1972), 14-25.

7251 Frenzke, Dietrich. New Czech-Soviet Alliance Treaty. Aussenpolitik. 21:3 (1970), 321-330.

7252 Freund, Michael. From Cold War to Ostpolitik in Germany and the New Europe. London: Wolff, 1972, 124 P.

7253 Frowein, Jochen Abr. Legal Problems of the German Ostpolitik. International and Comparative Law Quarterly. 23:1 (January 1974), 105-126.

7254 Gasteyger, Curt. The Fragile Balance of Power: Critical Aspects of European "Ostpolitik". German Tribune Quarterly Review. No. 14 (29 April 1971), 1-4.

7255 Gliga, Vasile. Extending Bucharest-Bonn Relations. Aussenpolitik. 24:3 (1973), 345-349.

7256 Goergey, Laszlo. Bonn's Eastern Policy, 1964-1971: Evolution and Limitations. Hamden: Shoe String, 1972, 191 P.

7257 Goergey, Laszlo. New Consensus in Germany's Eastern European Policy. Western Political Quarterly. 21:4 (December 1968), 681-697.

7258 Graefrath, Bernhard. Schulz, Joachim. Seiffert, Wolfgang. Bonn Must Face Historical Realities. German Foreign Policy (GDR). 9:1 (1970), 35-46.

7259 Hahn, Walter F. West Germany's Ostpolitik: The Grand Design of Egon Bahr. Orbis. 16:4 (Winter 1973), 859-880.

7260 Hauptmann, Jerzy. The Federal Republic of Germany and East Europe: The September 1969 Parliamentary Elections and the New "Ostpolitik". Central European Federalist. 17:2 (December 1969), 13-24.

7261 Hauptmann, Jerzy. The Meaning of the Chicago-Wiesbaden Experiment. Central Europe Journal. 22:6 (September-October 1974), 189-190. Report Followed By Papers (Pp. 191-225), on 9Th International Conference, Dealing With East-West Relations.

7262 Heathcote, Nina. Brandt's Ostpolitik and Western Institutions. World Today. 26:8 (August 1970), 334-343.

7263 Hirsch, Felix Edward. Ostpolitik in Historical Perspective. Current History. 62:369 (May 1972), 229-233.

7264 Hopper, Richard B. Changing Conceptions of German 'Ostpolitik.' Ph.D. Thesis, Johns Hopkins University, 1975.

7265 Keesing's Contemporary Archives. Germany and Eastern Europe Since 1945: From the Potsdam Agreement to Chancellor Brandt's "Ostpolitik". New York: Scribner's, 1973, 322 P.

7266 Kegel, Gerhard. Bonn's Eastern Policy: Substance and Illusions. World Marxist Review: Problems of Peace and Socialism. 11:12 (December 1968), 61-67.

7267 Kewenig, Wilhelm A. German Ostpolitik and Basic Law. German Tribune Quarterly Review. No. 16 (December 1971).

7268 Koppel, Thomas P. Sources of Change in West German Ostpolitik: The Grand Coalition, 1966-1969. Ph.D. Thesis, University of Wisconsin, 1972, 482 P.

7269 Korbel, Josef. West Germany's Ostpolitik: Intra-German Relations. Orbis. 13:4 (Winter 1969), 1050-1072.

7270 Korbel, Josef. West Germany's Ostpolitik: A Policy Toward the Soviet Allies. Orbis. 14:2 (Summer 1970), 326-348.

7271 Kryukov, P. Failure of Bonn's "New Eastern Policy". International Affairs (Moscow). (July 1969), 41-46.

7272 Lindemann, Eva. German Cultural Relations With Eastern Europe. Aussenpolitik. 25:4 (1974), 166-176.

7273 Luchsinger, Fred. A German Dilemma. Swiss Review of World Affairs. 17:12 (March 1968), 3-4. How Far Can FRG Go in Dealing With Eastern Europe Without Recognizing the GDR?.

7274 Mensonides, Louis J. European Realpolitic II: Bonn's Ostpolitik. The Future of Inter-Bloc Relations in Europe. Ed. Louis J. Mensonides and James A. Kuhlman. New York: Praeger, 1974, Pp. 162-180.

7275 Merritt, Richard L. From Reunification to Normalization: West German Policy Toward the East. Journal of International Affairs. 27:2 (1973), 268-273. Review Article of Five Books.

7276 Meyer-Landrut, Andreas. Fourth Year of the Moscow Treaty. Aussenpolitik. 25:1 (1974), 23-30.

7277 Moeller, Dietrich. The Understanding Between Bonn and Prague. Aussenpolitik. 24:3 (1973), 331-344.

7278 Muhlen, Norbert. Germany's New "Ost-

Politik": An American Dilemma. Interplay. 3:8 (April 1970), 4-10.

7279 Noetzold, Juergen. East-West Cooperation and Communication. Aussenpolitik. 25:3 (1974), 293-302.

7280 Novoseltsev, Y. Bonn's Eastern Policy and European Security. International Affairs (Moscow). (July 1968), 27-33.

7281 Oppermann, Thomas. Renunciation of Force in International Law. Aussenpolitik. 21:3 (1970), 253-271.

7282 Ostpolitik. Current Notes on International Affairs. 41:6 (June 1970), 317-321.

7283 Petrocelli, Peter. Old Realities and New Myths: Ostpolitik and the Americans. Sais Review. 15:2 (Winter 1971), 13-19.

7284 Pinder, John. An Ostpolitik for the European Community. Survey. 17:3 (Summer 1971), 157-179.

7285 Poznanski, V. J. Brandt's Ostpolitik. Poland and Germany. 14:1-2 (January-June 1970), 3-7.

7286 Poznanski, V. J. A Bungled Job or How the Eastern Treaties Were Ratified. Poland and Germany. 16:2-3 (April-September 1972), 3-7.

7287 Poznanski, V. J. Profile of Willy Brandt and His Policies. Poland and Germany. 13:3-4 (July-December 1969), 8-18.

7288 Poznanski, V. J. The Ratification Battle in Bonn. Poland and Germany. 16:1 (January-March 1972), 3-13.

7289 Prittie, Terence C. F. Germany and Her Eastern Neighbors. Encounter. 28:2 (February 1967), 61-65.

7290 Richardson, James L. Germany's Eastern Policy: Problems and Prospects. World Today. 24:9 (September 1968), 375-387.

7291 Richthofen, Hermann Von. The Treaty Between Bonn and Prague. Aussenpolitik. 25:1 (1974), 42-49.

7292 Roberts, Frank. Is Germany's "Ostpolitik" Dangerous?. Encounter. 36:5 (May 1971), 62-68.

7293 Roberts, Geoffrey K. The West German Parties and the Ostpolitik. Government and Opposition. 7:4 (Autumn 1972), 434-449.

7294 Rose, Guenther. The "Ideological Offensive"--Nature and Methods of the Imperialist Ideological Diversion Against the Socialist Countries. German Foreign Policy (GDR). 7:6 (1968), 419-431.

7295 Saeter, Martin. Change of Course in German Foreign Policy. Cooperation and Conflict. 2:2 (1967), 82-101.

7296 Schack, Alard Von. The Next Stage in Federal Republic Eastern Policy. German Tribune Quarterly Review. No. 1 (4 May 1968), 1-5.

7297 Scheel, Walter. Europe on the Move. Foreign Policy. No. 4 (Fall 1971), 62-76.

7298 Seton-Watson, Hugh. The "Sick Heart" of Modern Europe: The Problem of the Danubian Lands. Seattle: University of Washington Press, 1975, 64 P.

7299 Sinanian, Sylva, Editor. Deak, Istvar, Editor. Ludz, Peter Christian, Editor. Eastern Europe in the 1970S. New York: Praeger, 1972, Ix and 261 P.

7300 Smith, Jean Edward. Convergence, Ostpolitik, and the Berlin Accords. Teaching Postwar Germany in America: Papers and Discussions. Ed. Louis F. Helbig and Eberhard Reichmann. Bloomington: Indiana Univeristy, Institute of German Studies, 1972.

7301 Sommer, Theo. Bonn Changes Course. Foreign Affairs. 45:3 (April 1967), 477-491.

7302 Sommer, Theo. Bonn's New Ostpolitik. Journal of International Affairs. 22:1 (1968), 59-78.

7303 The Soviet Bloc and West Germany: Survey of an Unfinished Peace. East Europe. 10:6 (June 1961), 3-10.

7304 Tatu, Michel. Something More Than an Interlude. Atlantic Community Quarterly. 9:1 (Spring 1971), 50-55. FRG's Eastern Policy and Detente.

7305 Tilford, Roger B. The Ostpolitik and Political Change in Germany. Westmead, Farnborough, Hampshire: Saxon House, 1975, Vi and 111 P.

7306 Voslenskii, M. S. The "Eastern" Policy of the Federal Republic of Germany. Springfield, Va.: Clearinghouse for Federal Scientific and Technical Information, 1970, 483 P.

7307 Wagner, Wolfgang. Basic Requirements and Consequences of the Government's Ostpolitik. German Tribune Quarterly Review. No. 12 (10 December 1970), 1-6.

7308 Wagner, Wolfgang. Basic Requirements and Consequences of the Ostpolitik. Atlantic Community Quarterly. 9:1 (Spring 1971), 20-33.

7309 Wagner, Wolfgang. Ostpolitik Prospects Following Conclusion of the Berlin Negotiations. German Tribune Quarterly Review. No. 18 (8 June 1972), 9-12.

7310 Wagner, Wolfgang. Towards a New Political Order: German Ostpolitik and the East-West Realignment. International Journal. 27:1 (Winter 1971-72), 18-31.

7311 Wesson, Robert G. German Policy Toward East Europe. Current History. 60:357 (May 1971), 295-301.

7312 Whetten, Lawrence L. Appraising the Ostpolitik. Orbis. 15:3 (Fall 1971), 856-878.

7313 Whetten, Lawrence L. Germany's Ostpolitik: Relations Between the Federal Republic and the Warsaw Pact Countries. London and New York: Oxford University Press, 1971, 244 P.

7314 Whetten, Lawrence L. The Role of East Germany in West German-Soviet Relations. World Today. 25:12 (December 1969), 507-520.

7315 Wiedmann, Christoph. New Europe or a New Yalta?. German Tribune Quarterly Review. No. 3 (5 October 1968), 1-4.

7316 Wieser, Theodor. Changing Emphases in the Federal Republic. Swiss Review of World Affairs. 21:7 (October 1971), 4-5.

C.6.3. Soviet Union

7317 Albert, E. H. Bonn's Moscow Treaty and Its Implications. International Affairs (London). 47:2 (April 1971), 316-326.

7318 Bark, Dennis L. Changing East-West Relations in Europe: The Bonn-Moscow Treaty of August 1970. Orbis. 15:2 (Summer 1971), 625-642.

7319 Berezowski, Z. Russia and Germany. Poland and Germany. 7:3 (July-September 1963), 11-29.

7320 Bonn, Moritz J. Dr. Adenauer in Moscow. Contemporary Review. 188:1079 (November 1955), 290-293.

7321 Braunthal, Gerard. An Agreement With the Russians. Cases in Comparative

Politics. Ed. James B. Christoph. Boston and Toronto: Little, Brown, 1965, Pp. 256-287.

7322 Byrnes, Robert F. Soviet Policy Toward Western Europe Since Stalin. Annals of the American Academy of Political and Social Science. 303 (January 1956), 166-178.

7323 Clemens, Walter C., Jr. The Soviet World Faces West: 1945-1970. International Affairs (London). 46:3 (July 1970), 475-489.

7324 Cohen, Elliott A. Soviet Foreign Policy and West Germany. Social Science. 32:2 (April 1957), 90-95.

7325 Dallin, David J. Soviet Foreign Policy After Stalin. Philadelphia: Lippincott, 1961, 543 P.

7326 Deutscher, Isaac. Will Russia Make a Deal With Germany?. New York Times Magazine. (22 May 1949), 10+.

7327 FRG, Press and Information Office. The Policy of Renunciation of Force: Documents on German And Soviet Declarations on the Renunciation of Force, 1949 to July 1968. Bonn: Press and Information Office, 1968, 45 P.

7328 FRG, Press and Information Office. The Treaty of August 12, 1970 Between the Federal Republic of Germany and the Union of Soviet Socialist Republics. Bonn: Press and Information Office, 1970, 204 P.

7329 Federal Republic of Germany-Union of Soviet Socialist Republics: Non-Aggression Treaty. International Legal Materials. 9:5 (September 1970), 1026-1027.

7330 Fehling, Helmut M. One Great Prison: The Story Behind Russia's Unreleased Pow's. Boston: Beacon, 1951, 175 P.

7331 Frei, Otto. Germany Wooed By Soviet Propaganda. Swiss Review of World Affairs. 3:1 (April 1953), 3-4.

7332 Galkin, A. German Militarism and Soviet-West German Relations. International Affairs (Moscow). (July 1961), 81-83.

7333 Hall, Martin. Europe Puts Its House in Order: The Moscow-Bonn Treaty. New World Review. 39:1 (Winter 1971), 38-45.

7334 Hawtrey, Sir Ralph George. Russia and Western Europe. Political Quarterly. 22:1 (January 1951), 33-42.

7335 Hills, Denis C. Germans in Soviet Captivity. Contemporary Review. 181:1034 (February 1952), 82-86.

7336 Hudson, G. F. Soviet Soft-Line Toward the West. Current History. 45:266 (October 1963), 230-234.

7337 Hughes, William R., Editor. Those Human Russians: A Collection of Incidents Related By Germans. London: Gollancz, 1950, 128 P.

7338 Jaksch, Wenzel. Germany and Russia's European Policy. Elements of Change in Eastern Europe: Prospects for Freedom. Ed. David S. Collier and Kurt Glaser. Chicago: Regnery, 1968, Pp. 107-119.

7339 Karat, Johann. Soviet Union and the European Communities. Aussenpolitik. 23:3 (1972), 299-308.

7340 Klein, Johann K. The Soviet Espionage System in Germany. Military Review. 38:11 (February 1959), 77-79.

7341 Kohn, Hans. Germany and Russia. Current History. 38:221 (January 1960), 1-5.

7342 Korbel, Josef. German-Soviet Relations: The Past and Prospects. Orbis. 10:4 (Winter 1967), 1046-1060.

7343 Laqueur, Walter Z. Russia and Germany. Survey. No. 44-45 (October 1962), 3-11.

7344 Laqueur, Walter Z. Russia and Germany: A Century of Conflict. Boston: Little, Brown, 1965, 367 P.

7345 Laqueur, Walter Z. Russians and Germans. Encounter. 24:4 (April 1965), 81-89.

7346 Laukhuff, Perry. German Reaction to Soviet Policy, 1945-1953. Journal of International Affairs. 8:1 (1954), 62-72.

7347 Merzyn, Gerhard. The Soviet Union and the "Eastern Policy" of the Federal German Republic. Atlantic Community Quarterly. 7:2 (Summer 1969), 196-202.

7348 Middleton, Drew. Key Factor: Russian Fear of Germany. New York Times Magazine. (5 April 1959), 15+.

7349 Pabst, Alfred A. Soviet Perceptions of West Germany's Eastern Policy, 1964-1970. Ph.D. Thesis, George Washington University, 1972, 299 P.

7350 Petrov, V. Alarm in Bonn. International Affairs (Moscow). (August 1962), 57-62. Need for Agreement With Soviet Union.

7351 Quilitzsch, Siegmar. On the Position of the Ussr Towards the Aggressive Policies of the Kiesinger-Strauss Government. German Foreign Policy (GDR). 8:2 (1969), 108-114.

7352 Ropp, Stephen De. Between Germany and Russia. Eastern Quarterly. 4:4 (October 1951), 27-32.

7353 Sanakoyev, Sh. Ussr-FRG: A Turn Toward New Relations. International Affairs (Moscow). No. 8 (August 1973), 12-17.

7354 Schuman, Frederick L. The Soviet Union and German Rearmament. Annals of the American Academy of Political and Social Science. 312 (July 1957), 77-83.

7355 Smith, Jessica. The Ussr's 36Th Year--Questions of Germany and the Far East. New World Review. 21:10 (December 1953), 8-13.

7356 Sosnovskaya, T. Soviet Union-FRG: Possibilities and Prospects. International Affairs (Moscow). No. 2 (February 1974), 47-52.

7357 Soviet Union and Federal Germany: Cooperation for Peace. Moscow: Novosti Press Agency, 1973, 35 P.

7358 Soviet-West German Treaty. Current History. 59:350 (October 1970), 238, 246.

7359 Tetens, Tete Harens. Germany Plots With the Kremlin. New York: Schuman, 1953, 294 P.

7360 Treaty Between the Gfr and the Union of Soviet Socialist Republics. Poland and Germany. 14:3-4 (July-December 1970), 34-36.

7361 West German-Soviet Relations. Current Notes on International Affairs (Australia). 28:10 (October 1957), 782-795.

7362 West German-Soviet Treaty: CDU/Csu Has Reservations. Poland and Germany. 14:3-4 (July-December 1970), 40-42.

0.6.4. Poland

7363 Berezowski, Z. Germany, France, and Poland. Poland and Germany. 4:13 (July 1960), 8-20.

7364 Berezowski, Z. Overtures to Poland. Poland and Germany. 5:1 (January-March 1961), 1-7.

7365 Birdwood, Lord. Germany, Poland and the Future. Contemporary Review. 198 (December 1960), 671-673.

7366 Bregman, Alexander. German Interest in Poland. Poland and Germany. 7:4 (October-December 1963), 6-18.

7367 Bregman, Alexander. Poland and German Unity: Why Poles Want a Unified Germany. Modern Age. 6:2 (Spring 1962), 183-190.

7368 Bregman, Alexander. Polish-German Relations: A New Phase. East Europe. 12:11 (November 1963), 2-7.

7369 Bromke, Adam. Riekhoff, Harald Von. Poland and West Germany: A Belated Detente?. Canadian Slavonic Papers. 12:2 (Summer 1970), 195-210.

7370 Bromke, Adam. Riekhoff, Harald Von. The Polish-German Treaty. East Europe. 20:2 (February 1971), 2-8.

7371 Bromke, Adam. Riekhoff, Harald Von. The West German-Polish Treaty. World Today. 27:3 (March 1971), 124-131.

7372 Czechanowski, S. A New Phase in Polish-German Relations?. Poland and Germany. 13:1-2 (January-June 1969), 3-8.

7373 Czechanowski, S. The Polish-West German Treaty. Poland and Germany. 14:3-4 (July-December 1970), 3-9.

7374 Czechanowski, S. Reflexions After the Warsaw-Bonn Treaty. Poland and Germany. 15:1-2 (January-June 1971), 3-7.

7375 Declaration of the Federal Chancellor Concerning the West German-Polish Treaty. Poland and Germany. 14:3-4 (July-December 1970), 28-30.

7376 Drobnik, J. Thoughts on Polish-German Relations. Poland and Germany. 10:3 (July-September 1966), 7-17.

7377 Dross, Armin. German-Polish Complexes: Past and Present Relations of the Two Neighbouring Countries. Modern World: Annual Review of International Relations and Political Science. (1964-65), 35-51.

7378 Exchange of Letters Between the Catholic Hierarchy of Poland and of Germany. Poland and Germany. 10:1 (January-March 1966), 28-41.

7379 FRG, Press and Information Office. The Treaty Between the Federal Republic of Germany and the People's Republic of Poland. Bonn: Press and Information Office, 1971, 200 P.

7380 The Fruits of Work and Struggle. Poznan: Wydawnictwo Zachodnie, 1960, 85 P.

7381 Gamarnikow, M. Poland, West Germany and the Common Market. Poland and Germany. 9:1 (January-March 1965), 3-14.

7382 Gomulka, Wladyslaw. Policy of the Polish Peoples's Republic. Foreign Affairs. 38:3 (April 1960), 402-418.

7383 Grabowski, K. Lost Opportunities. Poland and Germany. 1:3 (Autumn 1957), 1-10. Gfr Vacillation Regarding Accord With Poland.

7384 Grabowski, K. The Polish Dilemma in German Policy. Poland and Germany. 3:10 (October 1959), 3-9.

7385 Grabowski, K. Polish-German Relations and European Integration. Poland and Germany. 8:3 (July-September 1964), 19-27.

7386 Gronowicz, Antoni. Pattern for Peace: The Story of Poland and Her Relations With Germany. New York: Paramount, 1951, 215 P.

7387 Grossmann, Kurt R. A Chapter in Polish-German Understanding: The German League for Human Rights. Polish Review. 15:3 (Summer 1970), 32-47.

7388 Heinsdorf, Helena. A Responsible German Policy Towards Poland?. Poland and Germany. 5:3 (July-September 1961), 12-20.

7389 Joesten, Joachim. Germany and Poland: Good or Bad Neighbors?. New York: Joachim Joesten, New Germany Reports No. 51, April 1961, 14 P.

7390 Katelbach, T. Pragmatism in Polish-German Affairs. Poland and Germany. 11:3-4 (July-December 1967), 29-35.

7391 Konieczny, Jozef. Poland and West German Plans for European Integration. Polish Western Affairs. 10:2 (1969), 286-310.

7392 Kozlowski, E. A New Chapter in Polish-West German Relations?. Poland and Germany. 15:1-2 (January-June 1971), 8-19.

7393 Kudlicki, S. First Attempts at Reconciliation. Poland and Germany. 10:1 (January-March 1966), 3-11.

7394 Kudlicki, S. Germany's Policy to-Day. Poland and Germany. 9:2-3 (April-September 1965), 15-30.

7395 Leslie, R. F. Germano-Polish Relations in the Light of Current Propaganda in the English Language. German Life and Letters. 15:2 (January 1962), 129-139.

7396 Lubomirski, S. Compensation From Germany. Poland and Germany. 6:1 (January-March 1962), 21-23.

7397 Markiewicz, Wladyslaw. Perspectives of the So-Called Versoehnung (Reconciliation) Between Germans and Poles. Polish Western Affairs. 7:1 (1966), 233-256.

7398 Michalowski, Roman. Poland and Europe: A German Appraisal. Polish Review. 2:4 (Autumn 1957), 65-88.

7399 Morawski, Kajetan. Realism in Polish-German Relations. Poland and Germany. 2:6 (September 1958), 1-7.

7400 Observer. Revisionism in Germany. Poland and Germany. 1:3 (Autumn 1957), 15-23.

7401 Ostoya, M. Elements of Settlement. Poland and Germany. 5:2 (April-June 1961), 1-7.

7402 Pact Between Poland and West Germany, 1970. Current History. 62:369 (May 1972), 259.

7403 Piszczkowski, T. The German Problem. Poland and Germany. 11:1-2 (January-June 1967), 21-39.

7404 Polish-American Conference of Illinois. German-Polish Relations and the Future of Eastern Europe. Poland and Germany. 6:2 (April-June 1962), 19-24.

7405 Polska Agencja Prasowa. Poland-G.D.R.; Materials and Documents. Warsaw: Department of Information for Abroad, 1963, 33 P.

7406 Sczaniecki, Michal. Wiewiora, Boleslaw. Nowak, Zdzislaw. Ziolkowski, Janusz. Manual of German Revisionism. Polish Western Affairs. 1:1 (1960), 64-109.

7407 Stein, Stanley. Realism in German-Polish Relations. Central European Federalist. 17:1 (June 1969), 31-33.

7408 Szulc, H. Alternative German Policies. Poland and Germany. 3:8 (April 1959), 5-13.

7409 Text of the Treaty Concluded Between the Gfr and Poland Concerning the Basis for Normalization of Their Mutual Relations. Poland and Germany.

14:3-4 (July-December 1970), 30-31.

7410 Tomicki, A. Pledges Not to Use Force. Poland and Germany. 1:3 (Autumn 1957), 11-14. Can This Pledge Be Believed If Germans Really Mean to Regain Eastern Territories?.

7411 Tomicki, A. A Polish-German Understanding. Poland and Germany. 3:9 (July 1959), 1-7.

7412 Tomlinson, A. K. Discrimination in Compensation. Poland and Germany. 11:3-4 (July-December 1967), 54-60.

7413 Tomlinson, A. K. Old and Young Germans. Poland and Germany. 3:10 (October 1959), 10-20.

7414 Uschakow, Alexander. Germany in Poland's Foreign Policy. Aussenpolitik. 21:3 (1970), 307-320.

7415 Wagner, Wolfgang. The Warsaw Treaty--A Fresh Start in Relations With Poland. German Tribune Quarterly Review. No. 13 (18 February 1971), 1-4.

7416 Wierblowski, Stefan. Germany Remains Chief European Problem. Poland of Today. 4:1 (November 1949), 3-5+.

0.6.5. Oder-Neisse Territories

7417 Arntz, Helmut. Interpretation of a Map. Bad Godesberg: Inter Nationes, 2D Ed., 1969, 60 P.

7418 Arski, Stefan. The New Polish-German Border: Safeguard of Peace. New York: Polish Embassy, 1947, 64 P.

7419 Aurich, Peter, and Others, Editors. Germany's Eastern Territories: A European Problem. Leer/Ostfriesland: Rautenberg, 1961, 46 P.

7420 Banasiak, Stefan. Settlement of the Polish Western Territories in 1945-1947. Polish Western Affairs. 6:1 (1965), 121-149.

7421 Berezowski, Z. Facing Realities. Poland and Germany. 6:1 (January-March 1962), 1-4. Protestant Ministers' Manifesto on Oder-Neisse Territories.

7422 Berezowski, Z. Policy of Make-Believe. Poland and Germany. 9:2-3 (April-September 1965), 3-6. German Policy on the Oder-Neisse Territory.

7423 Bierzanek, Remigiusz. Czakowski, Antoni. Lubojanski, Jozef. Zygulski, Kazimierz. "Heimatrecht": Instrument of Revisionism. Warsaw: Zachodnia Agencja Prasowa, 1963, 175 P.

7424 Brozek, Andrzej. The Germans in Post-War Poland. Poland and Germany. 9:1 (January-March 1965), 19-28; and 9:2-3 (April-September 1965), 31-44.

7425 A Discussion of the Oder-Neisse Line in the American Congress. Poland and Germany. 2:4 (March 1958), 34-44.

7426 Drzewieniecki, W. M. The German-Polish Frontier. Chicago: Polish Western Association of America, 1959, 166 P.

7427 Gayre, George Robert. Teuton and Slav on the Polish Frontier. London: Eyre & Spottiswoode, 1944, 76 P. Diagnosis of Racial Basis of German-Polish Borderlands, With Suggestions for Settlement of German and Slavic Claims.

7428 Gelberg, Ludwik. Poland's Western Border and Transfer of German Population. American Journal of International Law. 59:3 (July 1965), 590-593. Gelberg Is Professor of International Law, Polish Academy of Sciences; Response to Von Braun, 58:3 (July 1964), 747-750.

7429 Goettingen Research Committee. East Prussia. Goettingen: Goettingen Scientific Circle, 1947, 24 P.

7430 Goettingen Research Committee. The Eastern Part of Germany Beyond Oder and Neisse in the Polish Press, 1958-1961. Wuerzburg: Holzner, 1964, 155 P.

7431 Goettingen Research Committee. German Eastern Territories: A Manual and Book of Reference Dealing With the Regions East of the Oder and Neisse. Comp. Joachim Frhr. Von Braun. Wuerzburg: Holzner, 1957, 196 P.

7432 Goettingen Research Committee. The German Eastern Territories Beyond Oder and Neisse in the Light of the Polish Press. Wuerzburg: Holzner, 1958, 112 P.

7433 Goettingen Research Committee. The Polish Eastern Territories and Their Importance to Poland and Europe. Goettingen: Goettingen Scientific Circle, 1948, 25 P.

7434 Grabowski, K. Dangers of German Irredentism. Poland and Germany. 4:14 (October 1960), 1-9.

7435 Grabowski, K. Divided Views in Germany. Poland and Germany. 2:6 (September 1958), 8-13. on the Oder-Neisse Issue.

7436 Grabowski, K. Misplaced Intransigence. Poland and Germany. 3:8 (April 1959), 1-4. Insistence on Retaining Oder-Neisse Territories.

7437 Grazynski, Michal. The Odra-Nysa Line: A Frontier of Central Eastern Federation and a Guarantee of Lasting Peace. Eastern Quarterly. 5:1-2 (January-April 1952), 2-14.

7438 Hadfield, Jean. Germany's Eastern Frontier. Socialist Commentary. 11 (August 1947), 697-701.

7439 Heinsdorf, Helena. As the Germans See It. Poland and Germany. 5:1 (January-March 1961), 8-17.

7440 Jaenicke, Wolfgang A. Right and Freedom for Silesia. Goettingen: Goettingen Research Committee, Publication No. 215, 1959, 22 P.

7441 Jedrychowski, Stefan. The Recovered Territories an Integral Part of Poland. Warsaw: Ksiazka I Wiedza, 1952, 44 P.

7442 Jordan, Z. Oder-Neisse Line: A Study of the Political, Economic, and European Significance of Poland's Western Frontier. London: Polish Freedom Movement, 1952, 133 P.

7443 Kaps, Johannes, Editor. The Martyrdom and Heroism of the Women of East Germany: An Excerpt From the Silesian Passion, 1945-1946. Munich: Christ Unterwegs, 1955, 154 P.

7444 Kaps, Johannes, Editor. The Tragedy of Silesia, 1945/46. Munich: Christ Unterwegs, 1952-53, 576 P.

7445 Karch, John J. Oder-Neisse: Anachronism of World War II. World Affairs. 123:4 (Winter 1960), 102-104.

7446 Klafkowski, Alfons. The Polish-German Frontier and Two German States. Polish Western Affairs. 7:1 (1966), 109-124.

7447 Klafkowski, Alfons. The Polish-German Frontier in the Light of International Law. Poznan: Instytut Zachodni, 1964, 225 P.

7448 Klafkowski, Alfons. The Polish-German Frontier in the System of International Agreements. Polish Western Affairs. 1:2 (1960), 213-245.

7449 Kloskowska, Antonina. National Concepts and Attitudes of Children in a Middle-Sized City in the Polish Western Territories. Polish

Sociological Bulletin. No. 1-2 (1961), 43-56.

7450 Kokot, Jozef. The Logic of the Oder-Neisse Frontier. Poznan: Wydawnictwo Zachodnie, 1959, 289 P.

7451 Kokot, Jozef, Editor. The Miseries of the Prussian Eastern Provinces. Warsaw: The Western Press Agency, 1958, 115 P.

7452 Kokot, Jozef. The Oder-Neisse Territories After Twenty-Two Years. Poland and Germany. 12:1-2 (January-June 1968), 33-48.

7453 Kokot, Jozef. Brozek, Andrzej. The Policy of Misinformation in Publications of the Statistisches Bundesamt. Opole: Silesian Institute, 1966, 100 P.

7454 Kostanick, Huey Louis. Poland: Geography for Disaster. Current History. 36:212 (April 1959), 205-209.

7455 Kraus, Herbert. The Status Under International Law of the Eastern Territories of Germany. N.P.: N.P., 1963, 216 P.

7456 Kruszewski, Z. Anthony. The Oder-Neisse Boundary and Poland's Modernization: The Socioeconomic and Political Impact. New York: Praeger, 1972, 245 P.

7457 Kwilecki, Andrzej. Polish Western Territories in Sociological Research and Theory. Polish Sociological Bulletin. No. 18 (1968), 61-68.

7458 Lachs, Manfred. The Polish-German Frontier: Law, Life and Logic of History. Warsaw: Polish Scientific, 1964, 80 P.

7459 Lehndorff, Hans Graf Von. East Prussian Diary: A Journal of Faith, 1945-1947. London: Wolff, 1963, 252 P.

7460 Lesniewski, Andrzej, Editor. Western Frontier of Poland: Documents, Statements, Opinions. Warsaw: Western Press Agency, 1965, 302 P.

7461 Luchsinger, Fred. Christian Bridges Across the Oder. Swiss Review of World Affairs. 15:10 (January 1966), 6-7.

7462 Machrowicz, Thaddeus M. The Polish-German Boundary Settlement in the Light of International Law. Poland and Germany. 2:6 (September 1958), 23-31; and 3:7 (January 1959), 10-21.

7463 Malcuzynski, Karol. At the Peace Frontier. Warsaw: Ksiazka I Wiedza, 1953, 160 P.

7464 Marshall, Joyce. The German-Polish Boundary. Columbia Journal of International Affairs. 4:2 (Spring 1950), 77-79.

7465 Marzian, Herbert G. The German Frontier Problem: A Study in Political Interdependence. Goettingen: Goettingen Research Committee, 1969, 95 P.

7466 Meyer-Lindenberg, Hermann. Germany's Frontiers: The Evidence of International Law. Bonn: Atlantik-Forum, 1964, 16 P.

7467 Nowakowski, Stefan. Egalitarian Tendencies and the New Social Hierarchy in an Industrial-Urban Community in the Western Territories. Polish Sociological Bulletin. No. 10 (1964), 68-83.

7468 Nowakowski, Stefan. Social Integration in the Opole District in Western Territories. Polish Sociological Bulletin. No. 8 (1964), 58-66.

7469 Pagel, Karl, Editor. The German East. Berlin: Lemmer, 1954, 151 P.

7470 Pickett, Ralph H. Germany and the Oder-Neisse Line. Peace Research Reviews. 2:1 (1968), 1-109.

7471 Polish American Congress. In Defense of Poland's Western Boundary: An Economic Study. Chicago: Polish American Congress, 1948, 16 P.

7472 The Polish-German Frontier. International Relations. 1:1 (April 1954), 23-28.

7473 Powell, Robert. The German-Polish Frontier. Fortnightly. 159:952 (April 1946), 237-242.

7474 Raup, Philip M. The Agricultural Significance of German Boundary Problems. Land Economics. 26:2 (May 1950), 101-114. Oder-Neisse Line; Reply By K. O. Kurth and G. Heyn in 28:3 (August 1952), 264-270.

7475 Reece, B. Carroll. On German Provinces East of Oder-Neisse Line, and Economic, Historical, Legal and Political Aspects Involved. Washington: Government Printing Office, 1957, 32 P. Speech in House of Representatives, 16 May 1957.

7476 Rhode, Gotthold, Editor. Wagner, Wolfgang, Editor. The Genesis of the Oder-Neisse Line in the Diplomatic Negotiations During World War II: Sources and Documents. Stuttgart: Brentano, 1959, 287 P.

7477 Rosenthal, A. M. Forgotten Clue to Central Europe: Poland's Western Territories. New York Times Magazine. (26 April 1959), 9+.

7478 Sadler, Charles G. The Expendable Frontier: United States Policy on the Polish-German Frontier During the Second World War. Ph.D. Thesis, Northwestern University, 1971, 287 P.

7479 Sadowski, George G. The Coming Moscow Conference: Poland's Western Boundary Is on the Oder and Neisse Rivers. Washington: House Office Building, House of Representatives, 1947, 4 P.

7480 Schaffer, Gordon. A Frontier of Peace. New World Review. 20:12 (December 1952), 21-23.

7481 Scholz, Albert A. Silesia Yesterday and Today. The Hague: Nijhoff, 1964, 94 P.

7482 Skubiszewski, Krzysztof. The Frontier Between Poland and Germany as a Problem of International Law and Relations. Polish Western Affairs. 5:1 (1964), 311-362.

7483 Skubiszewski, Krzysztof. Poland's Western Frontier and the 1970 Treaties. American Journal of International Law. 67:1 (January 1973), 23-43.

7484 Stein, Barry N. The Boundaries of Eastern Europe With Emphasis on the Oder-Neisse Boundary. Ph.D. Thesis, New York University, 1969, 281 P.

7485 Stenzl, Otto. Germany's Eastern Frontier. Survey. No. 51 (April 1964), 118-130.

7486 Szaz, Zoltan Michael. Germany's Eastern Frontiers: The Problem of the Oder-Neisse Line. Chicago: Regnery, 1960, 256 P.

7487 Tomicki, A. German "Moral" Arguments. Poland and Germany. 4:12 (April 1960), 1-7. The Right to the Oder-Neisse Territories.

7488 Tomlinson, A. K. Public Opinion Polls on the Oder-Neisse Line. Poland and Germany. 7:3 (July-September 1963), 30-36.

7489 Tresp, Lothar L. A Compromise for the German-Polish Boundary. Georgia Review. 13:2 (Summer 1959), 117-134.

7490 US, Omgus, Civil Administration

Division. Germany's Eastern Boundaries. N.P.: Cmgus, Civil Administration Division, 1947, 9 and 24 P.

7491 Volz, Wilhelm. Eastern German Colonial Reservation. Warsaw: Western Press Agency, 2D Ed., 1957, 38 and 17 P. Reprint of Portions and Commentary on 1930 Edition.

7492 Wagner, Wolfgang. The Genesis of the Oder-Neisse Line: A Study in the Diplomatic Negotiations During World War II. Stuttgart: Brentano, 2D Ed., 1964, 192 P.

7493 Wagner, Wolfgang. Oder-Neisse Line. Marxism, Communism and Western Society: A Comparative Encyclopedia. Ed. C. D. Kernig. New York: Herder and Herder, 1973, Vol. 6, Pp. 151-157.

7494 Walczak, A. W. The Conception of Heimatpolitik in the Foreign Policy of West Germany. Polish Western Affairs. 3:1 (1962), 38-79.

7495 Wassermann, Charles. Europe's Forgotten Territories. Copenhagen: Roussell, 1960, 272 and 32 P.

7496 Watt, Donald C. British Opinion and the Oder-Neisse Line. Survey. No. 61 (October 1966), 118-128.

7497 Wiewiora, Boleslaw. The Attitude of the German Federal Republic to the Frontier on the Oder and Lusatian Neisse. Polish Western Affairs. 6:1 (1965), 25-58.

7498 Wiewiora, Boleslaw. The Polish-German Frontier in the Light of International Law. Poznan: Instytut Zachodnie, 2D Ed, 1964, 225 P.

7499 Wiewiora, Boleslaw. West German Territorial Claims Against Poland and International Law. Polish Western Affairs. 2:1 (1961), 3-30.

7500 Wilder, Jan Antoni. The Polish Regained Provinces: A Survey of a Year's Achievement. London: Hodge, 1948, 109 P.

7501 Wilpert, Friedrich Von. The Oder-Neisse Problem: Towards Fair Play in Central Europe. Bonn: Atlantic-Forum, 2D Ed., 1969, 167 P.

7502 Wirth, Guenther. The Churches and the Oder-Neisse Peace Frontier. German Foreign Policy (GDR). 5:2 (1966), 138-145.

7503 Zachodnia Agencja Prasowa. Falsification Beware! On the Methods Used by "Goettinger Arbeitskreis". Poznan: Wydawnictwo Zachodnie, 1959, 237 P.

7504 Zachodnia Agencja Prasowa. German Revisionism on the Move. Poznan: Wydawnictwo Zachodnie, 1960, 102 P.

7505 Zachodnia Agencja Prasowa. Western and Northern Territories of Poland: Facts and Problems. Poznan: Wydawnictwo Zachodnie, 1959, 50 P.

7506 Ziolkowski, Janusz. Demographic Changes in Polish Recovered Territories. Poland and Germany. 3:10 (October 1959), 21-35; and 4:11 (January 1960), 6-18.

7507 Znamierowski, Czeslaw. From Tuebingen to Goettingen. Polish Western Affairs. 5:1 (1964), 3-20.

O.6.6. Czechoslovakia

7508 Dean, Robert W. Bonn-Prague Relations: The Politics of Reconciliation. World Today. 29:4 (April 1973), 149-159.

7509 FRG, Press and Information Office. Treaty on Mutual Relations Between the Federal Republic of Germany and the Czechoslovak Socialist Republic of 11 December 1973. Bonn: Press and Information Office, 1974, 47 P.

7510 The German Problem and Czechoslovakia: Three Recent Documents. Prague: Orbis, 1961, 36 P.

7511 Haertling, Peter. The Lesson to Be Learnt From Prague. German Tribune Quarterly Review. No. 4 (21 December 1968), 13-16.

7512 Kotyk, Vaclav. New Features in Czechoslovak-German Relations. International Affairs (Moscow). (July 1961), 83-84.

7513 Treaty of Mutual Relations Between the Czechoslovak Socialist Republic and the Federal Republic of Germany. International Affairs (Moscow). No. 3 (March 1974), 103-104.

7514 Wolfe, James H. West Germany and Czechoslovakia: The Struggle for Reconciliation. Orbis. 14:1 (Spring 1970), 154-179.

7515 Zalyotny, A. F.R.G. and Developments in Czechoslovakia. International Affairs (Moscow). (November 1968), 22-27.

P. GDR: Foreign Policy

P.1. Institutions and Policies

7516 Badia, Gilbert. The German Democratic Republic and France. German Foreign Policy (GDR). 3:6 (1964), 425-431.

7517 Barth, Herbert. Common Sense and Good Will More Necessary Than Ever. German Foreign Policy (GDR). 3:2 (1964), 81-86.

7518 Feist, Manfred. Germans Abroad. German Foreign Policy (GDR). 3:1 (1964), 70-74.

7519 Fischer, Heinz. Consular Relations of the German Democratic Republic. German Foreign Policy (GDR). 2:1 (1963), 32-37.

7520 Florin, Peter. The International Position and the Peace Policy of the German Democratic Republic. German Foreign Policy (GDR). 9:6 (1970), 423-439.

7521 GDR. for Peace, Understanding and Reunification: Declarations and Statements to the Foreign Ministers Conference at Geneva. N.P.: N.P., 1959, 39 P.

7522 GDR, Council of State. A True Policy of Relaxation, Peace and European Security. Dresden: Zeit Im Bild, 1968, 15 P.

7523 GDR, National Congress. The Historic Task of the German Democratic Republic and the Future of Germany. Berlin: National Congress, 1962, 46 P. Document Accepted By Delegates at National Congress, 17 June 1962, in Berlin.

7524 GDR, State Council. on the Implementation of the Principles of Democratic International Law in the GDR. Dresden: Verlag Zeit Im Bild, Documents of the GDR No. 6, 1970, 12 P.

7525 Goetting, Gerald. Foreign Policy of the German Democratic Republic. German Foreign Policy (GDR). 6:4 (1967), 289-298.

7526 Goetting, Gerald. 20Th Anniversary of the GDR--20 Years of Christian Commitment to Peace and Socialism. German Foreign Policy (GDR). 8:5 (1969), 332-341.

7527 Hangen, Welles. The Muted Revolution: East Germany's Challenge to Russia and the West. New York: Knopf, 1966, 231 P.

7528 Hangen, Welles. New Perspectives

Behind the Wall. Foreign Affairs. 45:1 (October 1966), 135-147.

7529 Hartmann, Ralph. Instructive Days. German Foreign Policy (GDR). 7:1 (1968), 13-18.

7530 Heymann, Stefan. Krueger, Joachim. Some Aspects of the Struggle of the Socialist Unity Party of Germany for a National German Foreign Policy. German Foreign Policy (GDR). 2:1 (1963), 59-71.

7531 International Committee for Information and Social Activity. Militarists! BLITZKRIEG-PLOTTERS! Revanchists! WHERE?. Luxembourg: International Committee for Information and Social Activity, 1961, 25 P.

7532 Kitayeva, N. The GDR Strengthens Its International Position. International Affairs (Moscow). No. 4 (April 1973), 103.

7533 Klein, Peter. Seven Points for Peace and Understanding. German Foreign Policy (GDR). 2:5 (1963), 329-337. Statement Issued By 6Th Congress of Sed.

7534 Klein, Peter. The Socialist Policy of Securing Peace. German Foreign Policy (GDR). 7:5 (1968), 331-337.

7535 Koenig, Johannes. The German Democratic Republic: Bulwark of Peace in Europe. International Affairs (Moscow). (November 1961), 65-70.

7536 Koenig, Johannes. German Democratic Republic: Peaceful Foreign Policy. International Affairs (Moscow). (November 1963), 16-20.

7537 Kotov, Y. G.D.R., an Important Factor of Peace in Europe. International Affairs (Moscow). (March 1967), 50-54.

7538 Kuhlman, James A. European Realpolitik I: East Berlin's Westpolitik. The Future of Inter-Bloc Relations in Europe. Ed. Louis J. Mensonides and James A. Kuhlman. New York: Praeger, 1974, Pp. 145-161.

7539 Lemberg, Gerhard. For Peace on the Baltic Sea. German Foreign Policy (GDR). 1:4 (1962), 398-404.

7540 Lerch, Gerhard. International Sports Relations of the German Democratic Republic. German Foreign Policy (GDR). 7:5 (1968), 368-376.

7541 Livingston, Robert Gerald. East Germany Between Moscow and Bonn. Foreign Affairs. 50:2 (January 1972), 297-309.

7542 Markowski, Paul. The GDR and Peace in Europe. World Marxist Review. 15:5 (May 1972), 102-109.

7543 Mikhailov, Vladimir Ivanovich. The German Democratic Republic: An Important Factor of Peace. International Affairs (Moscow). (July 1959), 35-38.

7544 Milyukova, Valentina. GDR: International Position Strengthened. International Affairs (Moscow). (January 1970), 71-74.

7545 National Front of Democratic Germany. For Peace and Security in Europe and the Whole World. Dresden: Zeit Im Bild, 1969, 83 P. Speeches and Documents From Congress of National Front, Berlin, 21-22 March 1969.

7546 Norden, Albert. Appeal in a Grave Hour. Dresden: Zeit Im Bild, 1969, 20 P.

7547 Ott, Harry. The Class Character of the German Democratic Republic's Foreign Policy. German Foreign Policy (GDR). 11:3 (1972), 191-199.

7548 Ott, Harry. Peaceful Coexistence-- Basis of Our Foreign Policy. German Foreign Policy (GDR). 2:6 (1963), 464-470.

7549 Peace and Security for Socialist Construction. Dresden: Zeit Im Bild, 1968, 167 P.

7550 Peace Council of the GDR. "Every Cloud Has a Silver Lining..."--Ralph Abernathy Visits the GDR. Dresden: Peace Council of the German Democratic Republic, 1971, 20 P.

7551 Peace Initiative of the Community of Socialist States. Dresden: Zeit Im Bild, 1970, 45 P.

7552 Riege, Gerhard. Seidel, Karl. Foreign Policy Activities of the State Council of the German Democratic Republic. German Foreign Policy (GDR). 2:4 (1963), 263-275.

7553 Ruge, Wolfgang. German Working Class Foreign Policy. German Foreign Policy (GDR). 2:2 (1963), 118-126.

7554 Schaffer, Gordon. The German Democratic Republic: A New Force for Peace. Soviet Russia Today. 17:20 (December 1949), 12-13.

7555 Schaffer, Gordon. Germany and Peace. Labour Monthly. 51 (November 1969), 510-513.

7556 Schmidt, Gerhard. The Foreign Affairs Committee of the People's Chamber. German Foreign Policy (GDR). 3:6 (1964), 463-468.

7557 Schwabe, Ernst Otto. The Foundation of the G.D.R. League for Friendship Among the Peoples. German Foreign Policy (GDR). 1:1 (1962), 63-66.

7558 Schwabe, Ernst Otto. What Has Been Achieved and What Must Be Done?. German Foreign Policy (GDR). 1:4 (1962), 367-374. GDR Foreign Policy.

7559 Segre, Sergio. Italy and the German Democratic Republic. German Foreign Policy (GDR). 3:6 (1964), 421-425.

7560 Smith, Jean Edward. The German Democratic Republic and the West. International Journal. 22:2 (Spring 1967), 231-252.

7561 Smith, Jean Edward. The German Democratic Republic and the West. Yale Review. 58:3 (Spring 1969), 372-387.

7562 Szymanski, Zygmunt. A New European Vision. German Foreign Policy (GDR). 7:2 (1968), 123-126.

7563 Tisch, Harry. Peace and Security in the Baltic Coastal Area. German Foreign Policy (GDR). 11:4 (1972), 271-278.

7564 Tudyka, Kurt. The Foreign Policy of the Ddr. Survey. No. 61 (October 1966), 56-69.

7565 Ulbricht, Walter. Command of the Hour: Unity of Action Against Imperialism. Dresden: Zeit Im Bild, 1969, 39 P.

7566 Ulbricht, Walter. A Contribution of the German Democratic Republic to Peace in Europe. Dresden: Zeit Im Bild, 1967, 15 P.

7567 Ulbricht, Walter. The Lessons of History and the Struggle for the Preservation of Peace. Dresden: Zeit Im Bild, 1970, 26 P.

7568 Winzer, Otto. Fifteen Years of a German Policy for Peace. International Affairs (Moscow). (October 1964), 8-14.

7569 Winzer, Otto. Foreign Policy of the GDR: A Survey of Two Decades of Socialist Foreign Policy. United Asia. 21:5 (September-October 1969), 225-228.

7570 Winzer, Otto. G.D.R. Efforts for a Peace Treaty. World Marxist Review: Problems of Peace and Socialism. 4:10 (October 1961), 22-28.

7571 Winzer, Otto. On the Foreign Policy of the Socialist State of the German Nation. German Foreign Policy (GDR). 8:5 (1969), 323-331.

7572 Winzer, Otto. Socialist Constitution Confirms GDR Policy of Peace. German Foreign Policy (GDR). 7:3 (1968), 186-188.

7573 Winzer, Otto. Strengthen International Position of the GDR--A Goal in Battle for Peace and Socialism. World Marxist Review. 14:8 (August 1971), 99-106.

7574 Winzer, Otto. Ten Years of a Peaceable German State. International Affairs (Moscow). (October 1959), 28-34.

7575 Winzer, Otto. Twenty Years of GDR Foreign Policy. International Affairs (Moscow). (October 1969), 3-8.

P.2. USSR, Warsaw Pact, Other Socialist States (See Also J.7)

7576 Agreement Concerning Questions Connected With the Presence Of Soviet Forces on East German Territory, 1957. American Journal of International Law. 52:1 (January 1958), 210-215.

7577 Axen, Hermann. Peace Movement and Socialists Advance. German Foreign Policy (GDR). 5:1 (1966), 3-10.

7578 Baras, Victor. East Germany in Soviet Foreign Policy: The Objectives of The New Course and the Impact of the Uprising of June 17, 1953. Ph.D. Thesis, Cornell University, 1973, 240 P.

7579 Barth, Herbert. A New Stage of Brotherly Friendship. German Foreign Policy (GDR). 1:4 (1962), 361-366. GDR-Czechoslovak Relations.

7580 Binder, David. Ulbricht's Mission. East Europe. 12:4 (April 1963), 2-4.

7581 Bollinger, Klaus. The Ddr Treaty With the Soviet Union. Contemporary Review. 218:1260 (January 1971), 24-28.

7582 Brown, James F. The New Eastern Europe: The Khrushchev Era and After. New York: Praeger, 1966, 306 P.

7583 Brzezinski, Zbigniew K. The Organization of the Communist Camp. World Politics. 13:2 (January 1961), 175-209.

7584 Brzezinski, Zbigniew K. The Soviet Bloc: Unity and Conflict. Cambridge: Harvard University Press, 2D Ed., 1967, 599 P.

7585 Cattani, Alfred. Moscow and Ulbricht. Swiss Review of World Affairs. 21:2 (May 1971), 6-7.

7586 Croan, Melvin Czechoslovakia, Ulbricht, and the German Problem. Problems of Communism. 18:1 (January 1969), 1-7.

7587 Croan, Melvin. East Germany. The Communist States at the Crossroads Between Moscow and Peking. Ed. Adam Bromke. New York: Praeger, 1965, Pp. 126-139.

7588 Croan, Melvin. Reality and Illusion in Soviet-German Relations. Survey. No. 44-45 (October 1962), 12-28.

7589 Diessner, Gerhard. Schneider, Gerhard. Schoenherr, Hans-Jochen. Friendship and Co-Operation Between the GDR and the Cssr. German Foreign Policy (GDR). 12:1 (1973), 27-37.

7590 Draft of Peace Treaty With Germany. New Times (Moscow). No. 3 (January 1959), 33-40.

7591 East German Draft Treaty. Poland and Germany. 13:3-4 (July-December 1969), 40-42.

7592 Elsner, Joachim. Common Struggle of the GDR and the Ussr for European Security. German Foreign Policy (GDR). 6:6 (1967), 465-470.

7593 Esslin, Martin J. Peking-Pankow Axis?. China Quarterly. No. 3 (July-September 1960), 85-88.

7594 Fischer, Oskar. The GDR--Partner in the Struggle for Peace, Progress and Socialism. German Foreign Policy (GDR). 10:5 (1971), 363-371.

7595 Fischer, Oskar. The Role of the German Democratic Republic in the Socialist Comity of States. German Foreign Policy (GDR). 9:1 (1970), 17-26.

7596 Florin, Peter. Socialist Foreign Policy. German Foreign Policy (GDR). 5:2 (1966), 99-106.

7597 The GDR--A Firm Ally in the Struggle for Peace and Security. Dresden: Zeit Im Bild, 1970, 30 P. Speeches Given By Ulbricht and Stoph at the 21St Anniversary of the GDR.

7598 GDR-Ussr: Together on the Path of Peace and Progress. Dresden: Zeit Im Bild, 1967, 37 P.

7599 Graefrath, Bernhard. International Law and the GDR-Soviet Friendship Treaty. Law and Legislation in the German Democratic Republic. No. 1 (1965), 5-16.

7600 Grehl, Dieter. Ten Years of GDR-Yugoslav Diplomatic Relations. German Foreign Policy (GDR). 6:6 (1967), 478-482.

7601 Griffith, William E. Eastern Europe After the Soviet Invasion of Czechoslovakia. Santa Monica: Rand Corporation, P-3983, October 1968, 45 P.

7602 Grzybowski, Kazimierz. The Socialist Commonwealth of Nations: Organizations and Institutions. New Haven: Yale University Press, 1964, 300 P.

7603 Hartmann, Karl. Poland Under New Party Leader Gierek. Aussenpolitik. 22:3 (1971), 288-310.

7604 Hirsch, Felix Edward. The Poles and Eastern Germany. Current History. 8:44 (April 1945), 294-298.

7605 Huber, Gerhard. Sydow, Peter. Power Relations Are Changing in Favour of Socialism. German Foreign Policy (GDR). 1:4 (1962), 375-390.

7606 J. C. Relations Between Poland and Eastern Germany. World Today. 7:9 (September 1951), 370-376.

7607 Johnson, A. Ross. The Warsaw Pact's Campaign for "European Security". Santa Monica: Rand Corporation, R-565-Pr, November 1970, 102 P.

7608 Khrushchev, Nikita S. The New Content of Peaceful Coexistence in the Nuclear Age. New York: Crosscurrents, 1963, 48 P. Speech at 6Th Congress of Sed, Berlin, 16 January 1963.

7609 Kiesewetter, Wolfgang. German-Soviet Relations. German Foreign Policy (GDR). 3:3 (1964), 174-183.

7610 Korbonski, Andrzej. The Warsaw Pact. International Conciliation. No. 573 (May 1969), 73 P.

7611 Kroeger, Herbert. GDR Socialist Sovereignty and Proletarian Internationalism. German Foreign Policy (GDR). 9:1 (1970), 26-35.

7612 Kroeger, Herbert. The Socialist Unity Party of Germany and Socialist International Law. German Foreign Policy (GDR). 10:2 (1971), 83-97.

7613 Krolikowski, Herbert. Relations Between Yugoslavia and the German Democratic Republic. German Foreign Policy (GDR). 4:4 (1965), 269-276.

7614 Krueger, Joachim. The "Declaration for Peace, Security and Co-Operation in Europe"--A Democratic Program of Action. German Foreign Policy (GDR). 11:4 (1972), 279-289. Warsaw Pact Declaration at Prague.

7615 Krueger, Joachim. Friendship Treaty Between the GDR and the Romanian Socialist Republic. German Foreign Policy (GDR). 11:6 (1972), 462-469.

7616 Librach, Jan. The Rise of the Soviet Empire. New York: Praeger, 1964, 382 P., Esp. 176-180.

7617 Livingston, Robert G., Moderator. The Role of the German Democratic Republic Within Eastern Europe. Eastern Europe in the 1970S. Ed. Sylva Sinanian, Istvan Deak, and Peter C. Ludz. New York: Praeger, 1972, Pp. 242-257.

7618 Lowenthal, Richard. Expanding Empires: The Illusion of Stability. Twentieth Century. 165:987 (May 1959), 447-456.

7619 Markowski, Paul. Foreign Policy in the Spirit of Socialist Internationalism. German Foreign Policy (GDR). 6:4 (1967), 279-288.

7620 Meissner, Boris. Foreign Policy at the Moscow Party Congress. Aussenpolitik. 22:3 (1971), 270-287.

7621 Meissner, Boris. The Soviet Union and Collective Security. Aussenpolitik. 21:3 (1970), 272-284.

7622 Meissner, Boris. The Soviet Union and Germany's Right to Self-Determination. Studies on the Soviet Union. 3:3 (1964), 80-89.

7623 Moscow's Visible and Invisible Controls in East Germany. Swiss Review of World Affairs. 5:10 (January 1956), 7-9.

7624 Ott, Harry. Karlovy Vary--Alternative to Imperialist Global Strategy. German Foreign Policy (GDR). 6:6 (1967), 443-452.

7625 Peck, Reginald. Russia in Eastern Germany. Contemporary Review. 180:1028 (August 1951), 80-84.

7626 Petrushev, A. Cooperation in the World Socialist System. German Foreign Policy (GDR). 4:4 (1965), 301-307.

7627 Quilitzsch, Siegmar. Fraternal Alliance With the Soviet Union. German Foreign Policy (GDR). 7:1 (1968), 19-24.

7628 Remington, Robin Alison. The Warsaw Pact: Case Studies in Communist Conflict Resolution. Cambridge: Mit Press, 1971, 268 P., Esp. Pp. 134-164.

7629 Roberts, Henry L. Eastern Europe: Politics, Revolution, and Diplomacy. New York: Knopf, 1970, 324 P.

7630 Schmidt, Helmut. The Consequences of the Brezhnev Doctrine. Atlantic Community Quarterly. 7:2 (Summer 1969), 184-195.

7631 Simon, H. Paul. The Warsaw Pact and East Germany--Provocation or Response?. Queen's Quarterly. 71:3 (Autumn 1964), 345-364.

7632 Spittmann, Ilse. Soviet Union and Ddr. Survey. No. 61 (October 1966), 165-176.

7633 Stern, Leo. The Soviet Union and the G.D.R.'s Development. International Affairs (Moscow). (December 1966), 62-67.

7634 Through the Eyes of Friends: Correspondents of the Ussr and the GDR Report. Moscow: Novosti Press Agency, 1972, 150 P.

7635 The Treaty on Relations Between the German Democratic Republic and the Union of Soviet Socialist Republics of September 20Th, 1955. Berlin (East): Die Wirtschaft, 1955, 48 P. Speeches to Volkskammer By Grotewohl, Ulbricht, Bolz.

7636 Ulbricht, Walter. Friendship and Alliance With the Soviet Union: Lessons of German History. Dresden: Zeit Im Bild, 1967, 40 P.

7637 Vehres, Gerd. Consolidation of Socialist Comity of Nations. German Foreign Policy (GDR). 6:6 (1967), 460-465.

7638 W. K. East Germany: Soviet Rampart or Achilles' Heel?. Problems of Communism. 6:2 (March-April 1957), 38-42.

7639 Weiss, Grigorij. A Red Letter in the Calendar. German Foreign Policy (GDR). 3:6 (1964), 442-445. GDR-Ussr Relations.

7640 Wenning, Werner. The GDR and the People's Republic of Bulgaria. German Foreign Policy (GDR). 12:1 (1973), 14-26.

7641 Wettig, Gerhard. Community and Conflict in the Socialist Camp: The Soviet Union, East Germany and the German Problem 1965-1972. New York: St. Martin's Press, 1975, 160 Pp.

7642 Wettig, Gerhard. East Berlin and the Moscow Treaty. Aussenpolitik. 22:3 (1971), 256-269.

7643 Wettig, Gerhard. East Berlin in the Shadow of Moscow's German Policy. German Tribune Quarterly Review. No. 6 (24 June 1969), 7-12.

7644 Winzer, Otto. The Contribution of the GDR to the Strengthening of the Socialist World System. German Foreign Policy (GDR). Spec. Ed. 1 (October 1961), 48-56.

7645 Winzer, Otto. The German Democratic Republic Within the Community of Socialist States. German Foreign Policy (GDR). 10:6 (1971), 453-462.

7646 Wohlgemuth, Kaethe. Real Friendship. Dresden: Zeit Im Bild, 1971, 63 P.

7647 Wolfe, Thomas W. The Soviet Union's Strategic Stake in the G.D.R. World Today. 27:8 (August 1971), 340-350.

7648 Wolfe, Thomas W. The Soviet Union's Strategic and Military Stakes in the GDR. Santa Monica: Rand Corporation, P-4549, January 1971, 19 P.

7649 Yesterday and Today, 1917-1967: Contemporary Report on the Progress of German-Soviet Friendship. Dresden: Zeit Im Bild, 1967, 221 P.

7650 Zelt, Johannes. Reissig, Karl. Unity of National and International Elements in the Relations Between the GDR and the Ussr. German Foreign Policy (GDR). 6:5 (1967), 400-409.

P.3. Defense, Security, Arms Control

7651 Bender, Peter. East Europe in Search of Security. Baltimore: Johns Hopkins University Press, 1972, X and 144 P., Esp. Pp. 10-47.

7652 Bock, Siegfried. For Collective Security in Europe: The European Policy of The GDR. Dresden: Zeit Im Bild, 1968, 47 P.

7653 Buehring, Guenter. Who Is in Favour of a Conference for European Security?. German Foreign Policy (GDR). 6:1 (1967), 15-21.

7654 Doernberg, Stefan. Schirmeister, Helga. The Public Opinion Movement--A Major Factor in the Struggle for Security and Co-Operation in Europe. German Foreign Policy (GDR). 11:6 (1972), 456-462.

7655 Felber, Rolf. The Protection of the GDR State Frontier in the Light of International Law. German Foreign Policy (GDR). 5:2 (1966), 107-123.

7656 Florin, Peter. European Security and the German Democratic Republic. International Affairs (Moscow). (August 1965), 25-31.

7657 GDR, Council of State. New Initiatives of the German Democratic Republic for European Security. Dresden: Zeit Im Bild, 1968, 43 P.

7658 Graefrath, Bernhard. International Law Protects G.D.R. Air Space Sovereignty. German Foreign Policy (GDR). 1:1 (1962), 67-76.

7659 Hoeldtke, Siegfried. Safeguarding European Security. German Foreign Policy (GDR). 6:3 (1967), 220-224.

7660 Hoffmann, Heinz. The Military Policy of the Socialist Unity Party of Germany. German Foreign Policy (GDR). 10:4 (1971), 289-299.

7661 Klaiber, Wolfgang. Security Priorities in Eastern Europe. Problems of Communism. 19:3 (May-June 1970), 32-57.

7662 Kohl, Michael. The Borders of the G.D.R. Must Be Respected. German Foreign Policy (GDR). 1:6 (1962), 565-570.

7663 Krueger, Joachim. European Security-- Urgent Necessity. German Foreign Policy (GDR). 5:2 (1966), 124-130.

7664 Krueger, Joachim. GDR Support for Non-Proliferation. German Foreign Policy (GDR). 7:1 (1968), 33-39.

7665 Krueger, Joachim. The Struggle of the German Democratic Republic for Disarmament. German Foreign Policy (GDR). 4:6 (1965), 430-438.

7666 Schirmer, Gregor. International Law Protects Borders of the German Democratic Republic. German Foreign Policy (GDR). 2:5 (1963), 338-344.

7667 Steiniger, Peter-Alfons. Border Violation Means War Preparation. German Foreign Policy (GDR). 1:6 (1962), 571-581. Followed (Pp. 582-604) By Statements By GDR Officials.

7668 Ulbricht, Walter. Disarmament, Peaceful Co-Existence and Friendship With All Peoples. Berlin (East): N.P., 1960, 14 P.

7669 Vogl, Dieter. The Warsaw Treaty States and the European Security Conference. German Foreign Policy (GDR). 10:1 (1971), 15-29.

7670 Wandel, Paul. The G.D.R.--Pioneer of Disarmament in Germany. German Foreign Policy (GDR). 1:3 (1962), 241-248.

P.4. Third World

7671 Bernheim, Roger. Ddr Propaganda in Southeast Asia. Swiss Review of World Affairs. 9:4 (July 1959), 19-21.

7672 Diplomatic Relations GDR-India. Dresden: Verlag Zeit Im Bild, 1972, 6 P.

7673 GDR. Linked in Friendship. Berlin: Staatsverlag, 1965, 48 P. GDR-Egyptian Relations.

7674 GDR, Ministry of Foreign Affairs. The Anti-Imperialist Liberation Struggle of the Afro-Asian and Latin American Peoples and the German Democratic Republic. Dresden: Zeit Im Bild, 1964, 120 P.

7675 GDR, Ministry of Foreign Affairs. The German Democratic Republic and the United Arab Republic--Good Friends. Dresden: N.P., 1965, 120 P. Ulbricht Visit to Uar, 24 February-2 March 1965.

7676 The GDR: A Staunch Ally of the Emergent Countries. Dresden: Verlag Zeit Im Bild, 1971, 82 P.

7677 Goetting, Gerald. GDR Relations With the African Peoples. German Foreign Policy (GDR). 6:3 (March 1967), 199-206.

7678 Helbing, Hubert. Scientific Aid From the German Democratic Republic to Economically Less Developed Countries. German Foreign Policy (GDR). 2:4 (1963), 254-262.

7679 Kiesewetter, Wolfgang. Relations Between the GDR and the Union of India. German Foreign Policy (GDR). 6:5 (1967), 372-377.

7680 Kulitzka, Dieter. The Relations Between the GDR and the Latin-American Countries. German Foreign Policy (GDR). 11:1 (1972), 19-26.

7681 Marsh, William W. East Germany and Africa. Africa Report. 14:34 (March-April, 1969), 59-64.

7682 Perera, Reggie. Ceylon and the GDR. United Asia. 21:5 (September-October 1969), 313-314.

7683 Rennhack, Horst. Solidarity With Vietnam. German Foreign Policy (GDR). 6:4 (1967), 309-313.

7684 Samant, Bal. India in the GDR. United Asia. 21:5 (September-October 1969), 310-312.

7685 Scholz, Paul. Cooperation Between the German Democratic Republic and the United Arab Republic. German Foreign Policy (GDR). 6:4 (1967), 304-308.

7686 Schweinberger, Willy. G.D.R. Assistance to the Economically Underdeveloped Countries. German Foreign Policy (GDR). 2:1 (1963), 12-22.

7687 Sefrin, Max. Peaceful International Co-Operation in the Spirit of Mahatma Gandhi. United Asia. 21:5 (September-October 1969), 221-224.

7688 Sefrin, Max. South-East Asia and the Two German States. German Foreign Policy (GDR). 1:3 (1962), 292-300.

7689 Weiss, Gerhard. Political and Economic Relations Between the GDR and the Uar. German Foreign Policy (GDR). 6:1 (1967), 36-42.

7690 Zaostrovsky, Y. The GDR's Cooperation With Developing Countries. International Affairs (Moscow). (November 1972), 99-100.

P.5. International Organizations

7691 Bierzanek, Remigiusz. The Principle of Universality and Its Implementation in the United Nations Organisation. German Foreign Policy (GDR). 9:5 (1970), 360-372.

7692 Bolz, Lothar. Universality--Aim of the United Nations. German Foreign Policy (GDR). 4:1 (1965), 3-11.

7693 Fellhauer, Harry. Winklbauer, Ernst. The International Patent Organization (Ipo) and the Principle of Universality. German Foreign Policy (GDR). 6:2 (1967), 168-177.

7694 GDR, Council of State. The German

People and the United Nations. Dresden: German United Nations League, 1966, 61 p.

7695 GDR, Ministry of Foreign Affairs. German Democratic Republic and the Xvii United Nations General Assembly. Berlin: Ministry of Foreign Affairs, Press Department, 1962, 23 p.

7696 GDR, Ministry of Foreign Affairs. The German Democratic Republic and the United Nations Organization: White Book. Dresden: Ministry of Foreign Affairs, 1969, 171 p.

7697 The GDR and the Uno. Dresden: Verlag Zeit Im Bild, 1972, 21 p.

7698 German League for the United Nations. The German Democratic Republic and the United Nations. Dresden: Verlag Zeit Im Bild, Documents of the GDR No. 7, 1970, 78 p.

7699 Graefrath, Bernhard. The GDR Is Entitled to Un Membership. German Foreign Policy (GDR). 5:4 (1966), 288-294.

7700 Gruber, Hans. GDR Welcomes United Nations Resolution on Anti-Racism Year. German Foreign Policy (GDR). 11:1 (1972), 3-18.

7701 Hoehnel, Gerd. Bader, Lothar. Protection of Environment and Universality. German Foreign Policy (GDR). 11:5 (1972), 403-412. Un Declaration and Stockholm Conference.

7702 Kiermeier, Hildegard. The Contribution of the German Democratic Republic Towards The Work of the Social and Humanitarian United Nations Agencies. German Foreign Policy (GDR). 10:1 (1971), 29-37.

7703 Kroeger, Herbert. The Principle of Universality and the Efficacy of the United Nations. German Foreign Policy (GDR). 10:5 (1971), 400-409.

7704 Moldt, Ewald. Topical Issues of GDR Foreign Policy and the Tasks of Uno in the Struggle for Peace and International Security. German Foreign Policy (GDR). 11:6 (1972), 447-455.

7705 Olivier, Hans. The 18Th Session of the General Assembly of the United Nations. German Foreign Policy (GDR). 3:1 (1964), 42-58.

7706 Plischke, Elmer. East Germany's Quest for United Nations Membership. World Affairs. 130:2 (July 1967), 89-94.

7707 Poppe, Eberhard. The Un Declaration of Human Rights and the Constitution of The GDR. German Foreign Policy (GDR). 7:3 (1968), 203-210.

7708 Rose, Harald. The German Democratic Republic and the United Nations. German Foreign Policy (GDR). 8:5 (1969), 367-376.

7709 Rose, Harald. The Legal Claim Of The German Democratic Republic To Membership In The United Nations. German Foreign Policy (Gdr). 2:3 (1963), 165-174.

7710 Schirmer, Gregor. The Universality Of International Conferences. German Foreign Policy (Gdr). 3:5 (1964), 327-341.

7711 Schumanr, Hans. The German Democratic Republic And The United Nations. German Foreign Policy (Gdr). 11:5 (1972), 372-377.

7712 Steiniger, Peter-Alfons. The Gdr And The United Nations. German Foreign Policy (Gdr). 3:6 (1964), 446-453.

7713 Steiniger, Peter-Alfons. Position And Prospects Of The United Nations. German Foreign Policy (Gdr). 5:6 (1966), 420-431.

7714 Steiniger, Peter-Alfons. The Role And Prospects Of The United Nations. German Foreign Policy (Gdr). 2:1 (1963), 54-59.

7715 Steiniger, Peter-Alfons. The Universality Of The United Nations And The Application Of The Gdr For Admission. Law And Legislation In The German Democratic Republic. No. 2 (1966), 5-7.

7716 Ulbricht, Walter. For Peace And Equality--For The Universality Of The United Nations. Dresden: Zeit Im Bild, 1966, 52 p.

7717 Wuensche, Harry. The Principle Of Universality And The Right Of The Gdr To Membership In The United Nations. Law And Legislation In The German Democratic Republic. No. 2 (1969), 5-12.

Q. FRG-GDR: The German Problem

Q.1. German Problem: Unity (See Also D.4)

Q.1.1. Between East And West, 1949-55

7718 Adenauer, Konrad. German Reunion And The Future Of Europe. International Journal. 9:3 (Summer 1954), 173-176.

7719 Bitzer, Ronald. Soviet Policy On German Reunification In 1952. World Affairs (London). 132:3 (December 1969), 245-256.

7720 Brecht, Arnold. The Idea Of A "Safety Belt". American Political Science Review. 43:5 (October 1949), 1001-1009. Proposal For Supplementing The Atlantic Treaty.

7721 Brodrick, Alan H. Danger Spot Of Europe. London And New York: Hutchinson, 1951, 192 p.

7722 Burchett, Wilfred G. Cold War In Germany. Melbourne: World Unity Publications, 2Nd Ed., 1950, 258 p.

7723 Burmeister, Werner. The Struggle For Germany. Yearbook Of World Affairs. 7 (1953), 149-169.

7724 Burns, Emile. German Unity: The Key To Peace. Communist Review. 7:6 (June 1952), 163-169.

7725 Cahnman, Werner J. Frontiers Between East And West In Europe. Geographical Review. 39:4 (October 1949), 605-624.

7726 Carey, Jane Perry Clark. German Politics And The East-West Deadlock. Foreign Policy Reports. 25:2 (1 April 1949), 14-27.

7727 Carey, Jane Perry Clark. Germany Today: Security Versus Recovery. New York: Foreign Policy Association, 1949, 247 p.

7728 Chambon, Albert. The Problem Of Germany In Europe. How Can We The People Achieve A Just Peace? Selected Speeches. South Hadley: Mount Holyoke College, Institute On The United Nations, 1949, Pp. 50-56.

7729 Churchill, Winston S. European Unity And Settlement With Russia. Bulletin Of The Atomic Scientists. 6:6 (June 1950), 168-170.

7730 Cox, Henry B. The Struggle For German Unity. Department Of State Bulletin. 26:668 (14 April 1952), 563-568.

7731 Craig, Gordon A. Germany Between The East And The West. Proceedings Of The Academy Of Political Science. 23:3 (May 1949), 222-231.

7732 Dethleffsen, Erich. The Chimera Of German Neutrality. Foreign Affairs. 30:3 (April 1952), 361-375.

7733 Doenhoff, Marion Graefin. Germany Puts Freedom Before Unity. Foreign Affairs. 28:3 (April 1950), 398-411.

7734 Dorpalen, Andreas. Germany Between

East And West. Virginia Quarterly Review. 25:4 (Autumn 1950), 500-514.

7735 Epstein, Klaus. The German Problem, 1945-1950. World Politics. 20:2 (January 1968), 279-300.

7736 Frg, Federal Ministry For All-German Affairs. The Efforts Made By The Federal Republic Of Germany To Re-Establish The Unity Of Germany By Means Of All-German Elections: Papers And Documents. Bonn: Deutscher Bundesverlag, 2D Ed., 1954, 172 P.

7737 Fay, Sidney B. Germany: An Uneasy Buffer. Current History. 20:113 (January 1951), 16-21.

7738 Food For East Germany: Letters Exchanged By President Eisenhower And Chancellor Adenauer. Department Of State Bulletin. 29:736 (3 August 1953), 147.

7739 Fraenkel, Heinrich. A Nation Divided. London: Yates, 1949, 87 P.

7740 Frei, Otto. German Unity And International Law. Swiss Review Of World Affairs. 2:7 (October 1952), 9-11.

7741 Frei, Otto. Russian Policy In Germany: A Balance Sheet Of Success And Failure. Swiss Review Of World Affairs. 4:2 (May 1954), 3-4.

7742 Freund, Gerald. American-Germany-Russia. Occidente. 11:2 (1955), 149-160.

7743 Gdr, Information Office. The German Democratic Republic In The Fight For The Unity Of Germany. Berlin: Information Office, C.1952, 158 P.

7744 Geilinger, Eduard. On The Tortuous Course Of The Kremlin'S German Policy. Swiss Review Of World Affairs. 1:8 (November 1951), 7-9.

7745 The German Problem On The Eve Of The Four Power Talks. World Today. 11:7 (July 1955), 280-290.

7746 Germany: Problems Of Unity And Issues Of The Peace. Proceedings Of The Institute Of World Affairs. 26:5 (December 1949), 89-92.

7747 Gimbel, John. Cold War: German Front. Maryland Historian. 2:1 (Spring 1971), 41-55.

7748 Gottlieb, Manuel. The Quest For East-West Settlement In Germany. Ph.D. Thesis, Harvard University, 1953.

7749 Haffner, Sebastian. German Unity And Western Strategy. Twentieth Century. 180:898 (December 1951), 471-482.

7750 Hafter, Rudolph F. German Ideas On Reunification Have Matured. Swiss Review Of World Affairs. 1:1 (April 1951), 2-4.

7751 Hallstein, Walter. Germany'S Dual Aim: Unity And Integration. Foreign Affairs. 31:1 (October 1952), 58-66.

7752 Hartmann, Frederick H. Soviet Russia And The German Problem. Yale Review. 43:4 (June 1954), 511-524.

7753 Hasselmann, Erwin. Germany'S Desperate Dilemma. Twentieth Century. 157:935 (January 1955), 15-25. Reunification Vs. Western European Integration.

7754 Huston, James A. Germany, Another Korea?. World Affairs. 116:3 (Fall 1953), 69-71.

7755 J. F. A. W. Ten Years Of East-West Relations In Europe: The Struggle For Germany. World Today. 11:6 (June 1955), 246-254.

7756 Johnsen, Carsten Ingeman. Germany Unification Question Mark. Floral Park, N.Y.: N.P., 1954, 53 P.

7757 Kappelman, Glenn L. Germany Between East And West. Ph.D. Thesis, University Of Kansas, 1950.

7758 Kohn, Hans. Germany Between East And West. Current History. 28:164 (April 1955), 243-248.

7759 Kohn, Hans. Germany Between East And West. Occidente. 11:2 (1955), 138-147.

7760 Laukhuff, Perry. Warburg, James P. Germany: Rearmed Or Neutralized?. Foreign Policy Bulletin. 33:21 (15 July 1954), 4-6.

7761 Lichtheim, George. Germany, Center Of The "Peace Offensive"--Is An East-West Settlement Possible?. Commentary. 15:6 (June 1953), 584-592.

7762 Lohr, George. The Meaning Of A Unified Democratic Germany. Political Affairs. 30:6 (June 1951), 58-69.

7763 Lowe, John. Germany-- A Dilemma. Twentieth Century. 147:875 (January 1950), 12-16.

7764 Lowenthal, Richard. The Challenge Of Unification. New Leader. 38:10 (7 March 1955), 3-5.

7765 Lowenthal, Richard. German Unity And The Western Counter-Offensive. Twentieth Century. 150:897 (November 1951), 377-388.

7766 Lowenthal, Richard. The Germans In The Cold War. This Is Germany. Ed. Arthur Settel. New York: Sloane, 1950, Pp. 40-73.

7767 Matthews, George. Which Way For Germany?. Labour Monthly. 32:12 (December 1950), 561-568.

7768 Nettl, Peter. Economic Checks On German Unity. Foreign Affairs. 30:4 (July 1952), 554-562.

7769 Neumann, Sigmund. Germany: Promise And Perils. New York: Foreign Policy Association, Headline Series No. 82, July-August 1950, Pp. 3-53.

7770 Opie, Redvers. The Search For Peace Settlements. Washington: Brookings, 1951, 366 P., Esp. Pp. 199-271.

7771 Patch, Buel W. German Problem. Editorial Research Reports. (26 April 1950), 295-315.

7772 Perusse, Roland I. The Study Of The Problems Of Contemporary Germany, With Particular Emphasis On The Question Of German Reunification And German Integration Into The Western Community Of Nations. Ph.D. Thesis, American University, 1955.

7773 Platts-Mills, John. Where Do We Go From Here?--Some Thoughts On The Problem Of Germany. New Central European Observer. 2:25 (10 December 1949), 295.

7774 Purcell, Henry. Germany: Peace Or War?. Labour Monthly. 34:9 (September 1952), 402-407.

7775 Quaestor. Germany And Peace. Labour Monthly. 34:5 (May 1952), 219-226.

7776 Raman, K. V. Sri. The Future Of The Germanies. Foreign Review (Delhi). 9:12 (December 1950), 674-681.

7777 Ratazzi, Peter. A Marxist Prussia Or A Swiss Germany. Dalhousie Review. 29:1 (April 1950), 47-51.

7778 Reuter, Ernst. Germany And The Cold War. Political Quarterly. 22:1 (January-March 1951), 27-32.

7779 Scammon, Richard M. Germany And Europe: Battleground, Bastion, Or Buffer. Germany And The Future Of Europe. Ed. Hans J. Morgenthau. Chicago: University Of Chicago Press, 1951, Pp. 163-169.

7780 Schnitzer, Ewald W. Soviet Policy On The Reunification Of Germany, 1945-1952. Santa Monica: Rand Corporation, Rm-1119, 1953, 81 P.

7781 Schuetz, Wilhelm Wolfgang. German Neutrality?. Contemporary Review. 173:988 (April 1948), 211-216.

7782 Seton-Watson, Hugh. Eastern Europe And The German Problem. Twentieth Century. 153:913 (March 1953), 195-202.

7783 Seton-Watson, Hugh. Moscow And The West. Fortnightly. 1041 (September 1953), 147-153.

7784 Shell, Kurt L. The German Peace Settlement. Social Research. 28:2 (Summer 1961), 252-253.

7785 Shulman, Marshall D. Stalin's Foreign Policy Reappraised. Cambridge: Harvard University Press, 1963, 320 P., Esp. Pp. 64-73, 191-194.

7786 Smith, Jessica. Korea And Germany-- World Peace In The Balance. New World Review. 20:6 (June 1952), 3-5.

7787 Smith, Robert F. The Policy Of The United States Toward Political Unity In Germany, 1945-1953. Ph.D. Thesis, University Of Chicago, 1955, 250 P.

7788 Smogorzewski, K. M. Germany's Future Role In Europe. Fortnightly. 175:1049 (May 1954), 304-310.

7789 Sollohub, Nicolas. Germany's Dilemma: Problems Of A Divided Germany. Dublin Review. 228:463 (Spring 1954), 33-45.

7790 Stone, William T. Germany And The Balance Of Power. Editorial Research Reports. (15 June 1955), 399-416.

7791 Strang, William, Lord. Germany Between East And West. Foreign Affairs. 33:3 (April 1955), 387-401.

7792 Sweezy, Paul M. The German Problem. Monthly Review. 1:1 (May 1949), 37-43.

7793 Two Approaches To The German Question. New World Review. 21:9 (October 1953), 32-37.

7794 Un, General Assembly. Report Of The United Nations Commission To Investigate Conditions For Free Elections In Germany. New York: United Nations, General Assembly, 5 May 1952, 71 P. Covers Period From 11 February To 30 April 1952.

7795 Us, Department Of State, Office Of Public Affairs. Confuse And Control: Soviet Techniques In Germany. Washington: Department Of State Publication 4107, Government Printing Office, 1951, 107 P.

7796 Us, Hicog, Office Of Executive Secretary. Documents On German Unity. Bad Godesberg-Mehlem: Hicog, Office Of Executive Secretary, 4 Vols., 1951-53.

7797 Ussr, Ministry Of Foreign Affairs. The Soviet Union And The Question Of The Unity Of Germany And The German Peace Treaty. Moscow: Foreign Languages Publishing House, 1952, 86 P.

7798 White, Theodore H. Fire In The Ashes: Europe In Mid-Century. New York: Sloane, 1953, 405 P., Esp. Pp. 130-188.

7799 Willging, Paul Raymond. Soviet Foreign Policy In The German Question: 1950-1955. Ph.D. Thesis, Columbia University, 1973, 333 P.

7800 Wolf, Simon. The Problem Of German Unity. Contemporary Review. 181:1033 (January 1952), 10-14.

7801 Younger, Kenneth. The German Problem. London: Fabian, 1952, 20 P.

Q.1.2. Declining Hopes For Unity, 1955-61

7802 American-German Conference On East-West Tensions. East-West Tensions: The Present Status--Future Developments. Freiburg: Rombach, 2 Vols., 1960-61.

7803 Aptheker, Herbert. The German Question--Again. Political Affairs. 39:3 (March 1960), 36-47.

7804 Association For An Indivisible Germany. Our Youth Sees Germany. Munich: Langen And Mueller, 1961, 207 P. Prize Essays From 80,000 Submitted In Kuratorium Unteilbares Deutschland Contest.

7805 Barkeley, Richard. Effect Of Soviet Propaganda. Contemporary Review. 195:2 (February 1959), 105-107.

7806 Beach, Vincent W. Germany: East Or West?. Queen's Quarterly. 63:1 (Spring 1956), 34-44.

7807 Bonn, Moritz J. The End Of German Reunion?. Bankers' Magazine (London). 185:1366 (January 1958), 6-12.

7808 Bonn, Moritz J. Germany: An End To Illusions. Bankers' Magazine (London). 189:1392 (March 1960), 223-226. Reunification Will Only Come In Distant Future, If At All.

7809 Buchwitz, Otto. German Unity And The German Working Class. International Affairs (Moscow). (October 1959), 59-65.

7810 Campbell, John C. East Europe, Germany, And The West. Annals Of The American Academy Of Political And Social Science. 317 (May 1958), 153-163.

7811 Conant, James Bryant. Gaitskell, Hugh. Could We Accept A Neutralized Germany, United But Outside Nato?. Western World. No. 15 (July 1958), 35-48.

7812 Dulles, Eleanor Lansing. The Meaning Of The Division Of Germany. Department Of State Bulletin. 41:1066 (30 November 1959), 790-795.

7813 Embree, George D., Editor. The Soviet Union And The German Question, September 1958-June 1961: Documents. The Hague: Nijhoff, 1963, 330 P.

7814 Erfurt, Werner. Moscow's Policy In Germany: A Study In Contemporary History. Esslingen: Bechtle, N.D., 140 P.

7815 Erler, Fritz. The Reunification Of Germany And Security For Europe. World Politics. 10:3 (April 1958), 366-377.

7816 Erler, Fritz. The Struggle For German Reunification. Foreign Affairs. 34:3 (April 1956), 380-393.

7817 Feld, Werner J. Reunification And West German-Soviet Relations: The Role Of The Reunification Issue In The Foreign Policy Of The Federal Republic Of Germany, 1949-1957; With Special Attention Toward The Soviet Union. The Hague: Nijhoff, 1963, 204 P.

7818 Feld, Werner J. The Role Of The Reunification Issue In The Foreign Policy Of The Federal Republic Of Germany, 1949-1957, With Special Attention To Policy Toward The Soviet Union. Ph.D. Thesis, Tulane University, 1962, 357 P.

7819 Fleming, Denna Frank. The Cold War And Its Origins, 1917-1960. Garden City: Doubleday, 1961, 2 Vols., 1158 P.

7820 Freund, Gerald. Germany Between Two Worlds. New York: Harcourt, Brace, 1961, 296 P.

7821 Gdr. Questions And Answers On The German Peace Treaty. N.P.: N.P., C.1961, 30 P.

7822 Gatzke, Hans W. Reunification. Current History. 30:176 (April 1956), 206-212.

7823 German Peace Council. The German People Want A Peace Treaty: Material On The Proposals Of The Government Of The Ussr Towards A Peaceful Solution Of The German Problem And The Berlin Question. Berlin (East): German Peace Council, 1959, 20 P.

7824 Gleitze, Bruno. Economic And Social Problems Of A German Reunification. Free World Forum. 1:1 (January 1959), 51-54.

7825 Grewe, Wilhelm G. The Unification Of Germany. Annals Of The American Academy Of Political And Social Science. 324 (July 1959), 8-15.

7826 H. G. L. The Four Powers And Germany: The Reunification Issue. World Today. 11:11 (November 1955), 471-482.

7827 Hottelet, Richard C. Khrushchev's German Gambit. Orbis. 3:1 (Spring 1959), 13-25.

7828 Hudson, G. F. Khrushchev's Visit: The German Problem Remains; Possibilities For A Settlement. Commentary. 28:4 (October 1959), 277-285.

7829 Inter Nationes. The Reunification Of Germany: A Necessity For World Peace. Bonn: Inter Nationes, 1961, 15 P.

7830 Kryukov, P. A Peace Treaty And European Security. International Affairs (Moscow). (July 1961), 77-80.

7831 Laukhuff, Perry. The Problem Of Germany. Current History. 30:175 (March 1956), 159-165.

7832 Lewis, Flora. The Unstable States Of Germany. Foreign Affairs. 38:4 (July 1960), 588-597.

7833 Loewenstein, Karl. Unity For Germany?. Current History. 38:221 (January 1960), 37-45.

7834 Loewenstein, Prince Hubertus Zu. Berlin And German Reunification As International Problems. Pakistan Horizon. 13:4 (1960), 278-283.

7835 Lohr, George. The Two Germanys And The War Danger. Political Affairs. 37:7 (July 1958), 32-39.

7836 Luchsinger, Fred. The German Question And Summit Diplomacy. Swiss Review Of World Affairs. 9:9 (December 1959), 1-2.

7837 Luchsinger, Fred. German Reunification And The Lost Areas In The East. Swiss Review Of World Affairs. 6:5 (August 1956), 6-7.

7838 Luchsinger, Fred. Reunification: A Risky Topic Of Debate In Germany. Swiss Review Of World Affairs. 8:9 (December 1958), 3-5.

7839 Luchsinger, Fred. West Germany: The Reunification Controversy. Swiss Review Of World Affairs. 5:4 (July 1955), 7-9.

7840 Meissner, W. For A Peaceful Settlement Of The German Question. International Affairs (Moscow). (August 1959), 3-8.

7841 Midgley, John. Germany's Changing Environment. Western World. 3:1 (January 1960), 38-41.

7842 Mogens, Victor. The German Problem: Freedom, The Restoration. World Affairs. 124:2 (Summer 1961), 38-40.

7843 Morgenthau, Hans J. The Problem Of German Reunification. Annals Of The American Academy Of Political And Social Science. 330 (July 1960), 124-132.

7844 Mueller, Walter. The Struggle For Neutrality As A Factor Promoting Peace And Helping Advance The Solution Of The German Problem. Law And Legislation In The German Democratic Republic. No. 1-2 (1961), 37-50.

7845 Nelson, Harold I. The German Problem, 1955. International Journal. 10:3 (Summer 1955), 183-191.

7846 Neubroch, H. Germany Between East And West: The Reliability Of An Ally. Royal United Service Institute Journal. 103:609 (February 1958), 51-57.

7847 Nothomb, Pierre. Ambiguity On The Elbe. Western World. 2:3 (March 1959), 16-18.

7848 Prittie, Terence C. F. Germany Divided: The Legacy Of The Nazi Era. Boston: Little, Brown, 1960, 381 P.

7849 Prittie, Terence C. F. Khrushchev's Aim--A Divided Germany. New York Times Magazine. (6 August 1961), 7+.

7850 The Problem Of Germany And European Security: Background To The Forthcoming East-West Conference. World Today. 15:5 (May 1959), 205-220.

7851 Reconnaissance In Moscow: The Quest For A German Settlement. Round Table. 49:194 (March 1959), 103-105.

7852 Roberts, Henry L. Russia And America--Dangers And Prospects. New York: Harper, 1956, 251 P., Esp. Pp. 174-194.

7853 Sala, J. R. Rich, Grover. Capper-Johnson, Karlin. Jonas, Frank H. Pundeff, Marin V. Schutz, John A. Jones, Sybil E. Uniting Germany. Proceedings Of The Institute Of World Affairs. 35:5 (December 1959), 139-145.

7854 Schaffer, Gordon. Whither Germany?. Labour Monthly. 38:10 (October 1956), 473-477.

7855 Schuetz, Wilhelm Wolfgang. Germany In Europe: Political And Economic Problems. Pakistan Horizon. 14:1 (1961), 18-22.

7856 Schuetz, Wilhelm Wolfgang. New Initiatives For A New Age: A German View. Foreign Affairs. 36:3 (April 1958), 460-471.

7857 Schuetz, Wilhelm Wolfgang. Thoughts Regarding The German And European Questions. Confluence. 6:4 (Winter 1958), 302-310.

7858 Siegler, Heinrich Von, Compiler. The Reunification And Security Of Germany: A Documentary Basis For Discussion. Bonn: Siegler, 1957, 184 P.

7859 Soviet Policy And The German Problem. World Today. 15:7 (July 1959), 269-277.

7860 Spencer, Robert A. Divided Germany And The Thaw. International Journal. 14:4 (Autumn 1959), 250-258.

7861 Spencer, Robert A. Germany And The "Long Haul". International Journal. 11:1 (Winter 1955-56), 16-24.

7862 Stadtmueller, Georg. German Reunification And The Cold War. Free World Forum. 1:1 (January 1959), 36-39, 43.

7863 Steltzer, Theodor. The German Question. Foreign Affairs Reports. 8 (April 1959), 34-48.

7864 Strauss, Franz-Josef. Soviet Aims And German Unity. Foreign Affairs. 37:3 (April 1959), 366-377.

7865 Strausz-Hupe, Robert. The Future Of The Germany And The European Settlement. Russian Review. 17:3 (July 1958), 176-182.

7866 Thedieck, Franz. Self-Determination And Free Choice Of Homeland: Basic Concepts Of A Policy For Germany As A Whole. Bonn: Press And Information Office, 1961, 16 P.

7867 Uk, Foreign Office. Correspondence Between Her Majesty'S Government In The United Kingdom, The Federal German Government And The Soviet Government About The Future Of Germany. London: H.M. Stationery Office, Cmd. 29, 1956, 21 P.

7868 Ussr, Ministry Of Foreign Affairs. Gdr, Ministry Of Foreign Affairs. The Truth About Western Policy On The German Question: Historical Survey. Moscow: Ministry Of Foreign Affairs; And Berlin (East): Ministry Of Foreign Affairs, 1959, 141 P.

7869 Ulbricht, Walter. Prevent War! Arguments and Material on the Question of a Peace Treaty With Germany And A Solution Of The West-Berlin Problem. Berlin (East): N.P., 1961, 7 P.

7870 Ulbricht, Walter. Statement On The German Peace Plan. Berlin (East): N.P., 1961, 30 P. On Plan Adopted By Volkskammer, 6 July 1961.

7871 Waldman, Eric. The German Problem, 1959. Marquette Business Review. 3:3 (June 1959), 10-23.

Q.1.3. New Status Quo, 1961-69

7872 Adenauer, Konrad. The German Problem: A World Problem. Foreign Affairs. 41:1 (October 1962), 59-65.

7873 Agentstvo Pechati "Novost". Germany Qa: Thirty-Six Questions And Answers On The Ussr View On Germany. Chicago: Translation World, 1962, 62 P.

7874 Albrecht-Carrie, Rene. Europe And The German Problem. Orbis. 10:4 (Winter 1967), 1031-1045.

7875 Anderson, Evelyn. Germany In The Cold War. Survey. No. 58 (January 1966), 177-186.

7876 Aust, Hans Walter. Peaceful Coexistence And The Two German States. German Foreign Policy (Gdr). 1:2 (1962), 117-131.

7877 Aust, Hans Walter. Who Is Acting On Behalf Of The Nation?. German Foreign Policy (Gdr). 5:6 (1966), 407-419.

7878 Barzel, Rainer. The German Question Remains Paramount. Atlantic Community Quarterly. 4:3 (Fall 1966), 366-376.

7879 Baumgaertel, Werner. A Dangerous Model. German Foreign Policy (Gdr). 8:4 (1969), 257-265. Gerhard Schroeder Sees Frg As Model For Reunited Germany.

7880 Bloemer, Klaus. Eastern European Politics And Reunification. Atlantic Community Quarterly. 5:2 (Summer 1967), 219-222.

7881 Blumenson, Martin. Two Germanies Or One?. Military Review. 46:4 (April 1966), 29-38.

7882 Brandt, Heinz. The Search For A Third Way: My Path Between East And West. Garden City: Doubleday, 1970, 333 P.

7883 Brandt, Willy. The Ordeal Of Co-Existence. Cambridge: Harvard University Press, 1963, 112 P.

7884 Breit, Peter Klaus. Case Studies Of West German Views On Reunification. Ph.D. Thesis, University Of Massachusetts, 1967, 336 P.

7885 Brundert, Willi. German Unification And The European Center. Elements Of Change In Eastern Europe: Prospects For Freedom. Ed. David S. Collier And Kurt Glaser. Chicago: Regnery, 1968, Pp. 95-97.

7886 Brzezinski, Zbigniew K. The Danger Of A German Veto. New Leader. 47:2 (20 January 1964), 13-15.

7887 Brzezinski, Zbigniew K. The Framework Of East-West Reconciliation. Foreign Affairs. 46:2 (January 1968), 256-275.

7888 Brzezinski, Zbigniew K. Russia And Europe. Foreign Affairs. 42:3 (April 1964), 428-444.

7889 Collier, David S., Editor. Glaser, Kurt, Editor. Western Integration And The Future Of Eastern Europe. Chicago: Regnery, 1964, 207 P.

7890 Cornides, Wilhelm. German Unification And The Power Balance. Survey. No. 58 (January 1966), 140-148.

7891 Croan, Melvin. The German Problem Once Again. Survey. No. 55 (April 1965), 171-176.

7892 Czechanowski, S. New Course In German Policy?. Poland And Germany. 10:2 (April-June 1966), 12-17.

7893 Dialogue On The Vital Question Affecting The German Nation. Dresden: Zeit Im Bild, 1966, 78 P.

7894 Doernberg, Stefan. The German Problem And The Future Of Europe. International Affairs (Moscow). (May 1966), 19-23.

7895 Dress, Hans. Czechoslovak Foreign Policy And The German Question (1945-1960). German Foreign Policy (Gdr). 1:2 (1962), 159-165.

7896 Frg, Federal Ministry For All-German Affairs. The Soviet Union And The Right Of Peoples And Nations To Self-Determination: A Contribution To The German Question. Bonn: Federal Ministry For All-German Affairs, 1962, 28 P.

7897 Frg, Foreign Office. Efforts Of The German Government And Its Allies In The Cause Of German Unity, 1955-1966. Bonn: Foreign Office, 1966, 61 P.

7898 Friedrich, Paul J. Germany: Reunification Through Detente?. Western Politica. 1:3 (Winter 1967), 22-31.

7899 Gdr, Ministry Of Foreign Affairs. How Germany Was Divided: Documentation. Berlin: Ministry Of Foreign Affairs, Staatsverlag, 1966, 176 P.

7900 Gass, Oscar. German Unification: Prospects And Merits. Commentary. 40:1 (July 1965), 25-38.

7901 German Institute Of Contemporary History. The Division Of Germany And The Road To Reunification: A Documentary Survey. Dresden: Zeit Im Bild, 1966, 115 P.

7902 Goetting, Gerald. Confrontation: Germany. German Foreign Policy (Gdr). 6:5 (1967), 382-385.

7903 Guttenberg, Karl Theodor Baron Von. German Reunification And The European Center. Elements Of Change In Eastern Europe: Prospects For Freedom. Ed. David S. Collier And Kurt Glaser. Chicago: Regnery, 1968, Pp. 98-106.

7904 Haenisch, Werner. Buehring, Guenter. The Gdr And The Solution Of The German Question. German Foreign Policy (Gdr). 5:1 (1966), 11-26.

7905 Haffner, Sebastian. Germany, Russia And The West. Encounter. 17:4 (October 1961), 62-67. Responses In 17:5 (November 1961), 47-55.

7906 Halle, Louis J. Myths And Hopes.

Encounter. 22:4 (April 1964), 25-27. Reunification Problem.

7907 Hanrieder, Wolfram F. German Reunification, 1949-63. Modern European Governments: Cases In Comparative Policy Making. Ed. Roy C. Macridis. Englewood Cliffs: Prentice-Hall, 1968, Pp. 116-139.

7908 Hartmann, Frederick H. Germany Between East And West: The Reunification Problem. Englewood Cliffs: Prentice-Hall, 1965, 181 P.

7909 Hauptmann, Jerzy. The Hopes And Fears Of German Reunification. Modern Age. 9:4 (Fall 1965), 378-386.

7910 Hauptmann, Jerzy. Hopes And Fears Of German Reunification: A Polish View. Western Policy And Eastern Europe. Ed. David S. Collier And Kurt Glaser. Chicago: Regnery, 1966, Pp. 141-154.

7911 Herzstein, Robert Edwin. Germany And The Future Of World Politics: An Interpretative Essay. Il Politico. 29:3 (September 1964), 547-553.

7912 Hinterhoff, Eugene. German Reunification And Poland'S Interests. Poland And Germany. 11:1-2 (January-June 1967), 7-13.

7913 Hinterhoff, Eugene. The Problem Of German Reunification. Poland And Germany. 10:3 (July-September 1966), 18-26.

7914 Hinterhoff, Eugene. The Question Of German Reunification. Poland And Germany. 13:1-2 (January-June 1969), 33-42.

7915 Hubatsch, Walther. The German Question. New York: Herder, 1967, 511 P.

7916 Kennan, George F. Polycentrism And Western Policy. Foreign Affairs. 42:2 (January 1964), 171-183.

7917 Khrushchev, Nikita S. Soviet Policy On Germany: "We Propose Peace". London: Soviet Booklets, 1961, 91 P. Khrushchev'S Speeches And Soviet Government Documents, June To September 1961.

7918 Khrushchev, Nikita S. The Soviet Stand On Germany--Nine Key Documents. New York: Crosscurrents, 1961, 157 P.

7919 Kissinger, Henry A. The Price Of German Unity. Reporter. 32:8 (22 April 1965), 12-17.

7920 Klafkowski, Alfons. The Legal Effects Of The Second World War And The German Problem. Warsaw: Interpress, 1968, 326 P.

7921 Klafkowski, Alfons. The Potsdam Agreement. Warsaw: Polish Scientific Publishers, 1963, 340 P.

7922 Korbonski, Andrzej. U.S. Policy In East Europe. Current History. 48:283 (March 1965), 129-134.

7923 Kownacki, L. The Contest. Poland And Germany. 7:4 (October-December 1963), 3-5. Between East And West Regarding Future Of Germany.

7924 Krause, Helmut. Twenty Years Of A National Policy In Germany. German Foreign Policy (Gdr). 5:4 (1966), 260-270.

7925 Kroeger, Herbert. The Potsdam Agreement And The Western Powers' Responsibility. German Foreign Policy (Gdr). 4:1 (1965), 23-31.

7926 Kroeger, Herbert. The Responsibility Of The Western Powers. German Foreign Policy (Gdr). 3:6 (1964), 404-412.

7927 Kryukov, P. The German Question And The Present Situation. International Affairs (Moscow). (February 1967), 11-16.

7928 Kuebler, Jeanne. German Border Question And German Reunification. Editorial Research Reports. (30 March 1966), 223-240.

7929 Kuebler, Jeanne. German Question. Editorial Research Reports. (1 July 1964), 481-500.

7930 Kulski, Wladyslaw W. German Reunification And Slavic Attitudes. Modern Age. 9:3 (Summer 1965), 262-271.

7931 Kulski, Wladyslaw W. German Reunification And Slavic Attitudes. Western Policy And Eastern Europe. Ed. David S. Collier And Kurt Glaser. Chicago: Regnery, 1966, Pp. 127-140.

7932 Kulski, Wladyslaw W. Soviet Views Of The German Problem. Canadian Slavic Studies. 3:1 (Spring 1969), 92-105.

7933 Kyle, Keith. The Final Price Of Munich. New Republic. 146:6 (5 February 1962), 12-16.

7934 Lall, Betty Goetz. Approaches To German Reunification. Bulletin Of The Atomic Scientists. 21:4 (April 1965), 41-44.

7935 Loewenstein, Karl. Berlin Revisited: Thoughts On Unification. Current History. 50:297 (May 1966), 263-268+.

7936 Lowenthal, Richard. Germany'S Role In East-West Relations. World Today. 23:6 (June 1967), 240-249.

7937 Luchsinger, Fred. German Restlessness. Swiss Review Of World Affairs. 17:10 (January 1968), 7-8.

7938 Luchsinger, Fred. German Uncertainties. Swiss Review Of World Affairs. 16:6 (September 1966), 1-3.

7939 Luchsinger, Fred. New Moves On Germany. Swiss Review Of World Affairs. 16:2 (May 1966), 1-3.

7940 Majonica, Ernst. East-West Relations: A German View. New York: Praeger, 1969, 240 P.

7941 Mclellan, David S. The Changing Nature Of Soviet And American Relations With Western Europe. Annals Of The American Academy Of Political And Social Science. 372 (July 1967), 16-32.

7942 Meier, Victor. Prague And The Two Germanies. Swiss Review Of World Affairs. 16:3 (June 1966), 5-7.

7943 Mieroszewski, Juliusz. One Road To One Germany. Atlas. 16:3 (September 1968), 25-27.

7944 Mikhailov, Vladimir Ivanovich. Eradicate Remnants Of World War Ii In Europe. Moscow: Foreign Languages Publishing House, 196-, 114 P.

7945 National Front Of Democratic Germany. The Division Of Germany And The Road To Reunification: A Documentary Survey. Dresden: Zeit Im Bild, 1966, 115 P.

7946 Neal, Fred Warner. The Unsolved German Settlement. Annals Of The American Academy Of Political And Social Science. 351 (January 1964), 148-156.

7947 Neal, Fred Warner. War And Peace And Germany. New York: Norton, 1962, 166 P.

7948 Neubert, Wolfram. German Reality And The "Indivisible" Mr. W. W. Schuetz. German Foreign Policy (Gdr). 7:2 (1968), 108-117.

7949 Ostoya, M. The German Problem In 1962. Poland And Germany. 5:4 (October-December 1961), 1-6.

7950 Ostoya, M. Germany'S Place In Grand Designs. Poland And Germany. 7:1-2 (January-June 1963), 3-9.

203

7951 Peet, John. The German Dialogue. Labour Monthly. 48 (July 1966), 316-319.

7952 Planck, Charles R. The Changing Status Of German Reunification In Western Diplomacy, 1955-1966. Baltimore: Johns Hopkins University Press, 1967, 65 P.

7953 Plischke, Elmer. Reunifying Germany-- An Options Analysis. World Affairs. 132:1 (June 1969), 28-38.

7954 Poeggel, Walter. Wagner, Ingo. Peaceful Coexistence In Germany. German Foreign Policy (Gdr). 2:6 (1963), 423-428.

7955 Pounds, Norman J. G. Divided Germany And Berlin. Princeton: Van Nostrand, 1962, 128 P.

7956 Prittie, Terence C. F. Again The Issue Of The Two Germanys. New York Times Magazine. (16 August 1964), 10+.

7957 Prittie, Terence C. F. Inquiry Into Germany'S Future. New York Times Magazine. (5 November 1961), 24+. Reunification Unlikely; Consequences For Frg And The West.

7958 Rabl, Kurt. Survey Of The German Problem Since 1944. Turkish Yearbock Of International Relations. 7 (1966), 121-138.

7959 Radmann, Martin. Potsdam Agreement And Twenty Years Later. Dresden: Zeit Im Bild, 1965, 48 P.

7960 Reece, B. Carroll. Peace Through Law: A Basis For An East-West Settlement In Europe. New Canaan: Long House, 1965, 114 P.

7961 Ritter, Gerhard. The German Problem: Basic Questions Of German Political Life, Past And Present. Columbus: Ohio State University Press, 1965, 233 P.

7962 Rostow, Walt Whitman. The Role Of Germany In The Evolution Of World Politics. Department Of State Bulletin. 49:1267 (7 October 1963), 536-542.

7963 Rostow, Walt Whitman. The Third Round. Foreign Affairs. 42:1 (October 1963), 1-10.

7964 Rubinstein, Alvin Z. The Problem Of Coexistence. Current History. 41:243 (November 1961), 273-279.

7965 Sawicki, Jerzy, Editor. Blocs, The German Problem And The Future Of Europe. Vienna: International Institute For Peace, 1968, 196 P. Conference Proceedings, Vienna, 6-7 March 1968.

7966 Schaffer, Gordon. Two Germanys. German Foreign Policy (Gdr). 4:2 (1965), 134-140.

7967 Schaffer, Gordon. Whither Germany?. Labour Monthly. 50 (April 1968), 182-185.

7968 Schenk, Fritz. The "Grey Plan": The Sed Campaign Against The Research Council For Problems Connected With The Reunification Of Germany. Bonn: Federal Ministry For All-German Affairs, 1967, 6 P.

7969 Schmitt, Hans A. Two Germanies: A Nation Without A State. Current History. 56:332 (April 1969), 224-229.

7970 Schoening, Ulrich. German Unity And European Integration: West German Attitudes. Internationale Spectator. 22:1 (8 January 1968), 34-63.

7971 Schuetz, Wilhelm Wolfgang. Rethinking German Policy: New Approaches To Reunification. New York: Praeger, 1967, 154 P.

7972 Schwarz, Siegfried. The Forces Behind The Splitting Of Germany, Past And Present. German Foreign Policy (Gdr). 7:1 (1968), 25-33.

7973 Seeberg, Axel. Hopes And Fears Of German Reunification: A German View. Western Policy And Eastern Europe. Ed. David S. Collier And Kurt Glaser. Chicago: Regnery, 1966, Pp. 155-165.

7974 Sibirtsev, Yu. What Are The Prospects For German Rapprochement?. International Affairs (Moscow). (March 1969), 38-42.

7975 Smith, Jean Edward. The United States, German Unity, And The Deutsche Demokratische Republik. Queen'S Quarterly. 74:1 (Spring 1967), 21-35.

7976 Speier, Hans. Germany: The Continuing Challenge. Santa Monica: Rand Coporation, P-3355, April 1966, 36 P.

7977 Speier, Hans. Germany, The Continuing Challenge. Texas Quarterly. 9:3 (Autumn 1966), 131-147.

7978 Stillman, Edmund. What Price Germany, Now?. New York Times Magazine. (4 December 1966), 54+.

7979 Strauss, Franz-Josef. The Grand Design: A European Solution To German Reunification. New York: Praeger, 1966, 105 P.

7980 Strauss, Franz-Josef. Prospects In Germany. United Asia. 19:6 (November-December 1967), 304-310.

7981 Strothmann, Dietrich. Bonn And The 'Moment Of Truth'. World Today. 21:11 (November 1965), 480-486.

7982 Suess, Herbert. Bollinger, Klaus. The German Question And International Law. German Foreign Policy (Gdr). 4:4 (1965), 289-300.

7983 Toeplitz, Heinrich. Time For A German Peace Treaty. Law And Legislation In The German Democratic Republic. No. 1 (1962), 5-31.

7984 Ulbricht, Walter. The German Democratic Republic Acts In The Interests Of The German Nation. Dresden: Zeit Im Bild, 1968, 21 P.

7985 Ulbricht, Walter. The Path To The Future Fatherland Of The Germans. Dresden: Zeit Im Bild, 1966, 85 P.

7986 Ulbricht, Walter. The Unity Of Germany Must Serve Peace. Dresden: Zeit Im Bild, 1966, 86 P.

7987 Ulbricht, Walter. The Way To The Completion Of The Socialist Construction Of The German Democratic Republic. Berlin (East): Staatsverlag, 1964, 76 P.

7988 Ulbricht, Walter. What Is At Stake In Germany?. Dresden: Zeit Im Bild, 1966, 46 P.

7989 Ulbricht, Walter. Whither Germany? Speeches And Essays On The National Question. Dresden: Zeit Im Bild, 1966, 439 P.

7990 Vaclav, E. Mares. Key To Europe: West Germany. Current History. 42:247 (March 1962), 148-153.

7991 Vali, Ferenc A. The Quest For A United Germany. Baltimore: Johns Hopkins University Press, 1967, 318 P.

7992 Verrier, Anthony. New Responsibilities For Bonn?. World Today. 20:6 (June 1964), 234-236.

7993 Wandel, Paul. A Peace Treaty Is Necessary And Cannot Be Postponed. German Foreign Policy (Gdr). Spec. Ed. 1 (October 1961), 6-12.

7994 What Kind Of Germany Is To Be?. Dresden: Zeit Im Bild, 1966, 61 P.

7995 Wheeler, George Shaw. Who Split Germany?--Wall Street And The West German Trade Union Leaders. Berlin (East): Tribuene, 1962, 111 P.

7996 Windsor, Philip. German Disunity. Western Europe: A Handbook. Ed. John Calmann. New York: Praeger, 1967, Pp. 276-288.

7997 Windsor, Philip. German Reunification. London: Elek, 1969, 140 P.

7998 Winzer, Otto. How Germany Was Divided. German Foreign Policy (Gdr). 6:1 (1967), 3-14.

7999 Wolfe, James H. German Reunification: Illusion Or Future Reality?. Ph.D. Thesis, University Of Maryland, 1962, 199 P.

8000 Wolfe, James H. Indivisible Germany: Illusion Or Reality?. The Hague: Nijhoff, 1963, 130 P.

8001 Women Strike For Peace. The German Problem: Roadblock To Disarmament. Washington: Disarmament Committee Of Washington D.C. Women Strike For Peace, 1964, 48 P.

8002 Wuensche, Kurt. New Developments In The German Question. German Foreign Policy (Gdr). 3:2 (1964), 131-138.

8003 Zelt, Johannes. For Socialism And A Peaceful German Settlement. International Affairs (Moscow). (January 1964), 29-33.

Q.1.4. Divided Germany, 1969-

8004 Blumenfeld, F. Yorick. German Reconciliation. Editorial Research Reports. (14 January 1970), 23-40.

8005 Boerner, Holger. Germany--Crossroads Of Europe. Aussenpolitik. 21:4 (1970), 425-433.

8006 Carroll, Berenice A. The Partition Of Germany: Cold War Compromise. The Politics Of Partition: Peril To World Peace. Ed. Thomas E. Hachey. Chicago: Rand-Mcnally, 1972, Pp. 81-131.

8007 Dulles, Eleanor Lansing. One Germany Or Two: The Struggle At The Heart Of Europe. Stanford: Hoover Institution Press, Publication No. 86, 1970, 315 P.

8008 Frg, Federal Ministry For Intra-German Relations. Policy For Germany. Bonn: Federal Ministry For Intra-German Relations, September 1970, 26 P.

8009 Frank, Elke. Divided Countries: East And West Germany. Conflict In World Politics. Ed. Steven L. Spiegel And Kenneth N. Waltz. Cambridge: Winthrop, 1971, Pp. 179-196.

8010 Frank, Paul. Bonn'S Voice In The West-East Dialogue. Aussenpolitik. 24:3 (1973), 275-284.

8011 Galtung, Johan. The German Problem: Some Perspectives. Cooperation In Europe. Ed. Johan Galtung. New York: Humanities Press, 1970, Pp. 85-96.

8012 Graham, Norman. Linkage Politics And Peace Settlements: East And West Germany And The Soviet Union In Search Of A Settlement, 1969-1974. From War To Peace: Essays In Peacemaking And War Termination. Ed. David S. Smith And Robert F. Randle. New York: Columbia University, International Fellows Program Policy Series, 1974, Pp. 125-170.

8013 Hennessey, John Russell, Jr. Partition As An Alternative To Great Power Conflict: The Case Studies Of Germany And Korea. Ph.D. Thesis, Georgetown University, 1971, 447 P.

8014 Herz, John H. Divided Germany. Divided Nations In A Divided World. Ed. Gregory Henderson, Ned Lebow, And John Stoessinger. New York: Mckay, 1973.

8015 Hess, Frederick W., Editor. German Unity: Documentation And Commentaries On The Basic Treaty. Kansas City: Park College, Governmental Research Bureau, 1974, 96 P.

8016 Munro, Gordon Douglas. Two Germanies: A Lasting Solution To The German Question?. Ph.D. Thesis, Claremont Graduate School, 1972, 325 P.

8017 Norden, Albert. No More War From German Soil: Drawing Up The Balance--25 Years After The Defeat Of Hitler Fascism. Dresden: Zeit Im Bild, 1970, 27 P.

8018 Remak, Joachim. Two Germanies--And Then? Journal Of International Affairs. 27:2 (1973), 175-186.

8019 Scheel, Walter. For German Unity And Peace In Europe. Central Europe Journal. 21:10-11 (October-November 1973), 249-254.

8020 Schoenberg, Hans W. The Partition Of Germany And The Neutralization Of Austria. The Anatomy Of Communist Takeovers. Ed. Thomas T. Hammond With Robert Farrell. New Haven: Yale University Press, 1974.

8021 Schuetz, Klaus. All-German Policy For The Seventies. German Tribune Quarterly Review. No. 8 (16 December 1969), 13-16.

8022 Schurer, Heinz. Germany In The Centre. Survey. 18:3 (Summer 1972), 54-55.

8023 Schweigler, Gebhard L. National Consciousness In Divided Germany. Ph.D. Thesis, Harvard University, 1972.

8024 Schweigler, Gebhard L. National Consciousness In Divided Germany. Beverly Hills, Calif.: Sage, 1975.

8025 Tomuschat, Christian. The Two Germanies. Legal Problems Of An Enlarged European Community. Ed. Maurice E. Bathurst, K. R. Simmonds, N. March Hunnings, And Jane Welch. London: Stevens & Sons, British Institute Studies In International And Comparative Law No. 6, 1972, Pp. 154-161.

8026 Ulam, Adam B. The Rivals: America And Russia Since World War Ii. New York: Viking, 1971, 405 P.

8027 Wagner, Wolfgang. German Question. Marxism, Communism And Western Society: A Comparative Encyclopedia. Ed. C. D. Kernig. New York: Herder And Herder, 1972, Vol. 4, Pp. 87-94.

8028 Zellentin, Gerda. Intersystemic Regionalism And Peace In Europe. Journal Of Peace Research. 10:3 (1973), 235-243.

Q.2. Conflicting FRG-GDR Claims

Q.2.1. FRG: Sole Representation

8029 Baur, Walter. On The Juridical Character Of The Bonn Government'S Presumptuous Claim To Exclusive Representation. Law And Legislation In The German Democratic Republic. No. 1 (1969), 5-26.

8030 Feige, Gerhard. Legal Position And Truth Concerning Name And Trademark Rights Of Zeiss/Schott & Gen. Jena. Law And Legislation In The German Democratic Republic. No. 1 (1964), 37-40.

8031 Feige, Gerhard. Observations On The British High Court Decision Of March 6, 1964, In Zeiss V. Zeiss. Law And Legislation In The German Democratic Republic. No. 2 (1964), 47-50.

8032 Gdr, Council Of State. Law And International Law In The Two German States; Documents On The Development Of Law In The Two German States And On The Juridical Arrexationist Efforts Of The West German Federal Republic. Berlin: Council Of State, Chancellery, 1966, 45 P.

8033 Germany--The Hallstein Doctrine. Current Notes On International Affairs. 40:8 (August 1969), 419-427.

8034 Huettner, Erich. The Presumption Of Sole Representation And The Grand Coalition. German Foreign Policy (Gdr). 6:2 (1967), 127-137.

8035 Kaul, Friedrich Karl. Graefrath, Bernhard. Expert Opinion On The Verdict Of The Stuttgart Assize Court (Schwurgericht) On October 11Th 1963 In The Case Of Franz Hanke, Accused Of Attempted Manslaughter. Law And Legislation In The German Democratic Republic. No. 1 (1964), 41-51. Former Gdr Border Guard Who Fired At Refugee.

8036 Kleyer, Hermann. Niethammer, Fritz.. On The Problem Of Legal Discrimination As An Instrument Of The Cold War. Law And Legislation In The German Democratic Republic. No. 1 (1964), 25-36.

8037 Kroeger, Herbert. Bonn Admits Failure Of Hallstein Doctrine. German Foreign Policy (Gdr). 3:5 (1964), 321-326.

8038 Kroeger, Herbert. Bonn "Doctrines" And International Law. International Affairs (Moscow). (February 1963), 28-32.

8039 Kroeger, Herbert. The Crisis Of Bonn'S Exclusive Representation Claim. German Foreign Policy (Gdr). 7:5 (1968), 347-358.

8040 Kroeger, Herbert. "Safe Conduct Act" Violates Constitution And International Law. Law And Legislation In The German Democratic Republic. No. 2 (1966), 35-38.

8041 Speier, Hans. The Hallstein Doctrine. Survey. No. 61 (October 1966), 93-104.

8042 Taylor, Thomas W. Effect Of Non-Recognition Of Foreign Governments: The Carl Zeiss Case. Harvard International Law Journal. 8:2 (Spring 1967), 373-388.

8043 Ulbricht, Walter. For Security In Europe; Against The Bonn Sole Representation Pretension; For Recognition Of The Gdr. Dresden: Zeit Im Bild, 1967, 40 P.

8044 Ullrich, Klaus. Hallstein Doctrine Condemned By The World Sports Movement. German Foreign Policy (Gdr). 2:4 (1963), 276-281. International Olympic Committee Decision On Joint German Team For 1964 Olympics.

Q.2.2. GDR: Recognition

8045 Commentator. A Historic Necessity. International Affairs (Moscow). (August 1961), 3-7. Recognition Of Gdr.

8046 Demand Of Political Common Sense. Dresden: Verlag Zeit Im Bild, 1971, 26 P.

8047 Goetting, Gerald. The International Reputation Of The Gdr. German Foreign Policy (Gdr). 3:3 (1964), 184-195.

8048 Haenisch, Werner. Problems Of The International Position Of The Gdr. German Foreign Policy (Gdr). 9:3 (1970), 176-186.

8049 In The Interest Of Europe: Recognize The Gdr Now. Dresden: Zeit Im Bild, 1971, 27 P.

8050 Kewenig, Wilhelm A. Recognition--An End In Itself Or A Means Of German Policy?. German Tribune Quarterly Review. No. 10 (16 July 1970), 11-13.

8051 Lyon, Peyton V. A Case For The Recognition Of East Germany. International Journal. 15:4 (Autumn 1960), 337-346.

8052 Peck, Joachim. The Potsdam Agreement: The Status Of The German Democratic Republic In International Law. United Asia. 21:5 (September-October 1969), 229-233.

8053 Pritt, Denis N. Is There A Need To Recognise The German Democratic Republic?. Contemporary Review. 219:1266 (July 1971), 13-18.

8054 Schaffer, Gordon. Cooperative Party Votes For Recognition Of The Gdr. German Foreign Policy (Gdr). 7:4 (1968), 301-302.

8055 Schaffer, Gordon. European Security And Diplomatic Recognition Of The Gdr. German Foreign Policy (Gdr). 11:3 (1972), 218-222.

8056 Steiniger, Peter-Alfons. The Potsdam Agreement: A Document And Instrument In Fighting Anti-Communism. German Foreign Policy (Gdr). 6:4 (1967), 299-303.

8057 Steiniger, Peter-Alfons. The Western Interpretation Of International Law With Regard To The Growing International Authority Of The German Democratic Republic. Law And Legislation In The German Democratic Republic. No. 2 (1963), 5-12.

8058 Wandel, Paul. The International Position Of The German Democratic Republic. German Foreign Policy (Gdr). 1:6 (1962), 557-564.

8059 Wuensche, Kurt. The Fiction Of The Non-Existence Of The Gdr Cannot Be Maintained. German Foreign Policy (Gdr). Spec. Ed. 1 (October 1961), 13-22.

Q.3. FRG-GDR Relations

8060 Albert, E. H. The Brandt Doctrine Of Two States In Germany. International Affairs (London). 46:2 (April 1970), 293-303.

8061 Bender, Peter. The Special Relationship Of The Two German States. World Today. 29:8 (August 1973), 389-397.

8062 Birnbaum, Karl E. East And West Germany: A Modus Vivendi. Lexington, Mass.: Lexington Books, 1973, 157 P.

8063 Blumenfeld, F. Yorick. German Reconciliation. Editorial Research Reports. (14 January 1970), 23-40.

8064 Bock, Siegfried. The Gdr, Bonn And Peace In Europe. German Foreign Policy (Gdr). 8:1 (1969), 23-36.

8065 Boyd, Andrew. Two Germanys In One World? Vista. 8:6 (June 1973), 22-23.

8066 Browne, E. Moxon. The Special Relations Agreements. The World Today. 29:8 (August 1973), 337-342.

8067 Croan, Melvin. Bonn And Pankow: Intra-German Politics. Survey. No. 67 (April 1968), 77-89.

8068 Deutsch, K. Deutsch, B. East German Irritations. Contemporary Review. 215:1246 (November 1969), 253-255.

8069 Ersil, Wilhelm. The Two German States And European Security. Dresden: Zeit Im Bild, 1967, 26 P.

8070 Frg, Bundestag. Humanitarian Imperative: Interpellation, Governmental Declaration And Resolution By The Bundestag Concerning The Situation Of The

People In The Soviet-Occupied Zone Of Germany. Bonn: Bundestag, 41St Session, 1 October 1958, 23 P.

8071 Frg, Federal Ministry For All-German Affairs. In The Heart Of Germany In The Twentieth Century: The Zonal Border. Bonn And Berlin: Federal Ministry For All-German Affairs, 1965, 94 P.

8072 Frg, Press And Information Office. Erfurt, March 19, 1970: A Documentation. Bonn: Press And Information Office, 1970, 94 P.

8073 Frg, Press And Information Office. Kassel, May 21, 1970: A Documentation. Bonn: Press And Information Office, 1970, 96 P.

8074 Frg, Press And Information Office. Treaty On The Basis Of Relations Between The Federal Republic Of Germany And The German Democratic Republic. Bonn: Press And Information Office, 1973, 69 P.

8075 Federal Republic Of Germany-German Democratic Republic: Treaty On The Basis Of Intra-German Relations. International Legal Materials. 12:1 (January 1973), 16-24.

8076 Gdr. Peace And Security In Europe Demand Normal Relations Between The Two German States. Dresden: Zeit Im Bild, 1967, 29 P.

8077 Graf, Rudolf. Mueller, Hans Gerhard. Stuebner, Siegfried. German Reality: Documentation On The Division Of Germany And The Relations Between The Two German States. Dresden: Zeit Im Bild, 1968, 86 P.

8078 Haeber, Herbert. The Gdr And The West Germans. German Foreign Policy (Gdr). 8:3 (1969), 163-168.

8079 Journalists, Scientists, Writers And Politicians From Both German States Discuss A Peace Treaty For Germany. German Foreign Policy (Gdr). Spec. Ed. 1 (October 1961), 23-47. Series Of Short Statements.

8080 Kegel, Gerhard. The Ground Wears Thin. German Foreign Policy (Gdr). 3:4 (1964), 261-270. Frg-Gdr Relations.

8081 Komarov, M. Co-Existence Of The Two German States And The Peace Treaty. International Affairs (Moscow). (July 1962), 6-10.

8082 Kroeger, Herbert. An Alibi That Failed. German Foreign Policy (Gdr). 5:4 (1966), 243-259. Frg Imperialist Policy Against Gdr.

8083 Kruczkowski, Adam. Revanchism Vs. Peaceful Co-Existence. International Affairs (Moscow). (July 1961), 76-77.

8084 Lasky, Melvin J. One Nation, Divisible. New York Times Magazine. (22 September 1974), 20+.

8085 Luchsinger, Fred. Two Germanies Confirmed. Swiss Review Of World Affairs. 22:9 (December 1972), 2-3.

8086 Lust, Peter. Two Germanies. Montreal: Harvest House, 1966, 238 P.

8087 Markgraf, Andre. The Organisation With The Misleading Name. German Foreign Policy (Gdr). 2:6 (1963), 446-451. Kuratorium Unteilbares Deutschland.

8088 Meinhardt, Hans. Normal Relations Between The Gdr And West Germany. German Foreign Policy (Gdr). 7:5 (1968), 338-346.

8089 Novoseltsev, Y. West-German Discussion. International Affairs (Moscow). (June 1966), 79-84. Must Be Government-Level Contacts Between Frg And Gdr.

8090 Piater, Willi. Normalizing Relations Between The Two German States. German Foreign Policy (Gdr). 6:5 (1967), 363-371.

8091 Prokop, Siegfried. Intrigues Of The West German "Forschungsbeirat" Against The Gdr. German Foreign Policy (Gdr). 4:2 (1965), 158-166.

8092 Przybylski, Peter. Terrorism A System. German Foreign Policy (Gdr). 3:5 (1964), 392-396. Sabotage In Gdr.

8093 Rzhevsky, I. Gdr-Frg Treaty: A Major Step On Europe's Path To Peace. International Affairs (Moscow). No. 3 (March 1973), 78-80.

8094 Shabecoff, Philip. Country Cousin Of The Berlin Wall. New York Times Magazine. (10 July 1966), 8+. Wall Between Gdr And Frg.

8095 Shears, David. The Ugly Frontier. London: Chatto & Windus, 1970, 231 P. Borders Between Gdr And Frg, Between East And West Berlin.

8096 Tern, Juergen. A Policy Of Peaceful Relations. German Tribune Quarterly Review. No. 21 (22 March 1973), 1-7.

8097 Treaty On The Bases Of Relations Between The German Democratic Republic And The Federal Republic Of Germany. Dresden: Verlag Zeit Im Bild, 1972, 28 P. Treaty Of 8 November 1972.

8098 The Two Germanies. Great Decisions, 1968. Ed. Norman Jacobs. New York: Foreign Policy Association, Inc., 1968, Pp.61-72.

8099 Ulbricht, Walter. For European Security And Relaxation Between The Two German States. Dresden: Zeit Im Bild, 1966, 46 P. Report, 13Th Session Of Sed Central Committee, 16 September 1966.

8100 Ulbricht, Walter. National Mission Of The German Democratic Republic And The Forces For Peace Of West Germany. Berlin (East): Council Of State Of The Gdr, 1965, 59 P.

8101 Ulbricht, Walter. On Questions Of Peaceful Coexistence Between The Two German States. Dresden: Zeit Im Bild, 1967, 29 P.

8102 Ulbricht, Walter. Three Questions To Federal Chancellor Ludwig Erhard. Dresden: Zeit Im Bild, C.1965, 14 P.

8103 Vetter, Gottfried. On The Development Of Intra-German Relationships. German Tribune Quarterly Review. No. 2 (20 July 1968), 6-11.

8104 Voigtlaender, Kurt. Workers' Discussions Will Solve The National Problem In Germany. German Foreign Policy (Gdr). 5:3 (1966), 179-186.

8105 Wagner, Wolfgang. A Modus Vivendi In Germany. German Tribune Quarterly Review. No. 21 (22 March 1973), 7-10.

8106 Wettig, Gerhard. The Sed-Spd Dialogue: Communist Political Strategy In Germany. Orbis. 11:2 (Summer 1967), 570-581.

8107 Winzer, Otto. Normal Relations Between The Two German States And Between The Gdr And West Berlin. German Foreign Policy (Gdr). 7:1 (1968), 3-12.

Q.4. FRG-GDR Foreign Policy: Comparisons

8108 Aust, Hans Walter. For And Against The Colonial Rulers. German Foreign Policy (Gdr). 1:4 (1962), 391-397. Gdr And Frg Views On Indian Takeover Of Goa.

8109 Aust, Hans Walter. The Germans And The United Arab Republic. German Foreign Policy (Gdr). 4:3 (1965), 179-184.

8110 Dievenow, Friedrich G. International Friendship Versus Neo-Colonialism--Two German States And The Lessons Of History. Dresden: Zeit Im Bild, 1966, 63 P.

8111 East And West Germany Compete In Africa. World Today. 17:2 (February 1961), 45-48.

8112 France-Union Of Soviet Socialist Republics-United Kingdom-United States: Declaration On The Question Of U.N. Membership For The Two Germanies. International Legal Materials. 12:1 (January 1973), 217-218.

8113 Gdr, Ministry Of Foreign Affairs. White Book On The Policy Of The Two German States: Peace Or Atomic War?. Berlin: Ministry Of Foreign Affairs, 2D Ed., 1960, 187 P.

8114 Georgiu, Thanassis. Greece And The Two German States. German Foreign Policy (Gdr). 3:6 (1964), 438-441.

8115 Joesten, Joachim. German Duel For Africa: How East And West Germans Vie For The Dark Continent. New York: Joachim Joesten, New Germany Reports No. 49, September 1960, 16 P.

8116 Joesten, Joachim. The Germans And Col. Nasser: West And East German Relations With Cairo, 1958-59. Great Barrington, Mass.: Joachim Joesten, New Germany Reports No. 41, June 1959, 18 P.

8117 Kebschull, Dietrich. Frg And Gdr In The Third World. Intereconomics. No. 5 (May 1971), 158-160.

8118 Merkl, Peter H. German Foreign Policies West & East: On The Threshold Of A New European Era. Santa Barbara, Calif.: American Bibliographic Center, Clio Press, 1974, X And 232 P.

8119 Muhlen, Norbert. German Anti-Americanism: East And West Zones. Commentary. 15:2 (February 1953), 121-130.

8120 Muhlen, Norbert. The Return Of Germany: A Tale Of Two Countries. Chicago: Regnery, 1953, 310 P.

8121 Peace Council Of The Gdr. Centres Of Conflict: The Attitude Of The Two German States To International Problems. Dresden: Zeit Im Bild, 1969, 77 P.

8122 Stoph, Willi. How To Tell Friend From Foe In Africa. German Foreign Policy (Gdr). 3:4 (1964), 249-260.

8123 Ulbricht, Walter. The Two German States And The Aggression In The Near East. Dresden: Zeit Im Bild, 1967, 29 P. From Speech Before Leipzig Electoral Assembly, 15 June 1967.

R. Berlin

R.1. General, East And West

8124 Moennig, Richard. Berlin Book List. Bonn: Inter Nationes, 2D Ed., 1963, 15 P.

8125 Armstrong, Anne. Berliners: Both Sides Of The Wall. New Brunswick: Rutgers University Press, 1973, Xxii And 463 P.

8126 Army Times Editors. Berlin: The City That Would Not Die. New York: Dodd, Mead, 1967, 127 P.

8127 Baedecker, Karl. Berlin: Handbook For Travellers. New York: Macmillan, 7Th Ed., 1965, 316 P.

8128 Bentwich, Norman D. Eastern Berlin Re-Visited. Contemporary Review. 207:1195 (August 1965), 71-73.

8129 Bentwich, Norman D. The Two Berlins. Contemporary Review. 202 (October 1962), 206-208.

8130 Berger, Alfred. Berlin, 1945-1963: A Postwar History Of Berlin. Munich: Gersbach, 1964, 80 P.

8131 Berlin, Central Office For Education In Politics. The Capital Of Germany Berlin. Berlin: Schmidt, For Landeszentrale Fuer Politische Bildungsarbeit, 1959, 30 P.

8132 Berlin, Press And Information Office. Berlin In Brief. Berlin: Press And Information Office, 2D Ed., 1967, 112 P.

8133 Berlin, Press And Information Office. Reference: Berlin. Berlin: Graphische Gesellschaft Grunewald, For Press And Information Office, 1963, 71 P.

8134 Berlin The Hub Of Germany. Berlin-Tempelhof: Ullstein, 1961, Pp. 137-243. Special Issue Of "Berliner Illustrierte".

8135 Berlin-Reinickendorf, Bezirksamt. Verwaltungsbezirk Reinickendorf. Berlin-Reinickendorf: Bezirksamt Reinickendorf, 1968, Unpaginated.

8136 Bilainkin, George. The Allies In Berlin. Contemporary Review. 168:960 (December 1945), 343-348.

8137 Boehl, Erich, Editor. Berlin At The Crossroads Of Europe, At The Crossroads Of The World. Berlin: Haupt & Puttkammer, 1961, 196 P.

8138 Boehl, Erich, Editor. Berlin, West And East. Munich: Thiemig, Grieben Guide Books Vol. 7, 1967, 201 P.

8139 Brett-Smith, Richard N. B. Berlin '45: The Grey City. New York: St. Martin's, 1967, 176 P.

8140 Butler, Ewan. City Divided: Berlin 1955. New York: Praeger, 1955, 187 P.

8141 Byford-Jones, W. Berlin Twilight. London: Hutchinson, 1947, 192 P. An Account Of Life In The German Capital.

8142 Daniell, Raymond. Berlin--City Of Ruins, Doubt And Fear. New York Times Magazine. (25 April 1948), 7+.

8143 Elkins, Thomas Henry. West And East Berlin In 1959. Geography. 44:4 (November 1959), 268-271.

8144 Faviell, Frances. The Dancing Bear: Berlin De Profundis. New York: Norton, 1954, 246 P.

8145 Fischer, Alfred Joachim. The Berlin Scene. World Affairs (London). 2:3 (July 1948), 261-270. Picture Of Chaos In Berlin, 1948.

8146 Fondiller, Harvey V., Editor. Four-Sector City: The Story Of The U.S. Army's Mission In The Occupation Of Berlin. Berlin: Omgus, 1946, 17 P.

8147 Frank, William. Impressions Of Berlin. Contemporary Review. 196 (July 1959), 22-24.

8148 Gilroy, Harry. Shopping In East Berlin--And West. New York Times Magazine. (5 August 1956), 15+.

8149 Gumbel, E. J. Impressions From Berlin, 1953. Social Research. 21:1 (April 1954), 62-84.

8150 H. G. L. Berlin Revisited: Impressions After Three Years. World Today. 12:3 (March 1956), 93-101.

8151 Haus, Wolfgang. The History Of Berlin As Germany's Capital. Berlin--Pivot Of German Destiny. Ed. Charles B. Robson. Chapel Hill: University Of North Carolina Press, 1960, Pp. 4-46.

8152 Hildebrandt, Dieter. A Wedding Guest Crosses "The Wall". New York Times Magazine. (22 November 1964), 36+.

8153 Hobman, D. L. Life In Berlin. Contemporary Review. 178:1016 (August 1950), 77-80.

8154 Knight, David C. The First Book Of Berlin: Tale Of A Divided City. New York: Watts, 1967, 96 P.

8155 Lange, Annemarie. Berlin, Capital Of The Gdr. Dresden: Zeit Im Bild, 1970, 151 P.

8156 Lewis, Flora. Berlin: A Trip On The S-Bahn. New York Times Magazine. (8 November 1959), 144.

8157 Mclaughlin, Kathleen. Gi Wives In Berlin. New York Times Magazine. (13 October 1946), 28-29.

8158 Murray, John. Some Impressions Of Berlin. Studies. 39 (March 1950), 51-64.

8159 Nelson, Walter Henry. The Berliners: Their Saga And Their City. New York: Mckay, 1969, 434 P.

8160 Powell, Robert. Berlin To-Day. Fortnightly. 158:946 (October 1945), 234-239.

8161 Schatvet, Charles E. Island In A Red Sea: An American Businessman In Berlin Where Soviet And Free Worlds Collide. New York: Guide-Kalkhoff-Burr, 1959, 239 P.

8162 Stern-Rubarth, Edgar. Berlin Revisited: After Two Decades. Contemporary Review. 188:1076 (August 1955), 82-84.

8163 Sullivan, Walter. The Two Berlins--The Two Germanys. New York Times Magazine. (31 January 1954), 7+.

8164 Tiburtius, Joachim. Cultural Policy On The Two Sides Of The Brandenburg Gate. Berlin--Pivot Of German Destiny. Ed. Charles B. Robson. Chapel Hill: University Of North Carolina Press, 1960, Pp. 156-173.

8165 Uk, Ccg, Court Of Enquiry. Report, With Plan; Berlin, 14Th-16Th April 1948. London: H.M. Stationery Office, Cmd. 7384, 1948, 13 P. Report Of Court Enquiry Into The Circumstances Of The Collision Between A Viking Airliner And A Soviet Service Aircraft On 5Th April 1948.

8166 Us, Hicog. A Survey Of Berlin. Berlin: Hicog, 1950, 18 P.

8167 Vanocur, Sander. The Fleshpots Of Berlin. Twentieth Century. 157:935 (January 1955), 26-31.

8168 Wechsberg, Joseph. Thoughts At Berlin'S Symbolic Gate. New York Times Magazine. (19 November 1961), 27+.

8169 Welch, Colin. A Day In Berlin. Encounter. 29:3 (September 1967), 74-76.

8170 Wells, Ingeborg. Enough, No More. London: Joseph, 1948, 194 P.

8171 Wieser, Theodor. Berlin In Divided Germany. Swiss Review Of World Affairs. 5:5 (August 1955), 5-7.

8172 Wolf, Simon. The Two Berlins. Contemporary Review. 181:1037 (May 1952), 262-266.

8173 A Woman In Berlin. London: Secker And Warburg, 1955, 284 P. Living Conditions And Social Problems.

R.2. Legal Context

8174 Baade, Hans W. Some Basic Legal Problems Underlying The Berlin Dispute. West Berlin: The Legal Context. Ed. Roland J. Stanger. Columbus: Ohio State University Press, 1966, Pp. 53-100.

8175 Bathurst, Maurice E. Legal Aspects Of The Berlin Problem. British Year Book Of International Law. 38 (1962), 255-306.

8176 Bishop, Joseph W., Jr. The Origin And Nature Of The Rights Of The Western Allies In Berlin. West Berlin: The Legal Context. Ed. Roland J. Stanger. Columbus: Ohio State University Press, 1966, Pp. 23-51.

8177 Bowie, Robert R. Carroll, Doris. The Legal Background Of The Berlin-German Crisis. The Issues In The Berlin-German Crisis. Ed. Lyman M. Tondel, Jr. Dobbs Ferry: Oceana, 1963, 1-29.

8178 Friedmann, Wolfgang G. Legal And Political Aspects Of The Berlin Crisis. Columbia Journal Of Transnational Law. 1:1 (1961), 3-8.

8179 Grewe, Wilhelm G. Other Legal Aspects Of The Berlin Crisis. American Journal Of International Law. 56:2 (April 1962), 510-513. Response To Quincy Wright, 55:4 (October 1961), 959-965.

8180 Heidelmeyer, Wolfgang. The Status Of The Land Berlin: A Commentary. Berlin: Press And Information Office, 1970, 51 P.

8181 Hostettler, John. Berlin: The Legal Rights. Labour Monthly. 44 (January 1962), 39-42.

8182 Jessup, Philip C. The Rights Of The United States In Berlin. American Journal Of International Law. 43:1 (January 1949), 92-95.

8183 Johnstone, Paul H. American Policy-Making Practices And The Origins Of The U.S. Commitment To The West Berlin Enclave. Arlington: Institute For Defense Analyses, Weapons Systems Evaluation Division, September 1966, 112 P.

8184 Kreutzer, Heinz. West Berlin: City And State. Berlin--Pivot Of German Destiny. Ed. Charles B. Robson. Chapel Hill: University Of North Carolina Press, 1960, Pp. 67-99.

8185 Legien, Rudolf Roman. The Four Power Agreements On Berlin: Alternative Solutions To The Status Quo?. Berlin: Heymanns, 2D Ed., 1961, 68 P.

8186 Lindner, Gerhard. The Illegal Occupation Of West Berlin. German Foreign Policy (Gdr). Spec. Ed. 1 (October 1961), 57-74.

8187 Loewenstein, Karl. The Allied Presence In Berlin: Legal Basis. Foreign Policy Bulletin. 38:11 (15 February 1959), 81-84.

8188 Lush, C. D. The Relationship Between Berlin And The Federal Republic Of Germany. International And Comparative Law Quarterly. 14:3 (July 1965), 742-787.

8189 Mendlovitz, Saul. A Relevant Legal Context For The Problem Of West Berlin. West Berlin: The Legal Context. Ed. Roland J. Stanger. Columbus: Ohio State University Press, 1966, Pp. 101-133.

8190 Merritt, Richard L. The Tangled Tie: West Germany And The Berlin Problem. Politics In Europe: Structures And Processes. Ed. Martin O. Heisler. New York: Mckay, 1973.

8191 Metzger, Stanley D. The Division Of Berlin And Of Germany. West Berlin: The Legal Context. Ed. Roland J. Stanger. Columbus: Ohio State University Press, 1966, Pp. 3-22.

8192 Nelson, Daniel J. The Allied Creation Of The Postwar Status Of Berlin: A Study In Wartime Alliance Diplomacy. Ph.D. Thesis, Columbia University, 1970.

8193 Pakuscher, Ernst K. The Legal Status Of Berlin: Its Implication On The

Division Of Germany. New York University Journal Of International Law And Politics. 1:2 (December 1968), 208-218.

8194 Plischke, Elmer. Government And Politics Of Contemporary Berlin. The Hague: Nijhoff, 1963, 119 P.

8195 Plischke, Elmer. Integrating Berlin And The Federal Republic Of Germany. Journal Of Politics. 27:1 (February 1965), 35-65.

8196 Plischke, Elmer. Erdmann, Elisabeth. Berlin: Development Of Its Government And Administration. Bad Godesberg-Mehlem: Office Of The U.S. High Commissioner For Germany, Historical Division, 1952, 257 P. Reprinted: Westport, Conn.: Greenwood, 1970.

8197 Simpson, John I. Berlin: Allied Rights And Responsibilities In The Divided City. International And Comparative Law Quarterly. 6:1 (January 1957), 83-102.

8198 Smith, Bruce L. R. The Governance Of Berlin. International Conciliation. No. 525 (November 1959), 171-230.

8199 Stanger, Roland J., Editor. West Berlin: The Legal Context. Columbus: Ohio State University Press, 1966, 133 P.

8200 Tunkin, G. The Berlin Problem And International Law. International Affairs (Moscow). 5:2 (February 1959), 36-43.

8201 Uk, Foreign Office. Memorandum On The Principles Governing The Relationship Between The Allied Kommandatura And Greater Berlin, May 26, 1952. London: H.M. Stationery Office, Cmd. 8564, 1952, 4 P.

8202 Us, Hicog, Office Of Executive Secretary. 1950 Berlin Constitution And Electoral Law. Berlin: Hicog, Office Of Executive Secretary, Policy Reports Secretary, 1951, 99 P.

R.3. Access To East And West Berlin

8203 Agreement Between The Government Of The German Democratic Republic And The Government Of The Federal Republic Of Germany On The Transit Traffic Of Civilian Persons And Goods Between The Federal Republic Of Germany And Berlin (West). Dresden: Verlag Zeit Im Bild, 1972, 16 P. Agreement Of 3 September 1971.

8204 Peil, Michael. A Step Of Common Sense. German Foreign Policy (Gdr). 4:2 (1965), 99-109. Pass Question For West Berliners.

8205 Franklin, William M. Zonal Boundaries And Access To Berlin. World Politics. 16:1 (October 1963), 1-31.

8206 Gdr, Ministry Of Foreign Affairs. Memorandum On The Traffic In Citizens Of The German Democratic Republic Conducted From West Germany And West Berlin. Berlin: Ministry Of Foreign Affairs, 1961, 21 P.

8207 Gdr Makes Gesture Of Good Will. Dresden: Verlag Zeit Im Bild, Documents On The Policy Of The Gdr No. 3, 1972, 7 P. Decrees On Visits To Gdr By West Berliners, 23 February 1972.

8208 Goerner, Gunter. Gdr Ensures Peaceful Transit Traffic To And From West Berlin. German Foreign Policy (Gdr). 8:1 (1969), 12-23.

8209 Institute Of International And West German Questions. The Allied Travel Office (Ato) In West Berlin: Illegal Obstruction On The Road To The Guarantee Of European Security. Leipzig: Karl Marx University, Institute Of International And West German Questions, C.1970, 29 P.

8210 Mcclelland, Charles A. Access To Berlin: The Quantity And Variety Of Events, 1948-1963. Quantitative International Politics: Insights And Evidence. Ed. J. David Singer. New York: Free Press, 1968, Pp. 159-186.

8211 Pauw, Alan D. The Historical Background Relating To Access Rights To Berlin. Ph.D. Thesis, University Of Southern California, 1965, 317 P.

8212 Peck, Joachim. On The Question Of The "Allied Travel Office" In West Berlin. German Foreign Policy (Gdr). 3:3 (1964), 196-204.

8213 Schroeder, Dieter. The Legal Status Of The Lines Of Communication To And From Berlin. Berlin: Press And Information Office, 1970, 23 P.

8214 Treaty Between The German Democratic Republic And The Federal Republic Of Germany On The Questions Relating To Traffic. Dresden: Verlag Zeit Im Bild, 1972, 28 P. Treaty Of 12 May 1972.

F.4. Social And Political Issues

8215 Allemann, Fritz Rene. Berlin In Search Of A Purpose. Survey. No. 61 (October 1966), 129-138.

8216 Berlin, Senator For Economics. Berlin Communications, 1968. Berlin: Senator For Economics, 1968, 48 P.

8217 Berlin, Senator For Public Health. Public Health In Berlin. Berlin: Senator For Public Health, 1965, 48 P.

8218 Berlin, Senator For The Interior. Eastern Underground Activity Against West Berlin. Berlin: Senator For The Interior, 1959, 71 P.

8219 Carr, William G. Up Against A Stone Wall. Nea Journal. 51:2 (February 1962), 12-15. Effect Of Wall On Schools In Berlin.

8220 Catudal, Honore Marc, Jr. Berlin's New Boundaries. Cahiers De Geographie De Quebec. 18:43 (April 1974), 213-226.

8221 Catudal, Honore Marc, Jr. The Exclave Problem Of Western Europe. Ph.D. Thesis, American University, 1973.

8222 Catudal, Honore Marc, Jr. Exclaves. Cahiers De Geographie De Quebec. 18:43 (April 1974), 107-136.

8223 Catudal, Honore Marc, Jr. Steinstuecken: A Study In Cold War Politics. New York: Vantage, 1971, 165 P.

8224 Catudal, Honore Marc, Jr. Steinstuecken: The Politics Of A Berlin Exclave. World Affairs (Washington). 134:1 (Summer 1971), 51-62.

8225 Friedensburg, Ferdinand. The Geographical Elements In The Berlin Situation. Geographical Journal. 133:2 (June 1967), 137-147.

8226 Fuerlinger, Friedrich. City Planning In Divided Berlin. Berlin--Pivot Of German Destiny. Ed. Charles B. Robson. Chapel Hill: University Of North Carolina Press, 1960, Pp. 174-189.

8227 Hans, Theodor. Soviet Terrorism In Free Germany. Washington: U.S. Government Printing Office, 1960, 39 P. East German Abductions From West Berlin.

8228 Hirsch, Felix Edward. Crisis And Decline Of West Berlin. Current History. 54:321 (May 1968), 293-297, 308, 320.

8229 Hofmann, Wolfgang. West Berlin--The Isolated City In The Twentieth Century. Journal Of Contemporary

History. 4:3 (July 1969), 77-94.

8230 International Association Of Democratic Lawyers. The Inquiry Committee Of Free Jurists Of West Berlin: A Documentary Study. Brussels: International Association Of Democratic Lawyers, 1957, 17 P.

8231 Klein, Heinrich. Mueller, Wolfgang. Berlin. Bad Godesberg: Institut Fuer Angewandte Sozialwissenschaft, 1963, 48 P.

8232 Kolarz, Henry. Is West Berlin Quietly Dying?. Atlas. 15:2 (February 1968), 29-32.

8233 Lichtheim, George. A Berlin Notebook--Parochial Capital. Commentary. 24:4 (October 1957), 292-301.

8234 Merritt, Richard L. Infrastructural Changes In Berlin. Annals Of The Association Of American Geographers. 63:1 (March 1973), 58-70.

8235 Merritt, Richard L. Noncontiguity And Political Integration. Linkage Politics: Essays On The Convergence Of National And International Systems. Ed. James N. Rosenau. New York: Free Press, 1969, Pp. 237-272.

8236 Merritt, Richard L. Political Division And Municipal Services In Postwar Berlin. Public Policy, Vol. 17. Ed. John D. Montgomery And Albert O. Hirschman. Cambridge: Harvard University Press, 1968, Pp. 165-198.

8237 Merritt, Richard L. Politics, Theater, And The East-West Struggle: The Theater As A Cultural Bridge In West Berlin, 1948-1961. Political Science Quarterly. 80:2 (June 1965), 186-215.

8238 Merritt, Richard L. West Berlin: Center Or Periphery?. Comparing Nations: The Use Of Quantitative Data In Cross-National Research. Ed. Richard L. Merritt And Stein Rokkan. New Haven: Yale University Press, 1966, Pp. 321-336.

8239 Possony, Stefan I. Germany: West Berlin. Yearbook On International Communist Affairs, 1973. Ed. Richard F. Staar. Stanford: Hoover Institution Press, 1973, Pp. 163-168.

8240 Robinson, G. W. S. West Berlin: The Geography Of An Enclave. Geographical Review. 43:4 (October 1953), 540-557.

8241 Stammer, Otto. The Berlin Situation As A Socio-Political Problem. Berlin--Pivot Of German Destiny. Ed. Charles B. Robson. Chapel Hill: University Of North Carolina Press, 1960, Pp. 100-133.

8242 Vogt, A. M. The Interbau Exhibit In Berlin. Swiss Review Of World Affairs. 7:6 (September 1957), 21-25.

8243 Walker, Peter J. One Hundred Years Of The Berlin Tramways. Croyden: Light Railway Transport League, 1966, 81 P.

8244 Wieser, Theodor. The New West Berlin: The Hansaviertel. Swiss Review Of World Affairs. 6:6 (September 1956), 14-17.

8245 Wright, William E. Ideological-Pragmatic Orientations Of West Berlin Local Party Officials. Midwest Journal Of Political Science. 11:3 (August 1967), 381-402.

8246 Wright, William E. Local Leadership In Two West Berlin Political Parties. Ph.D. Thesis, Vanderbilt University, 1966, 490 P.

R.5. Economic Issues

8247 Berlin, Senator For Construction And Housing Affairs. The Reconstruction Of Berlin From 1949 To 1963. Berlin: Senator For Construction And Housing Affairs, 1962, 36 P.

8248 Bulwark Berlin: The Reconstruction Of Berlin; Trade With Berlin. Berlin: Pandion, 1955-56, 95 P.

8249 Conditions And Possibilities For An Expansion Of West Berlin'S Economy During The Next Few Years. Berlin: N.P., January 1951, 40 P.

8250 Cornelsen, Doris. Krengel, Rolf. Structural And Tension-Related Elements In The Subsidization Of West Berlin. Santa Monica: Rand Corporation, P-4426, June 1970, 49 P.

8251 Kluge, Franz. The Economic Viability Of Berlin. Berlin--Pivot Of German Destiny. Ed. Charles B. Robson. Chapel Hill: University Of North Carolina Press, 1960, Pp. 134-155.

8252 Krzyzanowski, Walter. The Position Of The Economy Of West Berlin. German Foreign Policy (Gdr). 2:6 (1963), 457-464.

8253 Meimberg, Rudolf. The Economy Of West Berlin: Development, Problems, Tasks. Berlin: Duncker And Humblot, 1950, 86 P.

8254 Moetteli, Carlo. In Western Berlin: Progress Against Heavy Odds. Swiss Review Of World Affairs. 4:5 (August 1954), 13-18.

8255 Parkman, Henry. Berlin--Reconstruction And Achievements. International Markets. 9:4 (April 1955), 16+.

8256 Schattmann, Stephan. The Economics Of West Berlin. Banker. 109:401 (June 1959), 364-368.

8257 Schmidt, Hubert G. Erdmann, Elisabeth. Economic Assistance To West Berlin, 1949-1951. Bad Godesberg-Mehlem: Office Of The U.S. High Commissioner For Germany,Historical Division, 1952, 135 P.

8258 Schmidt, Willi. Banking In West Berlin. The Banker. 121:539 (January 1971), 69-79.

8259 Traeger, Ludwig. Berlin'S Place In The Electrical Industry Of Germany. International Markets. 9:4 (April 1955), 46.

8260 Us, Hicog, Berlin Element, Economic Affairs Division. Berlin Export Directory. Berlin: Hicog, Berlin Element, Economic Affairs Division, 1950, 114 P.

8261 Us, Omgus, Manpower Division. Employment, Unemployment, Displacements, Western Sectors Of Berlin, June 1948-January 1949. N.P.: Omgus, Statistical Bulletin No. 1, February 1949.

R.6. Blockade And Division (1948-58)

8262 Anthon, Carl G. The Berlin Situation. United States Naval Institute Proceedings. 80:4 (April 1954), 385-395.

8263 Barker, Dudley. Berlin Air Lift: An Account Of The British Contribution. London: Air Ministry, H. M. Stationery Office, 1949, 61 P.

8264 Bennett, Lowell. Berlin Bastion: The Epic Of Post-War Berlin. Frankfurt: Rudl, 1951, 263 P.

8265 Berkowitz, Morton. Bock, Peter G. Fuccillo, Vincent J. The Berlin Airlift, 1948. The Politics of American Foreign Policy: The Social Context of Decisions. Englewood Cliffs: Prentice-Hall, 1977, pp.39-53

8266 Berlin And The Soviet Recognition Of East German Sovereignty. World Today. 12:1 (January 1956), 4-7.

8267 The Berlin Crisis Before The Security Council. Current History. 15:88 (December 1948), 352-353.

8268 Berlin: The West In Trouble. New Central European Observer. 1:14 (13 November 1948), 130.

8269 Charles, Max. Berlin Blockade. London: Wingate, 1959, 175 P.

8270 Cherne, Leo. Mayor Reuter Of Beleaguered Berlin. New York Times Magazine. (15 March 1953), 15+.

8271 Colvin, Ian. Berlin And Europe. National Review. 131:786 (August 1948), 111-118.

8272 Copleston, Frederick C. A Visit To Berlin. Studies. 37 (December 1948), 409-420.

8273 Davison, W. Phillips. The Berlin Blockade: A Study In Cold War Politics. Princeton: Princeton University Press, 1958, 423 P.

8274 Davison, W. Phillips. The Berlin Blockade: Study Of A Population Under Stress. Ph.D. Thesis, Columbia University, 1954, 570 P.

8275 Donovan, Frank Robert. Bridge In The Sky. New York: Mckay, 1968, 209 P.

8276 Dulles, Eleanor Lansing. Berlin And Soviet Methods In Germany. Department Of State Bulletin. 36:938 (17 June 1957), 978-983.

8277 Four-Power Reply To The Berlin Proposal. Current History. 15:88 (December 1948), 354-357.

8278 Fox, William T. R. Morgenthau, Hans J. Reston, James B. The United Nations And The Berlin Crisis. University Of Chicago Round Table. No. 550 (3 October 1948), 1-34. Radio Discussion, With Excerpts From U.S. "White Paper".

8279 Frei, Otto. Berlin--Outpost Of Democracy. Swiss Review Of World Affairs. 1:11 (February 1952), 13-14.

8280 Friedrich, Carl J. Airlift Shows U.S. Aims To See Berlin Crisis Through. Foreign Policy Bulletin. 27:46 (8 October 1948), 3-4.

8281 Green, Leslie C. Berlin And The United Nations. World Affairs (London). 3:1 (January 1949), 23-42.

8282 Harrell, Edward J. Berlin: Rebirth, Reconstruction And Division, 1945-1948: A Study Of Allied Cooperation And Conflict. Ph.D. Thesis, Florida State University, 1965, 298 P.

8283 Herbert, E. O. The Cold War In Berlin. Royal United Service Institution Journal. 94:574 (May 1949), 165-177.

8284 Hertz, Paul. Berlin And U.S. Foreign Policy Toward Germany. Columbia Journal Of International Affairs. 5:1 (Winter 1951), 45-52.

8285 Herzfeld, Hans. The Splitting Of Berlin In 1948. Berlin--Pivot Of German Destiny. Ed. Charles B. Robson. Chapel Hill: University Of North Carolina Press, 1960, Pp. 47-66.

8286 Howley, Frank L. Berlin Command. New York: Putnam's, 1950, 276 P.

8287 I. D. Berlin, New Year 1950. World Today. 6:3 (March 1950), 101-110.

8288 J. E. W. H. G. L. The Breakdown Of Four-Power Rule In Berlin. World Today. 4:8 (August 1948), 322-331.

8289 Jessup, Philip C. The Berlin Blockade And The Use Of The United Nations. Foreign Affairs. 50:1 (October 1971), 163-173.

8290 Jessup, Philip C. Park Avenue Diplomacy--Ending The Berlin Blockade. Political Science Quarterly. 87:3 (September 1972), 377-400.

8291 Lewis, Arthur. A Berlin Notebook. New Central European Observer. 1:16 (11 December 1948), 153.

8292 Luethy, Herbert. Berlin: The Unhaunted City. Encounter. 2:2 (February 1954), 35-41.

8293 Maitland, Patrick. Peace By Might: The Berlin Blockade And After. Soundings. No. 27 (June 1949), 24-30.

8294 Middleton, Drew. He Holds The Berlin Bridge: Lucius Clay. New York Times Magazine. (4 July 1948), 6+.

8295 Middleton, Drew. Ivan Ivanovitch Meets The West In Berlin. New York Times Magazine. (5 September 1948), 8+.

8296 Middleton, Drew. New Courage Rises From Berlin's Ruins. New York Times Magazine. (15 August 1948), 11+.

8297 Middleton, Drew. Potsdamer Platz: Berlin Battleground. New York Times Magazine. (3 June 1951), 13+.

8298 Middleton, Drew. The Stakes In The Battle Of Berlin. New York Times Magazine. (9 April 1950), 11+.

8299 Moore, Lyford. The Man In The Goldfish Bowl: Lucius D. Clay. This Is Germany. Ed. Arthur Settel. New York: Sloane, 1950, Pp. 23-39.

8300 Morris, Eric. Blockade: Berlin And The Cold War. New York: Stein And Day, 1973, 278 P.

8301 Mulready, Brendan P. Berlin Airlift Proved Unification Can Work. Proceedings Of The United States Naval Institute. 76:3 (March 1950), 282-287.

8302 Orion (Pseud.). The Berlin Air Lift. Royal United Service Institution Journal. 94:573 (February 1949), 82-86.

8303 Orton, Peter K. Scholz, Arno. Outpost Berlin. London: Orton-Press, 1955, 26 P.

8304 Peet, John, British Journalist In Berlin--Writes To A Colleague. New World Review. 19:8 (October 1951), 22-24.

8305 Peet, John. Open Letter To A Journalist In West Berlin. Labour Monthly. 33:8 (August 1951), 386-388.

8306 Quaestor. Berlin And Beyond. Labour Monthly. 31:6 (June 1949), 177-182.

8307 Reuter, Ernst. Appeal To The Free World. Berlin: Pressestelle Des Senats Der Stadt Berlin, 1952, 26 P.

8308 Riess, Curt. The Berlin Story. New York: Dial, 1952, 368 P.

8309 Rodrigo, Robert. Berlin Airlift. London: Cassell, 1960, 240 P.

8310 Schaffer, Gordon. The Berlin Crisis. Soviet Russia Today. 17:5 (September 1948), 8, 28.

8311 Schaffer, Gordon. Berlin's Case History. New Central European Observer. 1:9 (4 September 1948), 90-91.

8312 Schaffer, Gordon. Prospects In Berlin. Labour Monthly. 36:2 (February 1954), 71-76.

8313 Schaffer, Gordon. The Truth About The Air Lift. New Central European Observer. 4:7 (31 March 1951), 106.

8314 Scheinman, Lawrence. The Berlin Blockade. International Law And Political Crisis: An Analytic Casebook. Ed. Lawrence Scheinman And

David Wilkinson. Boston: Little, Brown, 1968, Pp. 1-40.

8315 Smith, Gaddis. Visions And Revisions Of The Cold War: The Berlin Blockade Through The Filter Of History. New York Times Magazine. (29 April 1973), 13+.

8316 Smogorzewski, K. M. West Berlin--The Beacon In The Night. Fortnightly. 174:1043 (November 1953), 299-304.

8317 Soloveytchik, George. After The Blockade. Contemporary Review. 175:1002 (June 1949), 325-330.

8318 A Special Study Of Operation "Vittles": The Story Of The Berlin Airlift. Aviation Operations. 11:5 (April 1949), 1-120.

8319 Spencer, Robert A. Berlin, The Blockade, And The Cold War. International Journal. 23:3 (Summer 1968), 383-407.

8320 Spencer, Robert A. Berlin Report: Summer, 1952. International Journal. 7:4 (Autumn 1952), 274-277.

8321 Stringer, Ann. Berlin Today: One Family's Story. New York Times Magazine. (2 January 1949), 13+.

8322 Sullivan, Walter. Berlin, 1952: A Divided Island. New York Times Magazine. (24 August 1952), 12+.

8323 T. R. C. Life In Berlin Today. World Today. 4:12 (December 1948), 502-510.

8324 Tergit, Gabriele. The Russians In Berlin. Contemporary Review. 174:992 (August 1948), 84-87.

8325 Thompson, Elizabeth M. Harassed Berlin. Editorial Research Reports. (12 March 1953), 181-197.

8326 Three-Power Note In Soviet Actions In Berlin. Current History. 16:89 (January 1949), 40-42. Us-Uk-France, 5 December 1948.

8327 To The Conscience Of The World: Berlin Women's Appeal To Humanity. Berlin: Blanvalet, 1948, 16 P. Speeches Of Municipal Councillors Lucia Krueger, Annedore Leber, And Ella Barowsky In The Berlin Municipal Parliament, 29 June 1948.

8328 Uk, Ccg. Notes On The Blockade Of Berlin 1948 From A British Viewpoint. Berlin: Control Commission For Germany (Be), Hq British Troops Berlin, 1949, 85 P. Hq British Troops Berlin, Raf, Gatow, Hq Airlift, Btb, Mil. Gov'T, Btb.

8329 Uk, Foreign Office. Germany, An Account Of The Events Leading Up To A Reference Of The Berlin Question To The United Nations, 11Th October, 1948. London: H.M. Stationery Office, Cmd. 7534, 1948, 67 P.

8330 Us, Department Of State, Office Of Public Affairs. The Berlin Crisis: A Report On The Moscow Discussions, 1948. Washington: Department Of State Publication 3298, Government Printing Office, 1948, 61 P.

8331 Ussr, Ministry Of Foreign Affairs. Soviet Union And The Berlin Question. New York: Universal, 1948, 83 P.

8332 Van Hoek, Kees. Lord Mayor Reuter Of Berlin. Contemporary Review. 181:1035 (March 1952), 145-148.

8333 Van Wagenen, Richard W. Cooperation And Controversy Among The Occupying Powers In Berlin. Journal Of Politics. 10:1 (February 1948), 73-100.

8334 Western Powers Reply To The Soviet Proposals On Berlin (26 September 1948). Current History. 15:87 (November 1948), 298-301.

R.7. Soviet Ultimatum And The Wall, 1958-69

8335 Altena, John Van, Jr. The Flight That Failed. East Europe. 16:7 (July 1967), 2-11. American's Attempt To Help Gdr Friends To Cross Wall Into West Berlin.

8336 American Enterprise Association. Special Analysis: The Berlin Crisis. Washington: American Enterprise Association, Reports Nos. 14-16, 1961, 3 Pts., 168 P.

8337 Anthon, Carl G. The Berlin Crisis And Atlantic Unity. Current History. 42:245 (January 1962), 20-27.

8338 Ausland, John C. Richardson, Hugh F. Crisis Management: Berlin, Cyprus, Laos. Foreign Affairs. 44:2 (January 1966), 291-303.

8339 Aust, Hans Walter. The Berlin Question And The Interests Of Peace. International Affairs (Moscow). (January 1959), 46-52.

8340 Bailey, George. Under The Berlin Wall. Reporter. 33:8 (4 November 1965), 18-23.

8341 Baldwin, Hanson W. To Berlin--High Road And Low. New York Times Magazine. (29 October 1961), 22+.

8342 Barker, Elisabeth. The Berlin Crisis, 1958-1962. International Affairs (London). 39:1 (January 1963), 59-73.

8343 Beranek, Robert E. The Second Berlin Crisis And The Foreign Ministers Conference At Geneva (1959): A Case Study Of Soviet Diplomacy. Ph.D. Thesis, University Of Pittsburgh, 1966, 283 P.

8344 Berk, Alexander. The Misuse Of West Berlin By West German Militarists. German Foreign Policy (Gdr). 1:2 (1962), 132-143.

8345 Berlin, Press And Information Office. Berlin--Fate And Mission. Berlin: Press And Information Office Of The Land Of Berlin, 1959.

8346 Berlin, Press And Information Office. Berlin's Vitality. Berlin: Press And Information Office, 1965, 27 P.

8347 Berlin, Press And Information Office. A Great Day In The History Of Berlin, June 26, 1963: John F. Kennedy In Berlin. Berlin: Druckhaus Tempelhof, For Press And Information Office, 1963, 48 P.

8348 Berlin And The German Question: Editorial. Our Generation Against Nuclear War. 1:2 (Winter 1962), 23-34.

8349 Berlin: Crisis And Challenge. New York: German Information Center, C. 1962, 67 P.

8350 Berlin 1959: Eight Comments. Western World. 2:5 (May 1959), 15-20.

8351 The Berlin Question. Pakistan Horizon. 11:4 (December 1958), 291-295.

8352 Berlin: One Year Of The Wall. World Today. 18:7 (September 1962), 361-364.

8353 Bertsch, Herbert. West Berlin--Centre Of Revanchist Agitation. German Foreign Policy (Gdr). 1:6 (1962), 623-629.

8354 Blumenfeld, F. Yorick. Berlin Question. Editorial Research Reports. (4 May 1960), 321-337.

8355 Brandt, Willy. The Berlin Crisis. Pakistan Horizon. 12:1 (March 1959), 25-29.

8356 Brandt, Willy. Berlin's Mayor: "We Will Stay". New York Times Magazine. (6 November 1960), 25+.

8357 Brandt, Willy. Berlin's Special Tasks. Berlin: Press And Information Agency Of The Land Of Berlin, 1959, 47 P.

8358 Brandt, Willy. Lania, Leo. My Road To Berlin. Garden City: Doubleday, 1960, 287 P.

8359 Brandt, Willy. Tackle The Tasks Of Tomorrow. Berlin: Berlin Press And Information Office, 1963, 51 P. Statement Before Berlin House Of Representatives, 18 March 1963.

8360 Camp, Glen D., Jr., Editor. Berlin In The East-West Struggle, 1958-61. New York: Facts On File, 1971, 252 P.

8361 Camp, Glen D., Jr. City In The Middle: Berlin In The East-West Struggle. Ph.D. Thesis, Harvard University, 1964.

8362 Carthew, Anthony. West Berlin Has Grown Calluses On Its Nerves. New York Times Magazine. (28 July 1968), 8+.

8363 Chaplin, Dennis. The Berlin Wall--Ten Years In Retrospect. Contemporary Review. 219:1268 (September 1971), 125-131.

8364 A Chink In The Curtain: Significance Of West Berlin. Round Table. 51:204 (September 1961), 331-336.

8365 Clay, Lucius D. Berlin. Foreign Affairs. 41:1 (October 1962), 47-58.

8366 Collier, David S., Editor. Glaser, Kurt, Editor. Berlin And The Future Of Eastern Europe. Chicago: Regnery, 1963, 251 P.

8367 Commentator. West German Provocations In West Berlin. International Affairs (Moscow). (April 1968), 45-46.

8368 Conlan, William H. Berlin: Beset And Bedevilled; Tinderbox Of The World. New York: Fountainhead, 1963, 268 P.

8369 Dalma, Alfons. The Third Berlin Offensive Of The Cold War. Military Review. 41:12 (December 1961), 17-25.

8370 Deutsch, Harold C. New Crisis On Berlin. Toronto: Canadian Institute Of International Affairs, Behind The Headlines Series, Vol. 19, No. 2, 1959, 17 P.

8371 Donner, Joern. Report From Berlin. Bloomington: Indiana University Press, 1961, 284 P.

8372 Draper, Theodore. Beyond Berlin--Is There A New "Balance Of Forces"?. Commentary. 32:5 (November 1961), 382-390. U.S.-Soviet Relations Regarding Berlin Specifically And Europe In General.

8373 Dulles, Eleanor Lansing. Berlin: Barometer Of Tension. Detente: Cold War Strategies In Transition. Ed. Eleanor Lansing Dulles And Robert Dickson Crane. New York: Praeger, 1965, Pp. 121-137.

8374 Dulles, Eleanor Lansing. Berlin: The Wall Is Not Forever. Chapel Hill: University Of North Carolina Press, 1967, 245 P.

8375 Dulles, Eleanor Lansing. The Wall: A Tragedy In Three Acts. Columbia: University Of South Carolina Press, 1972, 105 P.

8376 Eschenburg, Theodor. Isolated Berlin. Bonn: Inter Nationes, 1963, 16 P.

8377 Frg, Federal Ministry For All-German Affairs. Barriers To Law And Humanity: Berlin, August 13. Bonn: Bundesministerium Fuer Gesamtdeutsche Fragen, 2D Ed., 1965, 64 P.

8378 Frg, Federal Ministry For All-German Affairs. The Flights From The Soviet Zone And The Sealing-Off Measures Of The Communist Regime Of 13Th August 1961 In Berlin. Bonn: Federal Ministry For All-German Affairs, 1961, 77 P.

8379 Frg, Federal Ministry For All-German Affairs. Violations of Human Rights, Illegal Acts and Incidents at The Sector Border in Berlin Since the Building of the Wall (13 August 1961-15 August 1962). Bonn: Federal Ministry for All-German Affairs, 1962, 27 P.

8380 FRG, German Embassy. To Keep Berlin Free. Washington: German Embassy, 1959, 16 P.

8381 Feinstein, Otto. Perspective on Berlin. Our Generation Against Nuclear War. 2:3 (Spring 1962), 72-76.

8382 Fleming, Denna Frank. The Future of West Berlin. Western Political Quarterly. 14:1 (March 1961), 37-48.

8383 Florin, Peter. The World Looks Upon Berlin. German Foreign Policy (GDR). 2:2 (1963), 85-94.

8384 Frei, Otto. The Barrier Across Berlin and Its Consequences. World Today. 17:11 (November 1961), 459-470.

8385 Friedman, Peter. Ulbricht's Wall. East Europe. 12:8 (August 1963), 2-9.

8386 Fuller, J. F. C. The Berlin Problem. Royal United Service Institution Journal. 107:626 (May 1962), 149-151.

8387 GDR. Memorandum of the Government of the German Democratic Republic on the Berlin Question. Berlin?: N.P., 1959, 21 P.

8388 GDR. The "Wall" and Humanity. Berlin: N.P., 1962, 16 P.

8389 GDR, Committee for German Unity. West Berlin--Stronghold of Reaction, Hotbed of Warmongers: A Documentation on the "Front Line City" Policy of the West Berlin Senate. Berlin: Committee for German Unity, 1958, 59 P.

8390 GDR, Ministry of Foreign Affairs. Documentation on the Question of West Berlin. Berlin: Ministry of Foreign Affairs, 1964, 284 P.

8391 GDR, Ministry of Foreign Affairs. The Problems of West Berlin and Solutions Proposed By the Government of the German Democratic Republic. Berlin: Ministry of Foreign Affairs, 1961, 3Rd Ed., 108 P.

8392 Gablentz, Otto M. Von Der. The Berlin Question in Its Relations to World Politics, 1944-1963: An Introduction. Munich: Oldenbourg, 1964, 43 P.

8393 Gablentz, Otto M. Von Der. Documents on the Status of Berlin, 1944-1959. Munich: Oldenbourg, 1959, 239 P.

8394 Galante, Pierre. The Berlin Wall. Garden City: Doubleday, 1965, 277 P.

8395 Galay, Nikolai. Berlin: on the Eve of the Denouement. Institute for the Study of the Ussr, Bulletin. 8:10 (October 1961), 21-31.

8396 Ganssauge, Guenter. A Wall of Peace. Dresden: Zeit Im Bild, 1968, 53 P.

8397 Gelman, Norman I. Berlin Crisis and German Reunification. Editorial Research Reports. (24 December 1958), 955-975.

8398 Geneva Conference, Closing Communique (5 August 1959). Current History. 37:218 (October 1959), 239.

8399 German Institute of Contemporary History. They Say So Themselves: Disturber of the Peace, West Berlin : Statements By Western Politicians and the Western Press on the Role of West Berlin as an International Centre of Provocation. Berlin (East): German

Institute of Contemporary History, 1962, 39 P.

8400 German Peace Council of the German Democratic Republic. A Central Problem: Documents on the West Berlin Question. N.P.: German Peace Council, 1961, 72 P.

8401 Grabowski, K. Germany and Berlin. Poland and Germany. 3:7 (January 1959), 1-9.

8402 Gradl, Johann B. The Stakes at Berlin: A German View. Free World Forum. 1:1 (January 1959), 47-50.

8403 Green, Leslie C. The Status of Berlin. Sydney: University of Sydney, 1962, 29 P.

8404 Grewe, Wilhelm G. Berlin and the Challenge to the West. Free World Forum. 1:1 (January 1959), 40-43.

8405 Grewe, Wilhelm G. Germany and Berlin: An Analysis of the 1959 Geneva Conference. Washington: German Embassy, Press and Information Office, 1959, 38 P.

8406 Haffner, Sebastian. The Berlin Crisis. Survey. No. 44-45 (October 1962), 37-44.

8407 Hall, Adam (Pseud.). The Berlin Memorandum. London: Collins, 1965, 254 P.

8408 Hamlett, Barksdale. Outpost of Democracy. Army Information Digest. 14:5 (May 1959), 2-11.

8409 Healey, Denis. The Case for Berlin Negotiations. New Leader. 44:33 (18 September 1961), 6-8.

8410 Heaps, Willard Allison. The Wall of Shame. New York: Duell, Sloan, and Pearce, 1964, 175 P.

8411 Heidelmeyer, Wolfgang, Editor. Hindrichs, Guenter, Editor. Documents on Berlin, 1943-1963. Munich: Oldenbourg, 1963, 373 P.

8412 Heller, David. Heller, Deane. The Berlin Crisis: Prelude to World War III?. Derby: Monarch Books, 1961, 190 P.

8413 Heller, Deane. Heller, David. The Berlin Wall. New York: Walker, 1962, 242 P.

8414 Henkin, Louis J. The Berlin Crisis and the United Nations. New York: Carnegie Endowment for International Peace, 1959, 30 P.

8415 Hester, Hugh B. Facts and Opinions About Berlin. New World Review. 29:10 (October 1961), 25-26.

8416 Hirsch, Felix Edward. Berlin--Symbol of Freedom. International Journal. 14:2 (Spring 1959), 111-121.

8417 Holbrook, Sabra. Capital Without a Country: The Challenge of Berlin. New York: Coward-Mccann, 1961, 121 P.

8418 Hottelet, Richard C. Berlin and Beyond. Orbis. 5:3 (Fall 1961), 267-291.

8419 Howley, Frank L. Berlin and the Western Cause. Western Integration and the Future of Eastern Europe. Ed. David S. Collier and Kurt Glaser. Chicago: Regnery, 1964, Pp. 130-152.

8420 Hudson, G. F. Berlin: The Menaced City--The Dilemmas Facing Our Diplomats. Commentary. 27:4 (April 1959), 310-316.

8421 International Commission of Jurists. The Berlin Wall: A Defiance of Human Rights. Geneva: International Commission of Jurists, 1962, 54 P.

8422 Kee, Robert. The Wall. Encounter. 17:5 (November 1961), 13-19.

8423 Keller, John W. Germany, the Wall and Berlin: Internal Politics During an International Crisis. New York: Vantage, 1964, 437 P.

8424 Kennedy, John F. The Berlin Crisis: Report to the Nation, July 25, 1961. Washington: Department of State, Office of Public Affairs, 1961, 21 P.

8425 Kertesz, Stephen D. Berlin and the Balance of Power. Current History. 37:218 (October 1959), 198-207.

8426 Khrushchev, Nikita S. Khrushchev Remembers: The Last Testament. Boston: Little, Brown, 1974, Xxxi and 602 P., Esp. Pp. 487-509.

8427 Kissinger, Henry A. "As Urgent as the Moscow Threat". New York Times Magazine. (8 March 1959), 19+.

8428 Kniestedt, Karlheinz. West Berlin: Anti-Imperialist Struggle. World Marxist Review: Problems of Peace and Socialism. 12:6 (June 1969), 57-60.

8429 Kotov, Y. West Berlin and Its Problems. International Affairs (Moscow). (April 1966), 47-49.

8430 Lang, Reginald D. Berlin, Germany, and East Central Europe. Central European Federalist. 7:1 (May 1959), 6-13.

8431 Lebed, A.I. Berlin: A Compilation of Analytical and Critical Materials. Munich: Institut Zur Erforschung Der Udssr, Soviet Affairs Analysis Service, Series 2:74, 1959, 101 P.

8432 Lewis, Flora. Berlin Beleaguered: Then and Now. New York Times Magazine. (30 November 1958), 11+.

8433 Lewis, Flora. Clay--Back at the Barricades. New York Times Magazine. (3 December 1961), 30+.

8434 Lewis, Flora. A Symbol, a Weapon, a Refuge: West Berlin. New York Times Magazine. (22 November 1959), 14+.

8435 Lewis, Flora. They Stay "Because It's Berlin". New York Times Magazine. (21 October 1962), 32+

8436 Lewis, Flora. West Berlin Waits, Uncertainly. New York Times Magazine. (1 October 1961), 26+.

8437 Lewis, Flora. What Berlin Means to the People of Berlin. New York Times Magazine. (27 August 1961), 24+.

8438 Liddell Hart, Basil H. The Berlin Squeeze--and a Solution. Royal United Service Institution Journal. 107:625 (February 1962), 45-49.

8439 Lowenthal, Richard. After Cuba, Berlin?. Encounter. 19:6 (December 1962), 48-55.

8440 Lowenthal, Richard. The Crossroads: Letter From Berlin. Encounter. 12:2 (February 1959), 3-9. Response By Fritz Rene Allemann in 12:3 (March 1959), 56-59.

8441 Lowenthal, Richard. The Impossible Defensive. Encounter. 17:5 (November 1961), 20-26.

8442 Luchsinger, Fred. at the Wall. Swiss Review of World Affairs. 16:7 (October 1966), 1-2.

8443 Luchsinger, Fred. The Berlin Pledge. Swiss Review of World Affairs. 18:4 (July 1968), 1-3. Will Brandt's Policies of Relaxation Work?.

8444 Mander, John. Berlin and Socialism. Socialist Commentary. (October 1962), 10-12.

8445 Mander, John. Berlin: The Eagle and the Bear. London: Barrie and Rockliff, 1959, 193 P.

8446 Mander, John. Berlin: Hostage for the West. Baltimore: Penguin, 1962, 126

P.

8447 Mason, John Brown. Next Steps in West Berlin. Foreign Policy Bulletin. 40:4 (November 1960), 29-33.

8448 Mcclelland, Charles A. Action Structures and Communication in Two International Crises: Quemoy and Berlin. Background. 7:4 (February 1964), 201-217.

8449 Mcclelland, Charles A. The Beginning, Duration, and Abatement of International Crises: Comparisons in Two Conflict Arenas. International Crises: Insights From Behavioral Research. Ed. Charles F. Hermann. New York: Free Press, 1972, Pp. 83-105. Berlin (1948-63) and Taiwan Straits (1950-64).

8450 Maccloskey, Monro. The Infamous Wall of Berlin: A Study of Its Political and Military Implications. New York: Rosen, 1967, 191 P.

8451 Mcdermott, Geoffrey. Berlin: Success of a Mission?. New York: Harper & Row, 1963, 147 P.

8452 Mcinnis, Edgar. Berlin: Case Study in Co-Existence. International Journal. 14:4 (Autumn 1959), 244-249.

8453 Meier, Victor. At the Crossroads of Two Worlds--Berlin. Swiss Review of World Affairs. 11:5 (August 1961), 3-7.

8454 Merritt, Richard L. The Berlin Wall: What Was It All About?. American Journal of Political Science. 17:1 (February 1973), 189-195. Review Article of Four Books.

8455 Merritt, Richard L. A Transformed Crisis: The Berlin Wall. Modern European Governments: Cases in Comparative Policy Making. Ed. Roy C. Macridis. Englewood Cliffs: Prentice-Hall, 1968, Pp. 140-173.

8456 A Message From Berlin: The Soviet Sea Around US. Berlin-Grunewald: Graphische Gesellschaft Grunewald, 1959, 25 P.

8457 Mezerik, Avrahm G. Berlin and Germany: Berlin Crisis, Free City, Separate Treaty, Cold War Chronology. New York: International Review Service, 1962, 93 P.

8458 Mezerik, Avrahm G. The Berlin Crisis: Free City Proposal; Postwar Germany; Reunification. New York: International Review Service, 1959, 57 P.

8459 Miksche, Ferdinand C. To Die for Berlin. Nato's Fifteen Nations. 6:2-3 (February-March 1962), 20-24.

8460 Molter, A., Rapporteur. Berlin (1944-1964): Brief on the Berlin Question. Paris: Western European Union, General Affairs Committee, 1964, 115 P.

8461 Montagu, Ivor. War Over Berlin?. Labour Monthly. 41 (March 1959), 127-130.

8462 Morgenthau, Hans J. Problem of Berlin. Politics in the Twentieth Century: Restoration of American Politics. Ed. Hans J. Morgenthau. Chicago: University of Chicago Press, 1962, Pp. 323-327.

8463 Mueller, Albert. Nato and Berlin. Swiss Review of World Affairs. 8:10 (January 1959), 3-4.

8464 Myers, Shirley. Berlin: Free City in a Communist Country. Johannesburg: South African Institute of International Affairs, 1966, 84 P.

8465 Neal, Fred Warner. And the Problem of Berlin. Our Generation Against Nuclear War. 1:2 (Winter 1962), 44-57.

8466 Neal, Fred Warner. War and Peace and the Problem of Berlin. Our Generation Against Nuclear War. 1:2 (Winter 1962), 44-57.

8467 O'Donnell, James P. The Brave "Buddelers" of Berlin. New York Times Magazine. (7 April 1963), 32+. Young People, Who Engineer Tunnel Escapes for GDR Refugees.

8468 Olsen, Arthur J. Breaching "The Wall": The Odds Grow. New York Times Magazine. (9 August 1964), 11+.

8469 Olsen, Arthur J. An "Uneventful Day" at the Berlin Wall. New York Times Magazine. (20 October 1963), 14+.

8470 Organski, A. F. K. Berlin and Two Germanies. Current History. 36:212 (April 1959), 200-204.

8471 Papadas, Panagiotis, Editor. The Wall in Berlin: Foreign Students Take a Look at Divided Germany. Kassel: Meister, 1964, 32 P.

8472 Plischke, Elmer. Resolving the "Berlin Question"--An Options Analysis. World Affairs. 131:2 (July 1968), 91-100.

8473 Possony, Stefan T. Berlin: Focus of World Strategy. Modern Age. 6:4 (Autumn 1962), 391-402.

8474 Possony, Stefan T. Berlin: Focus of World Strategy. Berlin and the Future of Eastern Europe. Ed. Davis S. Collier and Kurt Glaser. Chicago: Regnery, 1963, Pp. 21-42.

8475 Preece, Rodney J. C. The Berlin Wall--A Problem in Conflict Resolution. Contemporary Review. 212:1224 (January 1968), 20-24.

8476 Pritt, Denis N. What's This About Berlin?. Labour Monthly. 42 (July 1960), 305-310.

8477 Prittie, Terence C. F. What Berlin Means to Khrushchev. New York Times Magazine. (9 July 1961), 5+.

8478 Prowe, Diethelm Manfred-Hartmut. City Between Crises: The International Relations of West Berlin From the End of the Berlin Blockade in 1949 to the Khrushchev Ultimatum of 1958. Ph.D. Thesis, Stanford University, 1967, 312 P.

8479 Ramming, Hans. Berlin in the Lee of High-Level Politics. Swiss Review of World Affairs. 7:10 (January 1968), 8-10.

8480 Reif, Hans. Berlin--Pivot of German Destiny. Berlin--Pivot of German Destiny. Ed. Charles B. Robson. Chapel Hill: University of North Carolina Press, 1960, Pp. 207-226.

8481 Riesman, David. Dealing With the Russians Over Berlin. American Scholar. 31:1 (Winter 1961-62), 13-39.

8482 Ricklin, Alois. Berlin as a Problem in Power Politics. Modern World: Annual Review of International Relations and Political Science. (1964-65), 52-70.

8483 Robson, Charles B., Editor. Berlin: Pivot of German Destiny. Chapel Hill: University of North Carolina Press, 1960, 233 P.

8484 Rose, Jonathan William. The Berlin Crisis of 1958: The Calculated Risk of the Soviet Union. Chicago: Czechoslovak Foreign Institute in Exile, 1960, 53 P.

8485 Rosen, Edgar R. The United States and the Berlin Problem: An American View. Berlin--Pivot of German Destiny. Ed. Charles B. Robson. Chapel Hill: University of North Carolina Press, 1960, Pp. 190-206.

8486 Roucek, Joseph S. Berlin in

Geopolitics. Contemporary Review. 202 (August 1962), 119-124.

8487 Rovere, Richard H. Letter From Washington. New Yorker. 37 (23 September 1961), 82-88. Comment on Berlin Crisis.

8488 Rzhevsky, Yuri Sergeevich. West Berlin: A Special Political Entity. Moscow: Novosti Press Agency, C.1968, 100 P.

8489 Schaffer, Gordon. Background to Berlin. Labour Monthly. 41 (January 1959), 39-42.

8490 Schaffer, Gordon. The Lessons of History--Background of the German Crisis. New World Review. 29:10 (October 1961), 14-24.

8491 Schick, Jack M. American Diplomacy and the Berlin Negotiations. Western Political Quarterly. 18:4 (December 1965), 803-820.

8492 Schick, Jack M. The Berlin Crisis, 1958-1962. Philadelphia: University of Pennsylvania Press, 1971, 266 P.

8493 Schick, Jack M. The Berlin Crisis of 1961 and U.S. Military Strategy. Orbis. 8:4 (Winter 1965), 816-831.

8494 Scholz, Arno. Barbed Wire Round Berlin. Berlin: Arani, 1961, 104 P.

8495 Schwarz, Siegfried. The Events of August 13, 1961, and Their Impact on West German Foreign Policy. German Foreign Policy (GDR). 5:5 (1966), 372-381.

8496 Shell, Kurt L. Berlin and the German Problem. World Politics. 16:1 (October 1963), 137-146.

8497 The Siege of West Berlin: Fifteen Years of Divided Germany. Round Table. 51:202 (March 1961), 160-165.

8498 Slusser, Robert M. The Berlin Crisis of 1961: Soviet-American Relations and The Struggle for Power in the Kremlin, June-November 1961. Baltimore: Johns Hopkins University Press, 1973, 509 P.

8499 Smith, Jean Edward. Berlin Confrontation. Virginia Quarterly Review. 42:3 (Summer 1966), 349-365.

8500 Smith, Jean Edward. The Berlin Wall in Retrospect. Dalhousie Review. 47:2 (Summer 1967), 173-184.

8501 Smith, Jean Edward. The Defense of Berlin. Baltimore: Johns Hopkins University Press, 1963, 431 P.

8502 Smith, Jean Edward. Defense of Berlin. Ph.D. Thesis, Columbia University, 1964.

8503 Society for Cultural Relations With Foreign Countries. A Peaceful Solution of the Berlin Question Contributes to German Reunification: Official Statement of the German Democratic Republic on the Soviet Proposals for Berlin. Berlin (East): Society for Cultural Relations With Foreign Countries, 1958?, 23 P.

8504 The Soviet Proposal for a Free Berlin. Current History. 36:210 (February 1959), 107-114.

8505 Speier, Hans. Divided Berlin: The Anatomy of Soviet Political Blackmail. New York: Praeger, 1961, 201 P.

8506 Speier, Hans. The Soviet Threat to Berlin. Santa Monica: Rand Corporation, 1960, 67 P.

8507 Spencer, Robert A. Berlin: One Year of the Wall. International Journal. 17:4 (Autumn 1962), 420-425.

8508 Stolte, Stefan. The Berlin Problem and Peaceful Coexistence. Studies on the Soviet Union. 2:2 (1962), 5-13.

8509 Stone, Adolf. The Wall of Berlin. Social Education. 26:6 (October 1962), 292-294.

8510 Tanter, Raymond. Modelling and Managing International Conflict: The Berlin Crisis. Beverly Hills, Calif.: Sage, 1974, 288 P.

8511 Tanter, Raymond. Potter, William C. Modelling Alliance Behavior: East-West Conflict Over Berlin. Peace Science Society (International) Papers: Volume 20, the Rotterdam Conference, August 1972. Ed. Walter Isard and Julian Wolpert. Philadelphia, Pa.: Peace Science Society (International), 1973, Pp. 25-41.

8512 Toynbee, Arnold J. Symbols Men Live--and Die--for. New York Times Magazine. (20 November 1960), 13+.

8513 Trevor-Roper, Hugh R. Berlin: The Large and Basic Issue. New York Times Magazine. (25 February 1962), 13+.

8514 UK, Central Office of Information. The Meaning of Berlin. London: H.M. Stationery Office, 70-823, 1962, 24 P.

8515 US, Department of State. The Soviet Note on Berlin: An Analysis. Washington: Department of State Publication 6757, Government Printing Office, January 1959, 53 P.

8516 US, Department of State, Office of Public Services. Berlin: City Between Two Worlds. Washington: Department of State Publication 7389, Government Printing Office, Rev. Ed., 1960, 22 P.

8517 US, Department of State, Office of Public Services. Berlin--1961: Background. Washington: Department of State Publication 7257, Government Printing Office, Rev. Ed., October 1961, 48 P.

8518 The Vortex in Berlin: Divided Germany and European Security. Round Table. 49:194 (March 1959), 106-121.

8519 A Wall of Peace. Dresden: Zeit Im Bild, 1966, 63 P.

8520 Weyrauch, Erdmann, Compiler. Ulbricht's Wall. Bonn: Federal Ministry for All-German Affairs, 5Th Ed., 1965, 59 P.

8521 Windsor, Philip. City on Leave: A History of Berlin, 1945-1962. New York: Praeger, 1963, 276 P.

8522 Wiskemann, Elizabeth. Berlin Between East and West. World Today. 16:11 (November 1960), 463-472.

8523 Wright, Quincy. Some Legal Aspects of the Berlin Crisis. American Journal of International Law. 55:4 (October 1961), 959-965. Response By Wilhelm Grewe, Ajil, 56:2 (April 1962), 510-513.

8524 Ydit, Meir. International Territories From the "Free City of Cracow" to The "Free City of Berlin": A Study in the Historical Development of a Modern Notion in International Law and International Relations, 1815-1960. Leyden: Sythoff, 1961, 323 P.

8525 Young, Oran R. The Politics of Force: Bargaining During International Crises. Princeton: Princeton University Press, 1968, 438 P.

R.8. Normalization, 1969-

8526 Allemann, Fritz Rene. Berlin and the Four-Power Talks. German Tribune Quarterly Review. No. 12 (10 December 1970), 6-7.

8527 Bark, Dennis L. Agreement on Berlin: A Study of the 1970-72 Quadripartite Negotiations. Washington, D.C.: American Enterprise Institute for

Public Policy Research, 1974, 131 P.

8528 Bechtoldt, Heinrich. Berlin Agreement and Security Conference. Aussenpolitik. 23:1 (1972), 26-35.

8529 Birnbaum, Karl E. Pan-European Perspectives After the Berlin Agreement. International Journal. 27:1 (Winter 1971-72), 32-44.

8530 Bowers, Stephen R. The West Berlin Issue in the Era of Superpower Detente: East Germany and the Politics of West Berlin, 1968-1974. Ph.D. Thesis, University of Tennessee, 1975.

8531 Brandt, Willy. The Berlin Agreement. Atlantic Community Quarterly. 9:4 (Winter 1971-72), 493-495. Comment By Theo Sommer, Pp. 495-498.

8532 Doeker, Guenther. Melsheimer, Klaus. Schroeder, Dieter. Berlin and the Quadripartite Agreement of 1971. American Journal of International Law. 67:1 (January 1973), 44-62.

8533 Dulles, Eleanor Lansing. A New Berlin. Atlantic Community Quarterly. 11:1 (Spring 1973), 65-78.

8534 FRG, Press and Information Office. The Quadripartite Agreement on Berlin of September 3, 1971. Bonn: Press and Information Office, 1971, 119 P.

8535 Luchsinger, Fred. Berlin: A Test Case. Swiss Review of World Affairs. 20:10 (January 1970), 2-3. Possibility of Detente Tests Inner Strength of Western Cooperation.

8536 Mahncke, Dieter M. The Berlin Agreement: Balance and Prospects. World Today. 27:12 (December 1971), 511-521.

8537 Mahncke, Dieter M. The Berlin Problem at the Beginning of the Seventies. German Tribune Quarterly Review. No. 9 (March 1970).

8538 Mahncke, Dieter M. in Search of a Modus Vivendi for Berlin. World Today. 26:4 (April 1970), 137-146.

8539 Mattick, Kurt. The Berlin Agreements and Their History--A Look Back. German Tribune Quarterly Review. No. 17 (23 March 1972), 11-14.

8540 Merritt, Richard L. Divided Berlin: One Past and Three Futures. Journal of Peace Research. 9:4 (1972), 331-344.

8541 Poznanski, V. J. Agreement on West Berlin. Poland and Germany. 15:3-4 (July-December 1971), 3-7.

8542 Rush, Kenneth. The Berlin Agreement: An Assessment. Atlantic Community Quarterly. 10:1 (Spring 1972), 52-65.

8543 Text of Quadripartite Agreement on West Berlin--3 September 1971. Poland and Germany. 15:3-4 (July-December 1971), 34-47.

8544 UK, Central Office of Information, Reference Division. Berlin and the Problem of German Reunification. London: H.M. Stationery Office, 1970, 73 P.

8545 US, Department of State, Office of Media Services. Berlin: The Four-Power Agreement. Washington: Department of State Publication 8620, Government Printing Office, 1971, 14 P.

8546 Vysotsky, V. West Berlin. Moscow: Progress Publishers, 1974, 355 Pp.

8547 Wettig, Gerhard. The Berlin Policy of the USSR and the GDR. Aussenpolitik. 21:2 (1970), 136-149.

8548 Whetten, Lawrence L. The Problem of Berlin. World Today. 27:5 (May 1971), 222-227.

AUTHOR LIST

A Berlin Correspondent: 876
A Special Correspondent: 7118
A. D: 3442
A. H. H: 6728
A. W: 4703
Abbott, Edith: 5095
Abel, Elie: 537
Abel, Rein: 4005
Abosch, Heinz: 2725
Abraham, Karl: 5495
Abrahams, Frederick F: 5578
Abrams, Susan Diane: 5980
Abramson, Paul: 2047
Abs, Hermann J: 3726,3727,4318,4459,4490,6172
Acheson, Dean G: 1263,3612,6467,6898,7031
Achterberg, Erich: 3728
Adams, Carolyn Teich: 1473
Adams, Don: 5326
Addison, Lord: 910
Adebahr, Hubertus: 4319
Adel-Czlowiekowski, Ignatius J: 5670
Adelson, Joseph: 1710
Adenauer, Konrad: 2204,2599,2600,6174,6175,6468,6563,6899,6900,7718,7872
Adler, Elizabeth, Editor: 4971
Adler, Hans: 228
Adler, Margrit: 3098,6347
Adorno, Theodor W: 5789
Afheldt, Horst: 6975
Afro-Asian Solidarity Committee in the GDR: 4541,6773,6774,6784
Agar, Herbert: 298
Agentstvo Pechati "Novost": 7873
Agmon, Tamir: 4006
Agranat, Leon: 3397
Agricultural and Home Economics Evaluation & Info. Service: 3857,3858,3859,
    3860,3861,3862,3863,3864,3901,3902,3903,4071,5496,5830,5831
Ahlers, Conrad: 2374
Aica, Prodosh: 5724,5725
Aiken, Michael: 1615
Ainsztein, Reuben: 2239
Ajao, Aderogba: 5913
Albach, Horst: 3377,3835,5497
Albert, E. H: 7317,8060
Albert, Ernst: 6606
Albert, Lothar: 4704
Albertson, Ralph: 229
Albin, Felix: 2967
Albrecht, Karl: 7032
Albrecht, Ulrich: 1986
Albrecht-Carrie, Rene: 442,603,7874
Albright, Raymond J: 1918
Alden, A. J. L: 163
Alden, Robert: 3153
Alexander, D. J: 3867
Alexander, Edgar: 2205,4994
Alexander, H. G: 2726
Alexander, Lewis M: 129
Alexander, Thomas L: 6469
Alexandrov, V: 6348
Alexandrov, Vladimir: 3443,3444
Alexandrowicz, C: 4705
Alfert, Elizabeth: 2020
Allemann, Fritz Rene: 2240,2601,2602,2667,2727,2787,2815,2849,3154,7182,7228,
    8215,8526
Allen, Charles R: 2241
Allen, Claud G: 1877
Allen, Diane M: 514
Allen, Robert: 4921
Allerbeck, Klaus R: 4823,5671
Alley, Gary Lee: 6029
Allied Control Authority, Directorate of Economics: 3445,3446
Allied Forces, Supreme Headquarters, Chief of Staff: 735
Allied High Commission, Central Statistical Office: 200
Allied High Commission: 3587
Allison, Richard C: 3336
Allport, Gordon W: 2065
Allwood, Martin S: 4759
Almond, Gabriel A: 1322,2048,2277,2278,2279
Almond, Gabriel A., Editor: 689
Alperowitz, Gar: 515
Alson, Jacob: 2603
Alt, Herschel: 5096
Alt, Peter: 3613
Altbach, Philip G: 5579
Altena, John Van, Jr: 8335
Altenstetter, Christa: 5050
Althausen, Johannes: 4972
Altman, Wilfred: 4192
Ambrose, Stephen E: 587
Ambrosius, Wolfgang: 5081
Amen, Mary Zelime: 1424
American Committee on United Europe: 7033
American Enterprise Association: 8336
American Federation of Jews From Central Europe: 1084
American Historical Association: 443,444,911
American Institute of International Information: 4922
American Jewish Committee: 1211,1212,2462,2463,2464,2539,4923,4924,4925
American Jewish Congress: 4926
American Jewish Joint Distribution Committee: 1085,1086
American Ort Federation: 299
American University, Foreign Areas Study Division: 57
American-German Conference On East-West Tensions: 7802
Amerongen, Otto Wolff Von: 4388
Amery, Carl (Pseud. for Christian Mayer): 4874

Amery, Julian: 6336
Ames, Kenneth: 4706
Amnesty International: 3083
Amram, Philip W: 1746
An, Jack Young: 2507
Anderson, C. Arnold: 5663
Anderson, Eugene N: 5762
Anderson, Evelyn: 3155,3156,7875
Anderson, Graydon K: 3588
Anderson, H. Foster: 230
Anderson, Mosa: 604
Anderson, Nels: 2112,2135,4778
Andic, Suphan: 3799
Andrews, William G: 2788,2789
Andreyev, N: 6902
Andrus, Burton C: 912
Angelfort, Jupp: 1919
Anglo-Jewish Association: 2465
Anspacher, Heinz L: 231,300
Anspach, Ernest: 736
Anspacher, John M: 913
Anthon, Carl G: 2728,3157,3158,3159,5580,5914,6446,6564,7034,7035,8262,8337
Anweiler, Oskar: 5763
Apel, Erich: 4558
Apel, Hans: 2375,4594
App, Austin J: 343
Appleman, John A: 914
April, Nathan: 915
Aptaeker, Bettina: 4862
Aptaeker, Herbert: 6471,7803
Ardakyev, N: 4540
Arendt, Hannah: 2540
Arensberg, C. M: 5811
Arlt, Fritz: 5498
Armbruster, Wolfgang: 5499
Armstrong, Anne: 8125
Armstrong, John A: 1570
Army Times Editors: 8126
Armytage, Walter H: 5265
Arndt, Adolf: 1692
Arndt, Christian O: 5538
Arndt, Edward J: 5871
Arndt, Hans-Joachim: 1055,3836
Arndt, Helmut: 3911
Arndt, Herbert, and Others: 64
Arndt, Klaus Dieter: 3348,3837
Arnold, G. L: 2604,2605
Arnold, Hans: 6155,6156,6796
Arnold-Forster, Mark: 2954
Arntz, Helmut, Editor: 55
Arntz, Helmut: 51,53,54,7417
Aron, Raymond, Editor: 6869
Aronsfeld, C. C: 2508
Arski, Stefan: 7418
Arthur Andersen and Company: 1773
Artus, Jacques R: 4402
Arzinger, Rudolf: 3160,6349
Arzumanyan, A: 1965
Ashkenasi, Abraham: 2376
Assmann, Ingeborg: 5395,5581
Association For An Indivisible Germany: 7804
Association of Jewish Communities in the GDR: 4927
Astakhov, S: 6753
Atkinson, James T: 6903
Atlantic Bridge: 56
Aubert, Vilhelm: 5432
Aubrey, Henry G: 6447
Auburn, F. M: 6261
Audouard, Rolf: 4320
Audrieth, Ludwig F: 5832
Auer, Howard J. M., Jr: 5457
Auerbach, Philipp: 1837
Aufricht, Hans: 3730
Augstein, Rudolf: 979,1192,2206
Aurelius, Marcus (Pseud. for Walter Ernest Padley): 605
Aurich, Peter, and Others, Editors: 7419
Aurin, Kurt: 5396
Ausland, John C: 8338
Aust, Hans Walter: 2165,2729,3161,3912,4389,7123,7124,7876,7877,8108,8109,8339
Austin, Margretta S., Editor: 5751
Awni-Al-Ani: 4460
Axen, Hermann: 2968,3246,7577
Axis Victims League: 1087
Baade, Fritz: 3614
Baade, Hans W: 1179,1571,1676,8174
Bach, Julian, Jr: 757
Bachof, Otto: 1736,1737
Backer, John H: 3398,3399
Bader, Helmut: 1572,1762
Bader, Lothar: 7701
Bader, W. B: 1966
Bader, Werner: 2985
Badia, Gilbert: 7516
Baedecker, Karl: 8127
Baer, Theodore S: 3806
Baer, Werner: 4321
Baerwald, Friedrich: 3302,4875
Bahn, Eugene H: 6014
Bahr, Egon: 4491,6904
Baikalov, A: 1728
Bailey, George: 232,765,1920,2790,3674,8340
Bain, Trevor: 4254
Baker, James C: 4007,4008,4009
Baker, Kendall L: 2097,2098,4824,4825
Baker, Russell: 4322

Balabkins, Nicholas: 3400,3401,3402,3403,3404,4928,6754
Ball, Richard H: 2429
Baldwin, Charles C: 3447
Baldwin, Hanson W: 1921,6838,8341
Baldy, Francis H: 3448
Balfour, Michael: 517,691,1452
Balke, Siegfried: 4193,4267
Balling, Francis C: 445
Balogh, Thomas: 3383,3838,3839
Balow, Erich (Pseud.): 3162
Banasiak, Stefan: 7420
Bank for International Settlements, Monetary & Econ. Dept: 3732
Bank for International Settlements: 3731
Banks, Richard G: 5328
Bar-Zohar, Michel: 916,3449
Barach, Alvan L: 446
Baras, Victor: 3125,7578
Barclay, G. St. J: 6262
Barden, Judy: 4809
Baring, Arnulf M: 3126,6124
Bark, Dennis L: 7318,8527
Barkeley, Richard: 3163,7805
Barker, Dudley: 8263
Barker, Elisabeth: 8342
Barker, Ernest: 5726
Barley, Delbert: 344
Barman, Thomas: 6565
Barna, Tibor: 3913,3914
Barnes, Samuel H: 1323
Barnet, Richard J: 1703
Barnstorff, Hermann: 5764
Barnum, H. Gardiner: 130
Baron, Salo W: 4929
Barrett, Charles E: 4403
Barrister-at-Law: 917
Bartel, Walter: 2466,6350,6351
Bartels, H: 3349
Barth, Herbert: 6352,6905,7517,7579
Barth, Karl: 4973
Barth, Markus: 4974
Barth, Pius J: 5329
Bartl, Wilhelm: 4595
Bartlett, John L: 7125
Barton, Betty: 344
Barton-Dobenin, Joseph: 4010
Barzel, Rainer: 6906,7878
Bateman, Kenneth E: 5727
Bathurst, Maurice E: 1531,6907,8175
Batty, Peter: 3915
Baudissin, Wolf Graf Von: 1922,6908
Baudler, Paul G: 4011
Bauer, Edward F: 5981
Bauer, Leo: 4492,7126
Bauer, William Waldo: 5051,5052
Baum, Samuel: 4678
Baumann, Otto: 1967,1968,6353,7127
Baumert, Gerhard: 4784,4785,4793
Baumgaertel, Werner: 7879
Baumgart, Reinhard: 5982
Baumgarten, Peter: 3840
Baur, Fritz: 1747
Baur, Walter: 2242,3078,8029
Baxter, Craig: 2358
Baylis, Thomas A: 2909,2910,3247,4596,4597
Bays, Robert Alexander, Jr: 6030
Bazillion, Richard: 5257
Beach, Vincent W: 7806
Beal, Edwin F: 4194,4195
Beauchamp, George E., Editor: 5752
Bechtoldt, Heinrich: 6648,6785,6976,7128,8528
Beck, Carl, Editor: 4622
Beck, Earl Ray: 918,5458,5948
Beck, Elmer A: 5163
Beck, Maximilian: 447
Beck, Robert H: 5313
Becker, Egon: 6977
Becker, Frederick A: 7229
Becker, Hellmut: 5397,5521
Becker, Helmut: 4012,4043
Becker, Hermann-Josef: 4268,4269
Becker, Howard: 1180,4760,4761,4786,4826
Becker, Joerg: 2021
Beckner, Earl R: 4094
Bednareck, Horst: 6432
Bednarik, Karl: 4095
Beer, Francis A: 6909
Beer, Max: 2606,6804
Beer, R. R: 5949
Beglov, S: 6607
Beguin, J. C: 1738
Behrendt, Albert: 4118
Behrendt, Guenther: 3350,3868
Beigel, Greta: 4975
Beijer, G: 347
Beitzell, Robert, Editor: 518
Belding, Robert E: 5314,5500
Belgion, Montgomery: 692
Bell, Alan: 542
Bell, Daniel: 1324
Bell, Frank E: 5728
Bell, G. K. A: 3544
Bellstedt, Christoph, Editor: 4323
Beloff, Max: 1361,6805
Belth, Nathan C: 2603
Ben-David, Joseph: 5849

Bender, Peter: 3164,3248,7651,8061
Bendix, Reinhard: 2049,4059
Benecke, Theodor: 1987
Benes, Edward: 448
Benjamin, Hilde: 3019,3062,3063
Benjamin, Michael: 3064,3065
Bennett, Jack: 3567
Bennett, James V: 1838
Bennett, Lowell: 8264
Bennion, Sherilyn C: 5164
Benson, George C. S: 738
Bentley, Eric: 6062
Benton, Arthur: 1142
Benton, Wilbourn E., Editor: 919
Benton, William: 5330
Bentwich, Norman D: 301,345,846,847,1088,1089,1090,1091,1092,2668,3615,3616,
    4930,4931,4932,8128,8129
Beranek, Robert E: 8343
Berdes, George R: 2730
Berezowski, Z: 2731,2732,7183,7184,7319,7363,7364,7421,7422
Berger, Alfred: 8130
Berger, Don: 1802
Berger, Hans: 606
Berger, Joseph A: 302
Berger, Peter L: 1425
Berger, Stephen D: 1362
Berger, Wolfgang: 4598
Berghahn, Volker: 2467
Berghes, Ingeborg Von: 6729
Bergmann, Heinrich: 2437,2438
Bergo (Pseud.): 3450,3568,6566,7185
Bergstraesser, Arnold: 1426
Bergstraesser, Ludwig: 1325
Berk, Alexander: 8344
Berkes, Ross N: 607,1056,1213
Berkley, Eliot S: 6125
Berkley, George E: 1616
Berkowitz, Morton: 7036,8265
Berkowitz, William R: 4762
Berlin, Central Office For Education In Politics: 8131
Berlin, Press And Information Office: 8132,8133,8345,8346,8347
Berlin, Senator For Construction And Housing Affairs: 8247
Berlin, Senator For Economics: 8216
Berlin, Senator For Public Health: 8217
Berlin, Senator For The Interior: 8218
Berlin-Reinickendorf, Bezirksamt: 8135
Berndt, Siegfried: 5872
Bernheim, Roger: 7671
Bernitz, Alexander: 4634
Bernstein, Herbert L: 3337,5209
Berry, Wallace W: 2439
Bertram, Christoph: 7004
Bertsch, Herbert: 2140,8353
Besson, Waldemar: 6126,6127,6472
Besters, Hans: 3841
Bethell, Jethro, Editor: 1453
Bethell, Nicholas: 588
Bettany, A. Guy: 739,1181
Bettelheim, Bruno: 1182
Bettiza, Enzo: 5227
Bevan, Aneurin, and Others: 6839
Beveridge, William H., Lord: 193,608
Bevin, Ernest: 1214,1249
Beyer, Heinz: 2934
Beyer, Karl-Heinz: 3020
Beyme, Klaus Von: 5790,7230
Bialek, Robert: 3121
Bidault, Georges: 1215
Bidwell, Percy Wells: 1143,2541,3589
Bieber, Hugo: 4933
Bieberstein, Joerg: 1812
Biebl, Rudi: 3066
Biedermann, C: 4324
Biehl, Dieter: 171,3800
Bielfeldt, Claus: 172
Bierfelder, W. H: 5833
Bieri, Ernst: 346,4876,5165
Bierzanek, Remigiusz: 7423,7691
Biggs-Davison, John: 7129
Bilainkin, George: 8136
Billerbeck, Klaus: 4493
Billington, James H: 7231
Billoux, Francois: 6649
Binavince, Emilio: 1839
Binder, David: 2166,2167,7580
Birch, Lionel: 6840
Bird, Dillard E: 2280
Bird, Eugene K: 920
Birdwood, C. B: 2007
Birdwood, Lord: 7365
Birley, Robert: 848,5331
Birnbaum, Immanuel: 6263,7186
Birnbaum, Karl E: 7232,8062,8529
Birnbaum, Norman: 5950
Birrenbach, Kurt: 6448,6910,6911,7233
Bischof, Alfons: 4292
Bishop, Joseph W., Jr: 6180,8176
Biswas, K. P: 2733
Bittner, Horst: 3249
Bitzer, Ronald: 7719
Bizonal Economic Area, Admin. for Food, Agric. & Forestry: 3869
Bizonal Economic Area, Administration for Economics: 3451
Bizonal Economic Area, Administrative Council: 3405
Black, Hilary: 3250
Blackman, C. F: 6123

Blaettner, Fritz: 5433
Blank, Theodor: 5013
Bleimann, Robert: 3251,7234
Blessing, Karl: 3734
Blishchenkov, I. P: 6128
Bloch, Enid Greenberg: 233
Bloch, Max: 5014
Bloemer, Klaus: 7037,7880
Blow, Jonathan: 1264,6701
Bluecher Von Wahlstatt, Kurt: 234
Bluecher, Franz: 3570,3590,4494
Bluecher, Viggo Graf: 5250
Blume, O: 4091
Blumenfeld, Erik: 5672
Blumenfeld, F. Yorick: 2734,3165,8004,8063,8354
Blumenson, Martin, Editor: 740
Blumenson, Martin: 7881
Blumenthal, Henry: 5166
Blumenthal, Ralph: 4827
Blumenthal, Werner Michael: 4196,4197,4233
Blumenwitz, Dieter: 1677
Board of Deputies of British Jews: 4934
Boarman, Patrick M: 3617,4444
Boas International Publishing Company: 24
Bock, Peter G: 8265
Bock, Siegfried: 7652,8064
Bockelmann, Horst: 3785
Boden, Hans: 4325
Bodenheimer, Edgar: 1664
Bodenman, Paul S: 5639,5873,5874,5875
Bodungen, Thilo Von: 1803
Boeck, Klaus: 4053
Boeckenheuer, Jessie M: 5834
Boeckman, M. June: 6702
Boehl, Erich, Editor: 8137,8138
Boenle, Bernd: 25
Boenle, Karl-Heinz: 1183
Boehm, Anton: 6473
Boehm, Eric H: 449
Boehme, Hans: 4599
Boening, W. R: 4255,4256
Boelling, Klaus: 1454
Boenau, Arthur Bruce: 1947
Boening, Eberhard: 5582
Boeninger, Hildegard R: 1
Boenisch, Alfred: 3675
Boerner, Holger: 8005
Boerner, Manfred: 4707
Boettcher, Carl: 1783
Boettcher, Manfred: 4600,4657
Boetticher, Dietrich Von: 4461
Bohlen, Adolf: 5143
Bohlig, Robert: 4322
Bohndorf, Michael T: 1774,1867,1868,1888
Bohring, Guenther, Editor: 5915
Boldt, Karl: 3994
Bolen, C. W: 2669
Bolesch, Hermann Otto: 2168
Bolles, Blair: 7130
Bolling, Landrum: 3099
Bollinger, Klaus: 3263,7581,7982
Bolte, Karl Martin: 4763,4793
Bolten, Seymour R: 2304
Bolton, J. Harvey: 4270
Bolz, Lothar: 7692
Bond, Martyn A: 6015
Bondy, Curt: 5791
Bondy, Francois: 3100
Bonhoeffer, Emmi: 921
Bonn, Moritz J: 609,849,922,1404,2305,2306,2468,2542,2543,2544,2545,2546,2607,
  2735,3481,3571,3572,3970,4404,6181,7038,7104,7320,7807,7808
Bonner, Thomas N: 2608,2609
Bonnet, Henri: 7105
Boothby, Robert: 6182,6183
Borch, Herbert Von: 6265
Borchardt, Knut: 3719
Borgese, Giuseppe Antonio: 235
Borinski, Fritz: 5332
Born, Lester K: 5850
Bosch, William J: 923,924
Bosse, Hans: 4495
Bossenbrook, William J: 236,237
Botne, Michael: 2889
Botsas, Eleutherios N: 4257
Botsford, Keith: 5983
Boudin, Anna P: 303
Bouman, Pieter Jan: 347
Bourke-White, Margaret: 610
Bouscaren, Anthony T: 2359,2360
Boutros, Samir R: 1455
Bower, Blair T: 5107
Bowers, Stephen R: 8530
Bowie, Robert R: 2670,6474,6912,8177
Boyd, Andrew: 8065
Boylan, Marguerite T: 5040
Boyle, Kay: 611,2671
Boynton, G. Robert: 2050
Bracher, Karl Dietrich: 1456,2509,2736,6266
Brack, Hans: 5228
Bradley, Jack A: 4293
Brailsford, Evamaria: 6184
Brailsford, H. N: 1144,6184
Braje, Wilfried: 2377
Bramsted, Ernest K: 1457
Brand, Friedrich: 2378

Brand, G: 925
Brand, George H: 4976
Brand, Joel: 304
Brandes, O. Jean: 4787
Brandt, Alfred: 3735
Brandt, Edward R: 6475
Brandt, Gerhard: 6841
Brandt, Heinz: 7882
Brandt, Joseph A: 5167
Brandt, Karl: 741,742,6185
Brandt, Sabine: 6063
Brandt, Willy: 2169,2170,2850,2851,6267,6268,6269,6449,6450,6476,7005,7039,
    7236,7883,8355,8356,8357,8358,8359,8531
Brant, Stefan (Pseud. for Klaus Harpprecht): 3127
Brantley, Susan K: 2099
Brasch, Horst: 6042
Brass, Heinz: 4684
Brass, Paul: 1895
Brauer, Anna E: 5082
Brauer, Max: 1923
Braun, Heinrich: 5007,5033
Braun, Joachim Freiherr Von: 348
Braun, Joachim: 2171
Braun, Sigismund Freiherr Von: 7131
Braunthal, Gerard: 1813,1969,2281,2282,2312,2430,2672,2852,3676,4294,5229,6270,
    6271,7321
Brecher, Michael: 6755,6756
Brechling, Frank R. P: 3351,4326,4405
Brecht, Arnold: 450,1364,1405,1573,1574,1575,2172,7720
Bredow, W. Von: 1924
Bregman, Alexander: 7188,7189,7366,7367,7368
Brehm, Eugen: 451
Bremmer, Ekhard: 4406,4468
Breit, Peter Klaus: 7884
Breitenkamp, Edward C: 5144
Breitenlohner, Cynthia A: 3870
Breitenstein, Rolf: 6157
Breitling, Rupert: 1460
Bremen, Senator for Schools and Education: 5459
Brems, Hans J: 3352,4462,7132
Brentano, Heinrich Von: 6567
Breslauer, Walter: 1093
Bressensdorf, Erwin B. Von: 7006
Brett-Smith, Richard N. B: 238,8139
Bretton, Henry L: 1535,2379,2380,2610,2611,2612,5640,6477
Brezinka, Wolfgang: 5641
Brickman, Harry: 4119
Brickman, Myrtle: 3981
Brickman, William W: 5333,5876
Brickner, Richard M: 239,446
Bridge, F. H. S: 1814
Briefs, G. A: 785
Briggs, Herbert W: 6186
Bringmann, Wolfgang: 2035
Brinkers, Helmut: 1532
British Productivity Council: 3916
Brockway, Fenner: 612
Broder, Simon: 1775,1776
Brodie, Bernard: 6913
Brodrick, Alan H: 7721
Brogan, Denis W: 6650
Bromke, Adam: 7369,7370,7371
Brompton, Henry: 1572
Bronfenbrenner, Urie: 4789
Brookes, Marilyn: 2307
Brooks, Alfred Glenn: 6016
Brosse, Therese: 5074
Brouwer, Marten: 2113,2114
Brown, James A: 3008
Brown, James F: 3166,7582
Brown, Lewis H: 3545,3591
Brown, Macalister: 349
Brown, Michael Barratt, and Others: 4390
Brown, Michael Barratt: 3167
Brown, Ralph A: 6478
Brown, Thomas K: 6079
Browne, E. Moxon: 8066
Browne, George S: 5317
Brozek, Andrzej: 350,7424,7453
Bruecher, Horst, Editor: 4463
Bruecher, Horst: 4327
Brueckner, Leo J: 5334
Brundert, Willi: 7885
Bruner, Jerome S: 2115
Brunner, Guido: 6129
Brunner, Ronald D: 2510
Brunotte, Heinz: 4995
Bryson, Phillip J: 4496,4601
Brzezinski, Zbigniew K: 6479,6914,7190,7583,7584,7886,7887,7888
Brzezinski, Zbigniew K., Moderator: 7237
Buchan, Alastair, Editor: 6568
Buchanan, William: 2116,2117
Bucholz, Erich: 3021,3022,5128,5138
Buchwitz, Otto: 7809
Buckholts, Paul Omar: 131
Buckhout, Gerard Lee: 1427
Buckley, Dennis La Vern: 5480
Buechel, Hans Joachim: 4665
Buehring, Guenter: 7653,7904
Bullivan, Keith: 6008
Bullock, Alan: 6569
Bundschuh, Wilhelm: 452
Bundy, Mcgeorge, Editor: 6480
Bundy, Mcgeorge: 570
Bunn, Ronald F: 2283,2284,2285,2286,2287,5210,5211,5212,5539

Burchard, Hans-Joachim: 4328,7133
Burchardt, F. A: 3546
Burchett, Wilfred G: 7722
Burin, Frederic Siegfried: 1665
Burisch, M: 4497
Burkett, Tony: 2308
Burkhart, Sylvia Davis: 6031
Burkus, John: 5015
Burmeister, Werner: 2548,2549,2673,6570,7239,7723
Burn, Barbara B: 5583
Burns, Arthur R: 3618
Burns, Emile: 3168,7724
Burridge, Trevor David: 453
Burstein, Paul: 2051
Burtenshaw, D: 6703
Busch, Alexander: 5657
Busch, Benjamin: 1894
Busch, E: 4729,6354
Busch, Fritz: 4295
Buschbeck, Malte: 5584
Business Europe: 4013
Business International S. A: 3677
Bussche, Axel Von Dem: 6842
Busse, Gisela Von: 5851
Butler, Ewan: 8140
Butler, Harold: 850
Butz, Otto: 1423,6481
Byford-Jones, W: 8141
Byrnes, James F: 743,744,1216,1217,1249
Byrnes, Robert F: 7322
Byrnes, Robert F., Editor: 7191
Byroade, Henry A: 6482
C. A. M: 351
C. C. W: 4877
Cahan, J. Flint: 3619
Cahnman, Werner J: 7725
Cairncross, A. K: 3620
Calder, Donald B: 4464
Callender, Harold: 868,7106
Calleo, David: 6915
Callmann, H. William: 1094
Calmann, John, Editor: 58
Calvocoresh, Peter: 927
Calvocoressi, Peter: 928
Cameron, D. Ewen: 446
Cameron, James: 2511
Camp, Glen D., Jr: 8361
Camp, Glen D., Jr., Editor: 8360
Campbell, Angus: 6483
Campbell, John C: 6484,7810
Canine, Ralph J: 2550
Cantril, Hadley: 2052,2117
Capper-Johnson, Karlin: 7853
Carey, James B: 4120
Carey, Jane Perry Clark: 305,2288,7726,7727
Carleton, William G: 2551
Carlson, Howard K: 3592
Carmichael, Joel: 929,1057,6017
Carney, Brian: 3772
Carr, Albert Z: 3483
Carr, Robert A: 3406
Carr, William G: 8219
Carroll, Berenice A: 8006
Carroll, Doris: 8177
Carroll, Mitchell B: 4465
Carsch, Henry: 2022
Carsten, Francis L: 5916,6043
Carstens, Karl: 7240
Carter, Dorothy Jean: 2046
Carter, Frank T. C: 6044
Carter, Gwendolen M., Editor: 1477,3340
Carter, John P: 4296
Carthago, D. E. (Pseudonym): 454
Carthew, Anthony: 8362
Cartwright, Hilary: 1792
Cash, Webster C: 4730
Casper, Gerhard: 1840
Cassidy, Paul J: 2053
Cassidy, Velma Hastings: 1265,1326
Castberg, Frede: 1704
Castles, Stephen: 4258
Cate, Donald Francis: 4872
Cattani, Alfred: 2853,2854,3252,3253,6786,7585
Catudal, Honore Marc, Jr: 8223
Catudal, Honore Marc, Jr: 8220,8221,8222,8224
Caty, Gilbert: 5862
Cecil, Robert: 520
Celovsky, Boris: 2289
Center for Auto Safety: 3917
Cerf, Jay H: 5977
Cerf, Walter: 5585
Chablani, S. P: 353
Chalmers, Douglas A: 2381,2382,2390
Chamberlain, Joseph P: 306
Chamberlin, William Henry: 2243,2737,6272
Chambers, S. P: 3573
Champon, Albert: 7728
Chandler, William Mayhew: 2054
Chaplin, Dennis: 1948,8363
Chapline, Allen: 5315
Chapman, Brian: 1576
Chaput De Saintonge, Rolland A. A: 1577
Charisius, Albrecht: 2006,6916
Charles, Max: 8269
Chase, John L: 521,522

Chatterjee, Subrata: 5917
Chaumont, Charles: 6806
Cherne, Leo: 930,8270
Chester, T. E: 3678
Chettiar, L: 5586
Child, Frank C: 4407
Childs, David: 78,2173,2383,2384,2512,2791,2816,2817,2911,2969,2986,3169,3254,
3255
Childs, James Bennett: 2,3,4
Chinn, Herman I: 5832
Chiout, Herbert: 5540
Chmielewski, Mieczyslaw: 1095,1096
Chopra, H. S: 6651
Chopra, Maharaj K: 2987
Christen, Peter: 745
Christenser, Vagn A. C: 2385
Christian Democratic Union, Federal Secretariat: 2363
Christian Democratic Union: 2361,2362
Christie, Donald M: 32
Christofferson, H. C: 5335
Chuikov, Vasilii Ivanovich: 589
Churchill, Winston S: 590,1218,7040,7729
Ciolkosz, A: 2386
Cisar, Mary Ann: 4498
Civis Germanicus: 613
Clare, G. P: 132
Clarion, Nicolas: 2470
Clark, Dale: 746
Clark, Delbert: 931,6843
Clark, Joseph: 1266
Clark, Sydney Aylmer: 26
Clark, William: 747
Clarke, Eric T: 5729
Claude, Henri: 6652
Claude, Inis L., Jr: 354,355
Clausen, Oliver: 6018
Claussen, Wilhelm: 5016
Clay, Dorothy N: 5474
Clay, Lucius D: 748,749,750,6188,8365
Clayton, William L: 523
Clemens, Diane Shaver: 524
Clemens, Walter C., Jr: 7323
Clemens, Walter R: 1841,1842,1843,1844
Clement, Alain: 2792
Cleveland, Harlan: 6917
Clews, John: 3009
Cloe, Carl W: 3452
Close, Richard B: 1970
Clough, Shepard B: 7041
Cobb, Alice: 307
Cogan, Morris: 5316
Cohen, Benjamin J: 3484
Cohen, Elliot E: 2552
Cohen, Elliott A: 7324
Cohn, Ernst J: 1097,1643,1673,1748,1749,1768,3338,3519
Cohn, Ernst J., Editor: 1644
Cohn, Kurt: 932
Cohn, Thomas S: 2022
Coit, Eleanor G: 5501
Coker, J. A: 7107
Colby, Reginald: 1925,6704
Cole, G. D. H: 3485
Cole, John Alfred: 27
Cole, R. Taylor: 4199
Cole, R. Taylor: 1578,1678,1679,1680,1885,2290,2471,4198,5587
Coleman, Herbert J: 3934
Coles, Harry L: 751
Collester, Jerry B: 1524
Collier, David S., Editor: 7192,7889,8366
Collins, Ellen: 6705
Collins, Henry H., Jr: 693
Colvin, Ian: 1145,1219,1220,1268,8271
Colwell, Ernest C: 1146
Combs, Jerry W: 4678
Comfort, Louise K: 2055
Commager, Henry Steele: 525
Commentator: 6355,8045,8367
Commerce Clearing House: 4014
Commission for the Drafting of a Socialist Constitution: 2890
Committee Against Mass Expulsions: 356
Committee for Economic Development: 4329
Committee for the Protection of Human Rights of the GDR: 1705,1971
Common Council for American Unity: 6485
Communist Party of Germany: 1719
Comstock, Alzada: 3486,3520
Conant, Grace Richards: 3170
Conant, James Bryant: 2613,2614,2674,3303,6486,6487,7811
Confederation of Free German Trade Unions: 3023
Conference on Jewish Material Claims Against Germany: 1098,1099
Congress of East German Regional Representatives: 3171
Conlan, William H: 8368
Conley, Samuel Glenn: 6097
Conly, Robert Leslie: 2675
Connell, Brian: 2615
Connors, Michael F: 6274,6275
Conover, Helen F., Editor: 297
Conrad, Klaus: 4015
Conrad, Richard: 4977,5258,5259
Conradt, David P: 1507,2309,2431,2855,2881,5792
Constantine of Bavaria, Prince: 6189
Constantopoulos, Demetrios S: 1406
Contimart: 4331
Converse, Philip E: 5243
Cook, Alice Hanson: 4121,5502,5522
Cook, F. G. Alletson: 1147

Cookridge, E. H: 2008
Cooper, Carolyn C: 6996
Cooper, Elias: 2174
Copeman, George H: 4060
Copeman, H. W. M: 1753
Copleston, Frederick C: 8272
Cordes, Bernhard H: 1706
Cormack, Una: 5042
Cornell, Francis G: 5398
Cornelsen, Doris: 8250
Cornides, Wilhelm: 7890
Cornu, Auguste: 2387
Correns, Erich: 2955
Costrell, Edward S: 5336
Cotton, Clare M: 3918
Cottrell, Donald P: 5588,5589
Council for Education in World Citizenship: 485
Council for Protection of Rights and Interests of Jews: 1100,1101
Council for a Democratic Germany: 5337
Council of Europe, Consultative Assembly: 6706
Council of Europe, Council for Cultural Co-Operation: 5642
Coverdale and Colpitts, Consulting Engineers: 4297
Coverley, Harvey M: 2472
Cowan, Laing Gray: 6707
Cowles, Willard B: 933
Cox, Harvey: 4878
Cox, Henry B: 7730
Craddock, Walter R: 6708
Craig, Gordon A: 6130,6918,6919,7731
Cramer, Frederick H: 1148
Cramer, John F: 5317
Crane, Wilder W., Jr: 1458,1553
Crauford, W. G: 1793
Crawley, Aidan: 79
Credit Institute for Reconstruction: 4500
Crespi, Leo P: 2056,2057,2096,4016
Creuzburg, Harry: 3024,3067
Croan, Melvin: 877,2912,2935,2956,3172,3173,3174,3175,3256,3257,4978,6045,6953,
  7586,7587,7588,7891,8067
Cromwell, Richard S: 2432,2473
Crosfield and Sons, Ltd: 4560
Crossman, George R: 4200
Crossman, Richard H. S: 6191
Crotch, W. Walter: 870
Cruikshanks, Randal L: 3327,3331
Cullity, John P: 1579,1580,5399
Culver, Lowell W: 1617,1618
Culver, Wallace W: 2023
Cumming, Hugh S: 3176
Cumming, William P: 5590
Cunliffe, W. Gordon: 5984
Czakowski, Antoni: 7423
Czaya, Eberhard: 6775,6776
Czechanowski, S: 2856,7193,7241,7242,7372,7373,7374,7892
Czempiel, Ernst-Otto: 5793,6276
Czirjak, Laszlo: 4658
D'Arms, Edward F: 1146
D. F: 3101
Dagon, Roger: 4466
Dahl, Guenther: 2244
Dahrendorf, Ralf: 1429,1430,2141,2857,3304,4764,5408,5781,7134
Dalcher, Laurence P: 5168
Dale, Edwin L., Jr: 7135
Dallin, David J: 7325
Dalma, Alfons: 8369
Damm, Walter: 1815
Damner, H. W: 1988
Daniel, Anita: 4810
Daniel, Vera: 5664
Daniell, Raymond: 240,614,615,752,753,934,3971,3972,8142
Daniels, William G: 1794
Danton, J. Periam: 5852
Darby, Joseph J: 4391
Daspach, Anita Mallinckrodt: 5251
Dasbach, Fernando Louis: 5140
Dash, Shreeram Chandra: 1407
Daskiewicz, Krystyna: 935
Dautricourt, Joseph Y: 936
Daven, Angela: 4332
Davenport, John: 3621
Davidson, Basil: 1269,2474,2553,2676,3102,6844,6845,6846
Davidson, Eugene: 754,937,938,3177
Davin, Louis E: 3622
Davis, Earl: 2044
Davis, Franklin M., Jr: 755
Davis, Jerome: 878
Davis, Kathleen S: 5541
Davis, Melton S: 4122
Davis, Paul Ford: 5591
Davis, Robert Gorham: 4935
Davison, W. Phillips, Editor: 6152
Davison, W. Phillips: 2058,5145,5146,5147,5252,8273,8274
Dawidowicz, Lucy S: 308
Dawis, Rene V: 4768
Dawson, John P: 1795,1796
Dawson, John S: 6032
De La Malene, Christian: 6868
De Mendelssohn, Peter: 694,1896,6847
De Menil, Lois A. P: 6571
De Schweinitz, Dorothea: 4201
De Young, Chris A: 5340
Deak, Istvan, Editor: 7299
Dean, Robert W: 4333,4392,4750,7508
Dean, Vera Micheles: 526,756,1149,1221,1222,3409,3410,6488,7043
Debatin, Helmut: 3802

Debevoise, Eli Whitney: 757
Debrouwere, Jan: 6730
Deethardt, John Fred, Jr: 5542
Deforest, Walter R: 5053
Dehio, Ludwig: 6277
Delarue, Maurice: 6653
Delfiner, Henry: 5573
Delmer, Sefton: 2009
Delong, Vaughn R: 5266,5338,5339
Demetz, Peter: 5985,6064,6080,6094
Deming, Robert C: 5523
Deml, Ferdinand: 134,135
Deneke, Helena: 4811
Denmark, Ministry for Foreign Affairs: 1223
Dennis, Jack: 2059,2100
Denny, Harold: 1184
Denton, Geoffrey: 3842
Dernburg, H. J: 1989,3521,4334
Derrick, Michael: 851
Detaleffsen, Erich: 7732
Detlefsen, J. A: 4061
Detwiler, Donald S: 5592
Deuss, Hanns: 3737,3738
Deutsch, B: 8068
Deutsch, Harold C: 6489,6490,6654,8370
Deutsch, K: 8068
Deutsch, Karl W: 1459,1460,6131,6132,6133,6278,6279,6280,6281
Deutsch, Martin: 4936
Deutscher, Isaac: 7326
Deutschkron, Inge: 6757
Devereux, Edward C., Jr: 4788,4789
Devries, Henry P: 3522
Dewhurst, C. H: 879
Dewhurst, J. Frederic, Et Al: 3354
Dewitt, Charles M: 5481
Di Palma, Giuseppe: 2060
Diamond, Dorothy M: 4635
Dibelius, Otto: 4879,4880
Dicagans, Hans: 6572
Dick, Royer: 6282
Dickens, Arthur G: 852
Dickerman, Watson: 5524
Dickinson, Robert E: 120,121,122,136,137
Dickopf, Karl: 616
Dicks, Henry V: 241,242,2024
Dickson, Alec: 309
Diebold, William, Jr: 3973,7108,7109
Dieck, Margret: 3803
Dieckmann, Johannes: 6356
Diederich, Nils: 1508,2310
Diessner, Gernard: 7589
Dietrich, George Philipp: 4123
Dietrich, Helmut: 4708
Dietrich, Hermann R: 1365
Dietze, Constantin Von: 3871
Dietze, Gottfried: 1666,1693,1763,2677
Dievenow, Friedrich G: 8110
Diggins, John P: 2475
Dill, Marshall: 80,2616
Dill, Richard W: 6158
Dillard, Hardy C: 6451
Dirks, Walter: 7243
Dirnecker, Rupert: 1681
Disnaw, Frank H: 1534
Dittberner, Juergen: 2311
Dittmar, Henry G: 758,1270
Dittmer, Lowell: 2513
Divo-Institut: 4467,4501,4828
Dluski, O: 6357
Dobo, Maurice: 3487
Dobbert, Helga: 5153
Dobbins, Claude Edwin: 3872
Dobell, Peter: 4124
Dobias, F: 6358
Dobriansky, Lev E: 7194
Dobrich, Joseph J. R: 6848
Documents on Berlin, 1943-1963: 8411
Dodd, Thomas J: 939
Doeblin, Alfred: 617
Doeuring, Karl: 1707
Doeker, Guenther: 5230,8532
Doenhoff, Marion Graefin: 7244,7733
Doenitz, Karl: 940
Doering, Guenter: 2175
Doernberg, Stefan: 1972,7654,7894
Dohmen, Guentner: 5565
Dohnanyi, Klaus Von: 7136
Dohnke, Dieter: 4863
Dolff, Helmuth: 5525
Dolgilevich, R: 3355
Dolinin, V: 6655
Dolive, Linda Landers: 1619
Doman, Nicholas: 941
Domandi, Mario: 4829
Domorowski, Erich Franz Otto: 2142
Domdey, K.-H: 4685,4686
Domes, Alfred, Editor: 7245
Domke, Martin: 1878
Donaldson, Gordon: 2678,4937
Donelan, Michael: 6609
Donner, Joern: 8371
Donnison, F. S. V: 527,853
Donors Association for German Science: 5593,5594
Donovan, Frank Robert: 8275
Donovan, Herman Lee: 5595

Dorn, Herbert: 6797
Dorn, Walter L: 528
Dornberg, John: 3259,3305,3306
Dorpalen, Andreas: 1185,1224,5878,7734
Dorr, Harold M: 1535
Dorrance, Graemes: 4468
Dos Passos, John: 759
Douglas, A. Vibert: 28
Douglas, William A: 1897,2440
Dovifat, Emil: 5169,5674
Dovring, Karen: 4636
Dowell, Jack D: 1898,2364,2388,2793,4202,4203,4881,4882,7195
Dowling, Walter C: 3307
Draynich, Alex N: 1461,1462
Draper, Theodore: 8372
Draper, William H., Jr: 695,1252
Drath, Viola Herms: 2176
Dress, Hans: 7895
Dreyer, H. Peter: 6459
Dreyer, Heinrich M: 4259
Dreyfuss, Allan: 942
Driscoll, Justin A: 5267
Dronnig, Ulrich: 4687,4709
Drobnik, J: 7376
Droege, Heinz: 6807
Droller, Gerard: 1256
Dross, Armin: 7377
Drozdzynski, Aleksander: 2245
Drummond, Andrew Landale: 4996
Drummond, Gordon D: 2389
Drummond, Stuart: 1620,2818
Drutmann, D: 311
Drzewieniecki, W. M: 7426
Du Bois, Josiah E: 943
Dubrovin, Vi: 6360,6361,6656
Duchene, Francois: 7246
Duckwitz, Georg Ferdinand: 4469,7007,7247
Dudgeon, Ruth A: 529
Duebber, Ulrich: 2312
Duerrhammer, Wilhelm: 1816
Duesenberg, Albert: 5170
Duggan, Stephen: 618,1150,5318
Duker, Abraham G: 4944
Dulles, Allen Welsh: 1225,1366
Dulles, Eleanor Lansing: 3178,4679,6573,7812,8007,8276,8373,8374,8375,8533
Dulles, John Foster: 6491
Dunham, Chadbourne: 6098
Dunlop, Sir John Kinninmont: 81
Dunner, Joseph: 760
Duroselle, J. B: 6657
Dusanyck, Walter: 7196
Dutt, Vidya Prakash: 6283
Duverger, Maurice: 4812
Dworkin, Martin S: 6492
Dybwad, Gunnar: 5075
Dyson, Kenneth H. F: 1526,1527
Dziewanowski, M. K: 6658,7197
E. J. P. Publications: 4017
E. P. W: 455
E. W: 6709
Earl, Lewis H: 4181
Earle, Edward Mead: 6493
East European Fund: 4561
Easterly, B: 750
Eaton, J. W: 456
Eaton, Ken: 2554
Ebenstein, William: 82,457,619
Eberhardt, Karl-Heinz: 3025
Ebsworth, Raymond: 854
Eckert, Gerhard: 5231
Eckert, Heinz: 3919
Eckes, Wolfgang: 1581
Economic Commission for Europe: 4731
Edding, Friedrich: 357,5596,5597
Edelman, Murray: 4182
Eden, Anthony: 855,6610
Edenhofner, Siegfried A: 5503
Edinger, Lewis J: 1463,1509,1510,1973,2143,2144,2145,2177,2390,2858,6131,6132,
    6133,6280,6281,6920
Editors of German International: 4502
Edwards, Morris O: 761
Eec, Monetary Committee: 3740,3741
Egler, Gert: 2957
Ehard, Hans: 944
Ehrhardt, Carl A: 6494,7137,7138,7139,7140,7141
Ehrmann, Henry W: 1151
Eich, Hermann: 2738
Eichler, Willi: 620,1408
Eichler, Wolfgang: 1845
Eifler, Margret: 6065
Eilers, Rudolph M: 6192
Eilsberger, Rupert: 5598
Einhorn, Claere: 6978
Einhorn, Hans: 3026
Eisenhower, Dwight D: 591,6495,6496
Eisler, Robert: 1271
Eith, Wolfgang: 5599
Elder, Glen H., Jr: 4790,4791,4792
Eliasberg, Vera Franke: 2313
Eliot, George F: 458
Eliot, Martha M., and Others: 5076
Elkins, Thomas Henry: 1464,8143
Ellinger, Thomas R: 5400
Elliott, A. Randle: 5341
Elliott, James R: 4603

Ellis, Howard S: 7045
Elmer, Frank L: 4779
Elon, Amos: 2794
Elsholz, Konrad: 5017
Elsner, Joachim: 7592
Elsner, Lothar: 4260
Elstermann, Gert: 4282
Embree, George D., Editor: 7813
Emery, Walter B: 5232
Emmer, Robert E: 3742,3743
Emmet, Christopher: 2476
Emminger, Otmar: 4408
Ender, Gerhard: 2246,2247
Enderwitz, Herbert: 5409
Engel, Lyle Kenyon: 29
Engelhardt, Werner: 5600
Engelmann, Frederick C: 2819
Engelmann, Konrad: 4018
Engelmann, Susanne Charlotte: 5342
Englisch, Karl: 1667
Engledow, Jack: 4043
Engler, Robert: 6099
English, Mildred: 5343
Enzensberger, Hans Magnus: 243,2061
Eppler, Erhard: 3385,4492,4503,4504,5102
Epstein, Benjamin R: 2603,2683
Epstein, Fritz Theodor: 5,6497
Epstein, Julius: 592
Epstein, Klaus: 6,2178,2739,2820,7735
Erbe, Rene: 3920
Erdmann, Elisabeth: 3014,4380,5082,6116,8196,8257
Erdmann, Ernst-Gerhard: 2291,4193
Erfurt, Werner: 7814
Erhard, Ludwig: 2062,2795,2796,2797,3626,3627,3679,3680,3681,4125,4335,4336,
   6284,6574
Erhart, Rainer R: 3894
Erickson, Harold B: 5880
Erler, Fritz: 2391,2740,6498,6921,6922,7815,7816
Ermarth, Fritz: 7248
Ernestus, Horst: 5951
Ernst and Ernst: 1777,4019,4020
Ernst, A: 880
Ernst, Fritz: 83
Ersil, Wilhelm: 6362,6363,8069
Erusalemskii, Arkadii S: 4542
Eschenberg, Horst Hermann Heinz: 4445
Eschenburg, Theodor: 8376
Eser, Albin: 1846
Eser, Wolfgang: 5171
Esser, F. K: 4126
Esslin, Martin J: 6019,6081,6082,6083,6084,7593
Etinger, Y: 4543,4544,6159
Etzkorn, Peter K: 5730,5761
Eucken, Walter: 3574,3843
Europa-Archiv: 1899,1900,1901,1902,1903
Evangelical Churches in Germany: 5043
Evans, Frederic: 1152
Evans, Joseph E: 3488
Evans, Roger Warren: 1739
Evely, Richard: 4073
Everling, H: 4074
Evitt, H. E: 4411
Ewen, Frederic: 6085
Eyck, F. Gunther: 6160
Eyck, Frank: 2207,2208,2314,2315,2477,2617,2618,2680,2681
Eysenck, Hans J: 2025
Eze, Onyeabo: 6777
F. G: 621
F.A.V: 3308
FRG, Bundestag: 174
FRG, Council of Experts on Overall Economic Development: 4412
FRG, Federal Chancellor's Office: 2859,2860
FRG, Federal Constitutional Court: 1720
FRG, Federal Government: 5401
FRG, Federal Insurance Supervisory Service: 1817
FRG, Federal Ministry for All-German Affairs: 65,358,2891,3084,3085,3103,3129,
   3130,3131,4637,7736,7896,8071,8377,8378,8379
FRG, Federal Ministry for Economic Cooperation: 4506,4507
FRG, Federal Ministry for Expellees, Refugees & War Victim: 363,364,365,366
FRG, Federal Ministry for Expellees: 359,360,362
FRG, Federal Ministry for Federal Aff., Expellees, Refugee: 367
FRG, Federal Ministry for Food, Agriculture and Forestry: 3873,5835
FRG, Federal Ministry for Housing and Urban Construction: 5085
FRG, Federal Ministry for Housing: 5083,5084
FRG, Federal Ministry for Scientific Research: 3995,5856
FRG, Federal Ministry for the Marshall Plan: 368,3387,3593,3594
FRG, Federal Ministry of Defense: 1927,1928,2248,6815
FRG, Federal Ministry of Economics: 3357,5855,7046
FRG, Federal Ministry of Finance: 369,3804
FRG, Federal Ministry of Justice: 945
FRG, Federal Ministry of the Interior: 175,5104
FRG, Federal Railway: 4298
FRG, Federal Statistical Office: 201,202,203,204,205,206,207,208,209,210,211,
   212,213,214,215,370,3358,3359,3360,3874,4096,5054
FRG, Foreign Office: 1708,7897
FRG, Foreign Trade Information Office: 4337
FRG, German Diplomatic Mission: 59
FRG, German Embassy in Malawi: 6778
FRG, German Embassy: 2682,8380
FRG, German Information Center: 1398,2146,6499,6575
FRG, German Research Association: 5854
FRG, Press and Information Office: 60,61,1399,1400,1929,2063,2741,3132,
   4505,4508,4509,4939,6285,6286,6979,7142,7327,7328,7379,7509,
   8072,8073,8074
FRG: 173,1102,1103,1394,1395,1396,1397,1778,1779,1780,1804,1805,1806,1807,1847,

1848,1849,1850,3386,4204,4938
Fabricius, Fritz: 1818
Fackler, Maxim: 6659
Fagan, H: 2392
Fahle, Walter: 5504
Fahrenkrog, Heinz: 4604
Fahy, Charles: 762
Fainsod, Merle: 530
Fair, Gordon M: 3103
Fair, Thomas J. D: 176
Fairman, Charles: 763
Falk, Hans-Juergen: 3760
Falk, Mirna Regina: 84
Falk, Theodor: 2988
Falkenhausen, Bernhard Freiherr Von: 1808,3682
Fann, Willerd R: 7249
Fantl, Irving L: 3805
Farajo, Ladislas: 946
Farley, Miriam S: 785
Farnell, Werner P: 3744
Farnen, Russell F: 5543,5561
Farnsworth, Clyde A: 947
Farnsworth, Helen C: 3876
Farquharson, John E: 6660
Farr, Warren F: 1000
Farrell, Ralph B: 30
Fassbender, Karl: 4510
Fassbender, Siegfried: 5836
Fassnacht, Bertel: 4092
Faude, E: 4688
Faulwetter, Helmut: 4689
Faviell, Frances: 8144
Fay, Sidney B: 1272,1273,1327,1367,2555,2619,6452,6710,7737
Federal Reserve Bank: 3745
Federation of British Industries: 1781
Federation of German Trade Unions: 5505
Federn, Robert: 948
Fedorov, V: 4413
Fehl, Philipp: 949
Fehling, Helmut M: 7330
Feige, Gerhard: 8030,8031
Feil, Michael: 8204
Feilchenfeld, Ernst H., and Others: 6287
Feinstein, Otto: 8381
Feis, Herbert: 531,532
Feist, Manfred: 7518
Fejtoe, Francois: 4680
Felber, Rolf: 7655
Feld, Werner J: 1740,7817,7818
Felderer, Bernhard: 3921
Feldman, K. Frank,: 2064
Feldman, K. Frank: 1926,3922
Fellhauer, Harry: 7693
Fenzlein, Volkmar: 4545,6364
Ferber, Christian Von: 5658
Ferencz, Benjamin B: 1694,3523
Ferguson, Elva Claire: 5344
Ferne, Georges: 5862
Feron, James: 6758
Fertig, Norman: 6193
Fest, Joachim: 5675
Fetscher, Iring: 5765,5766
Ficatner, Paula Sutter: 2514,2515
Picker, Hans: 1869
Fiebelkorn, Joachim: 6046,6047
Fiedler, Ewald: 1582
Fiedler, Horst: 6661
Field, Mark G: 5055
Field, Peter: 4127
Fikentscher, Wolfgang: 1819,4128
Finch, George A: 950
Findorff, W. B: 7143
Fine, Benjamin: 5434
Finer, Herman: 1465,1466,6923
Fink, Donald E: 3934
Fischer, Alfred Joachim: 881,882,2557,6759,8145
Fischer, Andreas: 5601
Fischer, Guido: 4205
Fischer, Heinz: 7519
Fischer, Helmut: 138
Fischer, Louis: 3133
Fischer, Oskar: 7594,7595
Fischer, Per: 6779
Fishel, Jeff: 1536,1537,1538
Fisher, Burton R: 5432
Fisher, Joel M: 2861
Fisher, Paul: 4206,4207,5018
Fisher, Stephen L: 1511,2425,2426
Fishman, Jack: 951
Fitt, A. B: 6787
Fitzgibbon, Constantine: 85,1059,1186
Fitzpatrick, Edward A: 5659
Flanagan, Robert J: 4190
Flanders, June: 4338
Flannery, Harry W: 2821
Fleischner, Eva Maria: 4940
Fleming, Denna Frank: 7819,8382
Fleming, John G: 1750
Fleming, Robben W: 4182
Fleming, William: 1328
Flenley, Ralph, Editor: 459
Flenley, Ralph: 86,441,6194
Flerlage, Ellen P: 5422,5423,5676
Fletcher, George P: 1851
Pliess, Peter J: 5213

Fliess, Walter: 1904,6850,6851
Flitner, Wilhelm: 5268
Flores, John M: 6066,6067
Florin, Peter: 6365,7520,7596,7656,8383
Fluegge, Walter: 4075
Focke, Katharina: 7144
Foerster, Friedrich: 460
Fondiller, Harvey V., Editor: 8146
Fontaine, Andre: 869
Ford, Frederick: 2742
Foreign Tax Law Association: 1782
Forrester, Ian S: 1645
Forssmann, Werner: 5853
Forster, Arnold: 2683
Forster, Leonard: 5986
Forster, Thomas Manfred: 2989
Forsthoff, Ernst: 1695
Forstmeier, Friedrich: 1992,4898,5745,6101
Forsyth, Murray: 3842
Fosnay, Arthur W: 5767
Foster, Charles R: 1539,1709,2808
Foster, John G., Editor: 6611
Fota, Carlos: 2246,2247
Fox, William T. R: 8278
Fraenkel, Heinrich: 883,2684,3010,7739
France, French Embassy, Information Service: 3489
Francisco, Ronald A: 2975
Frank, Elke: 8009
Frank, Isaiah: 3454
Frank, Paul: 6134,6135,6788,7250,8010
Frank, William: 3147
Frankel, Max: 3179
Frankel, Theodore: 1187,5952,6033
Frankfurt Institute for Social Research: 5794
Frankfurt University, Institute for Social Research: 5237
Frankland, E. Gene: 1540
Franklin, William M: 8205
Franzen, Carl G. F: 5319
Fraser, Geoffrey: 870
Fraser, Lindley: 622
Fraser, R. A: 4564
Frederick, Pierre: 6183
Frederiksen, Oliver J: 764
Free Democratic Party: 2433
Free German Movement in Great Britain, Editor: 462
Free German Youth, Central Council, Student Section: 5602
Free, Lloyd A: 2147
Freed, Paul B: 5233
Freedman, Ronald: 4793
Freeman, Christopher: 3975
Frei, Otto: 371,2358,2990,3027,3086,3180,3181,3182,4690,4997,7331,7740,7741,
 3279,8384
Freidin, Seymour: 765
Frenkiel, Leon: 312
Frenzke, Dietrich: 7251
Freund, Gerald: 2743,7742,7820
Freund, Ludwig: 2393
Freund, Michael: 7252
Frey, John R: 6068
Freyar, Helmut, Editor: 72
Freymond, Jacques: 6711
Friauf, Karl Heinrich: 1696
Fricke, Karl Wilhelm: 2936,2959
Fricke, Weddig: 1870
Fried, Edrita G: 4830
Fried, Edward R: 6953
Fried, John H. E: 697
Friedeburg, Ludwig Von: 5269,5677
Friedensburg, Ferdinand: 8225
Friedlaender, Ernst: 7198
Friedland, Diepold K: 5482
Friedlander, Albert H: 5678
Friedlander, Paul: 4546,4547
Friedman, Peter R: 3068
Friedman, Peter: 4864,8385
Friedman, Philip: 1116
Friedman, Samy: 372
Friedmann, Karen J: 3875,3876
Friedmann, Tuviah: 952
Friedmann, Wolfgang G: 698,699,4129,4511,8178
Friedrich, Carl J: 766,767,768,1060,1274,1275,1368,1369,1409,1410,1411,3175,
 3306,7047,3280
Friedrich, Carl J., Editor: 66
Friedrich, Carl J., and Associates: 769
Friedrich, Gerd: 4660
Friedrich, Klaus: 4339,4340
Friedrich, Otto: 3923,4208
Friedrich, Paul J: 7898
Friemond, Hans: 5402
Fries, Guenter: 5483
Frigge, Peter: 2960
Frischauer, Willi: 2010
Friters, Gerard M: 3976
Fritz, Friedrich (Pseud.): 6288
Fromm, Ernst Ulrich: 7048
Frost, Norman: 5345,5391
Frowein, Jochen Abr: 7253
Fry, Geoffrey K: 953
Fry, Richard: 4470
Frye, Charles E: 1431,2316
Frykholm, Yngve: 5665
Puccillo, Vincent J: 8265
Fuehr, Christoph, Editor: 5410
Fuehr, Christoph: 5305,5435
Fuerlinger, Friedrich: 8226

Fuerstenberg, Friedrich: 4209
Fuhrig, Wolf D: 5436,5603,5604
Fulbright, J. William: 6500
Fulda, Carl H: 1889
Fuller, J. F. C: 8386
Fuller, Leon W: 770
Fyodorov, T: 6366,6501,6924
G. G. W: 4299
G. K. Y: 623
GDR, Central Statistical Office: 4605
GDR, Committee for German Unity: 2011,2148,2249,2250,2251,2252,2253,2254,2255, 2256,2257,3328,4548,4549,4941,6368,6369
GDR, Council of Ministers, State Office for Voc. Training: 5882,5883
GDR, Council of State: 2896,3184,7522,7657,7694,8032
GDR, German Central Pedagogical Institute: 5884
GDR, German Institute for Occupational Training: 5885
GDR, Information Office: 2914,3012,4565,4566,6370,7743
GDR, Institute for Planning and Organization of Pub. Health: 5122
GDR, Ministry for Agriculture and Forestry: 4639
GDR, Ministry of Agriculture: 4732
GDR, Ministry of Culture: 6048
GDR, Ministry of Education: 5886
GDR, Ministry of Foreign Affairs: 4732,6136,6371,6372,6980,7674,7675,7695,7696, 7868,7899,8113,8206,8390,8391
GDR, Ministry of National Defense: 2991,2992,2993,2994
GDR, Ministry of Postal and Telecommunications Services: 5260
GDR, National Congress: 7523
GDR, Office for Inventions and Patents: 4661
GDR, People's Chamber: 3029,4567,4606
GDR, State Central Administration for Statistics: 223,224,225,4607
GDR, State Council: 7524
GDR, State Secretariat for West German Affairs: 3261
GDR, State Secretariat for West German Questions: 5918
GDR, Supreme Court: 2258
GDR: 67,2892,2893,2894,2895,3011,3028,3183,3260,4638,4691,5253,5881,7521,7673, 7821,3076,8387,8388
Gable, Lee J: 4883,4884,4885
Gablentz, Otto M. Von Der: 8392,8393
Gabriel, Ralph H: 533
Gaddis, John Lewis: 534
Gagliardo, John: 5919
Gaitskell, Hugh: 6981,7811
Galante, Pierre: 8394
Galay, Nikolai: 8395
Galbraith, Evan G., Editor: 1809
Galbraith, John Kenneth: 771,3595,3596,3628
Galkin, A: 2516,6373,7332
Gallagher, Richard: 954
Gallatin, Judith: 1710
Gallup International: 2118
Galtung, Johan: 8011
Gamarnikow, M: 7381
Gandillac, Maurice De: 6663
Gangloff, Perry J: 5044
Ganssauge, Guenter: 8396
Ganzert, Frederic W: 3597
Garbuny, Siegfried: 3977
Gardiner, Rolf: 2620
Gardner, Lloyd C: 772
Gareau, Frederick H: 3455,3456
Gareis, Herbert, Editor: 5842
Garnett, John: 6925
Garten, Hugh F: 6020
Gass, Oscar: 7900
Gasteyger, Curt: 6576,7254
Gatterman, A., and Others: 31
Gatzke, Hans W: 6502,7822
Gaus, Guenter: 2179
Gauthier, David P: 6289
Gayre, George Robert: 7427
Gebauer, Werner: 4076
Gebhard, Bruno: 5123
Geck, Wilhelm Karl: 5679
Geffen, William: 6816
Gehlen, Reinhard: 2012
Gehlhoff, Walter: 6808
Gehrig, Hans: 5887
Gehrig, Norbert: 1541
Gehring, Michael: 5124
Geiger, Theodore: 6453
Geilinger, Eduard: 2441,3104,4130,6852,6853,7744
Geimer, Hildegard: 5857
Geimer, Reinhold: 5857
Geiss, Imanuel: 6737
Gelb, Leslie H: 6926
Gelber, Lionel: 6927,7110
Gelberg, Ludwik: 7428
Gellhorn, Martha: 2744
Gelman, Norman I: 8397
Gemmill, Robert Fleming: 4341
Geneva Conference, Closing Communique (5 August 1959): 8398
Genscher, Hans-Dietrich: 6290
George, D. E. R: 5768
George, Manfred: 6809
Georgiu, Thanassis: 8114
Gerber, William: 3684
Gerelli, Emilio: 3807
Gerhardt, Uta: 3134
Gerlach, Frederick H: 6738
Gerlach, Hans: 6817
German Academic Exchange Service: 5837,5838
German Bankers' Association: 3746
German Federation of Housing, Town- and Regional Planning: 5086
German Federation of Trade Unions: 3749,4210
German Industrial Institute: 3361

German Information Center: 5681
German Institute Of Contemporary History: 7901
German Institute of Contemporary History: 8399
German Labor Delegation in U.S.A: 464
German League for the United Nations: 7698
German National Committee for International Youth Work: 4831
German National Union of Students: 3087
German Peace Council of the German Democratic Republic: 8400
German Peace Council: 7823
German Society for Foreign Policy, Research Institute: 7
German, Daniel Bernard: 5543,5680
Germanicus: 4569
Gerns, Willi: 4131
Gerschenkron, Alexander: 3877
Gershon, Karen , Editor: 4942
Gerson, Louis L: 6503
Gerst, Wilhelm Karl: 6855
Gerstenmaier, Eugen: 1542
Gerwin, Robert: 3996
Gesellschaft Fuer Marktforschung, Hamburg: 4022
Geyr, Leo Freiherr Von: 1930
Ghiselli, Edwin E: 4063
Ghurye, Charlotte W: 5987
Gibbon, Monk: 1467
Gibbs, Philip: 2558
Giere, Eggert W: 535
Giersch, Herbert: 3844
Gilbert, Edmund W: 139
Gilbert, Felix: 626
Gilbert, Gustave Mark: 955
Gilbert, Horace N: 627
Gilbert, Milton: 3362
Giles, O. C: 1797
Gillen, J. F. J: 1621,3457,4272,6100,6101
Gillespie, James M: 2065
Gilroy, Harry: 3148
Gimbel, John: 773,774,775,776,777,1061,5214,7747
Giniewski, Paul: 6761,6762
Ginsburg, David: 3491
Glade, Henry: 6086
Glaeser, Ernst: 3632
Glaser, Kurt, Editor: 7192,7889,8366
Glaser, Kurt: 244,778,884,5795
Glasgow, George: 628
Glassgold, A. C: 956
Glazebrook, G. Det: 1226
Glazunov, N: 6375
Gleich, Albrecht Von: 6798
Gleiss, Alfred: 7162
Gleitze, Bruno: 7824
Glickman, David Lloyd: 3412
Glija, Vasile: 7255
Gluck, Gustav: 3750
Glueck, Sheldon: 957,958
Glueckauf, Erich: 2394,2395
Goergey, Laszlo: 2396,7199,7256,7257
Goerner, Gunter: 959,960,8208
Goeseke, Gerhard: 3363
Goetting, Gerald: 3186,4980,7525,7526,7677,7902,8047
Goettingen Research Committee: 68,373,374,375,7429,7430,7431,7432,7433
Goettner, Reinhard: 4608,4609,4663,4664
Goetzinger, Hermann: 5347
Gohlert, Ernst W: 2365,6818
Golay, John Ford: 1370
Golde, Guenter: 4887
Goldman, Guido: 1468,1469
Goldschmidt, Dietrich: 5682,5796
Goldschmidt, F: 1093
Goldschmidt, Hermann Levin: 4943
Goldschmidt, Siegfried: 1104
Goldsmith, M. K: 5380
Goldstein, Israel: 6197
Gollancz, Victor: 629,630,1227,3547
Gollnick, Heinz: 3378
Gollwitzer, Helmut: 4888,4889
Gomulka, Wladyslaw: 7382
Gong, Walter, Editor: 5234
Gooch, George P: 6612,6664
Gooch, George P., Editor: 245
Goodhart, A. L: 961
Goodman, Elliot R: 6455,6929
Goodman, Thomas H: 747
Goold-Adams, Richard: 6504
Goppel, Alfons: 140
Gorden, Morton: 2157,6982
Gordon-Finlayson, R: 246
Gorer, Geoffrey: 856
Gottfurcht, Hans: 4132
Gottlieb, Manuel: 3492,3633,6291,7748
Gottschalk, Max: 4944
Govier, Robert A: 5988
Grabley, Peter: 4665
Grabowski, K: 2685,2746,2747,2748,2749,7383,7384,7385,7434,7435,7436,8401
Grabowski, Z. A: 2686,5953
Grabska, Virginia: 6376
Grace, Alonzo G: 5270,5348,5349,5350,5605
Grace, Frank: 1323,2366
Gradl, Johann B: 8402
Graebener, Juergen: 5780
Graebner, Norman A: 2862
Graefrath, Bernhard: 7258,7599,7658,7699,8035
Graf, Herbert: 3073
Graf, Rudolf: 8077
Gragt, Frits Van Der: 4300
Graham, Malbone Watson: 1412

Graham, Norman: 8012
Graham, Robert A: 2621
Gramann, Ernst-August: 4415
Granger, G. B: 3634
Granick, David: 4062
Graper, Elmer D: 6505
Grass, Guenter: 2822
Graue, Eugen Dietrich: 1646,1769,1798
Grauhan, Rolf-Richard: 1583
Graupner, Rudolf: 1820
Gray, J. Glenn: 5606
Grazynski, Michal: 6577,7437
Greaves, Rex B: 701
Grebing, Helga: 4133
Gredel, Zdenka J. M: 87
Green, Georg W: 1583
Green, Leslie C: 2559,8281,8403
Greenberg, D. S: 5411
Greenberg, Harold J: 6751
Greene, Ernest Thomas: 178,179,180
Greenwood, H. Powys: 2560,3978
Grejor, Ulrich: 5954
Grejory, Paul R: 4733
Grenl, Dieter: 7600
Greinacher, Norbert: 4890
Grenfell, Russell: 1188
Grewe, Wilhelm G: 6292,7825,8179,8404,8405
Griesbach, Bernard: 1821
Grieschmann, Guenther: 4273
Grieves, Forest L: 1993,2317
Griffith, William E: 1062,1063,6506,7190,7601
Griffiths, Eldon W: 247
Grigoryan, Y: 6799
Grimes, Warren S: 4666
Grimm, Georg, Editor: 919
Grimm, Hans: 4891
Grinwood, Gordon B: 4446
Gringauz, Samuel: 314,315
Grishin, Nikolai: 4667
Grobe, Hans: 1871
Grober, Guenter: 4351
Groener, Helmut: 3686,3997
Groennings, Sven: 2861
Groll, Goetz Von: 7008,7009,7010,7011,7012
Groner, Franz: 4892
Gronowicz, Antoni: 7386
Groseclose, E: 3751
Gross, Franz B: 5215
Gross, Herbert: 3635,4345
Gross, Hermann: 3458,3459
Grossack, Martin: 2066
Grosser, Alfred: 88,1470,2622,2882,6665,6666,6667,6668,6669,7049,7050
Grossfeld, Bernhard: 3030
Grossman, Vladimir: 7200
Grossmann, Bernhard: 5769
Grossmann, Kurt R: 248,465,466,1905,3105,4945,6763,6764,6765,6766,7387
Grote, Gerhard: 4692
Grote, Manfred W. H: 7201
Grotewohl, Otto: 3187
Grotewold, Andreas: 181
Grothe, Peter: 5254
Groussard, Serge: 6767
Grubel, Herbert G: 5731
Gruben, Baron De: 6731
Gruber, Hans: 7700
Gruen, Walter: 5732
Gruson, Sydney: 249
Grzybowski, Kazimierz: 3031,7602
Guarnieri, Robert Louis: 4416
Guenther, Arno: 4301
Guenther, Eberhard: 1822,1823
Guerster, Eugene: 1371
Gumpel, E. J: 8149
Gumpel, Henry J: 1783,1784
Gumpert, Martin: 2561
Gunlicks, Arthur B: 2318,2319,2320,2321
Guradze, Heinz: 467,1329
Gurian, Waldemar: 468
Gurland, Arcadius Rudolph Lang: 2562,5797
Gust, Kurt: 4981
Guthrie, Edwin R: 631
Gutkind, Erwin A: 123
Gutmann, Rudolf: 4078
Gutschow, Harald: 5566
Guttenberg, Karl Theodor Baron Von: 7903
Gyorgy, Andrew: 3188,3189
H. D. W: 3548
H. G. L: 2563,6198,6856,7826,8150,8288
H. H: 702
Haavelsrud, Magnus: 2120
Habe, Hans (Pseud. for Jean Bekessy): 6507
Haberler, Gottfried: 7051
Habermas, Juergen: 5683
Hacker, Jens: 5770
Hadfield, Jean: 7438
Hadik, Laszlo: 7013
Hadley, Guy: 2067
Hadsel, Winifred N: 469,703,3549
Haeber, Herbert: 8078
Haeger, Robert: 779
Haenisch, Werner: 2937,7904,8048
Haertling, Peter: 7511
Haeuser, Karl: 3719,4734
Hafemann, Wilhelm: 2898,2957
Haferkamp, Wilhelm: 7126

Haffner, Sebastian: 6578,7749,7905,8406
Hafter, Rudolph P: 5955,6137,7750
Hagelberg, Gerhard: 2564,2565
Hagemann, Guenter: 3800
Hagen, Paul: 470
Hager, Johannes: 471
Hager, Kurt: 3190
Hahn, C. H: 141
Hahn, Erich: 4865
Hahn, Gerhard: 3263
Hahn, H. J: 1668
Hahn, Walter F: 2397,5412,5437,5484,5545,5607,5643,5644,5941,6456,6819,7259
Hain, Jack: 4946
Haire, Mason: 4063
Hajdu, J. G: 126
Halasz, Nicholas: 7202
Halbach, Guenter: 3364,4274
Haley, Harold: 5271
Hall, Adam (Pseud.): 8407
Hall, J. P. E: 5485
Hall, Martin: 2897,3191,3309,6983,7052,7333
Hall, Peter: 142
Hall, Robert D: 5733
Hall, Robert King: 5351
Halle, Louis J: 536,7906
Haller, Heinz: 3808
Hallett, Graham: 3687,3688,3878,5087,6613
Halley, Fred G., Compiler: 962
Hallstein, Walter: 5608,6457,6930,7145,7146,7147,7148,7751
Halpap, Paul: 4550
Halperin, Morton H: 6926
Halperin, S. William: 6923
Halpern, Henry: 2068
Halpern, Manfred: 6702
Halsall, Thomas: 5889
Hamburg, Superior Court: 1879
Hamburger, Ernest: 3555
Hamburger, Michael: 5989
Hamel, Johannes: 4973,4982
Hamilton, Richard F: 4097
Hamlett, Barksdale: 8408
Hammer, Udo: 4417
Hammerbacher, Hans L: 4023
Hammerschmidt, Ernst: 5771
Hammond, Paul Y: 780
Hampe, Karl-Alexander: 6800
Hancock, M. Donald: 3329
Handler, M. S: 2209,2210,2623,6508
Handlin, Oscar: 316
Handsaker, Morrison: 4183
Handy, Mary: 781
Hanf, Kenneth I: 1584,3330
Hangen, Welles: 7527,7528
Hannardt, Arthur M., Jr: 3264,3331,5890,5920,5942
Hanisch, G: 3349
Hankel, Wilhelm: 4418,4513
Hankey, Baron Maurice Pascal Alers: 963
Hanley, Charles: 3310
Hanrieder, Wolfram F: 6138,6139,6293,6294,7907
Hans, Theodor: 8227
Hanwehr, Wolfram Von: 6049
Harbeson, John W: 1471
Hardin, William Russell: 4866
Harich, Wolfgang: 2938
Harkort, Guenther: 3550
Harlinghausen, C. Harald: 32
Harmsen, Hans: 5056
Harpprecht, Klaus: 2180
Harrell, Edward J: 8282
Harrelson, Lawrence E: 2026
Harriman W. Averell: 537
Harrington, Eugene C: 4983
Harris, Alan: 143
Harris, Charles W: 3526,3527
Harris, Chauncy D: 376,3979
Harris, Lement: 4641
Harris, Richard L: 1585
Harris, Sam: 1000
Harris, Whitney R: 964
Harris, Wilson: 6199
Harrland, Harri: 5129,5130,5131,5141
Harsch, Joseph C: 6857
Hart, Adrian Liddell: 1372,6670
Hart, Eric G: 1271
Hart, Merwin K: 3636
Hartenstein, Wolfgang: 2101,5798
Hartfiel, Guenter: 4134
Hartjens, Peter G: 1432
Hartman, F. L: 6140
Hartmann, Frederick H: 1373,7752,7908
Hartmann, Heinz: 2069,2292,4064,4065,4211,4814
Hartmann, Karl: 7603
Hartmann, Ralph: 7529
Hartmann, Richard: 3032,3033,5137
Hartmann, Ruediger: 6931
Harvey, C. P: 704,857
Harwood, Ralph: 782
Hasan, K. Sarwar: 2624
Hasenack, Wilhelm: 3460
Hasenclever, Walter, Editor: 33
Hassel, Kai-Uwe Von: 6932,7014
Hasselmann, Erwin: 4079,7753
Hassner, Pierre: 6933,7053
Hastings, Lewis: 6183
Haubenreisser, Johannes: 4514

Hauck, Karl: 5115
Hauenstein, Fritz: 6740
Haupt, Lucie: 2398,2957
Hauptmann, Jerzy, Editor: 7245
Hauptmann, Jerzy: 2517,7260,7261,7909,7910
Haus, Wolfgang: 8151
Hauser, Heinrich: 250
Hausmann, G: 5461
Havemann, Hans A., Editor: 4515
Havens, R. M: 1064
Havighurst, Robert J: 1252,1277,5609,5646
Hawes, Vincent L: 5352
Hawgood, John Arkas: 89
Hawkins, Irene: 2876
Hawtrey, Sir Ralph George: 7054,7334
Hay, John: 6810
Hay, Peter: 7149
Hayman, Ronald, Editor: 6021
Hays, Arthur Garfield: 1712
Healy, Bruce: 1536
Heald, David: 5647,5648
Healey, Denis: 6200,6984,7055,7056,8409
Heaps, Willard Allison: 8410
Hearnden, Arthur: 5943,5944
Heath, Kathryn G: 783
Heathcote, Nina: 7262
Heberle, Rudolf: 2322,2323,2518
Heck, Bruno: 4832
Heclo, Hugh: 1473
Heer, Friedrich: 5684
Hegner, Manfred: 3034
Heidelmeyer, Wolfgang, Editor: 8411
Heidelmeyer, Wolfgang: 8180
Heidenheimer, Arnold J: 1472,1473,2149,2324,2325,2326,2327,2367,2368,2369,3809,
    4135,5008,5413,5799
Heigert, Hans: 5388,5685
Heilman, John Greene: 6801
Heilperin, Michael A: 1228
Heimburger, Artur: 4136
Hein, John: 3752,3753,3754
Heineman, Leopold: 7057
Heinrichs, Wolfgang: 4570
Heinsdorf, Helena: 7388,7439
Heinze, A: 5800
Heiskanen, Veronica Stolte: 4799
Helping, Hubert: 7678
Held, Colbert C: 377,6712
Helde, Thomas T: 5610
Helrich, Andreas: 1890
Hellack, Georg: 5148
Heller, Bernard: 1189
Heller, David: 8412,8413
Heller, Deane: 8412,8413
Heller, Maxine J: 965
Heller, Walter W: 3637,3845
Helm, Everett: 5956
Helmke, Henry C: 5990
Helmreich, Ernst Christian: 5574,5575
Helms, Andrea: 7058
Helmstaedter, Ernst: 3365
Hemdahl, Reuel G: 182
Hemken, Ruth, Editor: 705
Hemmerling, Joachim: 3035
Henderson, James L: 5261,5272,6614
Hendrick, Ives: 446
Hendrickson, Hildegard Roedig: 3755
Hendus, Heinrich: 4481
Heneman, Harlow J: 784
Henkin, Louis J: 8414
Henle, Guenter: 6789
Hennessey, John Russell, Jr: 8013
Hennessy, Jossleyn: 3638,7059
Hennig, Walter: 5138
Hennis, Wilhelm: 1543
Hensel, Walther: 1622,1623
Hensen, Bent: 3810
Herbert, E. O: 8283
Herbst, Axel: 4024
Herbst, Clarence A: 2370
Herbst, Fritz: 4212,4275
Herbst, Josef: 1931
Herding, Richard: 4213
Herlitzius, Erwin: 4610
Herman, Frederick: 706
Herman, Stewart Winfield: 4998
Hermann, Kai: 5686,5687
Hermberg, Paul G: 3413
Hermens, Ferdinand A: 538,632,2566,2687,2823,5172,6295,6579,6580
Herrmann, H. C: 6161
Herrmann, Joachim: 1751
Herrmann, K: 1932
Herschel, Wilhelm: 4214
Herspring, Dale Roy: 2996,2997
Hertel, Guido: 1752
Hertz, Paul: 8284
Herwarth, Hans Von: 6615
Herwig, Holger H: 1994
Herz, Carl: 472
Herz, John H: 1065,1474,1475,1587,1588,1589,2824,3192,8014
Herz, John H., Editor: 1477,2863,3340
Herz, Otto: 5611
Herzfeld, Hans: 90,8285
Herzog, Dietrich: 2150
Herzstein, Robert Edwin: 7911
Hess, Frederick W., Editor: 8015

Hess, Gerhard: 5612
Hess, Peter: 34,3265
Hess, Robert D: 2070
Hesse, Helmut: 4346
Hesse, M. Harry: 5613
Hesselbach, Walter: 4080,4081,4137,4419
Hester, Hugh B: 6509,8415
Hettlage, Karl M: 3846
Heuer, Klaus: 4611,4642,4643
Heuer, Uwe-Jens: 4612
Heuser, Frederick W. J: 5858
Heuser, Henry K: 3756
Heusinger, Adolf Ernst: 6934
Heuss, Theodor: 251,2688,6162
Heyde, Wolfgang: 1647
Heydecker, Joe Julius: 966
Heydte, Freiherr Von Der: 1669
Heym, Stefan: 1190,6050
Heymann, Hans, Jr: 785
Heymann, Stefan: 7530
Hickman, Warren L: 3598
Higgins, Marguerite: 1278
Hilberg, Raul: 4947
Hildebrandt, Dieter: 8152
Hildebrandt, Rainer, Editor: 6051
Hildebrandt, Rainer: 3135
Hilker, Franz: 5273,5274,5438,5439,5772
Hill, J. W. F: 1330
Hill, Leonidas E: 2182
Hill, Russell: 1279,3088
Hilldring, John H: 317,786
Hille, Hans G: 3892
Hille, Hans J: 1495,6115
Hiller, Kurt, Editor: 473
Hiller, Kurt: 474
Hiller, Rudolf: 3036
Hillhouse, A. M: 1753,3414
Hillmann, H. C: 3599
Hills, Denis C: 7335
Hilton, Ian: 6022
Hinderer, Hans: 5132,5138
Hindrichs, Guenter, Editor: 8411
Hink, Heinz R: 1891
Hinkson, Pamela: 4815
Hinterhoff, Eugene: 1974,2998,6616,6617,6985,7203,7204,7912,7913,7914
Hippel, Ernst Von: 1670
Hiriekar, Yamunabai: 5275,5506,5614
Hirsch, Felix Edward: 633,967,1229,1374,1906,2183,2211,2625,2626,2689,2690,
    3193,3551,3640,3641,4765,5173,5216,5957,7263,7604,8228,8416
Hirsch, Joachim: 5801
Hirsch, Martin: 7162
Hirsch-Weber, Wolfgang: 2293
Hirschmann, Ira A: 1375
Hirshleifer, Jack: 3642
Hiscocks, C. R: 2627,6201
Hiscocks, Richard: 710,1476,2691,2750
Hoag, Wendy Jane: 2434
Hobman, D. L: 8153
Hocaschwender, Karl A: 1590
Hocking, William Ernest: 1153
Hodgman, Donald R: 3757
Hoegen, Dieter L: 1754
Hoean, Elfriede: 318
Hoenne, Heinz: 2013
Hoennel, Gerd: 6811,7701
Hoeldtke, Siegfried: 7659
Hoenekopp, Joseph: 4276
Hoepcke, Klaus: 6052
Hoeping, Hubert: 2184,3924
Hoeping, Hubertus: 4302
Hoepker, Wolfgang: 1433
Hoeppner, Rolf-Roger: 6741
Hoffman, Lawrence A: 707
Hoffman, Michael L: 4473
Hoffman, Paul G: 6202
Hoffmann, Heinz: 7660
Hoffmann, Walther G: 1995,3925,4277
Hofmann, Erich: 5891
Hofmann, Helmut P: 5452
Hofmann, Josef: 5200
Hofmann, Manfred: 3069
Hofmann, Wolfgang: 2294,8229
Hogan, Willard N: 968
Hohnstein, Willard E: 7150
Holbik, Karel: 4516,4517,4751,4752
Holborn, Hajo: 539,787,2628,6510,6858
Holborn, Louise W., Editor: 540,1477,3340
Holbrook, Sabra: 3311,8417
Hollander, Arie N. J. Den: 5688
Holler, Joanne E: 378
Holm, Hans Axel: 3266
Holt, John B: 2295
Holt, Robert T: 5235,5236
Holt, Stephen C: 1478,6660
Holtermann, Ursula: 2528
Holthus, Manfred: 4347
Holthusen, Hans Egon: 5991,5992
Holtzclaw, Katharine: 5546
Holzer, H. Peter: 4025,4026
Holzschuh, Karl: 5097
Homann, Heinrich: 3267
Hommen, Willi: 634
Homze, Alma: 35
Homze, Edward: 35
Honig, Frederick: 969,970,971,6768

Hoover, Calvin B: 3552,3553,3643
Hoover, Herbert C., Jr: 3194
Hoover, Herbert: 3415
Hopfinger, K. B: 3926
Hopkins, L. Thomas: 635,5353
Hopman, A. N: 5526
Hopper, Richard B: 7264
Horchem, Hans Josef: 2442
Horecky, Paul: 8
Horecky, Paul L., Editor: 9
Horkheimer, Max: 5802
Horlick, Max: 5019
Horn, Klaus: 5803
Horne, Alistair: 2629
Hornsby, Lex, Editor: 3195
Hornstein, Erika Von: 3089,3196
Horst, Karl August: 5993
Horstmann, Lali Von S: 3197
Hostettler, John: 8181
Hotham, David: 2185
Hottelet, Richard C: 7827,8418
Houlihan, Jack: 5045
Hovde, Bryn J: 3644
Howard, Elizabeth Fox: 2567
Howard, John B: 3493
Howard, Michael: 6986
Howard, Wilbert Francis: 4999
Howe, Mark Dewolfe: 738
Howe, Quincy: 1280
Howes, Eric G: 5089
Howley, Frank L: 6511,8286,8419
Hrabyk, Klaudiusz: 7205
Huang, R. Chu-Kua: 7060
Hubatsch, Walther: 7915
Hubbert, Bernd: 4101
Huber, Gerhard: 7605
Huber, Heinz: 44
Huber, Ludwig: 5773
Huberman, Leo: 2630,6377,6859
Huddleston, John: 4138,5507,5527,5528
Hudson, G. F: 6204,7336,7828,8420
Huebener, Theodore: 5276,5277,5414,5415,5529,5547,5892,6069,6070
Huettich, H. G: 6087
Huettner, Erich: 8034
Hughes, Barry B: 7151
Hughes, Christopher: 1563
Hughes, H. Stuart: 2631
Hughes, Richard D: 1281
Hughes, William R., Editor: 7337
Hugot, Heinz: 5133
Huiskamp, J. C. L: 4571
Huizinga, J. H: 2915
Hull, Cordell: 541
Hunck, Josef M: 4518
Hunnius, F. C: 5689,5690
Hunt, Chester L: 5576
Hunter, David R: 5046
Hunter, Robert E: 7015
Hurley, Neil: 379
Hurter, Edwin: 144,1824,1996,1997,3341,3645,3998,4027,4098,4215
Hurwitz, Harold: 5691,5692,5693
Hussmann, Eibe: 171
Huston, James A: 7754
Hutcheson, Harold H: 3600
Huta, William P: 3889
Hutschenreuter, Klaus: 4551
Hutton, Oram C: 788
Hylla, Erich J: 5278,5279
Hynd, John B: 855,858,2186,6732
I. D: 8287
Iben, Icko: 5174
Ickler, Albert: 2568
Ifo Institute for Economic Research: 3879
Iggers, Georg C: 91
Ignotus: 3106
Ilgen, Hans-Michael: 1645
Ilyin, V: 1975
Imhoff, Christoph Von: 6742
Imperial War Museum, Foreign Documents Centre: 10
India, Directorate of Commercial Publicity: 4348
India, National Productivity Council: 3927,3928
Indian Institute of Public Opinion: 2151
Indo-German Chamber of Commerce: 4350
Infield, Henrik F: 4082
Ingenkamp, Karlheinz: 5462
Inglehart, Ronald: 2121,2122,2123
Ingrams, Harold: 1331
Institute Of International And West German Questions: 8209
Institute for Finances and Taxes: 1998,1999
Institute for International Politics and Economics: 2259,6378
Institute for Occupation Affairs: 2000
Institute for Research in Human Relations: 5734
Institute for the Sciences of Society, Berlin: 3269
Institute for the Study of Public Affairs: 380
Institute of Jewish Affairs: 1105,1106,1107,2478
Inter Nationes, Editor: 13
Inter Nationes: 11,12,7829
Inter-Allied Reparations Agency: 3495
Intergov'Tal Group on Safeguarding Foreign Interests in Ger: 3528
International Association Of Democratic Lawyers: 8230
International Association of Democratic Lawyers: 6296
International Chamber of Commerce: 3554,7061
International Commission of Jurists: 1648,1713,8421
International Committee for Information and Social Activity: 2916,7531
International Conference on German External Debts, London: 3529,3530

International Court of Justice: 1880,1881
International Public Opinion Research, Inc: 5237,5735
International Research Associates: 5736,5737
International Society for Rehabilitation of the Disabled: 5034
International Workshop on Guidance: 5463
International Workshop on Social Studies, Heidelberg, 1950: 5548
Investigation Committee of Free Jurists: 2917,3090
Irving, David: 593
Irving, R. E. M: 2435,2883
Isbary, Gerhard: 145
Issing, Otmar: 4474
Ivanyi, B. G: 542
Ivens, Hans: 6743
Iwanska, George M: 4447
Iyengar, H. V. R: 3496
J. C: 7606
J. C. C: 3013
J. E. W: 8288
J. F. A. W: 7755
Jackson, J. Hampden: 2632
Jackson, Joseph Harrison: 5000
Jackson, Robert H: 972,973,974,975,976
Jackson, William Eldred: 977
Jacob, Herbert: 1591
Jacobi, Claus: 2212,2633,5175
Jacobs, Walter Darnell: 1479
Jacoby, Gerhard: 4948,4949
Jaeger, Hans: 475,476,2479,2480
Jaeger, Martin: 4669
Jaeggi, Urs: 4028
Jaenicke, Martin: 3198
Jaenicke, Wolfgang A: 381,7440
Jaenicke, Wolfgang, Editor: 382
Jahn, Hans: 3107
Jahn, Wolfgang: 6379
Jaksch, Wenzel: 92,7206,7338
James, Eldon R., Editor: 1852
Janeczek, Edward John: 978
Janicki, Lech: 3342
Janossy, Ferenc: 3646
Janowitz, Morris: 1191,2102,4766,4842
Jantz, Kurt: 5020
Jarman, T. L: 5280
Jaspers, Karl: 979,1192,2634,2751,2798,5859
Jaworski, Leon: 980
Jay, Martin: 5804
Jebens, F: 636
Jedrychowski, Stefan: 7441
Jenkins, Clive: 6935
Jenkis, Helmut W: 383
Jenne, Michael: 5796
Jensen, Finn B: 7152
Jensen, Lloyd: 6820
Jensen, Wiebke: 4351
Jerome, V. J: 477
Jescheck, Hans-Heinrich: 1853,1854,1855,3037
Jeschonnek, Emil: 4710
Jeske, Reinhold: 6380
Jessup, Philip C: 8182,8289,8290
Jewish Black Book Committee: 319
Jewish Restitution Successor Organization: 1108,1109
Jewish Travel Guide: 4950
Jewish Trust Corporation for Germany: 1110
Jocaimsen, Reimut: 1592,1593
Joenssson, Algot: 4139
Joesten, Joachim: 146,478,885,1282,1332,1933,2014,2015,2152,2187,2188,2213,
  2214,2215,2260,2261,2481,2569,2692,2918,2919,3108,3136,3199,3200,3201,
  3312,3647,3759,3811,3929,3980,3999,4140,4303,4304,4352,4353,4354,4393,
  4572,4573,4574,5176,5177,5201,5615,5958,5959,5994,5995,6071,6141,6744,
  6745,6746,6860,7153,7389,8115,8116
Joetze, Guenter: 4753
Joffee, Josef: 6142
John, I. G: 6713
John, Otto: 2016
Johnk, James P: 6512
Johnsen, Carsten Ingeman: 7756
Johnson, A. Ross: 7607
Johnson, Alvin: 320,1230,3555,4644
Johnson, D. H. N: 3531
Johnson, Julia E., Compiler: 1283
Johnson, Nevil: 1544,1594,2329,2752
Johnston, Howard W: 789
Johnston, W. H: 2216,2217
Johnstone, Paul H: 8183
Joliet, Rene: 1825
Joll, James: 5960
Jonas, Frank H: 7853
Jones, Alan G: 252
Jones, Edgar M: 6102
Jones, Howard Palfrey: 1333,1624,3416
Jones, Joseph M: 3601
Jones, Russell: 1066
Jones, Sybil E: 7853
Jones, William Treharne: 2519
Jordan, Wayne: 5217
Jordan, Z: 7442
Joseph, J. J: 3602,3603
Josephson, Eric: 4833
Jouhy, Ernest: 1193
Joy, James L: 1934
Juenger, Friedrich K: 1770
Juergensen, Harald: 3847
Juettemeier, Karl-Heinz: 3800
Juettner, D. Johannes: 4015
Jungbluth, Adolf: 4216

Jungclas, Georg: 1907
Juretzko, Werner I: 3091
K. G: 226
K. B: 2443
Kachelmaier, Rolf: 3038
Kahler, Franz: 5255
Kahn, Arthur D: 790
Kahn, J. F: 2570
Kahn, Leo: 981
Kahn, R. F: 4448
Kahn, Siegbert: 479,6381
Kahn-Freund, O: 1872
Kahrs, Karl H: 4613,4614
Kaim-Caudle, P. R: 5021
Kain, Walter: 3930
Kairouz, Akl: 6671
Kaiser, Karl, Editor: 6619
Kaiser, Karl: 6297,6298,6513,6618
Kalandarov, S: 4552
Kallegg, A: 2027,5440
Kaldor, Mary: 3931
Kalow, Gert: 1194
Kaltefleiter, Werner: 1595,2865,6514,6515
Kamlah, Ruprecht B: 1714
Kanaar, A. C: 3895
Kantorowicz, Alfred: 480
Kantzenbach, Erhard: 3848
Kanzig, Helga: 2934,3270
Kapferer, Clodwig: 4475
Kaplan, Abbott: 5530
Kaplan, Benjamin: 1755
Kaplan, Lawrence S: 6936
Kaplan, Louis L: 321
Kapluck, Manfred: 2444
Kapp, William K: 5354
Kappelman, Glenn L: 7757
Kapralik, Charles I: 1111,1112
Kaps, Johannes, Editor: 7443,7444
Karanjia, Rustom Khurshedji: 2866
Karasik, Monroe: 1113
Karat, Johann: 7339
Karau, Guenter: 3271
Karbstein, Werner: 4669
Karch, John J: 7445
Karl, Willibald: 5695
Karr, Chadwick: 4794
Karsteter, William R: 791
Kartun, Derek: 4575
Kassube, Ruth: 3343
Katcher, Leo: 4951
Katelbach, T: 7390
Katona, George: 2071
Katzenstein, Peter J: 6733
Kaufmann, Francois Xavier: 5022
Kaufmann, Hugo M: 4420,4421
Kaufmann, Walter A: 5961
Kaul, Friedrich Karl: 982,983,8035
Kaupen-Haas, Heidrun: 4767
Kauper, Paul G: 1413
Kayser, Elmer Louis: 6581
Kebschull, Dietrich: 4422,4423,4424,7154,8117
Kecskemeti, Paul: 2072
Kee, Robert: 384,385,8422
Keefe, Eugene K: 69
Keeling, Ralph F: 3556
Keesing's Contemporary Archives: 7265
Kegel, Friedrich O: 5279
Kegel, Gerhard: 7266,8080
Kehr, Helen, Compiler: 14
Keilhacker, Martin: 5567
Keith-Smith, Brian, Editor: 5996
Kelber, Magda: 3576,5047
Kelleher, Catherine M: 1935,1976,1977
Kellen, Konrad: 2218
Keller, Franklin J: 322,5355,5508
Keller, John W: 2398,2693,6143,8423
Keller, Peter: 4233
Kellerer, Hans: 2073
Kellerman, Barbara: 2189
Kellermann, Erwin: 2520
Kellermann, Henry J: 4834,4835,6144,6206
Kelley, Douglas M: 984
Kellner, Hansfried: 1425
Kelly, Matthew A: 3812,4083,4141,4142,4184
Kelman, Steven: 3092
Kelsen, Hans: 543,985,1231
Kelty, Mary G: 5356
Kempner, Robert M. W: 986,987,1596
Kendall, Walter: 4143
Kennan, George F: 6516,6861,6987,7916
Kennedy, John F: 6517,8424
Kenny, John P: 938
Keohane, Robert E: 1154
Keplicz, Klemens: 544
Keren, Michael: 4615,4616
Kern, Helmuth: 4355
Kerr, Anthony: 5616
Kerr, Clark: 4144,4217,4218,4233
Kersten, Heinz: 6053,6054,6055,6056
Kertesz, Stephen D: 8425
Kertesz, Stephen: 386
Keutgen, Rene: 3813,3849
Kewenig, Wilhelm A: 6576,7267,8050
Keyserlingk, Robert W: 637
Khrushchev, Nikita S: 7608,7917,7918,8426

241

Khvostov, V. M: 3272
Kienn, Ludwig: 5617
Kiel University, Institute for International Economics: 3648
Kielmansegg, Johann Adolf Graf: 6937
Kiep, Walther Leisler: 4504,7062
Kiermeier, Hildegard: 7702
Kiesewetter, Wolfgang: 7609,7679
Kiesinger, Kurt-Georg: 2190
Kilachand, Arvind: 4356
Kilgore, Harley M: 3461
Killius, Juergen: 4029
Kimche, Jon: 6862,6863
Kindleberger, Charles P: 3649,4099,4357,4449
King, Anthony: 1434
King, Charles D: 4219
King, David Burnett: 6582
King, Edmund J: 5618,5893
King-Hall, Sir William Stephen Richard: 1559
Kirchheimer, Otto: 1512,1528,1545,1721,2330,2635,2694,2695,3039,3109,4145,4146, 4147,5218
Kirchhoff, Werner: 2753
Kirchner, Wolfram: 6780
Kirk, Dudley: 216
Kirkpatrick, Clifford: 638,2074
Kirkpatrick, Ivone: 6103
Kirkpatrick, Ursula: 5416
Kirkpatrick, William S: 5219
Kirkwood, Thomas W: 4148
Kirschhofer, Andreas Von: 2075
Kirst, Hans Hellmut: 594
Kiselyov, A: 5939
Kisiel, Chester A: 5441
Kisielewski, Stefan: 4893
Kiss, Sandor: 4681
Kissinger, Henry A: 2696,6518,6938,6940,7919,8427
Kitano, Tosinobu G. F: 4220
Kitayeva, N: 7532
Kitchen, Martin: 1936
Kite, St. Alban: 5098
Kitzinger, Uwe W: 1513,2697,2754,2755,6714
Klabunde, Hans: 4100
Klafki, Wolfgang: 5486
Klafkowski, Alfons: 989,990,7446,7447,7448,7920,7921
Klaiber, Wolfgang: 7661
Klarsfeld, Beate: 991
Klasek, Charles Bernard: 5487
Klass, Gert Von: 3932
Klatt, Werner: 3880,3881,4617
Klaus, Joachim: 3760
Klee, Josef: 4066
Klefisch, Johannes W: 7016
Klein, Alfons: 4221
Klein, Heinrich: 8231
Klein, Johann K: 7340
Klein, John J: 3761
Klein, Peter: 1722,1978,1979,6734,6988,7533,7534
Klein, Richard D: 5696
Kleine, Erwin: 4894
Klemme, Marvin: 323
Klemperer, Klemens Von: 2445
Klenner, Hermann: 1723
Klevorick, Alvin K: 5105
Kleyer, Hermann: 8036
Kliemann, Horst G., Editor: 2153
Klima, Rolf: 5805
Klimov, Grigorii Petrovich: 3093
Kline, James D: 5738
Klingemann, Hans D: 2103,2867
Klinger, Guenter: 4612
Kloeckner, Alfred J: 5660
Klopfer, Karl E: 4358
Klopstock, Fred H: 3577
Kloskowska, Antonina: 7449
Kloss, G: 5619,5649
Kloten, Norbert: 3689
Klotzbach, Kurt: 5202
Kluge, Franz: 8251
Klugmann, James: 6864
Klugmann, Werner: 147
Knapp, R. H: 2028
Knappen, Marshall M: 1155,5001
Knappstein, K. Heinrich: 7063
Knapton, Ernest J: 6672
Knauth, Percy: 639,5238
Knees, Adalbert: 1195
Kneese, Allen V: 5106,5107
Knieriem, August Von: 992
Kniestedt, Karlheinz: 8428
Knight, David C: 8154
Knight, Rose: 5620
Knipping, Franz: 5203
Knoke, Karl Hermann: 1882
Knoll, Joachim H: 5281,5531
Knop, Werner Gustav John: 886
Knudson, Charles A: 1284
Knusel, Jack L: 4519,4520
Koca, Susan J: 6673
Koehl, Robert: 93
Koehler, Gerhard: 4618
Koehler, Heinz: 4693,4694,4711,4712,5929
Koelle, Willi: 5464
Koellermann, Hans Werner: 5009
Koenig, Ernest: 4645
Koenig, Helmut: 4728
Koenig, Johannes: 7535,7536

Koenig, Peter-Michael: 1546
Koenig, Rene: 4795,5806
Koenigswald, Harald Von: 3202
Koetter, Herbert: 1625,4796
Koetzing, Kurt: 4278,4279
Koever, J. F: 7064
Kogon, Eugen: 7017
Kohl, Helmut: 7065
Kohl, Heribert: 5204
Kohl, Michael: 7662
Kohler, Wilhelm F: 3933
Kohlhase, Norbert: 6576
Kohlmey, Guenther: 4695,4696
Kohn, Donald L: 3762
Kohn, Erwin: 5894
Kohn, Hans: 94,95,253,254,255,481,2698,2699,6299,6520,6583,6584,7066,7341,7758,7759
Kohr, Leopold: 5417
Kokot, Jozef, Editor: 7451
Kokot, Jozef: 194,387,388,7450,7452,7453
Kolarz, Henry: 8232
Kolcum, Edward H: 3934
Kollatz, Udo, Editor: 7018
Kolmin, Frank W: 3763
Komarov, M: 8081
Kommers, Donald P: 1682,1764,2331,5220
Konieczny, Jozef: 2124,5549,7391
Konvitz, Milton R: 993
Kooy, Gerrit A: 4796
Kopp, Fritz: 2971
Kopp, William L: 5997
Koppe, Karlheinz: 7067
Koppel, Thomas P: 7268
Koppens, Hendrikus Wilhelmus: 4155
Koranyi, Karl H: 3981
Korbel, Josef: 7019,7269,7270,7342
Korbonski, Andrzej: 4713,7610,7922
Kordt, Erich: 2756
Kormann, John G: 1067
Koroljov, W: 6747
Kosack, Godula: 4258
Kosok, Paul: 96
Kosovac, Nikola Dz: 1114
Kostanick, Huey Louis: 195,7454
Koszyk, Kurt: 5178
Kotov, Y: 7537,8429
Kotyk, Vaclav: 7512
Koutek, J: 6358
Kowalewski, Jerzy: 1980
Kownacki, L: 7923
Koziolek, Helmut: 4576
Kozlowski, E: 3273,7392
Kraemer, M: 4476
Kramer, Gerald H: 5105
Kramer, Yale: 994
Krane, Jay B: 5179
Kranke, Rudi: 3070
Kranz, Guenter: 4101
Krasnopolsky, V: 3355
Krasnov, Y: 4477
Krasomil, Dean Harold: 2399
Kraus, Herbert: 7455
Kraus, Hertha: 5060
Kraus, Willy, Editor: 4515
Kraus, Wolfgang H: 1196,3137
Krause, Elfriede A: 3882
Krause, Erwin: 5509,5510,5839
Krause, Harry D: 1715
Krause, Heinz: 4714
Krause, Helmut: 7924
Krause, Roland E: 2636
Kraushaar, Otto F: 5621
Krauss, Paul G: 5962
Kravis, Irving B: 3362
Kreinheder, Walter R: 708
Kreinin, Mordechai E: 7068
Krekeler, Heinz L: 6941
Krengel, Rolf: 3690,3935,8250
Kresl, Peter K: 4450
Kress, Guenther Gerhard: 5650
Kressler, Diane A: 6942
Kreutzer, Heinz: 8184
Krieger, Leonard: 256,546,547
Kriesberg, Louis: 2125,7111
Krippendorff, Ekkehart: 7207
Krisch, Henry: 887,2972
Krispyn, Egbert: 6088
Krivine, J. D: 3604,4425
Kroebel, Gerhard: 7155
Kroeger, Herbert: 2899,7611,7612,7703,7925,7926,8037,8038,8039,8040,8082
Kroeger, Wilhelm: 1857
Kroener, Arnold F: 3691
Krolikowski, Herbert: 6382,7613
Kronstein, Heinrich: 4222,5782
Krould, H. J: 3138
Kruczkowski, Adam, Editor: 6383
Kruczkowski, Adam: 8083
Krueger, Joachim: 2937,7530,7614,7615,7663,7664,7665
Krueger, Marlis: 5651
Krueger, Werner: 4619
Krug, Mark M: 5945
Kruyer, Horst: 5921
Krusch, Werner: 49
Krusche, Heinz: 1981,6384,6385
Kruszewski, Z. Anthony: 7456

Krutzsch, Walter: 3071,5138
Kryukov, P: 2825,6386,6387,6388,7271,7830,7927
Krzyzanowski, Walter: 8252
Kubek, Anthony: 548
Kubitschek, Helga: 4867
Kuby, Erich: 888
Kuby, Heinz: 6300
Kudlicki, S: 2799,2826,7208,7393,7394
Kuebler, Jeanne: 1197,2800,7928,7929
Kuebler, Ulrich: 5023
Kuenlewind, Gerhard: 4261
Kuenne, Karl: 1826,1827
Kuennelt-Leddihn, Erik R. Von: 5002,6865
Kuehnl, Reinhard: 2521
Kuelz, H. R: 3110
Kuenzli, Irvin R: 4149
Kuhlman, James A: 7538
Kuhlmann, J. Caspar: 5427
Kuhlo, Karl Christian: 3366
Kuhn, Charles G: 5511
Kuhnen, Frithjof: 3883
Kuklick, Bruce R: 3417,3497
Kuklick, Bruce: 3498
Kulischer, Eugene M: 389,390
Kulitzka, Dieter: 7680
Kullmer, L: 3814
Kulski, Wladyslaw W: 1285,7930,7931,7932
Kunde, Thelma A: 4768
Kunz, Frithjef: 3040
Kunz, Josef L: 6207,6208,6209,6210,6866
Kunze, Juergen: 4551
Kunze, Kurt: 5134
Kurchatov, A: 6389
Kursanov, G: 5774
Kurth, Edmund A: 3692,4223,4224,4225
Kutscher, Hans: 1697
Kwilecki, Andrzej: 6585,7457
Kybal, M: 1334
Kyle, Keith: 7933
Kyre, Joan: 792
Kyre, Martin: 792
Laan, Reint, Jr: 4155
Lacey, David C: 1828
Lach, Donald F: 482
Lacas, Manfred: 7458
Lackner, W: 3349
Ladd, Edward T: 5550
Lahr, Rolf: 6301
Lall, Betty Goetz: 7934
Lamberg, Werner: 2939,3274
Lambert, Dwight: 2881
Lambilliotte, Maurice: 6390
Lamby, Werner: 4521
Lamm, Hans: 2076
Lamont, Thomas W: 483
Lamouse, Annette: 4797
Landauer, Carl: 2827,3418,3499
Landeen, William M: 1156
Landwehrmann, Friedrich: 1785
Lane, John C: 1480,1683
Lane, Robert E: 4836
Lane, Stephen K: 391
Lang, Kurt: 5149
Lang, Reginald D: 8430
Langbein, John H: 1756
Langbein, Thomas: 6391
Langdon, Frank C: 2327
Lange, Annemarie: 8155
Lange, Halvard M: 7069
Langley, Robert S: 148
Lanhoff, Arthur: 1414
Lania, Leo: 6367,8358
Lanner, J: 3764
Laqueur, Walter Z: 2522,4837,6748,7343,7344,7345
Lasby, Clarence G: 3462,3463
Lasky, Melvin J: 640,3938,4838,5698,6302,8084
Latten, Friedrich: 4279
Lattimore, Bertram Gresh: 392,393
Laubach, John H: 6715
Lauckner, Nancy Ann: 5998
Lauer, Quentin: 4226
Laukhuff, Perry: 7346,7760,7831
Laumann, Edward O: 2154,2155
Laumas, Gurcharan S: 3781,3782
Laun, Kurt Von: 6211
Lauret, Rene: 6674
Lauterbach, Albert: 3557,4067
Lauterbach, Herbert: 5035,5077
Laux, William E: 2884
Lavergne, Bernard: 6392,6675
Lawrence, R. M: 6989
Lawson, Robert Frederic: 5282,5357,5418,5419,5420,5551,5946
Lawyer: 995
Layton, C. W: 4426
Lazar, Arpad Joseph Von: 3139
Lazarcik, Gregor: 4646
League of Culture for Democratic Regeneration of Germany: 889
Leahy, William D: 549
Lebed, A.I: 8431
Leber, Georg: 4280,4305
Lebovitz, Solomon: 2332
Leder, Herbert: 5036
Ledwohn, Josef: 4150,4227
Lee, Guy A: 6104,6105,6106,6107
Lee, Guy A., Editor: 6108

Lee, Robert E. A: 4984
Legault, Albert: 6943
Legien, Rudolf Roman: 8185
Legler, Harald: 3800
Legvold, Robert: 7020
Lehman, Jon A: 1716
Lehmann, Guenter: 5135
Lehmann-Grube, Hinrich: 4262
Lehmann-Haupt, Hellmut: 6057
Lehmbruch, Gerhard: 2828
Lehndorff, Hans Graf Von: 7459
Lehrman, Hal: 4952
Leibholz, Gerhard: 1649,1671,1698,1699
Leicht, Hans Dieter: 2168
Leicht, Robert: 2333
Leifer, Walter: 6790
Leiper, Henry Smith: 5003
Leipold, I. Edmond: 36
Leiser, Ernest: 394,2191
Leites, Nathan C: 2072,6868
Lekschas, John: 996,997,5136,5137
Lellau, Willi: 3939
Lemberg, Eugen: 7209
Lemberg, Gerhard: 7539
Lemner, Ernst: 395
Lengyel, Emil: 6521
Lens, Sidney: 2400
Leo, Gerhard: 998
Leo, Walter: 3203
Leonard, Irene: 5999
Leonhard, Wolfgang: 890,2920,2940
Leonhardt, Hans: 999
Leonhardt, Rudolf Walter: 1481,5421
Leopold, G. Vernon: 4478
Lepinski, Franz: 4151
Leptin, Gerd: 4620,4621
Lerch, Gerhard: 7540
Lerj, Winfried: 5150
Lerner, Daniel, Editor: 6869
Lerner, Daniel: 2156,2157,6676,6982,7156
Lerner, Max: 484,2700
Leskov, Vlas: 891
Leslie, R. F: 7395
Lesniewski, Andrzej, Editor: 7460
Lesser, Jonas: 2701,3313,4953,6620
Leutz, G: 5061
Leventhal, Harold: 1000
Levi, Carlo: 2757
Levi, Edward H: 1001
Levi, Werner: 1157
Levy, David M: 1068
Levy, Hermann J: 3884,6621
Levy, Lillian: 4954
Lewan, Kenneth M: 1700,3204
Lewin, Daniel M: 6145,6146
Lewis, Arthur: 8291
Lewis, Flora: 249,257,1198,2192,2193,2194,2195,2219,2220,2221,2702,2758,2759, 2921,2922,3205,3693,3982,5666,6023,6677,6678,6679,7832,8156,8432,8433, 8434,8435,8436,8437
Lewis, Geoffrey W: 3140
Lewis, Harold O: 1415
Lewis, Roy: 4068
Lewison, Robert: 5358
Leyser, J: 1873
Libbert, Werner: 4281
Librach, Jan: 7616
Lichtheim, George: 2760,2761,7761,8233
Liddell Hart, Basil H: 8438
Liddell, Helen, Editor: 5360
Liddell, Helen: 5359
Lider, Julian: 6944
Liebes, Peter: 5180
Liepelt, Klaus: 2101,2510,2523,5798
Liepman, Heinz: 4955
Liesner, Hans Hubertus: 4359
Ligatfoot, Claude: 5895
Lightfoot, Georgia: 5361
Lilje, Frederic: 5896
Liljegren, S. B: 5922
Lilly, Claude Clifford: 4360
Limbert, Paul M: 4839
Lincoln, G. A: 6870
Lindberg, Leon N: 2059,7157,7158
Lindegren, Alina Marie: 5283
Lindemann, Eva: 7272
Lindemann, Helmut: 5699
Lindemann, Jens Richard: 4451
Linder, Willy: 4427
Linder, Wolf: 1583
Lindholm, Richard W: 3500
Lindner, Gerhard: 8186
Linn, Rolf N: 5465
Linsel, H: 4670
Linthe, Hans: 5037
Linton, John H: 4181
Linz, Juan J: 2104,2105
Lippitt, Ronald: 5739,5758,5759
Lippmann, Heinz: 2941
Liss, Samuel: 4152
Lissance, Marjorie Fiske: 4830
Lister, Louis: 7112
Lit, Theodore: 4735
Litchfield, Edward H: 550,1335,6212
Litchfield, Edward H., and Associates: 793
Litov, M: 1547

Littell, Franklin H: 4895,4896
Litwak, Eugene: 4798
Livingston, Robert G., Moderator: 7617
Livingston, Robert Gerald: 7541
Livneh, Eliezer: 2222
Loch, Theo M: 6522
Lochner, Louis Paul: 3940
Lockett, Edward 3: 6109
Lockwood, W. B: 4868
Loeffler, E: 5284,5285,5286,5362
Loeffler, Martin: 5181
Loehr, Rodney C: 3765,6107
Loesch, Dieter: 2405
Loesche, Peter: 4153
Loewenberg, Gerhard: 1548,1549,2050,2334
Loewenstein, Karl: 709,1482,1650,1651,1652,2637,3111,5661,6871,7833,7935,8187
Loewenstein, Prince Hubertus Zu: 97,1937,6945,7834
Loewenthal, Fritz: 892
Lohenbill, F: 3141
Lohr, George: 2262,3206,3207,4647,7762,7835
Lohse, Egon: 1949
Loir, Raymond: 7210
Lomeiko, V: 2524
Lompe, Klaus: 1597,1598
London International Assembly: 485
Long, Tania: 641,794,4816,4840
Long, Wellington: 2525
Loomis, Charles: 4780
Loram, Ian C: 6034
Lorenz, Jurgen: 2829
Lorig, Arthur N: 5512
Lottich, Kenneth V: 3227,5897
Loud, Frederick V: 7100
Lougee, Robert W: 258
Lough, Thomas S: 6821
Loughary, John W: 5568
Loveday, A: 7070
Low, Alfred D: 3208
Low, David: 1002
Lowe, John: 7763
Lowenfeld, Andreas F: 486
Lowenthal, Richard: 259,7618,7764,7765,7766,7936,8439,8440,8441
Lower, Arthur R. M: 2571,6458
Lowie, Robert H: 260
Lowrey, Lawson G: 487
Lowrey, Lawson G. (Chairman): 446
Lozier, Marion E: 1003
Lubojanski, Jozef: 7423
Lubomirski, S: 7396
Lubowski, Herbert: 5090
Luchsinger, Fred: 1199,1626,1938,2017,2077,2223,2638,2703,2801,2830,2868,2885,
    2923,3094,3142,4841,5221,5622,5700,6586,6587,6680,6681,6682,7211,7273,
    7461,7836,7837,7838,7839,7937,7938,7939,8085,8442,8443,8535
Luck, Herbert: 4595
Luckman, Thomas: 4897
Ludwig, Emil: 642
Ludz, Peter Christian, Editor: 7299
Ludz, Peter Christian: 2924,2925,2926,2942,2973,3209,3275,3276,3277,5142,5923,
    6303,6459
Luebchen, Gustav-Adolf: 3041
Luebke, Paul: 1510,2078
Luedicke, Heinz E., Editor: 3650
Lueke, Rolf E: 2762,3766,3850,4428,4429,4479
Lueschen, Guenther: 4799
Lueth, Erich: 2482,4956
Luethy, Herbert: 2483,6089,6872,7212,8292
Lukaschek, Hans: 397,398
Lumer, Bob: 3278
Lunau, Heinz: 643
Lunden, Walter A: 795
Lupescu, Amando: 6163
Lupri, Eugen: 4800,4801
Lush, C. D: 8188
Lust, Peter: 8086
Lutz, Burkhart: 4102
Lutz, Friedrich A: 3578,3694,4361
Lutz, Hermann: 6683
Lutz, Ralph H: 644,645
Luza, Radomir: 399
Lvov, M: 6684
Lvovitch, David: 324
Lydon, Roger M: 6035
Lynch, James: 5442,5443,5552
Lynx, J. J., Editor: 4957
Lyon, Peyton V: 8051
Lyubsky, M: 4553
M. R: 1724
M. Z: 3558
Mab, Mikhail: 4671
Maccloskey, Monro: 8450
Maccurdy, John T: 488
Macdonald, D. F: 2296
Macdonald, H. Malcolm: 3896
Maceoin, Gary: 4985
Machrowicz, Thaddeus M: 7462
Mackey, William Francis: 5466
Mackie, Norman S., Jr: 871
Mackintosh, Malcolm: 6822
Maclennan, Malcolm: 3842
Macmillan, Harold: 6622,6623,6624
Macrae, Norman: 3695
Macridis, Roy C: 6280,6281,6685
Madariaga, Salvador De: 648
Mader, Julius: 2018,2019,2263,2763
Magathan, Wallace C: 1908,6823,6824

Maginnis, John J: 797
Maguire, Robert P: 1286
Mahle, Walter A: 5152
Mahncke, Dieter M: 1982,8536,8537,8538
Mai, Ludwig H: 3636
Maier, Karl P: 4054
Maier, Kurt S: 6000
Maier, Lutz: 6393
Maier, W: 4683
Maillat, D: 4256
Mair, John: 691
Maitland, Patrick: 8293
Majonica, Ernst: 7940
Malcuzynski, Karol: 7463
Malecky, J. M: 3885
Maletzke, Gerhard: 5239
Malik, Rex: 3697
Malinkowski, Wladyslaw: 3651
Mallard, William D., Jr: 1004
Mallinckrodt, Anita M: 3291
Mallinson, Vernon: 5287,5321
Mally, Gerhard, Editor: 6460
Mally, Gerhard: 6523
Malone, Joseph J: 6749
Maltzan, Baron Von: 4336,4362
Mampel, Siegfried: 5115
Manchester, William: 3941
Mander, John: 2126,2401,2526,2764,2765,2802,2869,2870,2886,3210,8444,8445,8446
Mankiewicz, R. H: 1829
Mann, F. A: 1287,1883,3532,6304
Mann, Golo: 98,1416,2224,6461
Mann, Thomas: 261,262,2572
Mansfield, Don Lee: 3501
Mansfield, Michael J: 6588
Mantell, David Mark: 1435
Maraḥrens, Friedhelm: 4154
Marburg, Theodore: 4055
Marck, Siegfried K: 501
Marcuse, Herbert: 2484
Marcuse, Ludwig: 5963,6072
Margolies, Daniel F: 3652
Marigold, W. G: 5183
Marjolin, Robert: 3605
Markgraf, Andre: 8087
Markiewicz, Wladyslaw: 4769,7397
Markovits, Inga S: 3042,3344
Markow, W: 4554
Markowski, Paul: 7542,7619
Marks, Edward B., Jr: 325
Markus, H. B: 3815
Markus, Joseph: 4363
Marlio, Louis: 492
Marquardt, Paul: 4306
Marsh, William W: 7681
Marshall, A. H: 1337
Marshall, Joyce: 7464
Martel, Giffard: 6873
Martin, Alexander: 6394
Martin, Bernd: 6791
Martin, Denis: 400
Martin, Friedrich P: 2999
Martin, James Stewart: 785,798
Martin, Kingsley: 1159,3546
Martin, Laurence W: 6874
Martin, Robert Lee, Jr: 5740
Marton, J. H: 401
Marvan, M: 6358
Marx, Daniel, Jr: 4395
Marx, Hugo: 1115
Marx, Walter J: 799
Marzian, Herbert G: 7465
Mason, Edward S: 800,1232,6536
Mason, Henry L: 5652
Mason, John Brown: 15,16,711,801,1436,8447
Massing, Otwin: 1684
Massing, Paul: 1069
Matern, Hermann: 2974
Matny, Leonard G: 3606
Matthes, Heinz: 2962
Matthes, Joachim: 4899
Matthews, George: 7767
Mattaijssen, M. A. J. M: 4900
Mattick, Kurt: 8539
Matzat, Wilhelm: 143
Mauldin, W. Parker: 217
Maurer, Ely: 3533
Maurois, Andre: 99
Max, Alan: 6875
Maxson, Rhea F: 4817
Maxwell, John Allen: 2402
May, Arthur J: 5623
May, Jacques M: 5126
Mayer, Herbert C: 3607,5288
Mayer, Karl Ulrich: 4770,4771
Mayer, Lyle V: 5624
Mayer, Milton: 263
Mayhew, Alan: 3886
Maynard, Peter: 1288,1377,2264,2403,3419
Mayne, Richard, Editor: 6462
Mayntz, Renate: 1483,2371,5701
Mcalpin, Michelle Burge: 5731
Mccarthy, John J: 3942
Mcclaskey, Beryl R: 3014,4898
Mcclellan, Grant S., Editor: 3314
Mcclelland, Charles A: 8210,8448,8449

Mcclelland, Charles E: 6095
Mcclelland, David C: 2028
Mccloy, John J: 796,2573,2574,6524
Mcclure, Robert A: 5151
Mcclure, Worth: 5289
Mccormick, Anne O'Hare: 551,646,647
Mccormick, Joan: 264,3143
Mccrone, Donald J: 2059,2100
Mcdermott, Geoffrey: 8451
Mcdougall, Ian: 2575
Mcelheny, Victor K: 5964
Mcgeehan, Robert J: 6525,6876
Mcgill, V. J: 3464
Mcgoldrick, Frederick Ford: 4394
Mcgranahan, Donald V: 2029,4842,6024
Mcgrath, Earl J: 1158
Mchargue, Daniel S: 1514
Mcinnes, Neil: 2446,2943
Mcinnis, Edgar: 710,2639,6213,8452
Mckay, Llewelyn R: 5290,5625
Mckee, Ilse: 2704
Mckelvey, Raymond D: 552
Mckenzie, R. T: 6589
Mckesson, John A: 7113
Mckinnon, Thomas Ray: 4364
Mclaughlin, Kathleen: 1378,2225,8157
Mclellan, David S: 7941
Mcmeekin, Gordon C: 4375
Mcpherson, William H: 1886,4228,4229,4230,4231,4232,4233
Mcwhinney, Edward: 1685,1701,1702,1725,1856
Mead, A. R: 649
Mead, Nelson P: 489
Medical Research Council: 5062
Meguen, P.J: 1599
Megnin, Donald F: 4522
Mehnert, Klaus: 5702,6590,7071
Mehren, Arthur T. Von: 1653,1654,1686,1755,1799
Meier, Ernest: 5184
Meier, P. J: 5775
Meier, Victor: 7942,8453
Meijer, Hendricus Johannes: 4155
Meimberg, Rudolf: 4736,8253
Meinhardt, Hans: 8088
Meisel, James H: 718
Meissner, Alfred: 402
Meissner, Boris: 7620,7621,7622
Meissner, W: 7840
Meister, Charles W: 5363
Meister, Roland: 1730
Melby, Ernest O: 5364
Melby, Everett K: 403
Melchinger, Siegfried: 5965
Melnikov, D. E: 3698,6305,6306,6395,6396,6946,6947
Melsheimer, Klaus: 8532
Meltzer, Bernard D: 1001
Memorandum On The Traffic In Citizens Of The German: 8206
Menck, Clara: 650,1160
Menczer, Bela: 6214
Mende, Tibor: 651,1233,2079,3502,3898,4156
Mendershausen, Horst: 1983,1984,2080,2871,3367,3653,4365,4366,4367,4648,4737, 4754,4755,6463,6825,6826,6948,6949,7114
Mendlovitz, Saul: 8189
Menges, Constantine: 5218
Menshikov, V: 2766
Mensonides, Louis J: 6526,7274
Menzel, Walter: 2705
Mercado, Perla N: 3654
Merkatz, Hans Joachim Von: 62
Merker, Paul: 490
Merkl, Peter H: 712,1379,1380,1437,1484,1515,2226,2335,3816,6147,7159,8118
Merleker, Hartmuth: 32
Merriam, Charles E: 1158
Merritt, Anna J: 1070,2082,2872,5422,5423
Merritt, Anna J., Editor: 2081
Merritt, Richard L: 2082,2083,2127,2128,2872,2963,2975,5422,5423,5703,5947, 6280,6281,6990,7275,8190,8234,8235,8236,8237,8238,8454,8455,8540
Merritt, Richard L., Editor: 2081,2129
Merzyn, Gerhard: 7347
Mesa-Lago, Carmelo, Editor: 4622
Meskil, Paul S: 2485
Mestmaecher, E. J: 1830
Meszaros, Joseph W: 2084
Metcalfe, John C: 6527
Metraux, Rhoda Bubendey: 2030,4802,4803
Mettin, Harry: 5133
Mettler, Eric: 6950
Metzger, Stanley D: 8191
Metzner, Wolfgang: 62
Meyer, Alex: 1892
Meyer, Erich: 2227
Meyer, Ernst W: 2336,4523,5807
Meyer, Fritz W: 3574
Meyer, Henry Cord: 100,2640
Meyer, Henry J: 4781
Meyer, Ingeborg, Editor: 72
Meyer, Karl J: 4100
Meyer, Klaus: 7160
Meyer-Landrut, Andreas: 7276
Meyer-Lindenberg, Hermann: 7466
Meyerhoff, Hans: 1338,2337
Meynen, E: 149
Mezerik, Avrahm G: 8457,8458
Miaudet, Francois: 3699
Michaelis, Alfred: 4368
Michaely, Michael: 4452

Michalowski, Roman: 7398
Michalski, John: 6025
Michel, Aloys A: 4307
Middleton, Drew: 265,266,267,268,802,1005,1161,1289,1290,2228,2229,2486,2487, 2576,2577,2578,2579,2641,4843,4844,6307,6877,7072,7348,8294,8295,8296, 8297,8298
Midgley, John: 1485,3655,7841
Mieczkowski, Bogdan: 4623
Mieroszewski, Juliusz: 7943
Mies, Herbert: 2447
Mikes, George: 33
Mikhailov, Vladimir Ivanovich: 2001,2803,2831,2832,6397,7543,7944
Miksche, Ferdinand O: 554,6951,8459
Militz, Alfred, Editor: 76
Milfull, John: 6026
Miller, Alexander F., and Others: 2488
Miller, Barry: 3934
Miller, Dorothy: 4624
Miller, Moses: 2265
Miller, Robert W: 1339,2338
Miller, Robert W., Editor: 805
Millet, John A. P: 446
Milliken, Robert: 1234
Milroy, Nicholas R: 3534
Milyukova, Valentina: 2130,2489,3213,6591,7073,7544
Minssen, Frederic: 5291,5292
Mintz, Ilse S: 3379
Mirbach, Baron D. Von: 4524
Mire, Joseph: 4157
Mirus, Karl Rolf: 3767
Mischaikow, Michael K: 4000
Mischel, Walter: 5741
Mishin, A: 6684
Mittag, Guenter: 4625
Mittendorf, Herbert: 4480,4481
Mitter, Wolfgang: 5444
Moe, George R: 1950
Moehle, Horst: 5898,5924
Moehring, Dieter: 3389
Moeller, Dietrich: 7277
Moenkemeier, Karl-Ludwig: 150
Moennich, Martha L: 4986
Moennig, Richard: 17,18,19,6164,8124
Moetteli, Carlo: 3700,3701,3702,3703,3704,4056,8254
Mogens, Victor: 7842
Mohl, Kurt: 3214
Moldt, Ewald: 7704
Molotov, Viacheslav Mikhailovich: 1235,1236,6215,6216
Molter, A., Rapporteur: 8460
Moltmann, Guenter: 555
Mommsen, Hans: 5360
Monckton of Brenchley, Major-General the Viscount: 6952
Money-Kyrle, Roger Ernle: 269
Montagu, Ivor: 1255,3461
Montgomery, John D: 713
Mookerjee, Girija K: 1486,2339,6308,6792
Moore, Charles Henry, Editor: 1487
Moore, Lyford: 8299
Moore, William W: 2085
Moore-Rinvolucri, Mina J: 5899
Morawski, Kajetan: 7399
Morgan, D. J: 3656
Morgan, Edward P: 2490,5365
Morgan, John H: 1006,1007
Morgan, Roger P: 101,1488,2873,2874,6309,6528,6529,6625
Morgan, Roger P., Editor: 6619
Morgenthau, Hans J: 652,1008,1237,2580,2767,6530,6592,7843,8278,8462
Morgenthau, Hans J., Editor: 6593
Morgenthau, Henry, Jr: 556,653
Moritz, Gunther: 1951
Mork, Gordon R: 5925,5926
Morkel, Arnd: 1529
Moro Serrano, Sebastian: 1600
Morris, Bernard S: 2448
Morris, Eric: 8300
Morris, Stuart: 6878
Morrow, Felix: 557
Morstein Marx, Fritz: 1601
Mosely, Philip E: 558,559,6183
Moses, Fritz: 3503
Moses, John A: 102
Mosheim, Berthold: 4818
Moskowitz, Moses: 2340
Mosley, Leonard O: 654
Mosley, Oswald: 7074
Moss, John J., Editor: 1786
Motekat, Ula K: 4030
Motherwell, Hiram: 491
Mott, Rodney L: 3420
Moulton, Harold: 492
Mowat, Charles L: 6923
Mueckl, Wolfgang J: 3840
Muehlenberg, Friedrich: 5742
Muehlmann, W. E: 5808
Mueller, Albert: 2642,2706,2707,2708,2768,2769,8463
Mueller, Eberhard: 183
Mueller, Ernst F: 404
Mueller, Eva: 4577
Mueller, Gebhard: 1655,1687
Mueller, Gerd: 4031
Mueller, Gerhard O. W: 1857
Mueller, Gerry G: 3887
Mueller, Gordon H: 2804
Mueller, Hans Dieter: 5205
Mueller, Hans Gerhard: 8077

Mueller, Paul: 5108
Mueller, Peter: 3897
Mueller, Rudolf, Editor: 1809
Mueller, Rudolf: 1717,1787
Mueller, Walter: 4771,4772,7844
Mueller, Wilhelm Johann: 5063
Mueller, Wolfgang: 8231
Mueller-Freienfels, Wolfram: 1788,1789,1874
Mueller-Wieland, Marcel: 5861
Muench, Fritz: 5807
Muenchmeyer, Alwin H: 4369
Muggeridge, Malcolm: 270
Muhlberg, Dietrich: 3279
Muhlen, Norbert: 806,1939,2476,2643,2709,3113,3144,3943,4845,4958,5966,7278,
    8119,8120
Mulaern, James: 1162
Mulin, V: 6387,6388
Mullady, Philomena: 4181
Muller, Steven: 2833
Mulready, Brendan P: 8301
Multhoff, Robert: 5553
Munich, Reconstruction Department: 184
Munro, Gordon Douglas: 8016
Muralt, Anton Von: 1627
Murphy, John George: 5809
Murphy, L. E: 5054
Murphy, Michael E: 4482
Murphy, Patrick W: 6991
Murphy, Robert: 1291
Murray, John: 2644,2710,7076,8158
Murray, Michael Patrick: 1009
Muta, Wilfried Robert: 3380
Mutnesius, Volkmar: 3768
Myers, Henry Allen: 4517,4752
Myers, Paul F: 217
Myers, Shirley: 8464
Myrdal, Gunnar: 3657,3658
N. M: 1292,5927
Nadelmann, Kurt H: 714,1688,1757,3535
Nadich, Judah: 4959
Nagel, Heinrich: 1765
Nagle, John David: 2527,2528
Nahrgang, Wilbur Lee: 6036
Nakashidze, Niko: 7213
Nakropin, O: 7214
Nanes, Allan S: 6594,6827
Napoli, Joseph F: 1071
Narpati, B: 4263
Narr, Wolf-Dieter: 6148
Natarajan, B: 4637
Nathan, Hans: 3043,3044
Nathan, Paul: 4370
National Association of Manufacturers: 3659
National Conference on the Occupied Countries: 655
National Front of Democratic Germany: 2266,2267,2491,2834,6398,6399,6400,
    6401,7545,7945
National Peace Council, London: 656
Natorp, Klaus: 6750
Naumann, Bernd: 1010
Naumann, Hans Guenther: 1628
Naumann, Theodor: 4846
Neal, Fred Warner: 7946,7947,8465,8466
Nearing, Scott: 3215
Neef, Arthur: 4104
Nell-Breuning, Oswald Von: 3705
Nellessen, Bernd: 5704
Nelson, Daniel J: 8192
Nelson, Harold I: 7845
Nelson, Kenneth R: 5185
Nelson, Walter Henry: 3332,3944,8159
Nenno, William C: 1909
Nerlich, Uwe: 6954,6992
Nesselrode, Franz Von (Pseud. for Joachim Joesten): 3216
Nessi, Serge: 3145
Nettl, John Peter: 2645,3114,6217
Nettl, Peter: 893,3504,7768
Neu, Axel: 4282
Neubert, Wolfram: 7948
Neubroch, H: 7846
Neuloh, Otto: 4105,4234
Neumann, Erich Peter, Editor: 2087
Neumann, Erich Peter: 2086,2131,2230
Neumann, Franz L: 1011,1163,1293,1340,2581,4158,6218,6879
Neumann, Robert G: 807,1012,1341,1489,1490,2341
Neumann, Sigmund: 493,1438,1491,2342,7769
Neumark, Fritz: 3817
Neumeister, Hermann: 5554
Neunreither, Karlheinz: 1564,1565
Neuse, Werner: 3315
Neven-Du Mont, Juergen: 1492
Nevsky, Viacheslav: 894
New York, Committee on Nuclear Attack Recovery: 3660
Newhouse, John: 6953
Newman, Bernard: 2584,2646,3217,3316
Newman, James R: 1164,5366
Newman, Jean J: 326
Newman, Pauline M: 4820
Nichol, David M: 808
Nicholls, Anthony: 1318,2231
Nickel, Herman: 3706
Niebergall, Fred: 1013
Niebuhr, Reinhold: 2404,4987,6219
Nieduszynski, T: 406
Niehus, Rudolf J: 1790,4032
Niens, Walter: 5513

Niethammer, Fritz: 8036
Nikolsky, P: 6402
Nipperdey, Hans Carl: 4185,4186
Nix, Claire: 2343
Nixdorff, Peter W: 5424,5799
Nobleman, Eli E: 715,809,6110
Noell, Kurt: 5024
Noelle, Elisabeth, Editor: 2087
Noelle, Elisabeth: 2088,2230
Noelle-Neumann, Elisabeth: 2089
Noessig, Manfred: 6090
Noetzold, Juergen: 7279
Nolting, Orin F: 1629
Norden, Albert: 595,2268,2944,6403,6626,6955,7546,8017
Nordheim, Manfred Von: 1744,2297
Nordhorn, Karlhugo: 5028
Norman, Albert: 310,6531
Normanton, E. L: 1602
Norris, Betty: 4311
Norris, Grace: 4847
Northcott, Cecil: 4903
Northedge, F. S: 6627
Northrhine-Westphalia Planning Council for Higher Education: 5445
Nota, Ernst Erich (Pseud. for Paul Krantz): 3559
Notnardt, Fritz: 5293,5294,5295,5296,5297
Notaomb, Pierre: 7847
Nova, Fritz: 1493
Novoseltsev, Y: 6404,6405,6406,7280,8089
Nowak, Zdzislaw: 7161,7215,7406
Nowakowski, Stefan: 7467,7468
Nyitray, Margot S: 2344
O'Brien, William V: 811
O'Connor, Roger Day: 5489
O'Donnell, James P: 1015,2196,6687,8467
Oberdoerfer, Conrad W: 7162
Oberhauser, Alois: 3851
Oberlaender, Theodor, Editor: 407
Obermayer, Klaus: 5577
Observer: 2345,6686,7400
Obst, Maxwell: 7045
Oecd, Committee for Invisible Transactions: 4483
Oecd, Directorate for Scientific Affairs: 5405,5447
Oecd: 3369,3390,3769,3888,3945,3946,4106,5065,5109,5262,5322,5403,5404,5446,
  5488
Oeftering, H: 3818
Oels, Heinrich: 5110
Oettle, Karl: 3819
Offenberg, Maria: 5776
Ofodile, Gilbert: 3218
Ogletree, Earl J: 2031,2032
Ogmore, Lord: 560
Ogrizek, Dore: 39
Oidtman, Christoph Von, Editor: 1858
Old Liberal: 408
Oliver, Henry M: 4057
Olivier, Hans: 7705
Ollenhauer, Erich: 2647,2648,2711
Ollig, Gerhard: 4756,4757
Ollssner, Fred: 3219
Olsen, Arthur J: 2197,2198,2232,2927,3220,3465,5222,5667,6037,6111,8468,8469
Olsen, Erling: 4372
Onslow, C. G. D: 6880
Opie, Redvers: 3707,7770
Opoku, Kwame: 1859
Oppe, Hubert W: 4848
Oppenheim, A. N: 5561
Oppenheimer, P. M: 4432
Oppermann, Thomas: 7281
Organski, A. F. K: 8470
Orion (Pseud.): 8302
Ort, Alexandr, Editor: 6383
Ortlieb, Heinz-Dietrich: 2405,5706
Orton, Peter K: 8303
Osgood, Robert Endicott: 6956
Ost, Friedhelm: 4484
Ostoya, M: 6407,7401,7949,7950
Ostwald, Walter: 1417,4187
Ott, Harry: 7547,7548,7624
Otto, G: 4698
Ou, C. Chau-Fei: 4485
Oudegeest, J. J: 347
Owen, Francis: 271
P. W: 895
P. S. J. C: 4069
P. V. Z: 7115
Pabsch, Wiegand: 5743
Pabst, Alfred A: 7349
Pachter, Henry M: 1200,2406,2712,2875
Packman, Martin: 2713
Padover, Saul K: 812
Pagel, Karl, Editor: 7469
Paget, Reginald: 1940
Paikert, G. C: 409
Pakenham, Lord: 359
Pakuscher, Ernst K: 1741,1742,1766,8193
Palyleish, Donald D: 2269
Palmer, James O: 291
Palmer, Martha Ellen: 410
Pan, Stephen C. Y: 561
Panfilov, Y: 6409
Panic, M: 3381
Panten, Hans-Joachim: 3770,3771
Panter-Brick, Keith: 2714
Papadas, Panagiotis, Editor: 8471
Papanek, Ernst: 327

Pappi, Franz Urban: 2154,2155,2867
Parfitt, Trevor: 7163
Parias, Louis-Henri: 6688
Parker, Margaret: 657
Parker, William N: 3947
Parkin, Ben: 6881
Parkman, Henry: 3255
Parry, Albert: 3466
Parson, Ruby A: 5240
Pascholt, Eduard: 5025
Pastusiak, Longin: 6410,6532
Patch, Buel W: 658,7771
Paterson, William E: 2407,2883,6310
Patterson, William E: 7077
Pauck, Wilhelm: 484
Pauga, Alvis: 4254
Paul, H. W: 5256
Paul, Wolfgang: 6073
Paulding, C. G: 484
Pauls, Rolf Friedemann: 6533
Paulu, Burton: 5241
Pauw, Alan D: 8211
Pavlock, Ernest J: 3820
Pavlov, A: 6411
Payne, J. E: 3317
Peace Council Of The Gdr: 8121
Peace Council of the GDR: 7550
Peak, Helen: 1165
Pebworth, Robert: 3983
Peck, Joachim: 3345,8052,8212
Peck, Reginald: 196,7625
Peel, Doris: 6534
Peet, John: 2529,7951,8304,8305
Pelius, P: 6412
Pelster, H: 4084
Peltzer, Martin: 3772
Pen (International Writers Organization): 6408
Pentland, Charles: 6459
Perera, Reggie: 7682
Perlmutter, Howard: 2115
Perlmutter, Nathan: 2771
Perlo, Victor: 6413,6414
Pernica, Karel M: 4085
Perryman, J. Nelson: 5448
Perusse, Roland I: 7772
Peter, A: 4086
Peters, Hans: 1603
Peters, P: 6415
Peters, William: 659
Petersmann, Ernst U: 4525
Peterson, Hans Joachim: 1201
Petrashik, A: 5928
Petri, Alexander: 6993
Petrocelli, Peter: 7283
Petrov, V: 7350
Petrushev, A: 7626
Petterson, Harold: 4738
Peukert, Werner: 4396
Pfaffenberger, Hans: 5078
Pfannenschwarz, Karl: 1731,1860
Pfeffer, Karl Heinz: 5744
Pfeiffer, Gerd, Editor: 1726
Pferdmenges, Robert: 3773
Pfitzer, Albert: 1566
Pfotenhauer, David: 5810
Philipps, Eugene A: 4486
Phillip, Werner: 5626
Phillips, Eurr W: 5367
Phillips, Paul: 4159
Piater, Willi: 8090
Picht, Georg: 5111
Picaugin, B: 4555
Pick, Frederick Walter: 1238,1239,1240
Pick, Otto: 2835
Pickett, Ralph H: 7470
Picton, Harold: 272
Pilgert, Henry P: 4782,4819,5153,5368,5745,6112,6116
Pilkington, Roger: 40
Pillsbury, Kent: 5555
Pinder, John: 7234
Pines, Jerome M: 3422
Pinner, Frank A: 5707
Pinney, Edward Lee: 1567,1568,1569
Pinnow, Hermann: 103
Pinson, Koppel S: 104
Pipping, Knut: 2033
Pirro, Ellen B: 6990
Pirsch, Hans: 2492
Piszczkowski, T: 7403
Pitt, Felix N: 5369
Pittman, Margrit: 3221,3318
Planck, Charles R: 7952
Planck, Ulrich: 4849
Plath, Werner: 4033
Platts-Mills, John: 7773
Plehwe, F.-K. Von: 6812,7078,7079
Plischke, Elmer: 1072,1073,1494,1495,1884,2772,6113,6114,6115,6116,6222,6223,
    8828,7706,7953,8194,8195,8196,8472
Plochmann, Richard: 3904
Ploy, Stanley C: 2034
Poage, Oren J: 1386
Poeggel, Walter: 7954
Pogodin, A: 6416
Pohekar, G. S: 1486
Pohle, Wolfgang: 4487,4488

Pois, Robert A: 105
Polak, Karl: 3222
Poland, Embassy: 1294
Poland, Ministry of Preparatory Work Concerning Peace Conf: 494,495
Polanyi, Ilona: 2493
Polikett, George: 6994
Polish American Congress: 7471
Polish-American Conference of Illinois: 7404
Polligkeit, Wilhelm: 5048
Pollitt, Harry: 6882
Pollock, James K: 496,717,718,785,1277,1323,1480,1497,1516,1517,1630,2585,2649, 6535,6536
Pollock, James K., Editor: 1496
Polska Agencja Prasowa: 7405
Poltorak, Arkadii I: 6957
Polyanov, N: 6595
Polyzoides, Adamantios Th: 6224,6883
Pommerening, H. E: 1631
Pommernelle, Lothar: 5515,5516
Ponomarev, G: 6995
Ponto, Juergen: 3774
Popova, T: 1418
Poppe, Eberhard: 3045,7707
Porter, Lyman W: 4063
Porter, Rose Albert: 4850
Possony, Stefan T: 2449,3280,8239,8473,8474
Poste, Lester I: 5154
Postler, Fred: 5394,5900
Potter, Pitman B: 719
Pounds, Norman J. G: 124,151,190,3984,7955
Pounds, Norman J. G., Editor: 125
Pouyat, Anna-Juliette: 7164
Powell, Charles A: 2090
Powell, George L: 7080
Powell, Nicolas: 218
Powell, Robert: 2586,2587,2650,7473,8160
Powik, Gerhard: 2945
Poznanski, V. J: 7216,7285,7286,7287,7288,8541
Prakken, Lawrence W: 5370
Predoehl, Andreas: 3391
Preece, Rodney J. C: 1439,1505,1632,1732,2233,2530,2531,8475
Preston, Ralph C: 5467,5468
Preuss, Lawrence: 1419
Price, Arnold H: 20,21,22,77,1512,5066,5263,6702
Price, Coy H: 3505
Price, Hoyt: 1295
Price, M. Philips: 6225
Pridham, Geoffrey: 1518,2372
Primeau, John King: 6001
Pringle, Robin: 3775
Prinz, Joachim: 4960
Pritchard, Norris T: 3889
Pritt, Denis N: 1016,1017,1018,2532,2836,3948,6417,6418,8053,8476
Prittie, Terence C. F: 41,273,1550,1551,2199,2234,2373,2408,2588,2651,2715, 2773,3223,3985,6628,6629,7289,7848,7849,7956,7957,8477
Proebst, Herman: 6630
Prokop, Siegfried: 6419,8091
Pross, Harry: 274,2716
Proudfoot, Malcolm J: 328
Prowe, Diethelm Manfred-Hartmut: 8478
Pryor, Frederic L: 4715,4739,4740,5929
Przybylski, Peter: 1019,1733,1861,2298,3046,8092
Pucaala, Donald J: 2132,2133,6690,7081,7082
Pucaala, Donald J., Editor: 2129
Pueschel, Heinz: 3047,3048
Pulch, Dieter, Editor: 4463
Pulzer, Peter G. J: 2346,2347,2533,2774
Pundeff, Marin V: 7853
Pundt, Alfred C: 1166
Purcell, David W: 1875
Purcell, Henry: 7774
Putnam, John J: 42
Putnam, Robert D: 2158
Puttkamer, Ellinor Von: 6807
Quaestor: 3506,6420,6421,6422,6632,6633,7775,8306
Quilitzsch, Siegmar: 7021,7351,7627
R. J. W: 1343
R. S: 1910
R.S: 2450
Rabier, Jacques-Rene: 2134,7083
Rabl, Kurt: 7958
Rachocki, Janusz: 4236
Radcliffe, Stanley: 50
Raddatz, Fritz: 2948
Radice, Jonathan: 2876
Radin, Max: 1020,1021
Radmann, Martin: 7959
Radspieler, Anthony: 3708
Radspieler, Tony: 411
Raede, John W: 4870
Raetsch, Herbert: 4035
Ragnov, V: 1728
Rainwater, Lee: 4804
Raiser, Ludwig: 5425
Raman, K. V. Sri: 7776
Ramn, Th: 1887
Ramming, Hans: 8479
Rand, H. P: 3579
Randall, Earle S: 5426
Raphael, Joan: 896
Rapp, Don W: 4805
Ratazzi, Peter: 7777
Ratchford, Benjamin Ulysses: 3507
Rau, Heinrich: 3224
Raup, Philip M: 4649,7474

Rauschenplat, Helmut Von: 5517
Raven, Wolfram Von: 6958
Rawlings, E. H: 6716
Ray, Edward J: 3776
Raymond, Jack: 412,660
Razmerov, V. V., Editor: 6383
Read, James M: 413,5627
Read, Ralph R., Iii: 6027
Reade, Arthur E. E., Editor: 1858
Rebel, Karlheinz: 5532
Reddick, John: 6038
Redlow, Gotz: 2949
Reece, B. Carroll: 7475,7960
Reed, Douglas: 1022
Reel, A. Frank: 1001
Rees, Goronwy: 2775
Regnery, Henry: 5631
Reich, Donald R: 1689
Reich, Nathan: 4160,4161
Reich-Ranicki, Marcel: 6002,6074
Reichel, Hans: 4237,4238,4239,4240
Reichling, Heidi: 5723
Reichman, Felix: 6003
Reichmann, Eva G: 2494
Reif, Hans: 8480
Reijrotski, Erich: 2135
Reiner, Klaus: 4627
Reimann, Horst: 414
Reimann, Karl: 1241
Reimann, Max: 2451,2452,2453,2454,2805,3333
Reimers, H: 5298,5299,5300,5301
Reinemann, John O: 5079
Reiner, Conrad: 2928
Reinhardt, Rudolf: 5930
Reinhold, Otto: 2806,7165
Reinsch, Ruth H: 3580
Reischer, O. R: 6717
Reischock, Wolfgang: 5901
Reisener, Wolfgang: 4373
Reissig, Karl: 3270,7650
Remak, Joachim: 8018
Remington, Robin Alison: 7628
Remmers, H. H: 4851
Remmert, Wilhelm, Editor: 3467
Renneberg, Joachim: 996,997,5135,5138
Rennhack, Horst: 6793,7683
Renning, H. Dieter: 4741
Research: 6331
Reston, James B: 8278
Reuss, Frederick G: 3821
Reuter, Ernst: 7778,8307
Rexin, Manfred: 3225
Reyman, K: 6596
Reynaud, Paul: 7084
Rheinstein, Max: 720,1656,1657,5783
Rhode, Gotthold, Editor: 7476
Rhode, Gotthold: 7217
Rhodes, Edmund O: 3949
Rias Berlin: 5242
Rich, Bennett M: 1718
Rich, Fern: 4564
Rich, Grover: 7853
Richards, Hyrum E: 5452
Richards, Paul: 1296
Richardson, Hugh F: 8338
Richardson, James L: 2837,6959,7290
Richardson, Justin: 661
Richebaecher, Kurt: 3709,3710,3711,3712,3713,3714,3778,4433,4434,4454
Richert, Ernst: 2929
Richner, Edmund: 6634
Richter, Hans: 4716
Richter, Kurt: 7166
Richter, Rolf: 5152
Richter, Werner: 1167
Richthofen, Hermann Von: 7291
Ricklin, Alois: 8482
Riddy, Donald C: 1252
Ridley, F. F: 1440,1952,4308
Rie, Robert: 1023
Rieder, Guenther: 2035
Riege, Gerhard: 7552
Riegert, Robert A: 1800,5784,5785,5786
Riekhoff, Harald Von: 7369,7370,7371
Riemann, Tord: 2900
Riemeck, Renate: 6885
Ries, Wolfgang: 4704
Riesenfeld, Stefan: 6537
Riesman, David: 8481
Riess, Curt: 1168,8308
Riggs-Davidson, John: 7167
Rimestad, Idar: 6123
Rimlinger, Gaston V: 4162,4852,5010,5027
Rinck, Gerd: 1893,4309
Ringer, Franz: 4238
Ringleb, Waldemar: 3779
Ringwald, Siegfried C: 5302
Rippley, Lavern J: 275,6091
Ritter, Annelies J: 5475
Ritter, Gerhard: 1953,2589,7961
Ritter, Traudel: 3049
Rittershausen, H: 3780
Roberts, Benjamin C: 4188
Roberts, Frank: 6464,7292
Roberts, Geoffrey K: 1498,7293
Roberts, Henry L: 7629,7852

Roberts, Holland: 6424
Robertson, Brian, Lord of Oakridge: 2776
Robertson, Edwin Hanton: 4988
Robertson, W: 4455
Robinsohn, Saul B: 5427,5556,5777
Robinson, Cyril D: 1862
Robinson, G. W. S: 153,8240
Robinson, Harold, Editor: 5519
Robinson, Harold: 5518
Robinson, Jacob: 1116
Robinson, John P: 5243
Robinson, Nehemiah: 1117,1118,1119,1120,1121,1122,1123,1124,1125
Robson, Charles B: 5811
Robson, Charles B., Editor: 8483
Robson, Karl: 2807,2876
Robson, William A: 1344
Rockwell, Alvin J: 1658
Rodes, John E: 106
Roding, Horst: 6151
Rodnick, David: 276
Rodrigo, Robert: 8309
Roediel, Werner: 3319
Roejele, Otto B: 2652,6718
Roen, Klaus: 4526
Roeloffs, K: 5582
Roemer, Joseph: 5557
Roeper, Burkhardt: 2590
Roepke, Wilhelm: 662,663
Rogers, John M: 3986
Rogger, Hans: 3226
Rogmann, Klaus: 1954,1955
Rogin, Lawrence: 5372
Rogowski, Ronald Lynn: 1441,1442
Rokkan, Stein: 2106,2107,5432
Rolfe, Sidney E: 4036
Rommen, Heinrich: 1672
Romoser, George K: 1539,2808
Ropp, Stephen De: 7352
Rose, Guenther: 7294
Rose, Harald: 7708,7709
Rose, Jonathan William: 8484
Rose, Richard, Editor: 185
Rose, Saul: 6635
Rosen, Edgar R: 8485
Rosenberg, Alfons: 5471
Rosenberg, Ludwig: 4163,4241
Rosenthal, A. M: 7477
Rosenthal, Harry K: 416
Rosenthal, Walther: 3050
Roskamp, Karl W: 3370,3781,3782,3822,3852,3853,4374,4375,4672,4700,4742
Ross, Albion: 277
Ross, Arthur M: 4242
Ross, William D: 3507
Rossmiller, George E: 3890
Rostow, Eugene V: 1297,1298
Rostow, Walt Whitman: 6538,7962,7963
Roth, Guenther: 1074
Rothfels, Hans: 417,1202
Rothman, Stanley: 1499,2777
Rothschild, K. W: 5812
Rothweiler, Robert L: 3823
Roucek, Joseph S: 3227,5813,5814,8486
Roux, Rene: 3950
Rovan, Joseph: 278
Rovere, Richard H: 8487
Rowson, Sefton W. D: 1126
Royal Institute of International Affairs: 497,1262,3661
Royce, Hans: 63
Rozen, V: 3783
Rubin, Henry B: 4904
Rubinstein, Alvin Z: 7218,7964
Rubinstein, Aryeh: 3509
Rudelt, Walter: 3051
Rudick, Georg: 4669
Rudoi, G: 1941
Rudolf, Walter: 1443
Rudolph, Karl: 2534
Rudolph, Vladimir: 897,898
Rueckert, George L: 1552,1553
Rueckriem, Georg: 5569
Ruediger, Wilhelm: 3951
Ruegle, Juergen: 2950
Ruemmland, Ullrich: 3003,3228
Rueschemeyer, Dietrich: 4774,5815
Ruff, Gunther Hermann: 418
Ruge, Friedrich: 1942,1943,6960
Ruge, Wolfgang: 7553
Rugg, Dean S: 154,186
Rugh, William A: 5244
Ruhl, Lothar: 6459
Ruhm Von Oppen, Beate: 721,2778
Rumpf, Helmut: 7022
Rupp, Hans G: 1659,1690,1758,1767
Rupp-Von Bruenneck, Wiltraut: 1691
Rusa, Kenneth: 8542
Russ, William A., Jr: 813
Russell, Edward F. L., Lord of Liverpool: 2495,2653
Russell, Francis: 108
Russell, William F: 1169,1170,1171
Russett, Bruce M: 2002,6996
Russi, Bernard A., Jr: 5245
Rust, Val Dean: 5449,5747,5748
Rust, William: 664
Rutgaizer, V: 4717
Rutgers University, Department of Sociology: 3146

Rutherford, Malcolm: 6311
Ryder, A. J: 109
Ryle, G. B: 3905
Ryten, Eva: 5450
Rzheshevsky, O: 5939
Rzhevsky, I: 8093
Rzhevsky, Yuri Sergeevich: 2838,6425,8488
S. E. S: 2951
Saal, Hubert: 5967
Sabelnikov, L: 6735
Sach, Kurt: 4628
Sachar, Abram L: 1444
Sadler, Charles G: 7478
Sadowski, George G: 7479
Saeter, Martin: 7295
Safran, William: 5967,5068
Sagalowitz, Benjamin: 1203
Sahmer, Heinz: 4189,4283
Sala, J. R: 7853
Sale-Harrison, Leonard: 1299
Salin, Edgar: 2591
Salomon, Ernst Von: 1075,3147
Salomon, Jean-Jacques: 5862
Salowsky, Heinz: 3919
Saltzman, Charles E: 1345,3560
Salvin, Marina: 6997
Salwin, Lester N: 419
Samant, Bal: 7684
Sammet, Rolf: 4376
Samuel, Richard H: 126,2654,3115,5303
Samuels, Gertrude: 330,331,1204,2270,2655,4853
Sanakoyev, Sh: 6426,7353
Sanderson, Fred H: 3392
Sandgreber, John: 5863
Sandmann, Fritz: 3961
Sandulescu, Jacques: 3561
Sankaran, S: 43
Santelli, Cesar: 5373
Saposs, David J: 4164,4165
Sasse, Christoph, Editor: 6150
Sauer, Ernst: 5632
Sauer, Wolfgang: 4310
Sauermann, Heinz: 197,3581
Saur, Karl-Otto, Editor: 2159
Sauvant, Karl P: 7085
Savage, Paul L: 2535
Savory, Douglas L: 155
Sawer, G: 1445,2717
Sawicki, Jerzy, Editor: 7965
Sawicki, Jerzy: 6961
Scammell, W. M: 4435
Scammon, Richard M: 1519,2348,7779
Scanlon, David G: 5323
Scaperlanda, Anthony E: 4603
Scarangello, Anthony: 5324
Scarlett, Dora: 4650
Schacht, Hjalmar Horace Greeley: 3784
Schack, Alard Von: 7086,7296
Schadt, Armin L: 5533,5534
Schaefer, Friedrich: 2839
Schaefer, Hans-Dieter: 5931
Schaefer, Henry W: 4718
Schaefer, Max: 2455
Schaefer, Rudolf: 1755
Schaffer, Gordon: 899,900,1985,2496,2497,2656,2657,2718,3116,3117,3118,3148,
   3320,4377,4397,6427,6428,6429,6636,6637,6886,7480,7554,7555,7854,7966,
   7967,8054,8055,8310,8311,8312,8313,8489,8490
Schaffner, Bertram: 279
Schairer, Reinhold: 5778
Schalk, Adolph: 110,4961,4962,5186
Schalluck, Paul, Editor: 5968
Scharf, Carl Bradley: 4682
Scharff, Monroe B: 4243
Scharffs, Gilbert W: 4905
Scharmann, Theodor: 5038
Scharpf, Fritz W: 1483
Scharrer, Hans-Eckart: 4436
Schattmann, Stephan: 4579,4580,8256
Schatvet, Charles E: 8161
Schatz, Frederick C: 5374
Schaul, Hans: 5902
Schechtman, Joseph B: 420,421,422
Schecker, Theodor: 3953
Scheel, Walter: 4527,6312,6313,7087,7297,8019
Schein, Ernest: 1127
Scheingold, Stuart A: 7168
Scheinman, Lawrence: 8314
Schellenger, Harold K., Jr: 2409,2410,2411
Schelp, Guenther: 4284
Schelsky, Helmut: 4806
Schenk, Fritz: 4581,7968
Schenke, Klaus: 5028
Schepses, Erwin: 5099
Scher, Steven P: 6095
Scherpenberg, Albert H. Van: 6597
Scherpenberg, Albert H. Van: 4743
Scheuch, Erwin K: 1520,4773,4774,4807,5709,5969
Scheuner, Ulrich: 2877,6314
Scheurig, Bodo: 498
Schewe, Dieter: 5028
Schick, F. B: 1024
Schick, Jack M: 8491,8492,8493
Schieder, Theodor, Editor: 423
Schierz, Erich: 4627
Schiffgen, Werner: 5840

Schiffman, Edward Gottlieb: 3423
Schildmann, Gerhard: 4398
Schiller, Karl: 3393,3394,3854,4437
Schiller, Otto: 3891
Schilling, Frederick K., Jr: 860
Schilling, Hartmut: 4547
Schimansky, Stefan: 665
Schindler, M: 1743
Schindzielorz, Hubert Ludwig: 2930
Schirmeister, Helga: 7654
Schirmer, Gregor: 4556,6962,7666,7710
Schirokauer, Arnold: 2036
Schirrmacher, Herbert: 1604
Schlagintweit, Reinhard: 6165,6691
Schlamm, William S: 6539
Schlauch, Wolfgang: 562
Schleck, Robert W: 3321
Schlegel, Joachim: 3052
Schlegel, Roger: 3053,3054
Schleifstein, Josef: 6430
Schlesinger, Arthur M., Jr: 6540
Schlesinger, G: 5903
Schlesinger, Helmut: 3785
Schlesinger, Rudolf B: 3346
Schleth, Uwe: 2108,2160
Schliebe, Heinz Dieter: 6431
Schloenbach, Camilla: 3786
Schloenbach, Knut: 1944
Schloss, Bert P: 814
Schmahl, Hans-Juergen: 3395,4438
Schmid, Carlo: 6598,6599
Schmid, Karl: 1420
Schmid, Peter: 2658
Schmid, Walter: 6166
Schmidt, Dana Adams: 666
Schmidt, Friedrich: 5039
Schmidt, George P: 5668
Schmidt, Gerhard: 7556
Schmidt, Gerold: 7169
Schmidt, Gert: 5816
Schmidt, Heinz A. F: 4582
Schmidt, Helmut: 156,2003,4378,4379,6315,6316,6829,6998,7630
Schmidt, Hubert G: 3892,4380,8257
Schmidt, Hubert G., Editor: 3954
Schmidt, J. L: 4037
Schmidt, Joachim: 6167
Schmidt, Jutta: 6059
Schmidt, Karl: 2456
Schmidt, Manfred H: 2299
Schmidt, Max: 2175
Schmidt, Willi: 3787,8258
Schmidt, Wolfgang: 3072
Schmidtchen, Gerhard: 2088
Schmitt, Hans A: 2200,3281,6317,6692,7088,7969
Schmitt, Hans O: 3715
Schmitt, Karl: 5904
Schmitt, Matthias: 4038,4399
Schmitt-Ott, Dietrich, Editor: 5841
Schmitz-Esser, Winfried, Editor: 5842
Schmoelders, Guenter: 2004,3824,5817
Schmokel, Wolfe W: 4528,6781
Schneider, Carl J: 2349
Schneider, Dieter: 5749
Schneider, Erich: 3716
Schneider, Gerhard: 7589
Schneider, Hans, Editor: 1660
Schneider, Heinrich: 6720
Schneider, Horst: 7219
Schneider, Max: 3613
Schneider, Theodor: 1731
Schneider, Wolfgang: 3469
Schnitzer, Ewald W: 4311,5818,5819,6226,6887,6888,6963,7780
Schnitzer, Martin: 3371,3372,3825,4744
Schnyder, Sebastian: 171
Schoenbaum, David: 1025,1205,1521,2779,2878,5223
Schoenberg, Hans W: 424,425,8020
Schoeneberg, Karl-Heinz: 2901
Schoenfeld, Hanns-Martin: 4026
Schoenherr, Hans-Jochen: 7589
Schoening, Ulrich: 7970
Schoenke, Adolf: 1863
Schoenthal, Klaus: 6541
Scholz, Albert A: 7481
Scholz, Arno: 8303,8494
Scholz, Paul: 7685
Schoonmaker, Donald O: 2300
Schoonmaker, Donald O., Editor: 1500
Schorske, Carl E: 1295,1300
Schrader, Achim: 5780
Schrader, Erich: 6391
Schrader, Rudolf: 6830,6964
Schram, Glenn N: 1446,1447,1674,1864
Schramm, Friedrich K: 1554
Schreiber, Hermann: 7220
Schreiber, Wilfrid: 3373
Schreuder, Osmund: 4906
Schroeder, Dieter: 8213,8532
Schroeder, Gerhard: 6318,6319,6320,6321,6965,7089,7170,7221
Schubert, Richard S: 1759
Schuchat, Theodor: 321
Schueler, Herbert: 5304
Schuetz, Klaus: 8021
Schuetz, Wilhelm Wolfgang: 667,668,722,6322,7781,7855,7856,7857,7971
Schulmeister, Dieter: 4684
Schultes, Karl: 1448

Schultz, Heinrich: 2457
Schultz, Theodore W: 1277,3893
Schultz, Walter D: 499
Schultze, Walter: 5305,5451,5490,5779
Schulz, Eberhard: 6323
Schulz, Guenter: 4285
Schulz, Heinz-Friedrich: 4529
Schulz, Joachim: 997,6999,7258
Schulz, Peter: 157
Schulze, Rolf H. K: 4775
Schumacher, Carl: 4087
Schumacher, Kurt: 670
Schuman, Frederick L: 7354
Schuman, Robert: 6693
Schumann, Guenter: 960
Schumann, Hans: 7711
Schumann, Maurice: 6694
Schumann, Wolfgang: 6432
Schumm, Siegfried: 2301
Schuppe, Erwin: 5306
Schurer, Gerhard: 4629
Schurer, Heinz: 8022
Schuschnigg, Kurt Von: 2719
Schuster, Hans: 2887
Schutz, John A: 7853
Schuyler, Joseph B: 4166
Schwab, Hermann: 4963
Schwabe, Ernst Otto: 7557,7558
Schwada, John W: 723
Schwamm, Henri: 7090
Schwartz, Harry: 4776
Schwarz, George M: 7091
Schwarz, Hans-Peter: 6324
Schwarz, John B: 7151
Schwarz, Karl: 219
Schwarz, Leo Walder: 426,1128,4964
Schwarz, R. P: 3510
Schwarz, Siegfried: 6966,7092,7972,8495
Schwarz, Urs: 5187,6967
Schwarze, Hanns Werner: 3282
Schwarzenberger, Suse: 1301
Schwarzschild, Leopold: 500
Schwarzweller, Harry K: 4854,5469
Schweda, R: 4312
Schweigler, Gebhard L: 8023,8024
Schweinberger, Willy: 7686
Schweinfurth, Ulrich: 5112
Schweitzer, C. C: 1735
Schwelb, Egon: 724
Schwenk, Walter: 4313
Schwerin, Kurt: 1129
Scott, William H: 4286,4287
Sczaniecki, Michal: 7406
Searing, Donald D: 2145,2161
Searle, Ronald: 44
Sebald, Hans: 280
Seborer, Stuart J: 701,1256
Secher, H. Pierre: 1956,1957
Sedar, Irving: 6751
Seeberg, Axel: 7973
Sefrin, Max: 7687,7688
Segal, David R: 2102,2109,2110
Seger, Gerhart H: 45,46,501,2821
Segre, Sergio: 7559
Seibt, Arthur: 4039
Seidel, Dietmar: 3022
Seidel, Gerhard, and Others: 4651
Seidel, Karl: 7552
Seidl-Hohenveldern, Ignaz: 6736
Seif, N. S: 5558
Seifert, Karl Dieter: 3283
Seiffert, Wolfgang: 7258
Seifritz, Adelbart: 1449
Seligman, Harold: 3662
Semler, Hans-Joachim: 3073
Senger, W: 4699
Senghaas, Dieter, Editor: 5820
Sergeyev, V: 4583
Setaur, Frederick: 7116
Seton-Watson, Hugh: 2977,7298,7782,7783
Settel, Arthur, Editor: 1501,3424
Sevruk, Vladimir, Compiler: 596
Seydewitz, Max: 4965
Seydewitz, Ruth: 4965
Seymour-Ure, Colin: 5188
Shabecoff, Philip: 1026,2840,5710,6769,8094
Shafer, Susanne M: 5325,5470,5476,5477
Shafer, Suzanne M: 5559
Shaffer, Ralph G: 158
Shanor, Donald R: 3284
Sharfman, Peter J: 6968
Sharif, Regina S: 2136
Sharp, Elke, Editor: 72
Sharp, Samuel L: 2902
Sharp, Tony: 563
Shartel, Burke: 5787
Shaver, James P: 5452
Shaw, Charles B: 4288
Shays, Eugene: 281
Shears, David: 8095
Shears, Ursula Hahn: 2412
Sheehan, James J: 5821
Sheldon, Charles H: 1727
Shell, Curtis, Editor: 1082
Shell, Kurt L: 3229,5711,5712,5713,7784,8496

Shenayev, V: 4557
Shepherd, Robert James: 2137
Sheppard, Alexander W: 2498
Sherman, George: 3149,3150
Sherman, Heidemarie C: 4439,4440
Sherwin, Stephen F: 3788
Sherwood, Robert E: 564
Shevchenko, N: 6402
Shilling, Neil: 1810
Shils, Edward A: 332,652
Shirer, William L: 671,2592
Shick, Paul R: 1958
Shneiderman, Samuel L: 565
Shorris, Earl: 6075
Shub, Anatole: 2841
Shuchman, Abraham: 4244,4245,4246
Shulman, Marshall D: 7785
Shuster, George N: 672,1172,1237,2720,4990,5375,5633,6183,6889
Sibert, Edwin L: 282
Sibirtsev, Yu: 2903,7974
Siegler, Heinrich Von, Compiler: 7858
Siemsen, Hans: 5453
Sierakowsky, Heinrich: 4088
Sievers, W. David: 5970
Sigel, Roberta S: 283
Sigrist, Helmut: 6151
Silberman, L: 5822
Silveston, Peter: 5932
Simmons, M. M: 5376
Simmons, Stephen: 872
Simon, H. Paul: 7631
Simon, Walter M: 111
Simons, Hans: 1421
Simpson, J. A: 5535
Simpson, John L: 3536,3537,6907,8197
Simsarian, James: 3533
Sinanian, Sylva, Editor: 7299
Singer, Rudolf: 1959
Sinnhuber, Karl A: 127
Sisson, Charles H: 1605
Skolnik, Alfred M: 5019
Skoug, Kenneth N., Jr: 2413
Skubiszewski, Krzysztof: 7482,7483
Slanecka, Vladimir: 5933,5934
Sloan, Pat: 3230
Slotta, Peter L: 6695
Slover, Robert H: 1257
Slusser, Robert M: 8498
Slusser, Robert M., Editor: 901
Smallwood, Russell: 861
Smart, K. F: 5905
Smith, Bruce L. R: 8198
Smith, Gaddis: 6542,8315
Smith, Gordon: 2809,2888
Smith, Howard K: 2593
Smith, Jean Edward, Editor: 815
Smith, Jean Edward: 3285,3286,3287,7300,7560,7561,7975,8499,8500,8501,8502
Smith, Jessica: 6433,6434,6435,6890,7355,7786
Smith, Marcus J: 333
Smith, Rennie: 673
Smith, Robert F: 7787
Smith, Thomas V: 1158,1173,5377
Smith, Walter Bedell: 1302
Smith, Willard E: 1960
Smogorzewski, K. M: 3004,7788,8316
Snell, Bruno, and Others: 5634
Snell, Edwin M: 4745
Snell, John L: 112,566,568,2414
Snell, John L., Editor: 567
Snellings, Aubrey N: 3789
Snyder, Agnes: 5478
Snyder, Harold E: 5750
Snyder, Harold E., Editor: 5751,5752
Snyder, Louis L: 113,114,284,285,2499
Sobanski, Waclaw: 5560
Social Democratic Party of Germany: 2415,2416,2417,2418
Socialist Unity Party of Germany, Central Committee: 3151,3288,3289
Society for Christian and Jewish Cooperation: 6770
Society for Cultural Relations With Foreign Countries: 73,74,4584,6048,6060,8503
Sodeur, Wolfgang: 1955
Sodhi, Kripal S: 5823
Sohmen, Egon: 3717
Sohn, Karl-Heinz: 4481,4530,4531
Sokolov, Valentin: 3470
Solberg, Richard W: 4991
Sollman, William F: 502
Sollohub, Nicolas: 7789
Soloveytchik, George: 3663,8317
Sommer, Louise: 7117
Sommer, Theo: 6465,6794,7023,7024,7093,7301,7302
Sommerich, Otto C: 1894,3538
Sommerkorn, Ingrid N: 4873,5428,5578
Sonnenhol, G. A: 7094
Sontheimer, Kurt: 1502,2350,2810,5715,5716
Soper, Vera: 6039
Sorgenicht, Klaus: 2964
Sorio, Georges: 902
Sorrentino, Constance: 4108
Sosnovskaya, T: 7356
Southall, Sara: 4820
Southworth, Constant: 3539
Spaak, Paul-Henri: 6969,7095,7096
Spackman, Ellis L: 725
Spann, Raymond J: 5154

Spanner, Hans: 1606
Specht, Minna: 5307,5471
Spectator: 3471
Speidel, Hans: 7025
Speier, Hans, Editor: 6152
Speier, Hans: 286,1911,1912,1913,2811,6543,6544,6752,7976,7977,8041,8505,8506
Spencer, Frank: 6545
Spencer, Robert A: 710,2780,2842,7860,7861,8319,8320,8507
Spender, Stephen: 674,675,5717
Sperker, Heinrich: 6970
Sperlich, Peter W: 1323
Spilker, Hans: 159
Spindler, G. Dearborn: 2037
Spiro, Herbert J: 1411,1503,4233,4247,4248
Spiropoulos, Jean: 1027
Spittmann, Ilse: 3290,7632
Spitzer, H. M: 287
Spitzer, L: 2036
Spolton, Lewis: 5491
Spotts, Frederic: 4907
Spranger, Eduard: 5308
Sprigge, Sylvia: 2659
Springer, Axel Caesar: 5206
Springer, Ursula K: 5406,5429
Spulber, Nicolas: 4719
Srole, Leo: 334
St. Leon, R. P: 30
Staden, Berndt Von: 7171,7172
Stadler, Heinz: 6437
Stadler, K. R: 5378,5906
Stadtmueller, Georg: 7862
Stahl, Walter, Editor: 1504,5309
Stann, Eberhard: 4532,4533
Staikof, Zaharj: 4799
Stambuk, George: 1709
Stammer, Otto: 8241
Stamp, Maxwell: 3562
Stanger, Roland J., Editor: 8199
Stanley, Timothy W: 6546,6953
Starobin, Joseph R: 2458
Starrels, John Murry: 3291,5907
Stars and Stripes: 47
Steefel, Ernest C: 1771,1787,1831,4029,4041
Steefel, Ernst C: 1808
Steeger, Horst: 4618
Steel, Sir Christopher: 6638
Steele, W. Scott: 3889
Steffani, Winfried: 1555
Steger, Hanns-Albert: 5780
Steile, Hansjakob: 7222
Stehr, Nikolaus: 5824
Stein, Barry N: 7484
Stein, Stanley: 2879,7407
Steinberg, Jonathan: 3955
Steindorff, E: 1832
Steiner, George: 6004,6005
Steiner, Helmut: 3074
Steinert, Marlis G: 597
Steinhaus, Rolf: 6831
Steiniger, Peter-Alfons: 7667,7712,7713,7714,7715,8056,8057
Steinitz, Klaus: 4618
Steinkuehler, Manfred: 2459
Steinmetz, Hans: 1346
Steltzer, Hans Georg: 6168
Steltzer, Theodor: 7863
Stendenbach, Franz Josef: 5825
Stenzl, Otto: 7485
Sterling, Eleonore: 2271
Stern, Carola: 2931,3231,3232
Stern, Fritz: 288
Stern, James: 676
Stern, Leo: 7633
Stern-Rubarth, Edgar: 2235,3956,6600,6721,8162
Sternberg, Charles: 427
Sternberg, Fritz: 3563,3664
Sternberger, Dolf: 1530,2351,5826
Stets, Walter: 4289
Stettinius, Edward R: 569
Stettner, Edward A., Editor: 6601
Stevens, E. H., Editor: 1028
Stevenson, Henry G: 5865
Stewart, Rosemary: 4068
Stieber, Hans R., Editor: 4489
Stiefbold, Rodney P: 1522,2059
Stillman, Edmund: 7978
Stinson, Henry L: 570,1029
Stirk, S. D: 1304
Stoddard, George D: 1146
Stodieck, Helmut: 4456
Stoeckigt, Rolf: 4652
Stokes, William S: 4058
Stolper, Gustav: 3718,3719
Stolper, Wolfgang F: 227,3396,3720,4585,4586,4683,4700,4720,4746
Stolte, Stefan: 8508
Stoltenberg, Gerhard: 160,6169
Stoltz, Volker: 2436
Stonborough, John: 1174
Stone, Adolf: 8509
Stone, Gerald C: 4871
Stone, Shepard: 677,1076
Stone, Vernon W: 5080
Stone, William T: 3665,6891,7790
Stoodley, Bartlett H: 2038
Stoph, Willi: 8122
Storette, Ronald Frank: 5226

Stowell, J. D: 30
Straeter, Artur: 1077
Strang, William, Lord: 570,571,7791
Strasser, Otto: 1305,1306
Straus, Richard: 5189,6547
Strauss, Emil: 6639
Strauss, Franz-Josef: 6466,6602,6832,7097,7864,7979,7980
Strauss, Harold: 1307
Strausz-Hupe, Robert: 873,7865
Strawson, John: 598
Street, Jessie: 1914
Streich, Rudolf: 4673,4674
Streit, Josef: 3075,4966,6438
Streit, M. E: 4042
Streumann, Charlotte, Editor: 128
Strevell, Wallace H: 5379
Strickert, Hans-Georg, Editor: 1726
Strickland, Richard C: 2039
Stringer, Ann: 3321
Strognanov, A: 7214
Strohbach, Heinz: 4630,4701
Strong, Anna Louise: 599
Strong, Kendrick: 4992
Strothmann, Dietrich: 7981
Strubelt, Wendelin: 1583
Struve, Walter: 3666
Stuchtey, Rolf: 3957
Studd, Howard R: 5046
Stuebner, Siegfried: 8077
Stueck, Hans-Jurgen: 600
Stuper, Rainer: 3790
Sturmthal, Adolf: 4167,4249
Sturr, J. F: 2023
Sublett, Michael: 181
Sucu, Heinz: 4587
Suchenwirth, Richard: 1945
Suci, George J: 4789
Suess, Herbert: 7982
Sullivan, Walter: 8163,8322
Sulzbach, Walter: 3512
Sundberg, Norman D: 2040
Supranowitz, Stephan: 4675
Suri, Surindar: 3233,5908
Sutton, Horace, Editor: 5971
Sutton, John L: 1961
Swain, Harry S: 4002
Swanstrom, Edward E: 428
Sweezy, Paul M: 2630,6377,6859,7792
Sweigert, William T: 1661
Swiridoff, Paul: 2162,4070,5972
Swoboda, Richard A: 4314
Sydow, Peter: 7605
Sylvester, Anthony: 3292
Szalai, Sandor: 2041
Szaz, Zoltan Michael: 6230,7486
Szczesny, Gerhard: 6092
Szewczyk, Wilhelm: 6006
Szkibik, Heinz: 5128
Szulc, H: 2302,2721,7408
Szymanski, Zygmunt: 7562
Szymczak, M. S: 3425,3426
T. B: 335
T. R. C: 8323
Taborsky, Eduard: 4588
Tabouis, Genevieve: 503
Taeuber, Irene B: 429
Taft, Philip: 4168
Takezawa, Shin-Ichi: 2044
Talbot, Joanne Hines: 6028
Talensky, N: 7000
Tank, Kurt L: 6007
Tanter, Raymond: 8510,8511
Tanzi, Vito: 3826
Taplin, Michael Redvers: 4315
Tapp, J: 6813
Tarnow, Fritz: 4169
Tatu, Michel: 7304
Tauber, Kurt P: 2427,2500,2501,5669,7098
Taubert, Horst, Editor: 5915
Taussig, Andrew J: 1607
Taylor, A. J. P: 115,6722
Taylor, Donald L: 4808
Taylor, John W: 1252
Taylor, Richard W: 1744
Taylor, Ronald: 3322
Taylor, Stephen S., Editor: 2153
Taylor, Telford: 1030,1031,1032,1033,1206
Taylor, Thomas W: 8042
Technical Assistance Commission on Integration of Refugees: 430
Teichler, Ulrich: 5654
Teirich, Hildebrand R: 5061
Tempel, Gudrun: 289
Templer, G. W. R: 726
Tenbrock, Robert-Hermann: 116
Teplinsky, B: 6548
Terfloth, Klaus: 7173
Tergit, Gabriele: 8324
Terhune, Kenneth W: 2091
Tern, Juergen: 8096
Tetens, Tete Harens: 2272,7359
Textor, Gordon E: 5151
Thal, Steven H: 1833
Thalheim, Karl C: 3234,3235,4721
Thayer, Charles Wheeler: 2660
Thayer, James R: 2661

The Barrier Across Berlin and Its Consequences: 8384
The Future of West Berlin: 8382
Thedieck, Franz: 7866
Theis, Adolf: 1608,1609,1610
Thielicke, Helmut: 5004,5005
Thieme, Werner: 5662
Thiemeyer, Theo: 4089
Thomae, Hans: 2042
Thoman, Richard S: 161
Thomas, Basil E: 5492
Thomas, Elbert D: 727
Thomas, Helga: 5430
Thomas, Homer: 1497
Thomas, R. Hinton: 5303,6008,6009
Thomas, Siegfried: 2419,6439
Thomas, Stefan: 3236
Thomas, Stephan G: 6971
Thompson, Carol L: 290,504
Thompson, Elizabeth M: 2502,6893,8325
Thompson, Lawrence S: 5866
Thomson, Stewart: 3121
Thonger, Richard: 48
Thorburn, H. G: 2781
Thorelli, Hans: 4043
Thorner, Isidor: 2043
Thorp, Willard L: 1308
Thude, Guenther: 5120
Thumm, Garold Wesley: 3987,6723
Thut, I. N: 5326
Thwaites, J. B: 4381
Tiburtius, Joachim: 8164
Tietjens, Hans: 5536
Tietmeyer, Hans: 7174
Tijmstra, L. F: 5155
Tilford, Roger B: 1505,2835,2843,2844,2845,7305
Tilton, Timothy Alan: 2503,2504
Timmler, Markus: 5113
Tisch, Harry: 7563
Tisch, J. Herman: 30
Titel, Werner: 5121
Todi, Gaylord H: 6010
Toens, Hans: 5069
Toeplitz, Heinrich: 3055,3056,3057,3058,3076,3077,3078,3347,7983
Tomass, J: 3059
Tomberg, Valentin: 678
Tomicki, A: 7410,7411,7487
Tomlinson, A. K: 1034,1207,2273,7412,7413,7488
Tomuschat, Christian: 8025
Tone, Fred H: 5431
Torney, Judith: 5561
Tortora, Vincent R: 3237
Toussaint, Donald Ray: 7099
Toussaint, Hergard: 1760
Townroe, B. S: 6696
Townsley, W. A: 7119
Toynbee, Arnold J: 1237,2782,8512
Traeger, Ludwig: 8259
Traxler, Arthur E: 1175
Treeck, Joachim: 1834
Treick, Edward L: 6549
Treni, Harry G: 4624
Trescher, Karl: 1835
Tresp, Lothar L: 7489
Treue, Wolfgang: 117
Treuhaft, Gerd: 2662
Treuner, Peter: 162
Trevor-Roper, Hugh R: 679,903,1035,1208,2505,8513
Trial, George: 5380
Triandis, Harry: 2044
Tripartite Commission on German Debts: 3540
Tripathi, Krishna Dev: 728
Tritz, Maria: 4821
Tron, Rene A: 785
Trossmann, Hans: 1556
Troughten, Ernest R: 505
Trouvain, Franz-Josef: 3791
Truestedt, H: 4312
Truman, Harry S: 6550
Tuchtfeldt, Egon: 3667,3721
Tudyka, Kurt: 7564
Tugendhat, Georg: 5114
Tumlir, Jan: 3855
Tunkin, G: 8200
Tureen, Louis L: 291
Turgeon, Lynn: 4589
Turner, J. Neville: 1876
Turner, Joel: 4967
Turroni, C. Bresciani: 3792
Tussler, Anthony J. B: 163
UK, CCG, Information Services Division: 5973
UK, CCG, Internal Affairs & Communication Division: 220
UK, CCG, Military Governor: 1261
UK, CCG, University Commission: 5655
UK, CCG: 862,863,1130,1347,3513,4856
UK, Central Office of Information, Reference Division: 8544
UK, Central Office of Information: 6231,6232,6241,8514
UK, Foreign Office: 572,573,1258,1348,1388,3334,3541,3542,4250,5071,5655,6117,
    6233,6234,6235,6236,6237,6238,6239,6240,6241,6326,6327,6328,6329,6640,
    6894
UK, Hicog, Office of the Economic Adviser: 3609
UK, Hicog: 3722
UK, Ministry of Economic Warfare, Economic Advisory Board: 572,573
UK, O'Sullivan Committee: 1131
US, Business and Defense Services Administration: 3958
US, Chief of Counsel for Prosecution of Axis Criminality: 1036

US, Committee to Review Decartelization Program in Germany: 3472
US, Department of Commerce, Bureau of Foreign Commerce: 430,4044
US, Department of Commerce, Bureau of Int'L Commerce: 4382
US, Department of Commerce, Bureau of the Census: 23
US, Department of Commerce, Office of International Trade: 3427
US, Department of Commerce, Office of Technical Services: 3428
US, Department of State, Bureau of Intelligence &: 6331
US, Department of State, Bureau of Intelligence & Research: 2965,4265
US, Department of State, Division of Research for: 6332
US, Department of State, Division of Research for Europe: 1176,3430
US, Department of State, Historical Division: 576,577,578,6333,6334,6335,6552
US, Department of State, Historical Office: 6336
US, Department of State, Interim Research & Intell. Service: 3988
US, Department of State, Office of Intelligence Res. & Anal: 3827
US, Department of State, Office of Intelligence Research: 1557
US, Department of State, Office of Media Services: 8545
US, Department of State, Office of Public Affairs: 431,729,819,1401,3015,3016,
  3122,4857,6246,7795,8330
US, Department of State, Office of Public Services: 8516,8517
US, Department of State, Office of Research & Intelligence: 3514,4171
US, Department of State, Office of the Geographer: 164,165,166
US, Department of State: 75,574,575,816,817,818,1037,3429,5381,6242,6243,6244,
  6245,6330,6551,8515
US, Department of the Army, Civil Affairs Division: 820,821,822,823,3582
US, Department of the Army, European Command, Headquarters: 4858
US, Department of the Army, European Command, Hist. Div: 579,824
US, Department of the Army, European Command: 3906
US, Department of the Army, Public Information Division: 825,3583
US, Department of the Interior: 3907
US, Displaced Persons Commission: 336
US, Economic Cooperation Administration: 432,3374,3608,4045,4046
US, Embassy: 3375
US, Federal Reserve Bank: 4383
US, Foreign Economic Administration: 3473
US, Hicog, Berlin Element: 3095
US, Hicog, Commercial Attache Division: 5867
US, Hicog, Division of Internal Political and Gov. Affairs: 6119
US, Hicog, Education and Cultural Relations Division: 4914,4915,4916,4917,4918,
  5349,5382,5383,5384,5385,5386,5562
US, Hicog, Foreign Relations Division: 1558,2904
US, Hicog, Information Services Division: 4400,5190,5191,5246
US, Hicog, Land Commission for Bavaria: 5753
US, Hicog, Management and Budget Division: 6120
US, Hicog, Office of Administration: 4109
US, Hicog, Office of Economic Affairs: 3609,3668,3959,3960
US, Hicog, Office of Executive Secretary: 2352,2905
US, Hicog, Office of General Counsel: 6121
US, Hicog, Office of Labor Affairs: 433
US, Hicog, Office of Political Affairs: 6724
US, Hicog, Office of Public Affairs: 5247,5248,5754,5868,5974
US, Hicog, Public Relations Division: 6122
US, Hicog: 337,1038,2978,4912,5909,6118,6247
US, House, Committee on Foreign Affairs: 6248
US, House, Select Committee on Foreign Aid: 3610
US, Office of Geography: 167,191
US, Office of Political Adviser for Germany: 1309
US, Office of Strategic Services, Research & Analysis Bran: 198
US, Office of Strategic Services: 581,1081
US, Omgus, Armed Forces Division: 829,4316
US, Omgus, Civil Administration Division: 199,221,222,434,730,830,904,1078,
  1079,1259,1310,1311,1312,1313,1314,1349,1350,1351,1352,1353,1354,1389,
  1390,1402,1422,1423,1612,2353,5072,5755,7490
US, Omgus, Control Office: 831,832
US, Omgus, Economics Division: 905,906,3433,3434,3474,3475,3515,3564,3856,3899,
  3908,5157,5843
US, Omgus, Education and Cultural Relations Division: 1355,4859,4860,4913,4914,
  4915,4916,4917,4918,5387,5388,5389,5455,5479,5493,5537,5571,5844
US, Omgus, Finance Division: 907,3435,3476
US, Omgus, Information Control Division: 2045,2163,5158,5159,5193,5194
US, Omgus, Information Services Division: 833,5160,5161,5195,5249
US, Omgus, Interdivisional Reorientation Committee: 5756
US, Omgus, Internal Affairs and Communications Division: 4858,4919,5563
US, Omgus, Joint Export-Import Agency (Jeia): 3436
US, Omgus, Legal Division: 834
US, Omgus, Manpower Division: 1356,3376,4110,4111,4112,4172
US, Omgus, Military Governor: 731,835,836,837,1133,1134,1260,1261,1357,1358,
  2979,3437,3477,3478,3584,3909,3910,3989,4173
US, Omgus, Military Tribunals: 1040
US, Omgus, Office of Economic Adviser: 3427
US, Omgus, Omg Bavaria, Industry Branch: 3479
US, Omgus, Omg Bavaria, Monuments, Fine Arts & Archives Sec: 5869
US, Omgus, Omg Berlin: 838
US, Omgus, Omg Hesse, Economics Division: 3438,3439
US, Omgus, Omg Hesse, Public Safety Section: 1080
US, Omgus, Property Division: 3516
US, Omgus, Public Relations Service: 3517
US, Omgus, Pw & Dp Division: 435
US, Omgus, Transport Division: 4317
US, Omgus: 580,826,827,828,1039,1132,3431,3432,5030,5192
US, Senate, Committee on Armed Services: 6553
US, Senate, Committee on Foreign Relations: 839,3543,6249,6250,6334,6335,6336
US, Senate, Committee on the Judiciary: 582,3096,3097
US, Spec. Commission to Study Nutrition in Bizonal Germany: 5073
US, Strategic Bombing Survey: 601
Ucker, Paul: 3900
Uckert, Gerhart: 4631
Ueberreiter, Kurt, Editor: 5845
Ueberreiter, Kurt: 5846
Uhlig, Christian: 4534
Ulam, Adam B: 8026
Ulbricht, Paul Wolfgang: 1450
Ulbricht, Walter: 2460,2812,2906,2907,2952,2980,2981,3017,3238,3239,3240,3241,
  3293,3294,3295,3296,3297,3298,4590,4632,4654,7565,7566,7567,7636,7668,
  7716,7869,7870,7984,7985,7986,7987,7988,7989,8043,8099,8100,8101,8102,
  8123

Ule, Carl Hermann: 1611
Ulich, Robert: 5327
Ullmann, Richard K: 1391,1559
Ullrich, Klaus: 8044
Ulman, Lloyd: 4190
Ulrich, Franz Heinrich: 3793
Umrath, Oscar: 5070
Un, Economic Commission for Europe: 4001
Un, Economic and Social Council: 4264
Un, General Assembly: 7794
Ungerer, Werner: 4384,5156,6814,7001,7175
Union of Anti-Fascist Fighters: 2274
Union of Democratic Control: 506
United Restitution Organisation: 1135,1136
United States Steel Corporation: 3440
Urbscheit, Peter W: 168
Urwin, Derek W: 1523
Uschakow, Alexander: 7414
Uschner, Manfred: 6802
Ussr, Ministry Of Foreign Affairs: 7797,7868,8331
Utley, Freda: 1315
Utley, T. E: 7120
Vaclav, E. Mares: 7990
Vagts, Detlev F: 4047
Valentin, Veit: 680,2354
Vali, Ferenc A: 6338,7991
Valkenburg, S. Van: 7176
Vallance, Margaret: 6076
Van Abbe, Derek Maurice: 6011
Van De Graaff, John H: 5494,5656
Van Den Berk, L. J. M: 3005,3006
Van Der Werf, Dirk: 3382
Van Es, Johannes C: 4777
Van Hoek, Kees: 1560,6725,8332
Van Hoorn, J., Jr: 3828
Van Riet, Joseph: 3961
Van Riper, Paul P: 5757
Van Schaick, F. L: 3990
Van Voorst, L. Bruce: 5207
Van Wagenen, Richard W: 8333
Vandevanter, E., Jr: 6972
Vanocur, Sander: 8167
Vansittart, Robert G. V., Lord: 507,508,509,681
Vardys, V. Stanley: 2420
Vehres, Gerd: 7637
Veit, Otto: 3794
Vente, Rolf E: 3834
Verba, Sidney: 292,2048,2092,2093
Verbrugge, Lois M: 2155
Vergin, Heinz: 4290
Verkade, Willem: 2355
Vermehren, E. M: 5006
Vermeil, Edmond: 118
Vernant, Jacques: 437
Verner, Paul: 3299
Vernon, Raymond: 7121
Verrier, Anthony: 7992
Verrina (Pseud.): 293
Vetter, Gottfried: 8103
Veverka, Jindrich: 3799
Vida, George: 333
Viedebantt, Joachim: 5196
Viereck, Peter: 294
Vigers, T. W: 1915
Villard, Oswald Garrison: 785
Villmow, Jack R: 192
Vilmar, Fritz: 2303
Vincent, Jean-Marie: 2783,3242
Viner, Jacob: 510
Vinogradov, K: 4722
Vitger, Erhard: 3962
Vladimirov, N: 6555
Voelker, Gottfried E: 4266
Voelling, Johannes: 3795
Vogel, Rolf: 6771
Vogel, Rudolf: 5162
Vogelsang, Thilo, Editor: 76
Vogl, Dieter: 7669
Vogl, Frank: 4048
Vogt, A. M: 8242
Vogt, Siegfried A: 2428
Voigt, Fritz A: 864,908,3323,5827
Voigt, Johannes H: 6339
Voigtlaender, Kurt: 8104
Vollmer, Rainer: 3689
Volz, Wilhelm: 7491
Vorholzer, Jorg: 5902
Voslenskii, M. S: 7306
Voslensky, M: 7223
Voss-Eckermann, Helga: 6281
Vosshall, Gerhard W: 3796
Vossschmidt, Theo: 5847
Vrga, Djuro J: 2421
Vysotsky, V: 8546
W. B: 2663
W. Europe: 6332
W. H: 3585
W. K: 7638
W. U. K: 4591
Wachenheim, Hedwig: 4251
Wacke, Gerhard: 4291
Wadbrook, William P: 4457
Wade, D. A. L: 1041
Waehler, Jan P: 4687
Wagenfuehr, Rolf: 4174

Wagner, Helmut R: 2982,4113,6061
Wagner, Ingo: 7954
Wagner, Wolfgang, Editor: 7476
Wagner, Wolfgang: 583,584,7177,7307,7308,7309,7310,7415,7492,7493,8027,8105
Wahrhaftig, Samuel L: 6153
Waidson, Herbert M: 6012
Walbaum, O: 2461
Walbruck, H. A: 5975
Walczak, A. W: 7494
Wald, Salomon: 5862
Walleck, Rosie Goldschmidt: 295
Waldman, Eric: 1946,2005,7871
Walichnowski, Tadeusz: 6772
Walinsky, Louis J: 339,340
Walker, Patrick Gordon: 682
Walker, Peter J: 8243
Walker, Richard: 6556
Wallace, Donald D., Editor: 1791
Wallace, J. Allen: 189
Wallach, Hans Gert Peter: 2356
Wallenberg, Hans: 2664
Waller, Peter P: 4002
Wallich, Henry C: 1613,3669,3670,7100
Wallisch-Prinz, Baerbel: 5651
Waln, Nora: 683,684,4861
Walser, Martin: 6603
Walter, Gerhard: 3079
Walter, Hilde: 4968
Walter, Ingo: 7152
Walton, Clarence C: 6895
Walton, Henry: 2313
Wandel, Paul: 7670,7993,8058
Wangemann, Karl: 4401
Wansbrough-Jones, Ll: 3324
Warburg, James P: 1243,1244,6251,6252,6253,6254,6340,7122,7760
Ward, Barbara: 6255
Ward, Conor: 4799
Warde, William F: 3152
Ware, George Whitaker: 5520,5848
Warnecke, Steven: 1614,2536
Warninghoff, Hans: 5431
Warnke, Rudolf: 1962
Warren, Kenneth: 7178
Warren, Richard L: 5472,5473
Warren, Roland L: 1633
Waschke, Hildegard: 4819
Wasem, Erich: 5572
Wasnke, Hildegard: 5082
Waskow, Arthur I: 7002
Wassermann, Charles: 7495
Watkins, W. P: 4090
Watson, Gerald G: 1561,1562,1634
Watson, Jeanne: 5739,5758,5759
Watt, Donald C: 1635,2846,6154,6641,6642,6643,6644,7496
Wayne, Ivor: 6024
Webb, Robert N: 2201,2236
Weber, Alfred: 4749
Weber, August: 511
Weber, Bernd: 2953
Weber, Hans: 1865
Webster, Donald H: 296
Wechsberg, Joseph: 1042,3243,8168
Wechsler, Herbert: 1043
Wedderburn, Dorothy: 4114
Weede, Erich: 2108
Weeks, H. Ashley: 4781
Wegener, Thomas: 2422
Weichelt, Wolfgang: 2966
Weiden, Paul L: 1662
Weigend, Guido G: 169
Weigert, Oscar: 4191,4233,4252
Weil, Gordon Lee, Editor: 7179
Weinberg, Albert K: 751
Weinberger, Bruno: 1636,1637
Weir, Cecil: 3671
Weir, Patricia Ann Lyons: 1044
Weis, George, Editor: 4049
Weis, George: 1137
Weismann, Arnold: 4050
Weisner, Gerhard: 1717
Weiss, Edith Brown: 3080
Weiss, Gerhard: 4702,4723,7689
Weiss, Grigorij: 7639
Weiss, Martin: 1045,2492
Weissberg, Robert: 6341
Weisser, Gerhard: 4091,4092
Weitzel, Heinz: 1717
Welch, Colin: 8169
Weller, Eva: 5720
Welles, Orson: 2594
Wells, Guy: 5391
Wells, Herman B: 5390,5760
Wells, Ingeborg: 8170
Wells, Leon W: 1046
Wells, Roger Hewes: 1317,1333,1359,1360,1638,1639,1640,4175
Wells, W. T: 3565
Welsch, Erwin K: 5870
Weltz, Friedrich: 4102
Welzel, Karl: 4822
Wendt, H. W: 2028
Wendt, Paul F: 5093
Wendt, Peter D: 4066
Wengler, Wilhelm: 1138,1772,5788,6342
Wenke, Hans: 5264,5310,5311
Wennberg, Samuel G: 3441

Wenning, Werner: 7640
Wentzel, Fred D: 4908
Werkman, Casper J: 4051
Wernecke, Hanns B: 5407
Werner, Alfred: 5976,6040,6041
Werner, Fritz: 1745
Werner, Max: 3325
Werner, Philipp: 4909
Wertheimer, Robert G: 3829,5094
Wesley, Frank: 4794
Wesner, Charlotte: 5139
Wessels, Theodor: 4003
Wesserle, Andreas Roland: 187
Wesson, Robert G: 7311
West, Charles C: 4993
West, Rebecca (Pseud. of Cicily Isabel Fairfield Andrews): 1047
Westerfield, H. Bradford: 6557
Westphal-Hellbusch, Sigrid: 5828
Westphalen, Juergen: 6803
Wettig, Gerhard: 3007,7003,7641,7642,7643,8106,8547
Wetzel, Gerhard: 6782
Weymar, Paul: 2237
Weymouth, Anthony, Editor: 512
Weyrauch, Erdmann, Compiler: 8520
Weyrauch, Walter O: 1675,1761
Wheeler, George Shaw: 3123,7995
Wheeler-Bennett, John: 1318
Whetten, Lawrence L: 7312,7313,7314,8548
Whipple, William, Jr: 732
White, John: 4535,4536
White, Nathan I: 585
White, Theodore H: 2596,3991,6257,6258,6259,6697,6726,7798
White, William L: 685
Whiteside, Andrew G: 2202
Whitney, Craig R: 1209
Whitt, Darnell M: 6546
Whyte, Anne: 733,1245
Wickham, Denis A: 1177
Wieck, Hans-Georg: 1963,6833,7026,7027
Wiedemann, Herbert: 4028
Wiedemeyer, Wolfgang: 2203
Wiedmann, Christoph: 7315
Wiegand, G. Carl: 3830,3831,4592
Wiemann, Horst: 3060
Wiener Library: 686,1139,1140,2275,2506,4920
Wierblowski, Stefan: 7416
Wierling, L: 188
Wiese, Leopold Von: 5829
Wiesenthal, Simon: 1042,3300
Wieser, Theodor: 1964,2784,2847,5721,5977,6077,7316,8171,8244
Wiewiora, Boleslaw: 7224,7406,7497,7498,7499
Wightman, Margaret: 3326
Wignton, Charles: 2238
Wiking, Paula: 3244
Wilcox, Francis O: 1246
Wildenmann, Rudolf: 438,1506,1520,2094
Wilder, Amos N: 4910
Wilder, Jan Antoni: 7500
Wilhelm, Bernhard: 2932
Wilhelms, Christian: 4053
Wilke, Alfred: 5910
Wilke, Werner: 4724
Wilke, Willi: 6441
Wilken, David: 6123
Wilkening, Eugene A: 4777
Will, Frederic: 5636
Will, Wilfried Van Der: 5720,6009
Willener, Alfred: 4102
Willenz, Eric: 5197,6896
Willett, John: 6093
Willey, Howard David: 3965
Willey, Richard James: 4176,4177,4178
Willging, Paul Raymond: 7799
Williams, A: 5911
Williams, Alan Lee: 7028
Williams, Ewart: 4387
Williams, Frederick W: 2138
Williams, Geoffrey Lee: 7028
Williams, J. Emlyn: 2597,2598,2724,2785,2786,5198
Williams, John E: 2046
Williams, Lowell: 1811
Willick, Daniel H: 2139
Willis, F. Roy: 874,875,6698
Willner, Dorothy K: 5100
Wills, S: 5903
Wilmot, Chester: 586,6645
Wilms, Dorothee: 5498
Wilpert, Friedrich Von: 7501
Wilson, Francesca M: 687
Wilson, Harold: 6646
Wilson, O. Meredith: 652
Wilson, Roger Cowan: 341
Winckler, Heino: 4458
Windsor, Philip: 6345,7029,7996,7997,8521
Winegarten, Renee: 5722
Winfield, P. H: 1048
Winklbauer, Ernst: 7693
Winkler, Hans: 4093
Winnington, Alan: 3301
Winston, Victor: 4725
Winter, Herbert R: 2423,2424
Winter, K: 5936
Winter, K., Et Al: 5127
Winterhager, J. W: 5912
Winterhager, Wolfgang D: 5499

Winternitz, Josef: 688,1319
Winzer, Otto: 1916,2933,6442,7568,7569,7570,7571,7572,7573,7574,7575,7644,7645,
   7998,8107
Wippold, Werner: 2908
Wires, Richard: 1210,2814
Wirsing, Giselher: 6795
Wirsing, Werner: 5088
Wirth, Fremont P: 5391
Wirth, Guenther: 7502
Wirth, Joseph: 6604
Wirzberger, Professor: 5937
Wiscanewski, Hans-Juergen: 4537
Wise, James Waterman: 4969
Wiskemann, Elizabeth: 6727,7225,7226,8522
Wissell, Rudolf: 5031
Witte, Barthold: 6170
Wittich, Guenter J: 4115
Wittkopf, Eugene R: 4538
Wlotzke, Otfried: 4239
Woeltge, Herbert: 5938
Woetzel, Robert K: 1049
Wohlgemuth, Ernest: 4179
Wohlgemuth, Kaethe: 7646
Wohlrabe, Raymond A: 49
Woischnik, Bernhard: 3672,3724,7180
Wolf, Gotthard: 5978
Wolf, Herbert: 4633
Wolf, Simon: 170,2665,3992,7800,8172
Wolfe, James H: 2983,3335,7514,7999,8000
Wolfe, Thomas W: 7647,7648
Wolfers, Arnold: 6558,6559,6560
Wolff, Friedrich: 3081
Wolff, Karl-Dietrich: 5723
Wolff, Kurt H: 1074,5564,5730,5761
Wolff, Max: 513
Wolff, Salomon: 4442
Woll, Artur: 3797
Woller, Rudolf: 7030
Wollmann, Hellmut: 1641
Wollsey, John M., Jr: 1000
Women Strike For Peace: 8001
Wood, Cecil, Editor: 1082
Woodley, W. John R: 3592
Woodman, D. R: 866,867
Wooton, Richard C: 5392
World Confederation of Organizations of Teaching Profession: 5456
World Federation of Trade Unions: 4180
World Jewish Congress: 1141
Worsley, R. H. M: 440
Worsnop, Richard L: 2537
Wortman, John August: 2984
Wright, David M: 3673
Wright, Lord: 1050
Wright, Quincy: 1051,1052,1053,6260,8523
Wright, William B: 8245,8246
Wszelaki, Jan: 4726
Wucher, Albert: 119
Wuelker, Gabriele: 376,4117
Wuensche, Harry: 7717
Wuensche, Kurt: 3061,3082,8002,8059
Wuertenberger, Thomas: 5101
Wulf, Amandus: 6171
Wuliger, Robert: 5637
Wunderlich, Eva C: 6078
Wunderlich, Frieda: 4253,4655,4656
Wurzbacher, Gerhard: 4783
Wyman, Louis C: 3611
Wyndham, E. H: 1247
Wyschka, Gerhard: 4727,4728
X. Y. Z: 734
Yahraes, Richard A: 6561
Yakoubian, Arsen Lionel: 1393
Ydit, Meir: 8524
Yefimov, D: 7227
Yefremov, A: 2538
Yerofeyev, T: 5939
Yershov, Vassily: 909
Ylvisaker, Hedvig: 2095,2096
Yochelson, John: 6973
Yoder, Amos: 3993
Yondorf, Walter: 7181
Young, Edgar P: 3124,3245,4593,4676,5940
Young, Gordon: 3966
Young, Oran R: 8525
Younger, Kenneth: 6183,6605,6897,7801
Yuryev, N: 6443,6444,6699
Zaborowski, Jan: 2245,2276
Zachodnia Agencja Prasowa: 7503,7504,7505
Zahn, Peter Von: 6562
Zaitsev, Evgenii: 6957
Zalyotny, A: 7515
Zander, Ernst: 1320,1917,5199
Zaostrovsky, Y: 7690
Zauberman, Alfred: 4677
Zaunitzer-Haase, Ingeborg: 7101
Zawadzki, Sylwester: 1451
Zbinden, Hans: 1321
Zboralski, Dietrich: 6445
Zedler, John N: 6974
Zehm, Guenter: 6013
Zeimer, Siegfried: 2006,6916
Zeisel, Hans: 1840
Zeitel, Gerhard: 3832
Zelle, Arnold: 3967
Zellentin, Gerda: 7102,8028

Zelt, Johannes: 7650,8003
Zencke, Hans-Henning: 3798
Zholkver, A: 2880
Zhukov, Yuri: 6700
Ziebill, Otto: 1642
Ziegler, David W: 2357
Ziemke, Earl F: 602,6834
Ziercke, Manfred: 3725
Zilliacus, K: 6647
Zimmels, Hirsch Jacob: 4970
Zimmer, Thomas M: 1866
Zimmerman, Hans: 3833,3968,4004,4539,7103
Zimmermann, Rolf: 1054
Zink, Harold: 841,842,843,844,845,1083,1479
Zinn, Georg-August: 1663
Ziock, Hermann: 6346
Ziolkowski, Janusz: 7406,7506
Znamierowski, Czeslaw: 7507
Zoeller, Josef Othmar: 5979
Zoellner, Detlev: 5011,5032
Zohlnhoefer, Werner: 2111
Zolling, Hermann: 2013
Zook, George F: 1178,5638
Zschocher, Hanns: 4240
Zucker, A. E: 5393
Zucker, F: 5394
Zuckerman, Stanley B: 5312
Zuealsdorff, Volkmar Von: 6945
Zundel, Rolf: 2848
Zvegintzov, Michael: 3480
Zweigert, Konrad: 1801
Zygulski, Kazimierz: 7423